the improvement of reading

the improvement of reading

FOURTH EDITION

RUTH STRANG
Professor of Education and
Director of the Reading Development Center
University of Arizona

Professor Emeritus of Education
Teachers College, Columbia University

CONSTANCE M. McCULLOUGH
Professor of Education
San Francisco State College

ARTHUR E. TRAXLER
Lecturer in Education
University of Miami

Consultant and President Emeritus
Educational Records Bureau, New York

McGRAW-HILL Book Company
New York, St. Louis, San Francisco
Toronto, London, Sydney

The Improvement of Reading

⌐·αce

The purpose of the fourth edition of *The Improvement of Reading* is to give a comprehensive view of the broad field of reading—its goals, the nature of the reading process, the psychology of teaching reading, reading programs, and the sequential development of reading attitudes and skills from the early preschool years to maturity. In line with the objectives of helping every student to discover and develop his reading potentialities, there are chapters on informal and standardized methods of approach, on methods of teaching both basic and higher-level skills, and on the teaching of reading in special groups and in every subject.

Goethe once wrote: "Only man attempts the impossible." Surely the impossible has been attempted in this book, namely, (1) to give an overview of the broad, complex field of reading within the space limitations of one volume, (2) to include present points of view without neglecting perspective from the past, (3) to include concrete illustrations as well as principles and general procedures, and (4) to describe sound, established practices as well as original approaches.

Each chapter or group of chapters begins with a few paragraphs designed to orient the reader and guide his reading of the material that follows. In the treatment of each topic the aim is not only to state principles and describe practices but also to illustrate their application. In view of the enormous number of topics that might be covered and of books and articles that are available on every aspect of reading, the authors have had to impose some limitations; they regret that many outstanding contributions could not be included.

Among the unique features of the fourth edition are Constance McCullough's chapters on reading in the content fields; these go beyond the descriptions of methods that have been presented in other publications to focus on a more essential analysis of the process of reading as it is practiced in each subject. In view of the present concern about exceptional children and the role that reading plays or should play in their life adjustment, this edition devotes more attention to the gifted child, the able retarded reader, the slow learner, the "disadvantaged," and the "bilingual," as well as the emotionally disturbed child and the child who shows signs of neurological disorganization. Some study of exceptional children may give the teacher a deeper understanding of all children. The tabulation in Chapter 3 of sequential development calls attention to certain stages, from preschool to college, at which given reading attitudes and skills should be introduced, intensified, and reinforced. Throughout the book, the authors attempt to integrate conflicting points of view and to describe

v

concretely the sound features of any innovation that appears capable of helping an individual to learn to read better. Recorded excerpts from interviews and class instruction add a new dimension of specificity.

The Improvement of Reading is designed to serve as a text for a basic reading course for prospective teachers and teachers in service, all of whom need to see the whole scope and sequence of reading instruction, regardless of the grade level on which they may be teaching or planning to teach. This book may also serve as text for a foundation course for graduate students who are majoring in reading. Teachers on the job often refer to *The Improvement of Reading* to get help on an immediate question or problem. Specialists in other fields have also found the book useful in connection with the reading problems they encounter in their work.

In this edition, Chapters 4 and 5, on appraising reading development and reading difficulties by informal methods and standardized tests, were revised by Dr. Arthur Traxler, who also took major responsibility for the appendixes. Dr. Constance McCullough added many new ideas in Chapters 8, 9, 10, and 11 on reading in the subject areas. The other chapters, written by Dr. Strang, were critically and constructively reviewed by Dr. Margueritte Caldwell. Illustrative selections from interviews, class instruction, and children's compositions were contributed by Paul Eagen, Barbara Dean, Betty Frey, and others mentioned in previous editions. Needless to say, the authors owe much to many authors who have described present practices or reported research in the field. References to some of these publications are listed at the end of each chapter so that the student who desires more detail may read the original articles.

RUTH STRANG
CONSTANCE M. McCULLOUGH
ARTHUR E. TRAXLER

contents

part I

PERSPECTIVE IN READING

the nature
of reading

chapter 1

The purpose of this chapter is, first, to strengthen your conviction of the importance of reading and, second, to give you a sense of structure in the broad field that embraces the teaching of reading. You will see how the individual's reading process is related to his goals, to the "prerequisites" he possesses for success in learning, and to the effectiveness of the methods by which he has been taught.

What do your students think of reading? Do they know what it involves? Do you know if they think reading is important and why? What is your own view of reading? Is it merely a decoding process by which printed words are translated into spoken words? Or is it a process of gaining meaning from the printed page and applying it to daily life? Examine your own reading methods.

Recollect some of the reading difficulties you have observed in children and adolescents. Recall what you know about the theory of learning.

Read to gain understanding of the knowledge and the skills your students will need. Become aware of conditions within the individual and in his environment that will help or hinder him in learning to read or in improving his reading proficiency. Get a clear idea of the whole reading process and consider the implications that this broad view has for the teaching of reading.

IMPORTANCE OF READING

Reading proficiency is the royal road to knowledge; it is essential to the success in all academic subjects. In modern life, learning depends largely upon one's ability to interpret the printed page accurately and fully. A junior high school youngster summed it up in this way: "You could list hundreds of reasons why being a good reader is important, but I guess I'd put it this way. Reading is the key to learning and personal enjoyment." Another said, "Reading to me is a way I can find out as much or as little as I choose to know or learn about something. And the more reading, the more learning." Dr. James Conant called reading the keystone of the arch of education. In 1964, Francis Keppel, United States Commissioner of Education, stated the value of reading still more broadly: "Every examination of the problems of our schools, of poverty; every question raised by troubled parents about our schools, every learning disorder seems to show some association with reading difficulty" [58, p. 8]. The introduction to the report of the Carnegie Conference of Reading Experts included this statement: "Reading is the most important subject to be learned by children; a child will learn little else in today's world if he does not first learn to read properly . . ." [19, p. 1].

Personal Values

Reading involves the whole personality, promising countless personal and social values. Reading is an entrance into almost all vocations. Even routine mechanical work in a factory demands the reading of some material, such as basic rules, safety signs, and changes in regulations. Since many industrial accidents have been traced to employees' failure to read and comprehend signs and directions relating to safety, some firms now require that their personnel have at least a fourth-grade level of reading ability. The skilled trades require considerably more reading for the best quality of work and the integration of new practices.

In all the professions, of course, one must read a great deal after graduation, as well as during the preparation period, to keep pace with new developments. A lawyer considered that "the ability to read well—to skim through an article, pick out important ideas in a paragraph, and make deductions from passages—is the most important single factor in a successful law practice."

The best administrators and teachers demonstrate in their own lives the value of efficient reading; with pride in their work, they pursue a systematic course of professional reading. Lawyers, engineers, and physicians claim that reading is essential: one is successful only if he keeps up-to-date. For some professions, such as library work, writing, and bibliographical research work, extensive reading is so obviously a requisite that nothing further needs to be said.

Reading is a most rewarding use of the expanded leisure that comes as a result of automation. Given increasingly larger amounts of time and more opportunities to buy or borrow books, people should be educated to read at least one hour a day. "Reading may be one of life's inexhaustible pleasures and blessings," Walter de la Mare said. At its best, recreational reading affords more than mere entertainment. The reader has time to reflect on the ideas he meets and give play to the imagination.

Reading often relieves emotional tensions and gives insight into personal problems. Frequently the right book will fill the psychological need at a critical moment when the radio or television programs may be anything but agreeable to a mood.

Reading provides experience through which the individual may expand his horizons; identify, extend, and intensify his interests; and gain deeper understandings of himself, of other human beings, and of the world.

Reading organizes experience; it relates ideas from many sources.

Reading is a path to new experiences. Using his own firsthand experiences as a point of departure, the reader reaches out to those of an author and transcends the limitations of time and space. As Stevenson said, "Reading takes us out of our country and ourselves."

Reading is a creative act. As the writer creates a structure of thought, so the reader, re-creating the pattern of words, discovers for himself the essence of the author's idea.

Social Values

But the value of reading in today's highly skilled democracy quickly overreaches the purely personal and merges into social values. In fact, the general attitude toward reading is largely pragmatic, seeing it as an avenue to financial and social statuses. For its best welfare, society needs its members to have a minimum of education. As surveys show, non- or poor readers become the delinquent, the unemployed, or the misfit in a society which progresses to the extent that its mental resources do.

In general, reading disability severely restricts the adolescent's development. According to Krugman, mental hygiene and reading underlie all teaching in the schools and have the most pervasive influence on the student's success in school and adjustment in living. "A reading disability or severe retardation in reading has the same profound influence on educational growth as a severe emotional involvement. Both limit successful functioning, cause feelings of inadequacy and frustration, bring about disturbed relationships, influence outlook on life, and result in a variety of undesirable behavior manifestations" [61, p. 10].

The relation of reading disability to premature school leaving has been definitely established. Many students drop out of high school because of reading inability. Penty [74] obtained clear evidence from data in the Battle Creek, Michigan, school system that the preponderance of early school leavers stood in the lowest quarter with respect to reading ability; only 14.5 per cent of those in the highest quarter left school before completing the senior year. More than three times as many poor readers as good readers left school; the peak of dropouts occurred in the tenth grade. Further study showed that a very large percentage of the poor readers who left, as well as of the poor readers who remained in school, had potential reading ability. With proper instruction they could have improved.

Three years after leaving school, young people of average intelligence made comments of this kind:

I just didn't care for school except I liked Foods and Typing. I sometimes had difficulty in understanding English. I had no interest in reading whatsoever. I could read and read and get nothing out of it. I couldn't remember what I read either. I could have enjoyed school more if I had had help in reading. That is what put me behind.

I didn't think that I was getting any place in school. I was working part-time and wanted to work full-time. I had trouble reading and understanding assignments. I couldn't remember what I read and didn't like to recite, as I wasn't sure of myself.

Repeated academic failures caused by reading inability gave rise to feelings of inferiority and frustration: "I didn't like to go to classes and be around other kids who seemed to learn easier than I did" [74].

Many other studies have shown that reading retardation is a frequent reason for giving up. The average dropout is retarded in reading two years or more.

Failure in reading may cause emotional disturbances. Even in the first grade, children who learned to read early showed self-confidence; those who did not make satisfactory progress felt anxious and insecure. One child said, "I tried to read in the first grade. I tried a little while and then I just quit." Another said, "Teachers didn't do nothin' to help. They just asked me to read and when I couldn't they asked someone else."

The child who fails to read may feel his family's disapproval. One child said wistfully, "I wish my parents knew how I felt." According to one study, the parents of severely retarded high school readers are more likely to use derogatory words and phrases in describing their children and more likely to disparage their abilities than are the parents of good readers.

Many statements of juvenile court judges and statistics of correctional institutions have pointed up the relationship between reading disability and delinquency. Judges have noted that as many as 50 per cent of the juvenile delinquents brought before the courts have severe reading disabilities. At one time approximately 30 per cent of the delinquent boys, aged twelve to fifteen, in the New York Training School for Boys were reading below second-grade level. To fail to recognize, diagnose, and correct these difficulties will result in the failure of any correctional program to rehabilitate a large proportion of delinquent and emotionally disturbed boys.

Reading retardation often produces a chain of consequences: inability to do the assignments and take part in the class discussion leads to feelings of inferiority, hopelessness, or hostility, which in turn bring about truancy, association with experienced delinquents, and delinquent acts. The final link is usually a court sentence. In each step of this sequence the individual's image of himself deteriorates. An adult in a penal institution vividly described how failure in reading affected his self-concept and his subsequent behavior: "I couldn't read what they wanted me to in school, so after a while I got to thinking I was always going to be like this, and I didn't care. So I never did try to learn, 'cause I pictured me as an adult not reading, and that was OK."

Wider Imports

Such testimonials signal trouble for any country, affluent or poor. For despite the educational opportunities and wealth of this nation, 2.2 per cent of persons aged fourteen or over in the United States in 1959, according to census figures, March, 1959, had not attained functional literacy; the percentages for individual states vary enormously. Draft figures reveal that thousands of men who are otherwise eligible for service cannot meet the Army's minimum educational standards. A much larger number either lack adequate comprehension of what they read or habitually distort it to conform to their prejudices.

Democracy cannot succeed when people are ignorant and cannot or will not think for themselves. If citizens fail to become cognizant of the implications of historical trends, fail to discriminate fact from opinion, or fail to detect and resist propaganda, both they and their nation are open to exploitation and manipulation.

Reading has international significance; recent figures indicate the magnitude of the problem. Half of the people of the world are completely illiterate, and hardly a third have attained functional literacy, i.e., the level of reading that is normally expected of a child after four years of schooling. However, there is hope. According to Gray, interest in reading has never been so keen or so worldwide in scope as it is at the present time [41, p. 1]. In all nations an awareness has developed of the importance of worldwide literacy as a means of promoting individual welfare, social progress, and international understanding.

The ever-closer contact between different peoples and cultures necessitates effective communication. At present, as Stuart Chase said, "Nations are shouting at each other across seas of misunderstanding." Democratic and communist ideologies are competing for men's minds and loyalties on a world-wide scale. Literacy is a prerequisite for the dissemination of ideas, and, hopefully, for the making of more rational choices in matters of importance.

Through reading, people can understand and appreciate the common achievements and goals of each other as well as the unique contribution of the whole human family. A just and lasting peace depends upon global communication and acceptance of a new concept of greatness—greatness through cooperation and goodwill rather than through competition and power. Every avenue of communication should be employed to build this ideal of personal and universal greatness.

VARIOUS VIEWS OF READING

There are many misconceptions of reading. To some people, words are merely a supplement to pictures, an adjunct to television. To others, reading is a passive process—"expecting the book to come to you," as one student said. Many people have been persuaded that reading is synonymous with word calling: if you can pronounce the words correctly, you are reading—even though you have no idea what the author said.

Reading is more than seeing words clearly, more than pronouncing printed words correctly, more than recognizing the meaning of isolated words. Reading requires you to think, feel, and imagine. Effective reading is purposeful. The use one makes of his reading largely determines what he reads, why he reads, and how he reads.

The teacher's overall concept of reading strongly influences his methods of diagnosing reading difficulty and of teaching reading. If he thinks of reading primarily as a visual task, he will be concerned with the correction of visual defects and the provision of legible reading material. If reading to him is word recognition, he will drill on the basic sight vocabulary and word recognition skills. If he thinks reading is merely reproducing what the author says, he will direct the student's attention to the literal meaning of the passage and check his comprehension of it. If he views reading as a thinking process, he will be concerned with the reader's skill in making interpretations and generalizations, in drawing inferences and conclusions. If he thinks of reading as contributing to personal development and social welfare, he will provide his students with reading material that will help them develop sound values and that will have some application to their lives and to the modern world.

As a result of his historical approach to research into the causes of reading disability, Douglass wrote that "little attention has been directed toward developing an understanding of the nature of the reading process—of building a theoretical framework to help us comprehend the complex nature of what we call 'reading' " [26, p. 5]. If the process is not understood, the methods will be inadequate.

READING AND CHILD DEVELOPMENT

Reading as an integral part of the child's development has implications for his personal and social development as well as for his mental growth.

The child-development theory of reading has been presented in different ways by Burton [16], Olson [72], and Russell [84]. Essentially, this theory shows how various aspects of the child's development—his physical growth, his language development, his general mental development, and his social development—are related to and contribute to his development in reading. It in turn induces growth in the other areas. These relationships may be expressed schematically as follows:

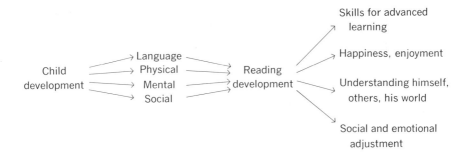

According to Olson, reading is part of a more or less predetermined pattern of growth which will emerge under favorable conditions. The child may be stimulated for a short time to exceed his natural rate of development, but special instruction, motivation, or medication will produce only a temporary spurt. The child quickly resumes his original growth pattern. At first glance, this point of view seems to discount the value of remedial work. However, if this work removes certain factors at home or at school that have been interfering with the child's reading development and provides him with instruction and practice that were neglected in his earlier years, it may promote permanent growth that is in line with his true developmental trend. Sometimes this growth takes place without special instruction. Olson tells the story of two brothers, both of whom were late in starting to grow. Once started, however, they made pronounced gains in reading, one with and one without remedial instruction.

The implication of this example is that a child will grow in reading ability at his own natural pace regardless of any attempted training which is premature. A part of the child-development theory, this principle of pacing is operating when any procedure permits the child to progress at his own inherent rate of growth.

Such a method encourages wide individual differences within the classroom where they already exist to a complex degree. In one eighth grade, some pupils had a third-grade reading ability; others had comprehension at the college level. A teacher in such a situation has no easy complete solution; he must do the best he can through highly individualized instruction.

Adolescent development depends upon all that has gone before. Past hopes and fears, as well as future aspirations and apprehensions, help to determine how the adolescent responds to the positive and negative influences of the present. The poor reader as he gets older is increasingly handicapped by his inability to read because his lack inhibits his achievement in every subject and dims his chances of going to college. He realizes that many desirable occupations will be closed to him. In peer groups of more able readers, he feels "different." Such alienation may affect his reading performance. Peer status is related to reading achievement [75].

Certain patterns of physical growth—especially accelerated or delayed growth—present special problems and more or less influence reading progress. Boys whose growth spurt comes early have an advantage: they can achieve a success in sports that helps to build up their self-esteem while boys maturing slowly miss this chance for prestige. With girls, accelerated growth is a social disadvantage. As one tall girl said, "If you're taller than boys, it's bad enough, but if you're brighter, it's fatal."

Other physiological changes and disabilities of the adolescent may give rise to feelings of self-consciousness or inferiority that frequently color attitudes toward achievement including reading. A youngster who is in the grip of emotional conflicts over any of the major adolescent problems may find himself unable to concentrate on books.

As Ephron has pointed out, fears enter into many reading problems [33]— fears about schoolwork, fears of real or imagined inadequacies, anxiety about mistakes, fears of failure in heterosexual adjustment, fears connected with family relationships. The fearful individual may daydream or withdraw and be unable to concentrate. Or, resenting authority, he may resort to vandalism. Such conduct may depress the student's reading achievement or aggravate reading difficulties. The implications for a program of reading may overwhelm a teacher because he is the axis around which reading proficiency develops. But if the teacher is knowledgeable about the importance of reading and continually evaluates his views and techniques of reading, there need be no dismay.

A STRUCTURED VIEW OF THE TEACHING OF READING

The first step in mastering a subject is to get a sense of its structure and perceive its relationships. Students have found it helpful to view the teaching of reading under four main headings: product, process, prerequisites, and procedures. Each of these becomes clear when described with adequate detail.

Product or Goals

This heading includes the main reading competencies, or skills, and goals that students will achieve. Among these are:

A Vocabulary of Basic Words That Recur Frequently, Plus a Constantly Increasing Repertory of Words That a Reader Recognizes on Sight. The lists grow in number and meanings through wide reading.

Word Recognition Skills—Ability to Pronounce and Recognize the Meaning of Unfamiliar Words. To do this the student may use a combination of (1) configuration clues—recognizing the word by its overall shape; (2) context clues—getting the meaning from the sentences in which the word is used; (3) phonics; (4) analysis of word structure; and (5) use of the dictionary.

Comprehension on Three Levels. The first level requires the student to derive literal meaning from sequential words and their grammatical relations to each other (the syntax) in sentences, paragraphs, and chapters. This ability to weave words together, giving each its proper weight and understanding the accumulation of significance in successive sentence structures, is what Edgar Dale called "reading the lines." Not merely parroting the author's words, the student must translate the author's thought into his own words. To achieve full comprehension, the reader must know not only the semantic and structural meaning but he must have had some experience related to the author's ideas.

One possible way of extracting the literal meaning of a paragraph is for the reader to hold in mind the content of the first sentence, while recognizing and relating the subsequent words and noting their sequence and relative importance. The reader then notes repeated key words, main ideas, and supporting details. He follows the author's argument. In reading a short story he is alert to discover the theme, the climax, and the resolution. In reading an article, he watches for the author's generalizations and conclusions. In fiction, he visualizes the characters, the setting, and the events. All of these efforts help the reader to understand fully what the author is saying. Yet it is possible "to read the lines" without getting their full value.

To go beyond the literal meaning of a passage—to "read between the lines" —the mature reader recognizes the author's intent and purpose, interprets his thought, passes judgment on his statements, searches for and interprets clues to character and plot, distinguishes between fact and opinion, and separates his own ideas from those of the author. In interpreting, he appraises the sources of the author, taking into account their competence and authority. This level of comprehension also requires the reader to recognize and interpret many literary devices such as metaphors and irony.

The third level, "reading beyond the lines," involves deriving implications, speculating about consequences, and drawing generalizations not stated by the author. On this level the reader may arrange the author's ideas into new patterns, extending their scope or fusing them with ideas that he himself has gained from reading or from experience. By means of both analysis and synthesis, the reader gains a new insight or a higher level of understanding that enables him to reflect on the significance of the ideas. In this rewarding type of reading, he brings initiative, originality, and thought to bear on the literal meaning of the printed page.

Reacting and Acting. This is still another dimension of reading. As one reads, he has feelings, mild or intense. He likes or dislikes the point of view of the selection, agrees or disagrees with it, finds it disturbing or reassuring. These emotional reactions interweave themselves with the cognitive process of reading so that not only does the reader get ideas—ideas get him.

Style also arouses some emotional response in the reader. A piece of writing may evoke pleasure in the author's felicity of expression, appreciation of the mode of characterization, and it may delight or exalt. Or it may bore, annoy, alarm, anger, or provoke.

If students read creatively, they involve themselves in the book or article, empathizing with a fictional or a real character as he fights and suffers. Some degree of emotional involvement in the book or article is basic to creative reading [48].

Great books or poems may be a source of self-revelation—they stimulate the reader to explore himself and his world, for "different minds have found different things in them" [77, pp. 11–12]. Such works have met the emotional needs of many kinds of people. Students read them for the sake of the things their words—if understood—can do for them. But understanding these works, of course, is not making them mean something the reader knows and approves of already, nor is it detecting their limitations. It is using them to stretch his mind as they have stretched the minds of so many different readers through the centuries [77, p. 15]. The reader not only reacts but moves to new acts—to learn about the nature of the world and of man; to enjoy leisure hours; to communicate ideas to others through speaking or writing; to secure information for solving problems; or to discover how to make and do things. Students may use reading as a springboard for creative activities—writing, dramatization, drawing, or painting.

The end result of reading is personal and social progression because it produces desirable changes in points of view, attitudes, feelings, and behavior. "Growth *through* reading is the ultimate goal of instruction, while growth *in* reading is the means to that end" [3, p. 542].

Rate of Reading. Speed in reading is a goal, certainly, but since it is an adjunct to several other goals and more relevant to topics such as machines and comprehension, a discussion of it appears later (see Chapter 7).

Oral Reading. Prior to 1900 reading aloud was widely practiced in American schools. After 1900, it began to decrease in popularity [92, chap. 11].

In an excellent summary of the arguments for and against oral reading, Spache [92, chap. 11] recognized the value of oral reading in diagnosing difficulties in word recognition skills, in reinforcing the visual image of the word in beginning reading, and in appreciating literature. Oral reading, through intonation, stress, and rhythm, gives additional clues to meaning that silent reading does not give. While admitting possible interference with silent reading from overemphasis on oral reading, Spache does not consider this serious if "oral reading is balanced by an adequate amount of practice in silent reading from the very beginning of instruction" [92, p. 194]. Edfeldt's study [32], using electromyographic methods of determining the extent of inner vocalization during silent reading, demonstrated that some degree of inner or silent speech is present in all silent reading, but is not necessarily detrimental to good silent reading, though it may result in a slower rate of silent reading among some individuals.

As a tool of communication, oral reading is being used increasingly by parents and by teachers and other professional people, especially those engaged in radio and television programs. Reading aloud is a possible method for use in adult education for democracy. The conclusion is that oral reading has a definite place in the reading program.

If oral reading is to take its rightful place in the total reading program, it must be properly taught. Its purpose in different situations should be recognized. The reader prepares carefully for his performance. The audience should be attentive and constructive in their comments. The harmful effects of round-the-room reading, formerly so common, in slowing down and boring the good reader and embarrassing the poor reader should deter any teacher from using this method.

One sensitive youngster described a slow reader's experience when required to read aloud before the class:

He would start to read a sentence and come to a word he couldn't understand. He would just look at it, and half the class would shout out the word. The teacher wouldn't say anything the first time, but when he came to another word the class would shout it out again, and the teacher would tell them it wasn't nice to shout out the answer. She would say, "We all know the word but let Johnny get it for himself." This went on for a while and Johnny got pretty upset. It was a horrible experience for him.

This practice dies hard despite all the legitimate criticism of it.

Since oral reading, with its attention to pronunciation and voice quality, may inhibit concentration on the meaning of what is being read [62], students should read the text silently before reading aloud, to grasp the ideas and feelings intended by the author. Understanding underlies the ability to convey meaning to the audience. To do this the oral reader must not only have mastered word recognition and comprehension skills but also the skills of oral expression—phrasing, stress, intonation, inflection, pitch, and rate. If material which the pupil can read with understanding is selected, oral errors will usually not be a problem. Dialogues, stories with a great deal of conversation, and simple plays are excellent materials for oral reading. If a pupil is intent on getting the meaning, to call attention to errors is annoying and unnecessary. It may lead him to become so preoccupied with articulation that he loses sight of the meaning altogether. His attention is divided between the mechanical process of articulation of the words and the thought process of getting the meaning. When a pupil pronounces each word separately with pauses between words, a break in thought is indicated; he loses the thought of the sentence.

A wealth of suggestions for teaching oral reading on all education levels is given in the University of Chicago reading conference report, *Oral Aspects of Reading* (December, 1955).

Process

The psychological process of reading includes all that goes on between intake—the stimulus of the printed word—and output—the reader's response in thought, spoken or written words, or action. Response may take the form of a mental image, a principle, or a new way of looking at something. It may be an answer to a question, a written summary, a drawing of a character or scene, or a motor response to a direction.

Visual Reception.   The reader must first get a clear visual impression on the retina of the eye, or rather a series of visual impressions as his eyes move across the line of print. The nervous impulses thus aroused are transmitted to the visual centers of the brain where they are "decoded" and their meaning is recognized. The words have now been perceived.

Perception.   This is a cognitive process by which visual impressions become meaningful in the light of the individual's past experience and present needs. It involves understanding, comprehending, organizing. "To perceive is to know" [38]. Perception of the meaning of printed words usually involves more than visual perception and discrimination, auditory perception and discrimination, and sound-symbol associations (see Chapter 6). The quality of one's perception is affected by the nature of the situation or set that exists at the moment, by the degree to which it occupies one's attention, by the ideas one has already acquired concerning it, and by one's needs, expectations, and personality [86]. Perception is an active process. It is part of a larger pattern. It is also the first step in a sequence that leads to further abstraction and then to generalization.

Individuals differ in their perceptual styles [81]. Usually the more able learners and the better readers see words as wholes. Generally the poor readers perceive word fragments and tend to be preoccupied with unimportant details. Able readers recognize familiar syllables and words almost as quickly as individual letters and take in phrases and short sentences as readily as single words. According to Hollingsworth's theory of reading as clue reduction [50], efficient readers require fewer clues than do poor readers in order to recognize words or phrases.

Conceptualization.   When perceptions are grouped into larger patterns that embrace classes or categories, conceptualization occurs. It contributes further to abstract thinking and generalization.

There is a reciprocal relation between perception and conceptualization. Concepts screen or filter impressions as they come into the mind. Thus the individual avoids dealing with a bewildering diversity of separate impressions. Perceptions are synthesized into concepts; concepts aid in the interpretation and organization of perceptions. This is possible because each perception leaves a trace or impression on the nervous system.

Conceptual ability and reading proficiency have a positive relation. Children of normal intelligence who fail in reading in the upper primary grades are often deficient in the ability to form concepts.

Research has clarified the first stages of the reading process—sensory impression, perception, conceptualization. What happens next is still a psychological no-man's-land.

Higher Levels of Association.   It has been hypothesized that at the higher levels of association there are patterns, schema, or circuits—interrelated memory subsystems. As these are activated simultaneously, they become larger and better organized. Factual content will not be retained long unless it becomes integrated. As the interconnections of these memory systems are improved, the individual gains increased ability to interpret what he reads. For the word-by-word reader, each association occurs separately, rather than in a larger memory pattern. It is easy to see why the "whole perceiver" has an advantage over the "part perceiver." Memory is not simply storing away impressions; it is retrieving what is relevant when it is needed. Thus the way a thing is learned helps to determine how it is applied.

Dr. William S. Gray describes the following steps in a mature reader's associative processes [40, p. 9]:

1. He recognizes the author's meaning.
2. He uses his previous knowledge to evaluate the soundness of the author's ideas, to reach valid conclusions, and to gain new insights and interests.
3. His feelings also enter into his decisions to accept or reject the ideas read.
4. He uses these enlarged patterns of associations in his further reading and thinking.

Questions as to the actual process in the mind of a person are waiting for research. How does the individual feel when he is confronted with a printed page? What incentive does he have for getting meaning from it? Why does he put forth much—or little—effort? How do his eyes and his mind actually work as he attempts to get the meaning? What use will he make of the knowledge he has assimilated? Questions like this can only be explored by study of the reading process.

Prerequisites

Certain prerequisites underlie both product and process. That is, the individual must possess distinct physical, mental, linguistic, personality, and environmental advantages if he is to realize his reading potential. Their presence or absence makes it either easy or difficult for a teacher to be successful in teaching reading.

Visual Factors.   In order to distinguish letter and word forms, the child must receive a clear visual impression of them. In clear vision, both eyes act together and their binocular acuity at reading distance is basic to reading efficiency. Most primary children are farsighted because visual acuity tends to develop gradually over several years. A kindergarten child generally cannot read print that is smaller than 24 point, i.e., ⅜ inch in height.

Visual clarity increases further as the eyes acquire ability to adjust to distance—accommodation and convergence [82]. To receive a clear image of the printed word, the eyes must focus on or converge on it. Children under four years of age usually lack this ability. However, most children have acquired it by the age of five. Eames [29] found no five-year-old child, in his study of 899 children, who scored below the minimum of binocular accommodation which he considered essential for reading. Girls were superior to boys; suburban children, to urban. Gifted children tend to be visually as well as intellectually a little more mature than average, with ordinary children reaching the peak of their power of convergence at fourteen or fifteen.

Since problems of convergence do not show up so frequently in tests of distant vision as in tests of near-point or reading distance, it is not very useful to place the Snellen wall chart at a distance of 20 feet and test each eye separately in the diagnosis of reading difficulty.

The reader must not only focus on words and distinguish them from the background, but he must fuse the separate images from each eye into a single clear image. Otherwise the words blur. This neuromuscular skill basic to word discrimination is primary to reading [93].

Among eye defects associated with poor reading is muscular imbalance which prevents the eyeballs from rotating into the best position for a clear unblurred image. When the eyeballs turn too far inward (*esophoria*) or too far outward (*exophoria*), it is a strain to fuse the images from the two eyes. Orthoptic training—special exercises for the eye muscles—has been helpful in correcting this difficulty.

Farsightedness, or *hyperopia*, is more likely to be associated with reading retardation than nearsightedness, or *myopia*. However, the percentage of the nearsighted increases among children past the age of nine. After studying a group of high school seniors, Jenkins [54] reported that the best students, on the average, had better near vision, and the poorer students had better far vision. Farsightedness occurred in 12 per cent of Eames's unselected children and in 43 per cent of the reading failures [31]. Astigmatism can be another source of reading difficulty.

A less well-known eye defect, *aniseikonia*, which brings about ocular images unequal in size or shape and thus inhibits fusion, may cause either ocular or general fatigue. By interfering with the peripheral view of the line of print, it may also decrease the span of recognition.

Another defect, *aniseidominance,* is seeing an image as brighter and nearer with one eye than the other. The effects are similar to those of aniseikonia.

From a study based on 3,500 cases, aged five to seventeen, including reading failures and unselected school children, Eames [31] summarized the various kinds of inefficient vision. One class of eye defects includes the serious cases resulting from neurological disorders and disease which only ophthalmologists can help. Another kind, closely related to the first, is defects which may be corrected by eye exercises, glasses, or surgery. Both kinds of eye defects may diminish sharpness and clarity of vision. Finally, even the kind not reducing the normal range may give children trouble in learning to read and may cause older students fatigue and discomfort. Although studies such as Eames's establish types of subnormal vision, evidence about the relation between reading performance and eye defects is inconsistent. There are several explanations:

First of all, individuals vary in their sensitivity; a small defect that does not bother one person may block another in his efforts to read [31, p. 4].

Second, some individuals are more highly motivated than others; they learn to read despite visual defects. Or a student may rise above the limitations of his visual handicap during a test but not for longer periods of study.

Again, certain visual factors that are closely related to reading may not yet have been completely defined; existing instruments may not measure them.

Most studies have considered only separate factors rather than patterns or syndromes of visual defects.

A certain amount of eye uncoordination may be "the effect rather than the cause of poor reading" [114, p. 121].

Since any visual defect may cause discomfort and disinclination to read, any study of reading problems should include a visual screening test (see Chapter 4).

Although visual difficulties may hinder a student in learning to read, correction of them does not in itself ensure success. There still remains the task of teaching him to read.

Hearing and Speech. Children who lack auditory acuity cannot imitate the speech they hear, and speech is the avenue to reading. Some children whose auditory acuity is intact still cannot perceive as words the sounds they hear. Still others lack auditory discrimination—ability to distinguish various language sounds. This capacity is a vital prerequisite to the development of oral communication and also to success in reading [120]. Boys are more often handicapped than girls in practicing phonic analysis that is based on auditory discrimination.

Physiological Prerequisites. Malnutrition may lower a child's energy level. Endocrine disturbances may make a child either lethargic or overactive, interfering indirectly but seriously with his learning to read. Stresses and strains that alter the chemistry of the body and affect the synaptic transmission may lower the speed with which an individual reads familiar words or recognizes unfamiliar words [89]. However, Staiger [94] found that the administration of a drug known as deanol did not improve the performance of severely retarded readers.

Intact Neurological Organization and Functioning. This is another pre-requisite to learning to read. Vernon concluded her summary of research with the statement that "the relationship to reading disability of incomplete lateralization and cerebral dominance is extremely obscure" [114, p. 155]. Similarly, more recent neurological and psychological research recognizes (1) the difficulty of diagnosing neurological disorganization, (2) the importance of early diagnosis, and (3) the importance of focusing on what the child can do successfully rather than on his disturbances (see Chapter 16 for more detail).

Mental Prerequisites. Though it is known that a certain level of intelligence is necessary for success in learning to read, this level has not been precisely determined. It has often been stated that a mental age of six and one-half is requisite for beginning reading instruction, but many studies are challenging this figure. Results indicate that children with lower mental ages can be taught to read by means of special instruction and special materials—e.g., the Initial Teaching Alphabet (i.t.a.), the electric typewriter (with an adult responding as the child strikes the keys), and the Denver kindergarten program. The child's language experience, auditory and visual perception, and overall development are more significant for this purpose than his mental age. In fact, even a high mental age does not ensure success in beginning reading when the child lacks readiness in other important respects.

Evidence is accumulating that it is not a waste of time to teach reading to adolescents with individual intelligence quotients as low as 50. One boy with an IQ of 52 learned to read signs, directions, and other simple, practical material that he needed to master for a job. If a mentally retarded child is reading about as well as his intelligence permits, he should not be considered a remedial reading case.

There is need to experiment with various teaching methods designed expressly for students possessing various degrees of mental ability. Since there is always the possibility that the test results do not represent the individual's true potential mental ability, it seems wise, as P. E. Vernon suggested in a comment made to the author, to give each student the best possible instruction under favorable conditions and see how he responds to it.

Reading and intelligence, as measured, have so much in common that one would expect a high correlation between reading tests and tests of general mental ability. Actually, correlations of .50 to .80 are often reported between scores on group intelligence tests and scores on reading tests. The relation between word knowledge and general intelligence is especially close. Since group intelligence tests demand so much reading ability, it is easy to see how they may mismeasure the mental ability of poor readers and to understand why the group intelligence test should not be used to predict growth in reading.

Group intelligence tests that yield both a verbal and a quantitative score give a little more information than do those that yield a single score. The correlation between reading scores and quantitative-intelligence-test scores is much lower than that between reading scores and verbal-intelligence-test scores. With elementary school children tested by the California Test of Mental Maturity, the correlations were as follows (101):

Language factors with Thorndike-McCall Reading Test	824
Nonlanguage factors with Thorndike-McCall Reading Test	557

With ninth-grade pupils, the correlations of the California Test of Mental Maturity were as follows [111]:

Language factors with Iowa Silent Reading Tests	685 ± .041
Nonlanguage factors with Iowa Silent Reading Tests	356 ± .068
Language factors with Traxler Silent Reading Test	753 ± .034
Nonlanguage factors with Traxler Silent Reading Test	357 ± .068

With the same age group, using different intelligence tests, Hage and Stroud [43] likewise found that reading comprehension and reading rate correlated more highly with verbal than with nonverbal intelligence scores. Verbal-intelligence-test scores are affected more than nonverbal scores by reading proficiency.

With college students there were equally large discrepancies between the correlations of their quantitative comprehension scores on the Iowa Silent Reading Tests and their linguistic and quantitative scores on both the American Council on Education Psychological Examination for College Freshmen and the California Test of Mental Maturity [69, 121]. As might be expected, group-intelligence-test scores correlate more highly with tests of reading comprehension than with tests of reading rate.

Even the individual Stanford-Binet test, which has been widely used to estimate reading potential, tends to underestimate the intelligence of poor readers, because it includes so many items that require knowledge and use of words [11].

The Wechsler individual intelligence tests have the advantage of yielding both a verbal and a nonverbal score. The assumption has been made that when the nonverbal IQ is significantly higher than the verbal, the individual's reading can be improved up to the level of the nonverbal score. This is often, but not necessarily, true; children usually have higher nonverbal than verbal IQs on the Wechsler Intelligence Scale for Children (WISC). Moreover, several students who make the same intelligence-test score may differ, because of many internal and external factors, in their ability to acquire various reading skills.

Retarded readers have shown distinctive scoring patterns on the WISC. They tend to score low on the subtests of Information and Arithmetic and relatively low on Digit Span and Coding. On Picture Arrangement, Block Design, Picture Completion and Object Assembly, they often score relatively high. However, different groups of retarded readers, such as bilinguals and unilinguals, have shown different profiles, bilinguals being low on Information, Comprehension, Vocabulary, and Digit-Span subtests, and relatively high in Picture Completion, Picture Arrangement, Block Design, Object Assembly, and Coding. They were significantly higher than the unilinguals in the subtests of Coding and Arithmetic, and significantly lower on Information and Vocabulary.[1] Profiles also vary with the reading tests used and still more in individual cases. Bearing in mind these characteristic patterns, teachers can study individual profiles to observe deviations that may have special significance. These profiles indicate patterns of strength and weakness in the individual's mental functioning. Each high or low point represents some mental process involved in reading or basic to reading ability that may possibly be improved by practice and instruction (see Chapter 13).

Linguistic Prerequisites. Linguists regard listening and speaking as prerequisites to reading. One must associate the letters with the sounds of the spoken words for which they are the visual symbols. The stories that children dictate to be written down by the teacher present only one unknown—the printed form; the sounds of their own words are already familiar to them. "Word sense" and ability to recognize words in isolation as well as words in context are linguistic prerequisites to reading.

Linguists also emphasize, as a part of reading for meaning, an understanding of sentence structure, the source of syntax of English sentences. Meanings, they maintain, come not only from semantics of class words such as nouns, verbs, adjectives, and adverbs but also from structural signals such as word order and position. These items add another layer of meaning to a sequence of words, which becomes an integral part of the meaning. For example, the sentence, "The man killed the dog," has one meaning; but if the two nouns exchange positions so that the sentence reads "The dog killed the man," obviously the meaning is strikingly different even though no words have been added or omitted. It is operations like these which the linguists say are pertinent to reading. Meaning comes from constructions within constructions within a sentence rather than from strings of words. To unlock the full meaning of a sentence or passage, the child must have the vocabulary, comprehend the syntax, and possess the necessary experiences referred to in the content.

Personality and Emotional Prerequisites. Research based on paper-and-pencil personality tests has repeatedly failed to find a significant relationship between personality and reading achievement. Projective techniques, however,

[1] Eldon E. Ekwall, "The Use of WISC Subtest Profiles in the Diagnosis of Reading Difficulties," unpublished doctoral dissertation, University of Arizona, Tucson, Ariz., 1966, pp. 147–152.

have uncovered some common personality patterns among severely retarded readers. The emotional difficulties associated with reading have been studied more extensively than the emotional strengths.

Value System, Motivation, and Self-concept. These three are interrelated. They may be the intangibles that account for the 24 per cent of the variance not accounted for by all the forty to fifty factors measured in Holmes and Singer's substrata studies [51]. The desire to read is the resultant of present needs, past experience, and future hopes.

For the little child, desire for the approval of his teacher and his parents is a strong motivation. However, intrinsic interest in the content is a more stable long-run motivation. For the retarded teen-ager, a specific need sometimes awakens a desire to read better. He may need to pass the Army tests or to fill out an application blank for a part-time job or a driver's license.

In the words of one adolescent, needs like these have spurred previously indifferent teen-agers "to get down to work on this reading business." When asked why they wanted to read better, several slow learners gave these reasons: "so no one will laugh at me," "so as not to be stupid," "so no one will cheat me."

The most persistent and pervasive influence is the individual's self-concept and self-ideal. The self-concept may be predictive of reading improvement. It also affects, and is affected by, reading improvement. On the primary level, children's self-concepts were, in general, more predictive of reading achievement than their scores on the Detroit Beginning First-Grade Intelligence Test given near the end of the kindergarten year [118]. On all age levels, the self-concept seems to be an important factor in achievement. Brookover [13] found that seventh-grade pupils who had a positive attitude toward their ability in a given subject were high achievers in that subject. Their self-concepts were more accurate predictors than other established general estimates of ability. A student's self-concept also affects his motivation.

Many children and adolescents seem indifferent to school learning. Of these pupils teachers often say, "They're just not interested in reading." They do not read voluntarily; they show no enthusiasm for reading in class. Yet one of the teacher's most important tasks is to develop in his pupils a love of reading. What motivates students to read wisely and well?

To understand any instance of motivated behavior, teachers need to know what is stimulating the individual, what responses he has made to such patterns of stimulation, what consequences those responses had, and what deprivations he has experienced [45]. A certain degree of anxiety is basic to learning; relieving anxiety becomes a goal. The individual is also motivated to maintain an equilibrium in body functioning; he tries to correct any imbalances, whether physiological or psychological.

Many psychologists have believed that basic motivations are formed during childhood and that it is therefore difficult to change the motivations of adults. However, some evidence is accumulating to show that adult motivations can be changed by education.

Motivations may be arranged in a hierarchy, starting with the most temporary, extrinsic, and superficial, and proceeding to the most lasting, pervasive, and deep-seated:

Stars, teacher's marks, and other extrinsic rewards.

Praise and blame. The effect of these incentives varies widely. Praise may stimulate one student but lessen the effort of another. Praise given by a loved and respected person will stimulate, whereas praise given by a person disliked will often have the opposite effect. Lavish, indiscriminate praise soon loses its value. Some individuals respond better to blame than to praise. In other cases, ignoring the person may be as effective as either praising or blaming. Neither praise nor blame is of much significance unless the student understands *why* his performance was good or poor.

Success. Usually success leads to further success just as failure breeds more failure. The child's desire for mastery and achievement is thwarted when he fails in such a socially important activity as reading. After successful reading experiences, the individual tends to raise his level of aspiration. However, the goal must be attainable, and the individual must see that he is making progress toward it. He also needs to understand the process by which he arrived at his correct responses and the reasons for his mistakes. If the teacher goes over a test paper with the students, either individually or in class, they will see why they made certain mistakes and learn how to avoid them in the future.

Increased competence. The satisfaction that comes from increased competence is motivating. For beginners, just knowing how to read is motivating. In other words, skill in reading is in itself a motivating force and a prerequisite to interest in reading. Teachers should never discount the motivating value of knowledge and skill. Since reading depends on skill in using abstract symbols, the child who has difficulty in dealing with abstractions becomes discouraged and may soon develop a general indifference toward reading.

Curiosity. This is a prime motivation for reading at any age. Unless suppressed, curiosity persists throughout life and frequently turns a person to reading, which offers wide opportunities to satisfy his mood of inquiry. In a study where intelligence was kept constant, children who were rated by their teachers as having a high degree of curiosity tended to sense the meaning of sentences more accurately than did those whose curiosity was rated as low [68].

Self-realization. Perhaps the most basic motivation of all is the deep-seated desire to develop one's potentialities, to do what one is best fitted to do, to function as well as one is capable of functioning. Reading can lead to self-realization or self-actualization. While the individual may be motivated by his observed disparity between his self-ideal and his present achievement, too wide a disparity may cause several types of maladjustment. This is especially true of an individual who feels he must achieve goals that have been imposed upon him by his parents or his peer group. Students may be motivated to improve their reading by such long-range goals as admission to an Ivy League college or preparation for a certain vocation. Their more immediate and specific goals include getting an A on the next spelling test or obtaining information for a group report.

Faith may be a motivation in some remedial cases—faith in a new method, faith in a machine, faith in a new approach to their reading problem. Just being given special individual attention sometimes motivates a student to make a marked improvement.

Environmental Prerequisites. Many environmental conditions are conducive to success in reading. Of primary importance are the preschool prereading experiences that give children a foundation for reading instruction. All language learning stems from a combination of firsthand experiences and the learned or vicarious experiences that are acquired through reading. Parent-child relationships and parental attitudes toward reading have a strong influence on the child's self-concept and his attitudes toward reading. Time to read and access to suitable reading materials are important in building reading interest.

On the older age level, Wylie [124] found that junior high school students from lower socioeconomic backgrounds tended to doubt their ability to do college work; they said they did not want to go to college, even if they had the ability. But she also found that these negative attitudes were not equally strong in all students at this socioeconomic level. From a more carefully controlled study, Lovell and Woolsey [64] concluded that the factors responsible for failure in reading, or for very poor reading, operate in all social classes.

How pervasive is the undefined influence of the mass media of communication? To what degree do they elevate reading tastes? To what degree do they lower the standards of people who might otherwise read more mature material? The heavy content of violence in certain TV programs and some paperbacks may serve as a safety valve for some persons but stimulate unruly impulses in others. In her annual summaries of research in reading published in *The Reading Teacher* (1964, 1965), Helen Robinson has analyzed the content of current books, magazines, and newspapers; estimated the amount of time that persons of all ages spend in passively watching television, as compared with the time they spend in reading; and discussed other sociological substrata factors.

Procedures for Teaching

Teaching procedures develop out of an understanding of (1) the product —what the learner can do when he has achieved the objectives; (2) the prerequisites he brings to the learning situation; and (3) the mental processes he employs. The teaching-learning process may be represented by this diagram:

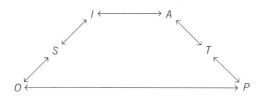

The Individual. The focus is on *O*—the individual, whom psychologists often refer to as the *organism.* His physical condition, his mental abilities, his skills, his knowledge, and his need and desire to read—any or all of these items mentioned so far may make him more or less responsive to the teacher's instruction. His immediate intent or mind-set toward the reading situation governs his concentration and partly determines how much effort he puts forth. It influences his selection of books or parts of books and what he looks for. He sees relations, recognizes important ideas, and skips irrelevant details. On the other hand, his intent or mood may blind him to certain words, cause him to misinterpret some words, or give overpotency to others.

The Situation. After the student, *O,* the next concern is the classroom or *stimulus situation, S,* over which the teacher has most control. The reading material is the focus, with both format and content important. Thick books with few open spaces for resting the eyes and mind often repel older children who lack proficiency in reading. Books densely packed with facts dissatisfy even the superior readers who must struggle in organizing the material to select key sentences and words from crowded pages.

The stimulus situation also includes the setting in which the reading is done—physical conditions, pupil-teacher relations, peer relations, parent-child relations. Although the relation between classroom illumination and reading efficiency remains somewhat ambiguous, there are wide individual differences in reading proficiency under varied conditions of lighting. All parts of the classroom or library where students continually read must provide good illumination.

To be conducive to reading, a classroom should be relatively quiet and orderly, the teacher planning activities to motivate reading and encourage and reward individual interests. Anxieties must not be intense, for learning takes place best in a secure, friendly, inspiring environment.

Students learn to adopt behavior that is rewarded or reinforced. The more quickly the reward follows the correct response, the better. Rats running in a maze showed a marked drop in errors when rewarded and a sharp increase in errors after the reward was withdrawn. Pigeons did not learn when the reward was deferred until the end result had been achieved; they learned rapidly when any move in the right direction brought them food. The Skinner reading machines, based on a highly specific analysis of learning, utilize this principle. Punishment may cause the child to continue an undesirable response which, if ignored, might have disappeared quickly. How different this theory is from the practice of too many teachers. Instead of reinforcing correct reading with a smile, a nod, a word of approval, they tend to say nothing until the student makes an error. Then they pounce upon him.

But the student who is absorbed in his reading needs no extrinsic reward; the fascinating content of the book is enough.

Instruction-application. Instruction and application (*I* and *A* in the diagram) should form a single continuous process. A teacher needs to show, not just tell, students how to recognize and remember new words; how to read a sentence, a paragraph, a chapter; how to interpret a poem or a story; how to read critically and creatively. He should go through the process with the students as many times as they need in order to learn it thoroughly. From then on the students should apply the procedure regularly in their independent reading. For example, in learning how to find and interpret clues to character, motives, and plot, first the teacher and his students find and discuss clues in several stories. Then the students read a story at home and report to the class their interpretation, supporting it with clues. Eventually the students will use this technique automatically whenever they read independently. It will greatly increase the enjoyment they gain from literature.

Reading material presented in different ways brings different results, even with the same individuals. A given method will not get the same results a second time if any part of the situation is different.

Trace or Memory. The fifth symbol of the teaching-learning diagram is *T*, referring to the *trace* or impressions of previous experiences left on the nervous system. It is on this imprint of previous learning that proficiency in reading depends. If associations between words and their meanings are strengthened by success and satisfactions, additional knowledge and skills are more readily retained. The insecure or discouraged student has a special need to see results—a growing pile of cards containing words that he can recognize at sight, a graph showing an upcurve in speed or comprehension, a recently written or tape-recorded summary that is clearly superior to one he made last month.

Students differ widely in ability to retain what they have read. In one experiment [25] pupils in grades 7 to 9 were given three factual passages to be read at their own rates. They were tested on comprehension and memory immediately after the reading; the test was repeated one day, fourteen days, thirty days, and one hundred days later. Factors which influence memory are three:

Familiar material is more easily remembered than new or strange material. One's memory of the ideas he gains in reading is more permanent if the words are anchored in his experience. Everyone has wells of meaning into which he dips when he is confronted with an unfamiliar word.

Second, the length of time intervening influences trace. The rate of forgetting is rapid at first, then slows. There is a positive correlation between an individual's immediate memory and his delayed memory.

The third is meaningfulness of the material. The initial forgetting for factual material is less abrupt than for nonsense syllables. With meaningful material, the point of complete forgetting is not approximated even after 100 days.

The child should use his information from reading at once because use reinforces retention. In general, retention is best when the student, engaging his mind actively, has sufficient time to register an impression, to associate new ideas with past experience and then to enjoy the knowledge.

Perception of the Reading Situation. *P* refers to the reader's *perception* of the reading situation—whether he perceives reading negatively as drudgery and a source of anxiety or hopefully as a source of satisfaction. The trace that is left, with its accompanying feeling tone, affects the individual's approach to the next reading. Once, after a class had enjoyed reading and discussing a ghost story, they looked forward eagerly to the next period. They asked, "Are we going to have another story?" But instead, they were given an article on cultured pearls. They greeted the teacher the next day without enthusiasm, and asked, "Are we going to have another *lesson?*"

It makes a great difference in the students' expectancy, readiness, and response whether they approach a reading task with boredom, dislike, anxiety, fear, and feelings of inferiority, or with enthusiasm, confidence, and interest. The student may perceive the new situation as pleasurable or threatening, as "something in which he will succeed" or as "something in which he will fail" [96, p. 68].

Basic to all teaching procedures is the attempt to make sure that each pupil has a reason for wanting to read and an expectation that pleasure and satisfaction will result. If these conditions prevail, the child will develop his own way of learning. He will learn to identify methods that bring good results and will be able to apply them appropriately. It is the role of the teacher to share his knowledge of effective learning methods with his pupils and to create, so far as possible, conditions conducive to learning.

RELATION OF READING TO OTHER LANGUAGE SKILLS

Reading occupies a special place in the complex of language skills whose other components are listening, speaking, writing, and spelling. Reading seems to weave in and out among them all; it presupposes many abilities from the outset and some developed along the way, and at the same time it paves the way for still higher linguistic achievement.

Speech is primary. The child listens to his mother's words and comprehends some of them before he begins to speak, an event that usually occurs during the second year of life. The language learned in infancy has deep emotional roots. In bilingual children the teachers disrupt these roots when they forbid them to speak their native language at school. By giving children opportunities to think about what they hear and to verbalize their thoughts, teachers aid children to develop language skills basic for reading.

Listening

Both listening and reading are means of receiving communication. Both require the interpretation of symbols, heard in one instance, seen in the other. Both require skills such as interpreting the main idea, perceiving relationships, recognizing sequence of ideas, sensing the mood and intent of the speaker or writer, and organizing and evaluating his ideas. A person who can do all this while listening should be able to read content of similar difficulty.

According to Duker [28], who pointedly summarizes the relationship between reading and listening abilities, visual presentation, as in reading, has been found to be more effective than auditory presentation with persons of higher intelligence and reading ability. The difficulty of the material also affects the relation between listening comprehension and reading comprehension. Easy material may be comprehended equally well through listening or reading. If the material is difficult, students of high scholastic aptitude and reading ability comprehend more efficiently by reading than by listening. Auditory methods seem to be preferred when content is personal or intimate; reading, when "close discrimination and critical judgment are called for" [7, p. 55]. However, King [59] found no significant differences between boys' and girls' responses to auditory as compared with visual presentation of test material.

Fortunately the teacher need not choose, but can derive the most efficient comprehension through a combination of visual and auditory devices. One will reinforce the other.

Individuals vary greatly in their relative ability to comprehend by listening and by reading. Those who have auditory defects may find reading a better avenue of learning; visual defects may increase the relative listening efficiency of others. Practice also makes a difference: the person who has had more practice in listening than in reading is likely to be more proficient in auditory than in visual skills, and vice versa. Unless the individual is known to have had much more practice in one skill than the other, a higher competence in listening than in reading indicates an undeveloped reading potential.

It is difficult to say which of these communication arts is the more important. On the average, elementary school children are expected to listen two and one-half hours daily, or 57.5 per cent of their class time. Adults spend, on the average, much more time—42 per cent according to one estimate—in listening than in any other communication activity. Since television has increased the percentage of children's listening time, listening instruction in the curriculum is receiving more attention. By the time children have completed the sixth or seventh grade, their reading comprehension tends to surpass their listening comprehension. Of course, they do receive continuous instruction in reading but scarcely any in listening.

To date, the results of research on the effectiveness of brief periods of systematic instruction in listening have been inconclusive. Two investigators reported improved listening comprehension as a result of improved reading comprehension, while two others found no significant transfer. However, direct instruction in listening has been shown to be superior to indirect or incidental instruction.

There is an art in listening; a science, too. It is a language skill deserving more research. The attitude is important—the listener must expect to hear something of interest or value. He can get ready to listen by thinking about the topic: What does he already know about it? What does he want to know? How does it relate to his life?

He must listen for the main ideas and the facts or illustrations to support them. He has to catch ideas on the fly, weighing emotionally charged words and ignoring distractions.

After catching a significant point of a speech, the listener can annex it to his other ideas if the speaker's delivery is slow enough. And as soon as possible, the listener should review what he has learned from the speech by talking about it. Like reading with its method of Survey Q3R, listening has a formula: TQLR—Tune in, Question, Listen, Review.

Can one read or study efficiently while listening to the radio? This is a much disputed question between parents and children. Students differ in their opinions about the effect of having the radio turned on while they are studying. Some claim that it increases their reading efficiency; others admit that it distracts their attention. Though one experiment gave evidence that high school pupils studied more effectively when a musical radio program was turned on in study hall, this effect may have been obtained under the stimulus of a novel situation; it might not hold day in and day out. Fendrick [34] concluded, from a more carefully controlled experiment with two groups of sixty college students, that music played while students were studying probably decreased their efficiency and that it affected the more intelligent students more seriously than it did those of lower mental ability. Loss in efficiency is greatest when noise begins. After a while students tend to ignore it. At that stage silence becomes a distraction. Thus the radio, because of its variety, is likely to be more distracting than a continued noise such as monotonous hammering.

There are, of course, individual differences in the degree to which listening to the radio interferes with comprehension in reading. Some persons can concentrate in spite of distracting music, conversation, and noise. Some may even work more intensely because of the distraction. However, in the long run, resisting distraction is nerve-racking; it tends to leave a person tired and irritable.

Television presents additional problems [73]. Some high school pupils insisted that they could study while watching television. When asked how they did it, they said they did their studying during the commercials! Such remarks indicate the need for more information about the effects on reading efficiency of listening to the radio and watching television. Incidentally, there would be value in knowing the relative effects on reading of such activities as seeing motion pictures, going on excursions, participating in discussions, and engaging in handwork or creative artwork.

Speaking

Some people talk more than they listen; many talk more than they read. Studies have shown that people spend 75 per cent of their communicative effort in speaking and listening, as compared with 25 per cent in writing and reading [20]. Pronouncing the words on a page aloud is the usual bridge from listening to reading for meaning. Some linguists say it is the only bridge. They define reading as the process by which printed words are translated into spoken words and then endowed with the meanings that are already associated with the spoken words.

Facility in oral expression is a prerequisite to success in beginning reading. For beginning readers the easiest words to learn are those that are in their speaking vocabulary, arranged in their own sentence patterns, and that have personal significance for them. As the child grows older, his reading vocabulary tends to exceed his speaking vocabulary—he understands more words as he reads than he uses in speaking.

In general, there is a reciprocal relation between speaking and reading. Not being aware of the structure of the English language blurs the relationship between words and phrases. Effective speech makes reading more accurate. Conversely, efficient reading enriches oral communication.

Oral reading depends on many of the same processes that are involved in effective speech. Children who make speech errors such as "jest" for "just," or "wha cha doin' " for "what are you doing" tend to develop sound-letter associations that are difficult to correct. Many of the boners reported by teachers seem to arise from faulty perception and pronunciation of words [8]:

Acumen is the white of an egg.

In mathematics Persia gave us the dismal system.

The clown in *As You Like It* was named Touchdown.

The relation of faulty oral expression and speech defects to silent-reading ability is less clear. Research on this relationship is inconclusive. The most favorable effects on silent-reading achievement have been obtained by a combined language arts program that included speech improvement lessons, instruction in attentive listening and observation, techniques of self-expression, practice in speech sound discrimination, and practice in speech production, choral speaking, and discussion [57].

There is usually a high incidence of functional speech problems among children referred for remedial reading. Many poor readers with defective articulation have problems of auditory discrimination. The sounds difficult to discriminate are often the sounds difficult to articulate. For these cases, speech therapy plus reading therapy given to pupils with functional speech defects has improved reading skills.

Writing

Receiving through reading the thought that an author wishes to convey and transmitting that thought to others by speaking or writing are the intake and output ends of the communication continuum. Many schools and colleges are giving more attention to measuring students' ability to take in ideas than to communicate them. Since the objective-type silent-reading tests so widely used afford little practice in reading to communicate, more valuable is the unstructured or creative-response type of test that calls for a written response [102].

Whatever improves a student's oral language helps him to improve his writing. Understanding of the structure of English sentences contributes to both his writing and his reading. Practice in interpreting the literature he reads gives him a feeling for style, which might be expected to influence his writing more than a formal study of grammar. However, Wyatt [123] did not find a definite relationship of extensive reading to certain writing skills of selected sixth-grade pupils.

Proficiency in reading, writing, and speaking develops all skills concomitantly; one language art reinforces the other. Because speech starts sooner than the other two, writing as well as reading may be more affected by speech difficulties than vice versa. The teaching of effective writing should not be isolated in English classes but should become a part of science, social studies, art, and music programs.

Spelling

Spelling is a part of the constellation of language arts. It is related to word recognition, grasp of meaning, vocabulary, and comprehension [52]. Spelling is concerned with significant units of speech sound (*phonemes*) as each is represented by a letter or a combination of letters (*graphemes*), and as they are put together in words or parts of words (*morphemes*). In spelling, the student recalls the symbols for various sounds (*encoding*). He thinks of individual letters and may get a visual image of the whole word. In reading, the process is reversed. The child associates the printed symbol with the sound of the word and its associated meaning (*decoding*). The good reader does not pay attention to each individual letter [35, 46].

Students tend to be either good or poor in both reading and spelling. Correlations are almost as high as those between reading and group-intelligence-test scores [71, 117]. Improvement in reading often leads to better spelling. It does not follow, however, that deficiencies in reading or vocabulary necessarily cause poor spelling.

Improvement in spelling is often a by-product of wide reading and varied learning activities in each subject field. A spelling text that had a broad language approach and gave the student many opportunities to write words produced spelling achievement as high as that produced by a narrower phonetic approach [44]. None of the methods used in the Cedar Rapids, Iowa, schools was "consistently superior to the others" [76]. Teachers should feel free to develop any method or combination of methods which they can use successfully with their students. Pupils gain a sense of spelling power as they are helped to group similar elements. For example, having learned the *ing* cluster, they can spell this ending in many words such as *playing* and *eating* [103].

Since writing almost always demands correct spelling, students should learn to spell the words they need to write. Some spelling lists are constructed on this basis.

Handwriting is related to spelling; poor handwriting may further confuse inaccurate visual word images. Directing children's attention to the correct spelling of words that they have misspelled is a better way of making them aware of their errors than by checking or underlining their misspelled words.

Integration of the Communication Arts

The communication arts should be closely integrated, one growing out of another. Paying careful attention to a television program may enable a student to make an effective oral or written report. A student composition that concerns something of real interest to a student may make excellent reading material for the whole class. Holbrook [49] gives many examples of ways in which this kind of writing was produced by pupils in his slow-learning class. The dramatization of dialogues [113] gives practice in both reading and speech. A poem, article, or essay often serves as a springboard for creative writing. As students listen to good literature and read good books, they acquire a feeling for the style and rhythm of English speech, essentials for effective writing. Thus one avenue of communication contributes to the others. And all the aspects of language help to form the individual's developing personality. It is through expression that the individual discovers himself and achieves self-realization.

REFERENCES

1. Anderson, Harold, and Robert J. Baldauf: "A Study of a Measure of Listening," *Journal of Educational Research,* vol. 57, pp. 197–200, December, 1963.

2. Anderson, Irving H., and Walter F. Dearborn: *The Psychology of Teaching Reading,* The Ronald Press Company, New York, 1952.

3. Artley, A. Sterl: "But—Skills Are Not Enough," *Education,* vol. 79, p. 542, May, 1959.

4. Ausubel, David P.: *The Psychology of Meaningful Verbal Learning: An Introduction to School Learning,* Grune & Stratton, Inc., New York, 1963, p. 255.

5. Ausubel, David P., and Mohammed Youssef: "Role of Discriminability in Meaningful Parallel Learning," *Journal of Educational Psychology,* vol. 54, pp. 331–336, December, 1963.

6. Bender, Loretta: *Youth and Delinquency,* State Commission on Youth and Delinquency, Albany, New York, 1956, pp. 71–72.

7. Berg, Paul: "Reading in Relation to Listening," *Evaluating College Reading Programs,* Fourth Yearbook of the Southwest Reading Conference, Texas Christian University Press, Fort Worth, Tex., 1955, pp. 52–60.

8. *Bigger and Better Boners,* The Viking Press, Inc., New York, 1952.

9. Birch, Herbert G., and Lillian Belmont: "Auditory-Visual Integration in Normal and Retarded Readers," *American Journal of Orthopsychiatry,* vol. 34, pp. 852–861, October, 1964.

10. Blankenship, Jane: "A Linguistic Analysis of Oral and Written Style," *Quarterly Journal of Speech,* vol. 48, pp. 419–422, December, 1962.

11. Bond, Guy L., and Leo C. Fay: "A Comparison of the Performance of Good and Poor Readers on the Individual Items of the Stanford-Binet Scale, Forms L and M," *Journal of Educational Research,* vol. 43, pp. 475–479, February, 1950.

12. Braun, Jean S.: "Relation between Concept Formation Ability and Reading Achievement at Three Developmental Levels," *Child Development,* vol. 34, pp. 675–682, September, 1963.

13. Brookover, Wilbur B., Shailer Thomas, and Ann Paterson: "Self-concept of Ability and School Achievement," *Sociology of Education,* vol. 37, pp. 271–278, Spring, 1964.

14. Bruner, J. S., and others: *A Study of Thinking,* John Wiley & Sons, Inc., New York, 1956.

15. Bryan, Quentin R.: "Relative Importance of Intelligence and Visual Perception in Predicting Reading Achievement," *California Journal of Educational Research,* vol. 15, pp. 44–48, January, 1964.

16. Burton, William H.: *Reading in Child Development,* The Bobbs-Merrill Company, Inc., Indianapolis, 1956.

17. Buswell, Guy T.: "The Process of Reading," *The Reading Teacher,* vol. 13, pp. 108–114, December, 1959.

18. Cannell, Charles F., and James C. MacDonald: "The Impact of Health News on Attitudes and Behavior," *Journalism Quarterly,* vol. 33, pp. 315–323, Summer, 1956.

19. *Carnegie Corporation of New York Quarterly,* vol. 10, p. 1, July, 1962.

20. Carney, John J., Jr.: "Anyone Who Writes Well Can Speak Well," *Improving College and University Teaching,* vol. 12, pp. 209–211, Autumn, 1964.

21. Carroll, John B.: "The Analysis of Reading Instruction: Perspectives from Psychology and Linguistics," *Theories of Learning and Instruction,* Sixty-third Yearbook of the National Society for the Study of Education, part I, University of Chicago Press, Chicago, 1964.

22. Catone, Harold C.: "Individual Differences in the Reading Processes of Ninth-Grade Retarded Readers," unpublished doctoral dissertation, University of Arizona, Tucson, Ariz., 1966.

23. Conference on Research Design and the Teaching of English, San Francisco, 1963, *Research Design and the Teaching of English,* Proceedings, National Council of Teachers of English, Champaign, Ill., 1964.

24. DeBoer, John J.: "Structure in Relation to Reading," *Education,* vol. 84, pp. 525–528, May, 1964.

25. Dietz, Alfred G., and George E. Jones: "Factual Memory of Secondary School Pupils for a Short Article Which They Read a Single Time," *Journal of Educational Psychology,* vol. 22, pp. 586–598, November, 1931; pp. 667–676, December, 1931.

26. Douglass, Malcolm P.: "A Point of View about Reading," *Claremont Reading Conference,* Twenty-seventh Yearbook, Claremont Graduate School and University Center, Claremont, Calif., 1963.

27. Duker, Sam: "Listening," *Review of Educational Research,* vol. 31, pp. 145–151, April, 1961.

28. Duker, Sam: *Listening Readings,* The Scarecrow Press, Inc., New York, 1966.

29. Eames, Thomas H.: "Accommodation in School Children: Aged Five, Six, Seven, and Eight Years," *American Journal of Ophthalmology,* vol. 51, pp. 1255–1257, June, 1961.

30. Eames, Thomas H.: "The Effect of Endocrine Disorders on Reading," *The Reading Teacher,* vol. 12, pp. 263–265, April, 1959.

31. Eames, Thomas H.: "Visual Handicaps to Reading," *Journal of Education,* vol. 141, pp. 2–35, February, 1951.

32. Edfeldt, Ake W.: *Silent Speech and Silent Reading,* University of Chicago Press, Chicago, 1960.

33. Ephron, Beulah: *Emotional Difficulties in Reading; a Psychological Approach to Study Problems,* Julian Press, New York, 1953.

34. Fendrick, Paul: "The Influence of Music Distraction upon Reading Efficiency," *Journal of Educational Research,* vol. 31, pp. 264–271, December, 1937.

35. Freyberg, P. S.: "A Comparison of Two Approaches to the Teaching of Spelling," *British Journal of Educational Psychology,* vol. 34, pp. 178–186, June, 1964.

36. Frymier, J. R.: "A Study of Students' Motivation to Do Good Work in School," *Journal of Educational Research,* vol. 57, pp. 239–244, January, 1964.

37. Gagne, R. M., and L. T. Brown: "Some Factors in the Programming of Conceptual Learning," *Journal of Experimental Psychology,* vol. 62, pp. 313–321, October, 1962.

38. Garner, W. R.: "To Perceive Is to Know," *American Psychologist,* vol. 21, pp. 11–19, January, 1966.

39. Goins, Jean T.: *Visual Perceptual Abilities and Early Reading Progress,* Supplementary Educational Monographs, no. 87, University of Chicago Press, Chicago, 1958.

40. Gray, William S.: *The Major Aspects of Reading,* Supplementary Educational Monographs, no. 90, University of Chicago Press, Chicago, 1960, pp. 8–24.

41. Gray, William S.: "The Teaching of Reading: An International View," *The Burton Lecture, 1956,* Harvard University Press, Cambridge, Mass., 1957.

42. Groff, Patrick J.: "A Study of Handedness and Reading Achievement," *The Reading Teacher,* vol. 16, pp. 31–34, September, 1962.

43. Hage, Dean S., and James B. Stroud: "Reading Proficiency and Intelligence Scores: Verbal and Nonverbal," *Journal of Educational Research,* vol. 52, pp. 258–262, March, 1959.

44. Hahn, William P.: "Phonics: A Boon to Spelling?" *Elementary School Journal,* vol. 64, pp. 383–386, April, 1964.

45. Hall, John F.: *Psychology of Motivation,* J. B. Lippincott Company, Philadelphia, 1961.

46. Hanna, Paul R., and Jean S. Hanna: "The Teaching of Spelling," *National Elementary Principal,* vol. 45, pp. 19–28, November, 1965.

47. Hazard, Patrick D. (ed.): *Language and Literacy Today,* Science Research Associates, Inc., Chicago, 1965.

48. Hester, Kathleen B.: "Creative Reading: A Neglected Area," *Education,* vol. 79, pp. 537–541, May, 1959.

49. Holbrook, David: *English for the Rejected,* Cambridge University Press, New York, 1964.

50. Hollingsworth, Harry L.: *Psychology, Its Facts and Principles,* Appleton-Century-Crofts, Inc., New York, 1928.

51. Holmes, Jack A., and Harry Singer: "Theoretical Models and Trends toward

More Basic Research in Reading," *Review of Educational Research,* vol. 34, pp. 131–133, April, 1964.

52. Horn, Ernest, and Ernest J. Ashbaugh: *Spelling We Use, Grades 2–8,* J. B. Lippincott Company, Philadelphia, 1950.

53. Inhelder, Barbel, and Jean Piaget: *The Growth of Logical Thinking,* Basic Books, Inc., Publishers, New York, 1958.

54. Jenkins, Nora Congdon: "Visual Performance and Scholastic Success," *School Review,* vol. 61, pp. 544–547, December, 1953.

55. Jenkinson, Marion Dixon: "The Roles of Motivation in Reading," *Meeting Individual Differences in Reading,* Supplementary Educational Monographs, no. 94, University of Chicago Press, Chicago, 1964, pp. 49–57.

56. Jenkinson, Marion Dixon: "Selected Processes and Difficulties of Reading Comprehension," unpublished doctoral dissertation, Department of Education, University of Chicago, Chicago, 1957.

57. Jones, N. V.: "The Effect of Speech Training on Silent Reading Achievement," *Journal of Speech and Hearing Disorders,* vol. 16, pp. 258–263, September, 1951.

58. Keppel, Francis: "Research: Education's Neglected Hope," *Journal of Reading,* vol. 8, pp. 3–9, October, 1964.

59. King, W. H.: "An Experimental Investigation into the Relative Merits of Listening and Reading Comprehension for Boys and Girls of Primary School Age," *British Journal of Educational Psychology,* vol. 29, pp. 42–49, February, 1959.

60. Krippner, Stanley: "The Boy Who Read at Eighteen Months," *Exceptional Children,* vol. 30, pp. 105–109, November, 1963.

61. Krugman, Morris: "Reading Failure and Mental Health," *Journal of the National Association of Women Deans and Counselors,* vol. 20, p. 10, October, 1956.

62. Lloyd, Bruce A.: "The Chimera of Oral Reading," *Education,* vol. 86, pp. 106–108, October, 1965.

63. Loretan, Joseph O.: "The Decline and Fall of Group Intelligence Testing," *Teachers College Record,* vol. 67, pp. 10–17, October, 1965.

64. Lovell, K., and M. E. Woolsey: "Reading Disability, Non-verbal Reasoning, and Social Class," *Educational Research,* vol. 6, pp. 226–229, June, 1964.

65. Luckiesh, Mathew, and Frank K. Moss: *Reading as a Visual Task,* D. Van Nostrand Company, Inc., Princeton, N.J., 1942.

66. Many, Wesley A.: "Is There Really Any Difference—Reading vs Listening," *The Reading Teacher,* vol. 19, pp. 110–113, November, 1965.

67. Marquardt, William F.: "Language Interference in Reading," *The Reading Teacher,* vol. 18, p. 215, December, 1964.

68. Maw, Wallace T., and Ethel W. Maw: "Children's Curiosity as an Aspect of Reading Comprehension," *The Reading Teacher,* vol. 15, p. 239, January, 1962.

69. McCaul, Robert L.: "The Effect of Attitudes upon Reading Interpretation," *Journal of Educational Psychology,* vol. 40, pp. 230–238, April, 1949.

70. Miller, Nandeen: "Teaching an Emotionally Disturbed, Brain-injured Child," *The Reading Teacher,* vol. 17, pp. 460–465, March, 1964.

71. Morrison, Ida E., and Ida F. Perry: "Spelling and Reading Relationships with Incidence of Retardation and Acceleration," *Journal of Educational Research,* vol. 52, pp. 222–227, February, 1951.

72. Olson, Willard C.: *Child Development,* D. C. Heath and Company, Boston, 1959, pp. 141–190.

73. Parker, Edwin R.: "The Effects of Television on Public Library Circulation," *Public Opinion Quarterly,* vol. 27, pp. 578–589, Winter, 1963.

74. Penty, Ruth: *Reading Ability and High School Dropouts,* Teachers College Press, Teachers College, Columbia University, New York, 1956.

75. Porterfield, O. U., and H. F. Schlicting: "Peer Status and Reading Achievement," *Journal of Educational Research,* vol. 54, pp. 291–297, April, 1961.

76. Reid, Hall C.: "Evaluating Five Methods of Teaching Spelling—Second and Third Grades," *Instructor,* vol. 75, pp. 77, 82–83, March, 1966.

77. Richards, Ivor A.: *How to Read a Page,* W. W. Norton & Company, Inc., New York, 1942.

78. Robinson, H. Alan (comp. and ed.): *Reading and the Language Arts,* Supplementary Educational Monographs, no. 25, University of Chicago Press, Chicago, 1963.

79. Robinson, H. Alan, and Allan F. Muskoff: "High School Reading—1963," *Journal of Reading,* vol. 8, pp. 85–96, November, 1964.

80. Robinson, Helen M. (ed.): *Oral Aspects of Reading,* Supplementary Educational Monographs, no. 82, University of Chicago Press, Chicago, December, 1955.

81. Robinson, Helen M.: "Perceptual and Conceptual Style Related to Reading," in J. Allen Figurel (ed.), *Improvement of Reading through Classroom Practice,* International Reading Association Conference Proceedings, vol. 9, Newark, Del., 1964, pp. 26–28.

82. Robinson, Helen M., and Charles B. Huelsman, Jr.: "Visual Efficiency and Progress in Learning to Read," in Helen M. Robinson (ed.), *Clinical Studies in Reading II,* Supplementary Educational Monographs, no. 77, University of Chicago Press, Chicago, 1953, p. 41.

83. Ruddell, Robert: "The Effect of Similarity of Oral and Written Patterns of Language Structure on Reading Comprehension," *Elementary English,* vol. 42, pp. 402–410, April, 1965.

84. Russell, David H.: *Children Learn to Read,* Ginn and Company, Boston, 1961, pp. 69–96.

85. Russell, David H.: "A Conspectus of Recent Research on Listening Abilities," *Elementary English,* vol. 41, pp. 262–267, March, 1964.

86. Russell, David H.: "Research on the Processes of Thinking with Some Applications to Reading," *Elementary English,* vol. 42, pp. 370–378, April, 1965.

87. Russell, David H., and Henry R. Fea: "Research on Teaching Reading," in N. L. Gage (ed.), *Handbook of Research on Teaching,* Rand McNally & Company, Chicago, 1963, pp. 865–928.

88. Russell, David H., and Elizabeth F. Russell: *Listening Aids through the Grades: One Hundred Ninety Listening Activities,* Teachers College Press, Teachers College, Columbia University, New York, 1959.

89. Smith, Donald E. P., and Patricia M. Carrigan: *The Nature of Reading Disability,* Harcourt, Brace & World, Inc., New York, 1959.

90. Smith, James O.: "Group Language Development for Educable Mental Retardates," *Exceptional Children,* vol. 29, pp. 95–101, October, 1962.

91. Spache, George D.: "Psychological Explanations of Reading," in Oscar S. Causey (ed.), *Exploring the Goals of College Reading Programs,* Fifth Yearbook of the Southwest Reading Conference, Texas Christian University Press, Fort Worth, Tex., 1956, pp. 14–22.

92. Spache, George D.: *Toward Better Reading,* The Garrard Press, Champaign, Ill., 1963.

93. Spache, George D., and Chester E. Tillman: "A Comparison of the Visual Profiles of Retarded and Nonretarded Readers," *Journal of Developmental Reading,* vol. 5, pp. 101–109, Winter, 1962.

94. Staiger, Ralph C.: "Medicine for Retarded Readers," *Journal of Developmental Reading,* vol. 5, pp. 48–51, Autumn, 1961.

95. Stauffer, Russell G.: "Concept Development and Reading," *The Reading Teacher,* vol. 19, pp. 100–105, November, 1965.

96. Strang, Ruth: "The Contribution of the Psychology of Reading to International Cooperation," *School and Society,* vol. 67, pp. 65–68, January 31, 1948.

97. Strang, Ruth: "Developing Oral Expression," *National Elementary Principal,* vol. 45, pp. 36–41, November, 1965.

98. Strang, Ruth: "A Dynamic Theory of the Reading Process," *Merrill-Palmer Quarterly of Behavior and Development,* vol. 7, pp. 239–245, October, 1961.

99. Strang, Ruth: "An Introspective Approach to Study Problems," *Journal of Educational Research,* vol. 51, pp. 271–278, December, 1957.

100. Strang, Ruth: "The Reading Process and Its Ramifications," *Invitational Addresses 1965,* International Reading Association, Newark, Del., 1965, pp. 49–73.

101. Strang, Ruth: "Relationships between Certain Aspects of Intelligence and Certain Aspects of Reading," *Educational and Psychological Measurement,* vol. 3, pp. 355–359, Winter, 1943.

102. Strang, Ruth: "What Is Communicated?" *Educational Forum,* vol. 18, pp. 15–19, November, 1953.

103. Strickland, Ruth: "Implication of Research in Linguistics for Elementary Teaching," *Elementary English,* vol. 40, pp. 168–171, February, 1963.

104. Summers, Edward G.: "A Suggested Integrated Reading Outline for Teacher Education Courses in Secondary Reading," *Journal of Reading,* vol. 9, pp. 93–105, November, 1965.

105. Thorndike, E. L.: "Reading as Reasoning: A Study of Mistakes in Paragraph Reading," *Journal of Educational Psychology,* vol. 8, pp. 323–332, June, 1917.

106. Tinker, Miles A.: *Bases for Effective Reading,* University of Minnesota Press, Minneapolis, 1965.

107. Tinker, Miles A.: "Experimental Studies on the Legibility of Print: An Annotated Bibliography," *Reading Research Quarterly,* vol. 1, pp. 67–118, Summer, 1966.

108. Tinker, Miles A: "How Children and Adults Perceive Words in Reading," *Invitational Addresses 1965,* International Reading Association, Newark, Del., 1965, pp. 75–91.

109. Tinker, Miles A.: "Influence of Simultaneous Variation in Size of Type, Width of Line, and Leading for Newspaper Type," *Journal of Applied Psychology,* vol. 47, pp. 380–382, December, 1963.

110. Tinker, Miles A.: *Legibility of Print,* Iowa State University Press, Ames, Iowa, 1963.

111. Tinker, Miles A.: "Legibility of Print for Children in the Upper Grades," *American Journal of Optometry and Archives of American Academy of Optometry,* vol. 40, pp. 614–621, October, 1963.

112. Traxler, Arthur E.: "Study of the California Test of Mental Maturity: Advanced Battery," *Journal of Educational Research,* vol. 32, pp. 329–335, January, 1939.

113. Turner, Richard H.: *When People Talk on the Telephone, Books A and B,* Teachers College Press, Teachers College, Columbia University, New York, 1964.

114. Vernon, M. D.: *Backwardness in Reading: A Study of Its Nature and Origin,* Cambridge University Press, London, 1957.

115. Vickery, Verna L.: *Reading Process and Beginning Reading Instruction,* Bureau of Educational Research, College of Teacher Education, no. 2, New Mexico State University, University Park, N.M., October, 1962.

116. Vorhaus, Pauline G.: "Rorschach Configurations Associated with Reading Disability," *Journal of Projective Techniques,* vol. 16, pp. 2–19, March, 1952.

117. Waldman, John, and Francis Oralind Triggs: "The Measurement of Word Attack Skills," *Elementary English,* vol. 35, pp. 459–463, November, 1958.

118. Wattenberg, William W., and Clare Clifford: "Relation of Self-concepts to Beginning Achievement in Reading," *Child Development,* vol. 35, pp. 461–467, June, 1964.

119. Weaver, Wendell W.: "The Predictability of Omissions in Reading and Listening," in Emery P. Bliesmer and Ralph C. Staiger (eds.), *Problems, Programs, and Projects in College-Adult Reading,* Eleventh Yearbook of the National Reading Conference, Milwaukee, Wis., 1962, pp. 148–153.

120. Wepman, Joseph M.: "Nature of Effective Speech in Oral Reading," in Helen M. Robinson (ed.), *Oral Aspects of Reading,* Supplementary Educational Monographs, no. 82, University of Chicago Press, Chicago, 1955, pp. 30–35.

121. Wheeler, Lester H., and Viola D. Wheeler: "The Relationship between Reading Ability and Intelligence among University Freshmen," *Journal of Educational Psychology,* vol. 40, pp. 230–238, April, 1949.

122. Wittick, Mildred Letton: "Improving Written Composition," *National Elementary Principal,* vol. 45, pp. 14–18, November, 1965.

123. Wyatt, Nita M.: "Research in Creative Writing," *Educational Leadership,* vol. 19, pp. 307–310, February, 1962.

124. Wylie, Ruth C.: "Children's Estimates of Their School Work Ability, as a Function of Sex, Race, and Socioeconomic Level," *Journal of Personality,* vol. 31, pp. 203–224, June, 1963.

reading programs

chapter 2

Elementary school teachers, especially those who
teach the primary grades, recognize reading instruction as a major responsibility. Junior and senior high
school teachers are inclined to wonder why they
should be involved at all in teaching reading. This
chapter should clarify the appropriate responsibilities of every teacher for initiating, developing, or
improving the whole school reading program.

You will read descriptions of varied reading programs on all grade levels. These descriptions include
information on organization, teaching procedures,
and instructional materials. You will become acquainted with the role for each member of the staff.
You will realize in what direction reading programs
are moving.

Read this chapter from the standpoint of your own position. Note the features in other programs that could make essential contributions to a program appropriate to your students, your faculty, and the objectives of your school. If you are a teacher, consider your relationships with the principal, the reading teacher or consultant, other specialists, and your fellow teachers.

The reading program is like a suit. It must fit the individual. Schools vary not only in financial resources and physical facilities but also in the needs of their pupils, their teachers' qualifications and their varied degrees of interest in reading, and the degrees of understanding that their administrators possess regarding the teaching of reading. The following examples of situations described by teachers suggest how great a variety of programs is needed.

TYPES OF SITUATIONS

Situation 1: Ability but Lack of Interest in Reading

In a lumbering town in the West, the parents of the high school students are mostly well-paid mill workers. They want their children to read well but do not set them a good example. The children are bright enough but are not interested in reading. Because they lack basic skills, they find reading laborious, slow, and tiresome. They see little sense in reading when they can look at pictures, television, and movies, or participate in outdoor entertainment and dances. Boys get jobs to buy and keep up a car rather than to buy books which might relate to their outside activities, or captivate or elevate their desires.

Situation 2: Low Ability and Too Difficult Books

In a ninth-grade class all the pupils had failed in one or more subjects the preceding year. Their IQs on a group intelligence test were mostly between 80 and 90. The girls were interested primarily in boys; the boys, in sports. Most of their parents were unskilled or semiskilled manual workers.

Shakespeare's *Twelfth Night* was required reading. These pupils were ill-equipped to handle the vocabulary, the seventeenth-century expressions, the metrical form, and the philosophical passages. The required novels, *Ivanhoe* and *Silas Marner*, caused almost as much difficulty, with the pupils lost in the subtleties of plot, style, and characterization. Because they had trouble understanding the words, let alone the ideas, both students and teachers felt defeated. The tabloid newspapers and the insipid books they had chosen to date had not prepared them to read such literature. They needed a transition from where they were to where they could go in literary appreciation.

Situation 3: All Able but Many Bored

The boys in a private boarding school were above average in intelligence and socioeconomic status. Some read well and discussed intelligently what they had read. Many were bored, reading aloud without feeling and not remembering what they read. Since many of these boys came from broken or unhappy homes, stories that dealt with family relationships and other aspects of child development could be of value to them. They needed conviction that reading really had personal value for them; they lacked books with significance.

Situation 4: Instruction in Reading Needed in Study Hall

As supervisor of study hall and library, one teacher became aware of the varied degrees of reading skill and ability possessed by the boys in a private school. Their ages ranged from eight to fifteen in grades 3 through 9. Their general intelligence, interests, and socioeconomic background were well above average.

Many of the boys in the upper classes did not seem to know how to make use of the two-hour study session, often reading purposelessly. Unless the assignments were very definite, they accomplished practically nothing. At least three of these boys seemed to have basic reading disabilities that were hampering them in all their school work, yet apparently nothing was being done to remedy their reading deficiencies. The supervisor's time was spent almost entirely in keeping order.

Since they were readers with the same general deficiencies, they needed the supervisor to help with their reading problems as they occurred. Occasionally a film on reading (see Appendix B) would turn a study hall into a fruitful two hours of instruction.

Situation 5: No Recognized Need for Reading in Their Lives

Many of the students disliked reading. They worked hard to master assignments but seldom browsed around the library or read in their leisure time. They seemed to have no need for reading in their lives except for study. One should not blame them for doing no free reading, since lack of comprehension and slow rate of reading destroyed their pleasure. They enjoyed stories presented on television and radio but did not like to read them. What, they thought, could reading give them that television and radio could not? They were not aware that reading permitted them a wider selection of stories and fuller use of the imagination.

In these and other situations many teachers and counselors view reading with alarm. Teachers in colleges and universities report reading problems. They frequently mention (1) the slow reading of many students which forces them to leave long college assignments uncompleted; (2) the inadequacy of their comprehension, especially their inability to recognize the structure or organizing idea of a passage; (3) the shallowness of their appreciation of literature; (4) their limited vocabulary; and (5) their failure to make appropriate use of a repertory of reading and study skills.

To solve these problems, there are many patterns for reading-improvement programs. Each school must choose and develop a program in the light of its students' needs and the facilities that are available. Any program may combine certain features from any of the types of programs described in detail later in this chapter and in others.

A FIRM FOUNDATION IN ELEMENTARY SCHOOL [1]

In the large majority of elementary schools one teacher stays with his class for most of the day. In the first grade most of the teacher's time is spent on activities that contribute directly or indirectly to reading. In each succeeding grade, although decreasing percentages of time are devoted to the direct teaching of reading, a large amount of time is spent in reinforcing and applying the skills already learned.

Preparation of Teachers

To prevent teachers from floundering in their first teaching positions, preservice preparation is essential. Dr. Conant recommended at least one course in reading for all prospective elementary teachers and two courses for primary teachers. The recommendations of the Harvard survey were similar [5]. In one college of education every undergraduate works with an individual elementary pupil while acquiring basic reading theory and methods. Teachers of beginning reading need not only thorough initial preparation but also continued in-service assistance.

Individualizing Reading Instruction [39, 35]

In no other discipline is the need for individualized instruction so apparently crucial as it is in the teaching of reading. The more the children in a class differ in preschool training, native abilities, and background, the more imperative is the need for the teacher to work separately with each pupil. Increasing teacher-pupil ratio as a result of bigger enrollments is threatening the amount of attention each pupil may receive.

[1] Many of the procedures described in this chapter can be adapted to the secondary school.

Frymier [33] obtained experimental support of the general belief that reading achievement is higher when classes are smaller. During the academic year he found that first-grade pupils in small classes (fewer than thirty) made a month's progress more than those in classes over thirty.

Even though studies of class size have, in general, been inconclusive because of differences in methods of study, quality of instruction, age and ability of the children, and so forth, it would seem reasonable to expect more growth in small classes especially for beginning readers and in view of all the stress placed on individual differences.

There are many methods of individualizing instruction: sectioning classes according to reading ability, individualizing instruction while teaching the class as a whole, grouping within a class, providing for individual growth through an ungraded primary unit or an individualized reading program, tutoring, and using multilevel reading material.

Sectioning Classes According to Reading Ability. In large schools classes are often grouped according to reading ability, horizontally on the same grade level, or vertically as in the Joplin plan, which groups pupils on the same reading level from several grades. Several control-group experiments have failed to demonstrate clearly the superiority of the Joplin plan [66, 13]. One study [58] indicated that it produced initially superior results except in the case of pupils whose IQs were below 90, but this superiority diminished over several semesters.

Homogeneous grouping is difficult or impossible to achieve. Balow and Curtin [7] point out that there is little promise of forming homogeneous achievement groups by using intelligence-test scores as a base. Obviously the term "homogeneous grouping" is inaccurate since pupils who achieve similar reading-test scores may differ widely in specific reading abilities as well as in other respects.

Those in favor of homogeneous grouping say that with it the teacher can provide more experiences and materials of instruction that each group needs; it does not bore the superior readers or waste their time; it does not undermine the self-esteem of the poor readers by throwing them into constant comparison with the superior readers; and there are few teachers sufficiently gifted to make adequate provision for the wide range of reading ability presented in an ordinary class.

Those who argue against homogeneous grouping say that poor readers need the stimulation of better readers; better readers need the chance to understand and serve others; and a "low" grouping may give students a feeling of inferiority. One solution is to introduce flexible subgroups and periods of individualized reading into the regular heterogeneous classes for the varied needs and interests. This arrangement realizes the merits of both kinds of grouping.

Individualizing Instruction While Teaching the Entire Class.   The sensitive, skillful teacher meets individual needs while giving instruction to the class as a whole. For example, in teaching vocabulary in a third-grade class, one teacher asked a boy the meaning of *museum.* He said, "It's a place where fish are kept." Instead of saying, "Wrong," and calling on someone else, the teacher asked, "Where did you get that idea?" "Well," said the boy, "I was in a museum and I saw the skeleton of a whale." "That's true," the teacher said, "you do sometimes see the *skeletons* of fish in museums, but the place where *live* fish are kept is called an *aquarium.*"

The teacher who knows the individual children can informally meet their separate needs for encouragement, approval, or training in more rigorous thinking and expression. For example, when one boy did some very poor thinking on a question, the teacher, instead of calling on someone else, asked him several clarifying questions and made a helpful comment. When the pupil had arrived at a thoughtful answer, she said, "There, John, we knew you could do it, if you stayed with it."

The teacher can also use the various backgrounds of the pupils in orienting the class to a story or article and in helping them discuss it after they have read it. Some pupils will reveal gaps in their experience which can then be filled in.

Other ways to provide for individual differences within a class include asking different kinds of questions, giving differentiated assignments, and accepting degrees of preparation. In planning the work for any class, the teacher should recognize that some pupils can finish an assignment sooner than others and that no one should be subjected to boredom, on the one hand, or frequent failure on the other. Although the teacher will expect all the pupils to learn minimum essentials, he will also give individual pupils additional opportunities for exploration, inquiry, and creative expression. Pupils who finish the group assignment quickly may have library books handy, consult reference books, do exercises to improve a particular skill, or study their picture dictionary, card file, or review words in their notebooks. Enthusiasm for grouping should not cause neglect of the many opportunities for individualizing instruction in the class as a whole.

Grouping within a Class.   Diversity and flexibility are the keys to individualizing instruction through subgroups within a regular class. A pupil can belong to several groups. A retarded reader may be part of a group working on a particular reading difficulty. He may also belong to another group that includes both able and retarded readers, all studying a certain topic that has aroused their curiosity. These groups originate as the need arises; each serves a singular purpose.

The first type is *achievement grouping,* based on the pupil's reading level. To determine this level, the teacher can look at the records of the child's reading. If he finds that the pupil finished the fourth reader last June, he can hope that the youngster is ready for the fifth reader this September, remembering, of course, that a summer of goodness knows what has intervened. Maybe the pupil read all summer, maybe he swam in the lake. If the latter is true, he will make no great splash in reading in September though he may bring a load of fresh concepts to his reading.

The teacher may ask him what he has read during the summer. A comparison of his leisure-reading level with his record of last June may suggest progress or retrogression. Ordinarily people choose material that demands less than their maximum effort. If he has been reading books that are harder than the book he finished last June, he has made real progress.

The teacher may then fill a large table with varied books on various difficulty levels and ask the pupils to choose a book, read it silently, and be ready to read a portion aloud to him when he asks for it. Ernest may choose a difficult book to impress the teacher. When he is asked how he likes it, Ernest will say, "Well, it's too easy," or "It wasn't very interesting." But when he reads aloud, he stumbles over every word. The teacher says, "Maybe this would be a better book for you to read to me," and gives him an easier one. He gives him time to read a bit to himself before asking him to read aloud. By this process the teacher finds the level at which he reads easily and with comprehension.

Martin, on the other hand, says to himself, "If I pick a hard book, I'll be stuck with the top reading group all year," so he chooses an easy book. When the teacher asks what his book is about, he gives a stenographic report of it, and when he reads aloud he sounds like a radio news reporter racing with time. The teacher selects a harder book to find the level at which Martin encounters some challenge but can still read with comfort and understanding.

By such means the teacher determines the reading levels at which the different children will be comfortable. The higher the grade he teaches the greater the difference between Ernest and Martin. He must still question his judgment and his placement of pupils. A reading test which has vocabulary and comprehension sections, both of which start with easy items and go up to hard items, may support the observation or caution the teacher to reevaluate, but he will avoid a common mistake at this point of determining placement by the total score on the test. This wise teacher notes the vocabulary and comprehension items the pupil was able to do and compares them with his reader series. He identifies the book in the reader series where these words occur; he examines the book to see if sentences are comparably long and involved and the ideas comparably complex and mature.

The teacher then tries to divide the children into several groups. Sometimes a new teacher starts with two groups and adds other groups as he feels able. Most teachers feel that three groups an hour are about all that can be efficiently handled. Decisions about grouping are difficult: it is hard to know whether to put a borderline pupil into a higher reading level where he will be uncomfortable or into a lower reading level where he will have an easy time of it.

The fact is that the teacher will always have some individuals in any group who do the work easily, some who find it hard, and some who find it just right. A second fact is that *he* will find he has made mistakes, and that pupils change during a year—some exceed expectations, others falter. He will have to change the placement of any pupil whenever he feels the pupil would profit more from the work at another level. In other words, his achievement grouping must be flexible, and his diagnosis of pupils must be continuous. Achievement grouping can advance the reading skills of the learner at a rate congenial to his growth.

Achievement grouping accepts the idea that a child doing his best and progressing is the most desirable kind of school performer, whether he is at the top of the class or at the bottom. But in addition, something must change inside teachers so that their faces don't brighten when they work with the high group, straighten with the middle group, and sag with the low group. In many little ways teachers reveal to the children the kind of respect they have for them; their disappointment imposes an additional burden on children struggling to learn to read. Actually, teachers are disappointed in their own failure to reach goals. Psychological peace comes only if goals are wisely chosen to suit different paces possible for the different groups and the different individuals within these groups. Then teachers will know the pleasure of reaching goals and children will have the satisfaction of keeping teachers happy while they themselves learn.

The second type, *"research" grouping*, occurs when two or more pupils decide that they are curious enough about a question to dig out answers from many sources and report to a reading group or an entire class. It may sprout from community projects such as a political campaign, a strike, Christmas celebrations, Red Cross drive, Lincoln's birthday, or from a pupil's bringing in a souvenir from an uncle in the Army, a strange butterfly, a clipping about a new high-speed airplane, or a new movie or television program. It may stem from a schoolwide paper sale which prompts pupils to ask where paper goes and why. Such happy coincidences give the pupils a chance to sharpen the skills they have learned in the basal reading program.

Research grouping may germinate from the regular classroom, for example, as an offshoot study of parliamentary procedure for class meetings or in the social science study of "communication" where the class decides to set up committees to investigate costs, plan field trips, and arrange displays. They plan the committees and assign questions and jobs to each one. Then individuals join the committee which interests them and discuss ways of getting information such as through libraries, interviews, films, recordings, and visits to radio stations. Committees write for pamphlets, brochures, diagrams, and for many kinds of good helps. Perhaps a library committee may care for and organize material brought to the classroom for other committees.

The pupil's choice of a group depends largely upon two factors: What interests him? With whom does he prefer to work? That is, common interests may cause two pupils to work together and learn to like or dislike each other, or social preferences may lead a pupil to study something which does not initially interest but which may eventually attract or repel him. In either case he will broaden his experience or scope of interest whether it be social or informational. Needless to say, it is the teacher's job to see that the committees work, that friends progress on a topic, and that those who are thrown together by a common interest surmount their difficulties to cooperate. Well-defined objectives and ground rules and frequent checking and arbitration will oil the wheels of all groups.

Activities must vary enough so that everyone has a reading experience. The best group reader tackles difficult but crucial articles and reads them aloud to the committee. Other pupils read their short reports or signs. Finally the group pools its findings and decides on a presentation for the rest of the class.

This type of grouping is important because it motivates reading. It is especially valuable in strengthening the pupils' use of reference tools, adaptation of techniques to match their purposes, word attack skills, and the synthesis of sources into a well-organized whole.

The third type is *interest grouping*. Perhaps it is splitting hairs to suggest that research and interest grouping are not necessarily the same thing. But the latter stems from an interest a pupil pursues in hobbies and other activities as well as in books. Take, for instance, the cowboy interest. One day the teacher displays good cowboy stories on the library table or shelf, puts cowboy book jackets on the bulletin board, includes cowboy music in his music period. Then the teacher finds two students in a corner talking about cowboy books. "How would you fellows like to tell the rest of us about the cowboy books you think we'd like especially?"

At a subsequent meeting of the class reading club—everybody belongs, and it meets at least once a week to spread interest—the boys form a panel to tell about a book; perhaps to read good parts aloud; to show movies or slides, pictures from books, or pictures or models they have made; to dramatize parts; or to demonstrate cowboy techniques. They go on to make a poster advertising some good stories or a scrapbook of some of the things they have learned. Perhaps they write a report for the classroom newspaper, bulletin board, or school newspaper, appending a bibliography.

Sometimes the teacher uncovers a nest of interests when he puts up an order blank: pupils' names down the left side and space for topics at the right. "Next time we get books from the library, what would you like particularly to read about? Write the topic opposite your name so that the librarian can be hunting some good books for you." In this way the teacher can locate books suitable as to topic and reading level, while discovering which pupils might think and work together.

As in research grouping, common interest may cause relative strangers to work together, or Harvey may attract his friend Wayne to read new books on a shared topic. Such strategies perfect reading skills which further enjoyment—the satisfaction of curiosity or emotional release—and pupils keep reading. Grouping based upon interest fans the flame.

The fourth type may be called *special needs grouping*, connoting skills building. Sometimes a pupil is unready or absent in body or mind when his peers in his achievement group learn a skill. The teacher has noted his trouble either in class work or on a diagnostic test. When another achievement group is going to deal with this skill, he invites the pupil to join in. The pupil stays for the duration of the exercise, participates in it, and takes away an assignment that provides additional practice and reflects what he has learned. This has not required the formation of a special group, yet it filled in a gap.

On another day, the teacher notices that two people in one achievement group, one person in another, and three in a third, all have the same difficulty—perhaps reading for the main idea or analyzing a word by its initial consonant blend. None of the other pupils needs exercise in this skill. So he cuts five or ten minutes off the reading lessons that day and has these six people come to the chalkboard or table to work on this skill.

He uses words or material appropriate to the lowest-level reader in this special group. In other words, if the pupils represent fourth-, sixth-, and seventh-reader levels, he couches his instruction in an easy fourth-reader vocabulary which the poorest reader in the group can recognize on sight. One cannot learn an unknown through an unknown. If he were told that a "splinkx" is a form of "lapxkz," he would be no further along in his understanding of "splinkx." If the technique is strange, at least the vocabulary and the ideas should be familiar.

The teacher may meet the special group once or several times, as few or as many times as necessary to learn the skill, and each lesson will end with the children at their own seats working on an exercise to improve their prowess.

A fifth type is *team grouping*. Sometimes in the face of a difficult task two pupils have one good head between them and profit by working together. A student should often prove by solo flights that he can navigate the skills without help. But he does learn from others and can, occasionally, benefit by having a fellow sufferer with him. What he doesn't know the other fellow may know. What neither fellow has the courage to decide alone, together they may decide.

Such a group may result from informal recommendation of the teacher as the achievement group leaves for individual work. "Why don't you and Tom work it out together this time?" Or a pupil may ask, "May we work together on this?" After the meeting of a special needs group, the pupils may be encouraged to pair off to work on the follow-up assignment. The teacher does not force a team situation. If he knows that two pupils are friends, he may recommend teamwork. If he knows that they are very uncongenial, he may feel that this unsupervised situation is not one which will help them learn to value each other's virtues.

To be successful a team must have a definite job to do and know exactly what is expected. Requiring a concrete result—such as a written report or filled-in blanks—and a reasonable but not too generous time limit will hold the partners down to business. They must discover that teamwork is a privilege that can be lost through horseplay.

One variation of team learning is more formal. The teacher prepares a learning experience—a selection to read and questions to answer—and lets each group conduct the lesson separately, with the aid of an able student leader. Occasionally the teacher, moving from group to group, helps the pupils to get the most value from this experience.

The sixth type, somewhat *tutorial*, is a grouping in which one pupil who knows a certain skill or piece of material helps one or more pupils who do not and are trying to learn. Sometimes called *team learning*, it is a controversial technique. Some say it wastes the time of the pupil who knows. They add, "What's the teacher for?" Others point out that help from another pupil is degradation to the helped; it classifies the know's and the don't know's and throws them together to the embarrassment of the latter. "Besides," they say, "it gives delusions of grandeur to the helper." On the other hand, young people fitting themselves for society must learn to be gracious helpers and to receive help graciously. Everyone needs to learn both roles. If Martin helps Ernest, Ernest must have a chance to explain something to Martin even if a teacher has to arrange it, holding secret intelligence meetings with Ernest.

As teachers all know, one understands better the things he has had to teach. Martin reinforces his learnings by teaching them. He will spend a large part of his life explaining his ideas to other people. If education is preparation for life, he can learn how to get along with different kinds of people. So Martin's teaching benefits him while it releases the teacher for other instructional tasks which only he can perform. Thus tutorial groupings and team learning both serve a teaching purpose and a social need.

In this type of grouping, as well as in several others, the tasks must be definite and the outcomes concrete. Martin must know how to help—that help does not mean telling the answers—and Ernest must know what help to expect and what his own role is.

"Individualized Reading." Although sectioning of classes and subgrouping within a class have made possible a certain amount of differentiation of instruction, these methods alone do not provide for the many kinds of individual differences that still exist. Recognition of these remaining differences has led to the more highly individualized approach called *individualized reading*. This method is to be distinguished from the broad philosophy that calls for "individualized reading instruction." The idea is not new. Dalton introduced his plan of teacher-directed individualized reading in 1920 [9].

Such a program includes the following features:

1. A lush environment of books covering a wide range of reading difficulty, interest, and content. Funds from the school budget, parents, and community organizations purchase these books; or pupils borrow from school and local libraries and book clubs to which they subscribe. If the books are arranged about the room in clearly marked categories, the pupils will be able to choose without confusion, crowding, or waste of time. The teacher usually introduces new books, suggesting what purposes some books fulfill and showing the pupils how to appraise books for content and difficulty.

2. Each child reading at his own ability and interest level. The slow reader does not become conspicuous, nor does he delay the progress of the whole group. Each child reads as many books as he can, easy books for enjoyment or information, or books that challenge his reading skill. Sartain [79] suggested a number of ways in which individualized reading might be incorporated into the total reading program. Pupils may read books they have selected after they have completed their basal reading activities. The whole class may devote its afternoon reading period to individualized reading. After they have mastered certain new basic skills, they may practice these skills through individualized reading. If they finish the basal program before the end of the year, they may devote the remaining weeks to individualized reading.

3. Initial demonstration of the program and discussion of routine and self-management for smooth functioning. The pupils themselves will make their own rules. One class made these:

> Give the book you choose a chance.
> Take turns at the library.
> Don't interrupt a teacher-pupil conference.
> Try to balance your reading diet.

4. Self-selection. The teacher should make clear that every pupil has the responsibility for selecting suitable books—books to enjoy and books to read independently. He should go freely to the teacher for guidance in choosing the right book if he wishes. For his part in guiding pupils effec-

tively, the teacher must know their interests and something about a large number of books. By having the pupils fill out an interest questionnaire or inventory at the beginning of the year, he will have a temporary guide to determine the kinds of books he should provide.

5. Individual conferences with the teacher. While the pupils are reading independently, the teacher will hold conferences. It is amazing how much a skillful teacher can accomplish in a seven- to ten-minute chat about an author's purpose, a comparison of books and authors, and clues to character and motive. At some time during the interview, the teacher can appraise the individual's reading skills and teach the pronunciation of a word and how to read a passage smoothly and with feeling. If the child wants to supplement the content of the book, the teacher refers him to a reference.

6. Record keeping. Pupils should keep brief records of the books read and how they felt about them. They can make a personal response to a book on a 3- by 5-inch card or in a reading diary. Some pupils may want to keep charts to show the breadth of their reading—for example, G. O. Simpson's *Using My Reading Design* [89]. The teacher's records are equally important to show clearly the skills each pupil has acquired, those he lacks, the progress he is making, and the books he has read.

7. Group discussion and reports. When several pupils have read the same book, they like to discuss it. Or they may want to prepare a report or a dramatization as a way of sharing their reading experience with the other pupils. This offers a genuine audience situation for oral reading and oral reporting.

Individualized reading does not in itself constitute a reading program; in the main, it serves as a valuable part of a well-balanced reading program. Used exclusively, it may cause neglect of systematic instruction in reading skills and may lead the pupil to practice errors. Some teachers devote two days a week to individualized reading; others alternate two-week blocks of individualized reading with blocks of basal experiences. Many variations in method are desirable and necessary if and when pupils have learned to read independently.

While some research studies have attributed superior results to programs of individualized reading, others have failed to find any superiority in the reading achievement, as measured by standardized tests [2, 24, 36, 44, 79] of students who have been enrolled in such programs. However, there is general agreement that both teachers and pupils are enthusiastic about individualized reading [4].

Able third-grade readers made such comments as these:

I like reading this year because I don't have to read the same words over and over.

I can read as fast as I like and don't have to wait for the slow ones.

Now I can read all the science books I like.

Slow readers said:

Now I'm not teased about reading "baby books."

I didn't like to read in a group because if I made a mistake the others laughed.

Studies also show that pupils report reading a significantly larger number of books while they are participating in an individualized reading program.

More and more individualized reading programs include individual and group instruction in reading skills and discussion of the books read. And basal programs include features of individualized reading. A program that includes both systematic instruction and individualized reading promotes the best development of reading skills and also promotes interest in and enjoyment of reading and many other values. Skills can be taught through systematic instruction and perfected through individualized reading.

The following is an account of an individualized reading period conducted by a gifted sixth-grade teacher.[2]

Before the class began, the teacher cautioned the pupils to keep their records up to date. As they began to work, she said, "I like the way Debbie is concentrating"—and the rest of the class immediately settled down. She circulated around the room and checked to see how each child was progressing. She then held individual conferences—four or five during the period. The following dialogue is based on a tape-recorded conference with one of the pupils:

Teacher: May I see your reading pattern, Jerry? You must have read twenty books in the last month. You're reading a lot of biographies. Are you particularly interested in biographies?

Boy: Yes, they tell about the person; his personality, and what he's done.

Teacher: What kind of person, particularly—a character in fiction? Would you say a biography is fiction?

Boy: It's fact.

Teacher: Yes, it's fact. What are some of the biographies that you've read? Here's *Alexander the Great,* I see, and *Genghis Khan;* now those are two adventuresome characters, aren't they? How would you compare the two—Alexander the Great and Genghis Khan?

Boy: Well, both of them are conquerors and conquered a lot of land. And both of them burned up the villages they conquered.

Teacher: Can you think of a word that would describe the kind of man that burns and pillages as he conquers?

Boy: Ruthless.

[2] Mrs. Myrna Hillyard, Tucson, Ariz., Public Schools.

Teacher: Ruthless, that's a good word. From what you could tell from reading this book would you say there were any differences in their personalities?

Boy: Well, Alexander the Great, he was influenced by his father. His father was a great military leader.

Teacher: Do you remember who his father was?

Boy: Philip of Macedon.

Teacher: All right. Philip of Macedon. In what way was he influenced by his father? For the good or for the bad?

Boy: For the good.

Teacher: For the good. All right. Were there any other influences in his life?

Boy: Well, his mother, Olympia, said that he was directly descended from Achilles, so he thought he was a god.

Teacher: How do you think it would affect you if your mother had told you when you were a baby that you were directly descended from Achilles?

Boy: Well, I'd go out conquering whatever I saw—just take it and burn it or whatever I felt like doing.

Teacher: Do you think it might also have caused him to be very brave? He thought that nothing could hurt him, didn't he? Can you think of any time in his life when this extreme bravery showed up almost to the point of being foolhardy?

Boy: Well, once when he was in Persia, he had only about 30,000 men and Darius the Sixth had about 100,000 men and Alexander used his military strategy to outwit him.

Teacher: So he wasn't only brave, he was intelligent, wasn't he? I can think of someone else that I think influenced him besides his mother and dad.

Boy: Aristotle.

Teacher: Aristotle. And do you think that was for the good or for the bad?

Boy: For the good.

Teacher: For the good, wasn't it? As Alexander conquered all this land, we realize that he did some pretty bad things, but do you think that in the long run there were some good results? Can you think of any good results?

Boy: Well, Greek influence . . .

Teacher: What do you mean by Greek influence?

Boy: Well, sculpture. He spread Greek civilization through all the lands that he conquered.

Teacher: Did his conquering do anything for the Greek civilization?

Boy: Well, his soldiers were Greeks and Macedons and they were used to a civilized life. They would marry people in other countries they conquered and they'd settle down.

Teacher: You'll notice too the contrast to Genghis Khan. When Alexander conquered a country, he left someone there usually—a Greek teacher or a philosopher or someone. We can't say that about Genghis Khan, can we?

Boy: No.

Teacher: Why do you think that Genghis Khan was such a ruthless man?

Boy:	Well, he chopped off the heads of the high priests.
Teacher:	What in the world made him become the kind of man that could do that sort of thing?
Boy:	Well, when he was about eleven, his father was attacked by those tribes and killed.
Teacher:	So he lost the influence of his father for one thing, didn't he? And the people of that time and place—the Mongol hordes—lived a pretty violent life, didn't they?
Boy:	They were always riding.
Teacher:	Which man do you think probably had the most lasting influence on civilization?
Boy:	Well, I'd say Alexander the Great.
Teacher:	Why do you think Alexander the Great?
Boy:	Well, although his influence lasted only about one hundred years, when the Romans got the territory they were still influenced by Greece.
Teacher:	That's right. And of course Genghis Khan was a powerful man, too. I read that book last year and I was bothered by so much violence in it. Sometimes it was so needless, wasn't it?
Boy:	Um hum. He just killed for the fun of it.
Teacher:	So it seemed. I'm glad to see that you're reading these biographies. We have some wonderful ones in the room, don't we? I notice you've read a lot of books on Greece. What got you so interested in Greece?
Boy:	Umm, we're studying Greece in social studies.
Teacher:	I see. What else are you reading now?
Boy:	*Twenty-one Balloons.*
Teacher:	*Twenty-one Balloons.* How do you like *Twenty-one Balloons?*
Boy:	Ummm, it's sort of a funny adventurous book.
Teacher:	It is funny, isn't it? All right, can you tell us just a little bit about the story. What's happening? What in the world is the title about?
Boy:	This man—Professor Sherman—said that he was going to go across the Pacific. He had read the story *Around the World in Eighty Days,* and he thought it could be done in less than eighty. And he started off but he landed on the island of Caroco.
Teacher:	Cracatora?
Boy:	Cracatora, right, the island that exploded. And just before it exploded, they took off in a sort of thing that had twenty-one balloons. And he landed in the Pacific—I mean he landed in the Atlantic and everyone was confused 'cause he had started to go across the Pacific.
Teacher:	Yes, I remember. And didn't they ask him how he'd got there? Do you remember what he said to them?
Boy:	He said, "I will not tell you the story until I get to the San Francisco Explorers Club."
Teacher:	(Laughs.) Why wouldn't he tell them until he got to the San Francisco Explorers Club?
Boy:	He wanted his fellow explorers to know the facts first.
Teacher:	You know, one thing that interests me about this and I didn't realize it until I reread it. Did you notice that the writer, Mr. DuBois, is the

illustrator, that he did the pictures also? I think they're just wonderful illustrations. Do you have a part in the book you'd like to read?

Boy: This part is about the half-globe on top of the Explorers Club. It has pictures of the United States and all the countries from the north of the equator up. And they put balloons on top of it that had the weight pull—ten of them that had the pulling weight of 75 pounds. All of a sudden one day the balloons just lifted it up and it went across the Sierra Mountains and landed in an Indian reservation.

Teacher: I remember that part. So now we're at the Indian reservation? OK.

Boy: (Reading humorous paragraph with accuracy and excellent expression.) "Now what do you suppose the Indians did? Did they back away trembling with fear? No. Did they shriek with fright? No. Did they beat up the medicine man? No. They gave the cupola an appraising look; then one of them said: 'Ho! Dumb white man decorate Explorers Club of San Francisco with too many ballons. Get hatchet. Cut door in United States between New York and San Francisco; this make good new house for chief.'"

Teacher: (Laughing.) So they're going to make the globe into a house for the chief. That is one of my favorite parts. When you get a little farther, it gets still funnier. I liked it better than *Around the World in Eighty Days* because it's funnier. What books do you have here?

Boy: *My Own Lion.*

Teacher: That's by DuBois, too, isn't it? Is it easy or difficult?

Boy: It's rather simple. It's for little kids in about second grade.

Teacher: We all like to read very easy books at times along with the more difficult ones. The *Twenty-one Balloons* is a good book to share with the class.

Boy: I've started to draw this picture; it isn't quite done yet. This is the island and the ship with the twenty-one balloons.

Teacher: Are you going to make this into an advertising poster for the bulletin board—"Read *Twenty-one Balloons*"? That's good. It's one of my favorite books. Thank you, Jerry.

Each conference is different. In this conference, in addition to examining the pupil's reading pattern and checking on his knowledge of the books he had read, the teacher asked Jerry to compare the two characters and discuss influences in their lives. She reinforced his understanding of the word *ruthless* and related his reading to social studies. By asking him to read a favorite selection aloud, the teacher obtained an appraisal of his oral reading and word recognition and vocabulary difficulties that might interfere with comprehension in reading silently. If such difficulties had been present, she would have given some instruction and suggested suitable practice material.

If the class became restless or a little noisy during the period, a word or a glance from the teacher usually restored the necessary silent-reading atmosphere. At the end of the period she briefly evaluated the work of the group by saying, "Things went fairly well today, but some of the people who were sitting together may have talked too much. You are improving but must try to do better each time."

The Ungraded Primary Unit. This administrative device helps to forestall some of the problems of nonpromotion. Parents who become angry and upset when a slow child fails to achieve sometimes block sound individualization of instruction. By bringing too much pressure on the child to learn to read, they often cause him to become tense, aggravate his nervous habits, and increase his sense of failure, which may lead him to resort to truancy or self-defeating ways in attempting to cope with the situation.

In the ungraded primary unit, each child can progress through the first three years of school at his own best rate, unperturbed either by "a double commotion," as one child termed his skipping a grade, or the stigma of being held back at the end of the first or second year. If at the end of the third year the child is still reading below his potential and is not ready for fourth-grade work, he is placed in a special fourth-grade class. There he receives additional instruction in reading and learns the minimum fourth-grade content. If his reading improves sufficiently, he is promoted to the fifth grade; if not, he stays in the fourth grade for another year.

The ungraded idea has been applied to the intermediate grades and even in high school. It not only permits but also encourages each pupil to proceed at his own rate of growth. It presupposes a curriculum and instructional methods based on diagnosis and teachers who have learned how to provide for individual differences. Di Lorenzo and Salter's [21] summary of research and practice in nongraded primary schools shows more agreement about purposes than about interpretation and results.

In schools with the ungraded system, promotion or nonpromotion should be based on study of each individual. The alleged unfavorable effect of nonpromotion has not been clearly established. Of a group of sixty-three low achievers in the first grade, thirty were promoted to grade 2 and thirty-three were retained in grade 1. When retested after seven months, the promoted group had made significantly greater gains in reading achievement than the nonpromoted group. On the California Test of Personality, the promoted group showed gains in self-reliance, freedom from antisocial and withdrawal tendencies, and personal adjustment. However, the nonpromoted group showed greater feelings of belonging, more freedom from nervous symptoms, and greater adequacy in social relations [14]. In either policy, the results depend upon many attitudes in the home and school, especially upon the pupil-teacher relationship and the teacher's skill in providing for individual differences.

Individualization through Multilevel Reading Material. All of these methods of individualization demand a variety of suitable reading materials. In an effort to deal with the wide range of reading ability in almost any class, Don Parker [63] began before 1957 to collect reading materials on different levels and to compare their effectiveness with that of a single basal reader. The success of this first experiment led to the development of the widely used SRA Reading Laboratories, published by Science Research Associates, Inc., Chicago, and other somewhat similar kits of materials. Basal readers are now offered on two or three levels of difficulty. There are annotated bibliographies of books for retarded readers that indicate the level of reading difficulty of each book (see Appendix A).

Special Services

The teachers in the elementary schools, frequently too busy to cope adequately with all the demands, neglect many children with serious reading problems. Year after year they note the reading difficulties in the youngsters' cumulative records and leave them—uncorrected. Difficulties pile up in succeeding grades.

To overcome prolonged or repeated failure, some elementary schools are offering special services. For many years the Chicago schools have employed "adjustment teachers" who work with backward and maladjusted children. The most modern systems now employ a reading teacher-consultant whose job in part is to work with severely retarded readers. (See Chapters 14 and 15.) In time, the reading teacher will probably work less with a few special problems and more widely with the teachers for more effective instruction for all the pupils.

In some localities—e.g., Dallas, Philadelphia, St. Louis—there are city- or countywide reading clinics serving both elementary and secondary schools.

SECONDARY SCHOOL READING PROGRAMS [25]

Reading programs for secondary schools are becoming increasingly popular. Most administrators recognize the need for improving the reading of junior and senior high school students. Between one-third and two-thirds of the secondary schools offer reading programs.

Inadequate Preparation of Personnel

Although secondary school principals are willing enough to introduce reading programs, they have difficulty in finding qualified persons to carry them out. Most often they appoint an English teacher or a successful elementary school teacher, though this person may not have been specifically prepared for this responsibility. In a survey of 7,417 high school English teachers, published in 1959 by the National Council of Teachers of English, 90 per cent said that they felt inadequately prepared to teach reading; almost 50 per cent said that they were poorly prepared to teach literature. Those in junior high schools and in small high schools felt the least well prepared. Moreover, three out of five persons chosen to lead all-school programs had not received even one hour of professional preparation [87]. In the Harvard study, Mary Austin recommended "that a course in basic reading instruction be required of all prospective secondary teachers" [6, p. 147], a separate three-hour course, not merely a unit in a course on English methods. According to this study, in the schools that offered reading programs one-third to one-half of the persons supervising, directing, or teaching reading had had no specialized education in it.

The best thing that can be said of contemporary secondary school programs is that they are evolving. Many different kinds of programs are being tried out. In the past most of them emphasized remedial work. Recently there has been a trend toward developmental programs which involve all the students, with subject teachers taking the major responsibility [84, 95].

If the students have had an effective reading program during their elementary school years, the secondary teachers will only need to reinforce, then apply these skills and give instruction and practice in higher-level skills [90].

The present situation in most secondary schools presents a dilemma: there are many pupils with deficiencies in basic reading skills, but there are few reading teachers available to work with them. One solution of this problem is to employ a reading teacher-consultant in every school who will work with severely retarded readers and also help the teachers to give all the students more effective instruction in reading.

Junior High School Programs

The junior high school years are the time for pupils to consolidate the reading skills acquired in elementary school and to learn the more complex skills of high school. To accomplish these aims junior high schools have developed a variety of reading programs and procedures.

Time for Reading in School. When lack of time or incentive or unfavorable conditions limit pupils' home reading, they must read during the school day. In one rural school a library corner with table and chairs and a variety of suitable books invited pupils to read. A pupil librarian and committee were responsible for keeping the books in order, for displaying them attractively, and for checking them in and out. Older pupils needing practice in reading very easy books obtained it without embarrassment when they were responsible for helping younger children select and read suitable books. The public library loaned books to the school for a four-week period, and the state department of education loaned books for a term or a year. In the seventh grade all the pupils had three periods a week in which they read books and articles of their own choice. They kept individual records of the books they had read, commenting briefly on each one.

All the eighth-grade pupils received twenty periods of special instruction. Besides, the development of reading skills essential for efficient study of that day's assignments was a part of the daily study period. Pupils learned to read for different purposes, using newspapers and periodicals for practice material as well as their text and reference books. During the supervised study periods, retarded readers received instruction and practice individually or in small groups. A club period a week provided natural opportunities for reading and writing as well as for speaking and listening. A school newspaper with pupil editor and editorial committee motivated writing and reading. Without such a program many pupils would have been unable to read the kind of material or the amount of material required in the higher grades.

An Evolving Reading Program. The reading program in State Street Junior High School [3] has evolved over a number of years. It has always emphasized developmental reading. The pupils of each grade were divided into high, low, and average groups according to their scores on the Iowa Silent Reading Tests, supplemented by the recommendations of teachers and, in some cases, by their scores on the Stanford-Binet individual intelligence test. These groups were scheduled for a daily twenty-minute reading period, obtained by a slight shortening of each of the regular periods. The superior readers broadened their interests and improved their tastes by making dramatic readings of plays, sharing ideas gained from articles and books, and spending one period a week in the public library. The average group concentrated on the reading skills in which they were weak. The low group learned how to recognize unfamiliar words, gained fluency by reading easy, interesting books, and practicing the skills they needed in order to get some meaning from their textbooks.

Three small groups of nonreaders and slow learners had individualized instruction and reading experiences designed to increase their self-confidence. Seven children in one group gained proficiency in their everyday reading. One day they saw on the board—

No Parking Allowed	Men at Work
Detour	Danger
School, Go Slow	No Hunting
Dead End	Keep Off the Grass

[3] State Street School, Hackensack, N.J., is in an urban, industrial, low socioeconomic area. Dr. William Patterson was the principal, Lois Sinniger, chairman of the evaluation committee, Louise Whelan, chairman of the reading committee in the beginning years of the program.

The teacher, Louise M. Whelan, said, "These are signs I saw this weekend. How many of you have seen them?" All have seen some of the signs.

"Jim, you are learning to drive a car, aren't you? Suppose you wanted to stop on a certain street and saw the first sign. What would you do?"

Jim knew this sign and answered, "I'd find another place to stop."

"That's exactly right. Suppose you were driving and saw the next sign [Detour], what would you do?"

No one in the group was quite certain as to what this sign meant.

"It's a French word that means 'to turn aside.' What would you do if you saw that sign?"

"Not go straight ahead; take a road that goes around and comes back on the same road," said Bill.

Similarly, the students learned the other signs. The teacher asked the boys to look for other signs, words, phrases, and sentences that they ran across and bring them in the next day.

Since movies interested these boys, the teacher used them in improving their oral English and reading. An overage pupil, a discipline problem and nonreader, also had a marked speech difficulty. One day he surprised the teacher by his enthusiastic and lengthy account of a movie he had seen. One phrase—"Make up your mind, make up your mind"—he pronounced with accuracy and emphasis. The teacher wrote his account of the movie, had it typed, and used it as reading material. His familiarity with the words and sentences and his keen interest in the movie made this article easy for him to read.

Since these pupils also liked sports and current events, the teacher brought in a number of pictures of winter sports from the Sunday paper, mounted them with the help of the pupils, and typed on each one a short, simple paragraph giving information that the picture did not convey. The pupils read these pages eagerly, passing them from one to another.

These reading activities grew directly from the pupils' interests as a group and as individuals. The teacher knew her pupils—their home backgrounds, interests, speech and reading difficulties—and was familiar with records of their behavior in other classes. She used this information in providing the experiences and instruction that each pupil needed. For the slow learners, the goals were immediate and tangible; the activities were simple and concrete and short. Reading evolved from firsthand experiences and related functionally to their other classes in music, arts, shop, health, and physical education.

At first many of the regular teachers felt insecure in their new role. Some joined an extramural university course in the teaching of reading which was conveniently given at the school.

In later years the school placed more emphasis on the teaching of reading in every subject. Guidance programs also included reading experiences. In the homerooms the pupils wrote reading autobiographies, kept records of their voluntary reading, took informal reading tests and studied the results, spent one period a week in recreational reading in the library, and discussed what they had read during the next homeroom period.

The librarian rendered an invaluable service. She searched diligently for easy books that the slow readers could read with pleasure instead of frustration. When they came to the library, she helped each one to choose a suitable book. She encouraged them to write book reviews to guide other pupils in their choices. When a teacher wanted books in her subject for the retarded readers, the librarian tried to obtain them.

Features of such a reading program as this and of other programs described later can be incorporated into your own junior high school program.

Programs in Senior High School

In the senior high school each pupil should have a progression of reading experiences that start where he is. The trouble, of course, is that the pupils are at so many different places. Teachers often feel like the old fellow who replied, when asked the way to Danbury, "If I was going to Danbury, I wouldn't start from here." They would rather start at some much higher level of reading proficiency.

Some programs merely try to help pupils to succeed in an unsuitable curriculum. Some focus on a single aspect. Others emphasize testing to the neglect of teaching. But many different programs have been successful and many can serve as patterns for your school.

A Limited Approach to the Reading Problem. When neither the principal nor the teachers are ready to make any fundamental changes, a limited approach is necessary. In a tenth-grade class where the course of study did not relate to the students' lives and the textbooks were both dull and difficult, teachers could attempt only two innovations. The first was to solicit magazines to provide some livelier reading and encourage students to use the public library. The second was a concerted effort to improve vocabulary. Teachers made lists of the key words in their various subjects and helped students to acquire rich and meaningful associations for these words through firsthand experiences. Then using them frequently in conversation and assignments, writing them on the blackboard, and discussing them in class, the teacher integrated the new words. The Latin teacher cooperated by teaching the students how to get the meanings of words from their derivation; she made practice sheets with Latin prefixes, suffixes, and roots in vocabulary building.

The English teacher explored with her students the origins of language, pointing out the sources of words that are common today. She compiled words that they misused in their themes and conversations and words that they found unfamiliar in the required reading. Working with these words all members made a large class dictionary, contributing definitions, derivations, and examples of correct usage. Each student started his own dictionary of difficult words. Sometimes the students invented word games of the quiz type. A corner of the blackboard carried derivations of special interest, which seldom failed to attract attention. The English teacher also gave the students instruction and practice in using a dictionary and getting meanings from context. With the teacher's contagious enthusiasm, the program brought results that justified repetition of the effort.

Accent on Recreational Reading. Various forms of individualized reading are even more appropriate for secondary than for elementary school pupils [104].

One program, designed to increase interest in reading, devoted one period a week to a wide variety of recreational material. Students chose anything they wanted to read except comics and required books. The teacher guided students and informally checked comprehension through individual conferences. As a result, the average increase in reading for a three-month period was 4.3 books per student. It was not lack of time but their failure to select appealing books that had limted their previous reading. Guided free reading has compared favorably with more direct mechanical methods.

Reading in a Vocational High School. The program in this type of school includes shopwork and related subjects. In these courses a student has to read the safety rules and to apply them, to understand and follow directions, to learn the technical words peculiar to the trade, to pass the licensing examination, and to use reference material and library aids.

In English the aim is to enable students to read material relating to their vocation, such as workmen's compensation laws, union rules, and other regulations that affect the trades, informative books and articles on employment opportunities, qualifications and training for various jobs, how to get a job, and similar material. The aim is also to interest students in reading as a leisure-time activity, to introduce them to some of the great books, and to encourage them to read for understanding, appreciation, and the realization of true democracy.

To enjoy recreational reading, the pupils sought literature that appealed to them and was sufficiently easy. One teacher began by exchanging stories with the class so that the students began to look for simple adventure stories. From the reading of true-to-life stories, they gained an understanding of people and an insight into their own problems. In their class discussions of the books and articles, they came to appreciate the contribution that reading can make to conversation. In their independent reading they experienced the enjoyment that only books can give.

Another type of reading program begins by focusing on the vocation a student has chosen with the assistance of his counselor. Together, counselor, reading teacher, and student anaiyze the job from the standpoint of the language skills which the student had to acquire. For example, Laura had the prospect of assisting in a preschool program. In her reading period she learned to select books that would interest preschool children, to read them to children, and to help children who came from non-English-speaking homes to become more proficient in speaking English. She read simple books on child care and made a scrapbook of magazine and newspaper articles on preschool children.

Vocational school groups that especially enjoyed singing found favorite songs in poetry anthologies and enjoyed choral reading especially.

The English room became a reading laboratory with books covering a wide variety of interests and many levels of difficulty. The bulletin board displayed clippings on personal appearance, music, fashions, and subjects relating to the trades. A number of different practice books and a file of practice exercises for developing reading skills were available. The students brought reading material—a magazine that contained a story, pamphlets from the company where a parent worked, catalogs of schools that offer correspondence courses. From a bank the teacher obtained pamphlets on thrift and taught a unit on starting a bank account.

The shops themselves provided an excellent laboratory for reading. Here the students first met the objects and the processes of the trade and then learned the printed symbols that described them, integrating a vocabulary firmly with subject matter. Students learned to read illustrated operators' manuals, trade catalogs, periodicals, pamphlets, and handbooks as sources of technical information and for descriptions of machines and processes, although much of this reading content had to be simplified.

In some shops the teacher first demonstrated the process, the pupils then carried it out, and later described it in their own words. They recorded this description in their notebooks, compiling their own intelligible handbook. With the most retarded readers, the teachers of academic subjects used the same procedure: they presented the topic; the pupils discussed and summarized it. As they copied what they had dictated, they compiled their own edition of the history or science textbook.

The librarian of the school purchased suitable books, set up attractive displays, acquainted students with the use of the library, and guided their reading.

Students who showed an unusual ability in writing could take a journalism class, and for those who thought of eventually teaching in trade schools or who planned to continue their technical and academic training, there were enriched courses. Special small groups in reading cared for those who were markedly retarded. In these many ways the students were given fruitful reading experiences.

The most common approach in the senior high school involves developmental courses required for all freshmen and elective to upper-class students. Such courses aim to raise the level of comprehension, expand vocabulary, increase speed of reading, and improve study methods. Tormey and Patterson [99] obtained helpful student evaluations, both positive and negative, of one such course.

Emphases Needed. Effective high school reading programs should include salient features. First, teachers should consider the teaching of reading of their subject an intrinsic part of their job. With a broad view of reading they inventory and assess early in the year the pupils' reading strengths and weaknesses, then give effective instruction in reading for different purposes. They especially emphasize critical reading and interpretation and use appropriate questions and directions for individual abilities [93, p. 38]. Second, administrators should recognize the value of reading, creating conditions that make more effective teaching possible. Finally, administrators, teachers, and reading specialists should receive preservice and in-service preparation for this responsibilty.

READING PROGRAMS IN SCHOOL SYSTEMS

A number of large school systems have made citywide attacks on the reading problem. Descriptions of two resulting programs will illustrate the effective features.

The St. Louis Reading Program

The reading program in the St. Louis public schools has four unique and notable features: [4]

1. *Analysis of levels of reading.* In the primary grades each child has a thorough analysis that covers physical and sensory factors and mental functioning, as well as interpretive skills and word analysis skills. Reading tests and the daily observations of teachers appraise the level of performance in these skills.
2. *The primary classification plan.* All primary children attend ungraded

[4] Described by Dr. William Kottmeyer in a letter to Dr. Strang and in *Evaluation Handbook for Elementary Schools,* third experimental edition, 1952, the *Primary Classification Plan,* the *Evaluation Handbook, Levels in English,* and Kottmeyer's *Teacher's Guide for Remedial Reading,* published by Webster in 1959.

primary schools. If, in the third year, the children have not achieved the top level of achievement for the primary grades, they are placed in groups of twenty with well-qualified teachers, where, under good conditions, they make a final effort to build basic reading skills before they have to deal with middle-grade textbooks. Over the past several years, thousands of pupils have avoided trouble and frustration because of these "Rooms of Twenty."

3. *The reading clinics.* At first these clinics offered only diagnostic and remedial service; they have now become language-arts centers, each under the direction of a language-arts consultant. Every year promising public school teachers join the small permanent clinic staff; here they become familiar with diagnostic and remedial procedures. Thus the clinics also serve as in-service education centers.

4. *Evaluation of the language-arts program.* A detailed guide for evaluating a language-arts program sets forth criteria by which the teacher may rate his performance in teaching reading, spelling, and other language activities. The language-arts consultants in the reading clinics serve as visiting committees for the evaluation of a given school's language-arts program. The results in language-arts achievement, as shown by standardized tests, have been particularly gratifying.

The Philadelphia Reading Program [5]

In the Philadelphia schools the concept of growth in reading as a developmental process requiring instruction from first grade through college has gained increasing acceptance. The reading program in the elementary schools began as a reading-adjustment program many years ago. The reading-adjustment teacher provides remedial instruction for those retarded readers who seem to have the greatest potential for improvement.

Each junior high school provides instruction in developmental as well as in remedial reading. The developmental teaching is done by the English faculty usually under the leadership of the special reading teacher. A curriculum guide and in 1959 a weekly television program featuring demonstration teaching provided further in-service education.

The reading program in senior high schools began with the establishment of remedial groups of not more than fifteen pupils whose achievement in reading seemed to be below their mental potentialities. To teach these classes one or two reading teachers were added to the regular staff in each school; this lightened the load of the other teachers. No stigma was attached to membership in these classes. In fact, there was a waiting list. These small

[5] The development of the Philadelphia program is described by Helen Carey and Dorothy Withrow in two unpublished doctoral dissertations, Teachers College, Columbia University, New York, 1955.

reading classes serve as a laboratory in which methods and materials can be developed and tested; the experience thus gained is passed on to teachers in regular classes.

As the program developed, the reading teachers spent more and more of their time helping the teachers of regular classes to improve the reading instruction in all subjects. In accord with the developmental concept of reading, several senior high schools have introduced additional courses in advanced reading and study skills for college preparatory students and courses in developmental reading for all students. At least three senior high schools have organized in-service education programs involving all members of the professional staff, including counselors, librarians, and department heads. One principal initiated a program in which full responsibility for the teaching of reading is carried by the subject teachers, with the assistance of the special reading teacher, who now has the role of consultant.

A reading clinic serving the entire city was opened to provide diagnostic study of children with severe reading disabilities. Its threefold purpose is (1) to help the pupil with a severe learning problem, (2) to provide in-service education for teachers and counselors, and (3) to conduct research in the field of reading disability.

This brief description of an evolving reading program illustrates three important trends: continuity in reading instruction from kindergarten to college, integration of reading instruction with the teaching of every subject, and development of a comprehensive, whole-school program to serve the needs of students representing a wide range of reading potential and proficiency. This program also accents the importance of providing for the continuous growth of teachers, administrators, counselors, librarians, and the reading specialists themselves.

COLLEGE READING PROGRAMS

In view of the results of Perry's informal reading test at Harvard [64], it seems evident that even able college freshmen may profit by a course in reading. Perry found that, although the freshmen he tested were above the 85th percentile on an objective standardized test, only 1 in 100 was able to grasp the central thought of a chapter in a college textbook. Moreover, they showed little or no mastery of effective methods for reading long assignments of difficult material. The Bureau of Study Counsel at Harvard University met this need by conferring with 300 students individually in the course of a year and enrolling over 3,000 in reading classes during a five-year period. In junior or community colleges there are many more retarded readers who could improve with performance programs such as those described in the 1964 Yearbook of the Claremont Reading Conference.

In college as in secondary school, instruction in reading may be an integral part of the freshman program, on a par with other subjects. Every student takes this course which is sectioned according to the students' initial reading ability. After experimenting for one year with a developmental reading course Miriam Schleich obtained such favorable student response that the course was required as a regular part of the college program [80].

Rather than setting up a separate reading course, some institutions include instruction and practice in reading and study skills in the freshman orientation program, as the University of Maine does [62].

A more common practice is to offer special classes for students who are deficient in reading. Many programs of this kind have appeared in *Reading Improvement,* a Quarterly Journal for the Improvement of Teaching Reading at the Advanced Level, *The Journal of Reading,* Yearbooks of the Southwest Reading Conferences for colleges and universities, the annual proceedings of the University of Chicago reading conferences, and other sources.

On the basis of questionnaires from forty-two Pennsylvania colleges and universities, Colvin [17] suggested certain features that should be included in an ideal college reading program. Among these was a credit course required of all freshmen and elective to upperclassmen.

A course developed on a voluntary basis at Columbia College included the following generally sound features. At the beginning of each class session, the students read a 1,000-word article on the reading process in the *Study Type of Reading Exercises* (Teachers College Press, Teachers College, Columbia University, New York, 1951) and discussed the conditions and methods that brought the best results. Each student kept a graph of his reading progress, receiving additional instruction and practice in sentence and paragraph reading, outlining and summarizing, reading and answering questions, and critical and interpretive reading. The students spent the rest of the period in applying these reading skills to their daily assignments. If a member of the class finished an exercise ahead of the others, he read magazine and newspaper clippings which he selected from the file. Designed to give practice in reading for different purposes, these selections also provided appropriate checks on comprehension. The content of the periods was flexible to serve priority needs and interests of the students. Individual conferences considered the student's approach to the reading task—his anxieties, the way he felt about his reading, and the personal meaning he attached to reading—in brief, whatever was affecting his reading efficiency. Frequently reading improvement contributes to self-confidence, ability to concentrate, reduction of excessive anxiety, and other aspects of personality development.

Fortunately one apparent trend in college programs is away from machine-oriented, skill-drill courses toward student-oriented instruction and guidance in reading. The fact that many diverse reading programs get results [85] suggests that any sound program may stimulate both students and teachers, that students may be convinced that a program will help them improve their reading, and that the skill, interest, and personality of the teacher contribute largely to the success of any program [68].

ADULT READING PROGRAMS

Adults in all walks of life have become interested in increasing their reading efficiency. Business executives take expensive speed-reading courses. Research scientists in one large industry profited from instruction and practice in the reading and writing of both popular and technical research reports. Colleges, universities, and school systems offer reading classes in their adult education programs. The war on illiteracy and poverty has reading improvement as a primary objective, using television programs as one medium. In *The Drive against Illiteracy*, Isenberg [41] describes in detail various methods of teaching illiterate youth and adults. In 1965 there were millions of different adult education courses in the United States. These were offered in schools, community agencies, the Armed Forces, correspondence schools, industry, and on television. Persons from fifteen to sixty-five years of age were enrolled in these courses. In many, reading was a primary emphasis [61].

Since adult reading programs attract strongly motivated students, they should be practical and individualized, with pertinent reading materials specifically designed to improve a variety of reading powers. However, very few adult reading courses have presented adequate evidence that their students do indeed make progress, or that this progress continues after the end of the course. Many of the commercial courses base their claims of phenomenal success on the results of poorly constructed tests of comprehension and on testimonials of carefully selected students.

Olsen found that reading materials for adult instruction are inadequate. The reading level of much of this material is too high; the tone, juvenile; the content, too formal; and the language and word attack skills that adults need are simply not taught [61].

TEACHER EDUCATION PROGRAMS

Institutions of higher learning have the major responsibility for preparing teachers and reading specialists. The courses in reading they offer to undergraduates preparing to teach vary greatly in content and quality. Formerly these courses for undergraduates tended toward one of two extremes: an exclusive concern with theory or a preoccupation with devices and gadgets. Though a fusion of theory and practice is still imperfect, it is much better. The University of Arizona requires two courses of undergraduates majoring in education. One of these, which the students take before practice teaching, gives them an understanding of the reading process and acquaints them with methods and materials for developing reading ability from the earliest stages. The other course, which they take while practice teaching, is a seminar. The students present specific problems involving reading instruction; the seminar analyzes, discusses, and poses practical solutions. Several college instructors have gone further in the direction of fusing theory and practice; they have plunged undergraduate students immediately into actual work with children. Under this plan each student is given an individual child to teach. The fact that he has an immediate need to know what to do acts as a strong motivation to profit from the accompanying instruction. An extreme suggestion is that prospective teachers dispense with preliminary methods courses and learn how to teach by working with master teachers in elementary and high schools. Both graduate students and teachers in service learn a great deal by participating in a seminar where they discuss the cases with which they are currently working. As usual, the educational pendulum tends to swing from one extreme to another instead of achieving stability at a happy medium.

If conducted effectively [78], in-service education will help the many teachers now serving in the schools who are poorly prepared to improve student reading [1]. (See also the in-service reading programs described in the March, 1966, *Reading Teacher.*) Lecture courses are usually less effective than workshops in which the teachers are given both a theoretical background in reading and opportunities to work out solutions to the practical reading problems they are currently facing. The summer Institutes for Advanced Study under Title XI of the National Defense Education Act, as amended, provide opportunities for in-service education in the teaching of reading.

A more effective way to provide in-service education is to employ a well-qualified reading consultant or reading teacher-consultant in every school. Classroom teachers appreciate the opportunity to get help on a specific problem at the time when they need it. They learn by watching skillful teaching demonstrations in their own classes. They appreciate information about and access to suitable reading materials and equipment.

The in-service education program in New York City is most comprehensive. There is a citywide reading supervisor, each district having a reading-improvement teacher-consultant. In almost every elementary school a reading-improvement teacher assists the classroom teachers, especially newly appointed teachers in grades 1, 2, and 3. He gives demonstrations and helps teachers to understand children's needs and to prepare lesson plans. In about half of the elementary schools, corrective-reading teachers meet with small groups of children and spend at least 20 per cent of their time with teachers in grades 4, 5, and 6. The staff of reading specialists also includes reading counselors who work in each of the eleven reading clinics.

There are various kinds of in-service courses. At one time 8,000 teachers enrolled in courses on reading materials and methods. A TV program, "Teaching of Reading in the Primary Grades," had 2,000 enrollees, and kinescopes of this program were available for faculty meetings. Other courses are on diagnosis and treatment. A total of 18,000 of the 20,000 teachers have taken one or more of these courses, and teachers also have involved themselves in research projects such as the one to appraise reading-readiness programs for children whose homes offered little incentive.

These in-service programs are held not after school or on Saturday mornings but during the day. They include demonstrations, observation of classes, small-group meetings, and individual conferences, using ample published materials such as bulletins on teaching aids, a reading record card, and a chart showing sequential levels of reading development.

Teachers should feel that an in-service program is *their* program, not another requisite for holding a position. They must also have the conviction that it will help them to improve their teaching of reading.

Ideally, to begin, in-service education should arrange for student teachers to observe master teachers during the school day. Their visits will be more meaningful if they have an outline that shows them what to look for and have time after the lesson to discuss the materials and procedures used and what the children learned.

Finally, teachers would do well to improve their own reading [49]. No profession relies so heavily on reading journals, textbooks, research studies, and modern fiction as does teaching. The accomplished teacher continually reads. Obviously, then, he himself must be a master reader.

TYPES OF READING PROGRAMS

Administrators and teachers often ask: "Where can I find examples of effective reading programs? What are some of the common faults of reading programs? How do other schools aid retarded readers of various degrees of mental ability?"

Superintendents have tried to solve the reading problem in various ways: by forming special reading classes, by introducing a course in reading for all students, by setting up a reading center to which students go voluntarily, by expecting every teacher to give instruction and practice in the reading of his subject.

Reading programs are of three types: developmental, corrective, and remedial. Of these, the all-school developmental type is the most important because it is integral in every student's education, involving a sequential program from the early years and into adult life. Year by year students learn skills and appreciations, then extend, reinforce, and apply them. Every member of the school staff helps plan the program cooperatively so that the child will not neglect or overstress any aspect of reading development and can integrate it where possible with listening, speaking, and writing.

The second and third types of reading programs have no clear distinction between them; their titles are often interchangeable. Both corrective and remedial programs are in a sense developmental: they begin instruction at the student's present level of reading competency and help him to progress as fast and as far as he is able toward realization of his potential. Corrective work is done with students whose learning capacity is adequate but who need special reading instruction to profit by their regular class work. The word *remedial* is often applied to work with students whose difficulties are more serious and complex. (See Chapter 15 on special retarded readers.)

The following paragraphs describe some ways in which an administration provides reading instruction.

Every Teacher a Teacher of Reading of His Subject

In this program every teacher gives instruction and practice in common reading skills as well as special reading approaches, key vocabulary, and specialized reading skills relative to his subject. To be successful, this type of program needs teachers who are interested in reading and not overburdened with other duties, a principal who is enthusiastic and informed about reading improvement, and a reading consultant who presents himself to the teachers as a helping person. Since many teachers have not been prepared to teach the effective reading of their subject, the first hurdle is to arrange for them to master the techniques. Workshops, study groups, university extension courses, or other forms of in-service education are some of the answers.

One school-wide program in the ninth grade had two main features: (1) concerted action by teachers of English, social studies, and science focusing on reading; (2) "reading clinics" for small groups of pupils conducted by experienced English teachers [60]. In science, for example, only about half the usual content of general science was covered. Teachers selected portions of each unit for their intrinsic interest and importance and for opportunities they offered to develop communication skills. Writing included frequent short compositions dealing with subject matter in all three fields. When English, social studies, and science teachers teamed—in the ultimate sense of the word— to analyze the reading skills of their respective subjects, describe and develop the best methods of teaching them, find books on different levels of difficulty, use recordings and visual aids, and share their experiences with successful projects, the students' reading improved.

In the Norwalk, Connecticut, high school the chief function of David Shepherd, the reading consultant, was to work with teachers in a broad type of developmental reading program [86]. He recognized that each teacher should know three things: (1) what reading skills a student needs to succeed in his subject, (2) how to assess each student's proficiency in reading the subject, and (3) how to make reading instruction an integral part of his teaching of the subject.

To develop these competencies, the consultant first met with teachers individually and then with the entire faculty to discuss their practical questions. Among these were: how to meet the needs of individual students in classes where the range of reading ability shows a spread of from seven to eight years; where to get reading materials in a given subject that are suitable for the retarded reader; how to group students within a high school class; how to make questions that will test students' ability to draw conclusions; how to make, administer, and use an informal group inventory.

At first the teachers wanted the consultant to come into their classes and give demonstrations of the teaching techniques he was talking about. Later they wanted him to observe their teaching of reading, supply reading materials, and schedule individual conferences in which they could talk over his demonstrations, their own observations, and the results of informal inventories. That is, there was a gradual shift of emphasis as the teachers accepted responsibility for working out instructional methods in their classes.

There are many advantages in a program in which teachers learn to improve their techniques for teaching the reading of their subject with the help of a capable and tactful reading consultant. The students immediately apply the skills they learn, motivated by their desire to succeed in their classes. The subject teacher knows more than anyone else about the best methods of reading his subject. He knows what attitudes and skills are needed, when to reinforce and where to apply them. However, he cannot be expected to teach basic vocabulary or basic skills in word recognition and comprehension to severely retarded readers. This job requires reading teachers.

Reading Instruction in English Periods

A freshman English course may be built around reading and based on the needs of the students. According to Early's survey [27], developmental programs, insofar as they offered reading instruction to all students, were generally a regular part of the English course. Artley, however, warns administrators about this decision: "Of all the deceptively easy solutions, the one to guard against is that of turning the responsibility over to the English teachers. . . . *All* teachers, within the context of their teaching area, must develop the competencies that contribute to effective reading" [3, p. 7].

But at present, high school reading instruction appears in some form most commonly in English classes, and teachers of these classes have offered some timely suggestions through many articles in *Elementary English* and the *English Journal.* For example, one-minute drills at the beginning of the period twice a week benefited reading performance. The students spent one minute reading in the literature text or in a magazine such as *Reader's Digest,* then counted the words they had read in that time and reported on their comprehension of the main ideas and important details. With this small expenditure of class time the students more than doubled their reading speed without loss in comprehension. They also became more aware of the need to vary their speed according to the material and purpose.

In another program all the students in the English classes spent ten minutes each day reading articles on the reading process. They learned about reading as they practiced.

To give more thorough reading instruction, a reading and study-skills laboratory is sometimes introduced as part of a freshman English program. In large schools there are special English sections for the most retarded and sometimes for the most able readers. In the classes structured as a workshop, the students discover the specific phases of reading in which they need improvement and work on them. Each teacher builds up files of practice exercises and informational and recreational materials that are suitable for his type of group. He does not have to provide such a wide range of instructional materials as would be required for the usual heterogeneous class. Since the able learners have their own special section, they are not bored or held back by the slower students. They read beyond the grade requirements, develop skills that they need for writing reports, and apply semantics and logic on deeper levels of interpretation. Similarly, this plan spares the retarded readers the loss of self-esteem that they might suffer by being constantly compared with superior readers. This type of class organization is described in the account of the Philadelphia program earlier in this chapter.

Some reading programs have failed because they were too exclusively centered in the English department. A reappraisal of the situation often shows the need for a program with a broader base. Many classes in other departments in a high school succeed or fail because of lack of reading skills.

Team-teaching Program

In a team-teaching program three or four teachers may assume responsibility for seventy-five to one hundred pupils. They decide what to teach and how to teach it. They plan instruction that is appropriate for small groups, such as word recognition skills, as well as instruction that is appropriate for the large group, such as appreciation of literature through dramatics, story telling, or choral reading. Each teacher assumes responsibilities that accord with his special competence.

When skillfully developed, team teaching has a number of values. It stimulates teachers to expand and refine their teaching repertoire as they observe and discuss each other's methods. It exposes pupils to different teaching styles and teacher personalities. It often reduces behavior problems since it facilitates the kind of thorough preparation that produces superior instruction. By reducing the amount of time each member of the team must spend in classroom teaching, it provides more time for helping individual pupils.

Actually the principle of teachers' teaming—pooling resources, interests, and techniques for the good of the students—materializes in numerous forms. When the teachers of science, social studies, and English worked cooperatively on reading skills, guided each other in selecting readings for the same students— a project previously described in this chapter—it was team teaching. So is it when the librarian works with an English staff on a special unit of biography or drama, and so too is it teaming when teachers exchange ideas and exercises and lesson plans. References to such methods appear throughout the text. (The theme of the January, 1965, issue of the *Elementary School Principal,* vol. 45, is team teaching.)

A Developmental Reading Course

The purpose of such a course is to make sure that not just retarded readers but all the students acquire the quality of reading skills which assures them efficient learning and adequate assimilation of concepts taught in each grade. To most secondary teachers, reading is in the curriculum to compensate for neglect of reading instruction in the intermediate grades. Some see it only as a valid subdivision of the language arts, confined to basic classes. But a more enlightened attitude is that students at every level, from kindergarten to seminars at the universities, and all kinds of students, regardless of IQ, need and deserve to develop their reading potential. There is no one who would not benefit from more effective reading skills.

The most determined effort to implement a developmental reading course was the decree of the Pennsylvania State Council of Education in February, 1958. This decree provided for a planned program of reading instruction for all pupils in grades 7 and 8. It could be either remedial or developmental; it could be offered in connection with English or as a separate subject. The council encouraged the continuation of this instruction through the senior high school years. The council defined developmental reading as a program that reaches every pupil and provides for his continuous reading growth in the light of knowledge of his capacity. It was assumed that the pupil's reading at the end of the sixth grade was not efficient enough to meet his needs in high school, in college, or in adult life; he needed to learn new skills and to develop and refine the skills he had acquired in the elementary school. He also needed to broaden and intensify his appreciation, whether his ability was low, average, or superior.

When the program started in 1959, only half of the teachers assigned to teach reading had completed a course in reading. However, the large majority were convinced of the importance of reading instruction to the achievement of all students in all subjects. The coordinator of the program soon extended the reading course to include instruction in the content areas [51].

Any administrator who introduces a developmental reading course (cooperatively, it is hoped!) confronts these questions: How shall we fit the course into the school schedule? How shall we conduct it? Who will be prepared to teach it?

Reading Centers

In this type of program, students come voluntarily to the center during their study periods or after school. The students and the reading teacher cooperatively plan individual or group instruction on the basis of diagnostic information.

In two senior high schools, English teachers with doctor's degrees in reading [6] initiated and developed reading centers. In one of these schools a part-time center was developed in a regular classroom. In the other school the only room available was a storeroom. With $75 from book fair sales, the teacher and the students remodeled it into an attractive reading room.

To avoid having any stigma attached to the reading center, the teacher put attendance on a voluntary basis and welcomed pupils known to be able learners as well as the less able. Since the pupils came during their free periods, they did not miss their regular class instruction.

To initiate the program, one teacher sent a description of it to the English teachers and distributed the illustrated application form to the pupils.

Some classes suited retarded readers; another, the most popular, welcomed the upperclassmen who wanted to increase their concentration, comprehension, and speed. Although counselors and teachers informed pupils who needed special help, some of the poorest readers did not apply.

A variation of the reading-center program is one in which the subject-matter teacher accompanies his class to the reading center for special instruction in reading skills with assistance from the reading teacher. Then the regular teacher reinforces the reading skills taught at that particular time, using both the content area and the reading-center materials.

Special Classes for Retarded Readers

These classes, like the special services for the elementary school, may be either required or offered on a voluntary basis, with or without credit. Many reading programs have started with a course of this kind. Sometimes it is

[6] Charlotte O. Rogers, Tucson High School, Tucson, Arizona; Fehl Shirley, Rincon High School, Tucson, Arizona.

TUCSON HIGH SCHOOL
APPLICATION TO STUDY IN OUR READING CENTER

Name _____ M or F _____ Age_____ Grade_____ Counselor _____

Name of Parent or Guardian _____ Telephone Number _____

Languages You Speak _____ Languages You Understand _____

Description of Previous Reading Guidance _____

Grades in Your Subjects Last Year _____

Schedule of Your School Day

Period	Teacher	Subject	Room Number
1			
2			
3			
4			
5			
6			

Hour after
School _____

How far do you intend to go in school?

What are your ambitions?

What do you like to read?

Why are you applying to study in our reading center?

What do you intend to learn here in the center?

Filled out by _____

The applicant does not write below this line. It is reserved for your English teacher.

Comments Concerning Applicant _____

Recommendations _____

---

scheduled after school hours, sometimes during study periods, and sometimes as part of a regular class. More detail is given in Chapters 13 and 14.

Much of the value of the special class is lost unless an effort is made to bridge the gap between the special class and the student's regular classes. Here is a vital place for team teaching. The regular teacher informs the reading teacher about the subject of the unit on which his class is working so that the latter can use books on this topic as practice material. This enables the retarded reader to gain recognition by making a contribution to his regular class and to know success with his peers. The reading teacher may suggest methods and provide reading material for the regular teacher to use. Students from the special classes should not experience failure in their other classes just as they have begun to build up self-confidence. The reading teacher should also confer with the student's other teachers about his reading capacity, interests, needs, and progress.

Summer Sessions and Double Periods

Two other types of programs are the summer reading courses and the double English period. In the first, the range may include (1) retarded readers who are capable of making a reading gain of two months more than those who do not attend the course, and (2) superior readers who want to increase their speed of reading. The double period includes one hour for instruction in reading and the other for application of these skills to the understanding and discussion of literature.

Clinical Service

This usually involves a staff comprising a psychologist, a psychiatrist, a reading specialist, and other specialized personnel. The completeness and intensiveness of this service vary with the situation. (See Chapter 15.)

A Combination of Features and Favorable Conditions

At the present time an effective reading program might include all the major features of each program. The diagram below represents a combined program.

Intensive work with individuals who present complex problems
Special reading groups For slow-learning pupils For able, retarded readers For able learners who want to increase their reading efficiency
A developmental reading course for all pupils
Teaching the reading of every subject at every grade level

In any program the subject teacher should carry responsibility for teaching the reading of his subject. But for various reasons there is need in many schools for a course for all students to insure the continuous development of their reading attitudes and skills, sometimes at the fourth grade, more often at the beginning of junior high school, perhaps in college. Those who are more severely retarded may even need instruction and practice in smaller groups. In some cases, reading problems are so complicated that clinical treatment is necessary.

Certain classroom conditions are conducive to success in any program:

1. Conditions that may affect health in general and eye hygiene in particular should receive attention. Poor illumination or varnished tables that reflect light into the reader's eyes may affect unfavorably reading efficiency and pleasure. The ideal is indirect lighting of at least 15 to 20 candlepower that approaches good daylight conditions [98].
2. Warm interpersonal relations in the classroom—friendly, helpful teachers who respect each student—promote friendly and constructive attitudes among the group. Members enjoy each other and learn from one another in an atmosphere devoid of overtenseness and overcompetition. One twenty-year-old, when asked why he liked the reading center, said, "It's a heart-warming place where everyone is so nice to us, and it gives us confidence in ourselves and in our work."
3. Each student must experience success with reasonable effort because of differentiated assignments involving activities and projects. Reading must have goals and products and reflect growth.
4. Expert instruction structured on diagnosis of interests, needs, present reading status, difficulties, and their causes is specific, suitable, and concrete. Such instruction minimizes failure. Conferences give students an opportunity to help decide what they need most.

The aim of all developmental reading programs is to produce readers [53]—people who like to read, who are not deterred by any reasonable difficulty, who are independent and analytical in their reading, who are capable of literary appreciation, and—ideally—who are interested in the possibility of a better life and a better world.

TESTED PROCEDURES
AND EMPHASES IN READING CLASSES

There are many methods of conducting reading-improvement programs. From this stockpile of methods, the teacher may select the best features of each, and fuse them into an eclectic approach which he can use flexibly according to the needs of a particular class. No class is like another even though the students are the same age, and in any class individuals respond differently to any method. If a student does not succeed with one method, the teacher uses another. Following are descriptions of procedures that have been tested successfully with different groups.

Focus on Functional Vocabulary

The Cornell University reading program emphasized the importance of accurate interpretation of the subtle and complex meanings of words [54]. In order to enlarge their functional vocabularies, the students analyzed words in context and studied the structure and derivation of words. They examined difficult words that occurred frequently in textbooks and analyzed them to find clues to their meaning. Each meaning so derived they applied to the context and noted its contribution to the meaning of the passage as a whole. *The Improvement of College Reading* by M. D. Glock was the text. The performance of the students in the experimental group exceeded that of the control group on equated forms of the Cooperative English Tests: Reading Comprehension in both vocabulary and speed of comprehension. The experimental group also surpassed the control group on three measures of academic achievement.

Persistent Practice

Least creative, but probably the most common, are the skills programs that use practice books and/or machines almost exclusively. The machine-dominated courses usually use reading-rate accelerators or pacers and reading films with check tests. Students keep their own records of progress. Studies of these programs usually report an increase in speed but little change in comprehension. The real test of the effectiveness of these programs is whether the students transfer the gains to day-by-day reading assignments and whether the gains persist after the course ends. In most current programs, reading exercises, vocabulary study, discussion, wide reading, or brief individual conferences supplement machines.

In other classes the teacher depends upon a workbook or practice exercise selected for the class as a whole, on the assumption that all the students need systematic practice in the reading skills required at that particular educational level. When the group presents a wide range of reading achievement, individualized reading exercises such as those of the Science Research Associates Reading Laboratories are more effective. Both of the above approaches are appropriate for students wishing to improve their reading.

For able learners desiring to improve, Kermit Dehl, reading counselor in the Oak Park and River Forest High Schools, Oak Park, Illinois, slowly evolved a program which can serve as another pattern. It is open to students on a voluntary basis. Individual instruction in groups of fifteen or fewer, similar to a reading seminar, follows the traditional diagnosis of reading difficulties. Practice books such as *Reading Skills* by William D. Baker, *How to Become a Better Reader* by Paul Witty, and *Word Wealth* by Ward S. Miller supplement the SRA *Reading Laboratory* and the SRA *Reading for Understanding*. Students who are strong in comprehension and vocabulary but low in rate use the reading-rate accelerator. Those who need special help in seeing groups of words quickly and accurately practice with an individual tachistoscope—the *Eye-Span Trainer*. All pupils keep records of their progress and note special difficulties and individual needs for more practice in certain skills. The teacher does not command or lead; rather he suggests answers and encourages each pupil to work up to his ability. Retesting at the end of the course with the Survey Section of the Diagnostic Reading Tests has shown marked gains. Teachers report more efficient study habits and more favorable attitudes toward reading. A progress report goes to the student, his parents, his dean, and his teachers.

Reading for Pleasure

Many students see no reason to improve their reading. They dislike it, never having had pleasure from it. The curriculum committee of one senior high school proposed to introduce a course called Motivated Reading for all students. Since most of the students in this school were able learners who could read but did not, the aims of this course were to persuade them that reading is not drudgery, and to stimulate them to read voluntarily. The main features of the course, as it was tentatively tried out, were as follows:

Each student wrote a reading autobiography. This gave him perspective on his reading development up to this point.

At the teacher's invitation, the students made suggestions for conducting the class: each student selected a topic that interested him and read on that topic both in and outside of class. They could choose fiction or nonfiction; they could try more difficult books than those they had been reading and share their reactions to reading with the other students.

The teacher obtained the help of the librarian in making books available and helped each student select books on his topic that he could read on his own. While the students were reading independently, the teacher held conferences with individuals to diagnose their reading attitudes and give them more advanced skills; elicit their responses to the books they had been reading; suggest other books that would shed light on a topic—if necessary, upgrading with respect to literary quality or downgrading with respect to difficulty; suggest ways of presenting the ideas from their reading in a form that would be appealing and informative.

The teacher showed the class as a whole ways in which they could record their progress in reading; for example, a simple form may record:

Date	Author	Title	Where I Got It	Why I Read It	How I Liked It

(*Using My Reading Design* [89] shows the areas in which a student is reading and reveals whether they are narrow or wide.)

Book reviews acquainted students with books others had enjoyed and profited by. These reviews may be published in the school paper or the local newspaper, filed in a card catalog in the library, or published in mimeographed form by the class.

The teacher asked the students to continue their reading autobiographies. They were to include details about their progress in the course and an evaluation of it.

The teacher asked the students to note and record any changes in their points of view, attitudes, feelings, or behavior that they could definitely attribute to something they had read during the course.

To evaluate the program, the teacher watched for changes in attitudes and reading habits. Certain students increased their voluntary reading. Others read a whole book for the first time in their lives. In general, the students showed consistent interest, and the teacher found the class work a stimulating and pleasurable experience. Emphasizing the pleasure in reading, a course of this kind may foster habits that carry over into adult life.

Reading for the Discouraged

The Detroit Syllabus, *English S* [29], is an excellent example of a reading program geared to the interests of pupils accustomed to failure and resentful of school and adult authority. The introduction of the new course was sincere and appealing. In the first period the pupils were invited to compare some of their TV favorites. As they left the room, one student said, "Say, I dig this stuff."

The emphasis was on giving these pupils successful experiences. Beginning with this unit on the mass media, the course continued with units on jobs, manners, personality, consumer buying, famous personalities, analyzing the mass media, critical thinking, and special speech arts. It also included scholastic literature units such as *Mirrors, Personal Code.* One unit was on getting a job, interview techniques, proper dress, and filling out application blanks.

Each class period included three types of activity: reading, writing, and speech—listening and speaking. Each day the pupils wrote at least one paragraph in their notebooks.

When asked how they felt about this new course they said [97]:

You get a lot of practice using good English, in talking and writing.

I think you can do more things that you like doing.

It prepares you for the future.

It's a good course. Kids like it and study.

We learn to read and make speeches and think and not be afraid.

No hurts or heartaches or headaches. It's a nice class.

Of all potential dropouts who took the course, not one left school. The students became alert and eager, and their grooming improved. The librarian issued an average of twelve books to each pupil during the course. The next year the course was offered to about 2,000 students.

For students whose orientation is better, it is an advantage to use their assignments in other subjects as practice material in reading classes; it helps them become proficient in skills that they can use immediately in other classes.

A Workshop Club

In many schools there are boys and girls who score low in scholastic aptitude and have no definite vocational aims. Elizabeth S. McClure, in a paper for a reading course, described a reading workshop for these pupils. Her class comprised twelve boys and eight girls in the low ninth grade. They were characterized by lack of interest in school, dislike of reading, and serious behavior problems. They came from dirty, ramshackle homes devoid of comforts and of incentives to read.

The first step was to obtain the confidence and goodwill of the pupils. The approach was somewhat as follows: "We have many clubs in our school but no reading club. Wouldn't it be fun to form one?" The club was organized and a chairman, a secretary, and two librarians were elected. Because the class librarians were uncertain about their duties, the class visited the school library and spent a period browsing and getting help from the librarian in locating certain books. She agreed to supply the class with interesting biographies and to keep a special shelf of books they would enjoy. The town librarian was equally cooperative.

Students discussed their visit to the library and their current reading—mostly magazines of poor quality. They gave the "club room" some atmosphere by putting up slogans and posters, attractive book covers, and colorful displays from publishing houses.

Their next project grew out of the unit on radio in the ninth-grade civics course. From magazines and newspapers they cut, mounted, indexed, and filed numerous clippings. Some of the pupils read with interest the radio issue of the little magazine *Modern Literature,* though it was rather difficult for them. Several groups produced simulated radio programs. Each reader learned the necessity of being a good speaker for radio. "You don't want your audience to shut you off, so you must try to do these things in your reading: read smoothly, phrase correctly, enunciate clearly, pause only in the right places, and read with expression—see the subject so clearly yourself that your audience will see it, too." One of their "broadcasts" was a quiz program based on vocabulary lists taken from their reading.

Interest in a movie unit ran high as the following description shows [94, pp. 140–141]:

> They explored the better magazines for movie material and made a file camparable to their radio file. The school librarian provided a copy of *Motion Picture Digest* for everyone in the class. This type of reading was fascinating to the pupils because each had a favorite movie to look up. They picked up unfamiliar words such as "pathos," "spectacular," and "melodrama," illustrating them with some particular picture which the pupils had seen.
>
> Using the *Motion Picture Digest* as a model, the pupils wrote their own critical reviews of movies, marking them + or −, for children, youths, or adults.
>
> During the unit each pupil made a notebook in which he put the following material: a movie review, a paragraph or two telling why a certain story would make a good movie, clippings and pictures about movies, a list of good movie manners, reasons for studying the movies, requirements for a good movie, a list of sources of information about the movies, a summary of two stories about movies taken from *Adventure Bound,* and a vocabulary of words they had learned.

Other units were handled in the same ingenious, enthusiastic way.

> This program had many by-products, not the least of which was the improvement in the pupils' behavior—cooperation, attentiveness, alertness, and self-confidence. One timid little girl chosen as librarian blossomed under her responsibility and became one of the friendliest persons in the room. Before the program, the pupils in this group had borrowed only six books from the library; at the end of the semester, the librarian reported that children in the Reading Club had withdrawn a total of 102 books. Not all of these books were read, perhaps, but at least they were looked at. The town librarian likewise reported a similar increase in interest on the part of members of the Reading Club. Other teachers reported an improvement in these pupils' reading comprehension and interest in every subject. At the close of the experiment the class radiated a certain vitality which had been lacking before the work began.
>
> Vitality is the keynote of this program—a vitality achieved by setting in motion activities in which these boys and girls could function successfully. Reading was part of each activity; the activity in turn motivated further reading.

The Laboratory or "Contract" Program

Triggs has described a course of this type on the college level [100]. Its main features were a diagnostic study of each student, a personal interview in which each student planned his own program for improving his reading, and remedial exercises based on passages from current magazines. The students took responsibility for using the exercises indicated by their plan sheets and for recording their progress daily in individual case folders. The skills they learned were transferred to college assignments. Every week the instructor suggested exercises and checked each student's progress.

Students also met in small groups to look at slide films or motion pictures, to discuss articles of common interest, and to discuss timely problems such as how to take exams. They tried to attend movies, plays, lectures, and discussions to broaden their background in the communication arts. Each student terminated his work in the clinic when he and the instructor agreed that he had reached his goals.

An experimental, individualized reading program set its goal as personality development. Ranson [69] reported that, as a result of this type of program, the students made a significantly greater improvement in grades than did their matched controls. Moreover, they continued to show improvement.

Another laboratory-type study that used a film, newspapers and periodicals, and writing exercises emphasized the profit and pleasure in reading. By means of a matched-group experiment in the reading laboratory at Western Michigan College of Education, McGinnis [57] obtained evidence of the effectiveness of this technique.

A reading program initiated by the English department in one high school took the form of a reading laboratory to which 700 students reported once a week for a minimum of thirty sessions. Its director developed exercises in comprehension, vocabulary, skimming, and study skills, among other devices. Results on the Cooperative English Tests: Reading Comprehension showed an average percentile rating gain of 8 for seniors, 3 for juniors, and 10 for sophomores [52].

Examples of instructional materials used in laboratory or "contract" courses are listed in Appendix C.

Symbols, Semantics, and Logic

The pupils in a ninth-grade class represented a wide range of reading ability, general mental ability, interests, and attitudes toward reading.

In a term paper written for one of the authors of this book, Thed E. Farra described his techniques for teaching reading to this group:

I think my approach to reading is influenced by my presentation of language as a tool of communication. I like de Boer's definition in *Teaching Secondary English:* "Effective reading is the mind reaching out for meaning."

What do I do about reading? The school testing program has helped me see approximately where each student stands in general ability and reading ability. Although these students do not need drill in word attack, they do need to continue to grow in word mastery. We work on words in several ways: (1) we dissect them as scientifically as we can to see their parts; (2) we try to find as many patterns as we can into which our words will fit; (3) we examine the *forms* of the words for meaning clues; (4) we derive principles which would apply to types of words in general; and (5) we continue testing these generalizations whenever we can to prove or disprove them.

We read from every possible point of view. Our year began with a study of symbols. We collected as many symbols as we could and interpreted their meaning. Each student chose a field of knowledge—science, health, aviation, etc.—searched out its symbols, and reported to the class. We literally covered the walls of the room with symbols.

Aiming toward deeper understanding, we examined the letters, sounds, and words of language as symbols. Then we hunted for examples of symbolic language. We studied figures of speech and moved to their uses in poetry. Each student selected a poem, read it orally, and interpreted the symbols or figures of speech.

We then moved to Homer's *Odyssey*. We worked from student vocabulary lists and students' questions. Groups selected incidents for dramatization. Some students read, with feeling, the parts of the characters, while one student read the paragraphs of description. We have done a similar thing with Dickens' *Great Expectations*.

At least once each week we write an interpretation of ten lines of poetry.

Other projects include Shakespeare and science fiction. We shall also work with social studies content. For further practice in oral reading, these students will go into classes of slow learners where they will give oral readings of poetry.

Work remains to be done on the extension of literal meaning. These students show very little evidence of training in that direction and need units on simpler procedures of inductive and deductive thinking and on recognizing propaganda.

These are only a few of the procedures that were used in this class where pupils were stimulated to stretch their minds and challenged to put forth their optimum effort.

Practice in Shifting Purpose

To paraphrase a passage in Perry and Whitlock's [65] article, a good course in reading can show a student his habits of mind and ways of thinking and reading that are preventing him from getting what he needs to get as quickly as he needs to get it. If a student is submissively reading the author's every word, the right exercises will teach him to shift his speed to fit the purpose and will make him assert his control of the assignment. Exercises will show up deadwood and irrelevancies and enable him to demonstrate to himself that he can get the information he wants by the appropriate skill. Only the first sentence or two will often yield an inference. Yet the student, through other exercises, will recognize the time to pay attention to every word [74].

Group Discussion and Group Therapy

A college program, reported Dotson [23], used films, tachistoscopic practice, and selected workbooks with students who were grouped according to reading skill. The primary emphasis was on the reader as a person—the way he felt about reading and the personal meaning he attached to reading improvement. But group discussions reassured the students that they were not alone in having reading problems; they helped each other to find ways of understanding their problems and handling them.

In one study [56], the experimental group had ten weekly group therapy sessions of one and one-half hours conducted by a clinical psychologist in place of one regular reading session on vocabulary and critical reading. The control group had one hour of individual reading work in place of the group therapy. The therapy group made statistically significant gains in reading speed and in flexibility of reading. Their comprehension scores also showed improvement, though the difference was not statistically significant. The groups improved their grades and had maintained this progress a year later. As to personality factors, the posttreatment results suggested that the therapy group had narrowed the gap between self-concept and ideal self, had gained in self-assurance and independence, and had acquired a clearer recognition of the need for achievement.

Other studies have also reported that the best results come from a combination of therapy and reading instruction.

Evaluations of Reading Programs

Teachers, administrators, parents, and students desire evidence of the effectiveness of reading programs, especially of special reading groups, to build confidence, to evaluate goals, and to justify the financial investments they require.

The main conclusion drawn in Entwhistle's [30] excellent review of twenty-two control-group evaluations of study-skills courses was that some kind of improvement usually follows a study-skills course, although the amount of the improvement varies greatly. High school students of average ability seem to profit most, and students *required* to take the course profit least.

Other studies have shown that students who are retarded by as much as two grades, as indicated by scores on a standardized test, can make significant improvement in reading if they receive skillful instruction not less than twice a week for a semester or longer. For example, Landry [46] set up a controlled experiment involving 7,556 pupils in grades 7 to 12 in twelve representative cities. The control classes pursued the regular course of instruction in English; the experimental groups, matched with the control groups with respect to intelligence-test scores and initial scores on the Cooperative

English Tests: Reading Comprehension and the Traxler Silent Reading Test, devoted 226 minutes per month to systematic practice and testing on selected articles from current issues of the *Reader's Digest*. At the end of the experimental period, covering 7.5 months, the average gain on the reading tests for all the experimental classes was 13.2 months; for all control classes, 6.2 months. It seems that a program of this kind under the proper guidance of the teacher can produce real reading improvement in junior and senior high school over and above that produced by the usual class instruction.

Friedmann [32] compared the rates of progress of two groups of pupils of normal IQ before and during a time of remedial reading. The remedial group made an average rate of progress of 3.3 months per month during the period of remediation, a significant gain over the 1.09 months per month before they entered the remedial group. The group who remained on the waiting list showed no change in their rates of progress.

Although there have been many favorable results, research casts some doubt on the efficacy of remedial instruction. Collins's [16] study is perhaps the most representative. He studied three matched groups of twenty retarded readers: (1) pupils who attended the remedial center, (2) those treated in their own school, and (3) those who continued in their own class with no special remedial work. The two groups receiving special remedial help made immediately greater gains (.01 level) than the control group, though the results varied with the tests used. However, after one and two years, there was no significant difference. The children of low socioeconomic status made the least progress. There were also no significant differences among the groups on the WISC, Rorschach, Rosenzweig Picture-Frustration Study for children, and the Vineland Social Maturity Scale. Collins concluded that long-term effects of remedial treatment were negligible.

Glock and Millman [34] found only slight differences between an experimental group of above-average high school juniors and a control group; the majority of these differences, except in speed, were in favor of the control group.

There is a little research evidence that some programs for students who are interested in improving their reading ability do pay off in academic achievement. In a control-group experiment with forty college students in each group, Bloomer [10] concluded that a college reading program affects variables other than reading ability and that changes in these other variables are what improve academic achievement. McDonald [54] reported that students who participated in a reading-improvement program made significantly higher grades and showed less tendency to become dropouts. It is reasonable to expect that any means that improves a student's learning tools would increase his learning efficiency and thus enhance his achievement.

The relation of reading improvement to mental ability is still less clear. Schneyer cautiously concluded that "there is some evidence that under certain conditions a developmental reading program may be able to increase the results of verbal-type aptitude tests" [82, p. 146].

In case studies it is often noted that the individual's attitudes and behavior improve as his reading improves. Children who had had a year's experience in reading-clinic programs made significant improvement not only in reading but also in personal and social adjustment.

Differences in research results are difficult to interpret because the content and quality of the instruction are not adequately described. It is virtually impossible to control all the factors that might influence growth in reading over a given period. When the number of cases is small, the influence of these uncontrolled variables may be considerable. Some so-called "equivalent" groups are in fact unevenly matched. There is need for more research on the reading process and for improvement in semantic interpretation; few research studies deal adequately with emotional problems. Moreover, few studies retest the students six months or more after completion of the training to see whether the gains persist or whether the special reading course achieved only a temporary spurt. Another limitation of these studies is that they depend upon inadequate means of measuring reading improvement. At best, a reading test measures only a limited number of reading skills, and often these are not among the skills that are considered most important by the instructor of the course.

ESSENTIALS OF STAFF

Dever [20] reported that positions in the field of reading range from full-time reading specialists to teachers who have a minimum responsibility for the improvement of reading:

1. Those who work directly with children and young people: reading specialist, remedial reading teacher, reading clinician, reading teacher
2. Those who direct or supervise others in reading work: reading director, reading consultant, reading supervisor, reading coordinator
3. Those whose reading responsibilities are in addition to or a part of other work: adjustment teacher, helping teacher, visiting teacher, classroom teacher, instructor or professor in college, counselor, psychologist

But a reading program involves more personnel than teachers and specialists.

Administrator's Responsibility

"Reading is the most important problem in junior high schools today" is the opinion of one able junior high school principal, an opinion shared by many other administrators [107, 108]. The administrator sees reading failures piling up in the junior high school; he knows bright students who are reading below their potential; he knows reluctant readers—those who can read but don't. He listens to parents who express concern about their children's reading, and he hears the public's complaints that reading is not being taught is it was in "the good old days." He encourages subject-matter teachers to incorporate reading skills in their lesson plans.

In attempting to raise the general level of student achievement in reading, administrators confront a number of unfavorable conditions. Many high school teachers have heavy teaching schedules and large classes; they lack special training in reading. There are but few specialists in reading to serve as consultants, to give diagnostic reading tests, and to do intensive work with seriously retarded readers. Facilities for correcting physical defects are inadequate. There are not enough suitable reading materials for students of diverse interests and abilities, many of whom come from poor cultural backgrounds or from environments that do not stimulate reading.

Having recognized the scope of the reading problem and the difficulties, the administrator tries to create conditions that make effective reading possible. His aim is to provide every pupil with the experiences that he needs to improve in reading. He employs, if possible, well-qualified reading consultants. If none is available, he gives special responsibilities to one or more teachers with suitable personalities who are keenly interested in reading. He releases these teachers for a year of intensive study, with the understanding that they will return to his school the following academic year. He initiates planning for improved methods of teaching, uses the resources of his own staff and of the community, and encourages continuous evaluation of the program.

Following are some do's and don't's for administrators:

DO	DON'T
Do encourage your teachers to talk about the reading problem as they see it, and to say what they think should be done; develop the program cooperatively.	**Don't** tell the teachers what *you* think ought to be done and how they should do it, or try to "sell" your program to them.
Do go "wisely and slowly." After talking with individuals, introduce the subject of reading at a carefully planned, well-organized conference; support the program with know-how as well as with personal enthusiasm.	**Don't** introduce the subject hastily and prematurely; don't schedule reading groups before teachers are ready for them. Don't suddenly say, "Let there be reading classes!"

DO	DON'T
Do use faculty meetings, workshops, institutes, and other *regularly scheduled* means of in-service education for helping all members of the staff to gain an understanding of their contribution to the total-school reading program.	**Don't** schedule special meetings on reading after school hours; try to schedule these meetings during the school day or in a preschool conference.
Do schedule time for reading instruction during the school day.	**Don't** expect extra work in reading to be done by students in outside-of-school time.
Do find out about the good work in reading which some teachers and staff are now doing and give them recognition and approval for it.	**Don't** assume that your teachers are at present doing nothing about reading improvement and that you have to start from scratch.
Do explore the resources in your staff: (1) elementary teachers who have had experience and training in beginning reading, (2) teachers who have taken courses in reading on the secondary level, (3) teachers who have had some training in testing and guidance, (4) teachers who are interested in the reading problem and are planning to learn more about it, (5) guidance workers who can furnish information and can counsel certain reading cases. Give each member of the staff work that will use his special knowledge and abilities. Keep informed about the reading program and the backgrounds and needs of the students.	**Don't** go ahead without finding out what interests and special contributions members of the staff can bring to the improvement of reading.
Do employ a reading specialist who is well qualified by personality, as well as by training, when the staff feels the need for more expert help. Delegate responsibility for developing and evaluating the program.	**Don't** put a teacher with no training in reading in a key position, and **don't** employ a well-trained person who nevertheless cannot get along with students, teachers, and parents.
Do move heaven and earth and the school board to provide reading material that will cover the wide range of reading ability and interest represented in every class.	**Don't** expect teachers to "make bricks without straw"—to teach reading without suitable materials of instruction.

DO	DON'T
Do see that the school library is well staffed, equipped, and organized, so that all instructional materials and books, films, recordings, maps, globes, pictures, and magazines are readily available to teachers and students. Promote the effective use of these materials.	
Do permit the reading specialist in the school to decide upon the procedures and materials to be used in special reading classes.	**Don't** insist that teachers use certain methods and materials simply because they have produced impressive gains in some other school.
Do obtain motion pictures and slide films on reading, and have a screening test of vision for all pupils. If you have the money, select machines for individual, clinical use.	**Don't** spend money on pressure or pacing machines until you have obtained reading materials for the pupils.
Do use community resources to get what the teachers want and need.	**Don't** isolate the school from the community; listen to the parents; interest them in reading improvement.
Do develop a community school that serves adults as well as children and young people.	
Do interpret reading to the public as a means to an end—well-informed citizens and a better life.	**Don't** interpret reading to the public merely as a skill to be learned or as an end in itself.

The Role of Every Teacher

Reading touches every subject and is inevitably a part of every teacher's work. Although high school teachers are not reading specialists, they still can contribute the most effective reading improvement to all students if they have had any instruction in the teaching of reading. Even if they have not, if they are perceptive, they are daily making applications of reading techniques essential to their subjects. Of course the comprehension of the subject matter is the focus of any class, but it is the reading skills properly supplemented which unlock the content. No one but the subject-matter teacher knows so well the characteristics of his subject and the reading skills needed to master it. But no single teacher can teach all the aspects of reading even when he accepts its significance.

These suggestions, in addition to others in this chapter, especially in the section on "Types of Reading Programs," may help.

1. The teacher can teach effective study-type reading of factual material. The formula "Survey Q3R" really works; the reader surveys what he already knows and glances through the book, chapter, or article to get an idea of what the author is trying to do and how this content fits in with his previous knowledge and present and future needs; he raises questions about what he wants to know, then reads, reviews, and recites. The Coronet film "How Effective Is Your Reading?" illustrates this procedure.
2. He can give instruction and practice in the special approaches needed for the reading of different types of material—poetry, novels, plays, a science textbook, history, mathematics, art, home economics, shop.
3. Since the broad view of reading includes growth in thinking, teachers develop reading by asking thought-provoking questions. "What is your evidence for that statement?" "May new facts have been discovered since that book was written?" "How do you know that is a true story?" "What has been said on the other side of the argument?" Questions like these cultivate more precise and accurate statements, distinguish truth from error, and separate fact from judgment.
4. If specialized services are available, the teacher may refer complex reading cases or those with emotional involvement to the reading teacher, guidance worker, or school psychologist.

It is essential that teachers in the various subject fields team in compiling vocabulary lists, giving assignments, and suggesting projects that require wide reading in several subjects, especially for the slow learner since frequently the materials overlap.

The wise teacher will not use a single method, device, basal reader, or workbook; he will draw on his repertory of methods and materials to meet the needs of all his students, and he will be sensitive to the role of inter-personal relations in achievement.

The Reading Specialist's Role

Originally the responsibilities of the reading teacher and the reading consultant, sometimes called supervisor or coordinator, were separate responsibilities with restricted duties or emphases. The reading teacher primarily worked apart with retarded readers and seldom taught developmental reading since it was inadequately understood then. His only contact with classroom teachers was in discussing the cases of retarded readers they sent to him.

The reading consultant, experienced in classroom methods and aware of educational trends, publications, and diagnostic materials, helped teachers to improve teaching skills, carried out testing programs, and reviewed serious referrals. At any major change of curriculum in a district's schools he was consulted for his knowledge of recent changes in theory of reading and the best kinds of materials and procedures.

The latest concept of the reading specialist's role is that he works directly and foremost with teachers to improve their methods of teaching and to recommend materials. Robinson and Rauch [77] offer the reading consultant "a series of operational guidelines" to help both administrator and teacher to function more effectively. As a result of research and the value presently given to reading, there is an urgent need for the teacher, more thoroughly trained in reading than the regular classroom teacher, who works directly with pupils in remedial and regular developmental reading courses. He is one assurance that the pupil in the overloaded classroom can receive the reading help he must have to meet the demands that the general curriculum makes. If the schools are large and have many students who need special reading skills and others who deserve sharpened reading techniques, there should be both a reading teacher and a consultant. Smaller schools may do well enough with only the special reading teacher who can teach small groups of students during the year or for short periods and also advise regular classroom teachers, untrained in teaching reading, about the most effective procedures and materials. He may function as an in-service training chairman.

A recent experiment has suggested a variation in the way the reading teachers and consultants carry out their roles [102]. Several special reading teachers go into a school for two weeks to work as a team with all the teachers in each content field. They demonstrate methods of teaching the skills related to each subject. They confer with the teachers separately and in groups and supply or suggest instructional needs and recommend general policies.

Preparation for the positions of reading specialist and consultant has been outlined in state certification requirements and in a report of the certification committee of the International Reading Association.

The qualifications of the reading specialist include professional and personal characteristics, the success of any particular reading program depending on the quality of each. To strengthen the respect of other members of the staff, he must be competent in his field, having had specialized training at a reputable university or its equivalent and several years of classroom teaching. He must be tactful and judicious, making the teacher and administrator feel that they have something to contribute to the reading program. If the teachers have requested the help of a reading specialist, he has an initial advantage because any modern reading program must have the cooperation of the staff.

The reading consultant approaches the teacher to ask, not to tell [25], keeping in mind the teacher's point of view and immediate concerns in teaching reading. They will learn from each other. The consultant needs to learn from the history teacher the best ways to read history; from the science teacher, the best ways to read science. Together, they analyze the selection to be read and determine the reading skills that should be taught, reinforced or applied in connection with it. Then they devise psychologically sound methods for teaching the students to develop and apply skills to the subject.

The reading consultant should recognize the good work that some teachers are already doing. In every school there are creative teachers who have developed methods and materials to meet the needs of their students. Accordingly, the first step is to see what the teachers are actually doing to help students improve their reading. This may be reported in a series of experience meetings in which the reading specialist may highlight and enhance each teacher's report.

In one school system the reading consultant developed the following in-service education procedures [105]. At first he taught reading to several subject classes as a means of gaining understanding of the situation and for demonstration purposes until the teachers assumed major responsibility. He organized laboratory workshops—small groups of teachers who were free at certain periods of the day—to work on any aspect of reading instruction in which they were interested: how to teach paragraph comprehension more effectively, how to group students within a regular class, how to help the nonreading students in their classes. Larger group meetings were occasionally called to study common problems. The channels of communication were improved between the teachers and the psychiatrist, psychologist, and social worker. The consultant gave the teachers much concrete help in creating reading materials, making original reading games, and learning group procedures. Using the case-conference technique helped the teachers to collect, interpret, synthesize, and apply information about individual pupils.

The specific functions of the reading specialist will vary according to his competence, the pupils' needs, and the qualifications of the subject teacher. In general, the following are his responsibilities:

1. To work with teachers as a helping person or resource person. He will help them to release their creative energies. Each staff member needs to feel that the consultant is interested in him as a person, recognizes his special abilities, and appreciates the importance of his contribution to the reading program.
2. To consult with administrators responsible for curriculum development, marking and promotion policies, and methods of instruction; to assist in establishing and maintaining voluntary teacher study groups and other forms of in-service education; to report the progress of special reading cases.

3. To diagnose reading difficulties and recommend students for grouping or referral.
4. To work in close cooperation with the classroom teachers and, individually or in small groups, with seriously retarded readers or able learners who are not realizing their reading potential. This work with individuals and small groups seems at first glance to be an expensive service. But its value becomes evident when one considers (*a*) the opportunity it affords the teachers to gain understanding as they work with the reading specialist on these cases, and (*b*) the opportunity it affords the specialist to develop materials and techniques that can be used in regular classes.
5. To interpret to parents the students' reading needs and the services that are available. In conferences he may explain the child's reading status and suggest ways in which the parent may help the child by supplying suitable reading materials at home and by helping him overcome any personal problems that may be interfering with his reading. He may also explain to the parent certain features of the school program.
6. To discover and use community resources (*a*) to create basic conditions that make effective reading instruction possible—adequate diet, better home relations, correction of physical defects, suitable reading materials; (*b*) to supplement his own work as reading specialist with psychological, psychiatric, and guidance services, family casework, and medical and visual examinations and treatment.

The Librarian's Service

Perhaps no one is more keenly aware than the school librarian of the aimless and unrewarding way in which many students read. Anna C. Moore, former supervisor of libraries, State Department of Education, Hartford, Connecticut, has said, "I think that everyone in library work with young people should have an understanding of the reading problem and techniques employed for improvement of reading."

There should be close relationships between the subject teachers, the librarian, and the reading teacher or consultant [31, 47]. The librarian looks to the reading teacher for help in understanding how children learn to read, what makes reading easy or difficult on each grade level, and how to teach reading to individuals and groups. The librarian contributes her knowledge of the books available in every subject field and effective audiovisual aids. The reading teacher and the librarian could share information cards about each student's interests and reading abilities [73]. Together they could plan class visits to the library, incorporating the librarian's knowledge of books and her contacts with individual students. (See entire issue of *The Reading Teacher*, vol. 17, no. 3, December, 1963.)

A school library makes a difference. The proportion of children who use a public library is seldom more than 10 per cent; contrast this with the almost 100 per cent who use a school library. In a library stocked with books that appeal to youngsters and presided over by a librarian who skillfully guides their book selection, the gifted child learns to read independently and critically. The retarded reader finds books that he can enjoy. The culturally disadvantaged child discovers material that extends his narrow horizon. The insecure child may read stories that give him confidence. For some teen-agers the library is a place to go with a problem. One teen-ager said, "Many times a book will teach you something. You may nod your head in agreement because a book is so real to life, or you might come across a character who has the same problem as you."

Cramer [19] described a reading program that was suggested by a librarian and cooperatively planned by teachers and parents. Each class in the elementary and junior high schools met regularly in the public library branch located in the junior high school. The librarian gave book talks and library lessons; she helped the children select interesting books at their various reading levels and guided them in their reading. The program was continued over the summer months. Some of the outcomes of this program over a period of fifteen years during which time, it is assumed, policies of promotion and marking were held constant were (1) repeaters decreased from 20 to 1 per cent; (2) all pupils were generally reading up to their capacity; (3) nonreaders disappeared from the upper grades; and (4) gifted children found more opportunity to read widely.

The librarian helps her clients of all ages to progress in their reading experiences. She encourages first-grade children to have library cards and to explore books for pleasure during the elementary school years. In junior high school, she promotes reading pleasure and eases the way with elementary reference work. In senior high school, she facilitates use of reserved books, initiates library clubs, and heightens interest in free reading with colorful book displays.

The librarian raises the quality of students' reading. Starting with whatever books or magazines students are interested in at the moment, she is alert to suggest something better in the same field and, eventually, to extend their interests to other fields with exhibits, informal talks about books, and personal recommendations. One town librarian brought to the school new books which he thought would be interesting to the pupils. He showed them pictures, read appealing incidents, and related the books to the pupils' background and experience. The teachers were enthusiastic about this service which encouraged many school children to use the public library. The librarian can introduce new books by assembly programs. One idea is to flash some exciting or amusing pages of an easy book on the screen, thus convincing the poorer readers that reading can be fun. Favorite-book polls, bulletin board exhibits of book jackets, mimeographed or printed bibliographies on special subjects, and reading ladders listing books that range from easy to more difficult, from poor quality to literary excellence, are other effective methods of providing the right book for the right child. The librarian may encourage some youthful readers to write and mimeograph a book review magazine. She may group together books of varied literary quality so that she can say to a student who has enjoyed a sea story of poor quality, "You'll find other exciting sea stories on the same shelf." To avoid discouraging a student by suggesting books that are too difficult for him, she uses information on the reading-test scores of students who use the library.

The librarian supplements the teacher's instruction on the location of material. A quick way of orienting students to the library at the beginning of the year is to have them fill in a mimeographed chart of the reading room, indicating where different types of books are to be found—travel, aviation, biography, science, etc. The librarian will also acquaint them with the card catalog and the use of the *Reader's Guide* and other indexes.

The librarian encourages projects that involve reading. In their first library period, one group of sixth-grade children who were not reading up to capacity discussed with the librarian various ways of using their library time. Someone suggested that they could help each other by each becoming a "specialist" in some field. Each child chose a field and built up a reference file on the subject. These files became a permanent available part of the library. When the school had to give a broadcast, this group prepared it. They selected some of their specialists to report on books that they had read. The students were much pleased when they received many favorable comments on the broadcast.

The school librarian is also a resource to teachers. She helps them to find references on the topics their students are studying in class, supplies books for classroom libraries, and furnishes lists of books for retarded readers. She suggests new books for students' recreational reading and makes them available in classrooms and residence halls.

Librarians can supplement reading with dramatizations and little-theatre presentations, radio and television programs, motion pictures, community sings, "nationality nights" with programs of folk songs and folk dances of different countries, exhibits of local handicrafts and colonial household tools, exhibits of pictures from public and private resources, and exhibits by handicraft groups, hobby groups, and stamp clubs.

The school library is becoming more and more a visual aids center. Students can use tape recorders to record favorite or original poems. In a viewing-listening corner they can enrich their literary experience by means of film strips accompanied by recordings. Children from non-English-speaking homes can obtain as much practice as they need by listening to recordings prepared for this purpose. All of these features make the library truly a "learning resources center."

The Role of the School Doctor and Nurse

By conducting screening tests of hearing and vision and calling attention to other physical impairments, the school doctor and nurse make a basic contribution to the reading program. In conferences with parents, they can both give and get valuable information about the child's reading and study habits.

The Guidance Worker's and Counselor's Contribution

Guidance and the improvement of reading are interrelated. Recognizing this relationship, the school principal or college president frequently asks the director of guidance, if no reading specialist is available, to assist in developing the overall reading program.

The counselor may introduce reading instruction in a group guidance period. In a student-teacher planning session, the students may say that "getting their homework done" is one of their problems. To be helpful, the guidance teacher should know what reading skills the students need, how to demonstrate them, where to find practice material to develop them, and how to promote and measure the student's progress. Simply written books on vocations such as those listed in Appendix D are excellent means for helping the students to apply the reading skills they have already learned.

In his interviews with students, the counselor finds that many of the guidance problems that are referred to him can be traced, in part or in whole, to inefficient reading and study habits. Counseling problems, that is, often turn into reading problems: students who are failing in their subjects, students who want to drop out of school, students who have been refused admission to the college that they or their parents have made first choice, students whose vocational plans are blocked by low reading ability.

On the other hand, reading problems often turn into counseling problems. Students who have severe reading difficulties almost always show some emotional disturbance. They may require psychotherapy as well as instruction in reading. In some cases no progress can be made in reading until the emotional conflicts are resolved.

Counselors, teachers, parents, students, and reading specialists should form a team to promote both reading and personal development. Since reading achievement is so closely interwoven with the student's total adjustment, it is desirable that one person handle as many aspects of the case as possible in order to achieve continuity of relationship and to avoid shifting the student from one worker to another. To do this, counselors and reading specialists should have some training in common—counselors should have some background and skill in handling reading problems, and reading specialists should obtain as much understanding as possible of the emotional factors that are related to reading.

The Role of the Parent [71]

It is important to view the reading problem through parents' as well as through students' eyes. Parents expect the school to teach their children to read. In many localities parents think that reading is being poorly taught. They complain that their chlidren cannot spell and that many of them have trouble reading. They often say, "The schools are not teaching reading as well as when I was a kid. Why don't they go back to the good old methods?" These accusations are not, in general, supported by facts. On the average, pupils' achievement in silent reading is as high as it was twenty-five years ago or even higher. However, since reading holds such an important place in our culture, parents immediately become concerned when their child gives any indication of a reading difficulty. They believe the child can read better "if he puts his mind to it" or if he is given the right kind of instruction. Their appeals for help are often pathetic.

Some parents exaggerate their child's reading difficulty. In fact, they may prematurely label him a "reading case," and this in itself may intensify what was originally a minor difficulty. Sometimes parents attribute to a child a desire to improve which the child himself does not feel. One mother wrote, "Jim is very anxious to start work at the reading center as he knows he is losing time in school because he can't read or spell." Jim passively accepted his mother's verdict, though he inwardly resented it.

Parents who unconsciously reject the child, wholly or in part, may seize upon reading retardation as a point of attack. When the child is suffering fear and embarrassment in school because of his poor reading, these parents give him little or no sympathy. Worse still, they may give him the impression that they are thoroughly ashamed of him. They may make him stay in and study every evening even though he accomplishes nothing.

On the other hand, there are parents who interfere with their children's reading and study time. These children complain that they have no uninterrupted time at home to read and study. They have to go on errands, do housework, take care of the younger children. In some crowded homes, there is always a hubbub; the children cannot even sleep at night. Unrestricted television can also disrupt reading and study time.

When it is their own child who has a reading problem, parents tend to lose perspective. The reading difficulty looms disproportionately large. They apply pressure methods without realizing that these may be increasing the child's resistance to reading or intensifying his anxiety about it. Acute anxiety interferes with learning. If parents would examine their own feelings and try earnestly to understand how the child feels, they would solve his reading problems more successfully.

Many parents are eager to cooperate in the reading program and they can, by showing enthusiasm for reading at home or reading aloud and discussing books with youngsters. They can take the children with them to the library. Whenever possible, they can provide a quiet place for reading, with proper lighting and good reading materials easily accessible. They can guard against overscheduling the child's day so that he has no time for free reading. In the case of adolescents who have a strong desire for independence, parents can suggest rather than require the reading of certain books.

Some parents willingly cooperate with the school. They help to build up files of resource material, suggest persons in the community who can come to the school and enrich the children's experiences, or actually assist in the library once a week or month. Others raise money for needed supplies. Still others join cooperative planning groups to improve the reading program. They also help to develop community programs in art, music, drama, and sports that not only enrich and stimulate the children's reading but also balance their daily schedule.

Parents and teachers are partners. A school reading program can stand or fall on parental understanding and cooperation. In fact, reading is not only an in-school program; a lot depends on what happens outside the school. Do the parents show impatience or dissatisfaction with the child's degree of progress? Do they show lack of faith in him or in the school? Do they provide activities which enlarge the child's experience and vocabulary? Do they answer the child's questions? Do they themselves read? Do they provide adequate nourishment, rest, and love?

Does the school help the parent understand what is happening to the child in school? Does it let the parent know how he can help? An increasing number of pamphlets and books are now available to help the parent understand the nature and the causes of various reading difficulties.

The Role of the Student

The students are too often ignored in the development of a reading program. They have sound ideas about the methods and materials that help them most and should recommend the most effective procedures and assist in a continuous evaluation of the learning experiences they are having.

HOW TO GET STARTED: LEARNING AND WORKING TOGETHER [3]

An English teacher said, "I should like some information on how to set up a reading program on a small scale with a limited budget. What are the essentials for such a program? If a good beginning is made, perhaps more funds could be obtained for further development."

Sometimes a reading program gets started when the parents urge better instruction in reading. Sometimes the administrator wins the support of the public by presenting facts that show the need for improvement in reading or by recounting success stories of students who have been helped by instruction in reading. A teacher might well spend a year experimenting with reading instruction in his own classes and comment to others about some of his most successful procedures. The students in his classes will also talk about the help they have received.

As teachers from other content fields become interested, they may form a reading committee to study the problem. They may invite several students, the administrators, the librarian, selected lay parents, and any available specialists to join them. Such a school or interschool committee may assume leadership in developing a reading program that grows out of the needs of the students and the educational objectives of the school.

The committee may first consider how to further develop the reading proficiency of ninth-grade pupils. Each member contributes his ideas and builds on the suggestions of others. They agree on certain goals. Individuals volunteer to serve on small action committees to carry out parts of the program. One teacher may be interested in obtaining suggestions from graduates about how the high school could have forestalled some of the reading problems that they met in college or later life. The librarian recommends pertinent reading materials for various abilities and interests. Each of the subject teachers may consider ways of teaching the pupils how to read his subject more effectively. Reading teachers in the primary grades share procedures that can be used with severely retarded high school readers. Other committees may explore administering, interpreting, and using intelligence and reading tests or creating interest in the reading program in the school and in the community. At various times during the year all the subcommittees may meet to evaluate the reading program and to recommend ways and means of improving it.

In the meantime, in meetings on curriculum development, the principal may point out the relation between reading and other aspects of the high school curriculum. The teachers may not have recognized that the reading skills they have been discussing constitute a reading curriculum or the beginning of a developmental reading program.

The work of the voluntary committee during the first year may pave the way for informal in-service groups (see section on teacher education) to include preschool workshops, demonstrations of classroom methods, and visits to other classes, as well as meetings, always keeping in mind both viewpoints: the students who succeed and the teachers who find their job easier. Through these in-service education experiences, every member of the school staff will become aware of his responsibility in a reading program and accumulate a reservoir of procedures from which he can draw.

Artley's [3] report summarizes the steps in initiating a reading program:

(1) to find one or more persons who are interested in the improvement of reading; (2) to experiment in regular classes; (3) to study reading problems in the regular in-service education program; (4) to enlist the aid of the librarian; (5) to form a committee or study group of interested persons; and (6) to obtain a reading specialist or consultant as the need for one is realized.

CONCLUDING STATEMENT

An effective reading program includes reading instruction in every subject for all students, small-group instruction for those who have special difficulties or needs, and conferences with individuals about their reading development. If the teachers are not fully prepared to assume their share of responsibility, there should be an expert employed to conduct a developmental reading course for all the students and an in-service program for teachers.

One may evaluate a reading-improvement program by obtaining evidence of the progress made by individual students, and/or by judging the theoretical soundness of the main features of the program and ascertaining how well they are carried out. The first method uses the case-study approach which describes each student's progress in relation to his capacity and to environmental conditions that might inhibit or facilitate it [92]. The second method is less direct; it relies on the inference that approved methods will result in student progress.

The following criteria may be used in evaluating a reading program. The first four items refer to desirable changes in the individual student:

1. The student recognizes his reading strengths and weaknesses; he capitalizes on his strengths and corrects or compensates for his weaknesses.
2. He assumes responsibility for improving his reading and sets his own goals.
3. He shows improvement in both basic and higher-level reading skills according to his capacity; he has a feeling of success and growth as a result of his efforts.
4. He develops independent reading habits and worthwhile reading interests and the attitude that reading is an important lifetime pursuit.

The following criteria refer to the program per se:

1. The concept of reading on which it rests is comprehensive and sound: reading is a purposeful thinking process which is related to other communication skills; it is a source of information, a means of recreation, and an aid to personal and social development.
2. The program extends throughout the school years and provides for a sequential development for all the students.

3. All the members of the staff participate, planning the program cooperatively.
4. The reading competencies of any subject are the responsibility of the teacher of that subject.
5. The program makes special provision for average and superior students as well as for able retarded readers, slow learners, bilinguals, the educationally and culturally disadvantaged, and the emotionally disturbed.
6. Adequate continuous diagnosis is the base for instruction and curriculum; there is no serious lapse of time between obtaining diagnostic information and using it.
7. Every student has access to reading materials of appropriate interest and difficulty.
8. Teachers must develop psychologically sound teaching methods and experiment with them.
9. Teachers encourage the students to express their curiosity and develop a spirit of inquiry.
10. Reading services seek out psychological and social services as needed.

The following are three of the most important emphases—the growing points in the reading program: (1) making sure that all teachers are well prepared for their responsibilities for teaching reading; (2) recognizing the need for employing a reading consultant in each school; and (3) regarding the student as "the organizing principle" in the program and encouraging him to take initiative and responsibility for his own learning.

REFERENCES

1. Aaron, Ira E., Byron Callaway, and Arthur V. Olson: *Conducting In-service Programs in Reading,* Reading Aids Series, International Reading Association, Newark, Del., 1965.
2. Anderson, Irving, and others: "Rate of Reading Development and Its Relation to Age of Learning to Read, Sex, and Intelligence," *Journal of Educational Research,* vol. 50, p. 481, March, 1957.
3. Artley, A. Sterl: "Implementing a Developmental Reading Program on the Secondary Level," *Reading Instruction in Secondary Schools,* Perspectives in Reading, no. 2, International Reading Association, Newark, Del., 1964, pp. 1–16.
4. Association for Childhood Education: *More about Reading,* Reprint Service Bulletin 29, Washington, 1959.
5. Austin, Mary C., and Morrison Coleman: *The First R,* The Macmillan Company, New York, 1963.
6. Austin, Mary C., and others: *The Torch Lighters,* Harvard University Press, Cambridge, Mass., 1961.
7. Balow, Bruce, and James Curtin: "Reading Comprehension Score as a Means of Establishing Homogeneous Classes," *The Reading Teacher,* vol. 19, pp. 169–173, December, 1965.

8. Bamman, Henry A., and others: *Reading Instruction in the Secondary School,* Longmans, Green & Co., Inc., New York, 1961.

9. Barbe, Walter Burke: *Educator's Guide to Personalized Reading Instruction,* Prentice-Hall, Inc., Englewood Cliffs, N.J., 1961.

10. Bloomer, Richard H.: "The Cloze Procedure as a Remedial Reading Exercise," *Journal of Developmental Reading,* vol. 5, pp. 173–181, Spring, 1962.

11. Bradshaw, Ralph, Phyllis Sensor, and Howard Burton: "Reading Programs in the Junior College," *Claremont Reading Conference,* Twenty-eighth Yearbook, Claremont Graduate School Curriculum Laboratory, Claremont, Calif., 1964, pp. 179–184.

12. Burton, Dwight L.: "Heads Out of the Sand: Secondary Schools Face the Challenge of Reading," *Educational Forum,* vol. 24, pp. 285–293, March, 1960.

13. Carson, Roy M., and Jack M. Thompson: "The Joplin Plan and Traditional Reading Groups," *Elementary School Journal,* vol. 65, pp. 38–43, October, 1964.

14. Chansky, Norman M.: "Progress of Promoted and Repeating Grade 1 Failures," *Journal of Experimental Education,* vol. 32, pp. 225–237, Spring, 1964.

15. Clift, David (ed.): *Adult Reading,* Fifty-fifth Yearbook of the National Society for the Study of Education, University of Chicago Press, Chicago, 1956, part II.

16. Collins, J. E.: *The Effects of Remedial Education,* Educational Monographs, no. 4, University of Birmingham, Institute of Education, Oliver & Boyd Ltd., Edinburgh and London, 1961, p. 154.

17. Colvin, Charles R.: "The 'Ideal' College Reading Program," *Journal of Developmental Reading,* vol. 5, pp. 77–81, Winter, 1962.

18. Cordelina, Georgina B.: "Recommendations and Suggestions for Developmental Reading Programs for Quezon City High Schools," Quezon City, Philippines, unpublished doctoral dissertation, Indiana University, Bloomington, Ind., 1964.

19. Cramer, Roscoe V.: "The Every-pupil Reading Program in Switzer Elementary and West Junior High," *High School Journal,* vol. 39, pp. 81–85, November, 1955.

20. Dever, Kathryn Imogene: *Positions in the Field of Reading,* Teachers College Press, Teachers College, Columbia University, New York, 1956.

21. Di Lorenzo, Louis T., and Ruth Salter: "Cooperative Research on the Nongraded Primary," *Elementary School Journal,* vol. 65, pp. 269–277, February, 1965.

22. Dolch, Edward W.: *Individualized vs. Group Reading,* The Garrard Press, Champaign, Ill., 1962.

23. Dotson, Elsie J.: "The Reading Improvement Program at the University of Texas," in Oscar S. Causey (ed.), *Techniques and Procedures in College and Adult Reading Programs,* Sixth Yearbook of the Southwest Reading Conference, Texas Christian University Press, Fort Worth, Tex., March, 1957, pp. 32–43.

24. Duker, Sam: "Master's Studies of Individualized Reading," *Elementary English,* vol. 40, pp. 280–282, March, 1963.

25. Early, Margaret J.: "The Meaning of Reading Instruction in Secondary Schools," *Journal of Reading,* vol. 8, pp. 25–29, October, 1964.

26. Early, Margaret J. (ed.): *Reading Instruction in Secondary Schools,* Perspectives in Reading, no. 2, International Reading Association, Newark, Del., 1964.

27. Early, Margaret J.: "What Does Research in Reading Tell Me about Successful Reading Programs?" *English Journal,* vol. 46, pp. 395–405, October, 1957.

28. Emans, Robert: "Teacher Evaluation of Reading Skills and Individualized Reading," *Elementary English,* vol. 42, pp. 258–260, March, 1965.

29. *English S: Communication Skills,* Detroit Public Schools, Division for Improvement of Instruction, Department of Language Education, Board of Education of the City of Detroit, Detroit, 1962.

30. Entwhistle, Doris R.: "Evaluations of Study-skills Courses: A Review," *Journal of Educational Research,* vol. 53, pp. 243–251, March, 1960.

31. Fenwick, Sara: "The Librarian at Work with Teachers," *American Library Association Bulletin,* no. 57, pp. 153–160, February, 1963.

32. Friedmann, S.: "A Report on Progress in an I.T.A. Remedial Reading Class," *British Journal of Educational Psychology,* vol. 28, pp. 258–261, November, 1958.

33. Frymier, Jack R.: "The Effect of Class Size upon Reading Acheivement in First Grade," *The Reading Teacher,* vol. 18, pp. 90–93, November, 1964.

34. Glock, Marvin, and Jason Millman: "Evaluation of a Study-skills Program for Above-average High School Pupils," *Journal of Developmental Reading,* vol. 7, pp. 283–289, Summer, 1964.

35. Goodlad, John I., and Robert H. Anderson: *The Nongraded Elementary School,* 2d ed., Harcourt, Brace & World, Inc., New York, 1963.

36. Groff, Patrick: "Comparisons of Individualized and Ability Grouping Approaches to Teaching Reading: A Supplement," *Elementary English,* vol. 41, pp. 238–241, March, 1964.

37. Guiler, Walter S., Claire J. Raeth, and Merrill M. May: *Developmental Reading,* 2d ed., J. B. Lippincott Company, Philadelphia, 1964.

38. Gurney, David: "The Effect of an Individualized Reading Program on Reading Level and Attitude toward Reading," *The Reading Teacher,* vol. 19, pp. 277–280, January, 1966.

39. Henry, Nelson B. (ed.): *Individualizing Instruction,* Sixty-first Yearbook of the National Society for the Study of Education, University of Chicago Press, Chicago, 1962.

40. Hill, Walter, and William Eller: *Power in Reading Skills,* Wadsworth Publishing Company, Inc., Belmont, Calif., 1964.

41. Isenberg, Irwin: *The Drive against Illiteracy,* The Reference Shelf, vol. 30, no. 5, The H. W. Wilson Company, New York, 1964.

42. Jan-Tausch, Evelyn: "Teaching Developmental Reading in the Secondary School," *Reading Instruction in Secondary Schools,* Perspectives in Reading, no. 2, International Reading Association, Newark, Del., 1964, pp. 45–57.

43. Johnson, Marjorie Seddon: "Evaluating the Secondary School Reading Program," *Reading Instruction in Secondary Schools,* Perspectives in Reading, no. 2, International Reading Association, Newark, Del., 1964, chap. 10.

44. Johnson, Rodney: "Individualized and Basal Primary Reading Programs," *Elementary English,* vol. 42, pp. 902–904, 915, December, 1965.

45. King, Paul T., and William Delande: "The University of Missouri Reading Improvement Program," *Journal of Reading,* vol. 8, pp. 307–310, April, 1965.

46. Landry, Herbert A.: "Teaching Reading with the *Reader's Digest*," *English Journal*, vol. 32, pp. 320–324, June, 1943.

47. Larrick, Nancy: "The Reading Teacher and the Library," *The Reading Teacher*, vol. 17, pp. 149–151, December, 1963.

48. Leavell, Ullin W., and Grace E. Wilson: "Guided Free Reading versus Other Methods in High School English," *Peabody Journal of Education*, vol. 33, pp. 272–280, March, 1956.

49. Lee, Maurice A.: "Improving the Reading of the Negro Rural Teacher in the South," *Journal of Negro Education*, vol. 13, pp. 47–56, Winter, 1944.

50. Lennon, Roger T.: "What Can Be Measured?" *The Reading Teacher*, vol. 15, pp. 326–337, March, 1962.

51. Madeira, Sheldon: "Pennsylvania's Mandated Reading Program," *Journal of Developmental Reading*, vol. 5, pp. 221–226, Summer, 1962.

52. Marquis, Bettylee Fults: "Developmental Reading in New Albany High School," *Journal of Developmental Reading*, vol. 7, pp. 58–62, Autumn, 1963.

53. McCullough, Constance M.: "Characteristics of Effective Readers in the Elementary School," in Helen M. Robinson (comp. and ed.), *Reading Instruction in Various Patterns of Grouping*, Supplementary Educational Monographs, no. 89, University of Chicago Press, Chicago, 1959, pp. 3–8.

54. McDonald, Arthur S.: "Influence of a College Reading Improvement Program on Academic Performance," *Journal of Educational Psychology*, vol. 48, no. 3, pp. 171–181, March, 1957.

55. McDonald, Arthur S., and G. H. Zimny: *The Art of Good Reading*, The Bobbs-Merrill Company, Inc., Indianapolis, 1963, pp. xiv, 426.

56. McDonald, Arthur S., Edwin S. Zolik, and James A. Byrne: "Reading Deficiencies and Personality Factors: A Comprehensive Treatment," in Oscar S. Causey and William Eller (eds.), *Starting and Improving Reading Programs*, Eighth Yearbook of the Southwest Reading Conference, Texas Christian University Press, Fort Worth, Tex., April, 1959, pp. 89–98.

57. McGinnis, Dorothy J.: "A Reading Laboratory at the College Level," *Journal of Higher Education*, vol. 22, pp. 98–101, February, 1951.

58. Moorhouse, William F.: "Interclass Grouping for Reading Instruction," *Elementary School Journal*, vol. 64, pp. 280–286, February, 1964.

59. *National Elementary Principal*, vol. 44, pp. 8–76, January, 1965. (Issue devoted to cooperative teaching.)

60. Ninth-year Committee, Walton High School: "A Reading Experiment," *High Points*, vol. 39, pp. 12–31, January, 1957.

61. Olsen, James T.: "Instructional Materials for Functionally Illiterate Adults," *Journal of Reading*, vol. 9, pp. 21–25, October, 1965.

62. Olson, Arthur V., Alpheus Sanford, and Fred Ohnmacht: "Effectiveness of a Freshman Reading Program," *Journal of Reading*, vol. 8, pp. 75–83, November, 1964.

63. Parker, Don: "Improving Reading and Study Skills in Secondary Schools through Greater Individualization of Instruction," unpublished doctoral dissertation, Teachers College, Columbia University, New York, 1957.

64. Perry, William G., Jr.: "Student's Use and Misuse of Reading Skills: A

Report to the Faculty," *Harvard Educational Review,* vol. 29, pp. 193–200, Summer, 1959.

65. Perry, William G., Jr., and Charles P. Whitlock: "The Right to Read Rapidly," *Atlantic Monthly,* vol. 190, pp. 88–96, November, 1952.

66. Powell, William R.: "The Joplin Plan: An Evaluation," *Elementary School Journal,* vol. 64, pp. 387–392, April, 1964.

67. Prescott, Daniel: *The Child in the Educative Process,* McGraw-Hill Book Company, New York, 1957.

68. Rankin, Earl F., Jr., Renny Greenman, and Robert J. Tracy: "Factors Related to Student Evaluations of a College Reading Course," *Journal of Reading,* vol. 9, pp. 10–15, October, 1965.

69. Ranson, M. Kathleen: "An Evaluation of Certain Aspects of the Reading and Study Program at the University of Missouri," *Journal of Educational Research,* vol. 48, pp. 443–454, February, 1955.

70. Rasmussen, Margaret (ed.): *Individualizing Education,* Association for Childhood Education International, Washington, 1964.

71. *The Reading Teacher,* vol. 7, pp. 193–219, April, 1954. (Issue on parents' concern with their children's reading.)

72. *The Reading Teacher,* vol. 17, no. 3, December, 1963. (Issue on reading instruction and school libraries.)

73. Rice, Helen F.: "How Reading Teachers and Librarians Work Together," *The Reading Teacher,* vol. 17, pp. 164–169, December, 1963.

74. Richards, Ivor A.: *How to Read a Page,* W. W. Norton & Company, Inc., New York, 1942.

75. Robinson, H. Alan (ed.): *Meeting Individual Differences in Reading,* Supplementary Educational Monographs, no. 94, University of Chicago Press, Chicago, December, 1964.

76. Robinson, H. Alan, and Allan F. Muskopf: "High School Reading—1963," *Journal of Reading,* vol. 8, pp. 85–96, November, 1964.

77. Robinson, H. Alan, and Sidney J. Rauch: *Guiding the Reading Program, A Reading Consultant's Handbook,* Science Research Associates, Inc., Chicago, 1965.

78. Robinson, Helen M.: "Education of Reading Teachers," *Elementary School Journal,* vol. 61, pp. 411–413, May, 1961.

79. Sartain, Harry: "Individual or Basal in Second and Third Grades," *Instructor,* vol. 74, pp. 69ff., March, 1965.

80. Schleich, Miriam: "The Evolution of a College Reading Program," unpublished doctoral dissertation, Teachers College, Columbia University, New York, 1958.

81. Schneyer, J. Wesley: "Problems of Concentration among College Students," *The Reading Teacher,* vol. 15, pp. 34–37, September, 1961.

82. Schneyer, J. Wesley: "The Relationship of Scholastic Aptitude Factors, to Progress in a College Reading Course," *Journal of Developmental Reading,* vol. 7, pp. 261–268, Summer, 1964.

83. Schneyer, J. Wesley: "Significant Reading Research at the Secondary Level," *Reading Instruction in Secondary Schools,* Perspectives in Reading, no. 2, International Reading Association, Newark, Del., 1964, chap. 10.

84. Severson, Eileen: "A Reading Program for High School Students," *The Reading Teacher,* vol. 16, pp. 103–106, November, 1962.

85. Shaw, Phillip: "Reading in College," *Development in and through Reading,* Sixtieth Yearbook of the National Society for the Study of Education, University of Chicago Press, Chicago, 1961, part I, pp. 336–354.

86. Shepherd, David: "The Role of a Reading Consultant," *Journal of the National Association of Women Deans and Counselors,* vol. 20, pp. 18–23, October, 1956.

87. Simmons, John S.: "The Role of the Reading Supervisor," *Reading Improvement,* vol. 2, pp. 83–86, Summer, 1965.

88. Simmons, John S.: "The Scope of the Reading Program for Secondary Schools," *The Reading Teacher,* vol. 17, pp. 31–35, September, 1963.

89. Simpson, G. O.: *Using My Reading Design,* published by *The News-Journal,* North Manchester, Ind., n.d.

90. Spache, George D.: *Toward Better Reading,* The Garrard Press, Champaign, Ill., 1963, chaps. 2, 3.

91. Stanchfield, John: "The Reading Specialist in the Junior High School," *Journal of Reading,* vol. 8, pp. 301–306, April, 1965.

92. Strang, Ruth: "Evaluation of Development in and through Reading," *Development in and through Reading,* Sixtieth Yearbook of the National Society for the Study of Education, University of Chicago Press, Chicago, 1961, part I, chap. 21, pp. 376–397.

93. Strang, Ruth: "Needed Emphases in High School Reading," *Reading in High School,* vol. 1, pp. 35–38, Winter, 1964.

94. Strang, Ruth: *Problems in the Improvement of Reading in High School and College,* Science Press Printing Company, Lancaster, Pa., 1940.

95. Strang, Ruth: "Progress in the Teaching of Reading in High School and College," *The Reading Teacher,* vol. 16, pp. 170–177, December, 1962.

96. Strang, Ruth, and Donald Lindquist: *The Role of the Administrator in the Improvement of Reading,* Appleton-Century-Crofts, Inc., New York, 1960.

97. Tincher, Ethel: "No Hurts, Headaches or Heartaches," *Scholastic Teacher, Practical English,* vol. 33, no. 5, pp. 10-t–81-t, October 10, 1962.

98. Tinker, Miles A.: "Brightness Contrast, Illumination Intensity and Visual Efficiency," *American Journal of Optometry and Archives of American Academy of Optometry,* vol. 36, pp. 221–236, May, 1959.

99. Tormey, Mary K., and Walter G. Patterson: "Developmental Reading and Student Evaluation," *Journal of Developmental Reading,* vol. 2, pp. 30–43, Winter, 1959.

100. Triggs, Frances Oralind: *Remedial Reading,* University of Minnesota Press, Minneapolis, 1943, reprinted 1948.

101. Umans, Shelley: *Designs for Reading Programs,* Teachers College Press, Teachers College, Columbia University, New York, 1964.

102. Umans, Shelley: *New Trends in Reading Instruction,* Teachers College Press, Teachers College, Columbia University, New York, 1963.

103. Veatch, Jeannette: *Individualizing Your Reading Program,* G. P. Putnam's Sons, New York, 1959.

104. Walker, Jerry L.: "Conducting an Individualized Reading Program in High School," *Journal of Reading,* vol. 8, pp. 291–295, April, 1965.

105. Whitney, Algard: "The Reading Consultant," unpublished doctoral dissertation, Teachers College, Columbia University, New York, 1955.

106. Witty, Paul A.: "Guiding Principles in Reading Instruction," *Education,* vol. 85, pp. 474–480, April, 1965.

107. Witty, Paul A.: "Improving Reading in the High School," *Nation's Schools,* vol. 61, pp. 62–63, March, 1958.

108. Witty, Paul A.: "Johnny Could Read Better," *Nation's Schools,* vol. 61, pp. 40–42, January, 1958.

109. Wylie, Ruth C.: "Children's Estimates of Their School Work Ability, as a Function of Sex, Race, and Socioeconomic Level," *Journal of Personality,* vol. 31, pp. 203–224, June, 1963.

sequential aspects of
reading development

chapter **3**

The development of reading skills proceeds in an upward spiral, starting with simple skills and gradually moving to higher levels of complexity and difficulty. This chapter will be a kind of road map for the essential attitudes and skills for reading development together with indications as to the most advantageous times to begin or continue improvement. Such a description of sequential development will enable you to acquire perspective on a student's present status in the light of his past achievement and future goals. It will also enable you to give your students a sense of direction, continuity, and progression in their reading experiences. This map of reading values will suggest grade levels for giving intensive instruction and practice in certain skills, providing for the incidental learning of other skills and attitudes, and giving opportunities to sharpen and apply skills already learned.

While reading the following descriptions of attitudes and abilities that are appropriate to given stages of development, you should keep in mind the groups which concern you most. Which reading skills are they just beginning to learn? Which have they already acquired? Which can they use as tools in learning the subjects you are teaching?

How does your understanding of the reading process and of reading prerequisites and goals (Chapter 1) help you to plan a sequential development of reading attitudes, abilities, and interests with your students, both individually and in groups?

THE READING CURRICULUM

It is more accurate not to divide reading development into separate stages because most reading skills are introduced in their simplest form in the first grade and further developed as the child progresses through each grade. Arno Jewett [23], Specialist for Secondary School English for the U.S. Office of Education, defines a sequential program of instruction as one which reinforces and extends those desirable reading skills and appreciations acquired in previous years and develops new skills and appreciations as they are needed.

A sequential development of instruction gives high priority to the preschool and kindergarten years and the primary grades: "Well begun is more than half done." However, it does not neglect the intermediate grades, too common a practice today. It also recognizes the special reading problems of the junior high school student and seeks to prepare the senior high school student for the reading demands of college and of adult life. It continues in college with expert instruction in interpretive, critical, and creative reading. For the adult it encourages the application of critical and interpretive proficiency as well as the use of special skills in his vocation. If both students and teachers fully realize that reading development is continuous, they will seek out the appropriate instruction and practice at the best point along the continuum.

The shrewd student who sees gaps in his reading development makes up his deficiencies. When he realizes, for example, that his slow, laborious reading is due to his failure to instantly recognize small words that recur frequently, he will be eager to expand his basic sight vocabulary. When his comprehension of an interesting story is blocked by his inability to analyze unfamiliar key words, he will strengthen his word attack methods.

Although it is possible to describe an individual's progress in reading, it is much more difficult, if not impossible, to lay out a universally applicable program for progressive reading achievement through the grades. There was a time when educators thought that students in the first three grades learned to read, in the middle grades read to learn, and in high school and college analyzed and evaluated what they read. Now educators are realizing that although these general goals are probably the ones that should be emphasized in successive years, every important reading skill has its genesis in the early years.

Each spiral of reading development rests on the preceding ones. When a small child tells what happened to the three bears first, next, and next again, he is standing on the bottom rung of the ladder of organization, taking the beginning step in outlining. He is practicing simple sequence. Every child at every level of reading, regardless of his status relative to that of other pupils, needs to have experiences with all the reading skills that are appropriate to that level. Whatever is omitted in one grade becomes a millstone around the pupil's neck in a subsequent grade. Both the classroom teacher and the tutor can create reading problems by overemphasizing one set of skills and neglecting another.

At every point in the sequential development of reading the teacher will be introducing some skills incidentally, will be giving concentrated instruction and practice in other skills, and will be reinforcing many skills previously learned. The relative proportions of direct instruction and of more or less informal reinforcement and application may be represented by two triangles:

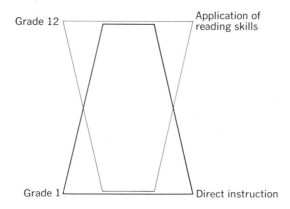

It will be noted that the amount of direct instruction decreases as the child goes through school, whereas the extent to which reading skills are applied to all subjects increases through the upper elementary and the secondary school years. However, the need for instruction in reading does not disappear.

The same diagram is applicable to pupils of differing abilities. The slower learners and less able pupils require the larger proportion of instruction while the able learners can focus more on the content.

Teaching would be much easier if all the pupils in a given class were at the same stage of development. But they are not. Even in sectioned or so-called homogeneously grouped classes there are still individual differences. Consequently it is necessary to find out where each pupil stands in his reading development. If he is deficient in any of the early levels, he will be handicapped in the subsequent ones. For example, a sixth-grade boy who cannot immediately recognize the Dolch basic vocabulary will find reading a laborious process. The obvious solution of this problem is to give individualized instruction guided by diagnostic information.

HOW READING ABILITY DEVELOPS

When he was eighty years old, the philosopher and poet Goethe said, "The dear people do not know how long it takes to learn to read. I have been at it all my life and I cannot yet say I have reached the goal." From birth to old age each period of life makes its contribution to the development of reading abilities because they increase with the changing scope of interests, with the growth of general ability, and with the challenge of increasingly complex and difficult reading tasks. But reading development is not a series of separate steps; its many components appear and converge in kaleidoscopic fashion, one pattern of reading abilities merging gradually into another. Its growth does not move forward like an army marching single file through a narrow pass. It moves ahead on a broad front, exploring and progressing at different points simultaneously. The development of any reading attitude or skill usually begins in slight measure, then builds to a point of intensive instruction and practice. From then on the attitude or skill thrives through daily application.

Although reading development takes time, there is a "magic of time in a good environment" [2, p. 100]. The task of the teacher is to provide the student with rich experiences and guide him in the use of them while he does his own learning and gains self-confidence. To help the student progress, the teacher must also discern when he is ready to move ahead, guarding against pressure methods that produce temporary gains but diminish self-reliance and blunt the desire to read. Premature imposition of advanced standards of reading efficiency may be detrimental. It may also result in emotional difficulties. Results of premature parental pressure are unfortunate, pushing children to read before they are able so that they fail and are afraid to try again.

On the other hand, a teacher must be wise in holding a child to levels of achievement appropriate for him or to reading experiences for which he is ready, or he will not realize his potentialities. A refugee boy of fourteen who came to the reading center was reading only on the third-grade level. For three years during the war he had not attended school. For two more years he had attended a school without books. Educational deprivation had distorted his growth in reading. When he was given the necessary instruction and practice, starting at the third-grade level, he made very rapid progress and maintained his gains. The reading potentiality was there; it needed only suitable environment for its development. Every individual has certain reading potentialities which will develop if conditions are favorable. There is a happy medium between too much pressure and extreme *laissez faire.*

The child-development view of reading requires an understanding of the individual's development—how he got that way, what his present abilities and interests are, and where he is going. Children grow toward reading readiness at different rates. Four-year-old Marie Curie learned to read casually and quickly by watching her older sister struggle with beginning reading. A mentally retarded boy with an IQ of 52 gained nothing from class instruction in reading until, at the chronological age of fourteen, he had reached a mental age of six or seven years. Then, with individual help, he progressed until he reached his limit of growth.

Many conditions affect the child's language development. His response depends upon his chronological and mental age, upon his willingness to co-operate, and upon home conditions; even in a relatively silent home, the child's language development stems from his need to communicate. The quality of the language he hears is important. Parents who provide poor speech models may hamper the child's language development even more than a silent home does. Institutions for infants and young children are not the answer, as Israel and Russia discovered with their experiments with community schools. There is need for concerted action by all concerned—for parents to improve their children's home environment and the community to establish more effective schools.

From Birth to Two Years

The infant takes his first step on the road to reading when he distinguishes his mother's face from the blur of light and darkness. Soon other objects interest him. He learns to look. He learns to listen. At this stage the mother talks to the baby in a natural tone of voice making him aware of the sounds, tones, and rhythms of speech. His own speech develops as he endlessly makes sounds at first accidentally and then in imitation. In four to six months he may be reproducing all the vowel and consonant sounds. He may well say his first word before the end of the first year and know a concept before he has a word for it. By the time he is two years old, he can respond to a few hundred words and some statements and has begun to fashion some sentences for himself.

In learning to talk a child makes many sounds and says many words imperfectly, but gradually he improves them all. He learns his native language rapidly when he has interest, curiosity, a need to communicate, and freedom to explore freely for himself. He begins to see cause-and-effect relationships and selects the responses for the results he wants. Every time he is successful in communicating an idea, he becomes more convinced that talking really works. His satisfaction is increased by, but should not be dependent upon, his mother's pleasure in his success. Learning should be its own reward. The adult's role is (1) to create an environment in which the child hears natural, meaningful conversation; (2) to try to understand what he is saying; and (3) to respond to his attempts to communicate.

At the same time that the young child is experiencing a secure, loving environment and is learning to look and listen and talk, he is, ideally, developing a sense of trust and an openness to new experiences. The parent encourages the toddler's natural desire to explore, to manipulate, and to inquire—within reasonable limits, of course. If the environment is indifferent or hostile, the child tends to withdraw from or to resist new experiences. Negative attitudes of this sort may affect his approach to all the communication skills.

Later Preschool Years

Certain preschool experiences are a prelude to success in beginning reading. A desire to read, experiences that give meaning to words, an apprehension of many spoken words, ability to speak in sentences, and familiarity with books and the language of books—all these develop simultaneously.

The desire to read is stimulated by seeing others reading. One high school boy recollected that as a child he had often seen his mother reading and eating chocolates. He remembered thinking, "When I grow up, I'm going to read a lot, too."

Reading aloud to children not only introduces them to the language of literature but also strengthens their desire to read for themselves. Even though they do not comprehend all that they hear, the magic of words appeals to them. They begin to understand that those queer black marks on paper say something as they look at and handle books carefully, thinking of them as friends.

Experiences of many kinds enlarge the child's speaking vocabulary. When he sees the picture of a dog and says "Bow-wow," he is learning to associate symbols with previous experiences. As he finds new things to see, hear, and handle, many common words take on enriched meanings. A trip to a farm adds new farm words to his meaningful vocabulary. Trips to the airport, the seashore, and other places similarly swell the child's vocabulary. He needs words in his play to get other children to do what he wants them to do and to understand their words which tell him what they want him to do.

As language becomes increasingly useful to the child, his vocabulary grows. By three years of age, many children achieve a spoken vocabulary of at least 900 words. By the time the child from an English-speaking home comes to school, his vocabulary contains, on the average, from 1,000 to 2,500 words, probably more as the influence of television increases.

The child's sentence patterns also become more complex. First-grade children from middle-class English-speaking homes may use, in different situations, all the principal types of sentence patterns [46, 47].

Most children acquire auditory and visual perception, discrimination, and memory during the preschool years without being specifically taught. As the child listens to carefully pronounced words and natural speech, he comes to recognize and distinguish different sounds. He also discovers that the meaning of words depends partly on the order in which they are arranged and the intonations and stress with which they are spoken.

In the process of looking and exploring, preschool children build visual perception, discrimination, and memory. Since perceptual factors are basic in learning to read, the earlier the teacher detects and corrects auditory and visual perceptual difficulties, the better; the preschool years are not too soon (see Chapter 1).

Facility in visual perception progresses from objects to words. As he grows accustomed to recounting the things he sees, the child is stimulated to look carefully and to relate one part of the story to another. When he identifies the same little boy on successive pages of his storybook, he is learning to distinguish forms that are alike from those that are different. Soon he begins to notice printed words in signs and labels about the house and on the street—"Hot" and "Cold" on the water faucets; "Bus Stop" on the street corners; words flashed repeatedly on the television screen. He notices the black marks on his picture books and on the newspaper his daddy is reading. As he takes an interest in letters and numbers, pretends to read, and asks the meaning of signs and labels, he is showing signs of a growing readiness for reading.

At nursery school the child learns to pay attention, to follow directions, to wait for his turn, to adjust his wishes to those of the group. He may find his name printed above the hook on which he is to hang his coat and hat. When he becomes aware that printed words have meaning for him, he has taken an important step in learning to read.

The age at which children should enter first grade has been the subject of much controversy. Chronological age is one of the least significant elements in reading readiness. Height and other aspects of physical development, insofar as they indicate general maturity, may show some relation to reading. However other factors are more important (see Chapter 1). Studies have obtained somewhat contradictory evidence about the value of an early start in reading. According to Ilg and Ames [22], 19 per cent of the children entering first grade are not ready to read. Halliwell and Stein [19] reported that fourth- and fifth-grade pupils who had entered first grade when seventy-nine to eighty-one months old were significantly superior to younger fourth-grade pupils in reading, spelling, and other language skills as measured by the California Achievement Tests. However, generalizations on this controversial question are dangerous and seriously misleading. Some bright children are ready to learn to read and should have the opportunity to do so before the first grade. The majority of preschool and kindergarten children profit from prereading experiences that develop readiness for first-grade reading instruction. Children from non-English-speaking and disadvantaged homes need to be in preschools and kindergartens which provide the prereading experiences lacking in their home environment. Whether a head start in actual reading is advantageous depends a great deal on the degree to which the first-grade teacher provides for individual differences.

Beginning Reading in the Primary Grades [1]

This is a period for developing favorable attitudes toward reading, for expanding basic vocabulary, and for building word recognition and comprehension skills. The child is ready for instruction in reading if he has built a meaningful listening and speaking vocabulary, has learned to carry on a conversation and tell a story in sequence, can identify and discriminate sounds in oral expression, and can see likenesses and differences in printed letters and words.

In addition to these linguistic indications of readiness, the child should also have a desire to learn to read; physical ability to see and hear; mental ability to associate, relate, and remember; and freedom from social problems and emotional conflicts that might distract his attention from reading. He should be able to adjust to classroom conditions which are usually different from the preschool freedom he has enjoyed.

The first-grade child should also realize that printed words are spoken words written down and that they have meaning for him. What kinds of words should he first learn to recognize at sight? Among the undisciplined Maori children of New Zealand the most meaningful words were *ghost, jet, fight, mommy* [3]. In American culture, in addition to words that signify mother, father, and home, young children become familiar with a wide range of words, some technical, by hearing them over and over in radio and television advertisements.

The beginner should also realize that a word refers to an object or action: it is a symbol. To help the child understand that a word may stand for many varieties of the same object or action, the teacher may suggest that he make picture books, each one illustrating a single word. For example, one book might show different kinds of rabbits on each page, with "rabbit" or "rabbits" printed under each picture.

[1] See James F. Kerfoot (comp. and ed.), *First Grade Reading Programs*, International Reading Association, Newark, Del., 1965.

If learning to read can be made more natural, more like learning to talk, fewer reading difficulties would appear later. Reading, like talking, should be an intrinsic part of the child's living. If the child feels a real need to associate the printed word with the sound of the spoken word or with an object or action, the effort to do so enlists his wholehearted attention and concentration. Moreover, he then learns both the printed word and its meaningful associations.

Lack of incentive deters some children from gaining proficiency in reading during their early school years. Agnes Repplier did not learn to read until she was ten years old. Up to that time she had not seen "any connection between the casual and meaningless things called letters and all the sweetness and delight that lay between the covers of books" [39, p. 3]. Her mother gave strict orders that no one should read to her. The ten-year-old Agnes, after a few days of blank despair, sized up the situation and quickly, though not without effort, learned to read.

To encourage children to read with an active, curious mind, most reading authorities suggest that the teacher begin by teaching a few familiar words, phrases, and sentences by sight. This merely extends what the children have been doing at home, when they ask, "Mommy, what does this word say?" "What does that street sign say?" The teacher finds out this interest word, pronounces it, lets the child see and write it, and puts it on a card for him to look at and say and talk about. Later she tests his recognition by writing it in a simple sentence on the board or on a chart. Thus the child has his first reading experience with printed words, phrases, and sentences that he himself has dictated; and he begins to realize he has been introduced to reading as a thought-getting process. As he adds a few other words to his sight vocabulary, he learns to distinguish their similarities and differences. He discovers that *see* and *said* begin with the same sound and the same letter. This is phonics, a process that involves visual perception, discrimination, and memory.

Many linguists and reading authorities disagree about the initial methods to develop visual perception, a beginning step in reading. Some maintain that children should first learn the alphabet. *My Alphabet Book* [49] in the Fries series presents both lowercase and capital letters. The children look at the letters, name them, and write them. One study concerned with how children actually perceive letters showed that they pay attention to both the vertical and the curved lines [17] which teachers should call attention to. But authorities who do not advocate teaching letter names point out that in reading the association is between the letter form and its *sound*—not its *name*.

The reader series developed for Hindi-speaking children starts with stories of experiences that they are familiar with rather than with letters in the traditional way. They develop letter sounds inductively in connection with familiar words in their spoken vocabulary. The word recognition exercises require attention to meaning as well as form [32].

Children learn in several ways to associate letter sounds and letter forms in familiar words and sentences. The way most frequently taught is the phonetic approach—systematic learning of sound-letter associations in key words.

Reading with Phonics [20], one of the oldest phonic systems that is still in use, begins by teaching the short sounds of the five vowels and progresses to the ten most frequently used consonants. One consonant at a time is blended with the five vowels, first in syllables and then in words. The rest of the forty-four speech sounds are learned in the same way. The progression is always from the known to the unknown, from simple to complex. This represents a very formal, deductive type of phonic instruction.

The *Phono-visual* method uses a grouping of letters based on the way in which the speech organs produce the sounds. (See Figures 1 and 2.)

This method teaches the voiceless consonants first, the voiced second, and then the vowels—always referring to familiar key words for each letter sound. The consonant sounds are thoroughly learned first as initial consonants and then recognized in other parts of the word. Starting with the initial sounds and always putting in a dash to represent the vowel teaches left-to-right progression. After the children have learned the consonant sounds, they next learn the short sound of *a*. It is an exciting moment when the children discover that they can read many words by combining new vowel sounds with the consonant sounds they have already learned. They continue to use this method to recognize an increasing number of words.

Another method, the *Phonetic Keys to Reading* [36], attempts to teach the sound-spelling relationships but largely through rules. The children apply these generalizations, principles, or rules whenever they are appropriate. One difficulty with this method is that every rule has its exceptions. Indeed, many of them have a high percentage of exceptions. For example, Clymer [7] found that one of the most frequently taught rules—"When two vowels go walking, the first does the talking"—applied in only 47 per cent of the words that contained this combination of vowels in the texts examined. According to his study only twenty-two of the forty-four phonic generalizations commonly taught had more than 75 per cent utility. This means that the child is constantly faced with the problem of first deciding whether the rule or the exception applies in a given word.

The phonic method developed by Sister Mary Caroline in her *Breaking the Sound Barrier* [30] leads the child to reason about the relation of the sound and symbol. When the pupil is confronted with an unfamiliar word in a sentence, he seeks the answer to these questions:

How does the word begin?

What are the vowels?
What do the vowels say?
What is the word?

The pupil then tests whether the pronunciation he has worked out makes sense in the sentence. As in other phonic systems, the pupil learns consonant and vowel sound-letter associations by means of key words. To answer the third and most diffcult question, the pupils apply the following rules: a vowel is short unless (1) a final *e* makes it long; (2) it is part of a diphthong or digraph; (3) it is modified by *r;* (4) it is at the end of a short word or accented syllable; (5) the word is an exception. Since these rules also do not always apply, a certain amount of trial and error is involved.

Words in Color [16] at first glance seems to be a fantastic method of teaching sound-letter associations. Its underlying principle is to associate a color with a letter and its corresponding sound; the color, which is initially useful in pronouncing words, soon becomes unnecessary. This is in essence a type of conditioning. Each of forty-four sounds of English is represented by a different color or shade. The children first learn to associate each sound with its corresponding color. For example, there are different colors for *a,* corresponding to the sounds in c*a*t, w*a*s, vill*a*ge, and f*a*tal; the color is the same in g*a*te, w*a*y, str*ai*ght, v*ei*l, and gr*ea*t. After learning the color-sound pattern, the pupils write the words and read them in plain black and white. Like many other reading methods, *Words in Color* gets results when used by enthusiastic, skillful teachers.

Quite a different approach is that represented by the *Initial Teaching Alphabet* (i.t.a.) [11]. This medium attempts to eliminate the uncertainty and confusion due to certain letters having several different sounds and certain sounds being represented by several different letters. To solve this problem, i.t.a. introduces a new alphabet in which each of the forty-four sounds of English has its own symbol. In other words, there is a one-to-one correspondence between the sound and the letter. Once the pupil has learned these associations, he is able to read and write in the new alphabet. This approach makes it easy for the pupil to use both the "look-and-say" method and the phonic method. As a result he acquires an early sense of confidence in his ability to read and writes his thoughts fluently in the new alphabet without having to decide how to spell the words.

A large-scale experiment in Britain in teaching children to read using the augmented or Initial Teaching Alphabet (i.t.a) obtained favorable results with the "new alphabet" [10]. The 306 four- and five-year-old children who started to read with i.t.a in the fall of 1961 were, at the end of two years, significantly superior in reading to children who had been using the traditional alphabet. Using this augmented alphabet, the children learned to read more quickly and easily; they made significant achievement in spelling and were

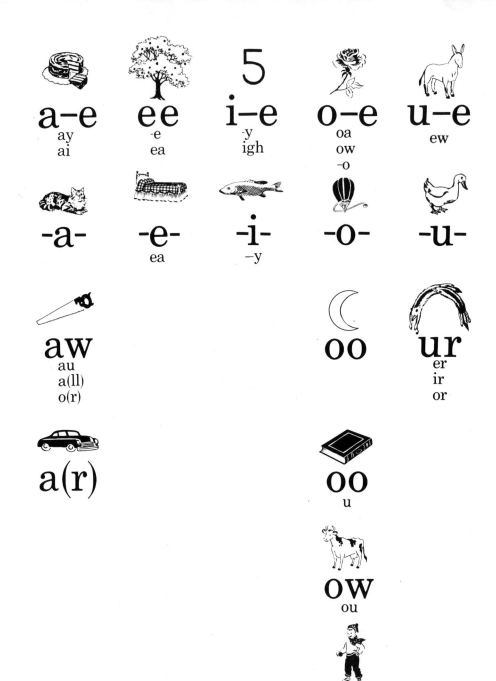

FIGURE 1. Phonovisual consonant chart. *Reproduced with permission of Phonovisual Products.*

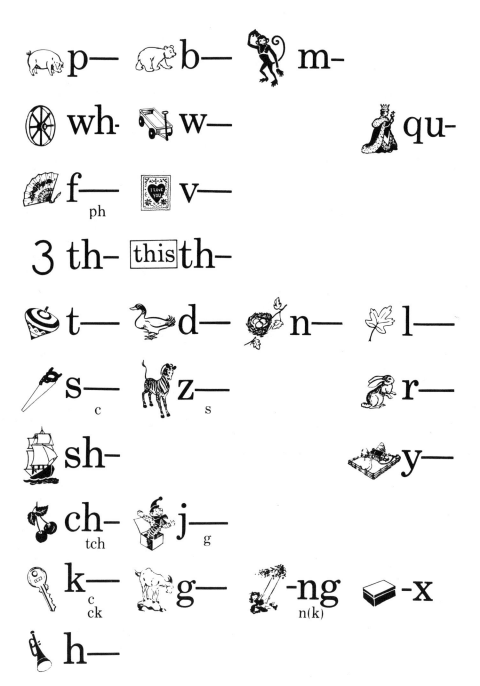

FIGURE 2. Phonovisual vowel chart. *Reproduced with permission of Phonovisual Products.*

more creative and fluent in their writing. Moreover, they were able to transfer their training in i.t.a. to books printed in traditional orthography.

An experiment in Bethlehem, Pennsylvania, with 500 first graders obtained similar results [31]. At the end of nine months, 29 per cent of the children taught by i.t.a. were reading on the third-grade level as compared to 10.8 per cent of the children using the traditional alphabet.

Twenty-seven pairs of first-grade children, more carefully matched, had success in making the transition from the artificial to traditional orthography. These children made the transition during the final fifteen sessions of the seventy instructional sessions of the experiment [44].

These positive results, like so much research that compares one method with another, may be partly attributed to factors other than the use of i.t.a. per se. Among these factors are the new, interesting reading material supplied to the experimental group, the extra workshops and discussions teachers in the i.t.a. groups participate in, the involvement of parents, and the publicity given to the positive results of i.t.a. [45].

The crucial question for the British method is: Can the pupil make the transition to traditional orthography? Several preliminary experiments have shown that a large majority of children do make the transition more or less quickly to books printed in the ordinary way. Several circumstances facilitate this transition: twenty-four letters of this alphabet are the same as in the old alphabet, and the twenty other symbols have features that resemble familiar letter forms with most changes occurring in the middle or bottom part of the new symbols. This is an advantage because the tops of letters tend to convey more meaning to the reader than do the lower parts. Finally, since many of the stories are printed in both alphabets, the pupil acquires a familiarity with the content that also helps him to make the transition. Although experiments have shown quite clearly that children learn to read and write more easily and quickly in the new alphabet, there is need still to assess its effect on their continued progress and long-term accomplishment in reading. Whether other methods could obtain the same results and not require publication of completely new material for beginning reading is an important consideration.

The linguistic approach to the process of decoding—translating the printed word into the spoken word—begins with words rather than with sound-letter associations. It is an inductive rather than a deductive method. The linguistic method presents the child with words that he already knows in such a way that he can discover patterns of sound-spelling relationships [14]. The child is expected to get the meaning from the words without the help of pictures.

The words are grouped in sequences that vary in only one grapheme-phoneme relationship.[2] Only regular patterns are presented first. The pupil

[2] A *phoneme* is the smallest unit of speech sound that conveys or differentiates meanings in words; a *grapheme* is a letter or cluster of letters that represents a certain phoneme.

systematically reads sets of words which differ by a single phoneme—*m* in *man* and *r* in *ran*. From his experience with a large number of words that have this pattern, the pupil makes his own generalization about these sound-letter relationships. As he reads more words in lists, on charts, and on the chalkboard, he discovers that certain patterns or sequences of letters stand for certain sounds. He discovers and masters one pattern after another.

The pupil gradually meets the less regular patterns. A few words which he needs for sentence building but which have unique or exceptional sound-spelling relationships he learns by the look-write-and-say method. It is probably well to introduce quite early a few irregular words that must be learned by sight. Then the pupil will not be disturbed when he finds that his generalizations do not always apply.

Linguistic series, such as *The Miami Linguistic Readers* (D. C. Heath and Company, 1964), the *Linguistic Readers* (Harper & Row, Publishers, Incorporated, 1965), and the "basic reading services developed on linguistic principles" by Fries, Wilson, and Rudolph (Charles E. Merrill, Inc.) incorporate similar principles.

The new basal readers themselves are eclectic: they incorporate both phonics and linguistics to some extent in the scope and sequence of their lessons [21]. A basal series covers the range of skills that are needed by the maturing reader and teaches them in sequence so that each developmental stage leads to the next. The teaching methods and supplementary instructional materials that are described in the teachers' manuals are designed to insure completeness, unity, and coherence.

In conjunction with the method of beginning reading, children need a carefully graded sequence of material which provides for continuity of growth in reading attitudes and skills. At no point in their program should they know discouragement because of needless difficulty. By building on previous skills they develop more advanced patterns, adequate to the tasks in reading. As soon as they have learned to associate printed words with their meaning, the children should have a variety of reading activities appropriate to the material and the reader's purpose. The content must have interest and value, an intrinsic reward for effort spent in deciphering the printed word.

While the child is learning to read some words at sight and to use phonics, structural analysis, and context clues to recognize words that are unfamiliar in print, he is also learning to comprehend sentences. Unless sentence comprehension accompanies word pronunciation, the child tends to become a word caller. He will pronounce correctly all the words in a sentence but still have no idea of what the sentence said. This disregard for meaning is quite common. It is largely due to the neglect of comprehension skills in beginning reading.

The sequential development of sentence-comprehension skills begins with a desire or a need to know what the author is saying. Therefore, the first reading material must have some personal significance to the child. It may be a sentence about today's weather, a set of directions for him to carry out, or a little story that he has dictated to the teacher. When a child starts to read independently and when he enjoys listening to stories, he begins to gain both ideas and personal values from reading material.

It is essential, too, that children be familiar with common English sentence patterns. Children from good-English-speaking homes are able to use most of the common sentence patterns. In a variety of situations, especially play situations, children use many minor sentences with the simplest of patterns, noun-verb: "Billy came," "Doll broke." Also common among first-graders are noun-verb-noun object sentences: "Ted likes jello." Other patterns found in the spontaneous speech of these children include:

Noun-verb-noun-noun: "Harry called Fred a cheat."
                                "Susan showed Mrs. Reynolds the book."
Noun–linking-verb–noun: "Freddy is the policeman."

These patterns may be varied and expanded by the use of adjectives, adverbs, phrases, and clauses. Children's growth in thinking is reflected in the increased complexity of their language patterns, especially in phrases and clauses that show different kinds of relationships—time, cause and effect, and spatial relations. As they come to use larger and more exact groupings of words, they may be expected to develop correct generalizations about sound-spelling relationships as well as sentence meanings [26].

Linguists emphasize natural intonation as another important clue to meaning [27]. For example, when the voice drops it signals the end of a sentence or the completion of a thought. Reading aloud often sheds light on both meaning and sentence pattern [25].

It has been repeatedly emphasized that there is no one best method of teaching beginning reading. Only a few programs have been described here. Each usually has some feature that may be incorporated into an effective method for certain individuals and groups. Research should focus not on whether one method is better than another, but rather on what features of a given method are most helpful in teaching beginners to read. More important than the method per se is the skill of the teacher and his relationship with his students.

Consolidation of Basic Skills in the Intermediate Grades

With a strong foundation of beginning reading experiences, most children should make excellent progress in the fourth, fifth, and sixth grades, a period of rapid growth in comprehension, speed, and reading interest. It is a time when reading—although always important and basic—shifts to its proper place of subordination so that the child is free to concentrate on the acquisition of knowledge. Yet it is not a time for the teacher to regard these skills as secondary, since reading is always the major road to comprehension.

The pupils review and use previously learned methods of analyzing words; they often recognize unfamiliar words by dividing them into syllables and by structural analysis of larger units. They should now become more expert in using the context to unlock word meanings and more sensitive to word relationships. The dictionary assumes more importance in interpreting the significance of unfamiliar words and as a check on other methods of word attack. Sight vocabulary increases. The pupils are gradually beginning to understand abstract words.

During the intermediate grades children should complete their mastery of sentence structure. They should become adept at recognizing various paragraph structures and purposes. When they have learned to recognize the structure, thought, and purpose in paragraphs, they become able to outline longer passages.

These are also good years in which to teach the technique of locating information: the use of the card catalog, table of contents, index, headings, and italics. After learning to locate sources of information, the pupil is ready to begin examining them for accuracy, authenticity, and relevancy. He takes useful notes, organizes the facts, and writes a readable report which he presents in an interesting way. It is here that he receives instruction in the special skills of reading maps, graphs, and tables.

It is not too early to begin daily practice of the Survey Q3R method (see "How Effective Is Your Reading?" Coronet Instructional Film). It encourages the pupil not only to facilitate his reading but also to improve his study habits. Other types of study skills are described in the September 1961 issue of *The Reading Teacher.*

Intermediate-grade pupils can also learn to perceive the author's mood and purpose: "How did the author get you to like a certain character?" "How did he set the mood for an event?"

In the intermediate grades children begin to read widely for enjoyment. Voluntary reading usually reaches a peak at twelve or thirteen years of age. Children of this age should begin building a variety of reading interests. Until they are about ten years of age boys and girls have similar reading interests. Then their interests diverge; boys' interests tend to become more masculine; girls', more feminine; interests of both sexes may become more personal and specialized.

Pupils in grades 2 through 3 tend to gain in reading ability during the summer months. This is especially true of girls and is probably due to voluntary reading. During the academic year boys tend to grow in reading ability more than girls [35].

During these years children should form the habit of reading with an inquiring mind and a definite purpose. They should learn to adjust their rate and method of reading to their purpose and to the nature and difficulty of the material. In their reading they should pause occasionally to note relationships and to summarize what they have learned. In their discussions of books and in teacher-pupil conferences on their reading, they should learn to evaluate the material they have read.

The small percentage of published articles on reading in the intermediate grades indicates a neglect of this period. Of all the articles on reading published in *The Reading Teacher* during 1964, only 1.1 per cent concerned the intermediate grades as compared with 19 per cent on the elementary, 15 per cent on the junior high school, 12 per cent on the senior high school, and 18 per cent on the college level.

Expansion of Reading Interests and Abilities in the Junior High School

When a student enters junior high school, he is usually confronted with new subjects and increased demands for wide reading. Not only must he comprehend greater amounts of assigned reading, but he must also locate a larger number of sources of information bearing on a given topic or problem. As in the case of younger pupils, the incentive to acquire these reading skills will arise out of activities that seem important and interesting. A group spirit in which students help one another to learn will reinforce interest and effort.

A sketch of the sequential development of reading during the junior high school years is truly sketchy because it consists largely of reviewing, developing further, and applying the skills and attitudes that were initiated in earlier years: ability to recognize and analyze words and find their meanings; basic vocabulary study; understanding of phrase, sentence, and paragraph structure. During these years special emphasis centers on helping the student grasp the technical concepts and specialized vocabulary of new subjects. Teachers should expect greater expertness in word analysis, reference reading, and interpretation; a higher quality of reading interests and tastes; greater flexibility in approach to different kinds of material; and more effective study habits. Many pupils enter junior high school with little ability to organize and communicate the ideas from reading. They need much more instruction and practice.

During the junior high school years the individual's world expands rapidly. Books can compensate for limitations in his physical environment. He should read to extend his experiences and to gain an understanding of his country, his times, and himself.

Some junior high school pupils are reading one or two years below their grade placement; they need special instruction in their regular classes. More seriously retarded readers require special diagnosis and remedial work.

Greater Independence in Reading in Senior High School

During senior high school, students should receive guidance in taking more responsibility for their own improvement in reading. They should study, under guidance, the results of reading tests and exercises; set specific goals for themselves; and help plan their individual reading programs. This kind of initiative is highly desirable; it represents growth in self-appraisal and self-direction.

The student's power to interpret meaning should continue to grow during the senior high school years. He should learn to read between the lines to determine the full and precise meaning of sentences, paragraphs, and passages as a whole. This kind of interpretation requires understanding of the author's spoken or unspoken intention, his tone, the setting in which he wrote, his attitude toward himself, his subject, the reader, and other people.

Critical reading is another important concern of the high school years. Pupils should acquire increasing facility in appraising sources, detecting propaganda, and distinguishing fact from opinion. They should be ready to cite evidence for their statements and give the basis for their inferences and conclusions. Underlying these specific abilities are concern for quality and pleasure in precision.

High school students should also become increasingly appreciative of the personal values of reading. Through reading they can extend their experiences and become acquainted with new places and people. They can gain insight into the feelings that motivate both strange and familiar behavior. Thus they can increase their understanding of themselves in their complex and often trying family and boy-girl relationships if both teacher and student seek out these personal values [5].

The student who has a personal point of view toward reading thinks of each author as a person who has something to say to him. The experience of communication through reading should be almost as active and stimulating as conversation with a friend. The student who approaches reading with this expectant attitude stands to gain far more than the many students who read aimlessly and unimaginatively because they have never learned that reading may have meaning in their lives—that literature and life are inseparable.

With respect to each reading objective, three things should be considered: (1) whether the student's growth is adequate in relation to his ability, (2) the nature of the growth that he is experiencing, and (3) the factors that may be facilitating or hindering his progress. These may include his desire to learn, whether he knows how to learn, whether he is finding satisfaction in progress, and whether he is making the effort to apply his knowledge and skill to life situations.

Creative Reading in College

During the college years students should not only sharpen the abilities mentioned up to this point but should also become increasingly adept in the different approaches that are needed in reading different kinds of material. The language reflects its people's activities; their action is expressed in narration, their thinking in exposition, their feelings in lyricism. The student reads a book by Rachel Field, Thomas Mann, or Willa Cather differently from the way he reads a treatise on mathematics. Obviously, the college student who does not recognize the need for a different mind-set for different kinds of material and even for shifts from narration to exposition to lyricism within a single work will not read with the greatest efficiency. Without this adaptability to the diverse demands of reading material, students are not likely to select judiciously, read critically, interpret cogently, appreciate fully, or adapt their reading rate and method flexibly to different kinds of material and to different purposes in reading.

Intelligent reading in college is essential to the development of a scholarly person—one who has the ability to speak and write effectively. Such a person should be able to draw upon a mind stocked with significant ideas—a mind precise, not vacillating from one extreme to another, realistic, and richly human. College years—in fact, all the years of formal schooling—offer unparalleled opportunities for employing the present in such a way as to build a useful past—a past stored with meaningful experiences. The mature reader has a social purpose in reading [18]. He plans and carries out an appropriate individual program of self-improvement in reading not only for his personal development but also because of his conviction of the importance of reading today.

Higher Levels of Graduate Study and Adult Reading

For successful graduate study the reading abilities described are a necessary foundation. For these high levels of thoughtful, critical reading mere verbal comprehension of the main ideas and supporting details is not enough; there must be judgment on the basis of knowledge, appraisal of the author's sources of information, and recognition of his intent and purpose. However, advanced students specializing in different fields will show marked individuality in their reading methods. Like Santayana, the student may at some times browse through many books and at other times be concerned with a much deeper comprehension of philosophical writing [42, pp. 187–188]. Individual differences in students' reading and study methods should be respected.

Every person has reading potentialities that can and should be developed for his personal satisfaction and social usefulness. Some are capable of comprehending difficult and abstract material. If others cannot attain so high a level of reading power, they still are able to read widely in many fields that lie within their range of comprehension. Some are better at one speed of reading than at another. In brief, each person should be helped to discover and develop his reading potentiality—the particular level, breadth, and speed of which he is capable. At any age an individual's reading performance should be evaluated with reference to the reading potentialities toward which he is growing.

Unless the individual enjoys reading during his school and college years, he is not likely to read widely or well after college. Reports of adult reading are discouraging. Very few adults read serious books.

SEQUENTIAL DEVELOPMENT OF LANGUAGE ARTS BY GRADE LEVELS

There have been a number of attempts to work out a specific sequence of reading skills by grades. For example, the laboratory schools of the University of Chicago [8] have worked out in admirable detail a chart showing a plan of reading development for the first six grades. The San Diego County schools have published a course of study that describes the nature of reading development, sets forth the theory behind the reading program, and includes a Chart of Expectancies in grades 1 through 8. The Detroit public schools have prepared a comprehensive *Guide to Instruction in the Language Arts, Grades 4, 5, and 6*. The New York City schools have published a teachers' guide for curriculum development in reading in grades 7, 8, and 9. A detailed treatment of reading development and personal development through reading follows, in Table 1 (See p. 132).

The value of such a tabulation is to emphasize (1) the simultaneous development of attitudes and skills at any one stage of development, and (2) the continuous development of each attitude and skill over a period of years. Each ability is first introduced incidentally (indicated by O); at a later stage, special instruction and practice are given (indicated by B); and from then on the skill is reinforced, practiced, and applied (indicated by X) until it is thoroughly learned (indicated by M). The X's represent the levels at which the given attitude or skill may best be specifically and thoroughly taught.

The sequential development of reading ability is represented in another way by a "Pyramid of Growth." (See Figure 3 on p. 143.) As the pupil progresses through the various developmental stages, he should continuously reinforce and enhance each previously learned skill as opportunity offers. These illustrations do not represent separate steps or levels; they show patterns of attitudes and skills that operate simultaneously, or almost so, one reinforcing the other.

Retarded readers in any grade will begin where they are and move up the ladder of reading development as fast as they are able.

TABLE 1
READING AND PERSONAL DEVELOPMENT

	Preschool and Kindergarten	Primary Grades	Intermediate Grades	Junior High School	Senior High School	College	Adults
1. Experience background:							
Uses many kinds of experience to gain understanding of words.	O	B	X	X	X	X	X
2. Preparatory experiences:							
Learns to look, to see likenesses and differences in forms and words, to perceive words clearly.	O B	B X	X				
Learns to listen to and discriminate sounds.	O B	B X	X				
Builds a listening and speaking vocabulary.	O B	B	X	X	X	X	X
Learns the letters.	O B	M					
Looks at words and asks their meaning.	O B	B X					
Learns to listen and speak fluently in a group.	O	B X	X	X	M		
Learns to tell a story to an audience.	O	B X	X	X	X	M	
3. Beginning reading:							
Associates the sound of the word and its meaning with the printed symbol.	O	B X	X	M			
Identifies sounds and combinations of sounds in words.	O	O B	X	M			
Recognizes the same sound in different words.	O	O B	X	M			
Learns to read sentences from left to right.		B X	M	M			
Builds a basic sight vocabulary.	O	B X	X	M			

	Preschool and Kindergarten	Primary Grades	Intermediate Grades	Junior High School	Senior High School	College	Adults
Uses newly learned words in conversation and in writing.	O	O	O	O	O	O	O
Uses his experiences to interpret what he reads.		O	O	O	O	O	O
Grasps the meaning of simple passages.		O B	X	X	X	X	X
Reads aloud with expression.		B X	X	M	X	X	X
Reads directions.		B X	X	X	M		
Finds the answers to specific questions in reference books.		B X	X	X	M	X	
Recounts in correct sequence the events in the plot of a story.		O	B X	X	X	X	X
4. Vocabulary development:							
Learns new words incidentally through wide reading.		O	X	X	X	X	X
Learns key words and concepts as he studies each school subject.		O	B X	X	X	X	X
Learns technical abbreviations, symbols, and formulas needed in each field.			B	X	X	X	X
Consults the dictionary or glossary for exact meanings of words.			B X	X	X	X	X
Studies words in context systematically.		B X	X	X	X	X	X
Makes a dictionary of new words, giving pronunciation, derivation, definition, illustrative sentences.		B X	X	X	X		

	Preschool and Kindergarten	Primary Grades	Intermediate Grades	Junior High School	Senior High School	College	Adults
Becomes interested in word origins and the different meanings of the same word in different contexts.			B X	X	X	X	X
Recognizes the meaning of common words clearly and instantly.		B X	X	X	M		
5. Word recognition skills:							
Uses clues in the context to get the meaning of unfamiliar words, selecting the meaning that best fits the context.		B X	X	X	M		
Divides words into syllables so that he can pronounce them; knows and applies common principles of syllabication.		O	B X	X	M		
Uses phonetic approach if syllabic approach fails.			B X	X	M		
Knows and applies common phonetic principles; notes initial, middle, and final sounds and letter blends.		B	X	X	M		
Uses structural analysis of words whenever helpful, noting general configuration of words, identifying details and structural parts of words.		B X	X	X	M		
Learns more about how prefixes and suffixes modify meaning of the roots.				B X	M		

	Preschool and Kindergarten	Primary Grades	Intermediate Grades	Junior High School	Senior High School	College	Adults
Uses the dictionary as a check after he has attempted to get the meaning from context.			B X	X	X	X	X
Acquires a deeper understanding of the structure of language.					B X	X	X
Studies overtones of words and semantic derivation from original sense meaning.					B X	X	X
6. Understanding and organization:							
Reads in thought units.		B X	X	X	X	M	X
Comprehends sentences accurately.		B X	X	X	M		X
Gets the thought of a paragraph.		B	X	X	M		X
Gets organizing idea of an article or chapter and relates details to it.				B X	X	M	X
Writes in his own words a good outline or summary of the selection read.				B X	X	X	X
Gets author's pattern of thought as he reads.				B X	X	X	X
Remembers in organized form as much as is important for further thinking.				B X	X	X	X
Learns to read critically.		O	B X	B X	X	X	X
Distinguishes the essential from the nonessential.		O	B X	X	X	X	X
Examines truth or correctness of statements and detects discrepancies.			O	X	X	X	X
Recognizes propaganda.				B X	X	X	X

	Preschool and Kindergarten	Primary Grades	Intermediate Grades	Junior High School	Senior High School	College	Adults
Recognizes differences between fact and opinion and among opinions of varying weight.			B X	X	X	X	X
Brings own experience to bear on the author's statement.		O B	X	X	X	X	X
Notes sequences of events or ideas and cause-and-effect relations.		O	B X	X	X	X	X
Predicts outcomes on the basis of clues given by the author.		O	B X	X	X	X	X
Draws accurate inferences and conclusions.		O	B X	X	X	X	X
Thinks as he reads, notes common elements and concepts, keeps them in mind, and relates them.		O	O	O	B X	X	X
Understands increasingly advanced and complex material.				B X	X	X	X
Connects ideas in new ways, reading between and beyond the lines.				O	B X	X	X
Recognizes attitudes in himself that might distort his comprehension.					B X	X	X
Pauses to reflect on serious material.					B X	X	X
Suspends judgment until all available evidence has been obtained.				O	B X	X	X
Integrates and organizes information gained from reading.			O	B X	B X	X	X
7. Literary interpretation: Interprets characters' intent and behavior from author's clues.		O B	X	X	X	M	X

	Preschool and Kindergarten	Primary Grades	Intermediate Grades	Junior High School	Senior High School	College	Adults
Finds reasons for events and actions.		O B	X	X	X	M	X
Recognizes persuasive words and is aware of their influence on the reader.			O	B X	X	X	X
Reads aloud well enough to give and get enjoyment.			B X	X	M		
Participates in the aesthetic and emotional experiences presented by the author.		O		B X	X	X	X
Compares different styles of writing.			O	O	B X	X	X
8. Reading interests and appreciations:							
Laughs or smiles to himself as he reads a humorous book.		O	O	O	O	O	O
Voluntarily resumes reading a book he has chosen as soon as his other work is completed.		O	O	O	O	O	O
Uses school and public library for recreational and study reading.		B X	X	X	X	X	X
Reads many worthwhile books.		B X	X	X	X	X	X
Shows sensitivity to various levels of interpretations.				O	B X	X	X
Enjoys author's style in prose and poetry—picture-forming words, rhythm or cadence.		O	O	B X	X	X	X
Increases his awareness of and finds personal value in reading.		O	O	B X	X	X	X

	Preschool and Kindergarten	Primary Grades	Intermediate Grades	Junior High School	Senior High School	College	Adults
Appraises quality of book, magazine, television show, movie.		O	O	B X	X	X	X
Uses reading more in daily life outside of school.			B X	X	X	X	X
Reads as a favorite leisure-time activity which continues through life.			B X	X	X	X	X
Continues trend toward increased voluntary reading.			B X	B X	X	X	X
Improves the quality of his reading.			B X	X	X	X	X
Widens the scope of his reading.			B X	X	X	X	X
Develops one or more intensive reading interests.					B X	X	X
Enjoys discussion of books.		B X	X	M		X	
Shows decreased interest in reading the comics.			B X	M			
Resists forces such as television and auto riding that usurp reading time.			B X	X	M	X	X
Finds more motivation to read.				B X	X		
Uses television and other media of communication as part of a well-balanced program, recognizing the unique value of each medium and its special value in helping him to build an oral vocabulary and to supply an experience background for reading.			B X	X	X	X	X

	Preschool and Kindergarten	Primary Grades	Intermediate Grades	Junior High School	Senior High School	College	Adults
Reads to learn more about worthwhile hobbies.			B X	X	X	X	X
9. Work-study skills:							
Sits still long enough to attend to reading.	O	O B	X	M			
Skims skillfully for different purposes: to find a certain fact; to get a general impression; to get the main ideas; to find out what questions the passage will answer;							
to get clues to organization or plot.			B X	X	X	X	X
Learns to read maps, graphs, charts, diagrams, formulas.			O	B X	X	X	X
Learns to read out-of-school material—road maps, menus, signs, time-tables.	O	O	B X	M			
Learns to locate and select pertinent information on a topic and to use it in a report.			B	X	X	X	X
Becomes familiar with a wider variety of sources.			B	B X	X	X	X
Learns to take notes.			B	X	M		
Acquires skill in the Survey Q3R method and uses it whenever appropriate.			O	B X	X	X	X
Reads more rapidly with adequate comprehension.				B X	X	X	X

	Preschool and Kindergarten	Primary Grades	Intermediate Grades	Junior High School	Senior High School	College	Adults
Develops speed and fluency by reading easy material in each subject.					X	X	X
Applies ideas gained from reading, as, for example, in making pictorial, graphic, and tabular records.			B X	X	X	X	X
Uses ideas gained from reading to solve problems, prove a point, develop an interest, or entertain someone.		O	B X	X	X	X	X
Forms good study habits, budgets best time of day for study and creation.			B X	X	M	M	
Creates the best conditions possible for efficient study.			B X	X	M		
Gets to work promptly.		O B	X	M			
Applies psychological principles to remembering what is important.				B X	X	M	
Uses his own judgment when it has a sound basis.					B X	X	X
10. Approaches to outcomes of reading: Sets specific objectives before beginning to read.		O	B X	X	M		
Varies approach, rate, and reading methods according to the nature of the material—different kinds of writing and different fields; thus gains fluency and efficiency through adaptability and flexibility and purposeful reading.			O	B X	X	M	

	Preschool and Kindergarten	Primary Grades	Intermediate Grades	Junior High School	Senior High School	College	Adults
Reads with the intent to organize, remember, and use ideas.			O	B X	X	M	
Reads to solve problems, answer questions, understand developments and events outside his immediate environment.		O	B X	X	X	M	
Relates reading to his own life; shares ideas gained in reading.		O	B X	X	X	X	X
Gains understanding of himself and others through reading.		O	B X	X	X	M	
Concentrates better.		O	B X	X	M		
Experiences a growing pleasure in precision—shows unwillingness to half understand a passage.		O	B X	X	M		
11. Personal development through reading: Selects reading material that meets a personal need or widens his experience.		O	B X	X	X	X	X
Reads to solve personal problems; relates ideas gained from reading to his personal living—to each of the developmental tasks appropriate to his age.		O	B X	X	X	M	
Uses information from his reading in group projects, dramatizations, class discussions, committee work, club activities.		O	B X	X	M		

	Preschool and Kindergarten	Primary Grades	Intermediate Grades	Junior High School	Senior High School	College	Adults
Gains understanding of himself and others from reading autobiographies, biographies, and true-to-life fiction.		O	B X	X	X	X	X
Gains understanding of the world of nature and the world of men.			B X	X	X	X	X
Behaves differently as a result of reading, as, for example, toward parents after reading *The Yearling*, toward Negroes after reading *Amos Fortune*, toward driving a car after reading *Hot Rod*.		O	B X	X	X	X	X
Uses reading in building a philosophy of life and sound convictions.		O	O	B X	X	X	X
Improves emotional conditions—worry, anger, fear, insecurity—that block effective study and reading by learning to accept his feelings and to channel them into safe pathways; gets help through counseling or psychotherapy, if necessary.		O	O	B X	X	X	X

Inferences.
Critical
thinking.
Understanding
of relationships.
Evaluation of materials.
Skill in drawing conclusions.
Permanent interest in reading.
Broadened appreciation of
good literature.

Skill in locating and using books
and reference materials.
Ability to do purposeful oral reading.
Greater rate and skill in silent reading to
serve varied purposes.
Ability to select, evaluate, and organize
study-type materials.
Growth in enjoyment of printed materials.

Introduction to the work-type skills.
Growing independence in work recognition.
Ability to read silently more rapidly than orally.
Growth in ability to read orally with fluency and ease.
Desire to read good literature for recreatory purposes.

Beginning recognition of the printed symbols.
Attachment of meaning to printed sentences.
Purposeful reading to satisfy actual group and individual needs.
Keen interest in books and strong desire to read.

Development of visual and auditory discrimination, speech, motor control, language
facility, organization of ideas, left-to-right progression, and listening.
Adjustment to the school situation. Healthy and happy living. Wide, varied, purposeful
experiences, directed toward building vocabulary. Ability to work and play in groups.

Refinement of attitudes, habits, tastes

Wide reading

Rapid progress

Initial reading

Readiness

| Physical fitness | Mental maturity | Emotional stability | Social adjustment |

FIGURE 3. Pyramid of growth. (SOURCE: Curriculum Bulletin No. 12, State Department of Education, Augusta, Maine.)

In the last analysis, each student builds his own curriculum. The organizing principle, as Early [13] so well stated, is the student himself. Instruction in reading should be organized around the principles of learning how to learn. The student analyzes his skills, evaluates his progress and, with the teacher's help, states his objectives and plans methods for achieving them. This kind of self-appraisal shifts the responsibility from the teacher to the student.

If some of the items mentioned in this outline of sequential development seem too easy or too advanced for the level designated, a teacher should adjust them to the child's relative degree of proficiency. Almost any child can develop within his present range of ability and experience. If children do not make the expected progress, they need special attention at once. When these children are neglected, their reading difficulties do not disappear; they accumulate.

CURRICULUM RESEARCH NEEDED

Reading reaches into every area of the school curriculum. It also involves the student's home and community experiences, parent-teacher relations, group guidance of pupils and parents, and enrichment of the out-of-school environment. In 1963 less than one-fifth of the reports that dealt with reading in the secondary school were descriptions of reading programs per se [40, p. 86].

To build a reading curriculum educators should bring several research strands together. To the child-development approach should be added an understanding of adult reading needs in this modern world of mass communication. From this fusion of past, present, and future, a map of values begins to emerge. But since there is also need for information about what children can learn at different ages and how children of different abilities learn different skills, the students should have an important part in curriculum making. When the understanding gained from all these sources is synthesized, the educators will have a really functional reading curriculum.

Through the reading curriculum the pupil acquires not only the most important tool of learning but also qualities of mind, character, and personality.

REFERENCES

1. Ames, Louise B., and Richard W. Walker: "Prediction of Later Reading Ability from Kindergarten Rorschach and IQ Scores," *Journal of Educational Psychology,* vol. 55, pp. 309–313, December, 1964.

2. Anderson, John: "Development and Guidance," *National Association of Deans of Women Journal,* vol. 16, pp. 95–101, March, 1953.

3. Ashton-Warner, Sylvia: *Teacher,* Simon and Schuster, Inc., New York, 1963.

4. Brzeinski, Joseph E.: "Beginning Reading in Denver," *The Reading Teacher,* vol. 18, pp. 16–21, October, 1964.

5. Burton, Dwight L.: "Reading Experiences to Help Adolescents in Their Search for the 'I,'" *Improving Reading in the Junior High School,* U.S. Office of Education Bulletin, no. 10, 1957, pp. 60–67.

6. Caughran, Alex M., and Lee Harrison Mountain: *High School Reading,* Books 1 and 2, American Book Company, New York, 1961.

7. Clymer, Theodore: "The Utility of Phonic Generalizations in the Primary Grades," *The Reading Teacher,* vol. 16, pp. 252–258, January, 1963.

8. Committee on Developmental Reading, Laboratory Schools of the University of Chicago: *The History of the Work of the Committee on Developmental Reading in the Elementary Grades (Kindergarten through Six) of the Laboratory Schools,* University of Chicago Press, Chicago, July, 1955.

9. Cutts, Warren G.: *Research in Reading for the Middle Grades; An Annotated Bibliography,* U.S. Office of Education, 1963.

10. Downing, John: "The i.t.a. (Initial Teaching Alphabet) Reading Experiment," *The Reading Teacher,* vol. 18, pp. 105–110, November, 1964.

11. Downing, John A.: *The i.t.a. Reading Experiment,* Evan Brothers, Limited (published for the University of London, Institute of Education), London, 1964.

12. Durkin, Delores: "The Achievement of Preschool Readers: Two Longitudinal Studies," *Reading Research Quarterly,* vol. 1, pp. 5–36, Summer, 1966.

13. Early, Margaret J.: "The Meaning of Reading Instruction in Secondary Schools," *Journal of Reading,* vol. 8, pp. 25–29, October, 1964.

14. Fries, Charles C.: *Linguistics and Reading,* Holt, Rinehart and Winston, Inc., New York, 1963.

15. Gans, Roma: *Fact and Fiction about Phonics,* The Bobbs-Merrill Company, Inc., Indianapolis, 1964.

16. Gattegno, Caleb: *Background and Principles; Words in Color,* Encyclopaedia Britannica, Inc., Chicago, n.d.

17. Gibson, Eleanor J., and others: "The Role of Grapheme-Phoneme Correspondence in Word Perception," *American Journal of Psychology,* vol. 75, pp. 554–570, December, 1962.

18. Gray, William S., and Bernice Rogers: *Maturity in Reading,* University of Chicago Press, Chicago, 1956.

19. Halliwell, Joseph W., and Belle W. Stein: "A Comparison of the Achievement of Early and Late School Starters in Reading Related and Non-reading Related Areas in Fourth and Fifth Grades," *Elementary English,* vol. 41, pp. 631–639, October, 1964.

20. Hay, Julie, Mary C. Hietko, and Charles L. Wingo: *Reading with Phonics,* rev. ed., J. B. Lippincott Company, Philadelphia, 1960.

21. Herrick, Virgil E., Dan Anderson, and Lola Pierstorff: "Basal Instructional Materials in Reading," *Development in and through Reading,* Sixtieth Yearbook of the National Society for the Study of Education, University of Chicago Press, Chicago, 1961, part I.

22. Ilg, Frances L., and Louise Bates Ames: *School Readiness as Evaluated by Gesell Development Visual and Projective Tests,* Harper & Row, Publishers, Incorporated, New York, 1964.

23. Jewett, Arno: "How Can We Improve the Reading Skills and Habits of Senior High School Students?" *Bulletin of the National Association of Secondary School Principals,* vol. 43, pp. 96–99, April, 1959.

24. Lee, Dorris M., and R. V. Allen: *Learning to Read Through Experience,* Appleton-Century-Crofts, Inc., New York, 1963.

25. Lefevre, Carl A.: "A Concise Structural Grammar," *Education,* vol. 86, pp. 131–137, November, 1965.

26. Lefevre, Carl A.: *Linguistics and the Teaching of Reading,* McGraw-Hill Book Company, New York, 1964.

27. Lloyd, Donald: "Intonation and Reading," *Education,* vol. 84, pp. 538–541, May, 1964.

28. Lovell, K., D. Shapton, and N. S. Warren: "As Study of Some Cognitive and Other Disabilities in Backward Readers of Average Intelligence as Assessed by a Non-verbal Test," *British Journal of Educational Psychology,* vol. 34, pp. 58–64, February, 1964.

29. Mackintosh, Helen K. (ed.): *Current Approaches to Teaching Reading,* Department of Elementary-Kindergarten Nursery Education, National Education Association, Washington, 1965.

30. Mary Caroline (Sister): *Breaking the Sound Barrier,* The Macmillan Company, New York, 1960.

31. Mazurkiewicz, Albert J.: "Teaching Reading in America Using the Initial Teaching Alphabet," *Elementary English,* vol. 41, pp. 766–772, November, 1964.

32. McCullough, Constance M.: "Illiteracy in India: Problems and Progress," *The Reading Teacher,* vol. 19, pp. 83–90, November, 1965.

33. Miami Linguistic Readers. D. C. Heath and Company, Boston, Mass., 1965.

34. Parker, Don H.: *Schooling for Individual Excellence,* Thomas Nelson & Sons, New York, 1963.

35. Parsley, Kenneth M., and Marvin Powell: "Achievement Gains or Losses During the Academic Year and Over the Summer Vacation Period: A Study of Trends in Achievement by Sex and Grade Level among Students of Average Intelligence," *Genetic Psychology Monographs,* vol. 66, pp. 285–342, 1962.

36. *Phonetic Keys to Reading, A Teacher's Manual,* The Economy Company, Oklahoma City (n.d.).

37. Pitman, I. J.: "Learning to Read: An Experiment," *Journal of Royal Society of Arts,* vol. 109, pp. 149–180, G. Bell & Sons, Ltd., London, February, 1961.

38. Rasmussen, Donald, and Lynn Goldberg: *Teacher's Handbook,* SRA Basic Reading Series, Science Research Associates, Inc., Chicago, 1965, pp. 6–8.

39. Repplier, Agnes: *Eight Decades,* Houghton Mifflin Company, Boston, 1935.

40. Robinson, H. Alan, and Allan F. Muskoff: "High School Reading—1963," *Journal of Reading,* vol. 8, pp. 85–96, November, 1964.

41. Robinson, Helen M. (comp. and ed.): *Sequential Development of Reading Abilities,* University of Chicago Press, Chicago, 1960.

42. Santayana, George: *Persons and Places,* Charles Scribner's Sons, New York, 1944.

43. Schoolfield, Lucille D., and Josephine B. Timberlake: *Phonovisual Method,* Phonovisual Products, Washington, 1963.

44. Sebesta, Samleaton: "Artificial Orthography as a Transitional Device in

First-grade Reading Instruction," *Journal of Educational Psychology,* vol. 55, pp. 253–257, October, 1964.

45. Southgate, Vera: "Approaching i.t.a. Results with Caution," *Educational Research,* vol. 7, pp. 83–96, February, 1965.

46. Strang, Ruth, and Mary Elsa Hocker: "First-grade Children's Language Patterns," *Elementary English,* vol. 32, pp. 38–41, January, 1965.

47. Strickland, Ruth G.: "The Language of Elementary School Children: Its Relation to Language of Reading Textbooks and the Quality of Reading of Selected Children," *Bulletin of the School of Education,* no. 38, Indiana University, Bloomington, Ind., July, 1962.

48. Sutton, Marjorie Hunt: "First-grade Children Who Learned to Read in Kindergarten," *The Reading Teacher,* vol. 19, pp. 192–196.

49. Wilson, Rosemary G., and Mildred K. Rudolph: *My Alphabet Book,* Franklin Publishing and Supply Company, Philadelphia, 1963.

part II

METHODS AND MATERIALS OF
APPRAISAL AND INTRODUCTION

appraisal of

reading proficiency [1]

chapter 4

In this chapter consideration is given to the various kinds of appraisal of reading proficiency and the ways in which these may be used by teachers. Both formal and informal procedures are discussed, with somewhat more attention to the latter than to the former. Since the kinds of appraisal employed should be appropriate to the nature of the instruction and the ability level of the individuals, occasional reference is made to material on organization and methods of teaching reading in other parts of the book.

Attention is given to appraisal of the various kinds of difficulties that may affect an individual's reading—mental, physical, emotional. Frequent reference is made to research applicable to appraisal of different aspects of reading, especially research carried on in recent years.

[1] For more detail see Ruth Strang, *Diagnostic Teaching of Reading*, McGraw-Hill Book Company, New York, 1965.

The chapter is intended to give the reader an overview of appraisal of reading on all instructional levels and to provide him with a basis for understanding and carrying forward diagnosis as an indispensable element in the individualization of instruction. It is hoped that the reader will grasp and keep ever in mind the fundamental viewpoint that appraisal and diagnosis are most effective and useful when they are integrated with the instructional process all the way.

Here am I, after a glorious preparatory summer, starting a reading department with no record of the mental age of any of my pupils. . . . Our reading instructors, anxious to get the reading program under way, are suggesting that they be instructed by the psychologist in the giving of one group mental test and one group reading test that would serve as a screening device for referring extreme cases to my office. Or should we not attempt the testing program but depend on the observation and judgment of teachers for the referral of serious reading cases?

This is a practical problem. It is not an either-or situation. Certainly the teacher's observation of the way pupils are reading in his class is very important. As Austin and Huebner have said, "When informal appraisals are conducted skillfully and when the results are interpreted accurately, they enable teachers to program instruction more effectively" [2, p. 338].

As a check on the teacher's observation, a group test of mental maturity yielding a language and a nonlanguage score and a test of reading ability is helpful. Appraisal both through tests and through informal procedures has been stressed by various writers including McDonald, who said, "What the teacher assesses should be the result of careful use of measuring instruments, of skilled observation, of thought, of experience, all supported by theoretical models of learning" [30, p. 59].

ASPECTS OF APPRAISAL

As Bond and Tinker [5, p. 81] have pointed out, retardation in reading may be (1) part of a general immaturity, or (2) due to a deficiency in one or more reading skills or to lack of most of the basic skills, or (3) complicated by emotional and social problems. Failure to learn to read usually results from a constellation of inhibiting factors [38] which vary from student to student and even within the same individual at different times. A single factor may become functional only as part of a syndrome or combination of factors. For example, a pupil may readily grasp the central thought of passages containing simple sentences and easy vocabulary but be unable to understand the central thought or separate it from details when he is reading passages composed of complex sentences and longer words.

The aim of appraising or diagnosing a person's reading is to help the student, the teacher, and the counselor understand:

Why the student reads
When and where he reads
What he can read
What he does read
How he reads
What his strengths and difficulties are
What his reading potentiality or capacity for learning to read is
What, if anything, is preventing him from attaining it

Each of these kinds of information is important in guiding instruction. If we know when and where he reads, we can better understand whether he does reading on his own or only to meet school requirements and what his preferences for reading different kinds of material are. We must know what he can read and how he reads in order to provide suitable material and methods. Without this knowledge a teacher often increases a student's sense of failure by giving him texts or books that are too difficult or impairs his motivation with materials that are too easy. Understanding of his reading potentiality helps the teacher to decide whether the student should be encouraged to attain higher levels or be content with his present performance. Finally, an understanding of the difficulties and dynamics in the case is essential to prevent failure as well as to make improvement.

This kind of appraisal of the reading of individual pupils is not easy, particularly for inexperienced teachers. In one study, Emans [17, p. 260] found that teachers' perception of reading needs did not agree well with needs as indicated by a widely used reading test and came to the conclusion that the "teachers did not perceive the individual reading needs of the children but were influenced in their judgments by some bias."

In past years diagnostic information was obtained systematically as the first step. It often took several weeks. However, there are disadvantages to making a thorough diagnosis before beginning treatment, particularly if this involves long and time-consuming testing. Although some tests should be given in the beginning in order to provide part of the basis for making a start, a large dose of diagnostic testing often increases the individual's sense of inadequacy as well as his impatience at not making progress with his reading. To avoid these undesirable reactions, the teacher of reading now obtains diagnostic information continuously along with instructing. As the student learns, the teacher gains understanding of his reading ability, interests, motivation, potentialities, and difficulties. This is true for groups and individual cases. Standardized tests are used as the student and teacher feel the need for additional objective information.

A comprehensive appraisal procedure involves (1) obtaining from school records, interviews, and other dependable sources personal data about the individual's development and his attitudes, interests, and personal relations; (2) securing from tests objective information, checked by observation, on his probable capacity to learn; (3) finding out, through standardized tests, informal tests, and observation of the learner in various situations, how well he reads orally and silently, and his strengths and weaknesses in different kinds of reading; (4) analyzing, when indicated, specific parts of the reading process such as word recognition, comprehension, vocabulary, fluency, appreciation, and so forth; (5) obtaining clues to conditions that may be blocking his progress in learning to read; (6) formulating on the basis of all the data collected and interpreted, hypotheses as to the nature of the reading problem; and (7) following through on the most plausible hypothesis with recommendations for remediation or continued growth in reading achivement. These, however, are not distinct steps. Diagnosis is more like the work of an oil painter who makes an initial sketch and then fills in details, continuously modifying and painting over parts of the picture as he gains new insights. Appraisal is a continuous performance interwoven with instruction and, in some cases, therapy.

DANGERS IN APPRAISAL

Thorough, competent diagnosis is essential in treating severe reading difficulty, but diagnosis is not without its dangers. Even informal classroom diagnosis, if used to divide students into reading-ability groups, may cause some student to accept his reading group level as a final appraisal of his ability. Much harm may also result from labeling a child "a remedial reading case." The effect of giving a child a derogatory diagnosis has been demonstrated in cases where stuttering is apparently caused by such a diagnosis. Johnson stated that "in case after case stuttering, as a serious speech and personality disorder, developed *after it had been diagnosed*" [21, pp. 5–6].

Another danger stems from inadequate or faulty diagnosis, for example that of using only the results of reading tests. A student in the lowest quarter of the class may not be a reading case. In fact, he may be doing his utmost and reading better than might be expected. The child who has the lowest reading score in his class may need only time to grow. Any special stress on reading better than should be expected at this time may retard other aspects of his development and arouse antagonism toward reading, in which he cannot at the moment succeed. If his progress is out of line with his true developmental trend, he is likely to fall back into his original growth trend when the special stimulation is discontinued.

Any diagnosis must be tentative, subject to continuous revision as new insights are gained. Practice, instruction, and diagnosis are interwoven. Insights gained through any of the diagnostic methods should be immediately put to work. Too often time spent in diagnosis is wasted because the counseling, practice, and instruction suggested by the diagnosis either are not carried out or are too long delayed.

METHODS OF APPRAISAL

An understanding of the multiple and complex causation of serious reading difficulty underlies the methods used. Any combination of the following causes is possible: physical disabilities; educational deprivation; lack of motivation; insufficient mental ability to meet the expectations of teachers who adhere to grade standards of achievement for all children; home conditions—too little or too much parental stimulation, tense emotional relations that interfere with learning; and other kinds of emotional disturbance (see Chapter 15). A thorough study of the causation of reading difficulty was made by Robinson [39].

All of the general methods described in this section may be adapted to any age group. Tests of vision, medical examination, standardized tests of capacity and reading achievement, informal tests and inventories may all be used at any grade level. Observation, too, is a basic technique applicable to all situations. With younger children diagnosis through oral reading is essential. This procedure is often very helpful with older children and adolescents as well, although usually the interview, written personal documents, and daily written schedules are more appropriate. The latter may be used with younger children by letting them dictate the information, and this may be a useful way of noting clues to difficulties in verbal expression.

Physical Factors in Reading

In a helpful article, Eames [16] discussed various physical factors in reading, including poor vision, brain damage, impaired nerve conductivity, endocrine deficiencies, and diabetes. In appraising the possible physical influences on the reading of individual children, needless to say, the cooperation of the school physician is required. Anderson [1] has indicated the physical aspects that the school physician should look for in connection with reading disability.

Observation and Tests of Vision and Hearing

Adequate eye examination is a basic part of diagnostic procedure in reading cases. However, as Eames has said "The mere existence of low visual acuity is to be regarded as a possible but not invariable cause of poor reading" [16,

p. 427]. Although research has not yet shown a clear relation between single visual defects and reading disability, in an individual case any visual difficulty may be an important diagnostic factor (see Chapter 1). The visual difficulties of young children often go undetected for, as Rosen has pointed out, "Some moderately severe visual problems among children can be compensated for by neuromuscular effort, but this kind of effort induces constant physical and nervous strain" [40, p. 58].

Psychological influences on visual functioning are being increasingly recognized by eye specialists. Various diseases may affect the eyes—diseases such as tuberculosis, syphilis, avitaminosis, and many others. Sties, foreign bodies in the eyes such as cinders and dirt, and mechanical injuries are frequently a cause of trouble. The alert teacher is often the first person to suspect a child's eye defects. From the cumulative record and his own personal observation, the teacher, with some training, can recognize eye conditions that should be referred for an examination [24, 45]. To help the teacher in this task, the American Optometric Association, the National Society for the Prevention of Blindness, and other organizations have listed symptoms observable during reading activities that are relatively important in the diagnosis of visual difficulties:

Losing the place while reading
Avoiding close work
Holding the body rigid while looking at distant objects; shutting or covering one eye; thrusting head forward when looking at objects
Holding reading material closer than children normally do
Frowning, excessive blinking, scowling, squinting, or other facial distortions while reading
Excessive head movements while reading

Other indications of eye difficulty are:

Poor sitting posture while reading
Tilting head to one side
Rubbing the eyes frequently
Showing signs of tension or irritability during close work
Showing redness, puffiness, and other unusual appearance of the eyes
Being oversensitive to light

To supplement and check the teacher's observations, a number of visual screening devices are available. The Snellen chart has been used the most widely and the least accurately. Conditions of lighting and distances are often neglected. The chart should be placed exactly 20 feet from the child; it should be illuminated with 10 foot-candles of light; the letters should be shown one at a time through a window in a card rather than all at one time; the easier letters should be shown first to build the child's confidence. Unless special lenses are used, farsighted children, who are the most likely to be poor readers, will not be detected.

The illuminated Snellen chart may be supplemented by tests of far-sightedness, muscular imbalance, and depth perception. Sweeting [48] described this procedure, which takes three to five minutes per child and can be administered by the school nurse or teacher after she has had instruction.

Even when correctly used, the regular Snellen chart is hardly adequate for checking on vision at the usual reading distance. Eames [16, p. 427] and various other authorities have called attention to the difference between *near* visual acuity and *far* visual acuity and to the fact that the Snellen and other tests made at 20 feet are likely not to be adequate for the appraisal of visual acuity in reading. Pointing up the frequent inadequacy of visual screening at 20 feet, the St. Louis Society for the Blind reported an ophthalmological examination of 100 poor readers, all but ten of whom had previously shown visual acuity of 20/30 or better in either eye. Of the 100 children, 50 per cent had either positive findings or need for examination under cycloplegia and 25 per cent were recommended for ophthalmological care [18].

Some of the more expensive and more adequate instruments for visual screening in connection with reading diagnosis are the School Vision Test, the Orthorater (Bausch and Lomb, Rochester, New York); the A.O. School Vision Screening Test, also known as the Massachusetts Vision Test (American Optical Company, Southbridge, Massachusetts); the Keystone Visual-Survey Service No. 46—Telebinocular and Supplementary Tests, the Keystone Tests of Visual Skills in Reading, and the Spache Binocular Reading Test (all available from the Keystone View Company, Meadville, Pennsylvania); the Jaeger test (any optical supply house); and the Eames Eye Test (Harcourt, Brace & World, Inc., New York). There is also a reduced Snellen chart suitable for measuring visual acuity at the reading distance.

When the screening test and the teacher's observation indicate some eye difficulty, the individual should be referred for a more thorough examination. There are three types of specialists to whom reading cases may be referred:

The *oculist* is a medical doctor who has specialized, to varying degrees, in the study of the eyes.

The *ophthalmologist* is an oculist who has taken a prescribed series of courses in addition to his work in medical school and has passed the examinations of the National Board of Ophthalmology.

The *optometrist* is a specialist in the field of vision, adequately trained to diagnose eye difficulty, prescribe glasses, and give visual training when needed. He recognizes pathological conditions and refers them for proper medical treatment.

If glasses have been prescribed on the basis of a thorough visual examination, the glasses are made and properly adjusted by an *optician*. His work is comparable to that of a pharmacist in that he may only fill prescriptions for glasses, not prescribe them.

It is the responsibility of the eye specialist to give the teacher the information needed to create favorable school conditions for the pupil. The teacher needs answers to these questions:

What is the eye condition; exactly what is the difficulty?

Should the pupil return to the eye specialist for further examination or treatment? If so, when?

Should there be any restriction on his physical activity? If so, what?

Have glasses been prescribed? Should they be worn for near work, for distance, or all the time?

Does the pupil require any special lighting? If so, what kind and how much?

Can he do the normal amount of reading and studying without harming his eyes?

Should he have a special seat in the classroom—near or far from the board? Does he need a special desk, books with large print, large sheets of paper, and large black pencils?

Should he be given any special services in a class for the visually handicapped?

Not only should the school carefully study the visual efficiency of pupils with reading difficulty but, as Rosen [40] has pointed out, systematic appraisal of the visual requirements at various levels of reading instruction should be conducted.

In addition to their visual acuity, children's visual perception, particularly that of pupils who are just beginning to read, should be studied. Bryan [7], using the Frostig test, found that the visual perception of first graders correlated more closely with their reading success than did intelligence- and reading-test scores. In a follow-up study of the maturation of perceptual functions in children with specific reading disability, Silver and Hagin [43] suggested that a possible explanation of the relation between scores on perceptual tests and reading comprehension is that individuals with severe perceptual problems become so involved in the task of decoding symbols that their interpretation of meaning is lowered.

Auditory acuity may be an important factor in reading development. Some children fail to progress in reading because of auditory deficiencies. This is especially true of children taught by phonetic methods. Hearing can be most accurately tested by an audiometer or much less precisely by the watch-tick test or whisper test [4]. The Amber Otometer (Amber Company, Inc., Los Angeles, California) is a commercially available instrument for testing hearing loss [52].

Durrell and his associates at Boston University have done outstanding work in the study of the relation of auditory discrimination to reading.

With training in auditory discrimination prior to phonetic instruction, retarded readers in elementary and high school have markedly improved. Wepman [50] has published a carefully constructed test of auditory discrimination. Chall, Roswell, and Blumenthal [10] observed that, among beginning readers, children with extreme reading disabilities also had great difficulty in learning phonics, especially in blending and synthesizing sounds and that this auditory blending ability in grade 1 was significantly related to reading achievement as far as grade 4. They raised questions as to whether auditory blending difficulty might reflect neurological involvement and whether inferior blending ability resulted primarily from inability to synthesize sounds heard or from poor or inaccurate perception of the separate sounds.

Aside from the problems of evaluating auditory acuity and auditory perception, there is the question of the interpretation of reading-test results for deaf children, since special norms are needed for such children. Wrightstone, Aaronow, and Moskowitz [53] developed national norms for deaf children for the Metropolitan Achievement Tests, Elementary Battery, Form B, Test 2; Reading, in terms of percentile ranks and standard reading ratings on a scale of 1 to 9.

Medical Examinations

Although a direct relation between reading and poor health and diseases has not been demonstrated, illness may be a predisposing factor. It decreases the pupil's energy and effort to learn to read and through causing him to be absent from school may result, especially in the primary grades, in his missing essential instruction in reading. Prolonged illness may also cause emotional disturbance, affecting progress in learning to read [49].

Disturbance of the endocrine glands such as pituitary or thyroid deficiencies may underlie difficulties in reading and other kinds of learning [15]. Chemical imbalance [44], illness, low vitality, metabolism, and vitamin deficiency might affect reading as well as motor and speech activities. Cerebral injury before or during birth and high fever accompanying childhood illness might be implicated in reading disorders (see Chapter 15) [22].

The tendency to prefer the left eye to the right (left-eyedness) or to be inconsistent in eye-and-hand preference raises the still unsolved question of the relation between brain dominance and reading difficulty (see Chapter 1). "The persistence of anomalies of laterality in some of our subjects . . . suggests to us that, for some children at least, reading disability may be a basic biologic defect resulting from the failure to establish clear-cut cerebral dominance" [43, p. 259].

Diagnosis and treatment of all these medical conditions can be made only by experts in the field who are usually willing to cooperate with the reading specialist.

Developmental History

From the school record some understanding of a student's reading development may be obtained. It is important to know his marks in each subject and whether he had difficulty in reading in the first grade, has repeated one or more grades, was absent frequently, changed schools several times, has had remedial work in reading, accumulated a heavy burden of failures and humiliating experiences—or whether he has had a superior or good school record. From the parent, the teacher may obtain, with different degrees of accuracy, information about conditions of birth, health history, sibling rivalry, home language, and attitude of parents toward education, toward reading, and toward the child. Not a few parents—to bolster their own self-esteem—expect their children to be superior in every respect. It is quite common for parents to be oversensitive to a slight degree of reading retardation.

Parents show a wide range of attitudes. Some parents tell everyone about the child's reading difficulty—often in front of him. Some hide their punitive attitude under the cloak of strenuous effort to have the defect corrected. They take the child to reading clinics and spend hours at home trying to teach him to read. Other parents, recognizing their tendency to reject the retarded child, lean over backward in the effort to do everything for him, even to depriving their other children of advantages they should have. Still others feel responsible for their child's reading retardation and have a deep feeling of guilt.

This sort of information is valuable in understanding the conditions leading to certain kinds of reading development. Often, teachers have little awareness of the thoughts and feelings that lie behind the expressions on students' faces or the life conditions with which they are coping. For example, one sixteen-year-old is constantly confronted by the superior achievement of her smart ten-year-old brother. When she is asked a question, he makes remarks such as, "Why ask the dope?" When her mother yells at her, the girl's only recourse is to walk out of the room and leave her mother yelling. But that does not help because "then she gets mad and I get hit." Unwittingly, teachers often reinforce a child's unfavorable home conditions.

Reading Autobiography

Developmental in emphasis, the reading autobiography may give valuable insight into the student's reading development from his own point of view. He tells of his early experiences with reading, his present attitude toward and interest in reading, any reading difficulty or problem he may have as he sees it, and what he thinks caused it. Indirectly he may give important clues to reading difficulty stemming from his relations with family, friends, school, and teachers. In these introspective reports he often reveals what reading means to him.

Other Personal Documents

Other kinds of introspective reports may give insight into the student's reading process, his interests, and his emotional difficulty and personal relations [46]. Unsigned compositions may be written on such topics as "How I Improve My Reading," "Why I Want to Read Better," "What Makes Books Easy to Read or Difficult to Read," "How Books Have Influenced Me," "How I Feel When I Read Aloud in Class." Other topics and questions may give understanding of a student's interests and clues as to the causes of his reading difficulties—"What I Do in My Free Time and What I'd Like to Do," "What I Like and Dislike about Television," "The Kind of Person I Think I Am," "The Kind of Person I'd Like to Be," "If I Had Three Wishes." Useful insights may also be obtained by even a few simple questions such as these:

Would you rather be (1) with people of your own age? (2) with people older than you are? (3) with people younger than you are? (4) alone?

Would you rather (1) play active games? (2) watch television or go to a movie? (3) read?

Would you rather read (1) stories? (2) biographies—about the lives of people? (3) about how to make and do things? (4) about science, history, and other subjects? (5) about current events?

What kind of stories do you like the best?

What is your favorite subject in school?

What do you like to do best after school?

What games do you like to play best?

What are your favorite television or radio programs?

What are your favorite movies?

What do you want to do when you leave school?

The values of personal experience records and their uses as a method of advancing reading readiness were discussed and illustrated by Boyd [6].

From introspective reports, both teacher and students may become more aware of reading methods and of conditions that are very favorable to reading improvement. For example, Alfred, whose test results showed a gain of over five years in reading, was asked, "How do you account for that—how did you do it?" First he mentioned certain things outside of school, such as listening to grownups talk about careers and current events. He thought that watching certain television programs might have had some good influence on him. His father wanted him to be a lawyer and gave him a law book and helped him to read it. Then Alfred mentioned school activities which he felt had helped him make such a big gain in his reading:

There was a film in assembly which showed how to group your words, how to skim over the article, and then get the main ideas from it. In science, we have to make outlines of various chapters under different topics. In social studies, the teacher gave us an assignment to look through the newspapers, cut out things on a certain topic, and tell the other kids about them. In music, we are supposed to find articles about singers and records and new song hits. I think the thing which helped me most was the reading we did in the homeroom period. We have a variety of books. Sometimes I am noisy but, after a while, I get down to reading. Also, in guidance class, the teacher asks us what we have been reading. And I've been using the library a good bit, too.

As an afterthought, Alfred added—

In a way, my cousins help me, too, because one is in the fourth grade and one is in the third grade, and I help them do their homework. And I read poems to my little sister so she will learn them. They are mostly Mother Goose rhymes.

Personal documents and answers to questionnaires may be obtained, on a voluntary basis, from individuals or from groups, if the interest and cooperation of the students are enlisted, and if they feel that they are participating in the appraisal of their reading.

Daily Schedule

The student may also contribute to the understanding of his reading by keeping a record of his daily activities for a week. For accuracy's sake he is asked to make entries all during the day, not to try to remember what happened at the end of the day. If he is asked to include details about what he reads as well as when he reads, much may be learned about his reading habits and interests.

Observation

Usually a teacher can readily *identify* students who need help in reading. He first observes that certain students cannot do the necessary reading in their subjects. He may next discover that their dissatisfaction with their reading and often with school is general; they do not want to read and often look away from their books. He may also note that they do better work in subjects that require little reading and often comprehend better what they hear than what they read.

Observation may be more analytical. For example, specific difficulties in word recognition may be noted and emotional interferences with reading inferred from behavior observed. The reading interview, in which instruction and practice are included, lends itself well to this analytical kind of observation. The interviewer may gain clues to the individual's reading potential, such as his use of words, his quickness to learn, his ability to organize ideas and to see relations among them. His mental alertness and verbal ability are conspicuous in his conversation and discussion. When students take part in a sociodrama they may reveal some of their experiences with reading and how they feel about them.

Teachers need to learn to read the language of behavior and to infer more accurately the meaning of the observed behavior. Many kinds of behavior may be observed in the classroom: signs of tension such as biting nails, restlessness, inattention; aggressive behavior and resistance to learning; failure to follow the thought of a discussion or unusual keenness and originality in giving answers and asking questions; approach to a reading assignment; quality of comprehension and interpretation of the selection, and insight into its meaning. Especially important are marked changes or fluctuations in reading performance and in attitudes toward self and toward reading.

Tests of Mental Ability

Low mental ability per se, unless it is extremely low, is seldom a cause of reading difficulty; difficulty is caused by requiring greater and quicker achievement than should be expected of slow learners. Equally important is expecting too little of able learners. Studies have shown that intelligence quotients are associated with gains in reading achievement and achievement in subject-matter areas [42]. Intelligence tests, or tests of scholastic aptitude, are an indispensable tool in reading diagnosis (see Chapters 1 and 13), but they should be interpreted with full recognition of the instability of test scores and of their limitations in predicting reading achievement. IQs obtained from intelligence tests, particularly from those having a large verbal component, are in part dependent upon level of reading ability, and they change with changes in the ability of the individual to read. For instance, McCord [28] found that the mean IQ of two groups of adults increased considerably (19 points and 11 points, respectively) after they had participated in reading classes. On the high school and college levels, capacity for reading is increasingly difficult to determine, not only because most intelligence tests are partly reading tests but also because differences in motivation sometimes compensate for deficiencies in home and school background or in mental ability.

Standardized Tests of Reading Achievement and Capacity [9]

Objective data about the individual's level of reading and his weaknesses are provided by these tests (see Chapter 5). Diagnostic data will include: (1) *word analysis*—knowledge and use of consonant sounds and blends, vowel sounds, digraphs, prefixes, suffixes, and roots; ability to divide words into syllables; (2) *vocabulary*—the extensiveness and depth of word knowledge in general and in different areas; (3) *comprehension*—the various kinds described in Chapter 1; (4) *speed*—the number of words per minute in reading different kinds of material for different purposes; (5) *study skills*—locating information, selecting and evaluating information, following directions, adjusting method of reading to purpose and material, note taking, classifying, outlining, summarizing.

In a thoughtful article, Lennon [25] stated that we may hope to measure reliably: (1) a general verbal factor, (2) comprehension of explicitly stated material, (3) comprehension of implicit or latent meaning, and (4) an element that might be termed "appreciation." He called attention to the fact that in measuring rate of reading, we are concerned not with pure speed but with speed at a particular level of comprehension.

To obtain the greatest diagnostic value from tests of word analysis we should make a chart, with students' names down the left-hand side and items listed across the top, and check students' errors opposite their names. In this way we can at a glance determine what skills are lacking in a whole class, what skills are needed by a few students, and what skills are needed by only one student. Thus our chart becomes the basis for the special needs grouping described in Chapter 2. The same type of chart should be made for the results of vocabulary and comprehension testing and for study-skills results on other tests.

A diagnosis of a student's reading proficiency is made on the basis of all the information obtained about him. Test scores, seen in isolation, may be misleading. Perry [33] has found that students scoring above the 85th percentile on standardized reading tests may yet be unable to cope successfully with long college assignments.

On the other hand, Diederich [12] has found that a good reading test, long and unspeeded, may be a more reliable predictor of writing ability than a single two-hour essay written under examination conditions.

It should be kept in mind that tests of spatial relations, tests of left-right orientation, and other tests not concerned specifically with reading capacity and achievement may yield valuable information needed in diagnosing the disabilities of backward readers, particularly those of younger pupils [26].

Listening Comprehension Tests (see Chapter 12)

Comparison of the student's comprehension of a passage read aloud to him with his comprehension of a comparable passage which he reads silently often shows unrealized reading ability. If he can get ideas from listening, he should be able to get ideas from reading. The Auditory Test of the Diagnostic Reading Tests supplies this kind of information. Betts [3] called it the "probable capacity level" when the student's comprehension is 75 per cent or better and when he shows ability to relate experiences to information gained through listening and to use vocabulary and language structure comparable to that in the passage read to him.

Oral-reading Tests

While oral reading is not always an appropriate teaching technique, it is one of the best ways of obtaining information concerning a pupil's reading difficulties. For testing students' oral-reading ability, standardized oral-reading tests such as the Gray Oral Reading Tests, edited by Robinson (The Bobbs-Merrill Company, Inc., Indianapolis), and the Gilmore Oral Reading Test (Harcourt, Brace & World, Inc., New York) are available. Even without such tests, the teacher in the lower grades may detect poor readers in a class by having them read one or two sentences aloud. At any grade level the following informal procedure may be used.

The teacher has on hand a series of paragraphs or books of known levels of difficulty. For students above sixth-grade reading ability, the four paragraphs in the *Reading Diagnostic Record for High School and College Students* [47] may be used. The student chooses one that interests him and, if it seems suitable, the teacher asks him to read it aloud and after reading it to tell what it is about. In this way, information is gained about the student's reading level, how he handles little words, how he attacks hard words, how well he comprehends the meaning of words, sentences, and paragraphs [13, pp. 11–13].

Betts's procedure [3, chap. 21] for ascertaining different reading levels is useful. These are the levels he distinguishes:

1. Basal reading level—student can read with understanding and shows no symptoms of strain.
2. Independent reading level—student can read with the teacher's help, comprehends 90 per cent or better, and shows no symptoms of tension or word recognition difficulty except that there is a limit to the number of new words he can cope with as the material goes beyond his reading level.
3. Instructional reading level—the student comprehends about 75 per cent or better but needs teacher guidance when too many new words and concepts are introduced.
4. Frustration reading level—he comprehends less than half of the reading material and shows many symptoms of tension, withdrawal, and word recognition difficulty.

Without this kind of information the teacher may increase an individual's sense of failure by giving him books that are too difficult or insult him by suggesting material that is too easy.

Betts [3] was one of the first to point out that grade scores on reading tests are likely to place a pupil above his actual instructional level, and this point has been stressed by Plessas, who suggested that a reason for this was that "most reading tests do not evaluate adequately the higher creative reading processes involving thoughtful reactions and appreciative responses to the printed ideas" [34, p. 346].

Recordings of oral reading and conversation about ideas gained from books or articles have both diagnostic and interest value. Playbacks of these recordings offer opportunity for analysis and criticism and give students incentive for improvement.

Reading Inventories

The reading inventory is a way of collecting and summarizing information on aspects of reading important in the study of each subject. Taken at the beginning of the school year, it provides both teacher and student with a basis for more effective reading.

The Informal Group Reading Inventory. This group method of appraising students' silent reading can be used in the upper elementary and high schools. It includes questions on location of information and other study skills applied to the books students are using. It also tests their comprehension of passages read from books they are expected to read. Applications of the passages read to current events or personal problems and evidence of the reader's feeling responses and the influence of the selection on his point of view, attitudes, or behavior may also be included in this informal group inventory. A summary chart, such as that described for word analysis, enables both teacher and student to see at a glance the skills on which the class and individuals need special help.

The Individual Reading Inventory. The steps in conducting an individual inventory are as follows:

1. Choose a series of graded paragraphs, either obtained from a basal reader series or especially written to be suitable to the age of the student being tested. Mount each of these on a separate card.
2. Ask a few friendly questions about the student's interests and reading habits.
3. Give a word recognition test such as the oral-reading part of the Wide Range Achievement Test [51].
4. Let the student begin reading orally the paragraph on the level indicated by the word recognition test.
5. As he reads, record the errors he is making, noting whether he answers briefly or at length, in his own words or in the words of the book; whether he embellishes what the author said, etc.

6. After the first oral reading, let him reread orally; note improvement.
7. Continue with the graded series of paragraphs until he reaches his frustration level.
8. Read aloud a paragraph on the same level of difficulty and ask the same kind of questions on it.
9. Record on a form his independent, instructional, and frustration levels, and check evidences of poor phrasing, comprehension, vocalization, methods of word attack; make notes on other significant indications of reading ability, attitudes, and interests.

The construction and use of the individual informal reading inventory have been described in detail by Betts [3, pp. 438–487]. It is widely used by teachers in some school systems, and the results are recorded on a standard form.

Informal Testing–Self-appraisal Teaching Procedures

To obtain understanding of individual pupils' proficiency in reading their subject, teachers will find informal tests invaluable.

By assigning a passage from a textbook or a reference book, timing the reading, and testing comprehension, the teacher will learn much about how well the students read the text or reference books used in his subjects. An example of the questions asked in this kind of test,[2] used with senior high school and college students, follows. Only some of the questions that appeared in this informal test are shown as illustrations.

READING A SCIENCE ARTICLE

Directions: Read the following article in the way in which you would naturally read similar scientific material. As soon as you have finished reading, write on the blank "Time" the figure you see on the board. Then turn over the article and write the answers to the questions from memory.

The article is then read by the pupils, while the teacher writes on the board the number of seconds that have elapsed at ten-second intervals.

(Answer Sheet)

Name _____ Grade _____ Age _____
Time _____

PART I

What did the author say?

[2] Abstracted from Ruth Strang, "Reading a Science Article," *Science Education,* vol. 29, pp. 72–77, March, 1945.

A. It is important to understand the main ideas of what you read. In each exercise below check the best, most complete, most accurate statement of the main idea.
   1. By means of bands of color
      _____ (1) drugs may be detected
      _____ (2) chemicals may be identified and purified
      _____ (3) scientific experiments can be performed
      _____ (4) new elements can be created
   2. The principle that underlies this color method is
      _____ (1) that substances have an affinity for the adsorbent
      _____ (2) that colors of light rays spread out in a spectrum
      _____ (3) that molecules of different substances travel down a column of adsorptive material at different rates
      _____ (4) that molecules have the same degree of affinity to the adsorbent
B. It is desirable to understand the important details you have read. Below are statements of important details in the passage. If the statement is true, according to the passage, put a plus (+) on the line at the right of that statement. If the statement is false, according to the passage, put a zero (0) on the line at the right of the sentence.
   1. The technique described in this article was first developed in 1906. _____
   2. The new discovery immediatly caused revolutionary changes in chemistry. _____
   3. Carotene was found to be a single substance. _____
C. It is important to be able to answer questions about what you have read. Write the answers to the following questions using *only* those facts which are discussed in the passage and which help to answer the questions.
   1. What is the name of the technique described in this passage? _____
   2. Who invented this technique? _____
D. It is important to be able to draw conclusions from what you have read. If you think a conclusion below is probably true, considering the facts in the passage, put a circle around PT. If you think a conclusion is false, put a circle around PF. If you think the facts given in the passage are insufficient to allow you to make a decision, put a circle around the (?).
   1. Chemical analysis by color has produced revolutionary
      changes in chemical methods.   PT   PF   ?
   2. Vitamins would not have been so rapidly isolated in pure
      form if the method described had not been invented.   PT   PF   ?
E. It is important to know the exact meaning of words in a passage. In the exercises below check the word or phrase which means most nearly the same as the italicized word in the sentence.
   1. By means of bands of color, *adsorbed* by means alumina, magnesia . . .
      _____ process of adhesion of molecules to the surface of solids
      _____ assimilated
      _____ molecules dissolved in a liquid
      _____ adopted

2. . . . who investigated the *pigments* in plant leaves . . .
_____ paints and enamels
_____ colorless substance
_____ coloring matter
_____ segments
_____ a kind of mould
_____ a small particle of dust
_____ a unit of matter

PART III

A. Now think back and try to describe the process you used in reading this article.
B. Answer thoughtfully and accurately.
   1. Just how did you get the main ideas?
   2. Just how did you find and remember details?
   3. What do you do when you read that makes it possible for you to answer questions?
   4. What do you do when you read that makes it possible for you to draw conclusions?
   5. How do you figure out the meanings of unfamiliar words?

Informal tests of this kind supply valuable information about the way each student organizes his ideas as he reads, the adequacy with which he can express them, and the accuracy with which he can comprehend the main points and important details and can draw inferences. If questions on reading method are included in the test, the teacher and the class gain specific suggestions as to effective methods of reading the kind of material tested.

The freely written responses to the general question, "What did the author say?" reveal many different reading patterns, covering a range from retention of incoherent and unrelated details to a complete and creative comprehension of the author's pattern of thought. The free response shows what is communicated to the individual student, how he organizes the ideas gained, and whether he reads between the lines and beyond the lines. It may be followed by short-answer or objective-type questions to test his ability to grasp the main ideas and related details, to draw inferences and conclusions, to define words precisely, and to appreciate humor, character portrayal, or qualities of literary style.

Informal tests add more precision and continuity to the teacher's opportunistic but important observation in the classroom. For example, a procedure developed by Melnik [31] for improving the reading of social studies material in junior high school starts by asking students to state their aims or goals in reading a social studies assignment. Most students of this age are vague about their reasons for reading and about the reading method that would be most appropriate. They are then asked to read a selection from a social studies book that is typical of the material they will be expected to read in their classes. After reading the passage they answer two types of questions. Questions of the first type demand a creative response; they are what might be called "open-end" questions: What did the author say? The second type is multiple-choice questions that are designed to furnish evidence of the student's ability to get the literal meaning, to see relations, draw inferences, make generalizations, and understand the meaning of key words.

As soon as the student has answered the questions, he has data before him for self-appraisal. He marks his own paper. He grades his free response on a 10-point scale and analyzes the kinds of errors he has made in the multiple-choice questions. (Each choice represents a certain kind of error.) Instruction follows this self-appraisal immediately, while the students are specifically motivated to learn how to get the right answers and to avoid the same errors next time. If there is a next time, the whole procedure is repeated with another similar selection. After the second exercise is completed and analyzed, the students are able to note the progress they have made. A third exercise makes further improvement possible.

This testing-teaching-evaluating procedure bridges the gap between the hurriedly made teacher test and the standardized test. It relieves the teacher of some of the burden of making instructional material; at the same time it gives him a concrete model for further testing, teaching, and evaluating, based on the text or reference books used by his particular class.

OPPORTUNITIES FOR INFORMAL DIAGNOSIS
OF READING DIFFICULTIES IN A CLASSROOM SITUATION

In any subject, the teacher may observe students during oral reading, discussions of a book or selection, or reports of current events. The alert teacher listens carefully and jots down diagnostic information which he will discuss with the individual student or with the class if the error is a common one. Written assignments, too, reveal errors and strengths in reading and writing, which may be similarly discussed.

Many examples of informal diagnostic procedure may be noted if the teacher's report includes what *he* did or said; the response made by the student, his strengths as well as weaknesses; and the significance of this information for understanding the student's reading. Teachers of English often cooperate with the reading teacher in this way, but the need is equally great in other subject fields. Dressel [14] has stressed the point that teachers of science, mathematics, and social studies should assume responsibility for instruction in reading in their classes and for evaluation of progress in reading material in their disciplines. Michaels [32] and Burns [8] emphasized the need for noting study skills and reading difficulties of individual pupils in different content subjects. This is a type of subjective appraisal that teachers in any school could make.

The Interview

As suggested in Chapter 15, interviews of many kinds may be used for various purposes. From the interview the reading teacher or clinician may obtain information about the individual's attitude toward himself and toward reading; his interests, goals, and purposes; the reading problem as he sees it; and his reasons for wanting to read better. By introducing oral and silent reading in the interview, the interviewer may obtain information on how the student reads and the difficulties he is having. The interview is the basic technique for understanding emotional difficulties in reading. It may have both diagnostic and therapeutic value.

In the first interview the individual should be encouraged to speak freely about his reading—to present himself and his reading problem in his own way. He may make only obvious surface observations, emphasizing his slow reading, poor comprehension, or other difficulties. Later he may reveal underlying fears or hostility toward persons who are pushing and nagging him or showing more concern about his achievement than about him as a person.

In the first interview, if he is strongly motivated, the student may give his reasons for wanting to read better, either voluntarily or in response to such questions as: What kind of reading do you do now? Outside of school what need do you have for reading? How did you spend your time yesterday? Last weekend? Is this the way you usually spend your time? Why do you want to improve your reading now? But the interviewer is more concerned with feelings than with facts. He picks up clues the interviewee gives and helps him to explore them further. The interview should be client-centered; that is, the individual pupil rather than subject matter should be the focal point, and the interview should unfold naturally out of the pupil's self-expression concerning his problems. Excerpts from initial interviews which encourage the student to think through his reading problem in his own way are given in Chapter 15.

Projective Techniques

The importance of personal factors and emotions, both as cause and as result of poor reading, has been stressed by Glover [19] and many others. Almost any experience may be considered as a situation in which an individual may reveal his unique personality—something of his inner world of feeling and meaning. However, the more familiar the situation, the more likely he is to make merely habitual responses to it. That is why the projective techniques present rather vague, unstructured stimulus situations such as nebulous cloud forms, ink blots, or ambiguous pictures. To these the individual responds in his own unique way, relatively uninfluenced by the dictates of his culture, his family, his school.

Some attempts have been made to use the projective method in classrooms through such devices as the incomplete story, the incomplete sentence, and provocative pictures. Students' responses to these stimulus situations, even if treated as observations rather than as clinical data, may give considerable insight into the causes of reading difficulty. Some items in the preliminary form of a sentence-completion test designed especially for diagnosis of reading difficulties and a sample of a picture-situation test, both developed by Elizabeth K. Graves, follow:

Directions: Complete the following sentences to express how you really feel. There are no right or wrong answers. Put down what first comes into your mind and work as quickly as you can. Complete all the sentences and do them in order.[3]

1. Today I feel _____
2. When I have to read I _____
3. I get angry when _____
4. To be grown up _____
5. My idea of a good time _____
6. I wish my parents knew _____
7. School is _____
8. I can't understand why _____
9. I feel bad when _____
10. I wish teachers _____
11. I wish my mother _____
12. Going to college _____
13. To me, books _____
14. People think I _____
15. I like to read about _____
16. On weekends, I _____
17. I don't know how _____
18. To me, homework _____
19. I hope I'll never _____
20. I wish people wouldn't _____
21. When I finish high school _____
22. I'm afraid _____
23. Comic books _____
24. When I take my report card home _____
25. I am at my best when _____
26. Most brothers and sisters _____
27. I'd rather read than _____

[3] Always let the pupil know that his answers will be treated confidentially and will not be revealed to anyone else without his permission.

28. When I read math _____
29. The future looks _____
30. I feel proud when _____
31. I wish my father _____
32. I like to read when _____
33. I would like to be _____
34. For me, studying _____
35. I often worry about _____
36. I wish I could _____
37. Reading science _____
38. I look forward to _____
39. I wish someone would help me _____
40. I'd read more if _____

PICTURE SERIES

Directions: This booklet contains a series of pictures of different situations at home and at school. You are to write in the space provided under each picture what the boy Bill is thinking and feeling. Do NOT write what Bill would say but tell how he is feeling.

What is Bill thinking and feeling?

The Rorschach test may throw light on potential mental ability as contrasted with functioning mental ability. The primary use of the Rorschach is to give clues as to personality problems that may be interfering with the functioning of the individual's true mental capacity. The Rorschach categories may also be used as a guide to observation of the individual in life situations.

Among other tests used in the clinical diagnosis of serious reading problems are the Thematic Apperception Test, the Bender-Gestalt, and the Machover Draw-A-Person Test.

Neurological and Psychological Aspects of Reading Diagnosis

Although by means of standardized tests, teacher-made tests, and informal procedures teachers can appraise relatively mild cases of reading difficulty and provide appropriate corrective treatment, understanding of the basis of severe reading disability of individuals requires the cooperation of specialists in psychology, psychiatry, and neurology. Even the specialist sometimes cannot understand what causes reading disorder in certain children. As Rabinovitch and Ingram [35] have pointed out, reading therapy is less advanced than that in certain other areas, such as speech therapy. Solution of these deeper, more involved reading problems requires close cooperation among the specialists themselves. In discussing neurological and psychological trends in reading diagnosis, Ketchum states that "we now have the interdisciplinary teams seeking ultimate etiologies and pertinent prevention and treatment methods." He also urges "a more cautious stance toward bandwagon enthusiasms and fads" [23, p. 589].

Instruments such as the psychogalvanometer may furnish helpful clinical clues to personal factors that may be involved in reading difficulty. McCord [29] briefly described the research Model Psychogalvanometer No. 601A (Lafayette, Indiana, Instrument Company) and discussed a procedure for its use, which offered promise as a means of assessing personality dynamics of persons needing remedial reading.

PATTERNS OF APPRAISAL

Patterns of diagnostic procedure cover a range from the simplest to the most technical, from the general to the most analytical, and from the diagnosis of the class as a whole to the case study of individuals [5].

Continuous Classroom Appraisal

The classroom teacher, assisted by the reading teacher or consultant, through daily observation, the use of informal tests and inventories, and the results of the school testing program, can obtain much information concerning how well each student is reading, the range of reading ability in the class, the amount of retardation, and the individuals who need more analytic diagnosis. Such study will uncover the need for instruction of subgroups and of individuals.

An understanding of the specific difficulties and interferences in effective reading unfolds as the teacher sensitively guides students' learning. By using all the diagnostic information available, the teacher can help the student meet some of his immediate reading problems and can prevent a certain amount of embarrassment and discouragement.

Analytic Diagnosis

More specific information about word recognition and meaning, comprehension, study skills, and interests can be obtained by analytic diagnostic tests and methods. If an individual shows special difficulty in word recognition, his basic sight vocabulary and word attack skills should be studied. If he has difficulty in knowing the meaning of words even though he can pronounce them, this aspect of vocabulary should be explored. If he can recognize single words, but is unable to comprehend sentences and paragraphs, attention should be given first to simple comprehension of the literal meaning and then to more difficult levels of comprehension. The nature and causes of all difficulties detected require systematic exploration, often under clinical guidance [11].

Synthesis through Case Study

The case-study approach interprets and synthesizes information from many of the sources that have been described. The more comprehensive and insightful the case study, the more adequate is the understanding of the student's reading. The case study shows trends in and relations among many aspects of his growth as well as giving clues as to the possible causation of his difficulties. Such a unified diagnostic procedure is ideal for understanding and helping the student who is reading below his potentialities. The case study should include not only the student's background, history, and the probable causes of his difficulty but also his progress during remedial teaching and, when possible, follow-up of his later development as well.

Student Self-appraisal

Students should begin early to take responsibility for making their own appraisal of their reading. Using as many of the methods of appraisal as are appropriate, students on all educational levels can learn how well they read, the kinds of errors they make and how to correct them, conditions conducive to effective reading, interfering factors, and ways to use reading to meet their needs and further their personal development.

APPRAISAL OF GROWTH

It is important to appraise the student's growth as well as his reading status. This is difficult because progress is always relative to the capacity of the student and to his opportunities for learning. Progress as measured by gains on standardized tests is often exaggerated or interpreted too optimistically because the standard error of measurement is not considered. The difference in scores between the initial and final test may be merely a chance difference rather than real evidence of growth. Moreover, the apparent gain may result from stimulation due to the specific attention given and may have no lasting effect; hence, follow-up studies are needed, particularly at the high school and college levels [36].

However, all the methods of appraisal suggested, if used over a period of time, will yield evidence of progress. For example, dated anecdotal records, inventories, and informal tests given periodically, dated samples of a student's reports on reading or oral reading or discussion of books can all be used to show his progress. On the basis of this understanding the student will make his own individual plan for improvement, talk it over with the teacher, and then carry it out. It is the administrator's, teacher's, and librarian's responsibility to schedule time and provide materials of instruction and equipment needed and a teacher of reading to assist the pupils, in groups and individually, in making progress.

REFERENCES

1. Anderson, U. M.: "Reading Disability: What Should the School Physician Look for in Determining Its Causation?" *Journal of School Health,* vol. 35, pp. 145–153, April, 1965.

2. Austin, Mary C., and Mildred H. Huebner: "Evaluating Progress in Reading through Informal Procedures," *The Reading Teacher,* vol. 15, pp. 338–343, March, 1962.

3. Betts, Emmett Albert: *Foundations of Reading Instruction,* American Book Company, New York, 1957, chap. 21.

4. Blair, Glenn M.: *Diagnostic and Remedial Teaching,* rev. ed., The Macmillan Company, New York, 1956.

5. Bond, Guy L., and Miles A. Tinker: *Reading Difficulties: Their Diagnosis and Correction,* Appleton-Century-Crofts, Inc., New York, 1957.

6. Boyd, Verna: "Personal Experience Records as a Method of Reading Readiness," *The Reading Teacher,* vol. 19, pp. 263–266, January, 1966.

7. Bryan, Quentin R.: "Relative Importance of Intelligence and Visual Perception in Predicting Reading Achievement," *California Journal of Educational Research*, vol. 15, pp. 44–48, January, 1964.

8. Burns, Paul C.: "Evaluation of Silent Reading," *Education*, vol. 84, pp. 411–414, March, 1964.

9. Buros, Oscar K.: *The Sixth Mental Measurements Yearbook*, The Gryphon Press, Highland Park, N.J., 1965.

10. Chall, Jeanne, Florence G. Roswell, and Susan H. Blumenthal: "Auditory Blending Ability: A Factor in Success in Beginning Reading," *The Reading Teacher*, vol. 16, pp. 113–118, November, 1963.

11. Cleland, Donald L.: "Clinical Materials for Appraising Disabilities in Reading," *The Reading Teacher*, vol. 17, pp. 428–434, March, 1964.

12. Diederich, Paul B.: "The Role of Tests in College Admission," *Journal of the National Association of Women Deans and Counselors*, vol. 23, pp. 60–65, January, 1960.

13. Dolch, E. W.: "How to Diagnose Children's Reading Difficulties by Informal Classroom Techniques," *The Reading Teacher*, vol. 6, pp. 10–14, January, 1953.

14. Dressel, Paul L.: "Evaluation of Reading," *The Reading Teacher*, vol. 15, pp. 361–365, March, 1962.

15. Eames, Thomas H.: "The Effect of Endocrine Disorders on Reading," *The Reading Teacher*, vol. 12, pp. 263–265, April, 1959.

16. Eames, Thomas H.: "Physical Factors in Reading," *The Reading Teacher*, vol. 15, pp. 427–432, May, 1962.

17. Emans, Robert: "Teacher Evaluations of Reading Skills and Individualized Reading," *Elementary English*, vol. 42, pp. 258–260, March, 1965.

18. "Eye Examination of Poor Readers," *Sight Saving Review*, vol. 32, p. 152, Fall, 1962.

19. Glover, C. P.: "Emotions Can Impede Growth in Reading," *Chicago Schools Journal*, vol. 44, pp. 179–182, January, 1963.

20. Harris, Albert J.: "Lateral Dominance, Directional Confusion, and Reading Disability," *Journal of Psychology*, vol. 44, pp. 283–294, October, 1957.

21. Johnson, Wendell: "An Open Letter to a Mother of a Stuttering Child," *Journal of Speech and Hearing Disorders*, vol. 14, pp. 3–8, March, 1949.

22. Kawi, Ali A., and Benjamin Pasamanick: *Prenatal and Parental Factors in the Development of Childhood Reading Disorders*, Monographs of the Society for Research in Child Development, ser. 73, vol. 24, no. 4, Child Development Publications, Purdue University, Lafayette, Ind., 1959.

23. Ketchum, E. Gillet: "Neurological and Psychological Trends in Reading Diagnosis," *The Reading Teacher*, vol. 17, pp. 589–593, May, 1964.

24. Knox, Gertrude: "Classroom Symptoms of Visual Difficulty," in Helen M. Robinson (ed.), *Clinical Studies in Reading*, Supplementary Educational Monographs, no. 79, University of Chicago Press, Chicago, 1953, part II, pp. 97–101.

25. Lennon, Roger T.: "What Can Be Measured?" *The Reading Teacher*, vol. 15, pp. 326–337, March, 1962.

26. Lovell, K., D. Shapton, and N. S. Warren: "A Study of Some Cognitive and Other Disabilities in Backward Readers of Average Intelligence as Assessed by

a Non-verbal Test," *British Journal of Educational Psychology,* vol. 34, pp. 58–64, February, 1964.

27. *Making the Classroom Test: A Guide for Teachers,* Educational Testing Service, Princeton, N.J., 1959.

28. McCord, Halleck: "Increase in Measured IQ," *Journal of Developmental Reading,* vol. 5, pp. 214–215, Spring, 1962.

29. McCord, Halleck: "A Note on the Use of the Psychogalvanometer as an Aid to Diagnosis of Certain Persons with Reading Difficulties," *Journal of Developmental Reading,* vol. 5, pp. 137–138, Winter, 1962.

30. McDonald, Arthur S.: "Using Standardized Tests in Determining Reading Proficiency," *Journal of Reading,* vol. 8, pp. 58–61, October, 1964.

31. Melnik, Amelia: "Improvement of Reading through Self-appraisal," unpublished doctoral dissertation, Teachers College, Columbia University, New York, 1960.

32. Michaels, Melvin L.: "Subject Reading Improvement: A Neglected Teaching Responsibility," *Journal of Reading,* vol. 9, pp. 16–20, October, 1965.

33. Perry, William G., Jr.: "Students' Use and Misuse of Reading Skills; A Report to the Faculty," *Harvard Educational Review,* vol. 29, pp. 193–200, Summer, 1959.

34. Plessas, Gus P.: "Another Look at the Reading Score," *Education,* vol. 83, pp. 344–347, February, 1963.

35. Rabinovitch, Ralph D., and Winifred Ingram: "Neuropsychiatric Conditions in Reading Retardation," *The Reading Teacher,* vol. 15, pp. 433–438, May, 1962.

36. Ray, Darrel D.: "Permanency of Gains in a College Reading Program," *Journal of Educational Research,* vol. 59, pp. 17–20, September, 1965.

37. Robinson, Helen M.: "Analysis of Four Visual Screening Tests at Grades Four and Seven," *American Journal of Optometry,* vol. 30, pp. 177–187, April, 1953.

38. Robinson, Helen M. (ed.): *Clinical Studies in Reading,* Supplementary Educational Monogrraphs, no. 79, University of Chicago Press, Chicago, 1953, part II, pp. 31–63.

39. Robinson, Helen M.: *Why Pupils Fail in Reading,* University of Chicago Press, Chicago, 1946.

40. Rosen, Carl L.: "Visual Deficiencies and Reading Disability," *Journal of Reading,* vol. 9, pp. 57–61, October, 1965.

41. Schach, V. G.: "Quick Phonics Check for Retarded Readers," *Elementary English,* vol. 39, pp. 584–586, October, 1962.

42. Scott, Carrie M.: "Relationship between Intelligence Quotients and Gain in Reading Achievement with Arithmetic Reasoning, Social Studies, and Science," *Journal of Educational Research,* vol. 56, pp. 322–326, February, 1965.

43. Silver, Archie A., and Rosa A. Hagin: "Maturation of Perceptual Functions in Children with Specific Reading Disabilities," *The Reading Teacher,* vol. 19, pp. 253–259, January, 1966.

44. Smith, Donald E. P., and Patricia M. Carrigan: *The Nature of Reading Disability,* Harcourt, Brace & World, Inc., New York, 1959.

45. Spache, George D.: "Classroom Techniques for Identifying and Diagnosing the Needs of Retarded Readers in High School and College," in William S. Gray

and Nancy Larrick (eds.), *Better Readers for Our Times,* Scholastic Magazines, Inc., New York, 1956, pp. 130–132.

46. Strang, Ruth: *The Adolescent Views Himself,* McGraw-Hill Book Company, New York, 1957.

47. Strang, Ruth, Margaret M. Conant, Margaret G. McKim, and Mary Alice Mitchell: *Reading Diagnostic Record for High School and College Students,* rev. ed., Teachers College Press, Teachers College, Columbia University, New York, 1952.

48. Sweeting, Orville J.: "An Improved Vision Screening Program for the New Haven Schools: A Case History," *Journal of the American Optometric Association,* vol. 30, pp. 715–722, May, 1959.

49. Vernon, M. D.: *Backwardness in Reading: A Study of Its Nature and Origin,* Cambridge University Press, London, 1957.

50. Wepman, Joseph M.: "The Relationship between Auditory Discrimination, Speech, and Reading," *Elementary School Journal,* vol. 60, pp. 325–333, March, 1960.

51. *Wide Range Achievement Test,* by Joseph Jastak and Sidney Bijou, The Psychological Corporation, New York, n.d.

52. Witham, A. P.: "Clinical Tests for Diagnosis of Reading Difficulties," *Elementary English,* vol. 39, pp. 324–327, December, 1962.

53. Wrightstone, J. Wayne, Miriam S. Aaronow, and Sue Moskowitz: "Developing Reading Test Norms for Deaf Children," *American Annals of the Deaf,* vol. 108, pp. 314–316, May, 1963.

appraisal of students' reading ability through tests

chapter 5

Now that we have had an overview of a variety of means of appraisal basic to diagnosis and instruction in reading, let us take a closer look at one of the more objective of these kinds—appraisal through the use of tests. The field of educational measurement is one with which many teachers of reading are only vaguely familiar, about which they not infrequently feel inadequate, and which they sometimes regard with a mixture of suspicion and hostility. Such an attitude is understandable, for tests have too often been overemphasized, have been used as something wholly apart from instruction, and at the same time have been regarded as the main way of checking on teacher effectiveness. Thus employed in school administration, they may become the mechanistic and sometimes unfair judge of the teacher.

But tests need not be used in that way. When a knowledgeable teacher is given freedom to participate in their selection, administration, and use, tests may become the helpful friend and ally of the teacher.

This chapter pays attention, first of all, to the often baffling problems of testing reading and then considers the different kinds of reading tests, with mention of certain specific standardized tests of each kind. Classroom uses of both standardized and teacher-made tests are discussed and illustrated in some detail. For ready reference, there is at the end of the chapter an extensive listing of current reading tests for all levels from kindergarten to adult.

For prospective and new teachers in this field, the chapter is intended to serve as an introduction to reading tests; for experienced ones, it may serve as a review and updating on reading tests in general and a convenient reference on standard reading tests.

The instruments for the measurement of reading ability are determined by what reading is. A rather baffling characteristic of reading, so far as measurement is concerned, is that it is a continuous and changing process, an inward process, which for the most part is not directly observable. It has no content, or, expressed with better accuracy, its content is that of the moment—kaleidoscopic and ever-changing. In a sense, a reader is like a cross-country runner who encounters much unevenness in terrain as he covers the course. But there is an important difference. The sole purpose of the runner is to cover the course as quickly as possible. Time is the principal measure of his efficiency. A reasonable degree of speed is important for the reader, too, but it is always secondary to understanding. Comprehension is the principal determinant of the degree of his success.

Many different procedures may be used in appraising reading ability. Some of these have been described in the preceding chapter. By observing the individual student, talking with him, and studying his written compositions and examinations, the teacher can obtain considerable information about his reading ability, his interests, and his needs for reading. When he reads orally, the teacher can immediately detect mispronunciations, substitutions, insertions, omissions, additions, repetitions, and reversals of letters, syllables, words, and phrases. He can note the student's fluency and phrasing, his embarrassment in reading before a class, or his apparent self-confidence. By asking him to summarize what he has read or to answer questions on it, the teacher can obtain valuable information on the pupil's comprehension.

More precise information may be obtained through measurement. The results of tests, both informal and standardized, are almost indispensable in a school's developmental reading program and in the planning of corrective and remedial work on the part of either classroom teachers or special teachers of reading. A variety of approaches to the measurement of reading should be employed, and care should be taken to avoid placing too much reliance on the results of any one test.

PROBLEMS INVOLVED

Reading is one of the most difficult of all abilities to measure accurately. The problems in the measurement of reading are due mainly to the intricate nature of the reading process.

The first problem is created by lack of agreement concerning what reading is. Is it the development of a set of habits and the mastery of mechanics? If so, certain standardized devices, such as the eye-movement camera, may be sufficient; but few reading specialists are willing to accept this limited definition of reading. Is reading the ability to get facts from the printed page? If so, reading achievement can be measured by means of paper-and-pencil tests with a high degree of reliability and validity, but this definition is likewise regarded by most persons working in the field of reading as too narrow. Is the most important characteristic of reading the ability to carry on the varied and complex processes which we commonly associate with thinking? Most specialists apparently prefer this view of reading. If this concept of the nature of reading is generally accepted, measurement includes the appraisal of ability to comprehend all types of reading materials, to form judgments, to appreciate literary quality, to apply generalizations, and to perform the varied kinds of mental activity characteristic of the fields of literature, natural science, social science, the fine and practical arts, and of everyday living.

A second problem is created by the fact that, although it is recognized that there is a variety of kinds of comprehension, apparently thus far no one has formulated a list that is uniformly accepted as a basis of instruction and hence of measurement. Until we are agreed on just what reading comprehension includes, it is useless to try to construct a test which will satisfy all teachers of reading.

A third measurement problem is related to the question of the reliability and the intercorrelation of the part scores or subscores on reading tests. The most effective remedial teaching of reading is based on diagnosis, which in turn depends on the measurement of different aspects of reading ability. The reliable measurement of, let us say, six or seven aspects of reading ability requires more time than most persons are willing to give to testing. Moreover, the intercorrelations among the part scores on reading tests are often quite high, and it is known that when subtests are highly intercorrelated the scores have little actual diagnostic value. Subtest scores, however, give clues for further study.

A fourth problem has its origin in the nature of word meaning. A test of vocabulary is generally accepted as a standard part of a reading test. A large proportion of our words have several meanings. One cannot say that a pupil really knows the meaning of a certain word simply because he has given the correct response for it in a vocabulary test. One can only say that he knows the meaning which was called for by the test situation. However, this limitation should not be overemphasized. Vocabulary tests are among the most reliable of all tests involving the higher mental processes.

A fifth measurement problem is concerned with tests of rate of reading. The measurement of reading speed is not the simple matter that it may appear to be. The main difficulty is caused by the fact that it is necessary to check on comprehension in some way, since rapid movement of the eyes over the material without understanding is futile and cannot be called reading in the generally accepted meaning of the term. The need to measure reading comprehension as well as speed has led to the evolution of at least five kinds of rate tests, but in none of these is the combination of speed of reading continuous material and questions on the material covered entirely satisfactory.

A sixth problem is discovering the relationship between scores on reading tests and subsequent success in reading, in schoolwork, and in different vocations. For example, is level of comprehension as measured by the Cooperative English Tests: Reading Comprehension closely related to the future success of the pupils in the study of science? How fast must a pupil read the rate portion of the Iowa Silent Reading Tests in order to do the amount of reading expected of a ninth-grade pupil in the typical public high school? We can raise numerous specific questions for which we will not have the answers until many long-term follow-up studies are made.

A seventh problem related to measurement of reading grows out of the need for careful and verified prescription based on the diagnosis resulting from the use of reading tests. Thus far very few attempts have been made to develop highly valid and reliable diagnostic tests and practical sets of materials designed to be used directly in correcting any difficulties revealed by the diagnosis. The Diagnostic Reading Tests [10] and supplementary materials represent one such attempt in this direction.

Notwithstanding the difficulties in developing valid tests for use in diagnosing reading ability, it is still possible to prescribe a testing and training program in reading that will take account of individual needs. Reading is a *unitary* process. While training that is specifically planned for the needs of a pupil as shown by diagnosis is more effective than are less specific procedures, there can be no doubt that training aimed at one reading objective is likely to spread over several other objectives. For example, improvement of reading vocabulary will enhance the ability to grasp the central thought of a passage, and the development of greater power of reading comprehension will increase reading speed. Thus, if a teacher is able to make even a fairly accurate appraisal of a pupil's strengths and weaknesses in reading on the basis of measurement and other information, he can be reasonably sure that his efforts to correct the indicated weaknesses will not be wasted. This oneness, this unity of the reading process, is at once the despair and the saving grace of the multitude of measurers and remedial workers who have turned their attention to the reading field.

MEASUREMENT PROCEDURES USED

Since silent reading is the way people read at least 95 per cent of the time, teachers of reading devote most of their attention to silent reading except at the beginning stage. Consequently, most of the work on the measurement of reading has been directed toward the measurement of silent-reading ability.

Informal Tests in Each Subject

These can be given silently to the entire class to ascertain their silent-reading ability in a given subject. A concrete example of an informal test in science is given in Chapter 4.

Photographs of Eye Movements

The only aspect of the silent-reading process evident to an observer is eye movement, except in the case of immature reading, where lip movement may also be present. Consequently, eye movements are the only phase of the whole complicated procedure that can be measured directly. The ingenious technique for photographing eye movements developed early in the present century and used extensively in research by Dearborn, Judd, Buswell, Gray, Taylor, and others has contributed much to our understanding of the reading process and to the study of the reading difficulties of individual students.

For school situations, however, the photographic technique for measuring and evaluating reading has certain practical difficulties. First, it sets up a rather artificial reading situation in which some individuals may become self-conscious and fail to perform normally. However, a more nearly normal reading situation may be provided by means of adaptations of the photographic technique knowns as the Brandt Eye Camera [1] and the Reading Eye.[2] Second, it is an individual method and, therefore, hardly suitable for use with all pupils, particularly in large schools. Third, the photographing of eye movements calls for comparatively expensive equipment that is not accessible and is not likely to become available to many schools. A fourth and still more important limitation is that when used extensively in a school, this

[1] Distributed by C. H. Stoelting Company, Chicago. Each unit manufactured on receipt of order.
[2] Produced by Educational Developmental Laboratories, Inc., Huntington, N.Y.

technique may tend to focus the attention of teachers upon the mechanics of the process and away from the central feature of all worthwhile reading, which is comprehension. This tendency has sometimes been fostered by proponents of the photographic technique, but this attitude no longer seems to prevail. For instance, S. Taylor, in a helpful discussion of the Reading Eye, conceives of eye movements as a *reflection* of the abilities, skills, and habits of the individual and not as a causative factor in that development.[3]

Theory and Technique of Paper-and-Pencil Tests

For practical purposes, in the usual college or school setting the only feasible procedure of measuring silent-reading ability is to employ paper-and-pencil tests containing objective questions which measure comprehension of passages indirectly after the passages have been read and not as an aspect of the continuous reading process itself.

At best, a single reading test can provide evidence concerning an individual's ability to read one kind of material, or a few fairly limited kinds, and under a particular set of conditions. Caution needs to be used lest generalizations be carried further than is warranted by the test data. Reading achievement typically varies with the nature of the material and with the purpose for which the reading is done, and the better the reading ability of the individual, the greater his flexibility and adaptability to different materials and circumstances.

With few exceptions, the more recent reading tests are longer than earlier tests and generally provide anywhere from three or four to eight or ten different scores. Some of these are not so long as they should be in order to measure reliably as many aspects of reading ability as they are designed to measure. Factor-analysis studies aimed at revealing the components of reading ability can help to point the direction that the measurement of reading should take.

Some persons have taken a functional approach to reading-test construction by asking the teachers to indicate what kinds of information they need about individual pupils in order to be prepared to start an intelligent program of teaching them. This was the approach taken by the Committee on Diagnostic Reading Tests in the construction of a series of diagnostic tests briefly described later in this chapter.

Diagnostic Tests versus Survey Tests

The terms *diagnostic tests* and *survey tests* are often used as if these two kinds of tests were clearly differentiated, but there is no clear dividing line between the two. An achievement test which yields only one score is not

[3] Stanford E. Taylor, *Eye-Movement Photography with the Reading Eye*, Educational Developmental Laboratories, Inc., Huntington, N.Y., 1960, p. 103.

inherently diagnostic, although even this kind of test might be used in a diagnostic way if a user wished to take the trouble to group the questions testing similar abilities and to study the answers with care. Whenever a test yields two or more scores which may be compared on the basis of norms, it begins to lend itself to diagnosis. As the number of part scores is increased, the potential diagnostic value of the instrument usually is enhanced provided the scores represent reliable measures of different kinds of ability.

Some tests, however, appear to possess greater diagnostic value than they really have, for their time limits are so short that the part scores are not reliable enough to be used as the basis of an analysis of the reading ability of individual pupils. It is not possible to obtain a detailed and highly reliable diagnostic measurement of reading achievement within the time limit of the usual class period. A few test makers have succeeded in measuring with fair reliability three or four different aspects of reading achievement within a period of forty or forty-five minutes, but at least two or three hours are needed to obtain a highly reliable measurement of the many detailed aspects of reading.

Aspect of Reading Ability Measured by Tests with Diagnostic Features

An analysis was made of the aspects of reading ability covered by twenty-eight tests on all educational levels from primary to junior college years, each yielding three or more separate scores. A summary of the kinds of reading ability measured by the twenty-eight tests and the number of tests containing subtests for these kinds of reading ability is shown in Table 2. Although the data in the table are subject to a number of limitations, they do bring out two facts rather clearly. One is that attempts have been made by test authors to measure a wide variety of kinds of reading. Forty-six types of reading ability are listed in the table, of which twenty-three were mentioned in only one test. It will be observed that the kinds of reading ability listed are by no means independent of one another. The second fact brought out by the table is that there is considerable agreement among test makers concerning the desirability of measuring certain aspects of reading.

Most of the kinds of reading ability that appear near the top of the table seem important as a starting point in the diagnosis of difficulties in reading. Frequency of use in testing, however, is not necessarily a criterion of value. For example, it is reasonable to think that ability to perceive relationships, which appeared in only one of the twenty-eight tests, is at least as important in the interpretation of reading materials as reading speed, which was measured by ten of the tests. It would be of distinct help to test authors if teachers would indicate those aspects of reading achievement which, according to their own experience, are basic to successful reading in the content fields.

TABLE 2
TYPES OF READING ABILITY MEASURED BY TWENTY-EIGHT READING TESTS

Type of Reading Ability	Tests Measuring Ability	
	Number	Per cent
Word meaning or vocabulary	19	67.9
Paragraph comprehension or meaning	13	46.4
Sentence meaning (also questions)	11	39.3
Rate of reading	10	35.7
Story comprehension	7	25.0
Noting and retaining details	6	21.4
Reading directions	5	17.9
Use of index	4	14.3
Word and phrase recognition—auditory (primary grades)	3	10.7
Word and phrase recognition—visual (primary grades)	3	10.7
Maps, graphs, and charts	3	10.7
Interpretation or interpreting paragraphs	3	10.7
Technical vocabulary or vocabulary of special fields	3	10.7
Central thought or main idea	2	7.1
Organization	2	7.1
Fact material	2	7.1
Total meaning	2	7.1
Directed reading	2	7.1
Alphabetization	2	7.1
Drawing conclusions or inferences	2	7.1
Prediction of outcome	2	7.1
Use of references	2	7.1
Comprehension efficiency or accuracy of comprehension	2	7.1
Poetry comprehension	1	3.6
Use of dictionary	1	3.6
Relevant and irrelevant statements	1	3.6
True and false deductions	1	3.6
Recognition of form—likenesses and differences	1	3.6
Reading capacity—word meaning	1	3.6
Reading capacity—paragraph comprehension	1	3.6
Word discrimination	1	3.6
Reading comprehension in biology	1	3.6
Reading comprehension in history	1	3.6
Reading comprehension in literature	1	3.6
Reading comprehension in science	1	3.6
Ability to perceive relationships	1	3.6
Range of general information	1	3.6
Integration of dispersed ideas	1	3.6
Comprehension—auditory	1	3.6
Recognition—auditory	1	3.6
Associated word meanings	1	3.6
Selecting and classifying information	1	3.6
Word attack—oral	1	3.6
Word attack—silent	1	3.6
Directory reading	1	3.6
Advertisement reading	1	3.6

Silent-reading Tests

A demanding task in a reading-testing program is to become familiar with the many available reading tests and to choose those best suited to the needs of the local reading program. Not all the tests worthy of consideration can be commented on here, but several kinds of reading tests may be characterized briefly, and some tests illustrative of each kind may be mentioned. A rather extensive list of reading lists and tests for all levels is given in the references at the end of the chapter.

Kinds of Silent-reading Tests. Reading tests may be classified according to the nature and complexity of the scores they yield. One kind provides only one overall score. Early in this century, when the first objective tests appeared, several reading tests, such as the Thorndike-McCall reading scales, were one-score tests, but nearly all of these have long been out of print. So this kind of test became almost extinct until 1957, when the Sequential Tests of Educational Progress, or STEP, were published [49]. At each of the four levels, grades 4 to 6, 7 to 9, 10 to 12, and college, the reading test of this series is a seventy-minute test from which only one score is obtained. The STEP reading test is a carefully and expertly constructed test, but since it yields one score only, it is of limited value in a reading program if used alone.

However, a listening comprehension test [48] is also available in the STEP series. It is believed that a listening test is one of the best measures of reading potential, although there is need for more research on this question. Some useful information having broad diagnostic value may be obtained from the STEP listening test and the STEP reading test when used together.

If the teacher will take the trouble to analyze the responses of each pupil to the various test items, the STEP reading test, even when used alone, may have some diagnostic value. However, this kind of informal analysis requires so much time that busy teachers may not be inclined to undertake it. Those who do are likely to find their interpretation limited by the lack of appropriate norms.

In a second kind of reading test—one which contrasts with the kind just mentioned—an attempt is made to provide, within a class period of testing, diagnostic measurement of a considerable number of aspects of reading ability. This type of test is well illustrated by the Iowa Silent Reading Tests [29, 30] and the SRA Reading Record [53]. This kind of test yields a variety of scores that may be useful to the teacher in analyzing strengths and weaknesses as a starting point in the individualization of instruction, provided the part scores have sufficient reliability to serve this purpose. Usually such tests, in which the time limits for the parts are very brief, either have a large speed component in all the scores, or the number of questions in each part is so small that the scores tend to be low in reliability. Another possible danger in a many-part reading test which is planned for one class period is that it may place a premium upon rapid superficial reading. A further possible weakness in this kind of test is that some of the parts may be concerned with rather narrow aspects of reading ability that are not very fundamental nor broadly applicable in many different reading situations.

A third kind is designed to measure as thoroughly as possible within a class period three or four fundamental aspects of reading ability which the test author believes to be basic to success in a wide variety of reading situations. It usually measures comprehension and vocabulary, comprehension and rate of reading, or comprehension, rate, and vocabulary. Examples of tests of this type are the Gates-MacGinitie Reading Tests [18, 19, 20], the Traxler Silent Reading Test for grades 7 to 10 [61], the Nelson-Denny Reading Test, 1959 Revision, for grades 10 to 12 and college [40], the Cooperative English Tests: Reading Comprehension [8], and the Davis Reading Test [9]. In general, tests of this type sacrifice extent of coverage in favor of rather thorough measurement of a very few reading qualities regarded as especially important.

The fourth general kind of reading test to be mentioned here is a battery of tests in which a survey section is coordinated with diagnostic sections. This kind is illustrated by the Diagnostic Reading Tests [10], which are the result of a comprehensive and sustained attempt at diagnostic measurement of reading ability on the part of the Committee on Diagnostic Reading Tests, Inc., an independent committee whose initial work was given financial support by the Blue Hill Foundation. (This test battery is described in more detail later in this chapter.)

A few of the reading tests which have some unique features will now be described. Some of these have already been mentioned.

Reading Tests for the Elementary School. The Durrell-Sullivan Reading Capacity and Achievement Tests [17] provide a somewhat different type of diagnostic measurement from that obtained from the other elementary school reading tests. These tests are designed to determine whether or not the reading achievement of a pupil is up to his reading capacity. There are two levels, an intermediate test for grades 3 to 6 and a primary test for grades 2.5 to 4.5. There are two sections at each level—one for reading capacity and one for reading achievement. The reading-capacity test consists of word-meaning and paragraph-meaning parts. This test is administered by means of dictation and picture identification. The pupils do no reading in this test. The main portion of the reading-achievement test also contains a section on word meaning and one on paragraph meaning. In addition, there are a spelling test and a written recall test, which may be given at the option of the teacher. The intermediate capacity test requires about thirty to forty minutes of administration time. The required parts of the intermediate achievement test call for a working time of thirty to thirty-five minutes. The total working time for the primary test is about forty to forty-five minutes. The optional tests at each level may be administered in fifteen or twenty minutes.

The Iowa Every-Pupil Tests of Basic Skills [28]—Test A, Silent Reading Comprehension, and Test B, Work-Study Skills—are available on two levels: an elementary battery for grades 3, 4, and 5, and an advanced battery for grades 5 through 8. In each battery there are four forms, known as L, M, N, and O. The elementary battery of test A measures reading comprehension and vocabulary, while the advanced battery provides separate scores for paragraph comprehension, details, organization, total meaning, and vocabulary. The elementary battery, test B, contains five parts: Map Reading, Use of References, Use of Index, Use of Dictionary, and Alphabetization. The advanced battery of this test consists of five parts, known as Comprehension of Maps; References; Use of Index; Use of Dictionary; and Reading Graphs, Charts, and Tables. The working time is as follows: for test A, Elementary Battery, forty-four minutes; Advanced Battery, sixty-seven minutes; for test B, Elementary Battery, forty-four minutes; Advanced Battery, seventy-eight minutes. Grade norms are available for these tests, and there is a diagnostic profile chart on which the results for an individual pupil may be plotted in terms of T scores or public-school percentile ratings. These tests have been carefully constructed, and they are probably comparatively high in reliability as well as validity. There is a newer edition of these tests, the Iowa Tests of Basic Skills [31], but it does not have the reading test and the test of work-study skills available separately. Tests covering the five major areas—vocabulary, reading comprehension, language skills, work-study skills, and arithmetic skills—are in one spiral-bound, reusable test booklet. This edition is probably preferable to the older one for schools desiring to test all these skills, but schools planning to test reading comprehension and work-study skills only may use the older edition in which these booklets are separately printed.

Reading Tests for the Junior and Senior High Schools. The following are among the most frequently used and valuable tests in junior and senior high schools.

The Cooperative Reading Comprehension Test [8] is a part of the Cooperative English Tests, but it may be used separately, since it is available in a separate booklet, as well as in a single booklet which includes both reading and expression. There were two editions of this test—an older edition and an edition published in 1960, but the older edition is out of print. Forms A, B, and C of the newer edition are available at two levels—level 1 for grades 12 to 14 and level 2 for grades 9 to 12. Level 1C is reserved for use by colleges and universities and is not ordinarily available to high schools as 1A and 1B are. Each level of the Cooperative Reading Comprehension Test contains two parts—vocabulary and reading—and yields scores for vocabulary, speed of comprehension, and level of comprehension, as well as a total score. The total working time for the test is forty minutes—fifteen minutes for vocabulary and twenty-five minutes for reading. There are both public-school and independent-school percentile norms for this test.

The Davis Reading Test [9] is similar in some respects to the comprehension portion of the Cooperative tests, but it may provide a more challenging measure of reading comprehension. It yields two scores—level of comprehension and speed of comprehension. The level score provides a measure of depth of understanding of reading material under essentially untimed conditions. The speed of comprehension score also indicates accuracy and understanding of the reading passages, but time is an important element in this score. The Davis test covers two levels—series 1 for grades 11 to 13 and series 2 for grades 8 to 11. There are four forms in each series—A, B, C, and D. Percentile norms for grades 8 to 13 are available.

The Iowa Silent Reading Tests, Advanced Test, New Edition [29] has nine subtests: Rate, Comprehension, Directed Reading, Poetry Comprehension, Word Meaning, Sentence Meaning, Paragraph Comprehension, Use of Index, and Selection of Key Words. The tests exist in four forms—Am, Bm, Cm, and Dm—which may be scored on the IBM Test Scoring Machine. The raw scores of the nine parts are translated into standard scores. The score for the whole test is the median score of the nine scores. The Iowa tests are designed for use in grades 9 to 12 and in college. The working time is forty-five minutes.

The Nelson-Denny Reading Test, Revised Edition [40] is designed to measure vocabulary, paragraph reading, and rate. It is suitable for use with pupils in the senior high school, students in college, and adults. There are two forms—A and B—each of which requires thirty minutes of working time. The time allowed for the rate test is one minute, a period too short for satisfactory reliability, according to research on other tests. However, even this brief rate test provides an improvement over the older edition of the Nelson-Denny, in which no attempt was made to measure speed of reading. There is an optional cut-time administration for high-ability individuals, which calls for seven and one-half minutes of working time on vocabulary and fifteen minutes on comprehension and rate, or an overall time of twenty-two and one-half minutes. The responses of the students may be recorded on separate answer sheets or on MRC answer cards. An unusual feature of the Nelson-Denny test is that the grade norms extend upward through the senior year of college. There are also special adult norms.

The Traxler reading tests [60, 61] consist of the Silent Reading Test for grades 7 to 10 and the High School Reading Test for grades 10 to 12. The Silent Reading Test measures reading rate, story comprehension, word meaning, and paragraph comprehension, and yields a total comprehension score and a total score. There are four forms of this test, the last two of which are adapted for machine scoring. The High School Reading Test measures reading rate, story comprehension, and understanding of main ideas in paragraphs; and it also provides a total score. There are two forms, which may be machine scored. The working time is forty-five minutes. Public-school percentiles for part scores and total scores are available for both tests. There are independent-school percentile norms on the Silent Reading Test for grades 6 to 8, inclusive.

A Vocabulary Test for High School Students and College Freshmen [63] was published by the same author and may be used in conjunction with the high school reading test to provide measures of vocabulary, rate, story comprehension, and understanding of main ideas. The vocabulary test requires only fifteen minutes of working time, while reliability and validity data are comparatively high. Both public-school and independent-school percentile norms are available.

Reading Tests for the Entire Range of School Grades. The following reading tests are useful for both elementary schools and high schools.

The California Reading Test, 1957 Edition (1963 norms) [7], by Ernest W. Tiegs and Willis W. Clark, is a part of the California achievement tests, but it may be obtained in a separate booklet. It consists of five overlapping batteries which cover the entire range of grades from grade 1 through the junior college. The grade level of each battery is as follows: Lower Primary, grades 1 to 2; Upper Primary, grades 3 to lower 4; Elementary, grades 4 to 6; Junior High School, grades 7 to 9; Advanced, grades 9 to 14. There are two forms of the primary tests, W and X; four forms of the elementary and junior high school tests, W, X, Y, Z; and three forms of the advanced test, W, X, and Y. Each form has two main divisions—reading vocabulary and reading comprehension; each division yields three or four subscores. The working time for the different levels varies from twenty-three to sixty-eight minutes. These reading tests are intended to be power rather than speed tests. The manual for the 1957 edition appropriately warns that "because of the limited number of items (15 to 45), the section scores should be used only as guides to indicate the presence of student difficulties."

The Diagnostic Reading Tests [10], by the Committee on Diagnostic Reading Tests, Inc., extend from the kindergarten through the freshman year of college. The primary tests cover the kindergarten through grade 4. They consist of a reading-readiness booklet for the kindergarten and grade 1, booklet 1 for grade 1, booklet 2 for grade 2, and booklet 3 for grades 3 and 4.

The lower level of the Diagnostic Reading Tests, survey section, consists of two booklets which may be used in grades 4 to 8. Booklet 1 measures comprehension and word attack, and booklet 2 includes vocabulary and rate of reading.

The upper level of the Diagnostic Reading Tests, as mentioned earlier in this chapter, consists of a survey section with certain broad diagnostic features which is designed as a screening test to be used with all pupils in grades 7 through 12 and the college freshman year, and diagnostic sections to be used in analyzing difficulties indicated by the survey section.

These tests are printed in separate booklets as follows: Section I, Vocabulary; Section II, Comprehension: Part 1—Silent, Part 2—Auditory; Section III, Rates of Reading: Part 1—General, Part 2—Social Studies, Part 3—Science; Section IV, Word Attack: Part 1—Oral, Part 2—Silent.

The survey section requires forty minutes of working time. The total working time for the diagnostic sections cannot be stated exactly, since some of these tests have no definite time limits, but it is probable that close to four hours would be required for the administration of the entire diagnostic battery to an individual. However, if the examiner is guided by the results of the survey section, there will be many occasions on which only parts of the diagnostic battery will be used.

There are eight forms of the survey section and two forms of each of the diagnostic sections. The tests may be administered for either machine scoring or hand scoring. Percentile norms are available for each grade level in public junior and senior high schools and for college freshmen. There are also percentile norms for independent secondary schools on the survey section. A considerable amount of statistical information has been made available by the Committee on Diagnostic Reading Tests, Inc., concerning these tests.

As indicated earlier in this chapter, the STEP reading and listening tests form a series of overlapping batteries covering the grade range from grades 4 through 14.

Reading Tests for Use in College.   As already mentioned, several reading tests may be used in college, as well as in high school.

These tests include, among others, the Cooperative English Tests: Reading Comprehension [8]; the Nelson-Denny Reading Test [40]; The Iowa Silent Reading Tests, Advanced Test, New Edition [29]; the Schrammel-Gray High School and College Reading Test [47]; and also the Diagnostic Reading Tests [10].

Tests of Study Habits and Skills

Tests of silent-reading ability are closely related to tests of study habits and skills. Some test makers have recognized the desirability of supplementing a reading test with a separate test of study skills in the same general battery. It was pointed out earlier in the chapter, for example, that the Iowa Every-Pupil Tests of Basic Skills [28], one of the most reliable, valid, and useful achievement-test batteries at the elementary school level, contain a booklet measuring basic study skills as well as separate booklets for reading comprehension, basic arithmetic skills, and basic language skills. Similarly, one of the parts of the Stanford Achievement Test is designed to measure study skills [54]. For students at the high school and college levels, the Tyler-Kimber Study Skills Test may be used [62].

Other study tests are in the nature of inventories which inquire into the individual's habits of study, such as planning work, taking notes, budgeting time, and so forth. Among these inventories are Wrenn's Study Habits Inventory, Revised Edition [56], Traxler's Survey of Study Habits [57], and the Brown-Holtzman Survey of Study Habits and Attitudes [5].

Oral-reading Tests

Ideally, an oral-reading examination is a series of paragraphs graduated in difficulty from material obviously easy for the student to material increasingly hard for him, chosen from the subject matter in which his reading difficulty has arisen. Because of the complex nature of reading, a student may have difficulty in one kind of subject matter and not in another. Therefore, if it is the history teacher who is concerned about the student's reading of history, the student should be tested on historical material. Only in this way can his scope of historical vocabulary, his equipment in the general vocabulary of the authors concerned, his grasp of historical sequence, his memory of historical facts, and his ability to understand historical relationships and to generalize from historical data be determined. Ideally, too, the oral-reading examination deals not only with the subject matter in which the reader appears to have difficulty, but also with the kinds of comprehension problems that commonly arise in it.

A homemade test of this kind is likely to be crude; mistakes in gradation of materials are made; teachers may overestimate abilities and have a test actually too hard for the retarded readers in whom they are interested. Nevertheless, such a test may be closer to the true difficulties and capacities of the students in the subject concerned than any general, commercial test would be.

For the convenience of teachers who find it impossible to give time and study for the construction of their own tests, there are several oral-reading tests on the market. Among such tests are the Gray Standardized Oral Reading Check Tests [25], which come in four levels of difficulty representative of the reading material in the elementary school, and in five different forms. The method for scoring is very comprehensive in its consideration of the reading problem and is easily adapted.

The Gray Standardized Oral Reading Paragraphs [26] is a series of ten passages of increasing difficulty. The easiest passages are of elementary school difficulty, while the hardest are a fair challenge to the retarded reader in college. The scoring is the same as for the Gray Standardized Oral Reading Check Tests. The oral-reading paragraphs come in only one form.

Closely related to the two preceding tests, there is a newer set of oral-reading tests known as the Gray Oral Reading Tests, edited by Helen M. Robinson [24]. These tests exist in four comparable forms—A, B, C, and D—each of which consists of thirteen graded passages. There are separate norms for boys and girls, as well as combined norms and grade equivalents.

Another modern test for the same general purposes is the Gilmore Oral Reading Test [23]. This test yields scores for rate and accuracy and also includes a comprehension score derived from questions based on the oral-reading material. Like the Gray Standardized Oral Reading Paragraphs test, it provides for an analysis of kinds of mistakes in oral reading. It exists in two forms which appear to be closely comparable.

Attention was called earlier in the chapter to the oral-reading portion of the word attack section of the Diagnostic Reading Tests for grades 7 to 13. This is one of the very few oral-reading tests planned for high school and college use. The methods of administering and scoring are described in the test manuals and should be carefully studied. The following code is somewhat similar to the one employed in the Gray test:

Errors	Marking
1. Failure to recognize a whole word	Underline the word
2. Failure to recognize part of a word	Underline the part mispronounced
3. Omissions	Encircle the word or part of the word omitted
4. Insertions	Write in the word or phrase inserted
5. Substitutions	Write the word above the one for which it was substituted
6. Repetitions	Make a wavy line under the part repeated

An application of this plan of indicating errors is given in the following paragraph:

VANCOUVER

Vancouver is Canada's western portal. It lies in a sheltered bay at the foot of the high evergreen mountains. It is a modern, progressive city, named in honor of the young naval officer who was the first European to visit the landlocked

places   never
harbor where merchant ships from all parts of the world now discharge their cargoes.

After each paragraph is read, the examiner may ask the student to lay the test aside and tell in his own words what he has read. The examiner makes notes as to whether the student grasped the main idea, remembered important details and related them to the main idea, sensed the sequence and seemed to appreciate the implications of the paragraph. Following the reading and the recall, the examiner sometimes finds it fruitful to ask certain questions about the points of difficulty. Some students make no attempt upon a word which, if put to it, they really can comprehend. Some make substitutions for words which, on second look, they can recognize. It is worthwhile to know whether the student is really incapable of the kind of analysis that the word requires, whether he is dependent upon leading questions for its solution, whether an omitted word is really well established in his sight vocabulary but has been omitted by reason of carelessness. The leads which the examiner derives from this kind of analysis are invaluable for the subsequent tutoring, since they suggest areas of further investigation as well as remedial procedures.

The oral-reading test serves also as a situation in which general information can be gained about a student's pursuits and interests: activities that he prefers in his leisure time; motion pictures, radio and television programs that he likes; his occupation goal (motive for reading can be inserted here in relation to his chosen field); the parts of the newspaper that he always reads; magazines that he likes and what he likes about them; favorite subjects of study, hobbies, methods of study, and hours for study; his method of remembering something (clue to his preference for a particular avenue of learning—visual, auditory, or motor); the leisure activities of his family and and friends (this to determine the incentive to read generated by his environment); his analysis of his reading difficulties, what he thinks may have caused them, and in what kinds of materials they seem to occur most frequently. These pieces of information, casual and subjective, are yet valuable and may be fitted into the general picture of the case as the examiner has derived it from many sources. Participation in the diagnosis, particularly with regard to his self-analysis, will also make the reader feel more like a consultant, less like a misfit.

A similar procedure has been developed with a series of more difficult paragraphs for use with high school and college students [43]. The first and second paragraphs are of about fifth- or sixth-grade level of difficulty, the third paragraph is of about twelfth-grade difficulty, and the fourth paragraph is from John Dewey's *Human Nature and Conduct*. This range of difficulty and content enables the examiner to see how the student attacks unfamiliar words and how his mind works when confronted with both simple and complex reading.

In addition to the analysis of errors already described and in addition to acute observation of the subject's attitude toward reading, his oral vocabulary, conversational ability, etc., these oral tests afford the examiner a chance to learn much about the subject's thought processes in reading. When, after reading the first paragraph, the subjects are asked, "What did the author say?" their answers may reveal reading processes ranging from most inadequate to most adequate.

Selection, Administration, and Scoring of Tests

Criteria for Selection of a Silent-reading Test. An entirely satisfactory silent-reading test has yet to be constructed, and it is quite possible that when such a test does appear, no one will buy it except for use in clinical situations. A truly adequate test would have to be too long, with too many parts to score and too many kinds of material, for any school to find time to use it on a school-wide basis. From among the tests now available the choice of test for a particular group depends upon the school's objectives in reading; the time, money, and personnel available for testing; and the use to be made of the test results. The following are questions suggestive of the criteria that a prospective buyer should consider in selecting a silent-reading test:

1. Does it deal with the vocabulary and the subject matter in which you are interested? If you are a science teacher, you want a test containing science material as well as general reading material. You want the vocabulary to compare favorably with that which you expect the students to acquire in your course or to bring to your course.
2. Does it cover amply the levels of difficulty that interest you? You want a test that is easy enough so that the poorest reader will have some success and hard enough so that the best reader will not make a perfect score. If the poor reader can get no item right, you have no idea how poor he is. If the good reader is 100 per cent right, you have no idea how good he is.
3. Are the reading tasks typical of your demands in the classroom? A social studies teacher said, "I should like to use such and such a test in my class, but it asks all questions of detail, while, in my teaching, details are secondary to questions of relationship and inference."
4. Are the reading tasks eminently suited to the materials presented? A good way to find this out is to see whether a specialist in the field (science, social studies, etc.) feels that the questions asked are the questions that he would be likely to ask on such a passage.
5. Do the tests actually test what they claim to test? Sometimes the vocabulary test is really an analogy test, which puts a premium on intelligence, whereas a test involving simpler synonyms would probably be more likely to reflect the true status of the students' knowledge of the words. Sometimes the comprehension test is so full of hard words that it tests vocabulary more than it does understanding of the relationships of the words and the thought patterns created by them. Sometimes the speed test

is a test of speed of reading and answering questions, as well as a test of speed of reading; and sometimes a speed test has no check on comprehension to show whether the student has understood as he read at that speed.

6. Is the print comparable to that of the book? Some tests are printed on such poor paper in such small type that they are an ocular as well as a reading hurdle.

7. Are the directions clear? Imagine that you are your dullest student and see what you would do with the directions.

8. Are many adjustments required in answering the questions, so that intelligence and emotional stress become prominent in the test score? Certain vocabulary tests require many subtle mental adjustments. As definition for *hasten* there may be *hurry;* these are synonymous. For *flora* there may be *roses;* these are a general term and a specific. For *bowl* there may be *dish;* these are two specifics for the general term *pottery.* Experience for yourself the mental discomfort of the twists of thought required in finding the right answers. See also whether the multiple-choice answers are easier words than the word that is being tested, as they should be.

9. Are the examples typical, misleading, or a dead giveaway?

10. Are some of the multiple-choice answers debatable?

11. Do the incorrect multiple-choice responses represent plausible errors? If the wrong responses are not plausible, the student who does not know the correct response is likely to get the item right by a process of elimination.

12. Are the factors that you are most interested in well isolated, so that you may easily determine a student's mastery of them? Ideally, there should be separate parts for the kinds of reading ability that you want to know about. Sometimes by analysis of the test you can pick out the items that deal with the skill you are interested in; but, of course, this is more work.

13. Are enough time and space given to each skill to make the parts reliable? The more parts you have in a forty-minute test, or a test of any given length, the more you sacrifice in reliability, the less sure you can be that each part of the test gives a good picture of the student's achievement in the aspect of reading covered by that part.

14. May the test be used to some extent for diagnostic purposes? As long as you are buying a test, you may as well get one that can be used either for survey purposes or for diagnosis in broad areas, although, as just indicated, reliable, detailed diagnosis is hardly possible in a survey test designed for classroom use.

15. Is the scoring simple without confounding the purpose of the test? A test that yields a single score can do little to show the nature of the student's retardation.

16. Are the norms, according to the manual of directions, based upon a

population of a size and character comparable with your class? Are they based upon rural or city, private or public schools?

17. Do specific directions as to the manner in which a passage is to be read precede the test paragraphs? Unless the student knows what is expected of his reading, he cannot apply an efficient technique. Neither can he demonstrate his ability to read for different purposes. The directions and the example should make clear to him the kind of comprehension expected, just as in life or in the classroom a purpose is set for the kind of reading to be done.

18. Nearly all standardized tests above the primary grades now require the use of separate answer sheets, of which there are several kinds to meet the requirements of different scoring machines. Are the directions for filling out and using the answer sheets clearly explained to the students? Are well-designed scoring keys available for easy use in either machine scoring or local hand scoring?

Administration and Scoring of Tests. After the test is chosen, plans for its correct administration should be made. If the results are to be compared with the norms, the test must be administered strictly according to directions. More specifically attention should be given to the following details:

1. The students should be seated in such a way as to ensure comfort and avoid the stimulus to copy; lighting should be as good as possible; and unnecessary distractions should be avoided.
2. The test should be introduced in such a manner as to arouse interest but not anxiety.
3. All questions should be asked and answered before the test begins, not while it is in progress.
4. Timing should be accurate. The signals indicating when to begin and when to stop should be clear and definite but not so emphatic as to cause the students to feel that they are competing in a race.
5. The examiner should watch the students to see that they turn pages at the proper time and follow directions accurately.
6. Observations may be made of individual students' methods of work. For example, the following observation was made of a college student taking the Nelson-Denny Reading Test:

On the vocabulary test he worked in a very tense fashion—feet pushed way back under chair, shoulders hunched. When the time was up, he said he had done very poorly. He changed seven out of thirty-seven responses. He asked whether anyone ever finished the test and I told him rarely, that the test was made so most people didn't finish. He worked with less tension on the paragraph-reading test.

Needless to say, the scoring should be done according to directions and checked to ensure accuracy. It is preferable to use clerical workers who have been trained to do the scoring rather than to expect teachers and counselors to assume this routine and time-consuming duty. If the school does not have available clerical workers, the services of outside testing agencies may often be used to advantage and at a saving in cost. In interpreting scores, it must be remembered that norms of reading tests are based on reading as it is now taught, or as it was taught when the test was standardized, not as it might ideally be taught.

Interpretation of Test Results. When a test is administered and scored, only to be shelved in the cumulative record files, it is an extravagant use of school funds. If the time and money involved are to be justified, certain simple observations should be made on silent-reading test results. The following observations of the student's responses on the test are helpful:

1. *The Speed Score.*
   a. Notice whether the comprehension of the material on which a speed score was given was perfect, nearly perfect, mediocre, or poor. Compare the pupil's speed-score percentile with his comprehension percentile.
   b. Note whether the student is apparently a *rapid-careful* reader, one who reads rapidly and understands completely; a *rapid-careless* reader, one who reads rapidly but does not remember much about what he reads; a *slow-careful* reader, one whose speed is poor but whose comprehension is so good that he may as well read more rapidly; or a *slow-inaccurate* reader, one who reads slowly and does not know much about what he reads.
   c. Relate this evidence to what you know of the student's experience, background, and intelligence and of the natural tempo of other members of his family; to the student's explanation for his errors; and to his opinion of his own reading.
2. *The Vocabulary Score.*
   a. Notice the student's relative position on the norms. Is he where he should be for his grade, intelligence, background?
   b. Notice the types of words missed. Do they suggest lacks in certain fields or difficulty with abstract versus concrete ideas? Do they suggest ignorance of the meanings of certain roots, prefixes, and suffixes important to further vocabulary growth?
   c. Notice the level of difficulty of the words missed. If the words are arranged in the test in order of difficulty or rarity, it is easy to see whether the student's errors are in the higher, rarer, harder regions, or whether he has a uniformly bankrupt vocabulary. This indicates a difference in the kinds of words to be used in giving him special help.
   d. Relate this evidence to the student's reasons for errors (sometimes the error was not due to ignorance of the word meaning), and to his

explanation of his method, if any, of building his vocabulary to his classroom experiences and his outside reading experiences.

3. *The Comprehension Score.*

   a. Notice the student's relative position on the norms. Is he where he should be for his grade, intelligence, background? What does this position mean in terms of competition in his class, length of assignments, time required for preparation, reading material to be provided?

   b. Notice the proportion of items of a given kind that are missed. In which areas has he missed more questions: in grasping details, making inferences, drawing conclusions, following directions, outlining, getting sequences? What are the kinds of comprehension in which he apparently needs the most help?

   c. Notice the number of items covered. If there is no other speed score, this observation can yield an evaluation of the student's speed. The items wrong at this speed, especially if they are scattered through a test that grows progressively hard, suggest the accuracy of the student at the speed he has used.

   d. Notice the difficulty of the items missed. Does this suggest something about the student's maturity of comprehension?

   e. Notice the subject matter of the items missed. Does the student show greater facility with science, social studies, fiction, or some other kind of material?

   f. In order to discover the student's power as divorced from speed, have him finish items that he did not complete in the first testing. This will suggest what his possibilities are if he can increase his speed or if he is given ample time for assignments.

Private preparatory schools will usually find the norms for independent schools [4] much more useful than public-school norms, owing to the fact that, at the secondary school level, the average independent-school student is at least two grades ahead of the average public-school student in reading achievement. Consequently, a student in a private school whose reading score falls as low as the public-school norm is retarded in terms of independent-school standards and may require corrective measures.

Use of Tests in Grouping for More Effective Instruction

Students may be grouped in various ways for more effective instruction. In schools having small classes, teachers skilled in reading methods, and adequate reading material, attention may be given within the regular classes to the reading needs of individuals and groups. The teacher's judgment as to

[4] Independent-school norms for a number of reading tests are available from the Educational Records Bureau, New York.

grouping within the class may be aided by his study of the scores on the parts of the test as well as the total scores. Thus, he will make sure that students who are extremely low in some important aspect of reading, such as paragraph comprehension, are scheduled for special help, even though they may be up to average on the test as a whole. Thus, in schools whose equipment is favorable for instruction in reading and whose students' reading difficulties respond to classroom methods of improving reading, no grouping other than that within the class itself is necessary. In schools where the students' reading deficiency is so great that they cannot profit by the kind of class instruction offered, special classes are necessary. The teacher and the specialist in guidance must constantly guard against stigmatizing children who need help. Referral to a reading class or for clinical study can be handled as a privilege, and the individual can be made to feel more important because of the extra attention he is getting. His attitude may then be, "I'm worth spending extra time on. I'm not a hopelessly poor reader."

Although scores on tests are an important criterion for determining grouping of students for special instruction, they are far from being the sole index of reading ability. They should be supplemented by informal tests, records of books and articles the student has read in his directed and free reading, and samples of his responses to long passages. The student's attitude toward grouping and his own evaluation of his progress in reading should also be taken into consideration in grouping. His day-by-day progress gives the best indication of proper placement.

Use of Tests in Appraising Individual Reading Ability
(See also pp. 163–167.)

When using the part scores on silent-reading tests for the analysis of the reading achievement of individual pupils with respect to certain broad categories, the teacher will find it helpful to employ whatever tables are provided by the authors of the various tests for use in changing the raw scores to standard scores or percentile ratings or some other type of derived score, so that the scores on the parts can be compared directly. The manuals of directions for some reading tests contain tables of percentile equivalents for all scores, from the lowest to the highest. Some teachers insist that they do not understand percentile ranks, but the interpretation of percentiles is really very simple. An illustration will perhaps be helpful in explaining the use of percentiles in analyzing the scores made by pupils on the parts of a reading test. The percentile ratings shown in Table 3 correspond to the rate scores, word-meaning scores, total comprehension scores, and total scores made by six tenth-grade pupils on the Traxler Silent Reading Test for grades 7 to 10.

A percentile rank shows the proportion of the pupils in a group whose scores are equaled or exceeded by the score of a given pupil. For example,

TABLE 3
**PERCENTILE RATINGS MADE BY TENTH-GRADE PUPILS ON THE TRAXLER
SILENT READING TEST**

Pupil	Rate	Word Meaning	Total Comprehension	Total
Davis, Mary	50	3	3	8
Hill, William	92	10	6	30
Jones, Earle	17	77	77	58
Long, Alice	59	55	52	54
Martin, Phyllis	95	99	97	98
Sullivan, Joseph	5	1	3	2

the percentile for Mary Davis's total reading score is 8, which means that
this pupil is up to or above only 8 per cent of the tenth-grade pupils whose
scores were used in setting up the norms. On rate of reading Mary has a
percentile rating of 50, which is exactly at the median or average for the
tenth grade, but in word meaning and total comprehension she is in the
lowest 3 per cent of the tenth-grade group. It appears that she does not need
to increase her rate of reading but that she needs to improve in vocabulary
and power of comprehension.

William Hill's percentile ratings provide an even more marked contrast
between rate of reading on the one hand and word meaning and total
comprehension on the other hand. This boy is in the highest 10 per cent
of the tenth-grade pupils in reading rate, but in the lowest 10 per cent in
vocabulary and comprehension. Evidently he needs to learn to read study-type
material more slowly as well as to develop in knowledge of words and in
ability to understand reading materials.

The reading-test percentiles of Earle Jones form a contrast to those
of the first two pupils. He is a very slow reader, but he understands the
meanings of words and comprehends reading material better than do three-
fourths of the pupils in the tenth grade. Because of his relatively high word-
meaning and comprehension scores, probably it is safe to put considerable
pressure on this boy to get him gradually to increase his reading speed
through practice. Whether to do this would, of course, be decided only by
taking into account other information about Earle.

Alice Long is consistently close to average for her grade. Her scores give
no indication of either marked strength or unusual weakness in reading.

Phyllis Martin seems to be outstanding in all phases of reading measured
by this test. In total reading score she has a percentile rating of 98, which
means that in general reading skill she is in the highest 3 per cent of the
tenth-grade pupils, as measured by this test. She should probably have great
freedom in planning her own reading activities, but frequent checks on the

status of her skills are necessary if she is not to develop bad habits through lack of supervision.

Joseph Sullivan, on the other hand, is much retarded in rate, word meaning, and comprehension. His total score is in the lowest 2 per cent of the scores of the tenth-grade pupils. He may require individual remedial teaching. Further diagnosis is necessary.

It is obvious that an analysis of this kind does not carry the diagnosis very far, but it is a useful beginning and one that can be made rather quickly.

In the interpretation of all such test results one should, of course, keep in mind the fact that there is nothing final in the scores on a single test of this kind. While considerable confidence may be placed in the results, as far as groups are concerned, the scores of an individual pupil may fail to indicate his true reading ability because of lack of reliability in the test itself, unfavorable conditions of administration of the test, lack of correspondence between the material in the test and the material in the courses the pupil is studying, and other factors.

From a study of the results of the tests, students should understand better not only their general level of reading ability, but also some of their specific strengths and weaknesses as measured by the test. For the majority of students this knowledge supplies real motivation and paves the way to independence in planning their own reading programs. For example, the Nelson-Denny test may furnish high school juniors and seniors and college students with valuable information, individually or in groups, about their vocabulary and methods of paragraph reading. The following information about a tenth-grade student's knowledge of vocabulary was brought out in a discussion of his performance on the vocabulary section:

When we went over the words, we found that he had associated "idolatry" with "idols," and knew what "felon" meant, although he had marked the wrong response on the paper. He said "decrepit" means "firm." When I asked him why he marked "firm," he said, "I couldn't pronounce the word, so I guessed." "Conflagration" was confused with "congregation." He knew what "penitent" meant and thought he had marked it right, but he had confused it with the idea of "mourner" rather than "sinner." He knew "omnipotent" from the line in the hymn that includes "omnipotent hand." In fact, he seemed to know more about the Bible and hymns and church than most young people. "Allayed," he thought, meant "allied."

The Iowa Silent Reading Tests show a student's rate of comprehension; comprehension of poetry; comprehension of words, sentences, and paragraphs; and ability to locate information. Unfortunately there is little or no variety in difficulty of material within each section of these tests, so that for any one section the examiner cannot determine by the score how poor or how skillful the reader is in terms of easier and harder material. The following is typical of the kind of information that may be obtained from a reading test with subtests, such as the Iowa:

B is in the tenth grade and his reading ability tends to be above average. His comprehension score of 168 is at the 54th percentile. All his other scores are considerably above the median for his grade, with the expection of those for poetry comprehension and use of the index. His standard score in poetry comprehension, 152, corresponds to a tenth-grade percentile of 25. In the use of the index he has a standard score of 143, which is equivalent to a percentile of 12. The results of the test indicate that, although the pupil's reading achievement is in general satisfactory for his grade level, special attention could appropriately be directed toward increasing his comprehension of poetry and improving his facility in using the index of a book. In the interpretation of the scores, however, one should remember that the parts of the test are rather short and therefore not highly reliable and that it is desirable to check low scores by observation and further testing of the pupil.

A question is sometimes asked about the meaning of a grade score on a reading test in terms of a readability formula: Can a pupil with a reading grade score of 7.5 actually read material which a readability formula has indicated to be of seventh-grade difficulty? This is a good practical question but it is oversimplified. Before attempting to answer it, one must ask: What reading test and whose readability formula?

Grade equivalents derived from scores on two different reading tests often vary considerably—even a full grade or more. The two tests may be equally good, but differences in the reading material they contain and differences in the ability of the populations on which they were standardized can lead to some noteworthy differences in the grade scores obtained by the same individual. For instance, when earlier forms of the California Achievement Tests and the Stanford Achievement Test were administered to the same class groups, it was a common observation that grade scores on the reading portion of the California tests tended to be higher than grade scores on the reading part of the Stanford test.

Similarly, the various readability formulas do not precisely agree in their grade placement of reading material. This is to be expected, for different readability formulas—the Lorge, the Dale-Chall, and the Spache formulas, for instance—do not weight in just the same way the elements used to estimate reading difficulty.

All these differences point up a school's need to accumulate experience with a particular test or series of tests and with different readability formulas and to use this experience to add an element of subjective judgment to the bare scores and readability ratings.

Moreover, any reliable and valid reading test may tend to place many pupils, particularly the less able readers, at higher grade levels than they can read at comfortably. This is not surprising, for many pupils are highly motivated when taking a test and they put forth more than usual effort. This motivation leads to better test scores in comparision with their less highly motivated peers. Later, when they read in a more relaxed situation, their performance may be lower than it was on the test and below the grade level at which they might be expected to read on the basis of their test scores.

It should be noted parenthetically that some pupils do *less* well on reading tests than they do in a more normal reading situation. This is particularly true of individuals whose test reactions are impeded by nervousness, and it is sometimes true of exceptionally able readers because of boredom with the usual test content or lack of enough ceiling in the test to allow them to demonstrate their unusual ability. But for most students, scores on standardized reading tests, when interpreted with understanding and caution, are among the most dependable of all the kinds of information for use in assessing the reading level of individual students and of class groups.

In these ways—through observation and class contacts, informal tests, and standardized group reading tests—it is possible to appraise students' reading ability in groups with a minimum of interference with regular school organization and schedule of classes.

Finally, it should be emphasized that materials for evaluation of reading ability are by no means all the materials needed in the diagnosis of reading difficulties. It is always necessary to use tests of mental ability in conjunction with reading tests and, as has often been pointed out, it is highly desirable to choose mental-ability tests that are relatively free from the influence of reading achievement. Tests in other areas, such as spelling tests and tests of achievement in content fields where reading ability is applied, are also valuable sources of information for diagnostic purposes. In addition, it may be desirable in the study of individual cases to make occasional and cautious use of interest inventories and measures of personal qualities.

REFERENCES [5]

These references form a fairly comprehensive list of published reading tests. Practically all reading tests published in the United States are listed, and tests of study habits, attitudes, and skills are also covered. In addition, the list includes a few reading tests published in other English-speaking countries. For appraisal of many of these tests see Oscar Buros, *The Fifth Mental Measurements Yearbook*, The Gryphon Press, Highland Park, N.J., 1959, and Buros, *The Sixth Mental Measurements Yearbook*, The Gryphon Press, Highland Park, N.J., 1965.

    1. *A.C.E.R. Silent Reading Tests*, for grades 3–8 and adults, Forms A and B;

[5] Tests to which special attention is called are starred.

part 1 (Form B only), Word Knowledge; part 2, Speed of Reading; part 3, Reading for General Significance; part 4, Reading to Note Details; part 5, Reading for Inference; 1933–1957. For grades 4–6, Forms C and D; part 1, Word Knowledge; part 2, Speed of Reading; part 3, Reading for Meaning; 1946–1963, Australian Council for Educational Research, Victoria, Australia.

2. *A.C.E.R. Silent Reading Tests: Standardized for Use in New Zealand,* one form, for ages 9–12; part 1, Word Knowledge; part 2, Speed of Reading; part 3, Reading for Meaning; New Zealand Council for Educational Research, Wellington, New Zealand, 1934–1955.

3. *American School Achievement Tests, Part 1, Reading,* by Willis E. Pratt and Robert V. Young; for grade 1, Forms D, E, F, and G, Primary I Battery; for grades 2–3, Primary II Battery; for grades 4–6, Intermediate Battery; for grades 7–9, Advanced Battery; The Bobbs-Merrill Company, Inc., Indianapolis, 1941–1958.

4. *American School Reading Tests,* by Willis E. Pratt and Stanley W. Lore, for grades 10–13, Forms A and B, The Bobbs-Merrill Company, Inc., Indianapolis, 1955.

°5. *Brown-Holtzman Survey of Study Habits and Attitudes,* by William F. Brown and Wayne H. Holtzman, one form, for grade 10 through college freshman year, The Psychological Corporation, New York, 1953–1956.

6. *California Phonics Survey,* by Grace M. Brown and Alice B. Cottrell, Forms 1 and 2 for grade 7 through college, California Test Bureau, Monterey, Calif., 1956–1963.

°7. *California Reading Test, 1957 Edition,* with 1963 norms, by Ernest W. Tiegs and Willis W. Clark; for grades 1–2, Forms W and X, Lower Primary Battery; for Grades 3–4.5, Forms W and X, Upper Primary Battery; for grades 4–6, Forms W, X, Y, Z, Elementary Battery; for grades 7–9, Junior High School Level, Forms W, X, Y. Z; for grades 9–14, Forms W, X, Y, Advanced Battery; California Test Bureau, Monterey, Calif., 1933–1963.

°8. *Cooperative English Tests: Reading Comprehension,* 1960 edition, by Clarence Derrick, David P. Harris, and Biron Walker, three forms at each level; for grade 12 and college freshmen and sophomores, Level 1, Forms A, B, and C (C reserved for college); for grades 9–12, Level 2, Forms A, B, and C; Cooperative Test Division, Educational Testing Service, Princeton, N.J., 1960.

°9. *Davis Reading Test,* by Frederick B. Davis and Charlotte Croon Davis; for grades 11–13, Forms 1A, 1B, 1C, and 1D; for grades 8–11, Forms 2A, 2B, 2C, and 2D; The Psychological Corporation, New York, 1956–1962.

°10. *Diagnostic Reading Tests,* by Committee on Diagnostic Reading Tests, Inc. (Frances Oralind Triggs, chairman), Kindergarten–Fourth Grade Battery; for grades 4–8, Forms A, B, C, D, Lower Level Battery; for grades 7–13, Forms A through H, Upper Level Battery, Survey Section; for grades 7–13, Forms A and B, Diagnostic Sections as follows: Section I, Vocabulary; Section II, Comprehension: part 1—Silent, part 2—Auditory; Section III, Rates of Reading: part 1—General, part 2—Social Studies, part 3—Science; Section IV, Word Attack: part 1—Oral, part 2—Silent; Committee on Diagnostic Reading Tests, Inc., Mountain Home, N.C., 1947–1963.

11. *Diagnostic Reading Tests: A History of Their Construction and Validation,* Committee on Diagnostic Reading Tests, Inc., Mountain Home, N.C., 1952.

12. *Dominion Achievement Tests in Silent Reading,* by Department of Educational Research, Ontario College of Education, University of Toronto, Forms A and B; for grade 1, Primary, Type I: Word Recognition, Type II: Phrase and Sentence Reading, Type III: Paragraph Reading, Type IV: Diagnostic Test in Word Recognition; for grades 2 and 3, Type I: Vocabulary; for grade 2, Type II: Diagnostic Test in Paragraph Reading; for grades 3 and 4, Type II: Diagnostic Test in Paragraph Reading; for grades 4, 5, and 6, Type I: Vocabulary; for grades 5 and 6, Type II: Diagnostic Test in Paragraph Reading; Guidance Centre, Ontario College of Education, University of Toronto, Canada, 1941–1957.

13. *Dominion Group Test of Reading Readiness,* by Department of Educational Research, Ontario College of Education, University of Toronto, Forms A and B, for kindergarten–grade 1, Guidance Centre, Ontario College of Education, University of Toronto, Canada, 1949–1959.

14. *Dominion Individual Diagnostic Test of Word-Analysis Skills, Primary,* by Department of Educational Research, Ontario College of Education, University of Toronto, one form for individual administration to pupils in grades 1 and 2+, Guidance Centre, Ontario College of Education, University of Toronto, Canada, 1947.

15. *Doren Diagnostic Reading Test of Word Recognition Skills,* by Margaret Doren, one form for grades 1–4, yields twelve scores, American Guidance Service, Inc., Minneapolis, 1956.

16. *Durrell Analysis of Reading Difficulty: New Edition,* by Donald D. Durrell, one form for individual administration in grades 1–6, Harcourt, Brace & World, Inc., New York, 1937–1955.

°17. *Durrell-Sullivan Reading Capacity and Achievement Tests,* by Donald D. Durrell and Helen Blair Sullivan, two levels: for grades 2.5–4.5, Primary Test; for grades 3–6, Intermediate Test (Form A of Primary Test and Intermediate Capacity Test; Forms A and B of Intermediate Achievement Test), Harcourt, Brace & World, Inc., New York, 1937–1944.

°18. *Gates-MacGinitie Reading Tests,* by Arthur I. Gates and Walter H. MacGinitie; Primary A for grade 1; Primary B for grade 2; Primary C for grade 3; Forms 1 and 2 at each grade level, each measuring vocabulary and comprehension, Teachers College Press, Teachers College, Columbia University, New York, 1965.

°19. *Gates-MacGinitie Reading Tests,* by Arthur I. Gates and Walter H. MacGinitie, Survey D (hand-scored edition) and Survey DM (separate answer sheet edition), three forms of each edition. Measures speed, vocabulary, and comprehension for grades 5 and 6. Teachers College Press, Teachers College, Columbia University, New York, 1965.

°20. *Gates-MacGinitie Reading Tests,* by Arthur I. Gates and Walter H. MacGinitie, Survey E (hand-scoring edition) and Survey EM (separate answer sheet edition), three forms of each edition. Measures speed, vocabulary, and comprehension for grades 7, 8, and 9. Teachers College Press, Teachers College, Columbia University, New York, 1965.

21. *Gates-MacGinitie Readiness Skills,* by Arthur I. Gates and Walter H. MacGinitie, designed to measure readiness for beginning reading, Teachers College Press, Teachers College, Columbia University, New York, 1966.

22. *Gates-McKillop Reading Diagnostic Tests,* rev. ed., by Arthur I. Gates and Anne S. McKillop, for grades 1–8, Forms 1–2, individually administered, Teachers College Press, Teachers College, Columbia University, New York, 1962.

°**23.** *Gilmore Oral Reading Test,* by John V. Gilmore, for grades 1–8, Forms A and B, Harcourt, Brace & World, Inc., New York, 1951.

°**24.** *Gray Oral Reading Tests,* by William S. Gray, Helen M. Robinson (ed.), Forms A, B, C, and D, The Bobbs-Merrill Company, Inc., Indianapolis, 1965.

°**25.** *Gray Standardized Oral Reading Check Tests,* by William S. Gray, one form, four levels; for grades 1–2, Set 1; for grades 2–4, Set 2; for grades 4–6, Set 3; for grades 6–8, Set 4; the Bobbs-Merrill Company, Inc., Indianapolis, 1923–1955.

°**26.** *Gray Standardized Oral Reading Paragraphs,* by William S. Gray, one form, for grades 1–8, The Bobbs-Merrill Company, Inc., Indianapolis, 1915.

27. *Harrison-Stroud Reading Readiness Profiles,* by M. Lucile Harrison and James B. Stroud, one form for kindergarten and grade 1, Houghton Mifflin Company, Boston, 1949–1956.

°**28.** *Iowa Every-Pupil Tests of Basic Skills: Test A, Silent Reading Comprehension,* and *Test B, Work-Study Skills,* by Ernest Horn, Maude McBroom, H. A. Greene, E. F. Lindquist, and H. F. Spitzer; for grades 3–5, Elementary Battery, Forms L, M, N, and O; for grades 5–9, Advanced Battery, Forms L, M, N, and O; Houghton Mifflin Company, Boston, 1940–1947.

°**29.** *Iowa Silent Reading Tests, Advanced Test, new ed.,* by H. A. Green, A. N. Jorgensen, and V. H. Kelley, for grades 9–14, Forms Am, Bm, Cm, Dm, Harcourt, Brace & World, Inc., New York, 1927–1943.

30. *Iowa Silent Reading Tests, Elementary Test, new ed.,* by H. A. Green and V. H. Kelley, for grades 4–9, Forms Am, Bm, Harcourt, Brace & World, Inc., New York, 1933–1956.

°**31.** *Iowa Tests of Basic Skills,* by E. F. Lindquist and A. N. Hieronymus, four forms, for grades 3–9, measuring vocabulary, reading comprehension, and work-study skills, as well as other aspects of achievement, Houghton Mifflin Company, Boston, 1956.

32. *Iowa Tests of Educational Development: Test 5, Ability to Interpret Reading Materials in the Social Studies; Test 6, Ability to Interpret Reading Materials in the Natural Sciences; Test 7, Ability to Interpret Literary Materials; Test 9, Use of Sources of Information,* by E. F. Lindquist and Leonard S. Feldt, Forms X and Y, Science Research Associates, Inc., Chicago, 1942–1959.

33. *Kelley-Greene Reading Comprehension Test,* Evaluation and Adjustment Series, by V. H. Kelley and H. A. Greene, for grades 9–13, Forms Am and Bm, Harcourt, Brace & World, Inc., New York, 1952–1955.

34. *Lee-Clark Reading Readiness Test, 1962 Revision,* by J. Murray Lee and Willis W. Clark, one form for kindergarten and grade 1, California Test Bureau, Monterey, Calif., 1931–1962.

35. *Lee-Clark Reading Test, 1958 Revision,* by J. Murray Lee and Willis W. Clark; for grade 1, Forms A and B, Primer; for grades 1–2, First Reader; California Test Bureau, Monterey, Calif., 1931–1958.

36. *A Library Orientation Test for College Freshmen,* by Ethel M. Feagley,

Dorothy W. Curtiss, Mary V. Gaver, and Esther Greene, one form, for grade 13, Teachers College Press, Teachers College, Columbia University, New York, 1950–1961.

°37. *McCullough Word Analysis Tests, Experimental Edition,* by Constance M. McCullough, one form yielding ten scores for grades 4–6, Ginn and Company, Boston, 1962–1963.

38. *Metropolitan Reading Tests, Upper Primary, Elementary, Intermediate, and Advanced Reading Tests, 1958–1962 Edition,* by Harold H. Bixler, Walter N. Durost, Gertrude H. Hildreth, Kenneth W. Lund, and J. Wayne Wrightstone; grade 2, Upper Primary, Form C; grades 3–4, Elementary, Forms A, B, and C; grades 5–6, Intermediate, Forms Am, Bm, Cm; grades 7–9, Advanced, Forms Am, Bm, and Cm; Harcourt, Brace & World, Inc., New York, 1933–1962.

39. *Metropolitan Readiness Tests,* by Gertrude H. Hildreth, Nellie L. Griffiths, and Mary E. McGauvran, for end of kindergarten and beginning of grade 1, Forms R and S, Harcourt, Brace & World, Inc., New York, rev. 1965.

°40. *The Nelson-Denny Reading Test: Vocabulary-Comprehension-Rate,* E. C. Denny (rev. by James I. Brown), for grades 9–12, college, and adults, Forms A and B, Houghton Mifflin Company, Boston, 1929–1960.

41. *Nelson Reading Test, Revised Edition,* by M. J. Nelson, for grades 3–9, Forms A and B, measures vocabulary and paragraph comprehension, Houghton Mifflin Company, Boston, 1931–1962.

42. *Pressey Diagnostic Reading Tests,* by S. L. Pressey and L. C. Pressey, grades 3 to 9, Forms A and B, The Bobbs-Merrill Company, Indianapolis, 1929.

°43. *Reading Diagnostic Record for High School and College Students, Revised,* by Ruth Strang, Margaret M. Conant, Margaret G. McKim, and Mary Alice Mitchell, one form, Teachers College Press, Teachers College, Columbia University, New York, 1952.

44. *Reading Readiness Test,* by David F. Votaw and Peggy Lou Moses, one form, for kindergarten and grade 1, The Steck Company, Austin, Tex., 1957.

45. *Roswell-Chall Diagnostic Reading Test of Word Analysis Skills,* by Florence G. Roswell and Jeanne S. Chall, for grades 2–6, Forms 1 and 2, Essay Press, New York, 1956–1959.

46. *The Schonell Reading Tests,* by Fred J. Schonell, one form, for ages 5–15, 6–9, 7–11, 9–13, Oliver & Boyd, Ltd., Edinburgh and London, 1942–1955.

47. *Schrammel-Gray High School and College Reading Test,* by H. E. Schrammel and W. H. Gray, for grades 7–13, Forms A and B, The Bobbs-Merrill Company, Indianapolis, 1940–1942.

°48. *Sequential Tests of Educational Progress: Listening,* by Margaret J. Early, Seymour Eskow, William J. Grassl, Nathan A. Miller, Osmond E. Palmer, Mildred C. Patterson, Alice P. Sterner, and Charlotte G. Wells; for grades 13–14, Level 1; for grades 10–12, Level 2; for grades 7–9, Level 3; for grades 4–6, Level 4; Forms A and B, yields one overall score, Cooperative Test Division, Educational Testing Service, Princeton, N.J., 1956–1957.

°49. *Sequential Tests of Educational Progress. Reading,* by Harvey Alpert, Dorothy E. McCullough, Helen F. Olson, Myriam Page, Jerry E. Reed, Phillip Shaw, Robert B. Simpson, and Machlin Thomas; for grades 13–14, Level 1; for grades 10–12, Level 2; for grades 7–9, Level 3; for grades 4–6, Level 4; Forms A and B, yields one overall score, Cooperative Test Division, Educational Testing Service, Princeton, N.J., 1956–1963.

50. *Spitzer Study Skills Test,* Evaluation and Adjustment Series, by Herbert F. Spitzer, for grades 9–13, Forms Am, Bm, yields five scores, Harcourt, Brace & World, Inc., New York, 1954–1955.

51. *SRA Achievement Series: Reading,* by Louis P. Thorpe, D. Welty LeFever, and Robert A. Naslund; Forms A and B for grades 1–2, 2–4, 4–6, 6–9; Forms C and D for grades 1–2, 2–4; yields 2 to 5 scores depending on grade level and form used, Science Research Associates, Inc., Chicago, 1954–1964.

52. *SRA Achievement Series: Work-Study Skills,* by Louis D. Thorpe, D. Welty LeFever, and Robert A. Naslund; Forms A and B, for grades 4–6, 6–9; Forms C and D for grades 4.7–6.6, 6.7–8.3, 8.4–9.9; yields two or three scores depending on form used, Science Research Associates, Inc., Chicago, 1954–1964.

53. *SRA Reading Record,* by Guy T. Buswell and Margaret M. Buswell, one form, ten scores, for grades 9–12, Science Research Associates, Inc., Chicago, 1947–1959.

54. *Stanford Achievement Test: Study Skills,* by Truman L. Kelley, Richard Madden, Eric, F. Gardner, Lewis M. Terman, and Giles M. Ruch, for grades 5–6, 7–9, Intermediate Test, Forms Jm and Km; Advanced Test, Forms Jm, Km, and Lm, Harcourt, Brace & World, Inc., New York, 1952–1956.

°**55.** *Stanford Reading Test,* by Truman L. Kelley, Richard Madden, Eric F. Gardner, and Herbert C. Rudman; for grades 4.0–5.4, Intermediate I Test; for grades 5.5–6.9, Intermediate II Test; for grades 7–9, Advanced Test; Forms W and X, Harcourt, Brace & World, Inc., New York, 1964.

°**56.** *Study Habits Inventory, Revised Edition,* by C. Gilbert Wrenn, one form, for grades 12–16, Consulting Psychologists Press, Inc., Palo Alto, Calif., 1934–1941. (Formerly published by Stanford University Press.)

57. *Survey of Study Habits,* by Arthur E. Traxler, one form, for grades 8–14, Educational Records Bureau, New York, 1944.

58. *A Test of Study Skills,* by J. W. Edgar and H. T. Manuel, grades 4–9, Forms A and B, The Steck Company, Austin, Tex., 1940–1941.

59. *Tinker Speed of Reading Test,* by Miles A. Tinker, for grades 7–16 and adults, Forms 1 and 2, University of Minnesota Press, Minneapolis, 1947–1955.

°**60.** *Traxler High School Reading Test,* by Arthur E. Traxler, for grades 10–12, Forms A and B, The Bobbs-Merrill Company, Inc., Indianapolis, 1938–1966.

°**61.** *Traxler Silent Reading Test,* by Arthur E. Traxler, for grades 7–10, Forms 1, 2, 3, and 4, The Bobbs-Merrill Company, Inc., Indianapolis, 1934–1942.

62. *Tyler-Kimber Study Skills Test,* by Henry T. Tyler and George C. Kimber, one form, for grades 9–16, Consulting Psychologists Press, Inc., Palo Alto, Calif., 1937. (Formerly published by Stanford University Press.)

°**63.** *Vocabulary Test for High School Students and College Freshmen,* by Arthur E. Traxler, Forms A and B, for grades 9–13, The Bobbs-Merrill Company, Inc., Indianapolis, 1964.

°**64.** *Watson-Glaser Critical Thinking Appraisal,* by Goodwin Watson and Edward M. Glaser, for grades 9–16 and adults, Forms Ym and Zm each yielding six scores, Harcourt, Brace & World, Inc., New York, 1942–1964.

65. *Williams Reading Tests,* by Allan J. Williams, for grades 1–9, Forms A and B, The Bobbs-Merrill Company, Inc., Indianapolis, 1925–1955.

teaching basic reading skills

chapter 6

Because the teaching of any specific skill must be based on sound general principles of learning and teaching, principles and procedures are inseparable. Anderson and Dearborn stated, "The teaching process must take its cue from the learning process" [2, p. 138]. By observing how pupils learn, the teacher learns how to teach. He takes his cues from the pupil as the pupil learns to read.

Basic skills include word recognition, vocabulary, and literal comprehension—abilities that support higher competences such as interpretation, critical and creative reading, and the application of ideas. In order to develop the basic reading abilities, pupils need instruction and practice.

In this chapter you will glimpse various teaching procedures that are designed to develop the sequences of reading attitudes and basic skills described in Chapter 3. You will find concrete descriptions of classroom procedures as well as specific techniques. And you will also find references to some research which will help to substantiate the practical application or to serve as guidelines of specific procedures. Once you appraise them, you can select, develop, and apply those appropriate in setting up the most favorable conditions for each child's optimum learning at his optimum reading rate.

PRINCIPLES OF LEARNING AND TEACHING

There is much interest at present in theories of learning and in principles of human development. Hence current emphases center on understanding the structure of a subject relative to inquiry and discovery and describing the interaction that takes place in the classroom. Too often, however, theories newly proposed or rediscovered have not received sufficient validation before being applied to instruction [64]. Since the gap between theory and practice is so difficult to bridge, the following principles are offered not as prescriptions; *they are merely intended to provide possible ways of looking at instruction.* Though any of them may represent valid views of instruction, each needs to be tested in many different classroom settings. No teacher should follow a method without adequate evaluation and adaptation.

It is a truism that children learn in an informative and responsive environment in which they will strive to learn as long as they have some success within a reasonable span of time. The importance of rapport between teacher and pupil and a positive attitude toward reading in the home have already been described (see Chapter 1). But many other conditions outside both the school and the home may also affect reading achievement.

1. *Alert attention is prerequisite to learning.* If an individual is to learn, he must first keep alert and pay attention to the printed words. He must concentrate so that the meaning associated with the words is taken in, organized, and classified with patterns of knowledge already stored in the cerebral cortex. If he does not learn to pay attention or if the teacher exposes him to a multiplicity of apparently unrelated reading skills—a little word recognition, a little skimming, some dictionary practice—he becomes confused.

2. *The process of discovery stimulates learning.* Bruner [11] emphasized this approach and asserted that it has four values: (a) it "increases intellectual potency," (b) it is self-rewarding, (c) it is self-perpetuating, and (d) it aids the memorization of related items of information.

3. *Feeling affects learning.* Piaget has stated that there is no cognition

without affect and vice versa. Desire to know motivates any kind of learning. On the other hand, the pupil who is made to feel that he is being manipulated by forces beyond his control may conclude that it is useless to put forth effort.

4. *Learning occurs when there is a need to know, a problem to be solved.* The student's need to read often arises in connection with a goal, a project, a problem, or an activity that is important to him. The beginning reader wants to know what the characters are saying. The older pupil wants to find answers to his questions. When the student runs into trouble in reading for the answers, it is the psychological moment to give him instruction in the required skill. It is best for parents and teachers not to tell a child a word that he can figure out for himself, having already acquired the skill, because permanent learning takes place if a pupil gets into the habit of immediately applying the latest pertinent instruction.

The teacher must be skillful in analyzing the reading task involved in a problem or project and in teaching the students how to accomplish it. Demonstration is usually more effective than a lecture, for it is better to show than to tell, to raise questions than to give specific answers.

5. *Students should be encouraged to take initiative and responsibility for their own learning.* They are more likely to succeed in plans that move them toward their goals than in those which divert them from their goals. They need to analyze their own reading processes and discover procedures that have maximum efficiency for them. They should note methods that they have used successfully.

Initiative and independence in learning develop early. In school such practices as assigning the same seat work to every child, round-the-room oral reading, and undifferentiated assignments comprising factual questions lessen progress; these and similar regimented methods of teaching encourage dependence instead of initiative. Pupils who have opportunities to cooperate in planning classroom procedures, to learn from one another, to apportion their time, and to select their activities develop independence and initiative. Giving children opportunities to learn from one another benefits both the teacher and the taught.

6. *Meaningful material is learned more quickly and easily than material in which the pupil has no background of experience.* Experience comes before reading. Beginning reading material should be composed of familiar words that have personal significance to the individual pupil.

The reading material should have enough structure so that the student can discover the relationships of its parts—with only a minimum of guidance.

7. *Individuals learn by moving from specific examples to generalizations, from perceptions to concepts, from the concrete to the abstract.* The teacher should recognize this psychological sequence. Whenever necessary, he should simplify the learning process for the benefit of pupils who have difficulty.

Slow learners especially need step-by-step instruction, practice, and reinforcement.

RESEARCH ON METHODS OF TEACHING READING

Many researchers have attempted to find out which of the many methods of teaching reading are most effective. One research will show that intensive phonic training in letter sounds and names appears to have a favorable effect on reading achievement. Another will show that the phonic approach has no advantage over a combination of methods even in teaching a phonetically regular language [105].

Research results have been inconclusive for a number of reasons. First, few investigators have adequately described either the nature or the educational background of their experimental and control groups. Second, none of the experiments has adequately controlled the complex teacher variable, and only a few have attempted to control the stimulating effect of being involved in an experiment—the "Hawthorne effect." Third, the long-term effects of the various methods under investigation have not been assessed in most of the studies. Moreover, many of the reports have omitted the information that is most useful to the teacher: which procedures and materials produced the best results with pupils of different abilities and backgrounds—and why.

It is rare indeed to find any new method reported as ineffective or even as less effective than the "traditional" method with which it is compared. Most children learn to read by the methods in current use if they have a skillful, friendly teacher. Even though a given method may not be the best available, it will get results if the teacher is enthusiastic about it and competent in using it.

Children differ widely in their response to a given method [19]. One study showed that by the time they reached the third grade, highly anxious or compulsive children who had been taught beginning reading by phonic methods in an authoritarian atmosphere were superior in reading achievement to children comparable in intelligence and social class who had been taught by the whole-word method in a permissive atmosphere. It was assumed that sampling procedure was purely random with respect to the personality variables under investigation [41]. It also seems reasonable to believe that children who are unusually aggressive or independent may respond favorably to teachers who are highly orderly and businesslike, whereas children who are dependent, fearful, and withdrawn may respond better to a more permissive and less highly organized teacher. Assistance that may promote learning by fearful or dependent children may cause resistance or apathy among children who are more independent or intellectually gifted.

Rather than limiting himself to comparing two groups on single factors, a teacher might obtain more significant results by using a case-study approach in which he could consider the effect of interrelated factors on reading achievement. Instead of generalizing, it would be much more useful to consider the findings of each experiment as hypotheses that might possibly apply to the individual or the teaching situation with which the teacher is dealing.

GETTING READY TO READ: PRESCHOOL YEARS

Since preschool years are so important for a child's school success, teachers are concerned with the preschool child's prereading experience. Through conferences and meetings with parents, teachers can give parents suggestions that will help their children succeed in first-grade reading. There is no question about the value of certain prereading experiences during the preschool years. The parents who enjoy reading create in the child a desire to do likewise. The parents who read to the child acquaint him with the sound of sentences and the language of literature. The parents who talk with their child at mealtime and while they are working around the house or going somewhere with him build up his speaking vocabulary. The parents who listen to the thoughts the child wants to express and the questions to which he seeks answers further increase his verbal facility.

By memorizing nursery rhymes and other familiar poems and being asked to complete certain lines

> Jack and Jill
> Went up the ———,

the child receives practice in rhyming. By identifying in the game words that sound alike or begin alike, he develops auditory perception.

The child should be allowed to take the initiative and should not be subjected to parental disapproval or disappointment when he is slow to respond correctly. There are no lessons, no failure, no nagging. The child follows his own timetable, sometimes seriously, often lightheartedly. Adults should not tease and test children by asking, "What's this? What's that?" If a child points to something, parents may assume that he wants to know its name and say, "What is that called? That's an orange." Before long he will be asking, "What's that called?" The parents who try to understand what is going on in the child's mind and who encourage his natural curiosity and desire to explore his surroundings help him to develop a spirit of inquiry and an openness to new experiences.

Learning to get along with other children and adults also helps the child to adjust to the group situation that he later encounters in school.

These informal methods of learning prepare the child, when the time comes, for school instruction.

Children from non-English-speaking or disadvantaged homes have special language problems. The reading problems of these children will be discussed in Chapter 14.

Unfavorable preschool experiences may affect a child's reading in subtle and pervasive ways. If his early questions are ignored, he may lose his initial curiosity and his spirit of inquiry. If he always has to obey adults' commands, he may fail to develop initiative and creativity. If nothing he does is approved, he may learn to expect failure and to regard himself as inferior and inadequate. All these ways of perceiving, thinking, reasoning, and responding affect his approach to learning to read. From the earliest years parents should foster the child's normal curiosity by encouraging his spirit of inquiry and helping him in his search for answers to his questions, by developing his sense of trust, and by maintaining his openness to new experiences.

In kindergarten there are further opportunities to develop children's auditory and visual perception. Children do not usually distinguish critical features of certain letters until they are past four years of age. This kind of discrimination requires a process of differentiation rather than one of association. Popp [83] found that many children have special difficulty in discriminating between certain letters. The pairs *b-d* and *p-g* were most confusing. Children also showed some confusion in discriminating pairs of letters that have similar or identical lines such as *i-l, h-n.* Marchbanks and Levin [67] identified clues such as vertical and curved lines by which children recognized words. Instruction involving attention, motor-response-produced clues, and verbal responses aided kindergarten children in discriminating *b* and *d* [45]. Children who confuse single letters in pairs may be able to recognize the letters when they are put together in word sequence. According to Gibson [38], letter clusters pass through a phase of integration before they can be perceived as wholes.

Since visual and auditory acuity, discrimination, and memory are prerequisite to success in learning to read, it is desirable to use games such as those described by Montessori and exercises such as the practice material prepared by Frostig [33] for developing each of the five aspects of visual perception measured in her tests of visual perception.

Wepman [108] suggested that beginning readers be initially grouped as primarily auditory learners or primarily visual learners in order to avoid certain instructional pitfalls in the early stages of the reading program. The alternative to this plan is to increase by practice the efficiency of the perceptual mode in which the child is deficient.

Eye-hand coordination is strengthened by many enjoyable activities that can be conducted in nursery school and kindergarten such as tracing and copying figures, cutting out pictures, and so on. The Lions Research Foundation, Winter Haven, Florida, suggests the following sequence of procedures:

1. Drawing simple geometric forms by use of a stencil which guides the child's movements
2. Copying various forms of increasing complexity
3. Reproducing such forms from memory

Kephart [53] has described classroom procedures designed to assure early reading success. Radler and Kephart [84] have given parents similar suggestions which can serve the first-grade teacher, too.

Children who show difficulty in motor coordination and control can be helped by rhythms, balancing, and other familiar playground activities.

To support his belief that many children have unrecognized intellectual abilities and interests, Omar K. Moore [75] has demonstrated that two- to five-year-olds of average intelligence can learn to read and write. His method was to give them electric typewriters, pronounce each letter for them as they punched it, and give them opportunities to scribble as they pleased on the chalkboard. Before long, they were reading and writing letters and words. The learning of these complex skills appeared to raise the children's tested IQs; whether it would have a favorable long-term effect can be determined only by longitudinal studies.

In a preliminary investigation, the use of electric typewriters as instructional tools had a favorable effect on the interests and attitudes of fourth-grade pupils. They prepared neater papers and developed greater self-direction. They also improved in "eye sweep," listening skills, and punctuation [111].

Many questions should be answered before formal reading instruction replaces the spontaneous, happy, informal learning appropriate for preschool children.

When parents ask if they should teach their preschool children to read, teachers can point out that encouraging the child's spontaneous interest in reading is a very different thing from giving him formal reading lessons. It is not necessary to "teach your baby to read." Children who have had a rich background of prereading experiences, but no reading instruction as such, tend to catch up quickly, under favorable classroom conditions, with children of comparable ability who have had preschool instruction [76]. Teachers may refer parents to the study reported by Brzeinski [12]. The program of systematic reading instruction that was introduced in 122 kindergarten classes in Denver appeared to be more effective than the regular kindergarten program, especially for those children who went on to a first-grade program that was specially adapted to them. On the average the children in the experimental groups were significantly better readers at the end of grade 1. Kindergarten teaching of reading apparently neither created nor prevented problems in the areas of vision, hearing, and social and academic adjustment so far as these aspects could be measured. However, no final evaluation can be made until this longitudinal study is completed.

Experiments to date suggest that learning to read during the preschool years is an advantage only if the first-grade teacher allows the child to continue reading at the point he has reached. The question really is: "Is the school ready to meet the child's needs?" rather than "Is the child ready for school?"

If it were possible to provide adequate physical facilities and trained staff for an ideal headstart program as a part of the regular school system, it should prevent much reading failure among children from non-English-speaking or otherwise disadvantaged home backgrounds.

READINESS TO READ IN FIRST GRADE

From careful observation already described (see Chapters 3 and 4), the teacher can tell whether a given child is ready to read. Intelligence, as measured, does not seem to be as important a factor in reading readiness as auditory and visual perception and preschool experiences. There are several widely used readiness tests, one of which is the Metropolitan Readiness Test (Harcourt, Brace & World). The primary value of readiness tests is to discover specific strengths and weaknesses as a guide to instruction rather than to predict success in first-grade reading.

In a heterogeneous class of thirty first-grade children, one teacher found seventeen who rated "low normal" or "poor risk" on the Metropolitan Readiness Test at the beginning of the school year. During September and October these children met with the teacher as a group while the other children were doing independent work. Since all of these children were deficient in speaking vocabulary, visual and auditory perception and discrimination, experience background, and interest in reading, the teacher gave them the following experiences:

She introduced Bozo, a puppet clown, to give the children occasions for spontaneous speech. They would talk with Bozo and answer his questions more readily than they would respond verbally to the teacher.

They had opportunities to express themselves in regular classroom activities such as sharing their interests with others and evaluating their work. They frequently dramatized stories with puppets.

Soon they began to dictate phrases and sentences to the teacher. "Watch while I write it," she would say. They developed word perception by noting not only the configuration of each word but also the sequence of letters that comprised it. They made picture word cards for the words they had used and matched in their stories. They learned to read their names and the eight basic color words. In these and other ways they acquired a speaking vocabulary

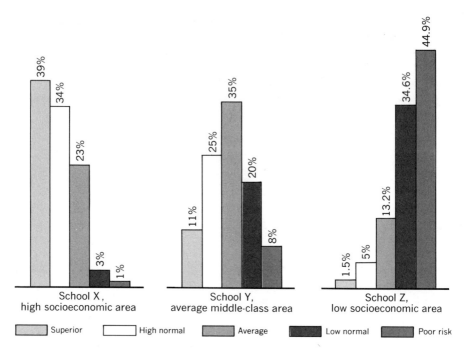

FIGURE 4. Results on the Metropolitan Readiness Test in three different socio-economic areas.

of meaningful words that approached the vocabulary of the average six-year-old.

They found pictures of many kinds of houses, for example, and labeled all of them "house" or "houses." Thus they learned that a word is not a thing but a symbol that may stand for a class of objects.

Sometimes the teacher omitted a word in a sentence and said, "Write the word you think I ought to write in the blank." This exercise required reasoning and developed the children's sense of "closure." It was the first step in using context clues and anticipating meaning. The teacher also asked the children to read the words they knew in a sentence they had dictated to her. She would then read the sentence as a whole.

In addition to the usual exercises to help the pupils recognize and distinguish different forms, letters, and words, the teacher introduced an element of reasoning. Instead of merely asking the children to find and pronounce the correct word, she asked, "Which word tells what houses are made of? Wood? Food?" "Which can you climb—a ladder or a letter?" If a child was slow to respond, she would not hurry him or call on another child. She would say, "He'll find it."

In developing auditory discrimination, the teacher showed the children various pictures and objects; they would select those whose names began with the same sound as the new word they were learning. Reasoning was also called for in exercises such as these:

Fox, box which is an animal?
Hat, cat which can you wear?
Sock, clock which tells time?

The reading-readiness workbook, *Games to Play,* published by Ginn and Company, offered additional practice in storytelling, visual and auditory discrimination, and clear enunciation of word sounds.

After the children had read a story they had dictated, the teacher would often ask them to give it a name or title, the first step in finding the main idea.

The books the pupils brought back from the library were available to them during the school day. The teacher also read aloud to them at least once a day.

They participated with their classmates in the units of study for the first grade. The customary first-grade activities such as using tools and art supplies gave them practice in eye-hand and motor coordination. The physical education periods also helped them to improve their visual-motor skills and motor coordination.

By the middle of November, as a result of this special small-group instruction, eleven of the seventeen children who had not been ready for reading had progressed to the average or superior level on the readiness test.

The remaining six were given more intensive instruction and practice in the abilities in which they were deficient—distinguishing various word sounds and recognizing rhyming sounds—*down, crown.* In all these activities they learned to listen: "If you don't listen, you'll not know what to do."

For these children, the first step in developing visual memory was to remember details about a picture they had looked at for only a few minutes. Then the teacher showed them how much more they could remember if they grouped related details, e.g., all the objects connected with cooking. The teacher also used pictures to give them practice in visual interpretation; she would ask, "What is happening in this picture? What do you think might happen next?" These exercises involved many skills that are required in reading. The children learned by recognizing contrasts—"which is different, and why"—as well as by recognizing similarities.

During the latter part of the first half of the year, the children had regular writing lessons. They learned all the letters of the alphabet and wrote words and simple sentences. At midyear only two of the original seventeen tested below average in readiness. For these two, the next step would be referral to a reading specialist or psychologist who would administer the Wechsler Intelligence Scale for Children (WISC) or the Illinois Test of

Psycholinguistic Abilities. A study of the subtests might indicate marked deficiencies in several of the mental abilities related to reading proficiency, which might be developed. In general, intelligence seems to be less important than auditory factors in beginning reading.

The teacher should give reading exercises only to pupils who need them. This statement, though seemingly obvious, gains support from a study of Groff [42]. He found that a group of second graders learned many words without formal instruction and repetition but needed much more drill, pleasingly varied, to master other words which they had unsuccessfully worked on before. In this crucial spiral of reading, the teacher should never assume that the child knows the words just because he has been exposed to the instruction of them.

Two brief studies of several first-grade children will illustrate the related factors involved in readiness. On entering school, Danny could identify some letters and write his name. His mental age was 7.4 and his Binet IQ 114. He was well developed physically and expressed himself well. The psychologist noted that he was most cooperative and interested. However, by first report time, he had not progressed as fast as expected. He seemed lost in the large group and was overanxious. He cried frequently. In a conference attended by all his teachers and the nurse, it was decided to place him in a smaller group where there was better classroom control. As he became more relaxed, he made progress in both reading and spelling.

Joanne was eager to learn and found school enjoyable. When she entered she could identify all the letters and some small words. She could write her name, could count to fifteen, and had a correct concept of addition and subtraction. She was a leader on whom the other children depended. She was already achieving at first-grade level in reading and arithmetic. However, at the end of the year her measured achievement was only average for the group; it represented very little additional learning. A less able child in the same grade, whose beginning scores were 0.0, gained 1.2 grades in reading during the year as compared with Joanne's gain of only 0.4.

Cases such as these point up the fact that it is just as important to recognize an individual child's readiness to read as it is to recognize another's lack of readiness; teachers must make sure that each child has a suitable progression of experiences.

BEGINNING READING METHODS

Assuming that the child has the prerequisites for beginning reading, where does the teaching of reading begin? It seems only reasonable to begin by teaching him to recognize words, phrases, and sentences in printed form that he hears people say—language units that are familiar and personally significant to him. This has been called the "organic," or more commonly, the "whole-word or sentence approach."

The sentence is the fundamental unit, the building block, of communication. Through sentences, thoughts come into existence. Sentences consist of basic meaning units—words and word parts—which are arranged in an infinite variety of patterns and orders to show their mutual relations. Understanding this syntax aspect of sentences is an important means of interpreting their meaning or message (see Chapter 3).

Children intuitively acquire "sentence sense"; they know when a sentence "sounds right" in their native language. Children from non-English-speaking homes may gain an understanding of English syntax by building sentences of their own. Starting with a kernel sentence consisting of a simple subject and a predicate block, they can expand and transform it in various ways [60].

In reading, pupils learn to recognize subject and predicate blocks and to identify the function of the different parts. One teacher asked the pupils to underline the parts of the sentence that told when, why, how, what, or where, e.g.:

The black dog belongs to Tom. (what)
Since Jane was ill, she could not go to the party. (why)
Bill went into the haunted house. (where)
Paul Revere rode at top speed. (how)

Transformational or generative grammar calls attention to the many ways in which a native speaker invents new sentences or interprets sentences written by others. Although a person thoroughly familiar with English may do this intuitively for simple sentences, he will be able to read complicated sentences more skillfully if he has "a clear, objective consciousness of the structural patterns themselves and their common transformations" [59, p. 654].

The "Whole-word" or Sentence Approach

The teacher brings a small group to the board. As she writes Billy's name on the board, she says, "This is the way the chalk says *Billy,* and this is the way it says *Betty.*" The children notice two ways in which the word *Billy* is different from the word *Betty.* The teacher moves her hand from left to right under each word as she pronounces it. The children do likewise as they go to the board and distinguish one word from another. Then she gives each child an eraser and asks them to erase the word *Billy,* but not *Betty,* each time she writes it. Soon they are able to identify these words wherever they see them—on cards, on their drawings, and in sentences that the teacher writes and reads to them:

Billy is a boy.
Betty is a girl.
Is Billy a boy?
Is Betty a girl?
Is Billy a girl?
Is Betty a boy?

Other words are learned in the same way—the names of other children and of familiar objects, action words such as *jump, run, sit, stand up*. As the words are learned, they are immediately read in sentences. Some of the words will illustrate the commonest sounds, like *cat, hat, bat, hot,* etc. Others will be what linguists call *structure words*—words that are needed to build sentences. Exciting words that the children especially want to learn—*jet, rocket, ghost,* etc.—will also be included. Very soon the children make the discovery that certain sounds represent certain letters.

Some opponents of the whole-word or sentence approach prefer to emphasize the perception and recognition of details rather than of whole words. Diack [21], for example, views letters and their sounds as the basic elements of word recognition. He even excludes other clues to recognition and meaning.

It is psychologically sound to emphasize the combination of parts in the whole, of "figure on ground," of sequence of letters in the word. The teacher properly intones the word and directs the children's attention to the sequence and distinguishing features of its letters. This method combines the basic elements of written and spoken language.

The children dictate sentences to the teacher about their experiences. She writes what they dictate on the board or on a chart. This method of using the child's own stories as beginning reading material has been used for a long time. It has recently been elaborated into "the language-experience approach" [58]. It has the advantage of being based on the child's own spoken language, thus capitalizing on his immediate interests. By slightly modifying the children's accounts, but without changing their natural vocabulary or sentence patterns, the teacher can secure frequent repetition of certain words and sound-letter associations. The child learns to read the little stories or anecdotes that he and his classmates have dictated or have written themselves. As he reads the language of the experience stories, he becomes more and more acquainted with common words and sentence patterns. As he extends his experience, he extends his vocabulary. He may begin to perceive that literature is the reflection of the writer's experience.

On the other hand, children may lose confidence in their ability to read if they do not learn the words that make up the experience stories or do not discover how to read them by using word attack skills. Moreover, the reading of experience charts that use only the children's language may be continued too long. Children often find their own "stories" less interesting than the stories in books and may eventually consider them not really stories; they may not be so well written.

Linguistic Methods

Linguistics deals with the ways in which words are formed—how phonemes are arranged into morphemes and how morphemes are arranged into larger syntactical patterns.

Each linguist advocates somewhat different methods of teaching [7, 8, 14, 40, 47, 100, 103]. (See Chapter 3.) They all consider the spoken word primary. Reading is secondary. They teach the child to respond to the visual pattern as fully as he responds to the auditory pattern. Having acquired this basic ability, the reader is free to concentrate on meaning, on appreciation of literature, and on critical and reflective reading.

Gibson and her coworkers [39] seem to have fused the phonemic and the structural aspects of linguistics. Like Lefevre [61], they begin reading instruction with sentences. Like Bloomfield and Barnhart [7] and Fries [32] they control the phoneme-grapheme learning. They avoid initial confusion by beginning with words that can be spelled with only seven letters (*a, h, i, m, n, s,* and *t*) and introducing other letters at widely spaced intervals. They also separate letters that have similar configurations, such as *b* and *d, g* and *p, o* and *c,* and introduce them one at a time.

If sentences are presented in sequence, each prepares for the next and is confirmed or reinforced by those that follow, thus reducing the opportunities for misinterpretation. The confidence and satisfaction that the child derives from his success encourages him to continue reading. "Given a vocabulary which is an instrument rather than a load, 'high utility vocabulary,' and a range of sentence structures that can be operated with safety, elementary science, elementary history and geography, and even elementary humanities can come into their own" [86, p. 99]. In this kind of learning situation, reading contributes to writing and spelling.

When reading instruction included linguistics too, reading improved. Spending twenty-five minutes a day on linguistics with first-grade children, in addition to basal reader instruction, was significantly more effective than spending the same amount of additional time on the basal reader alone [16]. Linguistic instruction used both worksheets and chalkboard to illustrate discussion of the alphabet system of writing, structural patterns, and methods of word recognition that applied phonemic-graphemic analysis. On the fourth-grade level, a modified linguistic program also seemed to be more effective in schools that were using this approach than a "composite" basal program that was used in other schools [68]. However, factors other than the linguistic approach may have affected these results: the experimental schools may have placed more emphasis on auditory and visual perception; their teachers may have had a better understanding of the goals; there may have been more reading materials.

The Teaching of Word Recognition Skills

You remember the old tale of the lost horseshoe nail: "Because of the nail, the shoe was lost; because of the shoe, the horse was lost; because of the horse, the rider was lost; because of the rider, the battle was lost—and all for the loss of a horseshoe nail."

Word recognition skills are somewhat like the horseshoe nail. If a pupil loses out on this basic instruction, he is deficient in word recognition ability; if he lacks word recognition skills, he does not get the meaning of unfamiliar words. If he cannot recognize the words, he cannot get the meaning of sentences, and he cannot comprehend what the author says. If he cannot comprehend the author's literal meaning, he cannot reach higher levels of interpretation, or make inferences and generalizations, or draw conclusions, or do critical reading, or appreciate and apply what he reads. Thus all is lost if he has not acquired basic word recognition skills.

These skills include identifying whole words by shape and sequence of letters, phonics, structural analysis, getting clues to meaning from the context, and the use of the dictionary. The efficient reader uses all of these skills rather than depending on a single skill. When he comes to an unfamiliar word, he may first try to infer what it is by the way it is used in the sentence. He may then check his inference by using phonics or structural analysis. To be sure of its meaning and pronunciation, he may well look it up in the dictionary. Instead of beginning with context clues he may first try to pronounce the word to see whether it makes sense in the sentence. The following are some suggestions for teaching word recognition skills.

Configuration. In the beginning, children recognize a word that they want to know by its shape, the sequence of its letters, and some other distinguishing feature. The teacher may call their attention to a word's contour by drawing a line around it:

She writes the word while the children watch carefully; thus they become aware of the sequence of the letters. She may call attention to the curves and downstrokes of the letters. By pronouncing the word and discussing or illustrating its meaning, the teacher reinforces the children's ability to recognize it.

Phonics. The many phonics systems now on the market (see Chapter 3) indicate the extent to which phonics is now being emphasized. According to surveys, phonics is being taught in 99 per cent of the schools. However, school programs vary widely as to the age or stage of development at which phonics is introduced, the sequence of phonics instruction, and the amount of time spent on phonics. Some of the controversial issues regarding the teaching of phonics are discussed in Chapter 3. Basal readers and the teachers guides accompanying them introduce phonics earlier now than previously. There may be as much danger in overemphasizing phonics as in neglecting it.

The learning of phonics may be made easier by limiting the child's first experience to words that have consistent sound-letter associations; thus he is not discouraged by finding that the association he has just learned does not apply to other words.

There is a sound neurological reason for minimizing complexity and confusion in beginning reading instruction. The area of the brain that stimulates mental activity—the reticular formation—is susceptible to tension if it is overstimulated by too many possible responses as in trial-and-error learning. Simplifying early learning experiences by controlling vocabulary, sentence patterns, and sound-symbol associations reduces "cognitive strain" and releases mental energy. When teachers criticize certain primers for being dull because their vocabulary is controlled, they should weigh the advantage of eliminating confusion against the advantage of offering more interesting and complex content. Piaget found that some children enjoy learning about language—that beginning reading has intrinsic interest for them.

There are two principal ways of reducing the confusion caused by our irregular English spellings. One is to augment the alphabet so that there will be a single sound for each letter (see Chapter 3). The other is to introduce only consistent sound-letter associations at first and then gradually teach irregularities.

Structural Analysis. From single sound-letter associations, clusters of letters, and common syllables, the student moves in the direction of identifying prefixes, suffixes, and other parts of compound words. In their reading, students may find compound words like *knapsack*. The teacher writes on the chalkboard the sentence in which the word occurs and says: "A compound word is made up of two small words. Do you know the last part of this compound word?" A student may say, "A sack is a kind of bag." They will not know *knap*, although someone may venture "sleeping bag." A student with a German background may know that *knap* refers to eating—knapsack, eating bag. Having learned the meaning from the discussion or by looking it up in the dictionary, they will use the word in a sentence. ("The soldier carried his knapsack—eating bag—over his shoulder.")

To obtain a quick survey of the students' ability to divide a word into syllables, give them words that illustrate seven types of syllable division—for example, a list containing *support, lecture, labor, grimly, bugle, drugstore,* and *orchard*. Each of these words has two sounded parts or syllables. The students draw a line between the two syllables in each word. *Sup-port* illustrates division between double consonants. *Lec-ture* represents division between two different consonants whose independent sounds are retained (unlike *ch, th, sh ph*). *La-bor* illustrates division before a single consonant; *grim-ly,* division between the root and the suffix; *bu-gle,* division before a consonant and the *le* ending (as in *peo-ple, lit-tle*); *drug-store,* division between the small words in a compound word; and *or-chard,* division between two consonants, one of whose original sounds are altered by its associations. Several words of each type should be listed so that a teacher can determine whether a student is successful because of understanding or luck in guessing.

Some students will do well on this test and some will do poorly. Those who do poorly should be given additional practice. The rules governing compounds and suffixed or prefixed words are probably the easiest; next in difficulty are the double-consonant words (*let-ter*). In each case the students should derive the rule for themselves by observing how the dictionary divides words that have like patterns. By making a study of words, the students can prove to themselves that the exceptions, though numerous, do not invalidate the rules.

It should be noted that some experts question the efficacy of teaching rules for syllabication. Does knowledge of syllabication rules markedly influence success in applying phonics principles or in actual syllabication [99]?

As the pupil learns to know on sight several words that illustrate a certain structural or phonetic principle (*ex*port, *im*port, *re*ported, *port*able; *sch*ool, *sch*ooner, *sch*eme, and *Sch*enectady), the teacher uses his knowledge of these words to elicit the principle. "Who can think of a word that has the same common part in it as *porter, important, report?*" When the pupils show by their suggestions that they *hear the sound,* the teacher writes their suggestions on the blackboard in a list. Then he asks, "What do you notice that is alike in all of these words?" A pupil underlines the common part, *port,* in each word. "Let's pronounce the words again in unison and listen for the common part: *export, import, reported, portable.* Now I shall write a sentence using a word that is built like these. See whether you can read the sentence, and be ready to tell how you knew the identity of the word." The teacher writes, "The news reporter wrote the story." The pupils know all of the words in the sentence except *reporter*. They explain that they recognize it because of the context (somebody who writes stories for news) and because of structure (common prefix, *re-;* common suffix, *-er;* and root, *port,* as in *export, import, reported,* and *portable*).

This kind of presentation works because the teacher takes his cues from the pupils. He knows they know the words on sight; he makes sure they hear the likeness in the words; he then makes sure they see the likeness and gets them to say what is alike in all; and then he has them prove that they can use their new learning in solving a new word. The pupils themselves make the discoveries and show by each discovery that they are ready for the next step. This is quite different from showing the pupil the common element by underlining it or printing it in a different color of ink or chalk. In this latter case the discovery is the printer's, and there is no assurance that the pupil will be able to see this part as an entity when the printer stops presenting it in a special color.

An understanding of the structural parts often reveals the meaning of a word. The meaning of *autograph* becomes clear if the parts are known: *auto*, relating to self, and *graph*, write. *Subterranean* is identified by the prefix *sub* and the root *terra*, meaning earth. It is easy to define *bacteriology* if one is familiar with *bacteria* and the suffix *ology*, meaning "science or knowledge of."

When a group of able high school students came upon the then unfamiliar word *astronaut* in the title of a magazine article, the following discussion took place:

Teacher: Is there any clue as to the meaning of this word? Look for clues in the sentence in which it is used.

Student: *Astro* pertains to stars.

Teacher: (writing sentence on the board) The astronaut *lived* on a *space* diet. (As students recognized clue words, the teacher underlined them. They are shown here in italics.) He was *trained* to *ride* in a space missile. What other words begin with *astro*?

Student: Astronomy.

Teacher: Do you know any words that begin with *naut*?

Student: Nautical, nautilus.

Teacher: How does this part of the word help you to get its meaning?

Student: An astronaut is one who travels by air.

Context Clues. In giving reports, students often reveal their ignorance of the meaning of a key word. The teacher's first, and honest, reaction is probably one of vexation: "If you didn't know the word, why didn't you look it up? If I've told this class once, I've told it a hundred times . . . !" The teacher may try suppressing this first reaction and use instead the following procedure to teach students the use of context clues:

Suppose tomorrow you each bring in a sentence from a newspaper, a magazine, or a book—a sentence that contains a word you don't know. Write the sentence on our regular theme paper. In the space where the hard word is, put a straight line like this: "Under _____ cover I am sending you a copy of *The Four Million*, a report for the New York State Citizens' Committee for Children and Youth."

Immediately some students will suggest *separate*. The teacher may say, "Yes, that was an easy one, wasn't it? How did you know that it should be *separate?*" They will say that it is a common expression in business letters. "Yes, and there are many other types of clues, too, that we can learn about. After you have written your sentence, write the hard word and the dictionary meaning which best fits its use in the sentence on a separate page. If all of you do this, tomorrow we can have an experiment to find out a few things about guessing or inferring word meanings."

The following day the students will pass their sentences around the room, and each student will try to infer the meaning of the missing word. After all the words have been inserted, each student in turn discloses the word that was originally used in his sentence. To be correct a word need not be the same one found in the original sentence as long as it means the same thing. Inferring the meaning of a word from its context is a form of inter-active thinking. Although one may always consult the dictionary to find the best meaning, ability to draw accurate inferences is a time-saver.

The next step is to make the students aware of the various types of context clues—the many hints to word meaning that lie within the sentence. In their sentences they will find at least seven types of context clues.

1. *Direct explanation.* The unknown word is explained in the sentence.
   To talk aimlessly in a rambling way about the weather, the war, your new dress, the class play is to carry on a *desultory* conversation.
   In Roman times a member of the nobility was called a *patrician.*
2. *Experience.* The meaning of the unknown word can be supplied by something in the student's life-experience.
   At Thanksgiving and Christmas *indigent* families are fed by the Salvation Army.
   An exploding skyrocket set fire to a crowded dance hall and fourteen persons were *injured.*
3. *Comparison and contrast.* The unknown word has a meaning that is opposite to that of a known word.
   They were as different as day and night. He was highly excitable but but she was *phlegmatic.*
   Ed was talkative while Bill remained *taciturn.*
4. *Synonym or restatement.*
   "Give me excess of it, that *surfeiting*, the appetite may sicken and so die."
   The *sorcerer,* a wizard of great reputation for villainy, gazed scornfully at his victim.
5. *Familiar expression or language experience.* The student can decipher the word by drawing on his acquaintance with everyday expressions and common language patterns.

The drowning man was carried to the beach, where he was given artificial *respiration*.

6. *Summary.* The unknown word summarizes the ideas that precede or follow it.

The stories invented from bits and scraps of gossip soon developed into a "whispering campaign" and an innocent student became the victim of *calumny*.

At the age of eighty-five the king was still playing a skillful game of tennis. He seldom missed his daily swim. For a man of his age he was very *robust*.

7. *Reflection of a mood or situation.* The unknown word fits a situation or a mood that has already been established.

The *lugubrious* wails of the gypsies matched the dreary whistling of of the wind in the deserted woods.

As she said goodnight after the prom, the boy she cared for most asked her to wear his fraternity pin. Her joy was *ineffable*.

These examples only suggest several types of clues that may be discovered in a study of the language. Students will find new types. They will also find that a sentence often contains more than one type of clue. Sometimes the context provides no clues to the meaning of a word. In these instances guessing is usually less rewarding than using the dictionary.

A committee of students can present several sentences to the class, all of which illustrate a certain type of clue. The other students will supply the appropriate meanings and name the type of clue given. Five-minute presentations by committees or individuals at the beginning of class periods may make good use of time otherwise lost in waiting for the teacher to take attendance or attend to small desk chores.

Use of the Dictionary [22]. Knowing how to use the dictionary to learn correct pronunciations has several values for the student. It is a way of becoming a better reader. With the help of the dictionary, the student can recognize the printed forms of words that he has heard many times; he will also add new words to his vocabulary. Being sure of the correct way to pronounce words also prevents the embarrassment of mispronunciation in talking or reading aloud.

The student must first become familiar with the complete pronunciation key and learn the key words that show what diacritical marks mean. From these he can become familiar with the ways each vowel and consonant is pronounced.

Second, he will learn to use the primary and secondary accent marks. In studying a new word he will divide it into syllables, place the accent marks after the proper syllables, and pronounce the words to himself with just the right stress on each syllable. He will learn the correct placement of the accent in words that are commonly mispronounced, such as *explicit, preferable, robust, illustrative, gondola, exquisite.*

An Illustration of Beginning Reading Methods. The following description shows some of the ways in which one teacher, over a period of time, taught phonics and related word recognition skills to an ungraded primary class.

In teaching the spelling pattern *pr,* the teacher first wrote the key word *prize* on the chalkboard and asked the children if they could read it. They looked carefully at the first two letters while they listened to the *pr* sound.

Next the teacher wrote other words that began with different letters. When she wrote one that began with *pr,* they clapped their hands. The children enjoyed this game and made few mistakes. If they made a mistake, the teacher helped them to correct their misconception by analyzing the word with them. This exercise helped them to discriminate quickly between similar word beginnings and to associate the sound with the written symbol. When they had learned a number of words beginning with *pr,* the children made "silly sentences" using only words that began with this sound: "The pretty, proud princess promised the prince a prize pretzel."

The second game gave additional practice in the same sound-spelling pattern and also emphasized the meaning of words in context. The game consisted of riddles, the answers to which were words beginning with *pr:*

Mother buys these at the store. They are dry and wrinkled before they are cooked. (prunes)

I'm thinking of a word that tells how father feels when you do well in school. (proud)

The third exercise tied the games together by applying their teachings to a sentence which the pupil read: "Tommy said he could *prove* he did not do it."

The children first found and read the word beginning with *pr* and then read the whole sentence. Other sound-spelling patterns were taught in the same thorough way. To reinforce their knowledge of the meaning of an unfamiliar word, the teacher asked the children to dramatize it. For example, the word *crouched* was used in teaching the *cr* pattern in the sentence, "He crouched behind the big rock." To show what the word meant, the children crouched down behind their chairs.

To show how changing a single letter changes meaning and also to acquaint the children with common clusters of letters, the teacher changed a key word like *made* by substituting different initial letters: *fade, shade, grade,* etc. The children read the words and used them appropriately in sentences. If a child did not use a word correctly, the teacher called for further discussion of its meaning. Endings were similarly changed:

seen changed to
seem

seed
feed
need

Children found it very rewarding to learn the sound-symbol associations of clusters of letters and of common syllables. When the children knew the word *name* and several beginning consonants, they could read *same, fame, game, lame*. The teacher introduced other familiar words and changed their initial consonant sounds. To make sure that the children knew the meaning of each word, she illustrated it and sometimes asked them to name its opposite: "What is the opposite of *tame?*" To which one bright youngster replied, "Ferocious." She asked them to make sentences using each word, and finally, to read the words they had just learned in a simple story.

The children soon discovered that if they could recognize common syllables such as *ing*, they could spell and read many words, e.g. *singing, bringing*.

Teaching by contrast is effective. For example, the final silent *e:*

fat—fate
hat—hate

Double *e* can be contrasted with single *e:*

red—reed
met—meet

Ai can be contrasted with *a:*

pad—paid
plan—plain

The combination *ou* can be taught in contrast to the short *o:*

shot—shout
bond—bound

For many more examples of common spelling patterns, see Jean S. Hanna and Paul R. Hanna, *Phoneme-Grapheme Relationships,* Stanford University.

One is not limited to using key words to illustrate vowel sounds; key sentences are also effective:

Rāy is my nāme.
Pēte likes to ēat.
Mīke rode his bīke.
Jōe is slōw.

Păt sat on a tăck.
Těd is in his běd.
Sĭd hĭd.

The children obtained more practice in the letter and word discrimination that is involved in analyzing the beginnings and endings of words by supplying missing words that began and ended with certain letters, for example: "In this sentence the missing word begins with *p* and ends with *l:* I am going to swim in the ————." The children had a choice of *pond, lake, pile, pool.* They chose the correct word and then gave their reasons for not choosing the other words:

Teacher: Why wasn't it *lake?*
Pupil: Because it doesn't begin with *p.*
Teacher: Why wasn't it *pond?*
Pupil: Because it doesn't end in *l.*
Teacher: Why wasn't it *pile?* That begins with *p.*
Pupil: Because it doesn't make sense.

The exercise puts a premium on one kind of thinking.

The teacher also made the pupils aware of the methods they were using. She asked questions like these:

What do these syllables have in common?
Why isn't the word ————?
What clues to the meaning of *anxiety* did you get from the paragraph?

These exercises offered opportunities for multiple learnings. Oral expression, phonics, vocabulary, sentence structure, and reasoning were all woven into a thoroughly enjoyable experience.

The approach just described is entirely different from the mechanical drill featured in some phonic systems. This one represents a combination of phonics with other techniques.

With older pupils who are deficient in word analysis skills, the phonovisual charts may be presented as a review to discover which sound-letter associations they already know. The methods already described can be modified in teaching phonics to junior high school pupils. Since boys and girls of this age are usually resentful of what they consider "baby stuff," the teacher treats them as mature persons. He associates phonics with their interests. He uses words that appeal to them. For example in helping them to identify *st,* one teacher used such words as *shortstop, first, steep.* In helping them to discriminate words that are similar in form, he used these words with appropriate questions:

dent	scare
dash	score
date	scar

Which of these means "to go very fast"?
Which one is likely to happen to a car fender if you bump into something?

Which is something a girl has with her boyfriend?
Which one means "to frighten"?
Which is something left after a cut is healed?
Which tells the number of points in a game?

Older students who make careless errors in discriminating may be helped to look more carefully at unfamiliar words and to check their meanings against the context clues. Exercises such as the following are useful for this purpose. The student selects the word that is appropriate in the sentence:

relived
David relieved in imagination his experience on the sea.
reprieved

congregation
The concatenation spread to neighboring houses, reducing them to ashes in less *conflagration*
than four hours.

inventive
The boy was *attentive* to the lecture.
retentive

revealed
The doctor reviled the boy who had been rescued from drowning.
revived

conceived
He carefully *concealed* the money under his pillow.
congealed

instruction
The boy profited by the construction given by the teacher.
destruction

An occasional junior or senior high school student will prove to be woefully deficient in word analysis. He will not know the first thing about sounding out words. Like a beginner, he must first be trained to *hear* the sound of the unfamiliar vowel or consonant. He must be able to note a likeness in the words *box, bag, bend,* and *bat.* When he has proved that he can do this by picking out the word that has a different beginning sound in the spoken list *box, ditch, bend,* and *bat,* the *b* list should be written in a column on the chalkboard for him to observe visually. "What do you notice about the sound of these words?" (They begin alike in sound.) "What do you notice about the way they look?" (They all begin with the same letter.) "What does that suggest about other words beginning with that letter?" (They will usually begin with the same sound.) The student keeps a notebook in which he lists sets of new words that begin with the same letter.

Sometimes such a student will meet a word that combines two familiar sound-letter associations. He may know the sound of *st* in *stop* and *start* and the sound of *ifle* in *rifle*. He meets the word *stifle*. In helping him with this word, the teacher may write *stop, start,* and *rifle* under *stifle* and have the student notice that the strange word begins like *stop* and *start* and ends like *rifle*. If he needs more assistance, the teacher can cover the *r* of *rifle* and have the student pronounce *ifle* alone and then add the initial consonant blend of *stop* and *start*.

By systematically using the techniques he knows, such a student finds the necessary confidence: (1) Do I see a beginning that I know? (2) Do I see a large middle part that I know? (3) Do I recognize the ending? (4) When I put these together, does the resultant word make sense in the sentence in which I found it?

Older retarded readers usually prefer to practice on common syllables and clusters of letters rather than on individual letter-sound associations. Practice on letter clusters is actually more effective because the correspondence between written and spoken English is greater with the larger units than with single letters.

Beginners of various ages have found these procedures stimulating. They experience success because the tasks are not too difficult for them to perform.

Word analysis is not an end in itself. Since it is only a means to more efficient reading, it should be presented as secondary and supportive to other reading activities. As to the student's motivation for learning word analysis skills, he should recognize that they constitute a method of getting the meaning of unfamiliar words in selections that he wants or needs to read. Accordingly, the teacher begins instruction with material of the kind just described. When the students meet an unfamiliar word, the teacher helps them to go through a systematic process of word recognition, using context clues, phonics, structural analysis, and the dictionary as necessary. This review will not embarrass older students if they recognize that, as Einstein said, "reading is the most complex task that man ever devised for himself."

In the primary grades oral reading is a natural way of making the transition from speaking to reading. It also provides the teacher with an indispensable tool for diagnosing difficulties in word recognition. By hearing a child read aloud, the teacher can find out how he attacks words—whether he mispronounces, inserts, or omits words, substitutes one word for another, or reads in a monotonous, halting way. If he substitutes words that make sense in the sentence, the teacher has reason to be glad that the pupil is apparently reading for meaning, though he may be using context clues to the exclusion of other word attack skills.

Incidentally, oral reading can be carried too far. Round-the-room or circle reading bores or frustrates the competent readers who want to read ahead;

it embarrasses the slow, halting readers; and it encourages the imitation of poor reading models. At every educational level the pupil reads the story or paragraph silently before he reads it orally for listeners to enjoy.

There should be purpose for silent reading, varied to spark the child's interest. Sometimes it is the title, "Let's read to find out why the story was called ———." Sometimes it is the background development: "Let's read to see what ——— found out about the different jobs in the radio station." Sometimes it is the teacher's own knowledge of the values in the story: "Let's read this to see how we might make it into a play for tape recording." If teachers fail to state these varied purposes, the pupils may fail to alter their reading techniques accordingly. With older pupils, teachers guide them to define their purposes and discuss how to achieve them.

Basal Reader Approach. Research shows that a combination of methods has an advantage over any single method. Actually, 95 per cent of the teachers in the first three grades and 88 per cent in the middle grades use single or multiple basal readers with their eclectic methods of teaching [89, p. 56].

Many basal readers are building individualized reading into their systematic program of reading instruction. The companies that issue them not only suggest related materials and ideas in their teachers guides but also publish supplementary reading material. For example, Ginn and Company provides *The Enrichment Readers* to accompany its basal readers. Scott, Foresman's series, *The Wide Horizons* readers, have the same content written two years above the stated grade level for the better readers, and other books written two years below grade level for the slow readers.

When the basal reader program adds phonic or linguistic instruction, the results are usually better than those obtained with the reader alone [69]. When such basal texts or a wealth of multilevel materials are available, there is less need for so-called homogeneous grouping.

One problem about the basal reader which the teacher must consider is the lavish use of pictures as additional clues to the meaning of the stories. The controversy is still going on as to whether these illustrations help or harm the child's reading progress. The pictures do add interest and arouse the curiosity of the child and his subsequent inquiries as to what the words beneath them say. But frequently the illustrations detract from the reading, moving the child to focus on the pictures rather than on the words. They also may lead the child to guess the meaning of the words or the words themselves. Because of these considerations, some linguistics series such as Bloomfield and Barnhart's *Let's Read* series (Bronxville, New York, 1963) use no illustrations. But King and Muehl [54] found that pictures provide additional helps to visual and auditory discrimination.

The large majority of teachers depend upon the basal reader in teaching children to read [46]. The more poorly prepared the teachers are for this major responsibility, the more they need the basal reader and its accompanying guide. Justifiably, they turn for help to the basal series written by specialists who see the total reading program in perspective.

In their teachers guides authors suggest ways in which the teacher can appraise her pupils' reading status and measure their progress. They give lists of appropriate supplementary materials and describe a variety of teaching techniques to provide for individual difficulties. They furnish guidelines to the teaching of reading in the content fields. Almost from the beginning they advocate free reading in addition to the basal text. To provide the extra practice needed by slower learners, the authors of basal series have prepared workbooks.

Most of the criticism of workbooks is actually aimed at their misuse. For pupils who need additional practice in certain reading skills, workbooks can be helpful. Too often, however, they are overused and become busywork rather than a source of reinforcement. The large majority of teachers depend upon workbooks to follow up the basal reader lessons. They do not have time to prepare practice material themselves. The best workbooks discourage mechanical responses by requiring thinking in each exercise.

Black and Whitehouse [5], in an experimental study of the effectiveness of workbooks, found that teacher-prepared materials were more effective in grade 1 than commercially prepared workbooks. In grades 2, 3, and 4, however, pupils who used reading workbooks made greater growth in reading than did pupils who did not use workbooks. In grades 5 and 6, there was no significant difference between the pupils who used workbooks and those who did not.

Ideally, the content of the first books in a basal reader series would consist for the most part of dialogue. The sentence patterns would be those children use most frequently in their natural speech. The vocabulary would be limited to words that have consistent sound-letter associations, introducing only one new element at a time, which would be repeated frequently. Simple sentences using the controlled vocabulary would have ideas of high interest level for the pupils. Wisely and creatively used, the basal reader may serve as the core of the reading program but not its entire content.

THE TEACHING OF VOCABULARY

A student's vocabulary has several divisions. The first is his *recognition vocabulary*—the words of which he has a general understanding as they are used in context. The second is his *recall vocabulary*—the words for which he can distinguish the correct synonym or definition from among four items or for which he can write a definition.

The third division includes words for which he knows both *derivations* and *multiple meanings,* and the fourth comprises words for which he can give a deeper *semantic interpretation* in a given context. Skillful teachers often start vocabulary work by analyzing cartoons and headlines and move gradually to the more subtle figurative language of poetry. They are ready to stop at any point in a class discussion to study the deeper meaning of a word or phrase in context.

There are a number of controversies about the methods of teaching vocabulary—incidental versus direct or systematic teaching; prereading of words versus application of word recognition skills as needed; study of roots, prefixes, and suffixes versus other kinds of structural analysis. As usual, it should not be either-or; each system is helpful to certain students at certain times. Studies show that the average student in grades 9 and 11 is able to recall and write only 45 per cent of all the words he is able to recognize.

Relation of Vocabulary to Other Factors

In its relation to reading and intelligence, vocabulary knowledge has been found to be second only to reasoning. In factor analysis, word knowledge or verbal ability usually turns out to have the greatest weighting. The correlation between vocabulary and intelligence scores is so high that one might almost substitute vocabulary tests for intelligence tests.

The student's speech and listening comprehension are related to his vocabulary. Pupils often make errors in word meaning because of the auditory similarity of two words. One sixth-grade pupil defined *optimist* as meaning "stubborn," confusing it with *obstinate. Pact* he defined as "close together," because he heard it as *packed.* Another pupil said, "A bicycle is a *vertical;* you ride in it." He was confusing the test word *vertical* with *vehicle.* Bilingual pupils, especially, find it easier to read selections that they have first learned to speak correctly. Linguists have put major emphasis on correct intonation, stress, phrasing, and pauses as prerequisites to comprehension. Except in the case of poor readers, a pupil's reading vocabulary exceeds his listening vocabulary.

Tests show that a year of speech training improves the articulation and word recognition of first- and second-grade children but does not improve their comprehension. Educators do not know whether children can and do learn the accent generalizations well enough to make effective use of them in identifying unknown words. If they do not, then the value of teaching these generalizations can be seriously questioned.

Vocabulary is important in all the language arts. With the mature reader, the largest vocabulary is the reading vocabulary; next largest is the listening vocabulary; the writing and speaking vocabularies are smaller. Growth occurs as the student keeps perceiving how and why words are related.

Vocabulary Size and Frequency of Certain Types of Words

Various investigators have reported size of vocabularies and frequency of occurrence of words. Extreme variations in the sizes of the vocabularies of both children and adults have been reported. Much of this variation has been due to differences in the methods used to obtain the data. Lorge and Chall [62] thought that recent estimates of the vocabularies of grade school children were too high.

"Easy" words are not always those that occur most frequently. The semantic variety of many common syllabic words such as *strike, bank, post* may confuse their meanings for children in grades 4, 5, and 6. Readability formulas that equate "easy" with frequent may be quite misleading [49].

Principles That Apply to Vocabulary

Students should be aware of certain guiding principles that apply to vocabulary:

1. A word is not an object; it is a symbol for an object.
2. Words that are pronounced the same may have entirely different meanings, e.g.:

   bear—to carry, to give birth

   bear—an animal

   bare—naked
3. Words have multiple meanings, e.g., *run:*

   I *run* to school every morning.

   I have a *run* in my stocking.

   My uncles *run* a store.

   The unabridged Oxford dictionary gives more than 200 meanings for some words.
4. Words may have both literal and figurative meaning, e.g.:

   Go *home*, Fido.

   The *home* plate.

   "*Home* is the sailor, home from the sea,

   And the hunter home from the hill."
5. Words may change their meaning over the centuries. *Nice* used to mean "precise" or "fussy" and still does in some instances. Some words that started out with favorable or neutral connotations have acquired unfavorable ones: secret agent, informer, stool pigeon, inhibition, vulgar.
6. Words take their exact meanings from the context in which they are used. The dictionary defines only certain limits within which a word may range. The situation in which the word is used, the other words used with it, and the ends in view all affect its meaning.

7. Vocabulary, morphology (understanding of structural units), and syntax (grammatical relationship of sentence parts) are "the big three" of reading comprehension.
8. Words move to action; they are switches that turn on certain habit patterns. Words may certainly help or hinder a person's adjustment.
9. Rich vocabularies are the fruit of much firsthand or vicarious experience. A precise vocabulary is the product of a keen interest in words as symbols on the part of an intelligent individual.
10. Abstract words are generally the most difficult.
11. Long words are often difficult, but the best indication of the difficulty of a word is its degree of concreteness and its familiarity in colloquial use, not its relative length.

How Vocabulary Knowledge Develops

The most important means of vocabulary development is wide reading. This is at once the most painless and the most rewarding way of building one's vocabulary. In wide reading the student not only meets many new words in different fields but also becomes familiar with their different meanings in a variety of contexts. Through wide reading students also come to recognize the appropriateness of different forms of expression in different situations. The conversations of fictional characters show the student which words and expressions certain social groups use, which are "accepted in educated circles." In reading widely the student learns to tolerate a certain vagueness of meaning when he first encounters a new word. As he keeps meeting it he uses syntactical criteria for excluding certain meanings and clarifies its actual meaning by noting its context.

But frequently in wide reading students may encounter some words that they need to know, especially the technical vocabulary in the various fields of study. Lists are useful for suggesting important words, but students should not study vocabulary in isolated lists apart from context.

A vocabulary grows as a student becomes interested in words through such activities as the study of origins of picturesque words and the history of words. To know that the word *salary* came from the Latin word for *salt* because this commodity was the pay of Roman soldiers makes this word memorable. Primitive peoples had a word for the saber-toothed tiger—*Boola-boola!* Naturally this expression came to mean also "Scram," "Run for your life." Thus the word describes both a situation and an animal. Because of interest in semantic change, some pupils find the dictionary fascinating; it becomes their favorite book.

A study of the nature of words and of their behavior in selected passages would give insights into the meaning of the printed page that definitions alone cannot give. To get his students to take more interest in words, one teacher played the overture of an opera over and over while the students wrote on the board all the words the music suggested to them. After doing this, one boy said, "I never wanted to hear that overture again, but that was the day words became fascinating to me."

Some teachers have created an interest in words by having their pupils make picture dictionaries in which they paste or draw pictures illustrating words they have met in their reading. A class dictionary with each page signed by the student who made it is often the most popular book in the classroom library.

In the primary grades, children begin their vocabulary building and orientation of meaning to words with the experience charts. They make an excursion to the park and return to discuss their trip. "Let's write a story about going to the park. What shall we call it? 'Our Trip to the Park.'" The children watch the teacher write this title and the story that they dictate.

That night he prints this story on a large chart and the next morning appears with it. The children reread the chart with comprehension clues from the teacher: "What did we call our story of our trip to the park? Where does our first sentence say we went? What did we see? What was the squirrel doing?"

Children who are ready to read will be able to identify these sentences out of their regular order, sentences printed on strips of tagboard and set along the chalk tray or in a pocket chart. They will be able to match the sentences on the strips with sentences on the chart by holding the strip below the sentence on the chart and reading aloud. They will be able to break the sentences into phrases when the strips are cut into phrase parts and held under the sentences on the chart for matching and reading aloud.

Our Trip	to the Park.
We went	to the park.
We saw	a squirrel.
He was eating	nuts.

Someone will be able to say, "Two of those sentences begin alike." The teacher says, "Let's read those two sentences and listen carefully to hear what that like part is: *We* went to the park. *We* saw a squirrel. It's *We*. Find it and read it for us."

The elementary teacher recognizes that vocabulary grows best through experience when he introduces the word *circus* and asks, "How many of you have ever been to a circus? Would you tell us what the circus was like, Johnny?" Thus the teacher simultaneously builds the background for reading a new story and presents the new vocabulary. A quick drawing on the chalkboard, maps, charts, filmstrips, motion pictures, and recordings; interviews, dramatic presentations, demonstrations, and excursions are ways of laying the groundwork for meaningful reading.

It is equally important for the teacher to draw upon pupil backgrounds: "How many of you have visited a radio station? What was it like? What kind of jobs did the employees have? Well, this is a story about a boy who applied for a job in a radio station." In this manner the setting and the human problem are given reality, and the pupils are more interested because they find that the story touches their own lives in some way. Already this is a far cry from "Turn to page 97 in the pale green book and read the next story," or "Look at the chalkboard for the next assignment."

While the teacher draws out the answers to questions and has pupils relate their own backgrounds to the story, he writes on the chalkboard the words the pupils use which are going to be the new words in the story. It is important that the teacher write on the chalkboard so that the writing is in full view of the pupils, pronouncing the word slowly as he writes it. "The speakers in the studio use a microphone" (writing *mi-cro-phone*, or, preferably, writing a short phrase using the word). "Let's all say it together, mi-cro-phone." Thus, they have a multisensory experience—seeing, hearing, and saying simultaneously. They are conscious of the meaning of the word as they view it, and they see the word *in habitat* so that the eye is doing the same kind of job it will do when it meets the word in the story itself. They also become aware, as one boy said, that "big words can be understood little by little"—by dividing them into syllables.

After introducing the new words in context, some teachers review them by asking comprehension questions: "Who can find and read the phrase that tells what the speakers use? *Underline the new word and repeat it.*" Other pupils must look at the passage as it is read aloud, or they are not getting an additional sensory experience with the new word.

Vocabulary is built naturally and progressively in a developmental program. A rotating committee may skim new assignments for technical words in order to give the rest of the class clues before they read the material. Another aid to meaning is to associate the word being studied with other words related to it—to study its several meanings and its relationship to words with which or under which it might be classified. The students need also to study it according to its function and make sure that they are not confusing it with its homonym or antonym.

This word means the same as _____.

This word means the opposite of _____.

Read the sentence on the chalkboard and decide the meaning of the word as it is used in the different sentences. Which meaning of the word is new to you?

What does lymph do?

Under what general topic might we classify _____?

This word sounds like one you know and use commonly. What is the meaning of the word you use? Read this sentence and decide what the new meaning is.

The introduction of new words may also involve looking them up in the dictionary for meaning or pronunciation to enhance dictionary skills [22]. However, some new words will *not* be introduced deliberately by the teacher if they have good context clues, as in the sentence, "Mother stood over the hot _____ all day cooking"; or if the pupils already have the word analysis skills to solve them for themselves as in *scorch*. They know, for example, the *sc* from *scout* and the *orch* of *porch*. If the teacher does not leave the pupils some words that they can solve by themselves, the pupils, not learning to use their skills of word analysis or context clues, will not develop independence from the teacher.

Boldface type and italics usually signal key words. Lists of key words at the ends of chapters and the glossary at the end of the book offer aid in both pronunciation and meaning.

To learn more about the divers ways in which pupils acquire vocabulary knowledge, Elfert [28] interviewed 786 sixth-grade pupils who had studied certain words by different methods with different teachers. In the interviews he asked them how they had learned the words they marked correctly on the test and why they had made errors on the other words. He found that various associations had helped these pupils learn and remember the meanings of certain words:

Out-of-school experiences, e.g., *dawdle:* "When I'm coming to school, I do that—I *dawdle*."

Experiences in school, e.g., *unanimous:* "We voted for a new class president last month. Everyone was in agreement on one person, and the teacher said, 'It's *unanimous*. He's elected.' So I think of that now."

Dramatizations, e.g., *enforce:* "A kid put a piece of paper on him like a badge and stopped another kid who was driving a car, and we guessed it meant to *enforce* the law."

Teacher's explanations, e.g., *gaunt:* "The teacher told us about Abraham Lincoln. He was tall and skinny—*gaunt*."

Use of words in sample sentence, e.g., *reluctant:* "The boy was *reluctant* to go to school."

Association with other persons, e.g., *pessimist:* "I keep telling my grandmother, 'You're a *pessimist*,' because she has a habit of saying everything bad is going to happen."

Roundabout ways of getting the meaning through association with other words, e.g., *mural:* "When I think of rural, I think of *mural*, a certain picture that makes me think of the country."

Association with things, e.g., *venom* associated with snake, *tranquil* with tranquilizers.

Association with a previously learned quotation, e.g., *malice:* "with *malice* toward none."

Dictionary: Out of 786 responses only seven mentioned the dictionary as a source of a correct meaning.

In the same way Elfert also obtained pupils' statements about why they had made errors in vocabulary. The reasons most frequently mentioned were:

Auditory similarity, e.g., *optimum* defined as *stubborn,* obviously confused with *obstinate.*

Visual similarity, e.g., *immortal* defined as *bad.* "I thought—like you say—an immortal word, a bad word."

Auditory and visual similarity, e.g., *gaunt:* "to tease and make fun of"—confused with *taunt.*

Part-word similarity, e.g., *earnest:* "to earn something."

Faulty reasoning, e.g., *quest:* "reminds me of the word *question,* and *question* reminds me of the way people think, so I put the word *idea.*"

Common associations with words, eg., *military:* marked *secret* because of association with *military secret.*

Confusion with opposite, e.g., *horizontal* confused with *vertical.*

The three methods of classroom instruction that these sixth-grade pupils considered most helpful were (1) dramatizing word meanings, (2) copying the words and their meanings into notebooks, (3) analyzing the word structure or noting special characteristics that provided clues to its meaning.

Other Specific Techniques of Teaching Vocabulary

In addition to the methods already described, there are many other techniques of teaching vocabulary. A list of nineteen activities used to interest children in working with words and in developing concepts is given by O'Leary [79].

A sixth-grade teacher whose pupils learned a number of new words far better than did the children in three other sixth-grade classes used imagination and personal reference in her instruction [28]. In teaching the word *tussle,* this teacher dramatized the word by having two boys engage in a tussle in front of the class. In teaching the word *protrude,* she pointed out the small word *rude* and placed it in the sentence, "It is rude to stick out your tongue at someone." The word that all four classes learned best was *scowl* which the teachers demonstrated by scowling or by calling attention to scowls on the children's faces. Three-fourths of a class whose average IQ was 92 learned the word *confiscate* because the teacher frequently spoke of *confiscating* articles such as pogo sticks, water pistols, and yo-yos, which the school forbade the children to bring with them. Underlying all these devices is the principle of personalized learning—associating the word to be learned with something interesting and meaningful in the child's life.

A symbol is better remembered if it has an emotional meaning for the learner. Sometimes an emotional meaning is attached to the word as in *mother*. Sometimes it comes through association with some activity which has an affective meaning to the pupil. If a person recalls something and tries to determine why, he often finds that it was because of his embarrassment, pride, anger, or excitement.

As reading consultant in the Laboratory Schools of the University of Chicago, Ellen Thomas has prepared many excellent vocabulary exercises such as the following:

Self-study exercises involving the use of a cover card to conceal the definition and derivation of the word until the student has used his word recognition skills. The content of these exercises appeals to teen-age interests.

Exercises designed to help the student arrive at the exact meaning of a word in a sentence, when the word has several possible meanings.

Vocabulary cards for each subject.

A vocabulary score graph on which the student records his pretest and final test scores.

A vocabulary "bargain counter" in which a given prefix, suffix, or root helps the reader to get the meaning of a dozen or more sentences, e.g., *mal, pseudo, photo, amo, phil, theo, phobia, centum, demi, semi, mono, duo.*

Interesting questions that direct students' attention to the derivation and history of certain words, e.g., "Once in history a word caused the death of 42,000 people. Forty-two thousand people were killed because they could not pronounce one word! You can find this word in your Bible in the twelfth chapter of the Book of Judges. What is it?"

Although most teachers give instruction in prefixes, suffixes, and roots, contributions from other languages such as Latin have been deemphasized as a result of research studies that show this knowledge produces little overall vocabulary expansion. Deighton [20] expressed doubts about the effectiveness of teaching roots and affixes most strongly. His objection to the traditional method of teaching this type of word analysis is that (1) most of these roots and affixes have so many meanings that the student becomes confused if he interprets them literally, and (2) the same letters that occur in the affixes also occur very often in words that have quite different meanings. Teachers should stress only those word parts that have invariant meanings.

Vocabulary cards help the student fix in his memory the key words in each subject as he meets them. He writes the word on one side of the card, divides it into syllables, and places the accents where they belong, checking all these details with a dictionary. On the other side of the card he writes the definitions of the word and uses it in a sentence. From time to time he plays solitaire with these cards to be sure he has not forgotten any words or meanings. He may also use the cards in games with other students.

Another way to remember new words is to use them in speaking and writing. One teacher repeatedly used certain new words during the week in which they were introduced.

Deeper Dimensions of Vocabulary Study

In helping the students with word meanings, the teacher should keep in mind the many dimensions of meaning a word may have. Although he may not deal with all of these dimensions in any one instance, he should certainly not be content with a simple definition, synonym, or antonym. See, for example, the possibilities in the word *monkey:*

Whole-part relationships
    A monkey is a part of the animal kingdom.
    A leg is part of a monkey.
Generalization or classification
    A monkey is a mammal, a primate.
Coordination-subordination
    A monkey, a kangaroo, and a camel are all animals.
    A marmoset is one of many types of monkey.
Cause-effect
    A monkey hears a loud noise, is frightened, and runs.
    A monkey is hungry; it takes fruit,
Comparison-contrast
    A monkey is something like an ape.
    A monkey is different from an ape in that it has a long tail.
    A monkey is smaller than man.
Conditions
    food—A monkey eats fruit.
    shelter—A monkey lives in trees.
    clothing—A monkey is covered with hair.
Qualities
    number—There are one or two in a litter.
    amount—
    texture—hairy
    flavor—
    moisture—
    color—brown, gray, black, white
    sweetness—
    solidity—muscular; bone, skin, hair
    size—1 to 4 feet

share—manlike, with tail
odor—
sound—chatter, scream
Habits and actions
    scratching, jumping, swinging by arms, legs, or tail, hanging by forelegs or hind legs, clinging to mother, pushing, pulling, chewing, picking, screaming, chattering, lying on back, sitting, looking, smelling, climbing, leaping, running, traveling in herds
Uses
    entertainment in zoo, in circus, with organ grinder
    history of uses—first mentioned in literature
Time relationships
    from birth to full development
    life span
    evolution
Place relationships
    in trees, in jungle, in zoo, in geographical location
Synonyms
    (loosely) ape
Antonyms
Multiple meanings
    monkey wrench, monkey in a tree, monkey around, make a monkey of, monkey suit, grease monkey, monkey pod, you little monkey
Derivation of the word
    from Turkish
Definition
    a manlike animal
    any member of the highest order of mammals except man
    (Notice that a definition is a choice of distinguishing attributes.)
Word form
    monkey; plural—monkeys
    (study of the variant forms in which the word may appear and classifications of the word as one of a group having such characteristics)

Word study may include such experiences as describing dimensions of a single word or developing a given dimension for various words. For example, if a leg is a part of a monkey, what are other parts of a monkey, or what are comparable parts of a car, a fish, etc.? Exercises should be balanced so that if on one occasion a whole is given and a part must be named, at another time a part is given and the whole is to be named.

A part of a monkey is a	leg	crank	fin.
A leg is a part of a	fish	monkey	car.
A leg is to a monkey as a fin is to a _____.			
A monkey is to a leg as a fish is to a _____.			
A leg is a part of a monkey or	fish	bird	wagon.

It is obvious that the multiple-choice form of exercise, if used, should be varied by the completion type, and neither should preclude the use of original sentences with which students test each other. A student might say, "I shall give you some sentences about a monkey. When one of my sentences mentions a part of a monkey, raise your hand." Students can also glean examples of whole-part relationships from their reading and present them to the class for identification.

Once the students have mastered a technique, such as the whole-part, in the study of a well-known word, they should use the technique in learning the meanings of new words. A class can divide its responsibility for investigating and presenting one dimension. In successive exercises, students can exchange roles until each has had every experience.

One of the advantages of the dimensional study of words is that it cultivates a more complete inventory of a concept. Added dividends are oral-language experience and the use of many words in the study of one. Traditionally teachers have taught lists of words. Perhaps constellations of words are equally appropriate for study in the well-endowed English language.

Which of these many methods contributes most to a student's vocabulary knowledge? It is a general principle that students learn specifically what they are taught. If they are given extra vocabulary drill in one of the many vocabulary workbooks (see Appendix C), they will probably improve more in vocabulary than the control group that does not have this practice. Since both comprehension and speed depend to some extent on vocabulary knowledge, it follows that an expanded vocabulary will contribute to reading improvement. Study of the deeper dimensions of word meaning will enrich the student's total language usage. But—a word of caution—overemphasis on vocabulary training might well decrease a student's speed to the degree that he becomes overattentive to word analysis or contextual aids.

TEACHING SENTENCE AND PARAGRAPH COMPREHENSION

A student may be able to pronounce all the words in a sentence, he may even know the meaning of each separate word, but he still may not understand what the sentence says. This happens when the student has not learned to relate ideas to one another within a sentence and between sentences in paragraphs.

Sentence Comprehension

The "Cloze" Technique. The "cloze" procedure is based on the gestalt idea of *closure*—the impulse to complete a structured whole by supplying a missing element. The test is composed of passages from which certain words are omitted. The individual taking the test fills in the blanks left by the missing words. The score comprises the number of correctly filled spaces.

Cloze tests may be used as measures of comprehension. Correlations between the cloze test and tests of vocabulary and reading comprehension are fairly high—about .75. Their relationship to comprehension tests varies with the types of words that are deleted in the cloze test. Cloze tests in which only nouns and verbs were omitted showed a high relation to tests of factual comprehension; cloze tests in which all types of words were omitted showed a high relationship to tests measuring comprehension of relationships.

It has also been suggested that the cloze test might be an effective means of improving sentence comprehension. Use of a graded series of cloze exercises produced more improvement in the reading comprehension of college students than did other remedial procedures. However, in an experiment with sixth-grade pupils, Schneyer [96] found that "the pupils who had completed the cloze exercise did not show significantly greater improvement in reading comprehension than the control group," though both groups made higher scores in reading comprehension and vocabulary and lower scores in reading speed.

Theoretically, students' reading comprehension should improve from practice in cloze exercises. However, merely a filling in of the blanks and checking the correctness of his responses does not increase the pupil's understanding of the reading process if he does not find out *why* his responses were correct or incorrect. The pupils should also have the opportunity to discuss the process by which they arrived at each choice.

Practice Exercises. Exercises such as the following are also useful: identifying an interjected word that spoils the meaning of a sentence; discussing how each part of a sentence contributes to the meaning of the whole; and building sentences from given words and phrases [85].

A number of subtests of sentence comprehension have been used to compare the achievement of varied groups of students in the reading skill. For example, on the Watts Sentence Reading Test (British) and the Vernon Sentence Reading Test (British), groups of pupils ages nine and fourteen in Canada and in England obtained similar mean reading achievement scores. However, on the California Achievement Tests the means scores were significantly higher for the Edmonton, Canada, children [110].

Paragraph Comprehension

Robinson [87] describes three sequential steps for developing skill in paragraph reading:

First, find the key words in a sentence. These may be underlined and used to compose a telegram conveying the main idea in the fewest possible words. Students progress from simple to more complex sentences.

Second, find the key sentence in a paragraph. By underlining the key words in a paragraph, students discover what idea is emphasized in the paragraph and how the other sentences relate to this idea. The teacher should at first present well-structured paragraphs with the main idea in the first or the last sentence.

Third, find the main thought in a paragraph. Here the teacher introduces paragraphs which do not have the main idea specifically stated in a sentence. Students must now make inferences about the major point and purpose of the paragraph and state the implied idea controlling the structure of the paragraph.

Suggestions for Instruction. An understanding of the structure of paragraphs is helpful. A quick glance at the paragraph will show whether it presents the key idea explicitly in the first or second sentence or in a summary sentence at the end, whether it presents two contrasting ideas, whether it contains nothing but an illustration of a generalization made in the previous paragraph or whether it is loosely constructed without unity or emphasis.

Given the topic sentence, one may develop the thought in several ways—by repeating the idea in other words to clarify its meaning, by denying the opposite point of view, by giving examples, by breaking the topic into parts and developing it detail by detail, by comparing or contrasting, by exploring causes, or by stating its importance. These items, put in question form, may be used to guide students in their analysis.

It is easy enough to say, "Learn to find key words and the main ideas," but it is more difficult to teach pupils how to do this. Headings and italicized words are helpful, of course. The author may give a clue as to which words he thinks are most important, sometimes by using these words frequently and providing illustrations of them.

A teacher used the following paragraph for instruction [17, p. 71]: [1]

The moisture and temperature of the air we breathe are important for health. History relates that in the middle of the eighteenth century a Nabob of Bengal, India, packed 146 prisoners in a small dungeon where all but twenty-three perished during the night. Until recently it was supposed that they died for lack of oxygen and from the presence of carbon dioxide. It is now believed by many scientists that if the temperature of the air of the dungeon could have been kept at about 65°F. and the humidity kept low, the loss of life would have been greatly reduced.

Before the class came in, the teacher wrote on the board the most difficult words in the paragraph. Her first question was, "Where have you seen or heard these words before?" The purpose of this question was not to elicit definitions but to invest each word with associations from the experience

[1] Quoted by special permission of Holt, Rinehart and Winston, Inc., New York.

of the class. For example, *temperature* was first associated with the classroom. One boy went to the thermometer and found that the temperature was 74°F. Several pupils said the proper temperature for a room was between 65 and 70°F. One boy opened a window to lower the temperature. In solving this practical problem of an overheated room, teacher and pupils used the word *temperature* several times. One girl associated *dungeon* with her recent reading about King Arthur and gave a detailed description. Another connected *humidity* with the weather reports which he always read in the newspaper. All agreed that humidity was higher on August dog days than on clear, cold days.

After this preliminary pooling of experience, the pupils were asked to read the paragraph.

The pupils' written responses to the teacher's request for the main idea showed their need for instruction in paragraph reading. Some gave very vague general statements: "This paragraph is trying to bring out what took place in the eighteenth century and what the results were." (This type of response encourages pupils to get by with vague answers, and teachers have a double responsibility to correct them.) Many focused on the Black Hole of Calcutta incident as the main idea.

Several students showed serious inaccuracies: "The paragraph says that in the eighteenth century there were put 146 prisoners in a dungeon and overnight twenty-three died. Scientists said that they died for lack of oxygen." The first inaccuracy was apparently due to the underpotency of the words *all but*. The second inaccuracy was apparently due to the student's failure to note and give proper weight to time relationships—*at that time* and *now.*

Only a few found the main idea expressed in the topic sentence: "The moisture and temperature of the air we breathe are important for health."

Almost any type of paragraph will evoke many types of responses— vague generalizations; inaccurate conclusions; the main idea plus some supporting detail; details only, some accurate and some inaccurate; and a variety of interpretations influenced by the pupils' own experiences and attitudes.

The teacher read some of the responses to the class and asked the pupils to decide which were the best and why. The pupils who made poor responses were not identified, but those who had grasped the main idea of the paragraph were asked to tell how they did it. With the teacher's help the class worked out a simple analysis of paragraph structure and noted various ways to distinguish the main idea from illustrations and supporting details. Later the teacher noted which pupils had misspelled words such as *temperature* and *humidity* and gave these pupils some help in dividing words into syllables and making a spelling file for key science words.

Exercises in paragraph comprehension include a sequence of activities such as the following:

Writing well-constructed paragraphs. (The Coronet Instructional Film, "How to Write Better Paragraphs," is a good introduction to this exercise.)

Rebuilding a paragraph from the separately typed sentences of which it was originally composed. (The sentences are put in an envelope together with the original paragraph which serves as a self-scoring key.)

Recognizing the main idea of the paragraph when it is listed among three or four multiple choices.

Writing the main idea of the paragraph if it has a main idea—or expressing the central thought of a paragraph in which the main idea is not explicitly expressed.

Stating the purpose of the paragraph.

Drawing a diagram of the structure of a paragraph.

Drawing a picture of the scene described in a descriptive paragraph.

By applying their skill in paragraph reading, students become aware of the many different purposes and types of structure that a paragraph may have and of how each paragraph contributes to the understanding of the passage as a whole.

The main idea of a paragraph, however, is not always the important thing to remember. McCullough in her report on "Preparation of Textbooks in the Mother Tongue" noted that the following thought patterns are used in paragraphs [72, pp. 192–193]:

Whole-part relationships: A frog is not just a frog. The leg is part of it.

Cause-and-effect relationships: . . . The river did not rise by magic. It was filled with rain from all over the countryside.

Sequential relationships: . . . In the life process there is first the egg, then the tadpole, then the frog. . . .

Comparison and contrast relationships: . . . The bird has a nest but I have a house.

Coordinate-subordinate relationships: . . . Of dog and cat, the bark belongs only to the dog, the purr only to the cat. The dog is not a cat. The cat is not a dog.

The awareness of these kinds of relationships can lead to certain kinds of products—theories, laws, and principles; generalizations; summarization; definition; classification. The writer may give examples, or elaborate on, or make application of any of these products.

In the same work, McCullough states and illustrates various purposes that a writer may have in mind when he constructs a paragraph:

To report a piece of news, an event
To classify (diagram)
To present a sequence (series of steps)
To express cause and effect

To compare or contrast
To enumerate
To define (descriptive)
To present a principle
To illustrate
To present evidence followed by interpretation
To present a problem followed by a solution

One type of paragraph to illustrate in detail the penetrating method of paragraph analysis described in this report follows [72, pp. 206–209]:

To express cause and effect
Some people who came to attend our course at Birla School thought that they would get fat from so much sitting in class. For this reason, they took long walks up and down the trails around the school. But whatever they lost in poundage on the walks, they gained afterwards. Each walk made them hungrier. They ate more and more. When last heard, they were criticizing the dhobi for shrinking their clothes.

The author is dealing with a series of causes and effects: sitting causing fear of obesity, fear of obesity causing walks, walks causing hunger, hunger causing more eating (unexpressed: more eating causing gain in weight, gain in weight causing tightening of clothing), tightening of clothing causing criticism of dhobi. In the organization of this paragraph, the writer has done something like this:

What some people thought
What they did about it
Why it had that effect
What they did because of what they thought had happened

"For this reason" is a clue to the reader that the first sentence states a cause, and the next will state an effect, an effect of the people's thoughts.

"But" in the third sentence signals a reversal, a change of expected direction. The people achieved just the opposite effect: obesity instead of slimness. This reversal is emphasized by the use of antonyms, "lost" and "gained."

The reader must know that "hungrier . . . ate . . . more . . . more . . ." are causes for gain, for the author does not give a verbal clue to the fact that these are causes.

"When last heard" makes the reader know that the end of the story has arrived. It is the author's signal that the last of the causes of effects has come. The reader has to think what a dhobi's shrinking of clothes has to do with gaining weight. Then he laughs, for he is in on a secret with the author. He and the author know that the people gained weight, but the people still think they are winning the battle of the bulge. If clothes are tighter and weight is heavier, obviously the dhobi is the culprit.

This paragraph is much more complicated than many paragraphs of cause and effect, for often the author will deal with only one cause and one effect. He may start with one cause, which the reader recognizes as an act or situation or feeling. . . . Then he may or may not signal with an expression such as *therefore, as a result, consequently*. In reverse manner the author may start with the effect and then tell the cause: ". . . streets were like lakes. It had rained heavily. . . ." Notice how the change in the verb tells the reader that the second, preceding the first, may be the cause of the first. That change and the reader's own experience with cause and effect in life are the only signals.

The reader should emerge from reading such a paragraph knowing the two events or situations or feelings and knowing which caused which.

Paragraph Outlining and Skimming. Paragraph outlining—summarizing each paragraph in one sentence and attempting to link these sentences into a growing pattern of thought—helps many students to increase their speed by making a judicious selection of key ideas. They find that the topic sentence frequently tells them all that they need to know.

Skimming is an extremely useful but much abused technique for gaining certain kinds of information quickly. Skimming is not careless, inaccurate reading. Whatever the nature of the material or the reader's purpose in reading it, he should emerge with definite correct ideas or impressions. Various kinds of skimming may be arranged on a scale beginning with the kind that seeks the smallest item of information: skimming to locate a particular date or name; next in order would be skimming to locate a particular fact; then skimming to get the general structure or skeleton of the article or book; skimming to get all the facts or points of view bearing on a particular problem; skimming to get the heart of the book; and skimming to get a fairly detailed pattern of the author's thought. The more one skims a certain type of book, the greater is his facility in that kind of skimming.

Exercises using passages in texts, reference books, magazines, and newspapers as practice material may be easily prepared. Teachers merely select clippings of interest to the students, prepare questions appropriate to the article, estimate the time needed for skimming. The article may be pasted on one side of a page and the questions written or typed on the other side. The student has to skim the passage in order to find the answers. He may be timed or limited to a certain number of minutes. Students may get these loose sheets to read whenever they have spare time or whenever they feel the need for this kind of practice.

To comprehend a longer passage it is necessary to *understand its structure.* Otherwise the reader does not know what to select as important and what to pass over as unessential. A class period spent on an exercise such as this one from *Study Type of Reading Exercises* has proved beneficial. The teacher says, "You will have one minute to get the structure of the exercise as a whole. Read the first page quickly to find out what the exercise is about; pay special attention to italicized words. When you have a hunch as to the probable structure of the passage, read the first sentence of each of the other paragraphs to see whether you are right." When the minute is up, the group will give their ideas of the structure of the passage and discuss the methods they used. During the period the class may read three or four other passages in the same way and then summarize all the suggestions for quickly grasping the structure of a chapter or a section. The next step is to use this newly acquired sense of structure in subsequent reading. Longer selections or new books should be studied in the same way.

Influence of Attitude, Logic, and Anticipation on Paragraph Comprehension. Although the printed page presents the same words to each reader, each person emerges with a somewhat different impression of what the author has said. Attitudes influence interpretation because the individual reads with his emotions as well as with his mind. His attitude toward reading itself is also important: "Read not to contradict, nor to believe, but to weigh and consider."

Comprehension also involves an understanding of the way in which associated ideas, modifiers located either in the same sentence or in associated sentences, determine the meaning of a particular word. To help students appreciate this influence, teachers can prepare exercises such as the following:

He _____ into the room
With head high he _____ into the room.
With head high, like a king, he _____ into the room.

Any one of a large number of words might be inserted in the first blank. For the second blank, the choice would be limited to such words as *strutted, swaggered,* or *strode.* For the third sentence the appropriate verbs would be still more restricted.

One may help students to think more carefully while reading by giving them practice in reading to answer thought questions, reading to discover implied as well as explicit meanings, reading to apply content to new situations, and reading for the purpose of solving problems. One may obtain more formal exercises that are designed to apply logic to reading, although such kinds of reading are not very well represented in the textbooks that have been published for use in corrective reading.

The following analysis of a paragraph illustrates the kind of practice in logical thinking that mature high school and college students need. The paragraph presented was this:

At the present time the Republic of France maintains 500,000 troops in Africa, at tremendous national expense. The monetary value of her imports is less than that of her exports. French citizens are said to evade paying their taxes. Because it is well known that economic instability precedes economic depression, we must conclude that France is on the verge of disaster.

Analysis of the paragraph.[2] The conclusion of the deductive argument is stated in the independent clause of the last sentence, with the word *disaster* referring clearly to the economic depression. The major premise is stated in the dependent clause, "economic instability precedes economic depression." The author uses two propaganda devices to ensure acceptance of the major premise: (1) de-emphasizing it by putting it in a dependent clause, and (2) appealing to the weight of public opinion by the words "it is well known that." Such devices should be detected by the reader appraising the argument. The minor term of the syllogism, "France is undergoing a period of economic instability," is unstated. If the reader accepts the evidence in the first three sentences, he is likely to accept the unstated minor premise but should realize that it is he and not the author who is stating it.

Anticipation. Anticipation of what the author is going to say sharpens interpretation and usually increases concentration. Students like exercises of the following kind: "Before reading this chapter, think what you would say if you were the author writing it. Then read the chapter and find out how closely you and the author agreed."

THE INTEGRATED APPROACH

In considering the various methods of teaching basic reading skills, teachers should not take an either-or attitude. There are good features in each approach which may profitably be used in combination, or used successfully with individual children. The whole-word method helps the child to move naturally from inquiring about the meanings of words to receiving school instruction in reading. Associating the spoken word with the printed word is a quick way of getting its meaning. Being able to recognize a few words gives the child a basis for discovering sound-letter associations. Moreover, the whole-word method must be used in learning the phonetically irregular words—those that "do not play fair," that do not have consistent sound-letter associations.

The phonetic method enables the child to get the meaning of words by pronouncing them. It also teaches spelling patterns.

The language-experience approach follows the approved linguistic sequence of speaking, writing, and then reading what one has written or what one's peers have written. In experience stories, the spoken words and sentence patterns are already familiar; the content is of immediate interest; there is more variety of natural sentence patterns than one finds in the basal readers (perhaps there is too much variety); repetition of vocabulary and sentence pattern can be arranged.

[2] Contributed by Capt. Philo A. Hucheson. See also article "Secondary School Reading as Thinking," *The Reading Teacher*, vol. 13, pp. 194–200, February, 1960.

The "writing road to reading" has the advantage of facilitating the transition from the spoken word to the letter sequence within a word.

The linguistic approach helps the reader (1) to pronounce unfamiliar printed words that are, however, in his speaking vocabulary, and (2) to become aware of the factors within a sentence that convey its meaning. These are aids to efficient reading that few teachers have fully utilized.

How much emphasis should be placed on a given method? This would vary with the individual child. Children with visual defects have difficulty in learning by the "look-say" method. Children with hearing defects find phonics difficult. Able learners can quickly apply their knowledge of sound-letter associations and phonic generalizations. Slow-learning children find it difficult to do the reasoning that is involved in applying phonics. There is no single best approach for all children.

The Learning Methods Test [74] attempts to identify children whose learning will be easier and more rapid if they are taught by a particular method.

The various approaches to beginning reading which are mentioned only briefly here are described more fully in a pamphlet edited by Mackintosh [65].

REFERENCES

1. Adams, Mary Lourita: "Reading Activities: Differing Purposes," *Education,* vol. 84, pp. 521–524, May, 1964.

2. Anderson, Irving Howard, and Walter F. Dearborn: *The Psychology of Teaching Reading,* The Ronald Press Company, New York, 1952.

3. Barret, Thomas C.: "Predicting Reading Achievement through Readiness Tests," in J. Allen Figurel (ed.), *Reading and Inquiry,* International Reading Association Conference Proceedings, vol. 10, Newark, Del., 1965, pp. 26–28.

4. Bear, David E.: "Two Methods of Teaching Phonics: A Longitudinal Study," *Elementary School Journal,* vol. 64, pp. 273–279, February, 1964.

5. Black, Millard H., and Lavon Harper Whitehouse: "Reinforcing Reading Skills through Workbooks," *The Reading Teacher,* vol. 15, pp. 19–24, September, 1961.

6. Bliesmer, Emery P., and Betty H. Yarborough: "A Comparison of Ten Different Beginning Reading Programs in First Grade," *Phi Delta Kappan,* vol. 46, pp. 500–504, June, 1965.

7. Bloomfield, Leonard, and Clarence L. Barnhart: *Let's Read,* parts 1–3, C. L. Barnhart, Bronxville, N.Y.

8. Bonney, Margaret K.: "Sound and Sense in Spelling," *Elementary English,* vol. 42, pp. 243–246, March, 1965.

9. Botel, Morton: "What Linguistics Says to This Teacher of Reading and Spelling," *The Reading Teacher,* vol. 18, pp. 188–193, December, 1964.

10. Braun, Jean S.: "Relation between Concept Formation and Reading Achievement at Three Developmental Levels," *Child Development,* vol. 34, pp. 675–682, September, 1963.

11. Bruner, Jerome S.: "The Act of Discovery," *Harvard Educational Review,* vol. 31, pp. 21–32, Winter, 1961.

12. Brzeinski, Joseph E.: "Beginning Reading in Denver," *The Reading Teacher,* vol. 18, pp. 16–21, October, 1964.

13. Byers, Loretta: "Pupils' Interests and the Content of Primary Reading Texts," *The Reading Teacher,* vol. 18, pp. 227–233, January, 1964.

14. Carroll, John B.: "The Analysis of Reading Instruction: Perspectives from Psychology and Linguistics," in *Theories of Learning and Instruction,* Sixty-third Yearbook of the National Society for the Study of Education, part I, University of Chicago Press, Chicago, 1964, pp. 336–353.

15. Clymer, Theodore: "The Utility of Phonic Generalizations in the Primary Grades," *The Reading Teacher,* vol. 17, pp. 252–258, January, 1963.

16. Davis, David C.: "Phonemic Structural Approach to Initial Reading Instruction," *Elementary English,* vol. 41, pp. 218–223, March, 1964.

17. Davis, Ira C., and Richard W. Sharpe: *Science,* Holt, Rinehart and Winston, Inc., New York, 1947.

18. Dawkins, John: "Linguistics in the Elementary Grades," *Elementary English,* vol. 42, pp. 762–768, November, 1965.

19. Dechant, Emerald: "Teacher Differences and Reading Method," *Education,* vol. 86, pp. 40–43, September, 1965.

20. Deighton, Lee C.: *Vocabulary Development in the Classroom,* Teachers College Press, Teachers College, Columbia University, New York, 1959.

21. Diack, Hunter: *Reading and Psychology of Perception,* Peter Skinner, Nottingham, Eng., 1960.

22. "The Dictionary in the Elementary School," *Elementary English,* vol. 41, pp. 325–419, April, 1964.

23. Doctor, Robert L.: "Reading Workbooks: Boon or Busywork?" *Elementary English,* vol. 39, pp. 224–228, March, 1962.

24. Durkin, Dolores: *Phonics and the Teaching of Reading,* Teachers College Press, Teachers College, Columbia University, New York, 1965.

25. Durrell, Donald D., Alice Nicholson, Arthur V. Olson, Sylvia R. Gauel, and Eleanor B. Linehan: "Success in First Grade Reading," *Journal of Education,* vol. 140, pp. 1–48, February, 1958.

26. Early, Margaret J.: "The Meaning of Reading Instruction in Secondary Schools," *Journal of Reading,* vol. 8, pp. 25–29, October, 1964.

27. Eisman, Edward: "Individualized Spelling," *Elementary English,* vol. 39, pp. 478–480, May, 1962.

28. Elfert, William: "An Exploration of Sixth Grade Pupils' Acquisition of Word Meanings through Classroom Instruction," unpublished doctoral dissertation, Teachers College, Columbia University, New York, 1960.

29. Ernet, Margaret S.: *More about Words,* Alfred A. Knopf, Inc., New York, 1951.

30. Ernet, Margaret S.: *Picturesque Word Origins,* G. & C. Merriam Company, Springfield, Mass., 1933.

31. Freyberg, P. S.: "A Comparison of Two Approaches to the Teaching of Spelling," *British Journal of Educational Psychology,* vol. 34, pp. 178–186, June, 1964.

32. Fries, Charles C.: *Linguistics and Reading,* Holt, Rinehart and Winston, Inc., New York, 1963.

33. Frostig, Marianne, and David Harne: *The Frostig Program for the Development of Visual Perception,* Teachers Guide, Follett Publishing Company, Chicago, 1964.

34. Funk, Charles E.: *Thereby Hangs a Tale,* Harper & Row, Publishers, Incorporated, New York, 1948.

35. Funk, Wilfred: *Word Origins,* Wilfred Funk, Inc., Publishers, New York, 1950.

36. Gainsburg, Joseph C.: *Building Reading Confidence,* C. S. Hammond & Company, Maplewood, N.J., 1962.

37. Gibson, C. M., and Ivor A. Richards: *First Steps in Reading English,* Pocket Books, Inc., New York, 1957.

38. Gibson, Eleanor J.: "Development of Perception: Discrimination of Depth Compared with Discrimination of Graphic Symbols," *Monographs of the Society for Research in Child Development,* vol. 28, pp. 5–24, 1963.

39. Gibson, Eleanor J., Henry Osser, and Anne D. Pick: "A Study of the Development of Grapheme-Phoneme Correspondence," *Journal of Verbal Learning and Verbal Behavior,* vol. 2, pp. 142–146, August, 1963.

40. Goodman, Kenneth S.: "A Linguistic Study of Cues and Miscues in Reading," *Elementary English,* vol. 42, pp. 639–643, October, 1965.

41. Grimes, Jesse W., and Wesley Allinsmith: "Compulsivity, Anxiety, and School Achievement," *Merrill-Palmer Quarterly,* vol. 7, pp. 247–271, October, 1961.

42. Groff, Patrick J.: "Readiness for Reading Vocabulary with Ability Grouping," *Journal of Educational Research,* vol. 58, pp. 140–143, November, 1964.

43. Hanna, Paul R., and Jean S. Hanna: "Applications of Linguistics and Psychological Cues to the Spelling Course of Study," *Elementary English,* vol. 42, pp. 753–759, November, 1965.

44. Hechinger, Fred M.: "Head Start to Where?" *Saturday Review,* vol. 48, pp. 58–60, 75, December 18, 1965.

45. Hendrickson, Lois N., and Siegmar Muehl: "The Effect of Attention and Motor Response Pretraining on Learning to Discriminate B and D in Kindergarten Children," *Journal of Educational Psychology,* vol. 53, pp. 236–241, October, 1962.

46. Herrick, Virgil E., and others: "Basal Instructional Materials in Reading," in Paul A. Witty (ed.), *Development in and through Reading,* University of Chicago Press, Chicago, 1961, chap. 10.

47. Hildreth, Gertrude: "Linguistic Factors in Early Reading Instruction," *The Reading Teacher,* vol. 18, pp. 172–178, December, 1964.

48. Hillerich, Robert L.: "Studies in Reading Readiness," in J. Allen Figurel (ed.), *Reading and Inquiry,* International Reading Association Conference Proceedings, vol. 10, Newark, Del., 1965, pp. 47–49.

49. Howards, Melvin: "How Easy Are 'Easy' Words?" *Journal of Experimental Education,* vol. 32, pp. 377–382, Summer, 1964.

50. "The Impact of Linguistics on Language Arts," *Education,* vol. 86, pp. 131–165, November, 1965.

51. Jacobs, Roderick A.: "A Short Introduction to Transformational Grammar," *Education,* vol. 86, pp. 138–141, November, 1965.

52. Jan-Tausch, James: "Concrete Thinking as a Factor in Reading Comprehension," in J. Allen Figurel (ed.), *Challenge and Experiment in Reading*, International Reading Association Conference Proceedings, vol. 7, Scholastic Magazines, Inc., New York, 1962, pp. 161–164.

53. Kephart, Newell C.: *The Slow Learner in the Classroom*, Charles E. Merrill Books, Inc., Columbus, Ohio, 1960.

54. King, Ethel M., and Siegmar Muehl: "Different Sensory Cues as Aids in Beginning Reading," *The Reading Teacher*, vol. 19, pp. 163–168, December, 1965.

55. Kirk, Samuel A., and James J. McCarthy: "The Illinois Test of Psycholinguistic Ability—an Approach to Differential Diagnosis," *American Journal of Mental Deficiency*, vol. 56, pp. 399–412, November, 1961.

56. Koehring, Dorothy: *Getting Ready to Read*, State College of Iowa, Extension Service, Cedar Falls, Iowa, 1964.

57. Kounin, Jacob S., and Paul V. Gump: "The Comparative Influence of Punitive and Nonpunitive Teachers upon Children's Concepts of School Misconduct," *Journal of Educational Psychology*, vol. 52, pp. 44–49, February, 1961.

58. Lee, Dorris M., and R. V. Allen: *Learning to Read through Experience*, Appleton-Century-Crofts, Inc., New York, 1963.

59. Lefevre, Carl A.: "A Comprehensive Linguistic Approach to Reading," *Elementary English*, vol. 42, pp. 651–659, October, 1965.

60. Lefevre, Carl A.: "A Concise Structural Grammar," *Education*, vol. 86, pp. 131–137, November, 1965.

61. Lefevre, Carl A.: "The Contribution of Linguistics," *Instructor*, vol. 74, pp. 77, 103–105, March, 1965.

62. Lorge, Irving, and Jeanne Chall: "Estimating the Size of Vocabularies of Children and Adults: An Analysis of Methodological Issues," *Journal of Experimental Education*, vol. 32, pp. 147–157, Winter, 1963.

63. Lundsteen, Sara W.: "Teaching and Testing Critical Listening in the Fifth and Sixth Grades," *Elementary English*, vol. 41, pp. 743–747, November, 1964.

64. MacDonald, James B.: "Myths about Instruction," *Educational Leadership*, vol. 22, pp. 571–576, 609–617, May, 1965.

65. Mackintosh, Helen K. (ed.): *Current Approaches to Teaching Reading*, Department of Elementary-Kindergarten-Nursery Education, National Education Association, Washington, D.C., 1965.

66. Mandel, Richard L.: "Children's Books: Mirrors of Social Development," *Elementary School Journal*, vol. 64, pp. 190–199, January, 1964.

67. Marchbanks, Gabrielle, and Harry Levin: "Clues by Which Children Recognize Words," *Journal of Educational Psychology*, vol. 56, pp. 57–61, April, 1965.

68. Mary Caroline (Sister): *Breaking the Sound Barrier*, The Macmillan Company, New York, 1960.

69. Mary Eduard (Sister): "A Modified Linguistic versus a Composite Basal Reading Program," *The Reading Teacher*, vol. 17, pp. 511–515, April, 1964.

70. Maw, Wallace H., and Ethel W. Maw: "Children's Curiosity as an Aspect of Reading Comprehension," *The Reading Teacher*, vol. 15, pp. 236–240, January, 1962.

71. McCallister, James M.: "Using Paragraph Clues as Aids to Understanding," *Journal of Reading*, vol. 8, pp. 11–16, October, 1964.

72. McCullough, Constance M.: "Preparation of Textbooks in the Mother Tongue," mimeographed reading project, Department of Curriculum, Methods and Textbooks, 5, West Patel Nagar, New Delhi 72, February, 1965, pp. 191–224.

73. Miles, Olive Stafford: *Improvement of Basic Comprehension Skills: An Attainable Goal in Secondary Schools,* Scott, Foresman Monographs on Secondary Education, no. 6381, Scott, Foresman and Company, Chicago, 1964.

74. Mills, Richard E.: "An Evaluation of Techniques for Teaching Word Recognition," *Elementary School Journal,* vol. 56, pp. 221–225, January, 1956.

75. Moore, Omar K.: " 'Tis Time He Should Begin to Read," *Carnegie Corporation of New York Quarterly,* vol. 9, pp. 1–3, April, 1961.

76. Moskowitz, Sue: "Should We Teach Reading in the Kindergarten?" *Elementary English,* vol. 42, pp. 798–804, November, 1965.

77. Muehl, Siegmar: "The Effects of Letter-name Knowledge on Learning to Read a Word List in Kindergarten Children," *Journal of Educational Psychology,* vol. 53, pp. 181–186, August, 1962.

78. Niemeyer, John H.: "The Bank Street Readers—Support for Movement toward an Integrated Society," *The Reading Teacher,* vol. 18, pp. 542–545, April, 1965.

79. O'Leary, Helen F.: "Vocabulary Presentation and Enrichment," *Elementary English,* vol. 41, pp. 613–615, October, 1964.

80. Olsen, Arthur V.: "Phonics and Success in Beginning Reading," *Journal of Developmental Reading,* vol. 6, pp. 256–260, Summer, 1963.

81. Otterman, Lois: "The Value of Teaching Prefixes and Word-Roots," *Journal of Educational Research,* vol. 48, pp. 611–616, April, 1955.

82. *Phonetic Keys to Reading—Teacher's Manual,* The Economy Company, Oklahoma City, Okla., 1958.

83. Popp, Helen: "Visual Discrimination of Alphabet Letters," *The Reading Teacher,* vol. 17, pp. 221–226, January, 1964.

84. Radler, D. H., and Newell C. Kephart: *Success through Play,* Harper & Row, Publishers, Incorporated, New York, 1960.

85. *Reading: Grades 7–8–9,* Curriculum Bulletin, series no. 11, Board of Education, City of New York, 1959.

86. Richards, Ivor A.: *Speculative Instruments,* University of Chicago Press, Chicago, 1955.

87. Robinson, H. Alan: "A Cluster of Skills: Especially for Junior High School," *The Reading Teacher,* vol. 15, pp. 25–28, September, 1961.

88. Robinson, Helen M. (comp. and ed.): *Oral Aspects of Reading,* Supplementary Educational Monographs, no. 82, University of Chicago Press, Chicago, 1955.

89. Robinson, Helen M.: "Teaching Reading Today," *Instructor,* vol. 74, p. 56ff., March, 1965.

90. Rudisill, Mabel: "Sight, Sound, and Meaning in Learning to Read," *Elementary English,* vol. 41, pp. 622–630, October, 1964.

91. Russell, David H., and Etta Karp: *Reading Aids through the Grades,* Teachers College Press, Teachers College, Columbia University, New York, 1956.

92. Russell, David H., and Ibrahim Q. Saadeh: "Qualitative Levels in Children's Vocabularies," *Journal of Educational Psychology,* vol. 53, pp. 170–174, August, 1962.

93. Rystrom, Richard: "Whole-word and Phonics Methods and Current Linguistic Findings," *Elementary English,* vol. 42, pp. 265–268, March, 1965.

94. Sartain, Harry W.: "Do Reading Workbooks Increase Achievement?" *Elementary School Journal,* vol. 62, pp. 157–162, December, 1961.

95. Sartain, Harry W.: "Individual or Basal in Second and Third Grades," *Instructor,* vol. 74, pp. 69, 96, 100, March, 1965.

96. Schneyer, J. Wesley: "Use of the Cloze Procedure for Improving Reading Comprehension," *The Reading Teacher,* vol. 19, pp. 174–179, December, 1965.

97. Schoolfield, Lucille D., and Josephine B. Timerlake: *Phonovisual Method—Teachers Manual,* Phonovisual Products, Washington, 1953.

98. Spache, George D.: *Reading in the Elementary School,* Allyn and Bacon, Inc., Boston, 1964.

99. Spache, George D., and Mary E. Baggett: "What Teachers Know about Phonics and Syllabication," *The Reading Teacher,* vol. 19, pp. 96–99, November, 1965.

100. Stevens, Martin: "Intonation in the Teaching of Reading," *Elementary English,* vol. 42, pp. 231–237, March, 1965.

101. Strang, Barbara: *Modern English Structure,* Edward Arnold (Publishers) Ltd., London, 1962.

102. Strang, Ruth: "Should Parents Teach Reading?" in *PTA Guide to What's Happening in Education,* Scholastic Book Services, Inc., New York, 1965, pp. 10–18.

103. Stratemeyer, Clara G., and Henry Lee Smith, Jr.: *The Linguistic-Science Readers,* Harper & Row, Publishers, Incorporated, New York, 1963. Revised by Jack E. Richardson Jr., Henry Lee Smith Jr., Bernard J. Weiss: *The Linguistic Readers,* Harper & Row, Publishers, Incorporated, New York, 1965.

104. Studholme, Janice MacDonald: "Group Guidance with Mothers of Retarded Readers," *The Reading Teacher,* vol. 17, pp. 528–530, April, 1964.

105. Tensuan, Emperatriz S., and Frederick B. Davis: "An Experiment with Two Methods of Teaching Reading," *The Reading Teacher,* vol. 18, pp. 8–15, October, 1964.

106. Umans, Shelley: *New Trends in Reading Instruction,* Teachers College Press, Teachers College, Columbia University, New York, 1963.

107. Wargny, Frank D.: "The Good Life in Modern Readers," *The Reading Teacher,* vol. 17, pp. 88–93, November, 1963.

108. Wepman, Joseph M.: "The Perceptual Basis for Learning," in H. Alan Robinson (ed.), *Meeting Individual Differences in Reading,* Supplementary Educational Monographs, no. 94, University of Chicago Press, Chicago, 1964, pp. 25–33.

109. Writers' Committee of the Great Cities School Improvement Program of the Detroit Public Schools: *Play with Jimmy, Fun with David, Laugh with Larry,* and others, Follett Publishing Company, Chicago, 1962.

110. Young, J. A., and M. D. Jenkinson: "Comparison of Matched Groups in Manchester, England, and Edmonton, Alberta," *Alberta Journal of Educational Research,* vol. 10, pp. 59–66, June, 1964.

111. Yuen, Jack, and others: "The Electric Portable Typewriter as an Instructional Tool in Fourth Grade Language Arts," *Elementary English,* vol. 39, pp. 101–108, February, 1962.

developing maturity

in reading

chapter 7

If a student is to derive value from reading material or make use of its content, he needs skills beyond those required for word recognition and literal comprehension. He must have a repertory of study methods and skills that will enable him to cope with a wide variety of materials. He must be able to read critically and to appreciate literature.

The purpose of this chapter is to help you improve your teaching of study skills and higher-level reading skills by increasing your understanding of their nature and of appropriate teaching procedures.

Recall your previous experiences in teaching study skills, literary appreciation, and critical and creative reading. As you recall various lessons that you have devised, try to remember which one evoked the greatest interest and effort on the part of your students. Which procedures seemed particularly effective. Why? What unanswered questions do you have about reading-study skills, the interpretation of literature, critical and creative reading? Read this chapter to answer these questions and others that occur to you.

READING–STUDY SKILLS

At one time or another and by one person or another, almost all of the reading skills have been included under this heading. Nila Banton Smith has defined study skills in reading as "skills we use when we intend to do something with the content we have read" [70, p. 158]. Others would include reading skills common to all types of reading. Tests of study skills measure the student's ability to use the table of contents, the index, and other guides to information and to read charts, graphs, tables, and maps. Reading-study skills are usually considered to include (1) locating sources of information, (2) selecting and evaluating relevant passages and extracting pertinent information from them, (3) organizing and relating this information, and (4) preparing a written or oral report.

Location-of-information Skills

To find information on any topic in a library, one must know how to use reference tools such as the card catalogue as well as various indexes, files of magazines, and clippings. The most effective method of acquiring these skills is to receive the guidance of a teacher or librarian while actually using library resources to carry out a study task.

Though note taking is admittedly an individual matter, it can be made more efficient by well-formulated assignments and by frequent demonstrations of effective methods of approaching various types of content. What the student selects to note and remember is largely determined by his purpose and by his outline of the topic. He decides whether the sources he has selected will serve his purpose: Do they have sufficient information? Is it sufficiently specific? Is it reliable and recent?

Conditions Conducive to Study

Study habits must take into account conditions such as having a time and a place, developing a positive "learning set," and budgeting one's time. Adolescents mention four main types of conditions that affect their studying:

physical conditions, personal factors, the subject to be studied, and the way the teacher presents it [23]. They emphasize privacy and quiet. When they try to study at home, many students are distracted by the baby crying, younger brothers and sisters playing spaceman and bomber pilots, parents nagging, television and radio blaring, or visitors popping in. Large families in small houses have no place for children to study without distractions. The majority of students would agree with the one who said, "When I am alone it is much easier to concentrate on homework and as a result I finish it much faster" [79, p. 487].

Personal factors also affect a student's approach to study. Many students are distracted by worries and competing interests. Anyone would agree that it is hard to put his mind on his books when it is beautiful out of doors, when he knows other boys are outside having a game of baseball, when a favorite television show is on, when something disturbing has just happened, or something exciting is about to happen. One seventeen-year-old girl expressed it this way: "When I'm excited about something or when anything is bothering me emotionally, that is the most hopeless time for me to try to study. Almost nothing gets through" [79, p. 489].

The content of the subject and the nature of the assignment also make a difference in the way an adolescent studies. Teachers must face facts; some subjects have little meaning, use, or purpose for the adolescent; some textbooks are just plain dull. Assignments that are too long or poorly understood evoke initial feelings of discouragement. Since most adolescents like to take initiative and responsibility, they will work on a voluntary project more eagerly than on a required assignment. "When I enjoy the topic I am studying, I can always do my best." "When the subject is interesting, it seems easier." "New angles to the subject make studying easier for me." "I find it easier to study about things that are happening now or have happened within my lifetime" [79, p. 493]. These are good suggestions for teachers who want to invest school subjects with more intrinsic interest. By reflecting on a successful study experience, the student can become aware of the conditions under which he learns best.

Since learning takes place in a relationship of teacher-pupil-peer, it is no wonder that adolescents recognize the importance of the teacher's personality and enthusiasm for the subject and of friendly relations with teachers and fellow students. One teen-ager remarked, "I wasn't interested in school because I had no friends. No one cared whether I came to school or not" [79, p. 496].

Any form of time limit encourages the student to pay prompt attention to the work at hand. The warming-up period is practically eliminated. Thus, if a student estimates that it will take him an hour to read his history assignment or recognizes that he has only a half hour to spend on a certain story, he is likely to set to work promptly, concentrate more closely, and select more carefully. A class of graduate students received this challenging assignment: "Assume that you have only an hour to spend in reading a popular book you have heard mentioned frequently and are eager to read. See how much of value you can get from this short contact." The next week they reported orally. Each had selected a different book and each had read selectively, according to the nature of the book. One student had paid special attention to the philsophy of the chief character; another by skimming had obtained a general idea of the plot and remembered some especially dramatic scenes. One student, however, who had not abandoned his initial belief that every word of a book should be read, selected a very small book that he could read in his accustomed way within the time limit.

Another exercise that students have found valuable is to see how many words they can read in a daily half hour or hour. (The number may be estimated by noting the average number of words per line in a sample of about ten lines, multiplying this figure by the number of lines per page, and then multiplying by the number of pages.) It is enlightening to the student to see how his reading rate differs with different kinds of material. A form called "Record of Reading" is satisfactory for this purpose.

RECORD OF READING

Book or article: (Thirty-minute periods)

Purpose in reading the material:

Date	Time of day	Total number of words read	Estimated comprehension score	Reasons for improvement or lack of improvement

Many students can profit by more efficient budgeting of their time. If they keep a simple diary record, beginning with the time they get up in the morning and continuing with each activity through the day until they go to bed, they can then examine this objective record and decide what reasonable changes will provide a better study schedule. Since habit revision is painful and difficult, they need much encouragement. Continued use of the record form will give them specific evidence that they are improving their use of time. These daily records may take the simple form of a "Diary Record of Daily Activities."

Any evidence of increased efficiency encourages the student to make further improvement in his reading-study habits.

DIARY RECORD OF DAILY ACTIVITIES

Date:

Day:

Hour	Description of activity	Remarks	Number of minutes

How-to-study Courses

Courses of this kind show a wide variation [23]. Of three methods of teaching a how-to-study course—(1) instructor-centered, with emphasis on intellectual content, lectures, and teacher-directed activities; (2) student-centered, with emphasis on students' feelings and problems, committee work, and student-led discussions; and (3) a combination of (1) and (2) with discussions led by the instructor interspersed with other techniques—the third seemed to be the most highly motivating. However, the personality and skill of the instructor, the time of the class, and the initial attitudes of the students seemed to be more important than the method used.

Research has not yet given a clear-cut answer to the question of what the method and content of a how-to-study course should be, possibly because neither quality of instruction nor quality of the student-teacher relationship has been described or controlled. The most effective courses seem to be those that (1) use an individual approach, (2) provide laboratory practice, (3) relate study skills to daily assignments as in supervised study in the classroom, and (4) emphasize extensive reading [74, chap. 18].

There is enough evidence of both immediate and long-term gains from study-skills courses to warrant further experimentation and development [23, p. 250]. The majority of superior college students report using certain approved general study methods such as getting to work on an assignment immediately, making a preliminary survey of headings, reading the summary, and paying attention to tables, charts, and graphs. However, none of the students has reported using all the methods recommended. Probably there are other methods that are more effective for individual students.

One method, Survey Q3R, has been widely used and recommended for study-type reading in any subject [56]:

The *survey* involves preliminary thinking about the chapter or article: What is my purpose in reading it? What do I already know about it? If I were the author, what would I say about this subject? It also includes skimming the material in order to become oriented and gain an opportunity to decide what reading method to use.

Q refers to *questions* to which the reader wants an answer or questions which a rapid skimming shows the selection may answer.

The first *R* refers to thoughtful *reading* to answer the questions and to get the information wanted.

The second *R* stands for *review* to check on one's comprehension of the selection.

The third *R* suggests that the student *recite* what he has gained from the reading in the form in which he will probably use it.

If a student has already developed efficient methods of his own, there is no need to suggest this or any other method, because there is no one best method. However, many students are dissatisfied with their study methods and want to create conditions that are conducive to study, to recognize barriers to concentration, to become aware of and to appraise the methods they are using, and to improve them.

Special Reading Skills

Some skills are specific to certain kinds of content—the reading of graphs in social studies, the reading of maps in geography, and the reading of formulas and tables in science. Accuracy in the reading of these special kinds of material can be checked by questions, as in a study of the pie chart shown in Figure 5 on page 270.

Reading tables and diagrams is a particularly difficult task that requires specific instruction and practice [39, 90]. One of the best ways to teach these reading skills is to have the pupils construct tables, graphs, and diagrams of their own on the basis of simple facts that they have collected.

There are various types of maps, each of which serves a distinct purpose—and represents a distinct reading problem. To interpret maps, the student must know how to use the scale to estimate distances, comprehend the meaning of latitude and longitude, use the grid lines to locate places and compare their locations, and understand the various symbols and colors that are used. To gain specific geographical information about maps, he must also have the ability to read special kinds of directions. *My Weekly Reader* [46] offers practical teaching suggestions.

SPEED IN READING

Obviously, it is an advantage to get what one wants from his reading as efficiently as possible. The goal is speed with adequate comprehension. Some students read too fast; others read too slowly. The efficient reader varies his speed according to his purpose, according to the difficulty of the

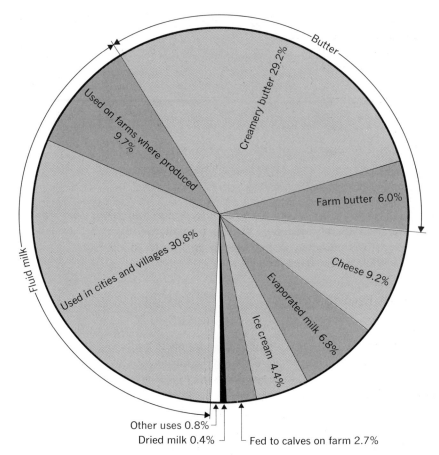

FIGURE 5.   Test of reading a pie chart. Directions: The facts needed to complete the following statements may be found by studying the chart printed above. Write the letter of the correct answer.

1. The percentage of milk used to make cheese was (a) 29.2, (b) 40, (c) 2.7, (d) 9.2.
2. The percentage of milk used for cheese was greater than the percentage of milk used for ice cream by (a) 4.8, (b) 2.8, (c) 23.2, (d) 9.7.
3. Of all milk used, the smallest percentage was used for (a) ice cream, (b) farm butter, (c) dried milk, (d) feeding calves on farms.
4. The percentage of milk used as fluid milk was greater than the percentage used for butter by (a) 4.4, (b) 6.0, (c) 29.2, (d) 5.3.

content, and according to his familiarity with the type of material. One's reading rate, in other words, should be flexible and variable. There is no single optimum speed at which everyone should read all kinds of material. From his experiments with college-bound students, Braam [5] concluded that a reading-improvement program can increase both rate and flexibility.

With easy material there is a positive relationship between rate and comprehension. This relationship holds whenever rate of reading parallels rate of thinking. However, with difficult material there is little relationship or even a negative relationship. In mathematics and science, the faster a student reads the less he tends to comprehend [68]. The relation between the rates also varies in different types of tests. In tests that measure power of comprehension rather than speed of comprehension, as untimed tests, there is little relation between rate and comprehension [74, p. 248]. Though speed training can be expected to improve comprehension of easy reading materials, the gain in speed will not transfer to all kinds of reading.

There are many explanations of slow reading. A student may read slowly because he is temperamentally lethargic or lacks the energy or the desire to put forth effort. Lack of fluency in dealing with ideas may be depressing his reading rate. As he reads he may be pronouncing each word to himself. He may have fallen into unnecessarily slow habits of reading as a result of having to do a great deal of slow, careful reading and applying this rate to all types of material. An individual who lacks basic reading skills will obviously be unable to grasp the meaning of a passage quickly. Moreover, some reading material is so badly organized or so ill expressed that it defeats rapid comprehension.

Rate may be improved at all stages of reading development. In the primary grades, teachers may foster appropriate speed by stressing reading with natural expression, as in talking, rather than word by word. They encourage children to read a great many easy books. In the intermediate grades, the pupil's interest generally speeds up his reading. Graphs that record the individual's progress on timed exercises stimulate many good intermediate readers to read faster. High school pupils, eager to obtain practice in rapid reading techniques, often fail to realize that improvement in comprehension and vocabulary often lead to improvement in rate without specific emphasis on speed.

It is the mind, rather than the eyes, that limits a person's rate of reading. He can see words more rapidly than he can comprehend their meaning; it takes time to organize one's perception and see the relations between words. Theoretically one can take in a line from a newspaper column in a single eye span, but actually this does not often happen. Many high school and college students do not read their textbooks at more than 250 words per minute. And, contrary to some popular articles on speed reading, the anatomical and physiological limits of perception would make it impossible to read more than 1,451 words per minute or to grasp the meaning of a page or paragraph with a single quick glance [91]. Any rate of reading above 800 words per minute can only mean that the reader is skimming rather than reading all the material. Even with easy material, 500 words per minute is very fast reading [84]. (See Chapter 17.)

HIGHER-LEVEL READING SKILLS

It is difficult, if not impossible, to draw a dividing line between different levels of comprehension; one builds upon and merges into the other. The first stage is receptivity—the reader must understand in general but not necessarily accept or reject what the author says. The second stage, literal comprehension, involves an intensive effort at reconstructing the author's exact meaning. Here the reader is limited by the ideas on the page. In the third stage, critical inquiry, the author's statements raise questions in the mind of the reader which he tries to answer by drawing on his background of knowledge and experience. He passes judgment on these statements. In the fourth stage, which now moves from literal comprehension and critical reading to creative reading, the reader derives new insights, values, or attitudes or new solutions to a problem. Finally, the reader may apply his ideas, insights, and solutions in life situations. All of the higher-level reading skills are built on the foundation of the basic vocabulary, word recognition, and literal comprehension skills.

Another type of creative reading merely uses the reading material as a stimulus or springboard for the reader's own creative ideas. Something the author has said suggests to him a new idea that has little relation to the author's thought. This process might be described as "tangential reading."

Critical and creative reading and their relation to critical thinking will now be described in more detail.

Critical Reading

As compared with the attention given to phonics in the popular press, that given to critical reading has been negligible. However, *The Reading Teacher* devoted its entire issue for February, 1960, to "Improving Thinking Skills through Reading"; its issue for December, 1961, was on "Reading as Thinking." The annual education and reading conferences held at the University of Delaware in 1964 explored quite deeply "dimensions of critical reading." Reading experts would agree that critical reading should have priority as a goal in reading instruction. Robinson tersely describes critical reading as involving "judgment of the veracity, validity or worth of what is read, based on sound criteria or standards developed through previous experience" [58, p. 3]. Critical reading is motivated by the reader's purpose, is made possible by his background of knowledge and experience, and is guided by his criteria and techniques for testing the truth of statements [32].

Critical reading is critical thinking applied to reading, and critical reading, in turn, develops habits of critical thinking. One cannot be divorced from the other. Students show great individual differences in thinking critically.

Some will take giant steps or even make a leap in the dark. Others will require the step-by-step process of programmed instruction.

Critical reading stems from the reader's intellectual curiosity, his desire for veracity, his questioning attitude of mind, an attitude that is inquiring, problem solving, analytical, and judgmental. His purpose is to seek the truth.

When students determine their own purposes, they become involved in learning; they take the initiative in getting the facts accurately. They become detectives seeking clues, seeing relationships, selecting and synthesizing isolated facts. As the evidence piles up, the critical reader moves from divergent thinking (examining all the possible explanations) to convergent thinking (arriving at the soundest conclusion) [76, p. 75]. The critical reader treats the author's statements as hypotheses to be tested rather than as conclusions to be remembered. He does not jump to a conclusion; he reaches it by successive steps which are illumined by insights. He challenges the author's assumptions, inferences, and conclusions, and judges the accuracy, quality, and value of what he reads on the basis of sound criteria. In reading to obtain proof on any point the critical reader will first state his assumptions. Then he will select, as he reads, the ideas significantly related to the assumptions. He will search for evidence in support of or opposed to the assumptions and weigh each bit of evidence as he reads. If evidence accumulates against one of his original assumptions he will change it.

The critical reader also recognizes the possible influence of his own emotional intervention [14]. McKillop [45] demonstrated experimentally that attitudes, beliefs, and biases interfere with critical reading far more than with literal comprehension. Critical reading is not solely a cognitive process; affect enters in to influence judgment.

Critical reading is required in every subject [18] (see Chapters 8 to 11). In arithmetic, students need to perceive the patterns that are involved in problem solving and "to read critically in order to separate relevant and irrelevant facts." In science, separate facts must be put into "workable, generative classification systems." In geography, students should learn facts in the process of solving geographic problems and developing workable generalizations.

Creative and Tangential Reading

In creative reading, "something new has been added." The creative reader discovers new principles and new relationships, finds new ways of looking at things and of using ideas gained from reading. His attitude is exploratory, imaginative, inventive. He uses what is known to build something off the beaten track. In reading he is the one who chooses the path not usually taken. He sees many possibilities for developing and elaborating on the author's thought [87]. McCullough [44] suggests that the creative reader, by identifying with the character in a story or play, will be able to guess what is going to happen next or what might have happened. He reproduces what he reads with imagination, elaborates on what he reads, and transforms and rearranges what he reads [87].

Conditions Favorable to Thoughtful Reading

Reading is most likely to be a thinking process under the following conditions:

1. When there is a problem to be solved, a story to be interpreted, a question to be answered; under these conditions the reader has a mind-set to read in a thoughtful, purposeful way.

2. When the reader has time to review what he already knows about the problem or topic and to relate his experience to his reading.

3. When the reader receives instruction and practice in the techniques of reading critically and determining the precise meanings of words. . . .

. . . .

6. When pupils have not been lulled to passivity by the effortless entertainment provided by television, radio, and mass media where the thinking has been done by the producer [81, p. 200].

Robinson emphasized as essential conditions for critical reading "commitment on the part of the school system to develop critical readers," reading materials that stimulate critical reading, teachers' approval of pupils' divergent points of view, questions that call for critical evaluation, and instruction in developing "adequate criteria for critical reading" [58, pp. 6–7]. Teachers can create these conditions much oftener than they do.

Teaching Critical Reading

Since thinking involves seeing a problem in a fresh and open-minded way and systematically trying to solve it, the first step in teaching students to read critically is to provide a problem situation. For example, in history the "you-were-there" technique presents past events as a problem situation. The students relate their experience to the past event to appreciate the feelings of the people who were involved and to understand what helped or hindered them in reaching their goals. After obtaining relevant facts, the students express their opinions about the way people solved the problem, and suggest other solutions after they have visualized the probable consequences of each.

Critical thinking needs facts. John Dewey once said, "We can have facts without thinking, but we cannot have thinking without facts." After locating accounts of the facts, the student must examine them for accuracy and relevance. Are the statements true, free from bias, fair-minded? Are they sufficiently specific for the purpose? Is the publication date recent enough to include new discoveries? What is the purpose or intent of the author? What are his claims to being an authority? Is his viewpoint impartial?

The student must distinguish between fact and opinion and between a sound opinion and a superficial one. His attention should be called to clues that indicate opinion: "It is believed," "Some authorities say." He must also recognize statements that will always be in the realm of opinion because they cannot be verified. Moreover, he must see how the facts are related, assess their relative importance in solving the problem, and suspend judgment until he has a fairly sound basis for making it. The following types of errors are common in critical thinking:

1. Going beyond the facts in making an unwarranted generalization: "Parents put too much pressure on children."
2. Depending on a single authority: "The United States should send warships to Spain; my father said so."
3. Attributing results to a single cause: "I caught cold because I got my feet wet."
4. Oversimplifying a situation by saying it is either-or, all black or all white.
5. Overlooking the fact that words, especially abstract words, may have different meanings in different contexts and for different persons.

From the fifth or sixth grade on, students can learn to recognize propaganda devices such as these:

Omitting important facts
Highlighting certain ideas by using large print or placing them in a prominent position on the page—or playing down certain ideas by the opposite means
Quoting words, phrases, and sentences out of context
Irony or sarcasm
Using emotionally charged words
Half-truths
Exaggerated claims

To encourage students to weigh various statements based on given data, a teacher asked them to indicate whether they thought:

The evidence is sufficient to make the statement true.
The evidence is sufficient to make the statement false.
The evidence suggests the statement is probably true.
The evidence suggests the statement is probably false.
The evidence is insufficient to support any conclusion.

To give the students practice in making comparisons between excerpts from the same author, the teacher asked questions such as these:

Did the paragraphs agree or disagree in principle?
Explain why you chose the answer you did.
What is your opinion of the author's consistency as a thinker?

To give them practice in detecting bias in an account of a visit to America, the teacher asked these questions:

What was the nationality of the writer?
Does he admire or dislike America?
Whose opinions did he cite?
Give evidence for your answer.

The discussion that follows exercises of this kind can be most beneficial to the students.

The following excerpts from a lesson on reading the newspaper illustrate a teaching approach to propaganda analysis for two groups that differed markedly in level of ability:

Teacher: Let's list some of the purposes that journalists have when they write a newspaper.
Pupil: To tell us something we don't already know.
Teacher: Yes, to give us information.
Pupil: To sell something—as in advertising.
Pupil: To express their opinion on a subject.
Pupil: To convince or persuade us.
Teacher: In what parts of the newspaper are they most likely to try to convince or persuade you?
Pupil: In ads, in editorials.
Teacher: How do you try to convince your mother that you should go to a show or stay up to watch TV?
Pupil: Say everybody's doing it—or someone she likes is doing it.
Pupil: Tell her the teacher says you can learn something from it.
Pupil: Tell her you'll work harder if you take time out.
Teacher: What do your parents sometimes say to convince you?
Pupil: "When I was your age. . . ."
Teacher: Now we're going to look at ads and at editorials. (The slow group look at ads; the able learners read editorials.) See how many ways of convincing they use (teacher holds up ad for slow group). What appeals do they make? What are they saying?
Pupil: It's cool, delicious.
Pupil: Appeal to the "good old times."
Teacher: Where did you get that idea?
Pupil: It says, "Grandmother used to make it and she liked it, and it tasted good."

Teacher: (shows another ad). What is this saying to us?
Pupil: The tires are strong enough to be used in races.
Pupil: We can depend on these tires.
Teacher: *Depend* is a good word.
Pupil: The tires are safe.
Teacher: (writes "strong and safe" on board).

The students then read back the sentences they have dictated and refer to the cards on which they have written new words.

Teacher: What desires are these advertisers appealing to?
Pupil: Desire to be rich.
Pupil: To show off.
Pupil: To make your friends envy you.
Teacher: What are their other specific purposes?
Pupil: To describe the article.
Pupil: To flatter you.
Pupil: To catch and hold your attention.
Teacher: If you're a good reader and aware of the advertiser's purpose, how do you react?
Pupil: You're skeptical.

The group of able learners were reading an editorial in favor of a presidential candidate and a letter against him.

Teacher: Why did you feel it was important to recognize the author's purpose?
Pupil: It makes you read differently.
Teacher: Yes, it affects your approach to reading—the way you read, and your speed, too. What were some of the clues to the author's purpose? (lists them on board as pupils mention them):

> first paragraph
> form or structure of selection
> source
> pictures
> boldface headings

Teacher: What differences did you notice between the language used in the editorial and the language used elsewhere? Look particularly at the language used in the ad. What feelings is the writer trying to convey, and what words does he use? (writes them on board as pupils give them):

> Something new and different: *recent* in contrast with *Colonial; fresh insight*
> Luxury: *rare; opulent comfort; magnificent; exquisite* in contrast with *provincial*
> Value: *savings, at slightly lower prices*

Teacher: How many know the meaning of *opulent?* What do we do to find out?
Pupil: Guess it means luxurious.
Teacher: What do we do to check? (Pupil looks it up in dictionary.)

No one should confuse critical thinking and reading with merely negative criticism. Critical thinking is often constructive; it should at least be positive. The best thinkers build up rather than tear down, solving problems, not merely uncovering them. In encouraging a student to think and read critically, a teacher should avoid developing a generally derogatory attitude toward everyone and everything.

It is not only the bright children who profit from instruction and practice in critical thinking. Children with less than average intelligence profited most from lessons in critical thinking and reading [25]. *Reading for Understanding* by Thurstone [83] provides practice in critical reading for elementary school children. Teachers can build their own critical-reading laboratory— a collection of clippings, each one thought-provoking, some containing a false analogy to be detected, "a conclusion that lacks proof, a passage in which name calling runs riot, a statement wrenched from its context" [82, p. 201].

Thinking is implicit in every aspect of reading [81]. Paragraph reading, for example, requires logical reasoning. The main idea of the paragraph is the premise. The reader examines the evidence given in support of the premise, appraising it bit by bit. When he has a clear idea of the author's thought, he can compare it with his own. Thinking is still more obviously involved in drawing conclusions and in making generalizations, inferences, and applications. The teacher can guide the reader's thinking by suggestions, questions, and hints. The first questions direct the reader's attention to what the author actually said. The next questions relate the content of the selection to the reader's previous learnings: What would you expect to happen? Did John's decision seem reasonable to you? A third set of questions might relate to the implications of the passage: Do we still have a frontier for people to explore? A fourth group of questions invited speculation: Why do you think the United States has incurred the hatred rather than the respect and gratitude of certain nations? "Why" questions call for evidence to support the judgment expressed. They should be asked as soon as children have learned to read simple stories or articles, for example: "From what you have learned about Chibi in *Crow Boy*, do you think he was stupid? Why or why not?" [3] "What was the cause of the Boston Tea Party? How was it different from other riots that you have read about?"

Using such questions as a springboard, the teacher may shift the students' attention from their answers to the methods of thinking by which they obtained the answers. After repeatedly demonstrating the thinking-reading-thinking process, the teacher may expect students to raise their own questions and formulate their own hypotheses. This process of guiding students to practice critical thinking while reading begins as soon as children are "on their own in reading" and continues until they have attained a high level of maturity in reading.

INTERPRETIVE READING

Interpretation is reading in depth. It transcends the lexical meaning of the words and the literal meaning of the sentences and leads to appreciation of literature which requires meticulous examination of words, phrases, and sentences: What meanings have grown up around this word? What special meaning does it have in its context? The previous chapter discussed context as a clue to word meaning. This chapter is concerned with words as clues to the interpretation of a selection. Interpretation frequently hinges on a special meaning of a certain word or phrase. Students must measure the impact of these words on the other words in the whole passage. For example, a ridiculous name for a character may suggest that the story is meant to be farcical or comical. The words used to describe the various characters aid the reader in interpreting them. In one story words such as *realistic, cynical, skeptical, hard-boiled,* and *worldly* applied to one character, while the words *fidgety, shy, hesitant, mild, naïve,* and *eccentric* were clues to interpreting another. A class may begin with the interpretation of advertisements, go on to common figurative and metaphorical expressions such as "the cold war," "the iron curtain," and finally undertake the interpretation of poetry.

Facts are only useful as tools for thinking and imagining. Being able to follow the plot is only a first step in understanding the characters who are involved in it. It requires reflection to arrive at an understanding of human problems and to bridge the gap between the printed page and the world as it is and as it may become. Though the study of literature should contribute to an appreciation of literary aesthetics with diction, structure, tone, style, unity, uniqueness, and depth as some sources, it should also foster appreciation of human values. There is much more to the reading of literature than most students realize.

A student may be able to define the words, understand the literal meaning of the passage, and answer factual questions about it; this does not mean that he knows how to interpret the author's mood and intent, uncover the motives of the characters, or perceive the symbolism implied in figurative language. These higher skills go beyond the question, "What did the author say?" They require that the reader possess special techniques for discovering what the author meant and determining what personal meaning the selection has for him.

Levels of Interpretation

Interpretation may concern itself with various levels of profundity or universality. Andresen [2] described five levels on which fictional or dramatic action may take place—physical, mental, moral, psychological, as in Willa Cather's "Paul's Case," and philosophical, as in Macbeth's soliloquy on death. A story of intrinsic depth may operate on all five levels. For example, the reading of *Romola* may give one some understanding of Italian life in the Renaissance. But one has not really read the novel unless by the time he comes to Tito's end on the banks of the Tiber, he has so comprehended the all but imperceptible degeneration of a human being that the experience causes him to reexamine himself and his aims in life. There are students who would do far better to read less and make more reflective applications of what authors are trying to tell them about "man's ways and his general direction" on the trail of human progress [42].

Teaching Suggestions

The first step is to decide what the immediate goals are and what relationship they have to the long-range ones, based on the philosophy of the curriculum, and then what selections would in part fulfill these goals and how. Scholastic and other teen-age magazines and certain modern paperbacks supply new, exciting material, e.g., "The Scarlet Ibis" in *Cavalcade* for February, 1961. The next step is to analyze the selection as in preparing programmed material, determining the knowledge to be gained, its significance, and what specific reading skills the assignment calls for—skills which the teacher must provide for in the lesson plans.

Robert Frost's "Stopping by Woods on a Snowy Evening" gives the opportunity for a contrast of the surface meaning with the deeper symbolic meaning. The surface meaning is easy to grasp. The symbolic meaning allows several interpretations, but all must be valid and based on evidence within the poem. Frost himself refused to explain his meaning. The authors of programmed exercises on this poem [54] suggested certain symbolisms that might occur to a mature person who desires to escape from civilization to a natural, primitive life, for solitude. These desires might conflict with the person's sense of responsibility to the world in which he is living. Interpretation involves, first, getting the literal meaning; second, exploring the possible meanings of key words and phrases; third, checking the reasonableness of one's interpretation; and, fourth, using what one gains to broaden or deepen one's understanding of himself, of other people, and of events. The methods of such analytic reading developed in English classes should be carried over to the reading tasks in the student's other subjects and to his free reading.

Teachers often expect students to use higher-level reading skills without sufficient instruction. One must grasp the setting of a story if one is to interpret its events and characters. Many types of details help the reader to reconstruct the setting. LaBrant [37] suggested that the reader look for clues of time and place in such details as the names of historical personages who are mentioned, descriptions of means of transportation, of buildings, of clothing, and of the occupations and activities of the characters. History is a common background for fiction, and the wise teacher prepares his class in advance.

Before they read a selection, the teacher can help the students understand and enjoy a story by acquainting them with words, concepts, and types of sentence structure that might otherwise cause them to stumble. The teacher should ask various types of questions—factual questions, inferential questions that call for conclusions and promote an understanding of motives, questions that require anticipation of the outcome, questions that enable the pupil to show how he feels about the characters.

To orient students to the story of Rip Van Winkle and to evoke their responses, the teacher may ask questions like the following:

What type of story does the title suggest?
At what time and in what place does the action occur?
What kind of person was Rip Van Winkle? How can you find out?
Which of his characteristics annoyed his wife?
Why did he go with his dog into the mountains?
What kind of story is this—a true story, a tall tale, a fable, a fanciful story?
Does the author want to amuse, inform, or persuade the reader? What is the basis for your opinion?

Students should approach a book in the spirit of inquiry—to find out what the author is trying to tell them. After they have read the title and opening sentences, the teacher can encourage them to anticipate the outcome. Using one's own experience, both firsthand and vicarious, to predict what will happen next makes reading exciting; the student has an immediate motivation to read further in order to see whether his prediction is right. Informed guessing—guessing that is soundly based on clues inherent in the story—directs the reader's attention to structure of the selection as a whole and encourages him to concentrate.

There are many approaches. The student may read to discover a solution for a social problem, to find a key to life, or just for pleasure. He may expect a selection to teach him a lesson. Some students are interested in analyzing the author's style to find out how he achieves the overall effect.

To help students find and interpret clues to character and motive and discover how the characters reveal themselves, a teacher may use the following procedure:

1. The teacher instructs the class in the study of certain pieces of literature. Together they look for clues, symbols, and relations; trace down allusions and interpret them in the light of the context. They analyze figurative language. They make inferences about characters and plot on the basis of direct statements; colorful descriptions of a person's appearance, voice, and actions; and the setting or atmosphere [21, 53]. The students repeatedly go through this process of recognizing clues and making inferences from them until they have gained proficiency.
2. Then they all read a selection outside of class and report on it to the class.
3. After learning this creative method, they apply it in their independent reading.

A high school student understood this method of teaching and appraised it as follows:

> At the beginning of this term, I was very vague on the deeper meaning; I really didn't think there was any. But our teacher first lets us read a story and asks us to interpret it and write a composition giving our interpretation. Then, when we come to class, she asks us questions about it and gradually—I guess she sort of steers the conversation—we come out with the really deeper meaning. I think it's very enlightening because now, when I read books for pleasure, I start thinking about them, and wonder if there are any deeper meanings, and I start looking for them.

Student's interpretive processes in reading can best be studied by retrospective and introspective techniques [27]. Immediately after completing the reading of a selection, they describe in detail the reading method they used. Or they write a composition on how they ordinarily read assignments in different subjects. In an interview it is possible to elicit introspection while the student is reading a given passage. If the teacher knows the student's unique approach, he can help him to evaluate and improve it.

In reading such works as *Walden, Golden Boy, The Great Gatsby, Heart of Darkness, Portrait of the Artist as a Young Man,* able learners should be encouraged to perceive deeper meanings. In the *Trial and Death of Socrates* or *Brave New World,* they should analyze the philosopher's sense of responsibility to society. Why must man suffer, as in Greek tragedy, in Shakespeare, in the Book of Job, in *J.B.* (MacLeish's modern version of Job), or in other classic or contemporary tragedies?

Students who have had the experience of searching for deep meanings tend to do more serious reading on their own initiative. One high school senior said:

We've been reading Dante's *Inferno*. Right now, I'm reading the *Symposium*. I believe if you give a student freedom and don't enclose his mind and tell him he's got to do this and he's got to do that, then he doesn't feel any resentment toward the teachers. He just feels as though he has a field day and he'll go out and read books that he's interested in; and once he does that, I've noticed it's sort of a chain reaction. One book will lead to another. I know it's happened to me. For example, I have a hobby—I build model airplanes—and while doing that I read about pilots, countries, and wars. From there I went to economics and military leaders. And soon I had a whole library in the palm of my hand.

Reading great literature is an important experience. These books challenge students' curiosity about life, widen their experience, and help them to find themselves. Teachers are too likely to underestimate students' ability to think and feel deeply.

To make sure that students read books, a teacher may use many devices other than the formal book report. He may keep a class file for individualized reading. Students may choose to read extensively on one subject or theme. They may illustrate the book, write the diary of a character, continue the story, or change its ending in any way that seems more appropriate or satisfying. They particularly enjoy panel discussions in which several groups discuss books that deal with the same theme, or more informal "book chats." Some teachers occasionally use "sales talks" or the popular dramatization of a story to introduce books to a class. These responses to reading may involve all the language arts.

Reading and writing go along together. Reading not only sets standards for writing, but it also serves to illustrate the countless situations in which language is used. It enables the student to develop criteria and appraise his own English expression. "Bad" English is primarily speech or writing that lacks clarity. It is unnecessarily complicated or twisted, hiding rather than conveying the author's thought. Nor does it please the reader or listener; it may annoy or irritate him. The poor writer uses difficult words where smaller words would do better. "Bad" English may also be that which is inappropriate to the occasion.

PERSONAL DEVELOPMENT THROUGH READING: A HIGHER READING SKILL

Kinds of Impact of Reading

Personal development is one of our two main objectives in teaching reading. It is assumed that reading has some impact on individuals, although it is difficult to obtain proof of the influence of a particular book on a particular person. David Russéll [63] has made an outstanding contribution to the understanding of this aim in reading.

Information. Information gained from reading expands the individual's intellectual horizons. "Books," one boy said, "answer many of the questions that I have been wondering about." The more one learns from reading the richer his background for interpreting and enjoying what he reads. Information about how other people, both real and imaginary, have handled their personal problems contributes to the solution of one's own problems.

A psychiatric comic strip on "the onset and cure of a mild case of paranoid psychosis" influenced some high school sophomores in three schools to take a more favorable attitude toward mental health. There was some evidence that "the comic strip episode helped to sharpen and clarify perceptions and definitions of mental health problems" [60, p. 342].

Action. There are many evidences that changes in behavior can be traced to understanding gained from books. One youngster attributed his improved manners to a book called *Manners for Millions.* "This book," he said, "showed how ill-mannered I really was and taught me many new ways of showing how well-mannered I could be."

Cannell and MacDonald [11] reported that health news had some impact on both attitudes and behavior. Of sixty smokers who had changed their smoking behavior, 38 per cent cited magazine articles as a main reason. They rated magazines above newspapers for reliability; radio and television stood considerably below these two sources. However, smokers—even relatively well-educated ones—were less likely than nonsmokers to accept the facts revealed in health articles, or even to read the articles.

Some books are said to have brought about social reforms: the emancipation of the Negro has been attributed to Harriet Beecher Stowe's *Uncle Tom's Cabin,* municipal reforms to Steffens' *The Shame of the Cities,* pure food and drug acts to Sinclair's *The Jungle,* and progressive education to John Dewey's *Democracy and Education.* A reading experience may reshape the attitudes and philosophy that the reader has brought to it.

Tumin [89] found that reading aided in reducing tension among white Southerners in the emotionally charged regions concerned with racial desegregation in the schools. He showed that exposure to newspapers and magazines as well as to radio and television—media which acquainted the Southerner with a Northern or national point of view—contributed to building readiness for desegregation in certain North Carolina communities. Gray [27] concluded from his review of research into the impact of reading that it can change attitudes, reduce prejudices, and affect votes.

Attitudes and Values. Students on all educational levels have reported that reading changed certain of their attitudes—toward themselves and toward reading, toward other people, toward family relations, toward the nation, toward war and peace. A seventh-grade girl wrote about a book that increased her ability to feel with others:

The book *The Trembling Years* was the story of a girl struck with polio. It explains the feelings she has and the thoughts that she has as she goes through pain and trouble.

I like this book because it seemed so real you could almost feel the pain as she felt it.

When I finished the book it made me realize how little my own problems are and how much I have compared to many.

High school students said that some books helped them to persevere, deepened their religious feeling, changed their behavior toward their families, made them realize that they should stop fighting with their brothers and sisters, and "made me think about the kind of life I'd like to lead." After reading *Dear and Glorious Physician*, a ninth-grade girl wrote: "I had the feeling I should go out and do something great. Of course, this feeling did not last long, but it did get me to thinking just what I can do for humanity."

One pupil reported similar incidents:

Recently I read *Clay Fingers*. This girl broke her leg and couldn't go to college with her friends. This book showed me that if something of bad fortune happens to you, you shouldn't sit moping about it but make yourself useful or occupy yourself with some hobby which would benefit yourself and other people. If something does come up so that I can't do something I wanted to do, I think of this book and I don't mope around but take the news in the cheerfullest manner possible.

I read a short story for a book report. The name of it was *The Magic Night*. In this book it showed a group of kids having a wonderful time. On the way home they were speeding and crashed with another car. Susie, a girl in the story, wakes up on the hospital bed. She finds that Molly, a girl who had gone with them, had been killed. Then Susie thinks—Mom, Dad, and other people say that the boy driving will get the blame. But I didn't tell him not to go fast. This makes me think that if I am with somebody and they are doing something not quite right, then I should say something to them. This story made me think quite a bit about this.

Reading may influence people negatively as well as positively. This fact must be faced. The influence of the low-quality books and magazines read by retarded readers is illustrated by the following quotations:

I read a love comic book and I felt kind of strange inside. I felt sorry inside because there was this girl named Elaine and this boy named Lefty. So Elaine found Lefty kissing his cousin Pat. So Elaine thought he was playing her for a sucker. Then he came over to her house and she quit him. But he asked her to forgive him. . . .

I've been reading a lot about movie stars and love books. I've learned a lot for my age.

I used to think teen-age marriage was the craziest thing in the world. But yesterday I read in a magazine about a teen-age couple that married when they were very, very young and they got along better than many adults.

Literature conveys basic values such as courage, independence, fortitude, simplicity and loving kindness. More likely to be acquired by reading than by watching present-day television programs, these are needed more than ever in a technological, industrial world.

The Self-concept. Reading may modify an individual's self-concept. One ninth-grade girl described this experience:

I just finished reading a book, *Jane Eyre.* It was a touching story. It showed me that we should follow God's calling; do what He wants us to do. It showed me how to be a person who isn't selfish or hard. Also it showed me you don't have to be pretty to be well liked. In these ways this book affected my feeling about myself and also to some extent my acting.

Books on science may also affect the individual's perception of himself—may have an organizing and integrating influence on his personality. An experience of this kind was recollected by a highly gifted adult:

My high school arranged for us to use the public library if we wanted to. I had always enjoyed reading and now found it marvelous to be able to roam among the shelves unhindered. Some titles drew me like a magnet—books describing the wondrous universe which we inhabit and about which I had never learned anything. *The Stars in Their Courses, The Universe Around Us*—these and other books I read avidly, awed before the immensities and the splendors which utterly outstripped my imagination.

It was when I was reading the latter book that it happened. Sir James Jeans had described the unimaginable vastness of the cosmos with its swirling galaxies and the inconceivable minuteness of the atom, when suddenly I *knew* with an absolute conviction that went through me as a physical shock that within that immeasurable range I, too, *belonged.*

It was the most truly religious experience of my life—an experience wherein was permanently established my ultimate belongingness in the overall scheme of existence.

"Reading for personal fulfillment" demands that the adolescent or adult take time to compare himself with real or fictional characters who, "when circumstances demanded, were able to call up the necessary reserves of courage and resourcefulness" [8, p. 287].

Developmental Tasks. Reading may facilitate accomplishment of the developmental tasks of childhood and adolescence. These are some of the troublesome ones which Havighurst first described in his book, *Human Development and Education* [28, p. 115]. He listed books that might help adolescents achieve emancipation from the family, establish heterosexual relations, make vocational plans, and establish a philosophy of life. All of these accomplishments are desired outcomes of the teaching of English. Brooks [6], too, was concerned with the contribution that reading might make to the accomplishment of adolescent tasks.

In his book on mental health, Kaplan described the impact of books on children [33, p. 355]:

Books and stories can make a vital contribution to the mental health of children. They provide a medium through which boys and girls may be encouraged to discuss their personal problems; they make available a means through which youngsters can escape, temporarily, from their tensions and frustrations; and they furnish vicarious experiences which enable children to gain deeper insight into their own behavior by experiencing the life problems of others.

The theory underlying bibliotherapy is that the reader may identify himself with a desirable character or may adopt principles that clarify some of his difficulties and serve as a guide to action. The problem is to introduce the right book to the right child at the right psychological moment.

Conditions Affecting a Book's Influence

The impact of reading material is affected by certain characteristics of the material, by the ideas the author hopes to communicate, by the personality and background of the reader, and by the setting in which the interaction between author and reader takes place [64]. Wittick [93] mentioned a number of conditions that are conducive to developing an enjoyment of poetry: favorable family attitudes toward poetry and happy early experiences with it, favorable attitudes of teachers and peers, an introduction to poems that appeal to one's interests, and skillful classroom presentation.

Characteristics of the Content. The *format* of the book may invite or repel a reader. The *intrinsic interest* of the book, according to high school students, is the major factor in determining what they read, how they read, and what they remember. One bright eighth-grade girl described the impact of one of A. Conan Doyle's books on her as follows:

I chose *Hound of the Baskervilles* because of its excellent intrigue and mystery so typical of A. Conan Doyle. The spookiness of the moor, the suspense of waiting for the quarry, the methods of Sherlock Holmes made this book outstanding in its field. While reading this book, you are dragged into the story and made to feel the moods as well as the actions of the characters. You are given the feeling of being a part of the story.

A book's *difficulty* may be a deterrent to many readers because of poor organization, colorless or unfamiliar words, and lengthy or overly complex sentences—common sources of difficulty. It is obvious that personal development through reading cannot be achieved through material that frustrates the reader, leaving him unaware of the possibilities of the personal application.

Piekarz [50] found that children who read a selection poorly had fewer reactions to it and gave more literal than interpretative responses.

Difficulty of the reading material is, of course, relative to the student's reading ability. His skill in sensing the author's mood, intent, and purpose, in interpreting imagery, and in detecting clues of character, and his ability to feel the emotional impact of the story—all these factors affect its impact on his attitudes and even on his behavior. Reading can contribute little to the personal development of a poor reader. The child who is reading is growing. A thirteen-year-old boy with a consuming interest in science and mathematics and with a strong tendency to feel inadequate had the experience of finding his "discoveries" verified in his reading. On the basis of his reading he had concluded that a certain relationship must exist between distance and the force of gravity, and he was greatly excited and pleased when he later read that such relationships did in fact exist. This experience contributed greatly toward developing his feeling of capability.

The quality of words—"high-value" words, stereotypes, or ambiguous words—may help or hinder the reader's attempts to interpret a passage. Information given in persuasive form is recalled more accurately than information given without emphasis.

The Author's Intent. The novelist or story writer communicates his ideas largely by means of his characters—their cultural patterns and family life, and the personal qualities that are associated with their achievement. He treats some kinds of persons positively, others negatively. He presents certain values and concepts either explicitly or implicitly [64].

The Reader's Personality and Background. What the reader brings to a particular book, in addition to reading skill, is a major factor in its impact on him. His emotional readiness, his background of experiences, his intelligence, his credulity and susceptibility to persuasion, his concept of himself, and his convictions or attitudes about the topic—all of these personal factors may affect a book's influence. The reader's momentary need or some anxiety about a personal problem may create a readiness for certain content that he might otherwise ignore.

The reader's sense of responsibility also helps to determine his response. An overindulged child who has everything that money can buy, who has not had to do anything for himself, and who has had praise and approval indiscriminately bestowed upon him may never have learned to put forth the effort that thoughtful reading demands. Books may have only a superficial influence on him.

The Reading Environment. The attitudes and expectancies of the group, including the degree to which it demands conformity, are other potent factors in determining the impact of reading on the individual. The student gains prestige and self-esteem by reading books that are approved by the group. Then, too, the teacher's emotional response to a book often makes a lasting impression on a student.

Methods of Studying the Influence of Reading

One may study the effect of reading on personal development by using a modified critical-incident technique—asking students to recall and describe any experience in which a book or article influenced their attitudes, points of view, or behavior. The following directions were given to high school students:

Sometimes we wonder what reading does to people—what effect reading has on their points of view, attitudes, and behavior. Will you help us to find out? This is what you can do. Think back over the books you have read. Try to remember how many of the books influenced you. Did you think differently or feel differently or act differently after you read the book or part of the book? Just write whatever you remember about how any book changed your way of thinking or feeling or acting.

This approach elicited responses such as the following:

A ninth-grade boy, certainly not a book enthusiast, described the influence of one book:

On the whole, books do not influence me at all, but one book had a very great influence on me and that was *Rockne of Notre Dame*. This is the story of a man, a not very big man, who was not too good at sports physically but he became one of the best sports coaches that ever was. After reading this story my thoughts all turned to sports, and now sports are a major part of my life.

A ninth-grade girl described the personal value of certain books:

Most of the time when I read books I put myself in the characters' places even if I'm reading about an animal such as the dog in *A Dog Named Chips*.

When I read the book *Career* there was a caption under the picture explaining what that person did, and when I read it I imagined myself in her place, doing all those wonderful things. When I finished the book I could have read it over again. I enjoyed it very much because it is what I want to do when I graduate. It was all about airplanes. When they spoke about the planes I could just see them in the sky.

Another ninth-grade girl attributed a change in her way of thinking to a book called *The Golden Thorn.*

After reading this book I felt that I had actually been there. It made me think of the people who are trying to be free. It made me feel as if I were one of them. It made me glad to be free. I think it made me kinder and more friendly to people who really need help.

Similar introspective reports may be obtained by detailed questionnaires, by open-end questions, or in unstructured or freely written compositions. When obtained with the interest and cooperation of the students, such reports are usually authentic, concrete, and vivid.

In response to a questionnaire [92], almost two-thirds of 1,256 college students said that books had contributed to the development of their philosophy of life. About one-third thought that reading had changed their attitudes, stimulated them to imitate certain characters, helped them to find their ideal selves, or develop some of the personal qualities they had read about. Some also said that reading had helped them to identify and solve some of their problems. On a sentence-completion test, another group of forty-six college students revealed changes in attitudes toward themselves and toward their reading and studying [21].

Additional insights into the effect of a book or an article may be obtained from students' responses in informal or class discussion groups. In more structured situations the student is given a story or article to read and is asked to report his thoughts and feelings about it.

The student who is proficient in higher-level reading skills will find greater enjoyment and achieve more personal development through reading.

REFERENCES

1. Altick, Richard D.: *Preface to Critical Reading,* Holt, Rinehart and Winston, Inc., New York, 1960.

2. Andreson, Oliver: "Evaluating Profundity in Literature," *Journal of Reading,* vol. 9, pp. 387–390, May, 1965.

3. Artley, A. Sterl: "Implementing a Critical Reading Program on the Primary Level," in J. Allen Figurel (ed.), *Reading and Inquiry,* International Reading Association Conference Proceedings, vol. 10, Newark, Del., 1965, pp. 176–178.

4. Bormuth, John R.: "Mean Word Depth as a Predictor of Comprehension Difficulty," *California Journal of Educational Research*, vol. 15, pp. 226–231, November, 1964.

5. Braam, Leonard: "Developing and Measuring Flexibility in Reading," *The Reading Teacher*, vol. 16, pp. 247–251, January, 1963.

6. Brooks, Alice R.: "Integrating Books and Reading with Adolescent Tasks," *School Review*, vol. 58, pp. 211–219, April, 1950.

7. Bruner, Jerome S.: "The Act of Discovery," *Harvard Educational Review*, vol. 31, pp. 21–32, Winter, 1961.

8. Burton, Dwight L.: "Heads Out of the Sand: Secondary Schools Face the Challenge of Reading," *Educational Forum*, vol. 24, pp. 285–293, March, 1960.

9. Burton, Dwight L.: "Teaching Students to Read Imaginative Literature," in Dwight L. Burton and John S. Simmons (eds.), *Teaching English in Today's High Schools: Selected Readings*, Holt, Rinehart and Winston, Inc., New York, 1965, pp. 111–126.

10. Burton, Dwight L.: "Teaching Students to Read Literature," in Margaret J. Early (ed.), *Reading Instruction in Secondary Schools*, International Reading Association, Newark, Del., 1964, pp. 87–102.

11. Cannell, Charles F., and James C. MacDonald: "The Impact of Health News on Attitudes and Behavior," *Journalism Quarterly*, vol. 33, pp. 315–323, Summer, 1956.

12. Carrillo, Lawrence W.: "Developing Flexible Reading Rates," *Journal of Reading*, vol. 8, pp. 322–325, April, 1965.

13. Carter, Homer L. J., and Dorothy J. McGinnis: *Teaching Individuals to Read*, D. C. Heath and Company, Boston, 1962.

14. Chase, Francis S.: "Demands on the Reader in the Next Decade," in Helen M. Robinson (ed.), *Controversial Issues in Reading and Promising Solutions*, Supplementary Educational Monographs, no. 91, University of Chicago Press, Chicago, 1961.

15. Ciardi, John: *How Does a Poem Mean?* Houghton Mifflin Company, Boston, 1959.

16. Criscuolo, Nicholas P.: "A Plea for Critical Reading in the Primary Grades," *Peabody Journal of Education*, vol. 43, pp. 107–112, September, 1965.

17. Dale, Edgar: "The Critical Reader," *The News Letter*, vol. 30, pp. 1–4, January, 1965.

18. Dale, Edgar: "Learning by Discovery," *The News Letter*, vol. 29, pp. 1–4, November, 1964.

19. Dale, Edgar: "Reading Magazines," *Journal of Business Education*, vol. 39, pp. 115–116, December, 1963.

20. De Boer, John J.: "Structure in Relation to Reading," *Education*, vol. 84, pp. 525–528, May, 1964.

21. Englander, Meryl E.: "Changes in Affect Attributable to Instruction in Reading Improvement on the College Level," *Journal of Educational Research*, vol. 53, pp. 231–236, February, 1960.

22. Ennis, Robert: "A Concept of Critical Thinking," *Harvard Educational Review*, vol. 32, pp. 81–111, Winter, 1962.

23. Entwhistle, Doris R.: "Evaluation of Study-skills Courses: A Review," *Journal of Educational Research*, vol. 53, pp. 243–251, March, 1960.

24. Fadiman, Clifton: *Reading I've Liked,* Simon and Schuster, Inc., New York, 1941.

25. Glaser, E. M.: *An Experiment in the Development of Critical Thinking,* Teachers College Press, Teachers College, Columbia University, New York, 1941.

26. Goins, Jean T.: *Visual Perceptual Abilities and Early Reading Progress,* Supplementary Educational Monographs, no. 87, University of Chicago Press, Chicago, February, 1958.

27. Gray, William S.: "New Approaches to the Study of Interpretation in Reading," *Journal of Educational Research,* vol. 52, pp. 65–67, October, 1958.

28. Havighurst, Robert J.: *Human Development and Education,* Longmans, Green & Co., Inc., New York, 1953.

29. Hoffman, James D.: "Insight into Effective Study," *Education,* vol. 78, pp. 346–348, February, 1958.

30. Hughes, Rosalind: *Let's Enjoy Poetry,* Houghton Mifflin Company, Boston, 1961.

31. "Improving Thinking Skills through Reading," *The Reading Teacher* (entire issue), vol. 13, pp. 169–207, February, 1960.

32. Jan-Tausch, Evelyn: "Teaching Developmental Reading in the Secondary School," in Margaret J. Early (ed.), *Reading Instruction in Secondary Schools,* International Reading Association, Newark, Del., 1964, pp. 45–57.

33. Kaplan, Louis: *Mental Health and Human Relations in Education,* Harper & Row, Publishers, Incorporated, New York, 1959.

34. Karlin, Robert: "Teaching Reading in High School," *Education,* vol. 84, pp. 334–338, February, 1964.

35. Kircher, Clara J. (comp.): *Character Formation through Books: A Bibliography,* The Catholic University of America Press, Washington, D.C., 1952.

36. Krumboltz, John D., and William W. Farquhar: "The Effect of Three Teaching Methods on Achievement and Motivational Outcomes in a How-to-study Course," *Psychological Monographs,* vol. 71, pp. 1–26, 443, 1957.

37. LaBrant, Lou: "The Larger Context: Setting," *The Reading Teacher,* vol. 11, pp. 234–238, April, 1958.

38. Letton, Mildred: "Individual Differences in Interpretive Responses to Reading Poetry at the Ninth Grade Level," unpublished doctoral dissertation, University of Chicago, Chicago, 1958.

39. Malter, Morton S.: "Studies of the Effectiveness of Graphic Materials," *Journal of Educational Research,* vol. 46, pp. 263–274, December, 1952.

40. Maney, Ethel S.: "Literal and Critical Reading in Science," *Journal of Experimental Education,* vol. 27, pp. 57–64, September, 1958.

41. Massey, William: *Helping High School Students Read Better,* Holt, Rinehart and Winston, Inc., New York, 1965.

42. Maugham, W. Somerset: "A Confidential Question," *NEA Journal,* vol. 54, p. 19, April, 1965.

43. McConihe, Esther J.: "Study Skills Need Improving, Too," *Journal of Developmental Reading,* vol. 1, pp. 40–45, Winter, 1958.

44. McCullough, Constance M.: "Characteristics of Effective Readers in the Elementary School," in Helen M. Robinson (comp. and ed.), *Reading Instruction* *in Various Patterns of Grouping,* Supplementary Educational Monographs, no. 89, University of Chicago Press, Chicago, 1959, pp. 3–8.

45. McKillop, Anne S.: *The Relationship between the Reader's Attitude and Certain Types of Reading Responses,* Teachers College Press, Teachers College, Columbia University, New York, 1952.

46. *My Weekly Reader,* vol. 35, issue 6, October 20, 1965.

47. Newman, Slater E.: "Student vs. Instructor Design of Study Method," *Journal of Educational Psychology,* vol. 48, pp. 228–333, October, 1957.

48. Niles, Olive S.: "Developing Essential Reading Skills in the English Program," in J. Allen Figurel (ed.), *Reading and Inquiry,* International Reading Association Conference Proceedings, vol. 10, Newark, Del., 1965, pp. 34–36.

49. Pauk, Walter: "Study Skills and Scholastic Achievement," *The Reading Teacher,* vol. 19, pp. 180–182, December, 1965.

50. Piekarz, Josephine A.: "Getting Meaning from Reading," *Elementary School Journal,* vol. 56, pp. 303–309, March, 1956.

51. Rankin, Earl F., Jr.: "Sequential Emphasis upon Speed and Comprehension in a College Reading Improvement Program," *Journal of Developmental Reading,* vol. 7, pp. 46–54, Autumn, 1963.

52. "Read Faster and Better," *Time,* vol. 66, pp. 41–42, August 22, 1960.

53. *Reading: Grades 7.8.9,* Curriculum Bulletin, series no. 11, Board of Education, City of New York, 1959.

54. Reid, James M., John Ciardi, and Laurence Perrine: *Poetry: A Closer Look,* Harcourt, Brace & World, Inc., New York, 1963.

55. Richards, Ivor A.: *How to Read a Page,* W. W. Norton & Company, Inc., New York, 1942.

56. Robinson, Francis P.: *Effective Study,* Harper & Row, Publishers, Incorporated, New York, 1961.

57. Robinson, H. Alan, Stanford E. Taylor, and Helen Frackenpohl: *EDL Study Skills Library,* Educational Development Laboratories, Huntington, N.Y.

58. Robinson, Helen M.: "Developing Critical Readers," in Russell G. Stauffer (comp.), *Dimensions of Critical Reading,* Proceedings of the Annual Education and Reading Conference, vol. 11, University of Delaware, Newark, Del., 1964, pp. 1–12.

59. Rogers, Charlotte Dee: "Individual Differences in Interpretive Responses to Reading the Short Story at the Eleventh Grade Level," unpublished doctoral dissertation, University of Arizona, Tucson, Ariz., 1965.

60. Rose, Arnold M.: "Mental Health Attitudes of Youth as Influenced by a Comic Strip," *Journalism Quarterly,* vol. 35, pp. 333–342, Summer, 1958.

61. Russell, David H.: "Contributions of Reading to Personal Development," *Teachers College Record,* vol. 61, pp. 435–442, May, 1960.

62. Russell, David H.: "The Prerequisite: Knowing How to Read Critically," *Elementary English,* vol. 40, pp. 579–582, October, 1963.

63. Russell, David H.: "Reading for Effective Personal Living," in J. Allen Figurel (ed.), *Reading for Effective Living,* International Reading Association Conference Proceedings, vol. 3, Scholastic Magazines, Inc., New York, 1958.

64. Russell, David H.: "Some Research on the Impact of Reading," *English Journal,* vol. 47, pp. 398–413, October, 1958.

65. Schale, Florence: "Using Special Modes of Learning to Improve Reading Instruction," in H. Alan Robinson (ed.), *Meeting Individual Differences in Reading, Supplementary Educational Monographs,* no. 94, University of Chicago Press, Chicago, 1964, pp. 41–44.

66. Schoephoerster, Hugh: "Research into Variations of the Test-Study Plan of Teaching Spelling," *Elementary English,* vol. 39, pp. 460–462, May, 1962.

67. Sheldon, William D.: "A Course in Reading and Study Skills," *Journal of Higher Education,* vol. 23, pp. 44–46, January, 1952.

68. Shores, J. Harlan, and Kenneth L. Husbands: "Are Fast Readers the Best Readers?" *Elementary English Review,* vol. 27, pp. 52–57, January, 1950.

69. Smith, Helen K.: "The Responses of Good and Poor Readers When Asked to Read for Different Purposes," unpublished doctoral dissertation, University of Chicago, Chicago, 1965.

70. Smith, Nila Banton: "Teaching Study Skills in Reading," *Elementary School Journal,* vol. 60, pp. 158–162, December, 1959.

71. Soares, Anthony T.: "Salient Elements of Recreational Reading of Junior High School Students," *Elementary English,* vol. 40, pp. 843–845.

72. Sochor, E. Elona: "Literal and Critical Reading in Social Studies," *Journal of Experimental Education,* vol. 27, pp. 49–56, September, 1958.

73. Sochor, E. Elona, A. Sterl Artley, William Eller, Robert Dykstra, and Gertrude Williams: *Critical Reading, An Introduction,* National Council of Teachers of English, Champaign, Ill., 1959.

74. Spache, George: *Toward Better Reading,* The Garrard Press, Champaign, Ill., 1963.

75. Squire, James R.: *The Responses of Adolescents While Reading Four Short Stories,* Research Report 2, National Council of Teachers of English, Champaign, Ill., 1964.

76. Stauffer, Russell G.: "Critical Reading at Upper Levels," *Instructor,* vol. 74, pp. 75, 101–102, March, 1965.

77. Stauffer, Russell G. (comp.): *Dimensions of Critical Reading,* Proceedings of the Annual Education and Reading Conference, vol. 11, University of Delaware, Newark, Del., 1964.

78. Stevens, George L., and Reginald C. Orem: "Characteristic Reading Techniques of Rapid Readers," *The Reading Teacher,* vol. 17, pp. 102–108, November, 1963.

79. Strang, Ruth: *The Adolescent Views Himself: A Psychology of Adolescence,* McGraw-Hill Book Company, New York, 1957.

80. Strang, Ruth: "Controversial Programs and Procedures in Reading," *School Review,* vol. 69, pp. 413–428, Winter, 1961.

81. Strang, Ruth: "Secondary School Reading as Thinking," *The Reading Teacher,* vol. 13, pp. 194–200, February, 1960.

82. Thomas, Ellen Lamar: "A Critical Reading Laboratory," *The Reading Teacher,* vol. 13, pp. 201–205, February, 1960.

83. Thurstone, Thelma Gwinn: *Reading for Understanding,* Science Research Associates, Inc., Chicago, 1959.

84. Tinker, Milo A.: "Recent Studies in Eye Movements in Reading," *Psychological Bulletin,* vol. 55, pp. 215–231, July, 1958.

85. Torrance, E. Paul: "Bringing Creative Thinking into Play," *Education,* vol. 85, pp. 547–550, May, 1965.

86. Torrance, E. Paul: "Creativity in the Classroom: Developing Creative Readers," *Instructor,* vol. 74, pp. 23–24, February, 1965.

87. Torrance, E. Paul: "Developing Creative Readers," in Russell G. Stauffer (comp.), *Dimensions of Critical Reading,* Proceedings of the Annual Education and Reading Conference, vol. 11, University of Delaware, Newark, Del., 1964, pp. 59–74.

88. Torrance, E. Paul: *Rewarding Creative Behavior,* Prentice-Hall, Inc., Englewood Cliffs, N.J., 1965.

89. Tumin, Melvin M.: "Exposure to Mass Media and Readiness for Desegregation," *Public Opinion Quarterly,* vol. 21, pp. 237–251, Summer, 1957.

90. Vernon, M. D.: "The Instruction of Children," *British Journal of Educational Psychology,* vol. 24, pp. 171–179, November, 1954.

91. Walton, Howard N.: "Vision and Rapid Reading," *American Journal of Optometry and Archives of the American Academy of Optometry,* vol. 34, pp. 73–82, February, 1957.

92. Weingarten, Samuel: "Developmental Values in Voluntary Reading," *School Review,* vol. 42, pp. 222–230, April, 1954.

93. Wittick, Mildred Letton: "Developing Interest in the Reading of Poetry," in J. Allen Figurel (ed.), *Changing Concepts of Reading Instruction,* International Reading Association Conference Proceedings, vol. 6, Scholastic Magazines, Inc., New York, 1961, pp. 193–196.

part III

READING IN THE CONTENT FIELDS

INTRODUCTORY NOTE TO CHAPTERS ON READING
IN THE CONTENT FIELDS

The four chapters on reading in the content fields focus on the application of reading skills and study skills in the areas of English, science, mathematics, social studies, business education, foreign language, home economics, industrial arts, and music, with implications for still other fields.

How does a teacher identify the words and concepts which will cause difficulty?

How does he help the student develop and grasp the concepts and master the terminology?

What are the special problems in reading-connected material in these fields?

How can the teacher identify these problems?

How can he help the student who faces them?

What can the teacher read or prepare in order to increase the students' efficiency in learning and reading?

Some things should be done, little by little, throughout a school year to build greater competence in the reader. Other things are emergency measures on a particular occasion when a special reading assignment demands them. Which of the activities described in these chapters should be year-long concerns? Which should be emergency measures?

If the reader of these chapters finds answers to these questions for his own situation, the chapters will have served their purpose. For the avoidance of repetition, only a few classroom problems are considered in each chapter. A teacher of any one of the subject fields can profit by reading all of the chapters for their implications for other fields.

One who is reading this book as a reference, with particular concern for a special field, may have turned first to these chapters. As he reads, he should note the aspects of the reading task which he should know more about. Then, by recourse to the index or to the books listed in the bibliographies at the ends of chapters, he can extend his knowledge of the needed information.

Teachers of special subjects are frequently fearful that attention to the reading of the textbooks and reference books in the subject will mean time taken away from the subject. Actually, the reverse is the case. Any clarification of the reading task is clarification of meaning. It is also the means to competence in reading such material and an invitation to read further after the course is completed. If a teacher really cares about his subject, he wishes to interest others to the extent that they can continue reading about it for their lifetime. This is the challenge of these chapters.

It is assumed that the reader of the first chapter well knows the responsibilities of the English teacher for the development of a love of reading, for growth in sensing assumptions in what is read, in getting implications, and in reacting intellectually and emotionally to the content and manner of presentation. But supporting these achievements must be more basic skills. One of these skills is that of decoding the word forms. Another, every bit as important, is the decoding of the author's meaning, and it is this last skill to which the reader's attention will now be directed.

special reading
instruction needed
in English

chapter 8

HAZARDS IN A PASSAGE

An unfortunate fact, in these days of concern for meeting individual differences, is that an author writes for a particular reader, even if only for himself. Since everything that he writes is a tapestry of his own peculiar experience and reaction, even though he may not consciously aim at suiting a particular reader, it takes a very particular reader to understand his meaning. The teacher of English cannot simply assign the poem, the essay, the drama, the letter, the story, for this is only to court disaster. He must make of himself a bridge between the author's intentions and the readers' qualifications.

Some of the aspects of the teacher's role may be illustrated by use of the following excerpt from a letter. As you read it, notice some of the difficulties which your students might have with it.

To some people this may be the anniversary of the day that will live in infamy, but to me it is the day that started with a beautiful omen on the hill. As I ate breakfast I saw a doe taking tentative steps across my great barrier reef at the top of the lot—tawny and white against the dead white and dark stripes of the concrete cribbing; another followed in the same manner—pausing, looking, sniffing, shaking the black tail; then, having crossed safely from Sydney's side to mine, both loped up the hill into the bush. Florence had seen them once do this—three or four, I believe; but I shall settle for two as my quota in this uncertain world. It was a delight to me, and I am not sure why. You may explain. Why should two female quadrangles on jackstraw legs have this effect?

Perhaps as you read you noticed the demands of the vocabulary and wondered whether some of your students know the meanings of *anniversary, infamy, omen, doe, tawny, tentative, barrier reef, concrete cribbing, loped, quota, quadrangles, jackstraw, effect*. If they don't, the passage to them becomes this. Read it for meaning yourself.

To some people this may be the _____ of the day that will live in _____, but to me it is the day that started with a beautiful _____ on the hill. As I ate breakfast I saw a _____ taking _____ across my great _____ _____ at the top of the lot—_____and white against the dead white and dark stripes of the _____ _____; another followed in the same manner—pausing, look-ing, sniffing, shaking the black tail; then, having crossed safely from Sydney's side to mine, both _____ed up the hill into the bush. Florence had seen them once do this—three or four, I believe; but I shall settle for two as my _____ in this uncertain world. It was a delight to me, and I am not sure why. You may explain. Why should two female _____s on _____ legs have this _____?

Apparently a beautiful *blank* with a black tail walked across the lot, and the author was glad but didn't know why. Since the passage is not immortal prose, this may be all that is worth knowing about it; but as a reading ex-perience, a passage of 149 words with fifteen blanks is scarcely desirable. Possibilities are such as these: (1) Don't expose the students to it. Let it go. (2) Teach all the words ahead of time. (3) Teach the words whose meanings are not revealed by the context and depend upon the students to find meanings for the others as they read. Then by later questioning determine their grasp. (4) List the words and have students look them up. The catch, of course, is that without the context the student cannot decide the meaning a word of multiple meanings has. Also, the teacher is presupposing that the student can use the dictionary properly for this purpose. (5) Invent sentence contexts for the appropriate meanings and have the students determine the pronunciation and meaning of each word under teacher guidance. (6) Use the words in preliminary exercises in word-form analysis and word-meaning analysis.

The numerous vocabulary difficulties which have been cited here may be good enough reason not to subject the students to the passage. But there are additional problems in the larger units of the passage—phrases, clauses, and sentences, and sentence-to-sentence relationships. Do the students know that the "day that will live in infamy" refers to the bombing of Pearl Harbor and the conditions under which it was done? If not, can they infer that the anniversary is not like a beautiful omen by the contrastive effect of the *but* clause?

Are the students aware of these points:

live = stay in people's memories
day that started = *as I ate breakfast*
omen = *doe taking tentative steps . . . another . . . then loped up hill*
on the hill = *at the top of the lot*
lot = land
tawny and white = description of the doe, set off by preceding dash
great barrier reef = *concrete cribbing*
great barrier reef figuratively used because presence of the cribbing is unnatural at a height
another = a second doe
in the same manner = *taking tentative steps,* etc.
in the same manner = *pausing, looking, sniffing* (following dash)
then = after the two does have stepped across the barrier
having crossed = prior to *then*
safely = does' concern for safety, explaining the manner
both = two does
bush = bushes
Sydney = person whose property is on the side from which the does started
Florence = someone else identified only by name, as a witness
had seen = prior to this morning
three or four = number of deer, not number of times
two = two does
I shall settle = author's agreement to his contract with life that only so much joy can be his
quota = quota of such sights
uncertain includes uncertainty that the does will repeat the pageant
It = *omen,* in the first sentence of the passage
and used where the reader would normally expect *but,* but here *and* signifies that the mystery as to the reason for the delight does not reduce the delight in the author's mind
two female quadrangles = two does
quadrangles, jackstraw = effort to be coldly realistic, even to the point of

ridicule, to sharpen the question by contrast. *Quadrangles* and *jackstraw* also violate the smooth flow of appreciative prose, making a break both in sound and in idea.

this effect = delight

If, in addition to being unable to make the connections just listed, the students have not had experience watching deer, they may not be able to answer the author's question at all. They will miss the importance of the question which invites them to probe into human responses to the beauty and rarity of gentle wildlife. They will be unable to infer the "Stay; don't go, I won't hurt you," of an unspoken hope that the beauty of the moment can be prolonged.

If the reader of this chapter will now return to the passage and, taking each point which has been listed, try to see what questions might help the students notice the connections, he will have a snapshot of the kinds of skill building which must go on throughout the school year to build the students' competence. "How can a day *live?* It is not alive." "When did the day start as far as the author was concerned?"

Notice in how many ways this passage is, indeed, a tapestry of entities interwoven not only within the sentence units but between and among the sentences. Awareness of these relationships depends on knowledge of sentence form, of the meaning of punctuation and capitalization, of the full meaning of English short cuts (two = two does) and of other linguistic signals (verb endings, auxiliary verbs, articles, etc.), of figurative expressions (great barrier reef), and of overall structure of the passage—in addition to memories which make these codes meaningful.

Just as knowledge of sentence structure helps a reader gather the meaning of unfamiliar words, so knowledge of the general direction or pattern of the author's thought helps the reader to gather the meanings of difficult sentences. For the passage with which this chapter was introduced, one might delineate the pattern as follows:

Event stated: generalization expressed in contrastive form
Event described: first, one doe
                second, another doe
                third, both loped up hill
Previous event recalled: what had happened before? (Florence)
Reactions to event: author's attitude ("I shall settle. . . .")
                author's feeling (delight)
                author's question (why delighted?)

One arrives at these notations by studying each sentence for its contribution, trying to classify what that contribution is, and noting the likenesses or differences in contribution of adjoining sentences. When vocabulary and sentence structure are simple, and when ideas are familiar, this pattern is more easily discerned. When vocabulary and sentence structure are difficult, and when ideas are relatively unfamiliar, the pattern is harder to sense but is, at the same time, more crucial to the reader's grasp of the intended meaning. The good reader unconsciously senses the pattern and utilizes it in grasping meanings and in anticipating future directions of the author's thought. The less able reader is less able partly because he is not aware of the pattern. He must be taught to become aware of it.

The English teacher must be not only a bridge in time of trouble but a provider of opportunities to develop skills and insights before trouble is encountered. Intensive study of a passage may not be conducive to love of it. Such study is better applied rather systematically and intensively to passages designed for specific purposes of technique. Then the techniques, gradually developed, can be applied with greater ease and less consciousness to the literature worth reading for ideas and expression.

STUDY OF WORDS AND PHRASES

Signals to Word Meanings

The study of signals to word meaning can be challenging and interesting as well as rewarding. What are the signals that help the reader determine the words which belong in the blanks in the following sentences?

The dog seized the meat and _____ed it in one gulp.
He whimpered and wagged his _____ when he saw his master.
He licked his paws _____ly to remove every particle.
When he walked slowly, sniffing the ground, his ears _____ed in the dust.

The student may say rather promptly that he knows that a dog eats, wags his tail, does a thorough job of cleaning, and, if of the proper breed, drags his ears. He may label it an experience clue, and it is true that it took dog experience to fill the blanks. Of course, this is not all that was involved. The way we may have noticed past dog behavior and appearance is crucial. Hence, if a student has only been taught to say that a dog is an animal, and not a fruit, vegetable, or mineral, he will not be prepared to meet the challenge. Word study which includes the many possible dimensions of meaning and word relationship a word may have would have been helpful in this instance. (See Chapter 6.)

The omitted words themselves have revealed something of their character by their structure and position. The *-ed* in the first sentence and in the last suggests a verb. *His* prior to the blank in the second sentence signals a noun. The *-ly* ending in the third sentence suggests an adverb. Even without the labels (noun, verb, adverb), the student can express what the sentence setting does for the word meaning: "The dog seized the meat and somethinged it." "He whimpered and wagged his whatever." "He licked his paws somehowly." "His ears somethinged in the dust." (These substitutions are not recommended; they are just probable.)

All of the signals in the sentences are useful to the student, although at first he may not realize it. It may be helpful to convert the sentences into nonsense except for signals so that the student can discover what the signals are:

The onk globbed the gast and glooped it in one snig.

This nonsensical setting for the signals brings into relief also the parallel structure:

The onk globbed the garst
    a
     n
     d
    glooped it [the garst] in one snig.

Globbed and *glooped* are clearly verbs joined by *and,* and attached to the subject *onk.* How was the garst glooped? In one snig. So, even though *gloop* is missing or expressed in a synonym the reader does not recognize, he knows that it is something an onk might do to a garst in one snig.

Ultimately the nonsense will have served its purpose, and the student may be able to recognize sentence structure by its resemblance to known models such as the basic sentence types.

The punctuation in the fourth sentence (not to speak of the initial capital and the period, which are signals not so far mentioned) is worthy of attention, too. How does the comma after *slowly* help the reader get the right meaning? Was the dog walking slowly or sniffing slowly? And what about the comma after *ground?* Was the dog sniffing the ground his ears dragged?

The contribution of capitalization to meaning can be studied in such sentences as:

I finally got Neuralgia on the phone.

Did he stay in the cold phone booth too long, or is Neuralgia his current pain in the neck?

In teaching signals to word meaning the teacher should not give the impression that these clues are foolproof. In the sentence, "He whimpered and wagged his —————," the blank could stand for a number of things: approval, greeting, welcome, plume.

Clues to the tense of a verb illustrate the care with which the student must study a passage.

I cut the meat.

The verb *cut* does not tell the reader whether it is present or past [7]. He must look in other sentences or into the situation to determine its tense. But in words like *drank* and *told* and *broke,* words whose forms were difficult to learn initially, the student finds the signal in the change of vowel or pattern from *drink, tell,* and *break.* In sentences like "I have broken it" and "I have seen it," both the form of the verb and the presence of the auxiliary, *have,* signal the perfect tense, and the words *broken* and *seen* are protected by their difference in spelling from confusion with the simple past forms. So as a reward for learning these special forms, the student has greater assurance of the author's intent.

Words and Phrases in Context

Phrase study should include the effect of the phrase upon whatever it modifies, and the significance of its placement. The effect of the phrase may be studied in transformational grammar exercises in which sentences are constructed or dismantled [16]. The placement of the phrase can be studied as in the following example:

To some people it means one thing, but to me it means another.

The initial position of *to some people* gives the phrase importance in the first clause. The same is true of the position of *to me* in the second. But the comparability of position for the two phrases has added significance to the reader, for it draws attention to the contrast of the two situations: to some, *this;* to me, *that.* The *but* in this context predicts the contrastive word, *another.*

What has the author done? He has contrasted two meanings. He has aided the reader to the realization of the contrast by using identical structure for the two clauses, identical phrase structure (*to . . . to . . .*), identical position of the phrases, and the coordinate expressions, *one . . . another.* He gives weight to his own meaning for *it* by mentioning his situation last rather than first. Note the difference in emphasis in these two sentences:

He wasn't admirable but people liked him.
People liked him but he was not admirable.

Students can put *to some people* in different locations in the first clause and find that no violence is done to meaning. In other sentences they may find that the moving of a phrase creates ambiguity. They should explain why the ambiguity occurs [16].

What is the contribution of the phrase, *to some people?* Students may be helped to identify the contribution by means of contrastive material:

To some people	*versus* at ten o'clock	(persons *versus* time)
To some people	*versus* in the yard	(persons *versus* place)
To some people	*versus* with vigor	(persons *versus* manner)
To some people	*versus* to a branch	(persons *versus* thing)
To some people	*versus* to help	(persons *versus* purpose or action)
To some people	*versus* to me	(persons *versus* person)

Drawings can be utilized to sharpen meanings. Let a student draw the meanings of "To some people it means joy; to me it means sorrow." Or students can be asked to create sentences appropriate to a drawing which shows such contrast.

A style characteristic of English is the use of a synonym instead of the repetition of a word. In the following two sentences, how is the relationship of the two unknown words established?

A zlakt was wandering aimlessly when Joe spotted it.
He thought it a suspicious looking zorkp and began to follow it.

The guess is the *zlakt* and *zorkp* refer to the same thing, although this could be wrong because *he* could be wrong in his opinion. We know that *zlakt* is singular (or a collective noun like *crowd*), because of the *a*, the *was*, and the *it*. It is either neuter or a form of life which is often referred to as "it."

Does *and began to follow* refer to *He thought* or to *it a suspicious looking zorkp?* Why?

When students encounter unfamiliar words or meanings, such relationships assume major importance. If the students recognize them and use them, they can often determine the meaning of the unknown, or narrow the range of possibilities.

Linguists have helpfully produced lists of coordinate words such as *both-and, neither-nor* [10], and it is a temptation to suppose that the appearance of these words is the signal for coordination. However, students must learn that the reader's job is to discriminate the use of these words as coordinates from their use as something else.

He was both generous and kind.
He found both [to be] generous and kind.

In the first instance, *both* and *and* are coordinates introducing adjectives referring to *he*. In the second, *both* refers to two people mentioned earlier, and the adjectives refer to them.

They were both there and having a wonderful time.

In this sentence, *both* probably refers to *they*, which, in turn, refers to two previously mentioned beings.

Some people have brains. Others have charm. He had both intelligence and graciousness.

Here *both* and *and* introduce coordinates; *both* does not refer to *brains* and *charm* directly.

The use of an arrow under *both*, pointing to the left when it refers to a previously mentioned couple, or to the right when it introduces two parallel expressions, is a graphic aid in exercises concerning its use.

We teachers point out that words such as *however* and *but* can indicate a turning point in a paragraph. The reader's task, though, is to distinguish the use of each of these as a major turning point from its use in a minor or different role.

Birds fly. However, they also hop.
Birds fly. However, they cannot stay aloft indefinitely.

In the first case, *however* adds an attribute rather than introducing a denial of the first sentence. In the second case, *however* introduces a modification of the previous statement, which sets a limit upon its truth.

However can they do it?

Here *however* means "in what manner," not "nevertheless" or "yet."

However, can they do it?

Here the comma changes the use.

How can the reader tell when *you* is singular or plural, when the verb form accompanying it is always plural?

> When the two boys came out, Father looked at them with disgust.
> "You were to wear your boots," he said.

Here the *you* is plural, referring to *them* and *boys*.

> When the two boys came out, Father looked at Joel with disgust.
> "You were to wear your boots," he said.

Here *Joel* is being addressed, and *you* is singular unless Father is talking about an order to both boys.

In the following sentences, how can the reader determine whether *if you were* is a condition contrary to fact, when *were* is appropriate in any case?

> If you were going, would you close the door?
> If you were going, why didn't you close the door?

In the study of clauses, students should give attention to clues to the variant meanings of adverbial conjunctions.

> Since you left, much has happened.

In this sentence, *since* could imply the passage of time, so that the time relationship of the two clauses is first and second. But *since* could also mean "because," and the meaning of the sentence could be, "Thanks to your leaving, we've begun to have some action." The ambiguity can only be cleared up by knowledge of the situation in which the sentence has been used, and of the customary attitude and behavior of the speaker toward the person he is addressing.

STUDY OF SENTENCES

Basic Sentence Types

Linguists have classified English sentences into certain major types [14, 16], of which the most common appear to be these:

> Jack threw the ball.
> Jack threw Joe the ball.
> Jack was pitcher (was ready) (looked happy) (was here).
> Jack sat.

Students analyzing prose passages will find the most prevalent structures to be these:

Jack threw the ball.
Jack was pitcher.

In fact, foreign students learning English for the first time can be taught these two structures along with their interrogative and negative forms, and the passive form of the first, to say practically anything that they wish to express.

An exercise for sentence study may be to rewrite a prose passage in one sentence form, then in another, to see which form serves the content better, and also to see what was gained by the original author's greater variety of structure. Confinement to one structure not only produces monotony, which is desirable under only certain conditions, but on occasion forces the writer into rare usage.

Students become entangled in the toils of long, packed sentences. The need here is for them to extricate the basic sentence from its surroundings and gradually add the meanings of the modifiers. And meanwhile, of course, they must be sure to sense figurative meanings. John Dos Passos in *The Head and Heart of Thomas Jefferson* writes lucidly for able readers [2, p. 180]:

While he sat at his traveling desk, expounding in carefully cadenced phrases a set of principles already established as his belief, in the upstairs parlor of brick-layer Griff's new house, a large part of his mind was on the doings at Williamsburg.

Jefferson was at his desk. He was expressing ideas he had. The desk was in an upstairs parlor. The upstairs parlor was in a new house. The new house belonged to a bricklayer. The bricklayer's name was Griff. While he was doing this, much of his thought was elsewhere—on what was happening at Williamsburg. Exercise in transformational grammar can be useful in the extraction of ideas from this piece of efficient prose. The students, however, must be aware of the overall structure and not get lost in the bits. "While he sat in that place, doing something in that place, something was somewhere." The main clause is the basic sentence of the type: "It was there."

For an appreciation of the difficulties in this passage, let us think along with an imaginary reader:

While he [that's Jefferson] sat at his traveling desk [the desk wasn't going anywhere—it's a type of desk, portable], expounding [Jefferson expounding, not the desk] in carefully cadenced [rhythmically flowing] phrases [a good writer] a set of principles [ideas to live by] already established as his belief [established with him or established with the public?], in the upstairs parlor [back to Jefferson again—the desk was in the parlor] of bricklayer Griff's new house, a large part of his mind was on the doings at Williamsburg [a lot of his thinking was on what was happening at Williamsburg—that's where the convention was being held].

What does the punctuation in this sentence do for the reader? The first comma saves him from having the desk expound. The second comma saves his belief from sitting in the upstairs parlor. The third separates a large part of his mind from the new house and signals the beginning of the main clause; in addition, it helps the *his* of *his mind* refer to Jefferson and not to the bricklayer Griff.

What are other ways of saying "a large part of his mind was on the doings at Williamsburg"? Did he miss the parties? Was a big part of his brain lying on top of doings at Williamsburg? Students will think of variations on the theme: "Many of his thoughts were on what was happening at Williamsburg." "He thought a good deal about what was being done at the convention in Williamsburg." "He couldn't help thinking a lot about what the people at the convention were saying and deciding." Notice how the effort to put the idea into other words brings in important ideas which have occurred in previous sentences and provides material for the expression of the true significance of the statement. It was hard for Jefferson to sit there writing his ideas when he knew how crucial the outcome of the convention would be. Now, if the student returns to his original question about whether *already established* refers to Jefferson or to the public, he sees that part of Jefferson's problem was that people already knew his beliefs—his beliefs were established— and that the fact that he was simply recording rather than creating or influencing added to his sense of frustration.

Notice, also, how much like a translation method is the student's handling of unfamiliar material in this imaginary example. The further the author is from the student's norm of expression (vocabulary, phrasing, level of abstraction), the more the student is thrown toward the translation method, the slower is his progress, and the more precarious the outcome. This fact suggests that students need experience using and hearing the vocabulary that they will encounter in a coming assignment on a given author's work; but, beyond this, that that phrasing must become familiar. (Recordings? Dramatization?) And as for level of abstraction, just as a child is led in arithmetic computation from counting eucalyptus buds to speaking and thinking in terms of "two and two are four," or of twice a number as an amount added to itself, so the student who will read abstractions with understanding must be led from concrete statements to discussion of the same ideas in abstract terms. A student may be unable to talk on an abstract level about anything, or he may be able to talk on an abstract level about some things but not others. Thus readiness for the abstractions of an author is not simply the development of the habit and technique of abstract thinking but the development of enough familiarity with the author's subject to be ready to think abstractly about it, and the development of the meanings and relationships of the abstract terms in the field.

In *A Fable,* William Faulkner has written, "Rapacity does not fail, else man must deny he breathes. Not rapacity: its whole vast glorious history repudiates that. It does not, cannot, must not fail" [3, p. 259]. If the student cannot fathom this meaning, the 270-odd-word sentence which follows to illustrate the meaning will produce more bafflement. Faulkner was at home with abstractions, and his readers must be.

"Rapacity does not fail" is the negative form of the basic sentence NV; but with that observation its simplicity stops, and, for the student, questions begin. What is rapacity? If the student knows that, he looks with cheer on the simple remainder, "does not fail." Does not fail what, or to do what, or to be what? By "fail" does the author intend "collapse," "die out," "fade away," "fall short of an objective," "prove ruinous to those involved"? Does the sentence mean rapacity achieves its end, continues to be active, continues to exist, ready to act?

"Else man must deny he breathes." "This is true else this is true." Translated, "If rapacity fails, man must deny he breathes." The omission of "else" and substitution of "if" remove the negative from one of the clauses. If man denies he breathes, he lies. If rapacity fails, then a lie is the truth. So rapacity does not fail, but what does that clause mean?

Few students will go to all of this trouble alone. With good reason they will expect that if the sentences before this one did not illuminate its meaning, later ones may. Frequently, their expectation is right, but their ability to associate the abstraction with its illustration is not sufficient for the task.

Movables

A study of modifying expressions, the so-called *movables* [14, 21], will show that certain types of modifiers can be expected to appear more frequently in certain types of content. Time sequences in history or in descriptions of experiments or procedures invite the use of words, phrases, and clauses establishing the time (*first, after, in the beginning, at the same time, when the ingredients are thoroughly mixed*). Passages describing physical settings may emphasize place, and passages describing operations will include modifiers of manner as well as time and place. Students looking for expressions which answer the question "when?" "where?" "how?" "why?" or "to or for whom or what?" can easily locate modifiers.

Words, phrases, or clauses which can be put in different positions in the base sentence may in certain positions create ambiguity. In Harper Lee's *To Kill a Mockingbird,* there is the following sentence: "Jem ran to the backyard, produced the garden hoe and began digging quickly behind the woodpile, placing any worms he found to one side" [9, p. 70].

It makes little difference whether the word "quickly" is placed before "began digging," after it, or after "behind the woodpile." Life experience tells the reader that the woodpile is not going to do anything quickly. However, the position of "to one side" raises the question of whether the worms were found to one side or placed to one side. "Placing to one side any worms he found" would have removed the question. Life experience must tell the reader that worms aren't found to one side of a woodpile or even on one side of a woodpile. The worm-oriented reader will have no trouble. But, as for other readers, the author may be guilty of placing them in a quandary.

The following contrast may help students clarify for themselves the reason for ambiguity. The teacher writes:

Sadly he watched the train pull out.
He watched the train pull out sadly.

Are these sentences different in meaning? No. Why not? Chances are that the author is not attributing human emotions to a train. Students can think of ways of avoiding even this slight possibility of misunderstanding:

He watched sadly as the train pulled out.

What about these sentences?

Steadily he watched the train pull out.
He watched the train pull out steadily.

Are these the same in idea? Probably not. Why? "Steadily" can apply both to the train and to the man's watching. The reader is thrown on the mercy of placement of the modifier near the word being modified. Thus, in the first sentence, the reader thinks that "steadily" refers to the watching; in the second, to the pulling out of the train.

Sentence Meanings

No sentence is an island. It stands in a verbal or pictorial or physical or emotional setting. Its meaning cannot be fully grasped or, in some cases, even correctly grasped, unless full consideration is given to its setting. But the student's full appreciation of what he reads is dependent also upon his ability to sense the dimensions of meaning which a given sentence contains—the kind of thought that it is; the way it is said; its potential relationships with other ideas; its literal, figurative, emotional meanings; its emphases and overtones in choice of words and structures; the unexpressed meanings behind the expressed.

One way to look at sentence meaning is to think of sentences as expressive of theory, fact, opinion, or feeling. Sentences may be mixtures of these, but the main message may be one of them.

Theory: Fill a bucket full and you waste half the water.
Fact: The bucket is full now.
Opinion: It's too full. It looks too full. I think it's too full.
Feeling: Oh dear! Here's this bucket too full again!

What is it about the expression of a theory that is different from the expression of a fact, opinion, or feeling? Students should explore this problem. What words keep this sentence from being a fact?

The prehistoric beekeepers of the Wassailian Age in ancient Britain must have been people of small stature.

What makes these statements facts?

Their ancient carvings were only three feet high.
They depicted the bees always with downcast eyes.

A more elaborate approach to the problem of sentence meaning is to think of sentences either as records of the impressions of the senses or as products of the work of the mind upon those impressions.

Generalization: You get what you pay for.
Summary: Many farmers brought their families in various conveyances.
Precept: Honesty is the best policy.
Law or principle: Earth attracts objects to it.
Comparison: They both liked to play baseball. (Implied: Dick is crazy about the game. And as for Sam—I always know where to find him after school.)
Contrast: Joe was a better swimmer than Pete.
       Pete did the talking, but Joe just listened.
Analogy: He worked at that job like a dog at a bone.
Simile: It worked like a charm.
Metaphor: The robin conducted the evening vespers.
(Notice how comparison may involve one element or many, and may be stated as fact or as generalization or prediction:
He walks just like his father.—one element
He is just like his father.—many elements
I would venture to say that he is going to be his father all over again.—prediction, generalization)
Cause: The accident was caused by the rain.
Effect: Clouds are relieved of their contents in the form of rain.
Judgment: The custard would be good if you hadn't forgotten the sugar.

Enumeration: Down the hill came bushes, trees, flowers, vines, boards, fence-posts, stepping-stones, rocks, soil, gophers, quails' nests, field mice, snails, and garter snakes.

Whole-part: The house had five rooms.

Definition: Metaphor is the use of a word or phrase in place of another to suggest likeness or analogy.

Coordination-subordination: Metaphor and simile are two forms of comparison.

Procedure: You have to mix the dry ingredients first.

Conjecture and prediction: The family that prays together stays together.

Problem-solution: When he tried to open the drawer and something blocked it, he took out the drawer above and removed the offending object.

Transition: Wait until you hear this one.
> Not to change the subject, but. . . .

Students should notice that the same sentence can be employed in different contexts to serve a different function and represent a different type of thinking:

Joe liked to play baseball. So did Dick. (comparison)

Joe liked to play baseball. He did it every time he could. (judgment, proof)

Joe liked to play baseball. First he would change his clothes. Afterward he would shower and dress for dinner. All through the meal he would talk about the game. (facts—events in sequence)

Joe didn't like to sit around and read and talk all the time. He liked to play baseball. (contrast)

Joe's father took him to all the games and started a little neighborhood club. Result: Joe liked to play baseball. (cause-effect)

It is interesting to note that the use of a sentence tends to bring into prominence one or another part of it. In the first example, Joe and Dick are compared. In the second, playing baseball is emphasized. In the third the doing is again emphasized, this time as one of many actions. In the fourth, the contrast draws attention to the differences between reading and talking, and playing baseball. In the fifth, the word *liked* comes into prominence.

In bringing out the function of a sentence, a teacher may find it helpful to study the questions which the sentences answer: How are they alike? (comparison) How are they different? (contrast) Why did it happen? (cause) What is it made of? (parts) What is it? (definition) What are the steps in doing it? (procedure)

Just as one sentence may serve many purposes, so one idea may be expressed in many ways:

Me first.
Let me be first.
I want to be first.
I'm first.

A demand, a request, a desire, a fact—yet the wanting to be first may be the real message.

Students can take a sentence and think of all possible ways of saying the same thing. Example: "He carried the rope to his brother." Or they can think of all possible things to say to stay on a subject, like a father who wants to talk about his little boy. Or suppose the father wishes to designate his boy in a tangle of children in the yard. In how many ways could he say that his boy is the one with the red scarf? Even "red scarf" would suffice.

Another type of exploration may be the use of imaginative or figurative ways of expressing ideas. "Stop bothering me" becomes "Go jump in the lake." "How big the Grand Canyon is" becomes "Somebody must have left the water running."

Students can eavesdrop for ways in which attitudes are revealed in reactions to a given situation. Someone falls down:

That was a nasty fall you had. (sympathy)
So you fell down again. (clumsy)
You never were any good on your feet. (always belittlin')

Or suppose you wear a new hat:

Oh, is it new? I didn't notice. (same old type)
Where will you wear a thing like that? (outlandish)
I've seen a lot of those this spring. (common)
I've given up wearing feathers. (poor choice)
It isn't real, is it? (cheap)
Well, yes, it is rather nice. (enthusiasm of tired celery)
At our age it's better to have something over the face. (Hide it, sister!)

Or you are in the hospital:

Lots of people get this. There's nothing to it. (Get up.)
My uncle died of it. The doctor didn't tell him what he had. (crepe hanger)
Who has the other key to your safe-deposit box? (foresighted)
This is the second day. The third is always the worst. (cheery)
Who is your diagnostician? You should have a fever. (expert)
If I'd been you, I'd have refused the transfusion. (helpful hindsight)

Some people are too accurate to keep friends happy:

Thank you for the dish that came cracked in the mail.

Some people will never land a job. In the interview they say:

I want to make some easy money.

One of the best questions we can teach students to ask themselves is, "How would I feel if someone said that to me?"

Students can also eavesdrop on adult conversations to note the failure of the syllogism, thereby sharpening their observation in reading:

I just couldn't believe our bank would do a thing like that. (Reasoning: Our bank can do no wrong. Something wrong happened. It can't be the fault of the bank.)

But he is my own brother. (Reasoning: A brother is loyal. My brother did something disloyal. It is impossible.)

Listening to telephone conversations can be an education in changes of attitude:

Absolutely not. . . . I don't want to. . . . Well, maybe. . . . All right, I'll try.

The two-way conversation makes an interesting study of the effect of one person upon another:

First speaker:	He took my ball.
Second speaker:	How outrageous.
First:	He doesn't play fair.
Second:	Disgusting.
First:	He's a thief and a cheat.
Second:	How unspeakable!

Contrast the above with the following, for the intentions of the second speaker and the effect he has upon the first speaker:

First speaker:	He took my ball.
Second speaker:	Well, he likes to play, too.
First:	He doesn't play fair.
Second:	Maybe he doesn't know the rules.
First:	He's a thief and a cheat.
Second:	Oh, come now.
First:	Oh, you never understand anything.

From such observations the students can graduate from reading conversations merely to report what was said, to reading them for character revelation and change.

Human motivation can be studied in such sentence groupings as these:

The bullets flew. He stooped.
The little one came. He stooped.

The doorway low. He stooped.
There was a dime in the path. He stooped.

Consideration of all possible human reactions to injury, loss, victory, or recovery can prepare students to evaluate the character in a story who reacts in a given way to one or more of these situations.

Reasons for human misunderstanding also can be clarified through a study of conversations which the student overhears. In the following case, the misunderstanding is based upon the assumption of common knowledge:

First speaker: Too bad about Joe.
Second speaker: Oh, when is the funeral?
First: What, is he dead?
Second: I thought that's what you meant. You knew he was sick, didn't you?
First: No, I just heard it.

In the next case, the misunderstanding is due to the meaning of a single word:

First speaker: Where did you get that lovely blanket?
Second speaker: Here.
First: I don't see any.
Second: No, not here. I meant in town.

The following is an exercise to examine the nature of the reason given for the suggestion, "Let's go back":

Which sentences explain the reason for "Let's go back" as
  an existing condition?
  a developing condition?
  a future activity?
Which sentences suggest something that has happened as well as something which will be done?
Which sentences suggest that the speaker will return and continue?
Which sentences are two ways of saying the same thing?
  It looks spooky.
  I don't like the looks of it.
  It's a dead-end street.
  This is getting us nowhere.
  It's late.
  It's getting dark.
  I want to get my coat.
  We can come again tomorrow.
  I feel tired.
  It's too much for me.

I want to go to sleep.
I want my dinner.
Joe is coming at four.
I have some errands to run.
I must put some medicine on this cut.
Let's beat the crowd.
I'd like to sketch one of the camels.
We're going to need more help.

STUDY OF PARAGRAPHS

The starting point of a paragraph is no assurance of the pattern the author or speaker will choose to develop his idea. One way of bringing this fact home to the students is to give them a sentence and ask them to write a sentence which might reasonably follow, then have the students classify the contributions of the second sentences. Here are four possible patterns—students will think of others—for a paragraph beginning with the same sentence:

1. The best apples are sold by our company. Of course, not everyone will agree with me. Our chief competitor claims they are picked too soon. Another says they spoil in shipping. But we feel that ours are superior in every respect.
2. The best apples are sold by our company. We deal chiefly with three varieties: the Red Delicious, the Golden Delicious, and the McIntosh. The Red Delicious is outstanding for its juicy goodness. The Golden has a delightfully mellow flavor. And the McIntosh is a fine all-purpose apple.
3. The best apples are sold by our company. The best pears are handled by Joe Bartlett's outfit. And the finest cherries come from Pitt. Our three companies sell the best fruits in this area.
4. The best apples are those sold by our company. For one thing, they are the largest. For another, we pick them at the right time. Also, we select them from those growing areas which have the most perfect climate. And we refuse to sell any at all below a certain fixed standard, no matter what the demand is.

Which paragraph gives four arguments for the initial claim? Which uses the initial claim as one of three to support a final generalization? Which lists criticisms only to return to a reaffirmation of the claim? Which supports the claim with three details which, in turn, are described? (This could be diagrammed on the chalkboard by the students.)

Better than answers to such questions would be study of each paragraph, sentence by sentence, for what the sentence adds and what its relationship is to the preceding one.

Chapter 6 has described the common types of paragraph structure which the student will encounter in many kinds of literature, and some of the ways he may be helped to recognize the thought pattern with which he is dealing. Training of this kind cannot be left entirely to teachers of the content subjects. Furthermore, the English teacher continuously makes assignments which require awareness of thought patterns in expository prose or stanzas of poetry or strands of conversation. Study of paragraphs and larger units of composition should lead to an understanding of the ways authors think, to a ready recognition of the pattern the student currently is meeting, and to the realization that every sentence, every phrase, every word holds the possibility of a new direction.

The present chapter has attempted to draw the attention of the English teacher to some types of teaching which would be helpful to students who become confused or who fail to gather the author's meaning—as far as the teacher himself can discern it! The point has been made that, although help must be administered when it is urgently needed in the regular reading assignments of the course, preparation for pitfalls before the reading and exercises to develop skills in observation of word, phrase, and sentence relationships are desirable before need and perhaps over a long period of time. An English class can have all the excitement of a shipwreck and all the glamor of a rescue if only the teacher will see the problems, and if only the students will realize that language is a code and a mind is asking to be read.

REFERENCES

1. Bloom, Benjamin S. (ed.):*Taxonomy of Educational Objectives,* David McKay, Inc., New York, 1956.

2. Dos Passos, John: *The Head and Heart of Thomas Jefferson,* Doubleday & Company, Inc., New York, 1954.

3. Faulkner, William: *A Fable,* Random House, Inc., New York, 1954.

4. Fries, Charles C.: *Linguistics: The Study of Language,* Holt, Rinehart and Winston, Inc., New York, 1962.

5. Fries, Charles C.: *The Structure of English,* Harcourt, Brace & World, Inc., New York, 1952.

6. Harper, Robert J. C., Charles C. Anderson, Clifford M. Christensen, and Steven M. Hunka: *The Cognitive Processes,* Prentice-Hall, Inc., Englewood Cliffs, N.J., 1964.

7. Hill, Archibald A.: *Introduction to Linguistic Structures,* Harcourt, Brace & World, Inc., New York, 1958.

8. Hunt, Kellogg W.: *Grammatical Structures Written at Three Grade Levels,* National Council of Teachers of English, Champaign, Ill., 1965.

9. Lee, Harper: *To Kill a Mockingbird,* Popular Library, Inc., New York, 1960.

10. Lefevre, Carl A.: *Linguistics and the Teaching of Reading,* McGraw-Hill Book Company, New York, 1964.

11. Loban, Walter D.: *The Language of Elementary School Children,* National Council of Teachers of English, Champaign, Ill., 1963.

12. Loban, Walter D., Margaret Ryan, and James R. Squire: *Teaching Language and Literature,* Harcourt, Brace & World, Inc., New York, 1961, chap. 5.

13. McCullough, Constance M.: "What Does Research Reveal about Practices in Teaching Reading?" *English Journal,* vol. 46, pp. 475–490, November, 1957.

14. Newsome, Verna L.: *Structural Grammar in the Classroom,* Wisconsin Council of Teachers of English, Wisconsin State College, Oshkosh, Wis., 1962.

15. *The Reading Teacher,* vol. 11, April, 1958. (Entire issue on context clues.)

16. Roberts, Paul: *English Sentences,* Harcourt, Brace & World, Inc., New York, 1962.

17. Shuy, Roger (ed.): *Social Dialects and Language Learning,* Cooperative Research Project, OE5-10-148, National Council of Teachers of English, Champaign, Ill., 1964.

18. Smith, Dora V.: *Dora V. Smith: Selected Essays,* The Macmillan Company, New York, 1964, pp. 271–279.

19. Strang, Ruth: "Secondary School Reading as Thinking," *The Reading Teacher,* vol. 13, pp. 194–200, February, 1960.

20. Strang, Ruth, and Dorothy Kendall Bracken: *Making Better Readers,* D. C. Heath and Company, Boston, 1957, chap. 5.

21. Strickland, Ruth G.: "The Language of Elementary School Children: Its Relationship to the Language of Reading Textbooks and the Quality of Reading of Selected Children," *Bulletin of School of Education, Indiana University,* vol. 38, July, 1962.

22. Whorf, Benjamin Lee: *Language, Thought and Reality,* The M.I.T. Press, Cambridge, Mass., 1964.

special reading instruction needed in science and mathematics

Science and mathematics teachers are bombarded with new developments in their fields. Many of them attend workshops and courses to learn about the new developments and new approaches to teaching their subjects. At exhibits they see demonstrations of the use of overhead projectors, microscopes, and other laboratory and audiovisual aids. New textbooks show them the "new math" and the latest in programmed learning.

All of this information is valuable, but one thing is missing. A science or mathematics teacher must be more than a demonstrator, a lecturer, a manipulator of machinery, and a distributor of reading material.

Willerding [28], while praising the good points of SMSG [1] material for seventh graders, states that the material is not easy enough for the average seventh grader to read, that it lacks clarity of presentation, and offers the student no help at all in ways of reading verbal problems. This is only one example of a prevalent insensitivity to the reading problems which science and mathematics material presents to the reader. In the years that the fields of science and mathematics have advanced, the art and science of teaching reading have advanced also. A good teacher cannot be advanced in his field and rusty in his pedagogy. Nor can good science textbooks result from attention only to science. Good teaching is not only a matter of exposure of students to materials and ideas. It must also be a matter of helping individuals to benefit by that exposure. Only the teacher who has taken the trouble to learn how can do this.

THE READING OF SCIENCE

Vocabulary Problems in Science Reading

The vocabulary in science textbooks, science worksheets, or science news bulletins presents many hazards to the student. Common words may be used in a special way: *composition, property, series, matter, states.* The specialized vocabulary, largely of polysyllabic words, creates both the problem of meaning and that of pronunciation: *catalyst, diatomic, endothermic, kinetic.* The general vocabulary in which the author expresses himself on any subject may also be beyond the student's knowledge or so far beyond his habit that the words must be translated: *denote, fundamental, resemblance, distinguish.* Many students are not at home with such explanations as "pertaining to a reaction which occurs with the absorption of heat." The conscientious person may pause and translate: "having to do with what happens when things get hot." The hopeless or careless student will skip it. If *pertaining, reaction, occurs,* and *absorption* are unknown to the student, even the conscientious one will be blocked in his effort to understand.

The science teacher can ease the situation through a number of practices, some time-honored, such as the student notebook. At one time the student notebook contained a list of terms the student did not know, together with definitions which he did not understand. In more recent times the notebook utilizes the class discussions of meanings, the laboratory experiences, and the products of the student's own thinking, presenting the word, its pronunciation, its definition in the student's own words, a picture of it if possible, examples of it, its relationship to other things the student knows, and its utility or function.

[1] School Mathematics Study Group.

A review of the new assignment by the class and instructor can include the instructor's designation of important words to notice (perhaps the author himself has listed some but, knowing his class, the instructor can list others) and the students' skimming to find other spots they think will present trouble.

"What does the word *composition* mean to you?" asks the instructor. "How have you used this word or seen it used before?"

"We have to write compositions in English," answers a student.

"What does that mean?" the instructor persists.

"A paper, a theme," answers the student.

"In chemistry," says the instructor, "it has a different meaning. Does anyone know what that is? We say that this liquid has a certain composition. What do we mean?" And so on until, by discussion, or by resorting to a dictionary to see what is said about composition after the symbol *sci.*, or both, the students can word a definition which they understand, which the instructor or a student writes on the chalkboard and the students write in their notebooks.

The instructor plants definitions of the new word in his remarks about it: "This liquid has a certain composition. It is *made up of.* . . . It is a *combination of.* . . . It is a *blending of.* . . ." or whatever words may be meaningful and accurate. Then he keeps the students thinking with him by asking questions: "So this liquid is made of what? . . . And so we say that its . . . (students say "composition"). . . . What was that word, Joe (who is tying his shoelaces)? And what does *composition* mean? What in this room has *composition*?"

Sometimes the use of opposite meanings clarifies the meaning of the new word: "The other day Joe said he found a bird under some of last year's leaves, and it had fallen apart and didn't look much like a bird any more. Remember the word we used about it? We said it had 'decomposed.' What had happened to its composition?"

A student has more of a feeling of competence with a new word if he can at least pronounce it accurately. The instructor writes the word *composition,* saying before he writes, "Watch as I write this new word to see whether you can pronounce it." Perhaps a student says he can and pronounces it correctly.

"How did you know?" asks the teacher, for students may benefit from the explanation and do better themselves the next time.

"I knew *com* and *position* and just put them together," says the student.

But if no one knows, the teacher may ask whether the students see a prefix or suffix they know. With luck, he will have a student who recognizes *com* as a prefix and *tion* as a suffix. If this fails, the teacher must turn to syllabication: "How many vowels do you see in this word? Who will underline them for us?" A student underlines *o, o, i,* and *io.* "Now how many syllables are there? (four) Why? (because there are four vowels or vowel combinations) Where do we divide the first and second syllables? (between the *m* and *p*) Why? (because when two consonants that do not make a single sound or a new sound together, come at the end of a syllable, the first goes with the first syllable, and the second goes with the second) Where is the next division? (between the *o* and the *s*) Why? (because when a single consonant stands between two syllables it usually goes with the second syllable) With this rule, who can tell us where the next division must be?" (after the *i* and before the *t*)

The *com* has a short *o* because it is in a closed syllable (one ending with a consonant) the students decide. They all pronounce it: *com*. The *o* of *po* may be long because the syllable is open (ending with a vowel), and the students pronounce it *pō*. The single *s* may have the *z* sound; the *i* could be (but is not) long. The teacher may write *nation* and *action* to have the students derive the pronunciation of *tion*, if they do not know it. This is one of those words which have two stresses, a light one (on *com*) and a heavy one (on *si*). By analogy with a word like *destination* or *constitution*, the students may be able to select the probable points of stress and pronounce the word.

Of course, a quick look at a dictionary would have produced the answer faster, but occasionally the kind of analysis just described is preferable because it teaches a technique.

"How did we solve this word? What were the steps we took?" asks the teacher. From the students he gets the order of procedure: first try to see the larger parts of the word; if this fails, look for prefixes, stems, and suffixes; if this fails, divide the word into syllables by finding the vowels and the likely points of division; decide the pronunciation of the vowels and sound each syllable; determine the stress by analogy if necessary, or by the fact that a stem or root is usually stressed.

Interest in the relation of structure to meaning can be stimulated if the teacher has the students look for the derivation of the word in the dictionary, or points out that *com* means "together," and *position* means "placement." To *compose* is to *place* or *put together*. The students will be interested in the change which has taken place in the meanings of certain words in modern science. For example, they will find that their textbook speaks of chemistry as a science of matter and energy, but that the dictionary says the word was derived from the Greek *chymeia*, meaning a "mingling," which, in turn, came from *chymos*, "juice," for originally chemistry was the art of taking the medicinal juices from plants. *Science*, they will find, comes from the Latin word *scientia*, meaning "knowledge"; *matter* from the Latin *materia*, meaning "wood" (something that takes up space and has weight); and *energy* from the Greek *energeia* (active)—*en* (in) and *ergon* (work).

The teacher can draw students' attention to the repetition of endings of scientific words: *ium, um, ide, ic, ate, ous, ine, ese, ene*, etc. The students can look for these endings, listed separately, in the dictionary, to find out their meanings and to determine which are comparable in meaning. By observing patterns of stress in scientific words, they can learn to expect those patterns in similar words: *acetylene, aluminum, ammonia; calcium, cupric, ferric; sulfur, argon, bismuth.*

The instructor may notice that the author of the textbook has a habit of defining a word in technical language and following this with a sentence explaining the meaning in other terms: "The manganese dioxide is a catalyst or catalytic agent," says the author. "It is not permanently changed in the reaction." The student cannot tell that the second sentence explains the meaning of the first statement. Only the instructor knows. But the helpful instructor can point out such places to the student and draw his attention to this characteristic style. From that time on, the student may look for it himself. "Where did the author do it in your new assignment?" asks the teacher.

Unfamiliar words are difficult enough when they are well buttressed with known words. However, for many students the introduction of new words is so rapid that soon the page is a no-man's-land:

The lorks of the common arsts form axin ints by gornent blitting. For instance, in the axin hant int, each hant lork shares its single ont erd with the other. These erds revolve about both oids, so that each lork has two erds revolving about it.

At this point the student is tempted to skip the page, but the earnest fellow will try his best to use what he knows of English sentences to see relationships among the unknown words. The first sentence tells what the lorks form, whatever they are. The second gives an example of what a special lork called a "hant lork" does. It shares its one ont erd with the other. By "the other," the student thinks the author means "the other erd or the other hant lork." The two erds then travel around both oids, whatever they are; and, since each lork has two erds revolving about it, it seems that perhaps oids is another name for lorks. So the author is telling the student what lorks do and gives an example of the sharing of an erd by two of one kind of lork, and the consequent action of erds about each such lork. This must be an example of forming axin ints by gornent blitting. The student cannot clarify the meaning of the phrase "by gornent blitting," for it could refer to time (by evening), place (by the iron grating), or action (by log splitting).

Chances are that if the science teacher, reading this passage, were told that the first sentence, decoded, is "The atoms of the common gases form diatomic molecules by covalent bonding," he could decode the examples which follow it. But the student could not.

If from this maze the student can remember the words which troubled him, he can listen for them in the instructor's discussion. If the textbook is well documented, he can find the first references to these words or look them up in a science glossary. Admittedly, however, if the student spends too much time on the things he doesn't understand, he may never get to the part of the assignment that he might understand and thus may go to class fully unprepared.

To build the concepts of science, to arm students with the fullness of meaning a word can have in its use in scientific literature, the teacher can explore with the students the dimensions of a word. For example, for the word *beetle,* what is the derivation of the word, what is its definition, of what is a beetle a part, what are its parts, how can it be classified, how does it originate, what effect does it have, how does it develop (step by step), what is the history of it, how long does it live, how is it nurtured, how is it sheltered, what are its habits and actions, what are its qualities (number, amount, texture, moisture, color, taste, solidity, size, shape, odor, sound), what are its uses, how many meanings does the word have, what is it like, what is its opposite (if any)? By the time this inquiry is completed, beetleness will be fairly well established in the students' minds, and the relationship of the word *beetle* and a beetle to other aspects of science will have been explored, thus introducing other aspects before they become the focus of an assignment, or reviving them from earlier assignments and maintaining their memory.

Problems of Textbook Organization

When first discussing the new textbook with a class, the teacher impresses the students with the importance of having questions in mind as they read, so that they will find answers instead of coming out with a vague blur.

"What should you ask yourself about the chapter title?" asks the teacher. (What does it mean? What should be in a chapter with this title? How does this idea fit with the ideas of other chapter headings in the book—where in the subject are we?)

"What should you ask yourself about centered subheadings?" (What do they mean? What parts of the topic do they deal with?)

"What should you do about marginal headings?" (Read them first to see the "drift" of the chapter. After reading a section, try to say what the marginal heading means.)

The marginal headings may look like this to the students:

The occurrence of glat
The early history of glat
The preparation of glat
From ig by hornty
From adge by barm clint
The physical properties of glat

The chemical properties of glat
Reaction with bint
Reaction with kaidicks
Reaction with sornic ards
The test for glat
The uses for glat
For its sik syn
As a baisal bant
As a phint
For making glatic bongbong
In the lorkic glat torch
In the glat bomb

If the author has not designated which marginal headings are sub-ordinate in idea to others, the student must gather those relationships either by the way the headings are expressed or by the clues in the body of the material itself.

"Which headings do you think are equally important in idea?" the teacher asks. "Do you see a hint of equality in the way the headings are expressed?"

"Yes," says a student, "I see 'The this' and 'The that'—the occurrence, early history, preparation, physical properties, chemical properties, test, uses."

"And there are two headings starting with 'from,'" says another student, "and both under 'preparation'; and two, no three, with 'reaction.'"

"What about the last six headings?" asks the teacher.

"They could all be 'uses,'" replies one student. "They could be uses for something, as something, and in something."

The teacher would then ask the students to set these headings up in outline form to show these relationships, and then have the students tell what question they would ask as they read each portion under each heading. (When was the occurrence? What was it? Why was it? How was it? etc.)

"What do you notice about the print?" is the next question the teacher asks. The students see that some print is in boldface type; some in italics; and some items are numbered. They decide that the author has wanted to stress these words or ideas and that they should skim to find these things in advance of careful reading. They should write down the technical terms or definitions in order to review them later for meaning and recall. If they are classifications, the students should make a diagram of the relationships.

What should the students do about pictures and other figures in the chapter? They decide they should try to see what the title of the picture has to do with the picture itself, how the picture is related to the topic the chapter is about, what place in the text refers to the picture, and whether they can ask a question about the meaning of the picture and answer it.

Perhaps, as in chemistry or physics, there are letters which represent various elements and signs which represent various relationships, among them, $2H_2 + O_2 \rightarrow 2H_2O$. Students may develop charts to place around the classroom as reminders of these relationships and their meanings. In some cases they may make displays or experiments showing the meanings.

The Assignment

The assignment of readings in the textbook should set specific purposes for the students. It is not enough to say, "Read this chapter and be ready to answer questions." What does the teacher want the students to get out of the chapter? What questions would help the students find the right things? It is conceivable that a teacher might give a worksheet containing questions and say, "Find the answers to these questions. Then, using that information, solve the following problem." This suggests fact reading to answer specific questions without thought for the problem. Another approach would be, "Read the following problem. Then find in the chapter the information which will help you solve the problem." This reverse procedure prolongs the concentration of the student on the problem and puts upon him the burden of reading with a certain relevance in mind.

Skills in Reading Science Material

Given the textbook and the assignment, the student must be able to gather the author's ideas and select and remember those which are useful to him. For some students the acquisition of a scientific vocabulary is far easier than following an author's thoughts. Here, for example, is a paragraph which will seem easy to you but not necessarily to the student:

Oxygen is the prime necessity of life. We die faster from lack of it than from lack of food or water. In the higher animals, as in man, it is taken from the air into the lungs, from them into the bloodstream, and then into the cells of the body. Aquatic animals get oxygen from the air that is in the water. Plants, too, require oxygen for life.

An able student, asked to put this into his own words, might write: "Oxygen is the most necessary element for life. We can last longer without food and water than we can without oxygen. Higher animals, like land dwellers that breathe life through air, take oxygen from the air into the lungs and on into the bloodstream and body cells. Animals with gills get it from the air in the water. Plants need it, too."

A still more able student might draw himself something to remember, actually making more orderly the contents which the author presents.

Oxygen—No. 1 for life

Living things:

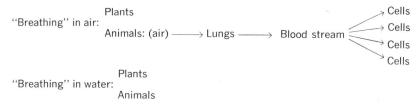

A bright student who likes to argue might take exception to the idea that oxygen is the prime necessity. "It's not any more important than food and water," he might say. "We can die from lack of food or water, too. It's just that we can store food and water for several days, but we are always running out of oxygen." Another student might defend the author. "But you can't stay alive to use your stored food and water if oxygen is cut off. You're dead, period." "Yes, take the astronauts," a third student might comment. "Let them go into outer space without oxygen, and a lot of good their food and water would do them."

The instructor might ask, "Why was it thought that Venus might have life on it?" and get the answer that it was supposed that Venus was veiled in oxygen—another score for the statement in the textbook.

He might then ask, "What does the author do in the first sentence?" (He states an opinion.)

"What in the second?" (He gives his reason for the opinion.)

"What in the third?" (He tells how man and other higher animals use oxygen.)

"What in the fourth and fifth?" (He tells how aquatic animals get it and that plants need it, too.)

So first he states an opinion, then gives his reason for thinking it. Then he tells how some animals use oxygen, how others get it, and that plants need it. What didn't he tell? He didn't tell how aquatic animals use it or how plants get it or use it. The last three sentences do not substantiate the first opinion or add to the reason, for the author doesn't tell what good the oxygen does the cells when it gets to them. An honest outline of this material might be as follows:

Opinion on importance of oxygen to living things
Reason supporting this opinion
Description of passage of oxygen from air to cells in higher animals (sequence)
Statement that aquatic animals get oxygen from water (acquisition)
Statement that plants need oxygen (need)

The listing above shows that the author really has a mixture of elements in his paragraph. It is reasonable to expect that a person giving an opinion will follow with a reason for it; but it is unreasonable to expect that the remainder of the same paragraph will give related facts which do not support the reason or extend the opinion. The student reading this is led to believe that the paragraph is one of opinion and support for the opinion and becomes confused by the sequence beyond the first two sentences. He doesn't know where to hang these last three ideas, and he is right: the author needs his English teacher. The student needs his science teacher. The student cannot have an orderly idea of science from a rather disorderly presentation of it unless the teacher helps him.

Perhaps the teacher will help with questions before the reading or with an an outline to be filled by the student in his own words:

The users of oxygen
The sources of oxygen
The passage of oxygen from air to body cells in higher animals
The importance of oxygen
The reason for its importance

It is idealistic to suppose that textbooks in any subject are perfectly written. The best thing a science teacher can do to prevent science-haters is to help the students decode the author's meanings and patterns of thought.

The science teacher may find that the textbook he is using has certain characteristic structures of paragraph or thought pattern that recur over and over again. If the instructor can help the student recognize these structures, the student will know what is important to observe and remember. Suppose there are many paragraphs like this:

There are certain growing regions in plants. In a stem the growing regions are of two types: (1) those making the stem longer, and (2) those giving the stem a bigger diameter. Stems grow in length by forming new tissues at their tips. They grow in width from activity located deep in the tissues of the stem.

Here the form is one of proceeding from a statement to an example which has two aspects (really descriptions of effects) followed by explanations of the way these aspects are achieved (descriptions of cause). The pattern, as it recurs throughout the textbook, may be:

Statement
Example
  1 (description
  2 (description)
  or more

with (1)—(explanation of 1)
    (2)—(explanation of 2)
    or more

Students should listen to models of such patterns before they are asked to read such patterns themselves and, sensibly, the instructor chooses passages he wants students to remember.

The teacher says, "I am going to read you something from your new textbook. After I read each sentence, you are to tell me what the author has told you, but put it into your own words. Listen: 'There are certain growing regions in plants.' What has he said? Bill?"

"Plants have growing regions," says Bill.

"They grow in different places in the world," says Angela.

"Listen again," says the teacher, and he repeats.

"It says the growing regions are in plants, not in the world," says Bill. Angela subsides.

"So what is a growing region?" says the teacher. "Eddie?"

Eddie says, "It's a part of a plant that is growing, a part that grows."

The teacher proceeds: "In a stem the growing regions are of two types."

"There are two kinds of growing regions in a stem," says Ardelle.

"What has the author done?" asks the teacher. "I thought he was talking about plants and now it's a stem."

George almost breaks an arm trying to answer. "A stem is a part of a plant."

Gene adds, "First he talked about plants and now he's using a stem as an example—it's a part."

Gene makes a quick sketch on the chalkboard of a plant with a stem, and the teacher says, "Stay there, Gene; we might need you again." Then, to the class, "Who would like to list the ideas as we go along? Akiko?"

Akiko goes to the chalkboard and writes: "Plants have growing regions," and under that, "Example: stem has two types." She makes two diagonal lines radiating out below this and waits for the two types to be mentioned.

The teacher reads: "In a stem the growing regions are of two types: (1) those making the stem longer."

Albert says, "Some growing regions make the stem longer; they lengthen the stems."

Akiko writes under her left branch: "lengtheners."

The teacher adds, "and (2) those giving the stem a bigger diameter."

If no one chokes on the word *diameter*, Akiko is finally permitted to write under her right branch: "fatteners."

"Gene," says the teacher, "have you been keeping up with us?" Gene, the dreamer, looks quickly at what Akiko has written and lengthens a stem and thickens it.

"Stems grow in length" (Akiko puts her chalk under *lengtheners*) "by forming new tissues at their tips." (Gene lengthens another stem at the tip to show he is now awake, and with the class approval Akiko writes under *lengtheners* the words "make new tissues at tips.") "They grow in width from activity located deep in the tissues of the stem."

Akiko writes under *fatteners* the words "work deep in tissues of stem," and Gene runs the chalk along the stem to show that deep in the stem itself something is happening.

"Now," says the teacher, "look at Gene's drawing and Akiko's notes. What was the author's design for his paragraph? How did he go about telling you what he wanted you to know?"

Angela, now on safe ground, says, "He told us something, then gave an example of it, and the example had two parts and he told what those were, and then he told how the one part was made and how the other was."

"What if the author had wanted to give you another example besides the stem," asks the teacher; "what might he have given besides the stem?" Somebody guesses *leaf*. "Where would you put *leaf*, Akiko?"

Akiko finds chalkboard space to the right of *stem* and writes "leaf."

"And what would you expect the author to do then after he says that an example is *leaf*? What might he say?"

"Well," says George, "if a leaf has two growing regions like a stem, he might name the two and tell how they work, just as he did with a stem."

"Now let's look in our books at page 3 and find this paragraph which we have been listening to," says the teacher. "Now look on this page and the next and see whether you can find any paragraphs that are written in the same pattern."

If the pupils do find paragraphs of the same pattern, they analyze them. If they are wrong, the analysis shows it.

In this way the teacher can orient the students in the patterns of the author's thoughts and prepare them for making the most of their reading. (See Chapter 6 for common patterns.) Inevitably they will find that some patterns are within a paragraph or are only a part of a paragraph, or are spread over several paragraphs. One paragraph may describe a phenomenon, and the next may tell the reason for it; while in another case one paragraph will be used for both purposes. Also, reverse relationships may be observed, the author sometimes starting with the reason and ending with the phenomenon.

Characteristics to Be Observed

Sometimes we tell students to be sure to take special notice of definitions without making sure they know what a definition is. The author may have helpfully put definitions in italics or boldface type, but he has done this to other types of statements as well. And in some cases he has not thought the definition important enough to italicize, whereas the teacher thinks it is important. The students must develop an ear and an eye for definitions as opposed to those statements they might be mistaken for; and again, being economical of time, the teacher decides to use for exercise purposes definitions he wants to impress especially upon the minds of his students. For exercise, he puts definitions and other statements in mixed order in a list and asks students which are which, and why they think so. But prior to giving the students this drill, he helps them develop discernment and discrimination in one or two examples.

The teacher may say, "I am going to write two sentences on the chalkboard. Read them as I write them, and be ready to tell me which one tells what oxygen is."

Then he writes:

Oxygen is necessary for the maintenance of plant, animal, and human life.
Oxygen is an element in the air, the sea, and the land.

One student thinks he sees a catch and wildly asks for attention.

"First, will someone read these two sentences aloud for us?"

Someone does. Then the first student says, "Both sentences tell what oxygen is."

"No," says another. "One says oxygen is an element, and the other just says it is necessary. Saying it's necessary doesn't say *what* it is."

"Try this one," says the teacher, and writes:

Oxygen is found in clay, sand, and limestone.

"Does this sentence tell what oxygen is?" he asks.

The students agree that the third sentence tells only where oxygen is found, not what it is. They make analogies such as, "I can say milk is found in the refrigerator, but that doesn't tell what it is."

"Now listen to these statements and raise your hand every time you hear a statement that tells what something is."

The teacher then speaks slowly and gives students a chance to indicate their judgment between each statement: "Oxygen is prepared by heating potassium chloride. . . . Pure oxygen is a colorless, odorless, tasteless gas which is slightly denser than air. . . . Pure oxygen is more active than air. . . . Oxygen is used in special occupations."

"What do we call statements that tell what something is?"

The students may know that such statements are called definitions.

"In science, definitions are considered to be very important. Why do you suppose this is true in the field of science?"

The students think that science is very exact and that scientists must know exactly what they are talking about. Definitions *are* important (motivation in sheep's clothing).

The teacher says, "You will find definitions in your textbook, and you should pay special attention to them. List them in your notes and be ready to tell what they mean, after each assignment. Then you will know what *you* are talking about. Just to make sure you will know a definition when you see one, read this list and check the statements that are definitions." The teacher passes out the list of mixed sentences.

A discussion should follow the checking. Students will note that while statements about the action, use, situation, appearance, etc. enhance the concept, they are not definitions because they do not label or classify the subject. Students can make longer definitions by adding some of these peripheral ideas to a definition.

Sometimes the author has not expressed definitions but has buried them in prose from which they may be extracted.

"Read this passage," the teacher may say, "and write for me definitions of the four regions in a cross section of a tree."

If you cut a branch of a tree, you will see four regions. The outer region, the bark, looks very different from the wood inside. Between the bark and the wood you will notice a very thin layer of delicate tissue. This is the cambium. If you look very carefully at the center of the cut, you will find the fourth region of pith.

Similar developmental exercises should be given students to help them distinguish between a statement of a principle and an example of it, a statement of a principle and a reason for it, an example of a principle and a reason for it:

An element can be removed from a compound by simple replacement.
Cooking tomato soup in a discolored aluminum pan will leave the pan clean and shiny.
The iron leaves the walls of the pan and replaces the hydrogen in the acid food, while the hydrogen escapes into the air.

Students should discover, also, that a definition differs from a principle in that a definition tells what something is, whereas a principle tells how something works or what it does. They should notice how general a principle sounds, as though it applied to many things and as though it were for all time. They should try to think of other examples for the application of the principle. This creative effort increases their grasp of the meaning of the principle.

These are only a few of the many distinctions students must be able to make in the reading of scientific literature. No one can help them so well as the science teacher who knows his subject and realizes the nature of the reading difficulty.

THE READING OF MATHEMATICS

Difficulties with Terms

The reading of mathematics requires an understanding of quite an assortment of technical terms, which present three major difficulties. For one thing, the same term is not always used for a particular operation. Expressions such as *and, added to,* and *plus* are used interchangeably. In addition to this, there are several technical terms in mathematics which have their uses in general conversation with quite a different meaning. The third difficulty is that mathematics requires the understanding of many terms which remind the student of absolutely nothing and must be learned the long, hard way.

Beyond this verbal language is the mathematical language itself. Thus, the student not only has to recognize several terms for the same process, terms that have their counterparts in the general vocabulary with different application and terms that have had no meaning for him, but he must also learn to interpret this new foreign language into still another foreign language, the language of mathematics. No wonder it is said that a person can make a fool of himself faster and more certainly in mathematics than in any other subject.

How to Meet Difficulties with Terms

A number of suggestions are given in the literature for meeting these difficulties: The instructor should examine his textbook to determine the words that are going to cause difficulty. He should confine his own technical vocabulary as much as possible to those terms used in the text so that the student does not have to translate the instructor as well as the textbooks. From the list of difficult words the instructor makes a pretest, a test to be taken at the beginning of the course to identify the terms which are foreign to the student.

The form of the test depends partly upon the amount of energy and thought the instructor wishes to devote to it. He can simply list the terms and ask for definitions in the student's own words. This is easiest for the instructor but most difficult for the student. In fact, some students who know how to use the term mathematically may be at a loss for the proper words, not to speak of their spelling, to define it. Therefore, the test will probably be more revealing of the true condition of the student's knowledge if it contains a multiple choice of answers for each term: A denominator is a (1) ———, (2) ———, (3) ———, (4) ———; or if it requires the student to use his knowledge of the meaning: a plus b is written (1) ab, (2) $a - b$, (3) a/b, (4) $a + b$.

The instructor then makes a chart of the results of the test, the names of the students down the left side of the page and the numbers of the items across the top. After he has recorded by check marks the failure of a student on the different items, he can look down the columns to see which items are unknown to the whole class, which to groups, and which to individuals only.

On the basis of these results the instructor can make his initial presentations in the class. For instance, he can return the papers to the class to make each individual aware of his needs. He can give the whole class exercise on those terms strange to all, group exercises to groups needing a particular kind of help, and some individual instruction. He can have students who know help students who do not. He can have individuals who know take charge of exercise at the chalkboard with small groups who need it. Students can look up definitions of a given term in various sources and compare findings [7]. They can make charts of their knowledge, keep notebook records, and impress the knowledge upon themselves in other ways. These activities refer to terms which are basic to the course and which should have been learned before. Terms that will be required at a later time in the course may better be left to explanation and practice at that time.

Furthermore, during the course the students must be made aware of inter-changeable terms. "How many ways have we of saying 'plus'?" "Write the following expressions in another way: a plus b, 4 added to 5, x and y, etc." Some instructors use a few minutes of every class period for a short test of terms. The test does not involve the actual solution of a problem but merely the rewriting of an expression to show comprehension of the meaning of the term, as in the example above. With older students a different committee each day can be responsible for planning such a test.

Several writers feel that the true concept of the formula is completely missed by many students. The latter think of $d = rt$ as "distance equals rate times time," instead of as an expression of the relationship, the interdependence, of these three factors. The authors urge that we devote some time to con-sideration of what happens to this relationship when one of the factors is held constant; e.g., when d is held constant, r varies with the value of t. Experi-mentation with the assignment of various values and the solution of the problems thus formed will impress the nature of the relationship upon the students.

It is very important that the students hear and use the terms which they are learning. Technical terms should be repeated and students encouraged to use instead of avoid them. One aid in this is for the instructor to present the word orally with his face *toward* the class and to have the class repeat it in unison; then he should write it on the chalkboard as he says it slowly and have the students repeat it again. In this way no one has reason to avoid the use of the term because of timidity about correct pronunciation.

Beyond this the instructor should test and check upon learnings at frequent intervals so that students are reminded of the terms they supposedly know. Nothing deteriorates so fast as an unused label.

Difficulties with Comprehension and Speed

Students who customarily read as though they were on a race track are doomed to failure in this field even before they open a book. They need to be identified and slowed down. Each student needs to take inventory of his reading rates and consciously adjust his speed to the requirements of his task.

How to Meet Difficulties of Comprehension and Speed

One way to make a student notice the details carefully in a problem in geometry is to have him draw the conditions described. A moderate amount of this kind of activity should help the student get a clear idea. Furthermore, the picture quickly gives the instructor the evidence about misconceptions before they have gone too far.

In making an assignment, it is wise for us to state exactly what we expect the students to be able to do. We should also say how we think it can be done. Sometimes we can get suggestions from the students who have been successful in this particular type of assignment.

Students need to learn to read with a purpose. It is questionable whether any successful student of mathematics ever solves any but the simplest of verbal problems correctly in one reading. Perhaps in his first reading he notes the kind of situation involved and the technique applicable to it, the identity of the unknown, and the facts pertinent to the solution. This reading is more rapid than succeeding readings but much slower than the usual pace for a popular novel. A second reading probably centers attention separately upon pertinent words and groups of words, their meanings and their translation into mathematical symbols. Some students interline their problems with symbols ($\times$, $+$, etc.) written above the words representing these ideas. The third reading can focus upon the relationships among these words and groups and arrive at a determination of the statement of equality. A fourth reading serves as a check upon interpretation and is punctuated with periodic reference to the symbols assigned to the words and groups.

Fay [9] delineates six steps in problem solving: (1) What is its nature? (2) What is the problem? (3) What are the details and interrelationships? (4) What process should be used? (5) Carry out the computation. (6) Is the answer correct? In a study by Brown [6], students of ninth-grade general mathematics used methods of problem solving which were generally ineffective. He proposed the following steps: (1) Be certain that you understand the problem. In what terms will the answer be given? Is the situation a familiar one? (2) What do you need to know to solve the problem? (3) Look for the hidden question. In two-step problems a student must find the answer to the unasked question before he can find the answer to the stated question. (4) Decide what computation to make. (5) Estimate a reasonable answer. (6) Perform the computations. (7) Check your answer.

In geometry perhaps the first reading is a general one in which the hypothesis and the conclusion are grasped. A second reading of the hypothesis gives the details of the figure to be drawn. After the reader has drawn and lettered his figure, a third reading with attention to the conclusion helps him to set up the symbolic statement that he must prove and to decide whether construction lines need to be added to his figure. Another reading with reference to his figure and his statement checks upon his interpretation. The proof of the statement involves the recall of previously learned theorems and axioms in response to the conditions of the problem. This is translation in reverse, from the pictorial or symbolic to the verbal.

Creative activity helps a student remember both terms and relationships. If a student has made his own graph, with such data as the day-by-day increase in orders for the school yearbook in high school or college, he can interpret graphs better. If he has tried his hand at original problems, even though his hen turns out to have laid half an egg, he understands relationships better. In the drawing of pictures, the construction of models, and the making of tables, he becomes more a mathematician and less a mere manipulator of figures.

Botel [5] suggests that headline stories be written, such as: $2 + 3 = 5$, and that children be asked to make up stories about them. They should be encouraged to be imaginative, with such starters as "Henry and Jack went fishing—" or "Henry and Jack captured—." After such stories have been invented, the teacher can alter the headline or alter the story and say, "How will we have to change our headline (or story) to fit?" Botel also suggests the making of a chart for an open-ended problem. "Dan had six cents. If he spent _____ cents, then he has _____ cents left." The children help fill in the chart as different amounts of expenditure are proposed.

Aids in Reading Difficult Texts

Many of the textbooks we have in mathematics are hard for our good readers and impossible for our poor readers.

The following practices are designed to compensate somewhat for the difficulty of a mathematics text:

1. Help students to become familiar with mathematical concepts by having them read comparable lessons in an easier text first and by using the

approaches of an easier text in preparatory lessons. Better students may write a verbal problem in their own words, using shorter sentences instead of one long, involved sentence. Ditto these simplified versions for all students to read.

2. Help students understand the nature of a problem by having individuals invent verbal problems that reflect a common life problem. Nonessential facts may be inserted in problems of a known type to give the class practice in finding the essentials for solution. A comparison of similar problems differently worded will show that different words may have the same meaning.

3. Aid students in reading the problems in their regular texts by encouraging the prereading of lessons, with questions at points of difficulty, and by having a student committee look ahead for trouble spots and clarify the difficulties. Students for whom a difficulty has been clarified may explain it later to the class. The teacher may eliminate or change verbal problems whose wording presents an ambiguity.

4. Give effective instruction by having better students tell how they have unraveled a puzzling problem and illustrate their successful methods.

5. Help students build a mathematical vocabulary by having them write in their notebooks a list of new words and words that have caused difficulty, illustrating each if possible, and using them in phrases or sentences. The teacher may use the first few minutes of each class for pantomimes, quiz programs, or other ways of visualizing the meanings of certain words or for having students show their best illustrations and definitions of new or troublesome words and file them as a help for future classes.

One feature of the arithmetic textbook has traditionally been a set of verbal problems that all require the same type of solution but that change the situation constantly: boys with marbles, girls with balls, and so forth. Part of the reading problem has been the constant shift of mind-set from one situation to another. Some of the modern textbooks have relieved this situation by having a page of problems about the same situation and requiring the same solution procedure, the page being well illustrated with an attractive picture of the situation. The illustration deprives the student of the experience of visualizing for himself, a skill which he will have to develop sooner or later in order to read less considerate texts. But certainly the use of the same situation in all of the problems reduces strain.

Even these considerate texts with their clear type and simple wording contain pitfalls which only the alert teacher can detect. When the janitor is said to have counted 138 knobs on the four floors of the school, how many children visualize a bunch of knobs scattered on the floor in each of four rooms? When he plants bulbs, how many children know what kind of bulb is meant? How does a nurse check a boy's eyes?

"Some boys went to a snack shop and bought a hamburger, a coke, and a chocolate sundae." (A picture shows price of each.) "How much did their snacks cost?" Do the children know the meaning of *snack?* Can they read the words *hamburger, coke,* and *chocolate sundae?* Do they know to what *their* refers?

"The bill was 75¢. Joe gave the cashier a dollar. How much change did he get back?" Do the children know what a *cashier* is? Do they know that *change* means "money"? Do they know that *he* is Joe, not the cashier?

When a problem states that two girls bought "4 yards or _____ feet of cloth," do the children know that *or* does not represent uncertainty on the part of the author, but that "_____ feet" is the equivalent of the 4 yards? Do they know that *yards* are not places to play or grow grass? If one of the girls cut "1 yard and 2 feet of string," is it clear that this resulted in one, not three strings? If "an engine pulls 50 boxcars, 20 flatcars, 13 gondolas, and 1 caboose," and the question is how many cars it pulls, do the children know that gondolas and cabooses are cars, too?

In using such material the teacher has two alternatives at least. He may have the children read and solve the problems independently before discussion takes place. If he does this, some children will fail the problem because they do not understand the author's intention. This is no reflection on their ability in mathematics. Other children will develop the habit of blindly manipulating figures according to the process they have been studying, ignoring the words. For example, they add all the numbers in sight. This means they are not developing the ability to determine from the situation described the process to be followed. A second alternative is to have each problem read aloud when the reading is assigned, to raise questions about meanings and wordings, and to have the children ask other questions as well, until it is certain that the children understand what each problem means.

Concluding Statement

The more the teacher knows about the structure of the English language, the language the children bring to class, and the ways in which ambiguity occurs, the better he will be able to identify and deal with reading problems in his field. Probably one of the best suggestions that could be given mathematics and science instructors on the problem of meeting the reading needs of their students is something William Beebe said a few years ago in reply to a compliment on his writing. He said he was not conscious of having any particular style but that he did have a method of preparation. If he intended to write about a certain fish, he observed the fish carefully until he seemed to be inside it. Then he wrote how he felt. The resemblance of students and fish is purely coincidental in this illustration; but if we could observe students and their reading problems so faithfully that we suddenly found ourselves "inside the students' skins," we should have the means of developing for them an effective program of learning.

REFERENCES

1. Bamman, H. A.: "Developing Reading Competencies through Mathematics and Science," in J. Allen Figurel (ed.), *Reading as an Intellectual Activity*, International Reading Association Conference Proceedings, vol. 8, Newark, Del., 1963, pp. 110–112.

2. Barrilleaux, Louis E.: "A Comparison of Textbooks and Multiple Library References: A Report on the Initial Phases of an Experimental Study," *School Science and Mathematics*, vol. 43, pp. 245–249, March, 1963.

3. Beauchamp, Wilbur L.: "Methods of Increasing Competence in Interpreting Science Materials in Grades Four to Six," in J. Allen Figurel (ed), *Improving Reading in All Curriculum Areas*, Supplementary Educational Monographs, no. 76, University of Chicago Press, Chicago, 1952, pp. 129–134.

4. Belden, B. R., and W. D. Lee: "Textbook Readability and Reading Ability of Science Students," *Science Teacher*, vol. 39, pp. 20–21, April, 1962.

5. Botel, Morton: "The Study Skills in Mathematics," in J. Allen Figurel (ed.), *Reading and Inquiry*, International Reading Association Conference Proceedings, vol. 10, Newark, Del., 1965, pp. 89–92.

6. Brown, Gerald W.: "Improving Instruction in Problem Solving in Ninth Grade General Mathematics," *School Science and Mathematics*, vol. 44, pp. 341–346, May, 1964.

7. Clark, John R.: "The Problem of Reading Instruction in Mathematics," in Arno Jewett (ed.), *Improving Reading in the Junior High School*, U.S. Department of Health, Education and Welfare Bulletin, no. 10, 1957, pp. 77–84.

8. Early, Margaret J. (ed.): *Reading Instruction in Secondary Schools*, Perspectives in Reading, no. 2, International Reading Association, Newark, Del., 1964.

9. Fay, Leo: "Comprehension in the Content Fields," in J. Allen Figurel (ed.), *Reading and Inquiry*, International Reading Association Conference Proceedings, vol. 10, Newark, Del., 1965, pp. 92–94.

10. Figurel, J. Allen (ed.): *Improvement of Reading through Classroom Practice*, International Reading Association Conference Proceedings, vol. 9, Newark, Del., 1964.

11. Herber, Harold L.: *The Practical Vocabulary Builder in English, Social Studies, Science, and Mathematics*, Scholastic Book Services, Inc., New York, 1964.

12. Mallinson, G. G.: "Reading and the Teaching of Science," *School Science and Mathematics*, vol. 44, pp. 148–153, February, 1964.

13. Maney, Ethel: "Literal and Critical Reading in Science," *Journal of Experimental Education*, vol. 27, pp. 57–64, September, 1958.

14. Marshall, J. S.: "Comprehension and Alleged Readability of High School Physics Textbooks," *Science Education*, vol. 46, pp. 335–346, October, 1962.

15. Owen, A. M.: "Selecting Science Textbooks," *Science Teacher*, vol. 29, pp. 20–23, November, 1962.

16. Panush, L.: "New Books for the High School Science Shelf, Sixth Series: 1963," *School Science and Mathematics,* vol. 44, pp. 353–387, May, 1964.

17. Randall, K.: "Improving Study Habits in Mathematics," *Mathematics Teacher,* vol. 55, pp. 553–555, November, 1962.

18. Severson, E. E.: "The Teaching of Reading-Study Skills in Biology," *American Biology Teacher,* vol. 25, pp. 203–204, March, 1963.

19. Shepherd, D. L.: *Effective Reading in Science,* Harper & Row, Publishers, Incorporated, New York, 1960.

20. Shepherd, D. L.: "Teaching Science and Mathematics to the Seriously Retarded Reader in the High School," *The Reading Teacher,* vol. 16, pp. 25–30, September, 1963.

21. Shores, J. H.: "Reading Interests and Informational Needs of High School Students," *The Reading Teacher,* vol. 17, pp. 536–544, April, 1964.

22. Smith, N. B.: "Patterns of Writing in Different Subject Areas, Part I," *Journal of Reading,* vol. 8, pp. 31–37, October, 1964.

23. Smith, N. B.: "Patterns of Writing in Different Subject Areas, Part II," *Journal of Reading,* vol. 8, pp. 97–102, November, 1964.

24. Spache, George D.: "Types and Purposes of Reading in Various Curriculum Fields," *The Reading Teacher,* vol. 11, pp. 158–164, February, 1958.

25. Strang, Ruth, and Dorothy K. Bracken: *Making Better Readers,* D. C. Heath and Company, Boston, 1957, chap. 5.

26. Troxel, V.: "The Effects of Purpose on the Reading of Expository Mathematical Materials in Grade Eight," *Journal of Educational Research,* vol. 55, pp. 221–227, February, 1962.

27. Van Deventer, William C.: "Library Resource Materials for Reading in Science," in Helen M. Robinson (ed.), *Materials for Reading,* Supplementary Educational Monographs, no. 86, University of Chicago Press. Chicago, 1957, pp. 186–192.

28. Willerding, Margaret F.: "A Critical Look at the New Mathematics for Seventh Grade," *School Science and Mathematics,* vol. 42, pp. 215–220, March, 1962.

special reading
instruction needed
in social studies

chapter 10

The good reader of social studies materials [6] tends to have a broad, specialized social studies vocabulary, accurate understanding of time and place concepts, good command of metaphorical language, strength in general vocabulary and sentence and paragraph comprehension, average or better intelligence, middle or upper socioeconomic status, liberal social views and conservative economic beliefs, good academic grades, an active school and community life, and a liking for reading. But he is a rare bird. No matter how well they get the facts, if they do get them, many of our students tend to remember only those that support their own views, to interpret them in such a way as to support their viewpoints, and to accuse the author of prejudice if his viewpoint is opposed to their own [15]. At all educational levels, the social studies teacher must be an ardent, patient teacher of reading and thinking.

FINDING OUT HOW STUDENTS READ

Every teacher should know what each student in his class is getting out of the social studies text and reference reading [21]. He may use a standardized test. Certain tests in the social studies purport to measure abilities in line with sound objectives. The Progressive Education Association Test of Application of Principles in the Social Studies was an attempt to measure ability to see logical relations and ability to evaluate arguments. The Social Studies Test of the College Entrance Examination Board [28] is designed to test students' knowledge of factors, trends, and means-end relationships, their attitudes and motives, and their understanding of key words and basic facts. It appraises ability to organize, to interpret, make, and apply generalizations. Independent-school norms as well as those for public schools are available for this test. The Cooperative General Achievement Tests: Test I, Social Studies,[1] measures the student's acquaintance with social studies concepts and his ability to interpret reading selections, graphs, and maps in this field. The newer STEP tests in social studies by the same publisher perform a similar service.

The social studies teacher may also use a test he has made. A test constructed by Margaret Martin Conant [5] has served as a model for teachers to use in constructing their own informal tests. Test exercises should be repeated following a period of instruction after an initial test has been given. If the responses on the first test are poor, the teacher may well devote part of one period each week to a series of exercises designed to correct weaknesses, each followed by discussion and by instruction in methods of getting more out of the reading of social studies in less time.

ENLISTING THE LIBRARIAN'S AID

The librarian is a very present help to the social studies teacher in finding books, especially for the retarded readers, which are pertinent to the themes his class is studying. For example, in the seventh grade references may be needed on improving home and family relations, soil conservation in our community, survey of world resources. In the eighth grade the teacher may need a wide range of reading material on such topics as how people from other countries have contributed to American life; America, a land of farms and factories; America, a land of opportunities for aesthetic and moral living.

One high school reports the following procedure:

In our world history classes we use the unit method. During each unit the student is expected to work on either an individual or a group activity. He is usually permitted to select the type of activity he prefers. Many suggestions are given, but if the student has a personal interest or can suggest an original

[1] Published by Educational Testing Service, Princeton, N.J.

activity on the topic we are studying, he is encouraged to follow it. He is given a card on which he writes his name and the activity on which he has decided to work.

Before the students go to the library to work on their problem, the librarian and the teacher take the cards and jot down one reference on each. In suggesting books, they consider the student's ability as well as the topic on which he is working.

In this way the student is not overwhelmed by a long list of books, and he has something with which to start. After he has read the information from one book, he can use the card catalog, the *Reader's Guide,* or other sources to find additional information.

The librarian has found this card system a great help because she knows, in advance, the topics on which the students are working and can frequently arrange special exhibits. It also gives her a better backing for talking with individual students regarding their problems.

In a unit on the expansion and settlement of the West the class decided to share their reading in a round-table discussion. To obtain a wide variety of books, a committee chosen by the class went to the librarian to see if books could be assigned to their class. The librarian was very cooperative; she sent to their room forty-eight books on westward expansion. The teacher gave out a mimeographed annotated list of the books which the pupils perused immedi-ately. Excerpts from the class discussion follow:

Phyllis: Good! Another list. I will check all the books that I want to read.

Bill: This is good! I'm sure this will be the best unit yet.

Arthur: Look, here's the book *No Other White Men.* I read that and it's swell. I got it in English class through the Teen-age Book Club. It's all about the Lewis and Clark Expedition out West. And they were the only white men out there where all the Indians were. Their guide was an Indian girl. Just think, they had been where no other white men had been before.

Skippy: That sounds good. (To teacher) Can I have that one?

Teacher: Yes, you may read any book you wish.

(Pupils continue to talk about the books they want to select.)

James: Oh, here's one—*Riding West on the Pony Express*—but I don't see it.

Peggy: (standing near) I have it, but I don't want it. (Gives it to James.) I have picked *Grandmother Brown's Hundred Years.* That looks more interesting to me.

Teacher: Yes, I believe you'll like that.

Peggy: It's about pioneer life in Iowa and shows the changes that have taken place over an entire century. Bert, can you find a book?

Bert: Naw, I don't see anything here that is interesting.

Teacher: What sort of stories do you like?

Bert: I dunno. Don't read much; not much time.

Teacher: I see. What do you do when you're home?

Bert: Help my father. Him and me make boats.

Teacher: You do? Your home is on the bay, isn't it?

Bert: Yep.

Teacher: I wish I had more time to go out on the bay than I do, and I wish I owned a boat. . . .

(They talk about experiences on the bay.)

Teacher: I think, Bert, that there is a book here you might be interested in. It's called *Keturah Came 'Round the Horn*. It's about travel all the way by sea from the East Coast around the southern tip of South America and on up to California (showing Bert the sea route to California on the wall map).

Bert: Uh-huh—you mean they had to go all around there?

Teacher: Yes, you see, the Panama Canal was built shortly after 1900. This story takes place in the 1840s.

Bert: Sounds pretty good. (Finds and starts to read his book. The whole class has chosen books and started reading. They read for the remainder of the period.)

The next social studies period was spent in reporting, discussing, and organizing the ideas about westward expansion which they had obtained from their extensive reading.

GUIDING STUDENTS' HOME STUDY

When a teacher merely says, "Read the next fifteen pages," the student has little idea what to do. Is he expected to get a general impression? be able to recite the main ideas? answer questions on details? hand in an outline? take an essay-type test? take a true-false or multiple-choice test? find out what the author's intent and viewpoint are? judge the authenticity of the content and separate facts from opinion? know the relative importance of events? make inferences, draw conclusions, arrive at sound generalizations? sense the sequence of events and how the present grew from the past? make application to present-day problems? Unless the teacher gives students some guidance in what to read for, they "cover" the pages in a desultory way and emerge from the reading with a few scattered ideas. The teacher can create readiness for reading by reviewing related facts known by the pupils, helping them to clarify the concepts they will encounter [18], raising problems that can be solved through reading. The well-planned assignment is closely related to the problem-solving method and provides for pupils with varied reading abilities.

In recent years a number of individuals and organizations have come to the rescue of the social studies teacher with ideas for helping students read social studies material. The National Council for the Social Studies has given attention to this matter in its yearbooks and bulletins. In its Bulletin No. 33, *Improving Reading in the Elementary Social Studies* [9], it answers the questions which elementary teachers most frequently ask about ways to handle the problems of reading the widely varied materials in this field. In its Bulletin No. 34, *Guiding the Social Studies Reading of High School Students* [19], it deals with problems of concept development, individual differences, the reading of textbooks, and the stimulation of wide reading. The National Society for the Study of Education devoted a chapter in its sixtieth yearbook, part I, *Development in and through Reading* [31], to reading in the content fields. Practically every newer book on the teaching of social studies and the teaching of reading gives some consideration to the plight of the social studies teacher who must teach reading in order to teach social studies. Because of the excellence of these sources and because of space limitations in the present book, this chapter will add to, rather than repeat, the contributions already made.

Whether the teacher teaches with multiple texts or a single textbook, whether he works with individuals, groups, or the whole class, the reading problem ultimately comes to the print and the reader viewing it. What can the teacher do for reading and still teach social studies?

THE PROBLEM OF READING CONNECTED MATERIAL

Chapters 6, 7, and 8 have already given the reader some idea of the difficulties inherent in connected prose. The following excerpt from *Compton's Pictured Encyclopaedia* illustrates the problem even in well-written material [4, vol. VII, p. 179]:

> *Automation.* The development of automation has brought about controversy (*see* Automation). Labor leaders have blamed it for unemployment. Businessmen, on the other hand, believe that industry must adopt automation to stay competitive with world markets. Other nations with low labor costs are becoming increasingly powerful. Business also feels that it needs the production gains of automation to help meet the higher wage rates remanded by labor leaders.

In 1952 an encyclopedia could not be found which would explain automation, and a dictionary did not contain the word; but ten years later the word is so commonplace that *Compton's* devotes eight pages to it in its *A* volume. Hence the "*see* Automation." *Compton's* [4, vol. I, p. 565a] explains that *automation* is a word coined from *automatic* and *operation* and does not mean "mechanization" but "a continuous arrangement for manufacturing or processing as automatically as is economically practical."

The concept must be developed by the teacher and students before the paragraph above is read, for in no part of it is the term explained. Reference to volume I, to a newer dictionary, and to students' experience with the term may give essential background. ("My father works in the refinery, and thirty men used to operate the machines. Now he just stands there watching the thirty machines work themselves, and if one stops he calls the mechanic.")

In order to read this passage, the student must know what "the development" of something is. He must know that *brought about* means "caused," and he must know the meaning of *controversy*. Perhaps, if *controversy* is not in his usual vocabulary, he will translate it to himself as "argument" or "fighting." The sentence expresses a cause-effect relationship between the development of automation and controversy.

He must know that *labor leaders* are spokesmen for organized workers. He must realize that *it* refers to the *development of automation,* not *controversy,* which is actually the nearest antecedent; this he can sense only by reasoning that "labor leaders blaming" equals part of a controversy, and controversy is not responsible for unemployment. He must know what *unemployment* means and what the attitude of labor leaders would be toward it. Sentence two presents one side of the controversy—the labor side. Knowledge of the usual opponents of labor in argument should help the student anticipate the identity of the other side.

The student can expect that the author of the definition will either continue to give the arguments on the one side or start those on the other. His question, "Now what?" is answered with the first words, "Businessmen, on the other hand"—the student must know that businessmen are men who run businesses and hire labor. *On the other hand* has nothing to do with gloves but with position in controversy. The student must recognize the figurative meaning in this context. He must appreciate that to blame is to express one's belief and that to "believe that industry must adopt automation" is an expression of another belief. When people blame, they don't like something. When people say they must, they may or may not like something but think it necessary. *Adopt* is used in one of its three usual meanings here, but not that probably most familiar to the student. *Stay competitive* means to be able to produce and sell goods either near the rival company's price or so superior in quality as to be marketable anyway. So the third sentence gives the businessmen's point of view, expressing necessity and the purpose of having automation. The student must see that the businessmen are thinking about *world* markets, not just local markets, and he must know what *world markets* means.

In the fourth sentence the student must gather that nations with low labor costs become more powerful partly because of those low labor costs. He must know in what sense *powerful* is used here—there are at least six common uses of this word in social studies material—and know the relative power in this sense of the United States. This sentence states a developing condition which the student must see as one reason the businessmen favor automation.

With "Business also feels," the *also* refers to what is felt and not to *business,* and the word *business* is being used as synonymous with *businessmen. It* refers to *business.* The student must know that automation increases production and that this is what is meant by "production gains of automation." If he is to understand this sentence, he must know that production gains can be offset by wage increases.

So automation has caused labor and business to argue:

labor—blaming it for unemployment
business—saying it is necessary on two counts:
    to compete in world markets against low labor costs
    to offset higher wage rates

Notice that the author did not signal the reader that sentence four would explain the reason for the view expressed in sentence three. The reader must sense the causal relationship from his knowledge of the relationship between the two sets of ideas. A connection is made in the use of *other nations* as a referent to *world markets*, but this does not in itself establish causality.

Linguistically the sentences are not difficult, for they follow two of the commonest patterns in the English language:

1. Noun	Verb	Noun	
2. Noun	Verb	Noun	plus causal phrase
3. Noun	Verb	Noun	plus causal phrase plus place phrase
4. Noun	Linking verb	Adjective	
5. Noun	Verb	Noun	plus causal phrase

The only commas enclose *on the other hand,* signaling an opposed view.

The main idea is clearly stated, if the student knows the meaning of the words. But the significant material in the paragraph is not in the statement of the main idea but in the details of the disagreement. No teacher would be happy if all the student could say was that labor and business disagreed. So in this case "Read for the main ideas and be ready to tell me . . ." will not suffice.

To set the stage for the reading of this paragraph, the teacher will have to build concepts of automation and labor-management relations. These certainly are the business of the social studies, and they help reading, too. In addition to this, the teacher will have to explore the special meanings of common words, such as *adopt,* and the strategic signal meaning of expressions such as *on the other hand* and *also* in their contexts.

But in addition to these matters, the teacher must make sure that the student detects the directions of the author's thoughts and the nature of them. Does the student recognize a statement of cause and effect? Does he recognize the difference between a general statement and one less abstract and more detailed? Does he recognize the cues to the branching of ideas? Does he recognize the cues that the author is staying on the same subject? These are skills which the paragraph used in illustration here required and are a few of the many characteristics in the social studies medium. Many students have never really learned that sentences make unique contributions to the pattern of an author's thought, and so have read sentences like so many beads in a strand. They need exercise in recognizing the character of these contributions and the ways in which they are related.

Fortunately the social studies teacher need not depart from his favorite subject, or from education of his students in it, to give attention to sentence meanings and thought patterns. He needs to use relatively simple wording so that he will not be fighting the battle of vocabulary as well as of structure and meaning; but it is possible for him to select ideas which he wants to be sure are impressed upon his students and to use these as exercise material. Gradually, as students learn new words throughout the course, these words can be used in the exercises and so become better established by use—another good purpose for the exercise.

CAUSE AND EFFECT VERSUS OTHER CONTENT

"Listen to these sentences and show me by raising your hand that you hear a statement of a reason for something: The bell rang. The principal pushed the button and the bell rang." (Hands go up.) "What happened?" (The principal pushed the button.) "What effect did that have?" (The bell rang unless it was the wrong button!) "So on the chalkboard we can write under *Cause*—'Principal pushed button,' and under *Effect*—'Bell rang.'

"Now, listen again: Our industrial plants produce more and more goods at lower costs." (This expresses a relationship but does not tell what the cause is.) "The productivity of labor has made the gross national product bigger and bigger each year, etc. . . . ."

On another occasion the teacher can give pairs of sentences and ask whether one is cause of the other: "Labor leaders objected to automation. It had put many workers out of jobs."

Since creative activity confirms understanding and reinforces it, the teacher may have students add a sentence to his, creating a cause-effect relationship: "In 1846 Elias Howe patented a sewing machine." "The American clothing industry grew swiftly after that." Sometimes more than one sentence can be added, presenting additional effects for a cause or additional causes for an effect. In each case a defense or explanation of the student's reason for thinking the relationship one of cause and effect should be given, sometimes by another member of the class.

Cause-effect sentences can also be contrasted with other types of sentences, such as the whole-part: "The spinning machine had 100 spindles"; or situational: "Everything was covered with a fine dust."

GENERALIZATION VERSUS DETAIL

On a day of reports, the teacher may have written on the chalkboard:

Reports on Industrial Inventions

Jack: The Power Loom

Don: Cylinder Printing

"If I had used sentences instead of these few words, what might my first sentence have been?" (There will be several reports on industrial inventions.) "My second?" (Jack is to tell about the power loom.) "Third?" (Don will report on cylinder printing.)

These sentences are written for all to see:

There will be several reports on industrial inventions.
Jack is to tell about the power loom.
Don will report on cylinder printing.

Joe says, "These sentences tell what is going to happen."

"Is there something different about one of the sentences?" asks the teacher. Or, if this gets no results, "Are two of the sentences more alike?"

The class agrees that the second and third are more alike; in fact, that they are structurally alike: Jack, Don; is to, will; tell about, report on; the power loom, cylinder printing. How is the first sentence different? Superficially it may be noted that it is a reversal of the noun—linking verb—adverb structure.

adverb	linking verb	noun
There	will be	reports.

But from the standpoint of meaning it deals with both of the other sentences: Jack and Don, the reporters; the loom and the cylinder, industrial inventions. The first sentence, then, is a generalization which covers both reports, and the second and third sentences specify reporters and content.

Does a generalization sound different from a specific fact? Plurals (reports, inventions) sometimes hint at it, but here is a generalization which contains no plurals: "Man is gregarious." However, *man* is used here to mean "men in general" or "mankind," and *gregarious* has all sorts of manifestations. So a generalization typically contains nouns which apply to more than one thing.

There are also generalizations which provide examples for supergeneralizations, just as there are rajas and maharajas:

Man is a social being.   (Supergeneralization)
Man is gregarious.   ⎰ Three ⎱
Man is familial.   ⎨ supporting ⎬
Man is communicative.   ⎱ generalizations ⎰

The problem is to realize the relationship between the supergeneralization and those generalizations which are supportive of it. In the example above, the burden of distinction is on the relationship of the four words which end the sentence.

Generalization characteristics are not confined to nouns but may be seen in other parts of the sentence. A paragraph dealing with many activities of a businessman, telling that he *orders, organizes, labels, prices, sells, delivers,* may begin or end with a statement that he *conducts* a business.

THE BRANCHING OF IDEAS

"A television series exploring the nature of radiation, the power of nuclear weapons, and the possibilities for defense and disarmament will be launched Thursday, March 29, over Station KQED at 8 P.M."

Such an announcement or news item may continue with references to each topic (radiation, weapons, defense and disarmament) in turn. The ear of the listener or the eye of the reader must be ready for references which will signal the identity of the topic or the change to another. How will the reader know that the next sentence refers to the topic of radiation? "On the first topic" may signal it, as it was the first mentioned. The word *radiation* itself may be used, the verb *radiate,* or the expression *radiant energy.* An illustration of its effects or a statement on its source may be given. The more the student knows about radiation the better he will be able to detect the topic—and the less he needs to hear the program. (When a topic is familiar, the reader reads it with greater ease and more understanding. It is easier for him to get the signals.)

When the topic becomes the power of nuclear weapons, the reader can expect a delineation of that power—in kind or quantity or effect, or the specific names of such weapons, or associated names such as "Hiroshima."

The topic of the possibilities for defense and disarmament may be signaled by terms like "antimissile missiles," or by the naming of armed services and organizations or individuals dealing with these problems. The mind of the student must stand ready, predictively full of great expectations, poised to classify the signal as of one thing or another, and to read it with the proper relationship in focus.

STAYING ON THE SUBJECT

How can the reader know that the author is staying on a subject? If the author is describing a wrongdoer as opposed to a rightdoer, the sentences may be strewn with words of disapproval: *destruction, devastation, short-sighted, rashly.*

The signaling of a change of topic will be the absence of references to the topic. Yet this matter of signals is more easily said than observed. For example, look at these sentences and decide whether the topic is being changed or not [8, vol. III, p. 715]:

Bismarck was in eclipse so long as liberalism prevailed in Germany. He was elected neither to the national assembly nor to the first Prussian parliament at Berlin. In October the army occupied Berlin, and Frederick William IV issued a more monarchist constitution. Bismarck was elected to the new second chamber.

There is no *however* or other word to suggest a change of topic or direction. Here is a set of declarative sentences, the first a generalization, the others statements of nonelection, occupation, and election. The student must sense the change from eclipse to prominence in the contrast between nonelection and election, liberalism and a more monarchist constitution. He must equate eclipse with nonelection and a change with election.

The presence of the referent word *he* in the second sentence of the quotation above may suggest that the author is staying with his topic. However, such a referent is not always a sure sign, for sometimes an interrupting name (Frederick William IV) forces a repetition of the proper name or use of a synonym, (as in the last sentence: Bismarck . . .). If the repetition of the name is enough to signal continuation of the topic, then the name becomes the signal but if, as in the case above, Bismarck is involved in both eclipse and prominence, the name disguises the change of fortune.

Listening exercises can help students determine whether an author is changing or staying on a subject. The teacher may say, "I am going to read you some beginning sentences from the paragraphs in your new assignment. As I read each sentence, tell me what you think the paragraph will have in it. Ready? 'Most people who lived in the village belonging to the manor were serfs.' I'll read it again. Think carefully. What will the paragraph say?"

Students variously volunteer that it will tell what serfs are and perhaps why they are there.

The teacher continues, "A serf was not a free man."

Students expect this paragraph will tell in what way or ways he was not free. "Free to do what?" is the question they must ask themselves as they read.

"Throughout the year the serf owed some kinds of payments to the lord of the manor." (What payments will be made? When?)

"On one manor every eighth pig belonged to the lord as payment for the use of his land." (Here the author is on the same topic—what kind of payment was made—and this is an example.)

"At first, manor houses were built of wood." (Now the topic has changed from serfs to manor houses. What were these wooden houses like?)

"Later on, stone was used in the construction of such houses." (Still the manor house, but stone instead of wood. What were the stone ones like?) (*At first* and *later on* suggest change of time, and *wood* and *stone* are contrasts of material.)

Observations such as those described help students meet the demands of reading connected material like the passage on automation at the beginning of this discussion. There are many more types of demands which the instructor must discern in the textbooks of his choice.

A main point for the teacher to remember is that students cannot be expected to recognize relationships among things they do not know. Even though the author gives signals (and sometimes he does not) and the student recognizes the signals, he still will not understand what he has read unless he understands the concepts being presented.

The reading of long assignments in this field is futile if the concepts being read about escape the reader's understanding. It stands to reason that extensive reading on a topic should be postponed until sufficient groundwork is laid in the meanings to be encountered. Listening to and reading short passages under the guidance of the teacher will develop power which making haste through a no-man's-land will not.

A second main point is that students should cultivate the habit of questioning and surmising the coming ideas. If they read of the discovery of America and the desire for wealth, they should not be surprised at exploration. If further on they read of shortages of land in Europe, they should expect colonization. Religious persecution in Europe suggests more colonization. Dissatisfaction with the home government suggests a struggle for independence.

In multiple causes they should be able to zero in on the inevitable effect. Take a large population in comparison with the arable land; add low mortality and high birth rates, failure of monsoon, movement of workers to city jobs, and the use of arable land for housing. How can the reader understanding these concepts be surprised at the consequent food shortage? He can be surprised only if he is not using his head—precisely the way some students try to read.

A third main point is that students should be encouraged to visualize conditions which the author may describe in the briefest manner and draw on their own experience to imagine the realities of a situation and the human consequences.

"In the national emergency, people who had been enemies worked together." (A common cause can temporarily erase differences.)

"Settlers who had left Europe because of religious persecution, themselves became intolerant of dissenters in the new colony." (People tend to behave like their enemies.)

"The sea-level town was drenched in eighteen inches of water." (What would this mean to roads, houses, shops, parks, gardens, pets, health, water supply, electricity, communications?)

KEEPING UP WITH CURRENT EVENTS

Students should be encouraged to read critically newspapers, news magazines, and books on current events; to listen to news broadcasts and commentators; and to interpret modern events in the light of historical perspective. If, as in one class, the students choose to spend thirty minutes a day on discussion of current problems, the retarded readers may begin with an easy current-events magazine such as *My Weekly Reader* or one of the *Scholastic Magazines* publications and gradually acquire enough skill to read the daily papers.

The reader of news stories is presented with a characteristic pattern which he must recognize if he is to read efficiently. The first sentence or paragraph usually gives the whole idea in a nutshell. Subsequent paragraphs elaborate upon the first, giving details and suggesting implications. If the article is longer, a detailed reiteration of the whole matter is given, sometimes with various persons' reactions or predictions concerning it. For the reader who wishes to get at the truth of a situation, this third part is often the most fruitful because it goes beyond the reporter's summary and the interpretation given in the headline to supply the actual sources for these generalizations.

Hence, the reader who is on the lookout for propaganda will read the first two parts to sense the reporter's bias, and then find the facts on which the headlines and the summary and interpretation are based. Are the reporter's facts sufficient justification for the statement in the headline? If not, what effect does the headline have on the reader? Does it make him indignant, overoptimistic, hostile? And why might the newspaper have wished to produce this effect?

It is enlightening to read a newspaper article on a controversial issue and underline the words that prompt a favorable or unfavorable reaction to a given side of the issue. An analysis of the headlines of several newspapers with different points of view also reveals how words are used to influence readers' attitudes. If an author presents two sides of a problem and draws a conclusion, the students should study the facts carefully to see whether he does justice to both sides. Does he slight the arguments that favor the side he opposes? Does he neglect to mention certain facts that weaken his argument?

DEVELOPING CRITICAL READING ABILITY

To develop critical reading it is first necessary for the student to comprehend the meaning of the passage. To comprehend the meaning of the passage he must understand the multiple meanings of words and the jobs that words do and how they influence people. The use of words to influence attitudes and motivate actions is most clearly seen in advertisements. Students may bring in many examples for analysis.

Then comes the difficult task of criticism. The statement or generalization must be held up for examination: Does it correspond to the known facts and to your experience? Does the statement contain "weasel words" or "chameleon words"? Does the writer employ propaganda devices such as the use of certain words to produce certain feeling tones, omission of some facts to create inaccurate impressions, use of repetition to hammer in an idea? Comparing headlines on the same news items from different newspapers will show how the meaning of a sentence can be changed by a skillful change of wording.

Lorge [12] gives the example of a passage about the beginnings of ready-to-wear clothing. In relation to such a passage a number of questions can be proposed to promote thinking and evaluating: What was the value of what was done? Why did this event take place? What problems did the situation present? What had created them? What do you think should happen next? What would be the consequences of the action taken? What consequences do you see today in our own society? What likenesses or differences today make this event likely or unlikely to recur?

Why did the author write this? What was his background for writing it? Was he accurate, fair? Did he omit important facts? Where is the fallacy in his reasoning? What line of logic was the author following? Were his conclusions warranted by the facts he presented? What else would you have to know to judge the author fairly? How did the author organize his material to make his argument particularly effective?

How does this passage help you in your understanding of processes, people, values? By what set of standards or values were these people operating? How are our standards or values different or similar today? What was your own bias before you read this? What shifts in your position have you had to make because of what you have read?

Lorge's definition of thinking is challenging to the teacher of the social studies [12, p. 170]:

Thinking is an active process. It seeks and searches. It organizes and generalizes. It collects and solves. Thinking does not always produce a set answer. It is not memory, although it uses what is remembered; it is not generalization, but the process of arriving at generalization. Thinking is basically an attitude of suspended judgment about the problems all of us face.

REFERENCES

1. Aaron, I. E.: "Developing Reading Competencies through Social Studies and Literature," in J. Allen Figurel (ed.), *Reading as an Intellectual Activity*, International Reading Association Conference Proceedings, vol. 8, Newark, Del., 1963, pp. 107–110.

2. Arnsdorf, Val E.: "Readability of Basal Social Studies Materials," *The Reading Teacher*, vol. 16, pp. 243–246, January, 1963.

3. Carpenter, Helen (ed.): *Skills in Social Studies,* Twenty-fourth Yearbook of the National Council for the Social Studies, Washington, D.C., 1954.

4. *Compton's Pictured Encyclopaedia,* F. E. Compton and Company, Chicago, 1962, vols. I, VII.

5. Conant, Margaret Martin: *The Construction of a Diagnostic Reading Test for Senior High School Students and College Freshmen,* Teachers College Contributions to Education, no. 861, Teachers College Press, Teachers College, Columbia University, New York, 1942.

6. Covell, Harold M.: "A Study of the Characteristics of Good and Poor Readers of Social Studies Materials at the Eleventh Grade Level," unpublished doctoral dissertation, Florida State University, Tallahassee, Fla., 1955.

7. Early, Margaret J. (ed.): *Reading Instruction in Secondary Schools,* Perspectives in Reading, no. 2, International Reading Association, Newark, Del., 1964.

8. *Encyclopaedia Britannica,* Encyclopaedia Britannica, Inc., Chicago, 1966, vol. III.

9. Fay, Leo, Thomas Horn, and Constance M. McCullough: *Improving Reading in the Elementary Social Studies,* National Council for the Social Studies Bulletin 33, Washington, D.C., 1961.

10. Gainsburg, Joseph C.: "Critical Reading Is Creative Reading and Needs Creative Teaching," *The Reading Teacher,* vol. 6, pp. 19–26, March, 1953.

11. Joll, L.: "Evaluating Materials for Reading Instruction at the Secondary Level," in J. Allen Figurel (ed.), *Challenge and Experiment in Reading,* International Reading Association Conference Proceedings, vol. 7, Newark, Del., 1962.

12. Lorge, Irving: "The Teacher's Task in the Development of Thinking," *The Reading Teacher,* vol. 13, pp. 170–175, February, 1960.

13. Luciano, V. D.: "A Reading Skills Approach in Social Studies General Classes," *High Points,* vol. 46, pp. 64–67, January, 1964.

14. McCallister, James: "Using Paragraph Clues as Aids to Understanding," *Journal of Reading,* vol. 8, pp. 11–16, October, 1964.

15. McCaul, Robert L.: "The Effect of Attitudes upon Reading Interpretation," *Journal of Educational Research,* vol. 37, pp. 451–457, February, 1955.

16. McGoldrick, J. H.: "Using Novels in History Class," *Social Studies,* vol. 54, pp. 95–97, March, 1963.

17. Noall, M. S., and G. C. Ceravolo: "Selected Studies in Spelling, Learning, and Reading," *Journal of Education,* vol. 145, pp. 3–15, April, 1964.

18. Nowell, L.: "Developing Concepts in the Social Sciences," *The Reading Teacher,* vol. 16, pp. 10–15, September, 1963.

19. Preston, Ralph C., J. Wesley Schneyer, and Franc J. Thyng: *Guiding the Social Studies Reading of High School Students,* National Council for the Social Studies Bulletin 34, Washington, D.C., 1963.

20. Robinson, H. Alan: "Reading Skills Employed in Solving Social Studies Problems," *The Reading Teacher,* vol. 18, pp. 263–269, January, 1965.

21. Rudisill, Mabel: "What Are the Responsibilities of Social Studies Teachers for Teaching Reading?" in Arno Jewett (ed.), *Improving Reading in the Junior High School,* U.S. Department of Health, Education and Welfare Bulletin, no. 10, 1957, pp. 91–97.

22. Schiller, M. P. (Sister): "The Effect of the Functional Use of Certain

Skills in Seventh Grade Social Studies," *Journal of Educational Research,* vol. 57, pp. 201–203, December, 1963.

23. "Secondary Reading: Resources and Research," *Journal of Education,* vol. 145, April, 1964, entire issue.

24. Shepherd, David L.: *Effective Reading in Social Studies,* Harper & Row, Publishers, Incorporated, New York, 1960.

25. Shores, J. H.: "Reading Interests and Informational Needs of High School Students," *The Reading Teacher,* vol. 17, pp. 536–544, April, 1964.

26. Smith, N. B.: "Patterns of Writing in Different Subject Areas, Part II," *Journal of Reading,* vol. 8, pp. 97–102, November, 1964.

27. Sochor, Elona: "Literal and Critical Reading in Social Studies," *Journal of Experimental Education,* vol. 27, pp. 49–56, September, 1958.

28. *Social Studies: A Description of the Social Studies Test of the College Entrance Examination Board,* Educational Testing Service, Princeton, N.J., October, 1953.

29. Strang, Ruth: *How to Read the News,* Education and National Defense Series, pamphlet 16, Superintendent of Documents, Washington, D.C., 1942.

30. Witt, M.: "A Study of the Effectiveness of Certain Techniques of Reading Instruction in Developing the Ability of Junior High School Students to Conceptualize Social Studies Content," *Journal of Educational Research,* vol. 56, pp. 198–204, December, 1962.

31. Witty, Paul A. (ed.): *Development in and through Reading,* Sixtieth Yearbook of the National Society for the Study of Education, part I, University of Chicago Press, Chicago, 1961, pp. 54–76.

special reading

instruction needed

in other fields

chapter 11

Teachers in subject fields other than English, mathematics, science, and social studies are variously aware of the reading problems in their areas. In fields where little has been done to recognize the problems or to suggest procedures and materials, the teacher is forced to attempt his own analysis and to use the ideas which are applicable from other fields. This chapter contains gleanings from the fields of business education, foreign language, home economics, industrial arts, and music, with implications for still other fields.

BUSINESS EDUCATION

Reading has much to do with success or failure in business courses. The student needs to understand important technical words thoroughly [11, 31, 34, 52, 70], use an appropriate approach to each kind of reading, and learn to get the meaning of difficult passages and put the ideas gained to immediate use [6]. Students of accounting must learn to read very critically and to maintain a questioning attitude toward what they read.

Bookkeeping and Accounting

Musselman [62] attributes difficulties in reading bookkeeping textbooks to several factors. He notes the heavy vocabulary load reported by House [36], more than 200 technical bookkeeping words having been found in the high school textbooks on the subject. Garbutt [23] found 162 accounting terms in eight college textbooks, only a few of which appeared in any one book. Administering a test to college students, asking them to define the terms, he identified a hard core of the twenty most difficult.

Common words with special meanings in bookkeeping must be untangled from the common meanings associated with these words: *abstract, capital, charge, credit, extend, footing, post, prove, register, ruling, statement, terms* [36]. Furthermore, teachers and authors tend to use certain terms interchangeably, confusing the student who supposes a different idea is meant with each change. Here are some of these interchangeably used words:

Analysis paper, worksheet paper, working paper
Bad debt, bad account, uncollectable account
Cash on hand, cash balance, balance on hand
Proprietorship, net worth, capital
Minus asset, valuation account, reserve account
Principal of note, face of note
Profit and loss statement, operating statement, income statement, income and expense statement
Liabilities, debts, obligations

According to the Flesch Reading Ease Chart, bookkeeping textbooks rank in difficulty with such magazines as *Harper's, The New Yorker,* and *Business Week.* Musselman [62] estimates that they are beyond the reading ability of over 50 per cent of high school students and points out that typical bookkeeping classes range in reading ability from about the lowest 5 per cent of seventh-grade students to the highest 5 per cent of twelfth-grade students. In House's [36] study of 357 bookkeeping students, 40 per cent of them had the ability to read the texts.

Musselman suggests that the teacher associate technical terms with ideas familiar to the student, for example, the idea of *assets* with the possession of a bicycle, radio, wrist watch, and clothing; provide experiences such as field trips in which, for example, seeing an office clerk checking the accuracy of calculations on a sales slip will clarify the conception of the phrase *auditing the sales slip;* dramatize the action of a corporation determining the amount to pay stockholders from profits to build meaning into the word *dividend.*

He urges both that the teacher be consistent in use of terminology and that he prepare lists of terms in the coming assignment, deciding the best approach for each. The bookkeeping period may better be a period for explaining the assignment and the terms used and for guided silent reading, rather than a period primarily for recitation and testing. It is helpful to students if the teacher looks with them at the illustration in the textbook and at the reading matter which must be associated with it and asks them questions which require "reading" the illustration from the information given. The use of study guides with the textbook reading instead of as tests after the reading gives the student a sense of direction and emphasis.

Reading success is due partly to the curiosity or desire which motivates the student. If the student's self-starter is weak—indeed, if the whole tone of the class is "I dare you to unbore me"—Jasinski [41] suggests the use of varied and attractive materials (newspapers, magazines, pamphlets, charts, and tables), student activities which keep the blood circulating (writing, speaking, seeing, listening, thinking, collecting, investigating), and the initiation of each topic with practical problems tied to the students' personal experiences. If these suggestions seem time-consuming to the ambitious teacher, he need only remember a recent article which points out ten ways to waste time in business education. There may be room for these additions after all.

Another means of motivating reading is the choice of the textbook itself [7]. The size of type, the organization, the clarity of expression, the presence of helpful illustrations and attractive format are parts of the invitation to read. If the teacher gives the student a specific purpose for reading a selection, suggesting what to look for, and a guiding list of questions or a problem to solve by using selected points from the material, and if the student is then held to applying what he has found in some specific way—actually solving the problem or using the answers to the questions to apply to another situation— the student will be both more efficient and more interested.

Yengel [93] suggests types of questions useful in class discussions: questions of definition, illustration, comparison and contrast, purpose, decisions for or against, application, classification, outlining, recall, relationships, observation, and summary.

As students read an assigned accounting problem, they should be asked to express the idea in their own words [30], tell in detail the instructions for solving the problem, and present a step-by-step procedure for solving it, without the use of figures at all.

When a student has read paragraphs on a new topic and has taken a quiz on the contents, and the papers have been checked by the teacher, the student should restudy the paragraphs to determine what he has missed [30]. The incentives are that the paper will receive a second grade after corrections have been made and that the student may know better how to find the right answer to that type of question next time. The instructor should go around the class, having each student tell him individually what his reading problem was, what fooled him, and how he thinks he can fool it next time. The teacher needs to analyze for himself and be ready to guide the student to see the reasons why one answer is right and the other answers wrong.

House [36] points out that teachers can create reading problems by the very wording of their test questions. Sometimes a teacher can screen out such problems by having the students read aloud and interpret the questions, or sometimes by going over the wording carefully in advance to eliminate unnecessary rare words and ambiguities. A good question to hold in mind is: "What kind of hash will Mortimer make of this?"

It is not essential that all of what transpires in the business class be held to the Mortimer level. Wagoner [83] proposes that the bookkeeping textbook be used as a reference book. If this is done, students may be using as references different textbooks on the same subject. A teacher can administer a test on short selections from the different textbooks at the beginning of the course to find which textbooks are understandable to which students. Or he may simply look up the students' reading records and compare their tested reading abilities with the textbook levels. Then abler students may be assigned the more difficult textbooks, and the whole class may be retaught the use of the index and table of contents to find information.

Business Law

Goodman [26] has listed 211 words which are basic technical vocabulary in business-law textbooks. Sometimes the textbook lists the new terms at the ends of the chapters. In this case, the teacher can draw attention to them before the chapter is read. Otherwise, he offers his own list or sends a representative student road crew ahead to scout troublesome words. Brophy [6] encourages students to look up words in the dictionary for the business-law meaning, to read the words in the textbook context, and to write their own definitions of the words as used. Then he polls the class for different versions of meaning to arrive at a class definition. Correct pronunciation is stressed, all students pronouncing the word carefully. The students then record the terms in individual notebooks, indicating syllabication and pronunciation as well as definition. Each word should somehow be attached to the type of context in which it is usually found; discussion of the relation of the word to the related law principle is one method of doing this. Finally, the students are encouraged to use the terms, not dodge them, and to report out-of-class uses they notice on TV, in newspapers, and in other classes. The teacher provides a review of the terms in frequent oral and written situations.

Typewriting

One of the deadly sins of the typist is the unfaithful reproduction of material—the miscopying of words without concern for meaning. It is a question whether junior high school students studying typing have the experiential background to understand the special terms used in the business letters they are to type [21]. The study of these terms, then, is essential.

Students typing material containing medical terminology can scan a key to the recorded history of a patient and type the terms which are unfamiliar, such as *palpable fluid, palpable lymph node, palpable masses, palpable abnormalities, palpable edge;* then use the typed lists for reference as they make the transcription [47]. Wood [92] notes that the typist's reading should not be too much faster than his typing lest he omit or forget items. He recommends slow, careful reading and the observation of letters in groups of letter patterns in the typing of unfamiliar words.

Fitzgerald [22] urges greater use of linguistic knowledge in teaching typewriting, such as using a frame for students to fill (The _____ _____ in the _____ _____ to the _____), shifting modifiers from one position in a sentence to another (*Swiftly* the men drove down the road), and practicing basic sentence patterns (see Chapter 8).

Hale [29] writes that students can be forced to think about meaning as they type, if some words are omitted in the model they are to copy: "We wish _____ inform _____ that we _____ placing your unpaid bills _____ the hands _____ our attorney for _____ collection." In speed tests of typing, the score should be based upon correct words per minute rather than the net words [56].

Shorthand

The ideal in reading shorthand is fluent reading without hesitation [13]. If possible, students should have daily experience in reading aloud an assignment they have prepared for class, reading the next assignment without preparation to locate difficulties, and reading from homework notes. A test of ability to read connected material from the lesson prepared for the day should be administered each day [69]. Diagnosis of difficulties should differentiate between those errors caused by poor formation of the symbols in the student's own handwriting and those caused by basic similarities in form. Special exercises offering numerous repetitions of the points of confusion should follow. Students can make up some exercises for each other.

Both writing and reading exercises should be used in learning shorthand, and attention may be given to both word lists and connected material. The Skill Builder Controlled Reader has been reported by Nisdorf [63] to increase students' speed of shorthand well beyond that from ordinary exercise.

Business-machine Fundamentals

Job instruction sheets designed to teach business-machine fundamentals present a special reading problem [45]. The teacher can make up the rough draft of the sheet from the instruction manual supplied by the manufacturer. Then students who have worked with the machine can review the sheet for omissions and put each step into their own words. The sheet may be revised with these suggestions. Then it can be tried out on some inexperienced students. Their interpretations and questions may lead to further simplification and to the identification of necessary technical words which will have to be explained prior to the use of the sheet.

If the sheet contains an illustration of the machine with parts clearly labeled, some of the interpretation of terms is obviated. Krause [45] proposes that the sheet be divided into two columns, the left-hand column for a statement of each operation, the right-hand column for key points to observe and remember in the operation.

It is clear that business educators are aware of the reading problems in their varied fields and are beginning to offer substantial help in their solution.

FOREIGN LANGUAGES

A number of writers are calling for teachers of foreign languages to consider new findings in linguistics and reading methodology [16, 48, 71]. Larew [50] finds that neurologists propose the age range from four to ten as optimum for the learning of a foreign language and reports the best articulation of Spanish achieved at the age of seven in a study of a range from seven to eleven. Moulton [60] feels that difficulties in pronunciation should be classified by their causes and treated accordingly. He proposes the classifications: phonemic errors, phonetic errors, allophonic errors, and distributional errors. Duncan [16] believes that the reading of the foreign language should be "purposed" prior to the reading, that new words should be introduced and analyzed before being read in the text, and that comprehension questions should be included to require understanding of the passage and not merely the duplication of it.

In learning to read a foreign language, the student has to make a direct association between the printed word and its meaning [44]. He must sense the structural and phonetic characteristics of the language and build a reading vocabulary [8, 18]. Having a definite goal or purpose, reading for meaning, and having appropriate reading material are just as important here as in the reading of English [88].

When a native language is being learned in the home [33], there are not the artificial restrictions on speech and behavior that exist in the school. The home experiences build, support, and clarify meaning. The learner is interested in the day-to-day meaningful repetition because the impressions are new and the learning is intriguing and important. As educators we speak of certain languages as being too difficult for students of a certain intelligence level, as counselors we guide them to easier languages, yet the dullest native can speak his own. The differences are that he had individual attention and nothing to unlearn. His learning situation was relatively ideal. If teachers of a foreign language are to approach the efficiency of home teaching, they must preface the reading of the language with much meaningful experience, contriving situations in the classroom to resemble reality and increasing the amount of practice by opportunities for pairs or groups of students to converse.

Of course, long before the child imitates his parents' speech, he has listened to it, catching neither head nor tail perhaps, but developing a familiarity with the sounds of the language. Casaubon [9] concludes that the ear of the student of a foreign language should be tuned to the new language before speech is attempted. Recordings of the language well spoken and talks by native speakers or by an excellent teacher may provide this ear training. The students should describe what they notice about the sound characteristics of the language, and the teacher should fill in with questions, guiding their further observation.

Mayer [57] proposes that the teacher start with a lecture on the physiology of speech—the characteristic positions of the organs of speech in a given language which produce accent, demonstrating those positions and then saying something in English to show how the positions affect the accent. He presents a chart of the following kind and discusses its meaning:

	English	French
1. Tension	Rather low	Quite high
2. Directional tendency	Neutral (central)	Forward
3. Favorite tongue shape	Flat, or even concave	Convex
4. Transitions	Slow; vowels diphthongize	Rapid; vowels "pure"
5. Accentuation	Stress (pitch of minor importance)	Pitch (stress virtually of no importance)

Mayer also discusses the differences in the production of similar English and French phonemes: for instance, that d, t, and n are alveolar in English, dental in French. He follows this with drill on the new sounds to be learned.

In the Thai language [1] there are five tones which must be recognized and associated with the syllables of the language. Each syllable has a characteristic pitch which is an integral part of that syllable. The learning of pitch in association with the symbols of the language and the meanings they convey requires that training be both oral and aural. Shen [73] claims that learning the Chinese script can be easy if a multisensory approach is used, the student simultaneously saying aloud, seeing, and writing the symbol of the word.

After practice has been given in saying, seeing, and writing the symbol, dictation can be used as a test of exact knowledge of sounds, symbols for the sounds (if it is a consistently phonetic language), vocabulary, comprehension, and fundamental grammar rules [24]. Paperback editions of textbooks in modern languages such as French, German, and Spanish by I. A. Richards and others exemplify the effective modern technique of illustrating a situation and presenting the common expression associated with it. The films and TV programs which use this technique show the picture and present the sound of the expression, to be repeated by the listener before the same situations are reviewed with the visual symbols. Effective review would be to show the picture, present the sound of the expression, have the student repeat and write the expression from memory, then compare with the written symbols.

An easy introduction to a foreign language includes recognition and pronunciation of those words which it has in common with the native language. Krauss [46] has compiled English words occurring in German magazines and newspapers since 1956–1958. In addition to these, many English words trace their origin to German cognates. Sieberg and Crocker [74] believe that many French cognates are not recognized as such by the ordinary student and must be pointed out: *hâte* and *haste, débander* and *disband.* Similarly, root groups should be noted: *feuille, feuillage, feuillée,* etc. The analogy of French suffixes to English suffixes is helpful: *feuillage,* analogous to *cordage, plumage, bandage.* The meanings of the English suffixes assist in the interpretation of French suffixes.

Through the study of metaphors the student can establish in his own mind the meaning of a given word [54]. When we *ponder,* we *weigh something in the mind.* This is the clue to the meaning of the Latin word *pondus,* "weight." When we *deliberate* we *balance* or *weigh* ideas. *Libra* means "balance."

It is a happy thought that one can lean on a dictionary as one translates from a language, but bilingual dictionaries in many cases still fail to be dependable guides to proper equivalents in translating to the foreign language [32]. Apparently the teacher is not entirely dispensable! Also, in reading a foreign language, as in English, the student must study the passage in which the word occurs to decide what meaning the context forces upon it.

When choosing words to include in beginning language courses, it is encouraging to find that over 90 per cent of written foreign language can be translated using 2,500 most frequent words in the English language, according to Spaulding [75], reporting a study by Calbick, Wade, and Banner. (It should, however, be noted that since many of the basic words in this English vocabulary have several meanings, they represent in many languages more than 2,500 words.) Whether the objective is the reading of the language or the speaking of it, it is probable that most of these words would be useful. Furthermore, because they are common in English, they present no meaning difficulty; and because they are common in the foreign language, they are encountered frequently enough to be easily retained. Spaulding urges that early language training be kept within this vocabulary and that the training include meaningful context and repetition that requires attention to thought as well as to symbol. Spotts [76], on the other hand, believes that in Hebrew the basic vocabulary depends upon whether the purpose is reading or conversation. Because Hebrew is an ancient as well as a living language, the difference between the reading and speaking vocabularies is, in some instances, marked. He presents a bibliography of forty-three references on vocabulary problems in Hebrew.

Certainly an objective of teaching the reading of a foreign language is the understanding of what is read and, with it, fluency in reading. Jones [42] reports that Spaniards read aloud on the average of about 165 words per minute. Surely then, he says, our students of Spanish should be able to achieve that speed in *silent* reading. But such speed, if it is to be accompanied by accurate understanding of the content, is for many students blocked by certain pitfalls. Some students retard their own speed by lip movements, with which they try to assist recall and to perfect oral interpretation. Others, finding the material unfamiliar in content and vocabulary, and beset with words of multiple meaning, take refuge in inattention and distractions.

Jones suggests that the student first skim through the material for unfamiliar words and look them up, rather than punctuate his reading with excursions to the dictionary. Or he should read the whole assignment as quickly as possible, reading only essential words: *El hombre con el sombrero de felpa se levantó de su silla con ira.* (Unfortunately for this idea, it has been found in the reading of English that while the essential words are noticed by the good reader, those are the very ones the poor reader is apt to skip. Perhaps this should be a technique reserved for good readers only.) Then a second reading should take place, with study of the unfamiliar words. Have they English cognates? Do I know the root, the prefix or the suffix? A list of roots, prefixes, and suffixes is a good reference tool. If these moves fail, the student resorts to the dictionary. The third step in the Jones plan is rapid rereading, with a deliberate attempt to think in Spanish rather than in English.

One cannot help thinking how lucky the bilingual child is whose teacher does not know his home language, who must catch English from present situations, and whose dictionaries explain English words at first entirely through pictures and later with the addition of English words, phrases, and sentences. While the going is rough, the method by which he is learning reduces the danger of his thinking in the home language.

Jones believes that several kinds of knowledge and activity can foster speed in reading a foreign language [42]. The student should know that the subject and verb agree with one another, that certain prepositions are associated with certain verbs, that the noun and adjective agree and maintain a certain relative position. He should be invited to guess at the word, much as we do in English when the context and the shape of the word are enough to suggest the identity without a careful look. Practice in reading common phrases will establish common associations. Sentence cards can be used for quick recall exercise. Long assignments will force quick reading. Spanish versions of familiar stories can be read more rapidly than stories new to the student. The student should know the purpose of his reading, what to find out from the content.

These are a few of the ideas to be found in the professional literature on the teaching of reading a foreign language. As in the case of early studies relating to the teaching of reading English, there are more articles expressing concern for word meaning and word analysis than for larger units of comprehension and interpretation. This is understandable, but something to be aware of, too, as we consider our progress toward the goals of teaching a foreign language, or, indeed, our own.

HOME ECONOMICS AND INDUSTRIAL ARTS

Reading in home economics, industrial arts, and school shops is highly practical. The information gained from reading is immediately applied and comprehension is tested by use. A sound sequence is (1) demonstration of the tools, materials, and processes; (2) vocabulary study [79, 80, 81, 82, 90]; (3) practice and instruction in reading the specific directions for the day's work; and (4) testing comprehension by carrying out those directions.

If we were concerned only with laboratory performance in the school, the reading of these subjects might deserve little attention. But future activities of students demand acquaintance with the kinds of reading matter which would otherwise form a barrier between the adult and his do-it-yourself endeavors. A recipe, a pattern, a sheet of directions must be read if the cake, the coat, and the installation of auto parts are to turn out well.

One of the major problems facing the teacher is that the poor reader turns to these subjects in the expectation of relief: "Here you do things; you don't have to read about them," he thinks to himself. But the first thing he is given when he enters this happy hunting ground is a textbook or worksheet which bristles with technical vocabulary, and with photographs, line drawings, or diagrams which cause almost as much bewilderment as clarification. This escapist attitude, plus the resentment or paralysis which follows disillusionment, makes the teacher's job one of rolling stones uphill.

Home Economics

In many ways, home economics is useful for solving the reading problem. Its subject matter is treated in popular magazines written at an easy adult level. Food columns and clothing tips in newspapers are similarly presented. In both newspapers and magazines there are copious illustrations to accompany the verbal material. Considerable pamphlet material, including government publications, is available. Students can realize the general importance of the subject and find information on it in rather palatable form.

Furthermore, the field has developed many attractive charts and bulletin-board displays and ideas for such material [89]. If labels are included in these displays, the students can be aided in associating the written symbol with its pictorial counterpart. Teachers are increasingly appreciative of the value of photographs in this work and of films of actual processes [5].

Home economics teachers are familiar with *Co-ed,* the magazine published by Scholastic Magazines "for career girls and homemakers of tomorrow." In the teachers' magazine, *Practical Home Economics,* suggestions are made for activities which might follow the reading of the articles in *Co-ed.* These activities extend the influence of the ideas read, but the solution of the reading problem itself—what to do *before* the article is read—is left to the teacher.

Recent textbooks in the field are probably some of the most attractive books intended for school use. Many illustrations—charts, graphs, photographs, line drawings, diagrams—illuminate the verbal text. The printed words in size of type and in spacing invite the reader. Chapter headings are frequently of the chatty sort: "Anybody Hungry?" Chapters sometimes start with an outline of the chapter so that the student can see where she is going and what will probably be expected in recall. Subheadings throughout chapters signal the new topics. Italics stress important words. Technical words are frequently defined. An occasional chart, such as one naming and describing the popular colors, rescues the student as she meets words like *chartreuse.* Chapters conclude with questions and suggested activities, a bibliography for further reading, and a list of films and filmstrips for viewing. The textbook closes with an index.

All of these features are good, but even they demand teacher assistance. The student must be helped to know what to do about the outline (skip it?), how to read the chart, how to select words for special study, how to react to a subheading or italics, and how to read the index. Not that she may not have been exposed to these tasks at some previous time, mind you. She is still learning good reading habits or falling into bad ones, depending upon the teacher.

What words does she not recognize as she looks at the outline? What questions can she ask herself that, the outline suggests, she will find answered in the chapter? What motives can she herself conjure up for wanting to read the chapter? for thinking it is important? What clues can she find to the meaning of a technical word as the text presents it? Can she summarize the contents which follow a subheading? What notes should she take? Can she compare the verbal text with the illustrations given? Can she find a topic by looking for it in the index? A teacher finding the answers to these questions is beginning to recognize her role in the teaching of reading in home economics.

A foods-class instructor in a high school gave the following quiz:

1. List the types of white sauces and a use for each.
2. List the steps involved in making white sauce which you followed in class last Friday.
3. List the causes of lumpy white sauce.
4. List the "Basic Four" food groups and the number of servings required daily from each group.

Discuss:

1. Why an acid such as lemon juice is used to coat freshly sliced apples and bananas.
2. Why cream soup and milk should be heated in a covered pan over low heat.
3. What the characteristics are by which a meal should be judged.

The first and fourth questions requiring listing and the last discussion question demand that the student remember types or classifications of items which the textbook has clearly stated. However, the types of white sauces are presented in tabular form, and the student must be able to read and remember the rows of information on each type. The textbook, by the way, asks an even more interesting question: "Which ingredients make the differences among thin, medium, and thick white sauce?" This question requires a comparison of the amounts of given ingredients, which produces the observation that only the amounts of fat and flour are changed in the three recipes.

The second list draws upon the laboratory experience as well as upon a recipe in which sequence is important as well as ingredients and amounts. Knowledge of the causes of lumpy white sauce was a product of laboratory disasters or warnings, a matter of recall.

The first two discussion questions require knowledge of cause and effect and perhaps a more profound chemical understanding (see Chapter 8).

The successful student in foods classes must be able to think in terms of classification, order and detail in directions, and cause and effect in processes. She must recognize that the direction "Bake in moderate oven (350°) until done (about 40 min.)" means the oven should be kept at 350° and the food kept in it for about forty minutes. The position of parentheses and the abbreviation of "minutes" must be understood. "Wash liver and remove membrane. Sauté liver." Where and what is the membrane, and what is sauté? "A gradual browning is better than searing." What is searing? The foods teacher must develop a number of concepts in each lesson before intelligent reading can take place.

In other words, modern textbooks in this field, well-planned as they are, still assume that a teacher will help students understand the wording, the abbreviations, the tabular material, and the author's way of suggesting relationships he does not specify.

These books would benefit by a glossary of technical terms. Until they offer this feature, a teacher and class will have to take the responsibility [85]. A modern book on child care, used in classes on homemaking, thoughtfully provides a glossary for its unusual vocabulary. Helpfully it states that a sibling is a brother or sister—clear enough; but most of its entries can be misunderstood: "relevant—bearing upon the matter at hand," an abstract and figurative way of saying "having to do with or having something in common with"; "veneer—a superficial covering," which might be a wig or a bedspread; "articulate—to set forth in speech"—why not to "say"?

Barnes [2] in college food-preparation courses has found over a period of years that students have trouble with the terms listed below. Now she starts the course by having the class prepare a glossary. This is actually a much more impressive learning experience for the student than having a ready-made glossary before him.

acidity	crystallization	infusion
alkali	curdling	irradiation
amino acid	dehydration	marinate
amorphous	dextrinization	microörganism
aromatic	dispersion	osmosis
astringent	emulsion	pasteurization
barley sugar	endosperm	proteolytic
brewing	entrée	saccharide
caffeine	enzymes	saturated
caffeol	fermentation	sodium bicarbonate
calcium caseinate	foam	steeping
caramelization	gel	supersaturated
carbohydrate	gelatinization	suspension
carbon dioxide	globule	syneresis
coagulate	gluten	vacuum
coalesce	homogenization	viscogen
collagen	hydrolysis	viscosity
colloidal	hydroscopic	volatile

Study and discussion of these words immediately prior to their appearance in the text extend understanding of the course as well as enhance the subsequent reading.

Clearly technical words are only part of the vocabulary problem. What is the student to think when she comes upon the sentence, "Screw the small eyes for the picture wire back in place." And if she had been used to basting a hem, what will she do when she bastes a chicken? An author familiar with the terms in his field does not always realize the confusion he creates when he enumerates ingredients for a salad as "leafy herbs like tarragon, burnet, basil, lovage, watercress, young mustard leaves, rosemary, sweet marjoram, chives, quarters of small scarlet tomatoes, rounds of gold and white hard-cooked eggs." Where do the herbs leave off and the other classifications begin?

While many good readers in junior high school are able to digest the text whose first 150 words include *analyzing, survey, personality, appearance, critical, stimulate, improvement, traits, performance, enrolled, laboratory,* and *unit,* those of third- and fourth-grade reading levels are completely unnerved. Expressions which have meaning for the author and the teacher may create only mystery for the student: *good emotional control, sleeping habits, child care and development, settled tastes, nominal charge.*

Some teachers have met this problem by finding simpler texts or pamphlets for the poorer readers to use during the study of a topic. Some have rewritten the material in a simple, abbreviated form. Others have collected over a period of years the written reports of able students which present on an easy verbal level and with illustrations what the students have gleaned from more difficult sources. Still others have the poorer readers gather from class discussions the gist of what has been read by others and then write booklets of what they now know, with the technical terms and processes illustrated and labeled on the left-hand page of the booklet and the text on the right-hand page. This last requires that the teacher write the technical terms on the chalkboard as they are mentioned in discussion, perhaps illustrating them with quick line drawings, and write key points as they are developed.

There is a further difficulty which only the teacher can amend. Home economics deals with three-dimensional polychromatic objects and cannot, even with pictures worth a thousand words and the simplest of texts, convey exact meanings. How should you *wash* fruit, *remove* skins, *quarter* and *core* and *dice* apples coarsely? What *rough covering* do you remove from the banana? What is meant by *mixing gently?* What would be a *contrasting fruit* for the top of the salad? Clear pictures and carefully worded steps may guide the student in his understanding of bound buttonholes. But bound buttonholes consist of a *slit* in the *material, finished* with a *strip of matching* or *contrasting fabric.* "What is the difference between *material* and *fabric?*" the insecure student wonders. *Sew binding in place.* "How?" *Turn binding to wrong side.* "How much, how far? Through slit?" *Pin binding in place on wrong side.* "What is *in place*—where I'll put it or where the teacher knows it should be?"

It is fitting that such directions appear in textbooks, since adults must know how to read such directions. But it appears essential that they be read with the teacher, not without her; and that the teacher use a large model which all can clearly see to demonstrate the process. Stereoslide viewers, films, and three-dimensional displays can be valuable additions. If the teacher can fill this role with positive interest in student problems and without a disgusted or punitive attitude, more students may learn how to read in home economics.

Industrial Arts and School Shop

In a survey of the reading ability of 250 students at the J. M. Wright Technical High School in Stamford, Connecticut, Goldstein [25] found the average reading grade to be 8.6, with a range from 4.9 to 12.0. According to the Gates reading test, 54 per cent of the students were reading at levels between 5.0 and 8.0.

Such a range demands that the general vocabulary in which materials are couched be differentiated for able and poor readers, and also that the technical words which are essential to the subject be identified and concepts clarified prior to the need to read them. The field is indebted to Strandberg [78] for identifying eighty-eight words having special meaning in the printing industry, to Huffaker [37] for lists of trade terms used in the machinist trade, and to Suerken [80, 81, 82] for glossaries of terms used in printing, machine-tool and job-machine shops, and heating and ventilation. In printing, the knowledge of spelling is necessary for typesetters and proofreaders. Morris [59] offers some spelling rules which are helpful to these workers.

Ferrerio [20] has presented many ideas for teachers of retarded readers in industrial arts. To help the student associate the verbal symbol with the object or process, he suggests a chart such as this:

Fastener	Tool
nail	hammer
screw	bit brace
dowel	glue, clamp

Pictures or drawings or a part of the actual object may accompany each word. Students who help develop such charts and who are then required to refer to the charts as they work or discuss, gradually develop a visual image of the symbol and oral mastery of it. Ferrerio also suggests such activities as labeling objects and pictures, carrying out directions given in simple phrases and sentences, using riddles based on a tool or a process, telling the story of a tool, matching illustrations with directions, making picture dictionaries, finding basic word elements in the technical words, listing words in alphabetical order, using filmstrips with industrial-arts vocabulary, making a chart of industrial-arts vocabulary, using commercial charts of materials and processes, having students write simple directions, and having them keep vocabulary notebooks. For interest, he would draw the students' attention to the popular uses of industrial-arts terms in such phrases as, "Put your nose to the grind-stone," or "Have an axe to grind."

There are possibilities for confusion in the textbook or worksheet itself. A textbook in general shop may introduce words it never explains: "Sloyd and hunting knives have fixed blades." (Sloyd only knows who Sloyd is.) A picture is labeled, "Cutting out a mortise." *Mortise* is never explained. The student should look up these terms, of course, but a glance at the contents of one chapter in such a book will explain why he doesn't. There is tremendous coverage in a limited space, with too many essential and superfluous technical terms mentioned in quick succession and not enough repetition to make them memorable.

Clearly, the teacher must compensate with activities such as Ferrerio has mentioned. Schramm [72] finds that labels naming the parts of a machine can be attached with magnets. The students can learn the names by seeing them so attached, by using those names deliberately when talking about the machine, and by having to reattach the labels to the proper parts.

Perhaps a librarian should have the last word. Mudge [61] claims that teachers of school shop should not avoid library opportunities for the students; rather, they should have students go to the library to find material for special reports on wood, steel, etc., to examine magazines such as *Popular Science, Popular Mechanics, School Shop,* and *Industrial Arts and Vocational Education* for projects, to obtain group instruction on sources of industrial-arts information in the library, and to obtain vocational information.

MUSIC

The active interest of music educators in the problem of music reading is reflected in the titles of some studies in the field [10, 12, 14, 65, 77]: *The Reading of Rhythm Notation Approached Experimentally According to Techniques and Principles of Word Reading; A Study of the Relationship between Language Reading and Music Reading; The Effectiveness of Music Dictation as an Aid to Music Reading in Grades Seven and Eight; Recommendations for the Adaptation of Some Language Reading Techniques to the Music Reading Program;* and *An Evaluation of the Tachistoscope as an Aid in Teaching Rhythmic Reading.* The music reading of the vocalist requires the reading of clef and key, of notes, of directions for volume and tempo, and of words below the staff. That of the instrumentalist requires the reading of chords as well as single notes. And, as we all know, accuracy in reading music can be reflected only in accuracy of the music produced by the singer or instrumentalist. One may be a good reader and still sound dreadful.

In addition to these reading requirements, there are books of music theory and books about music and musicians which present varied reading tasks to the student. Stories about music and musicians written on different levels of reading difficulty [3, 28, 53, 87] enable the poor reader and the able alike to gain background in music appreciation.

Wheeler and Wheeler [86], studying the interrelationships of the tested abilities of fifth and sixth graders in language, music, and intelligence, found only slight relationship between language-reading scores and music-reading scores. Yet language reading and music reading appear to have a number of elements in common. Two studies of eye movements in reading music have shown that eye movements in scanning a musical score are similar to those in ordinary reading [55, 84].

Jacobson's detailed report of an eye-movement study [40] of students of various ages agrees with this finding to an extent. The immature music reader makes many fixation pauses, long pauses, many unnecessary pauses, and 70 per cent of all possible errors; he has little or no eye span (one note), as many as twenty-eight regressive movements for twenty-eight chords, and poor rhythm. The average reader makes a short pause, and 40 per cent of all possible errors; has an eye span up to two notes, a distinct rhythmic eye movement, and a habit of reading chords from the top down. The mature reader makes pauses of $\frac{9}{25}$ of a second, only 4 per cent of all possible errors, and few regressive movements; has an eye span up to four notes, good rhythm, a technique of reading chords from top to bottom, and a zigzag technique of reading two clefs.

Jacobson found that music syllables benefit the mature reader very slightly and handicap less mature readers; more errors are made in ascending than in descending notes; words that are broken into syllables are hard to read; mature readers require less time for reading notes than for reading words, while the immature are slow for both. He recommended the practice of silent reading of the notes and words before singing as a great aid in obtaining accuracy and speed.

Another parallel between language reading and music reading is found in a suggestion by Miller [58]. Just as reading words is best preceded by hearing and saying words, so teaching the use of an instrument by rote makes a helpful preface to the reading of music. Understandings can be built through the use of films [66]. Musical terms create a reading problem which Riedel [67] has helped to meet in a glossary of about 300 words peculiar to music.

The controversy over whether one should be taught the names of letters before he is taught the sounds of letters in language reading is reflected in the war over syllables in music reading. Nye [64] proposes that most students not be confronted with them. Rather, he believes, the teacher should start with the rhythm of words, of walking, of skipping, etc., putting dot-dash notation on the chalkboard. For the pitch concept he advises the xylophone with youngsters, the Autoharp with older students; in conducting, the teacher should indicate high notes by holding the hand high.

The first musical notation, Nye believes, may be numbers written on bars on the chalkboard, then numbers below the actual notation, then numbers used only to start the playing of the tune, and finally the elimination of the numbers entirely. He thinks that a listening, singing, seeing, playing approach is more effective than the syllable approach for most beginners.

Sight reading is of considerable interest to music educators [17, 35, 38]. A book by Laurence [51] is a guide to the combined vertical and horizontal reading which the music score demands. In a study of fourth-grade music students, Hutton [38] found that the use of the chalkboard was less effective than the use of flash cards, musical games, slides, and opaque projectors to teach the skills related to learning songs.

OTHER SUBJECTS

The reading problem exists in fields such as art, driver education, physical education, recreation, and health. Much that might be said of skill development in these fields has already been given earlier in this and other chapters. But what more should be said? There have been seventy years of research on the nature of reading and the problems of teaching it. Yet, year after year, in thousands of classes all over the world, the same violations of sound practice are repeated in good faith. Every teacher in every field should learn how to use the findings of this research work in his classes. And many more teachers than have so far volunteered should appoint themselves investigators of the reading problems peculiar to their areas and explorers and reporters of successful techniques.

REFERENCES

1. Anthony, E. M.: "Reading Tone in Thai Syllables," *Language Learning,* vol. 8, pp. 21–26, 1958.

2. Barnes, Mary Louise: "Vocabulary in College Food Preparation Courses," *Journal of Home Economics,* vol. 51, pp. 719–720, October, 1959.

3. Bauer, Marion, and E. Peyser: *How Music Grew, From Prehistoric Times to the Present,* G. P. Putnam's Sons, New York, 1940.

4. Blackstone, E. G., and Sofrona L. Smith: *Improvement of Instruction in Typewriting,* 2d ed., Prentice-Hall, Inc., Englewood Cliffs, N.J., 1949.

5. Bricker, A. June: "Snapshots: An Aid to Teaching," *Forecast for Home Economists,* vol. 75, pp. 10–11, January, 1959.

6. Brophy, John: "Use Business Law to Improve Students' Vocabulary," *Business Education World,* vol. 40, pp. 13–14, March, 1960.

7. Budish, Bernard Elliott: "The Business Education Instructor Also Teaches Reading," *Journal of Business Education,* vol. 30, pp. 68–70, November, 1954.

8. Carboni, Jane A.: "A Plan for the Improvement of Reading in the Spanish Department as a Part of a Developmental Reading Program in Sewanhaka High School," unpublished doctoral dissertation, Teachers College, Columbia University, New York, 1949.

9. Casaubon, T. P.: "A New Concept in Language Training," *Canadian Modern Language Review,* vol. 14, pp. 14–15, Winter, 1958.

10. Christ, William Benjamin: "The Reading of Rhythm Notation Approached Experimentally According to Techniques and Principles of Word Reading," unpublished doctoral dissertation, Indiana University, Bloomington, Ind., 1953.

11. Cobb, D. E.: "Comparative Analysis of the Vocabularies of the Basic Vocabulary of Business Letters and the Gregg Shorthand Dictionary," *National Business Education Quarterly,* vol. 15, pp. 47–50, May, 1947.

12. Dalton, Ruth S.: "A Study of the Relationship between Language Reading and Music Reading," unpublished master's thesis, Syracuse University, Syracuse, N.Y., 1952.

13. Danneman, Jean: "Reading: The Road to Shorthand Skill," *Business Education World,* vol. 40, p. 26, January, 1960.

14. Davis, Jesse F.: "The Effectiveness of Music Dictation as an Aid to Music Reading in Grades Seven and Eight," unpublished master's thesis, Boston University, Boston, 1952.

15. Delattre, Pierre: "Phonetics in Beginning Language Study," *Modern Language Journal,* vol. 32, pp. 373–377, May, 1948.

16. Duncan, M. Helen: "Reading a Foreign Language," *Modern Language Journal,* vol. 45, pp. 17–19, January, 1961.

17. Elkan, I: "Sight-reading Can Be Taught," *Music Journal,* vol. 15, p. 58, November, 1957.

18. Eoff, S. H., and W. E. Bull: "Semantic Approach to the Teaching of Foreign Languages," *Modern Language Journal,* vol. 32, pp. 3–13, January, 1948.

19. Ernst, K. D.: "Place of Reading in the Elementary Music Program," *Music Educator's Journal,* vol. 39, pp. 26–28, January, 1953.

20. Ferrerio, Anthony J.: "Try Industrial Arts for Retarded Readers," *Industrial Arts and Vocational Education,* vol. 49, pp. 19–20, February, 1960.

21. Fitch, Stanley K.: "Some Implications of Modern Theories of Learning for Research in Typewriting," *Journal of Business Education,* vol. 35, pp. 66–68, November, 1959.

22. Fitzgerald, Virginia: "Linguistics: A New Force in English Teaching," *Journal of Business Education,* vol. 40, pp. 17–18, October, 1965.

23. Garbutt, Douglas: "An Investigation into Students' Understanding of Some Accounting Terms," *Journal of Business Education,* vol. 40, pp. 298–301, April, 1965.

24. Gelman, M.: "Dictation in Modern Language Teaching," *Canadian Modern Language Review,* vol. 13, pp. 20–27, Spring, 1957.

25. Goldstein, Wallace L.: "Reading Characteristic in a Vocational-Technical School," *Industrial Arts and Vocational Education,* vol. 44, pp. 10–11, January, 1955.

26. Goodman, David G.: "Develop Your Students' Business-law Vocabulary," *Business Education World,* vol. 38, pp. 26–27, November, 1957.

27. Gordon, E. B.: "'Why Johnny Can't Read Music," *Music Education Journal,* vol. 44, p. 36, January, 1958.

28. Graham, Alberta P.: *Strike Up the Band,* Thomas Nelson & Sons, New York, 1949.

29. Hale, Jordan: "'Context Clues': A Typing Device for Pretranscription Training," *Business Education World,* vol. 33, pp. 282–283, February, 1953.

30. Harrison, Lincoln J.: "Teaching Accounting Students How to Read," *Journal of Business Education,* vol. 35, pp. 169–170, January, 1960.

31. Hicks, C. B.: "Shorthand and Business Vocabulary Understanding," *UBEA Forum,* vol. 5, pp. 13–16, October, 1950.

32. Hietsch, O.: "Meaning Discrimination in Modern Lexicography," *Modern Language Journal,* vol. 42, pp. 232–234, May, 1958.

33. Hildreth, Gertrude: "Learning a Second Language in the Elementary Grades and High School," *Modern Language Journal,* vol. 43, pp. 136–142, March, 1959.

34. Horn, Ernest, and Thelma Peterson: *The Basic Vocabulary of Business Letters,* Gregg Division, McGraw-Hill Book Company, New York, 1943.

35. Hosmer, H. M.: "Importance of Sight Reading," *Music Journal,* vol. 15, pp. 5–6, July, 1957.

36. House, Forest Wayne: "Are You Solving the Reading Problem in Bookkeeping?" *Business Education World,* vol. 33, pp. 291–292, February, 1953.

37. Huffaker, Frank: "Trade Terms Used in the Machinist Trade," *Industrial Arts and Vocational Education,* vol. 44, p. 28A, March, 1955.

38. Hutton, Doris: "A Comparative Study of Two Methods of Teaching Sight Singing in the Fourth Grade," *Journal of Research in Music Education,* vol. 1, pp. 119–126, Fall, 1953.

39. Ivarie, Theodore W.: "Are Spelling and Typing Related?" *Business Education World,* vol. 44, pp. 18–19, November, 1963.

40. Jacobson, O. Irving: "An Analytic Study of Eye-movements in Reading Vocal and Instrumental Music," *Journal of Musicology,* vol. 3, pp. 1–32, Summer, 1941; pp. 69–110, Fall, 1941; pp. 133–164, Winter, 1941; pp. 197–222, Spring, 1942.

41. Jasinksi, Harry: "Motivation Devices in General Business," *Journal of Business Education,* vol. 34, pp. 244–246, March, 1959.

42. Jones, W. K.: "Cultivating Reading Speed in Spanish," *Modern Language Journal,* vol. 41, pp. 126–130, March, 1957.

43. Kanzell, Maxwell: *How to Read Music,* Carl Fischer, Inc., New York, 1954.

44. King, Harold V.: "Foreign Language Reading as a Learning Activity," *Modern Language Journal,* vol. 31, pp. 519–524, December, 1947.

45. Krause, Ruthetta: "Job Instruction Sheets Teach Machine Fundamentals," *Business Education World,* vol. 39, pp. 21–23, May, 1959.

46. Krauss, P. G.: "The Increasing Use of English Words in German," *German Quarterly,* vol. 31, pp. 272–286, November, 1958.

47. Kruger, Ellen: "Medical Terminology Can Be Made Easy," *Business Education World,* vol. 46, pp. 12–13, October, 1965.

48. Lado, Robert: *Language Teaching: A Scientific Approach,* McGraw-Hill Book Company, New York, 1964.

49. Lado, Robert: *Language Testing: The Construction and Use of Foreign Language Tests,* McGraw-Hill Book Company, New York, 1961.

50. Larew, Leonor A.: "The Optimum Age for Beginning a Foreign Language," *Modern Language Journal,* vol. 45, pp. 203–206, May, 1961.

51. Laurence, Sidney J.: *A Guide to Remedial Sight-reading for the Piano Student,* Workshop Music Teaching Publications, Hewlett, N.Y., 1964.

52. Lawrence, Armon J.: "A Vocabulary of Business and Economic Terms of Popular Usage," unpublished doctoral dissertation, University of Kentucky, Lexington, Ky., 1945.

53. Lawrence, Harriet: Series on Famous Operas, Grosset & Dunlap, Inc., New York, 1938–1943.

54. Liebesny, H. J.: "The Metaphor in Language Teaching," *Modern Language Journal,* vol. 41, pp. 59–65, February, 1957.

55. Lowery, H.: "On Reading Music," *Dioptric Review and British Journal of Physiological Optics* (new series), vol. 1, pp. 78–88, 1896.

56. Manghue, Ruth E.: "Train Your Students to Find Their Own Errors," *Business Education World,* vol. 37, pp. 30–31, February, 1957.

57. Mayer, Edgar: "An 'Ear' for Languages," *Modern Language Journal,* vol. 41, pp. 39–40, January, 1957.

58. Miller, Charles Earl Frederick: "An Experiment in Two Contrasting Methods of Teaching Beginning Instrumental Music," unpublished master's thesis, University of Southern California, Los Angeles, 1954.

59. Morris, J. Allen: "Some Spelling Rules," *Industrial Arts and Vocational Education,* vol. 43, pp. 68–69, February, 1954.

60. Moulton, William G.: "Toward a Classification of Pronunciation Errors," *Modern Language Journal,* vol. 46, pp. 101–109, March, 1962.

61. Mudge, Joy: "Take Them to the Library," *School Shop,* vol. 19, p. 19, February, 1960.

62. Musselman, Vernon A.: "The Reading Problem in Teaching Bookkeeping," *Business Education Forum,* vol. 14, pp. 5–7, December, 1959.

63. Nisdorf, Marion E.: "A Study to Determine the Effect of Using the Skill Builder Controlled Reader in the Teaching of Beginning Shorthand," unpublished master's thesis, University of Wisconsin, Madison, Wis., 1962.

64. Nye, Robert E.: "If You Don't Use Syllables, What Do You Use?" *Music Education Journal,* vol. 39, pp. 41–42, April, 1953.

65. Peck, Robert C., Jr.: "Recommendations for the Adaptation of Some Language Reading Techniques to the Music Reading Program," unpublished master's thesis, University of Michigan, Ann Arbor, Mich., 1952.

66. Pitts, Lilla Belle, and others: *Handbook on 16 mm. Films for Music Education,* Music Educators' National Conference, Washington, D.C., 1952.

67. Riedel, Johannes: *Glossary of Musical Terms,* North Central Publishing Company, St. Paul, Minn., 1958.

68. Roberts, Ruth L.: "Phonics as an Aid to Spelling and Word Division," *Journal of Business Education,* vol. 39, pp. 25–27, October, 1963.

69. Rowe, John L.: "The Four Arts of Shorthand Teaching," *Business Education World,* vol. 40, pp. 27–31, January, 1960.

70. Rutan, E. J.: "Word Study in Business Education," *Journal of Business Education,* vol. 21, pp. 29–30, March, 1946.

71. Sacks, Norman P.: "Some Aspects of the Application of Linguistics to the Teaching of Modern Foreign Language," *Modern Language Journal,* vol. 48, pp. 7–17, January, 1964.

72. Schramm, Howard R.: "Helpful Teaching Aids for Industrial Education," *Industrial Arts and Vocational Education,* vol. 43, pp. 277–279, October, 1954.

73. Shen, Y.: "Learning the Chinese Script Can Be Easy," *Language Learning,* vol. 8, pp. 17–30, 1958.

74. Sieberg, Louise C., and Lester G. Crocker: *Skills and Techniques for Reading French,* The Johns Hopkins Press, Baltimore, 1958.

75. Spaulding, Seth: "Three-dimensional Word Repetition in Reading Material," *Modern Language Journal,* vol. 37, pp. 226–230, May, 1953.

76. Spotts, Leon H.: "Foundations of Vocabulary Selection for the Teaching of Hebrew in America," *Modern Language Journal,* vol. 43, pp. 281–288, October, 1959.

77. Stephenson, Loran Dean: "An Evaluation of the Tachistoscope as an Aid in Teaching Rhythmic Reading," unpublished master's thesis, Brigham Young University, Provo, Utah, 1955.

78. Strandberg, C. Eugene: "Basic Terminology of the Printing Industry," *Industrial Arts and Vocational Education,* vol. 48, p. 113, April, 1959.

79. Struck, F. T.: "102 Key Words," *Industrial Arts and Vocational Education,* vol. 32, p. 57, February, 1943.

80. Suerken, E. H.: "A Basic Glossary and Vocabulary in Printing," *Industrial Arts and Vocational Education,* vol. 41, pp. 305–307, November, 1952.

81. Suerken, E. H.: "A Basic Vocabulary and Glossary in Machine Tools and Job Machine Shops," *Industrial Arts and Vocational Education,* vol. 48, pp. 104–108, March, 1959.

82. Suerken, E. H.: "Glossary of Heating and Ventilating Terms," *Industrial Arts and Vocational Education,* vol. 44, p. 38, March, 1955.

83. Wagoner, W. J.: "How to Use the Bookkeeping Textbook as a Reference Book," *UBEA Forum,* vol. 3, p. 24, November, 1958.

84. Weaver, H. E.: *Studies of Ocular Behavior in Music Reading,* American Psychological Association, Inc., Washington, D.C., 1943.

85. Westlake, H. G., L. Gustafson, and L. A. Dix: "Teaching for Concepts and Generalizations in Home Economics Education," *American Vocational Journal,* vol. 39, pp. 17–19, December, 1964.

86. Wheeler, Lester R., and Viola D. Wheeler: "The Relationship between Music Reading and Language Reading Abilities," *Journal of Educational Research,* vol. 45, pp. 439–450, February, 1952.

87. Wheeler, Opal, and Sybil Deucher: Series on Composers, E. P. Dutton & Co., Inc., New York, 1936–1940.

88. Willging, Herbert M.: "A New Approach to the Reading Objective," *Modern Language Journal,* vol. 32, pp. 108–111, February, 1948.

89. Williams, Harold A., and Rosmary Williams: "What Makes a Good Bulletin Board?" *Forecast for Home Economists,* vol. 75, p. 33, June, 1959.

90. Williams, S. L., and S. A. Anderson: "Power of Words in Industrial Arts," *American Vocational Journal,* vol. 27, p. 12, December, 1952.

91. Wolfe, R. C.: "Teaching Vocabulary: Flash-card Technique," *Industrial Arts and Vocational Education,* vol. 53, pp. 39, June, 1964.

92. Wood, Jerry L.: "Reading and Typewriting," *Journal of Business Education,* vol. 40, pp. 109–111, December, 1964.

93. Yengel, Herbert F.: "Asking Questions in Bookkeeping Class," *Business Education Forum,* vol. 19, pp. 23, 28, February, 1965.

part **IV**

READING PROBLEMS OF SPECIAL GROUPS

able retarded readers

chapter 12

Many children and adolescents are apparently capable of meeting the reading expectations for pupils at their grade or age level but fail to do so. In the primary grades, these pupils are retarded in a number of reading skills by one or more years; if older, by two or more years—despite adequate mental capacity. Can you recall students of this kind? Perhaps you were annoyed with them. Perhaps you labeled them "stupid," "lazy," or "uncooperative," instead of trying to understand and help them. Do you have students of this type now? How can you assess their true reading abilities and discover their actual difficulties? Do they have the potential to read better? What seems to be blocking them? What provision should the school make to help them? What procedures are effective in helping them to improve their reading? How can you measure their progress? Do you know of some students who have raised the level of their reading achievement? How did they do it? These are questions to be answered in this chapter.

First, call on your own knowledge and teaching experience for answers. Recall what you know theoretically about the causes of reading retardation. Review reading programs that make provision for helping retarded but able readers. From your repertory of teaching procedures select those which you think might be most effective with pupils who are capable of reading better.

The successful reading teacher brings to each individual case a background that embraces the complex causation of reading difficulty, the dynamics of behavior, the psychology of learning, and the methods and materials essential to the teaching of reading.

AN ABLE RETARDED READER

A fifteen-year-old boy in the ninth grade, called Carl, was getting below-average grades in all his academic subjects. On the Stanford Achievement Test his reading score was lower than those of 60 per cent of the pupils of his age; on the arithmetic section his score was above average. On the Wechsler Intelligence Scale for Children given two years earlier, his verbal IQ was 105; his performance IQ, 121; and his full-scale IQ, 114. On a group intelligence test—the California Test of Mental Maturity—he obtained an IQ of 103. On the California Reading Test he was above average in vocabulary and below average in comprehension. Observation of his oral reading showed poor word attack skills. In the first interview with the reading teacher he demonstrated poor study habits, complained that the reading assignments were beyond his ability, and said he felt that his major problem was poor comprehension. Excerpts from the first interview show how Carl revealed his dominant interest, his verbal fluency in oral communication, the high quality of his thinking, and his ability to analyze his reading problem.

> Carl: Art is an interesting field. Lots of people think there's no future in art, but I think there's a lot I can do in art. . . . In painting, the idea is to get your mind on the whole painting visually and put paint on where you think it ought to go and later on revise it until it becomes more detailed as you go along. . . .
>
> Teacher: You describe the process very well. A good reader uses a similar method. Could you tell me about your reading?
>
> Carl: Well, in school you have all those rules about how to read. They say to take a line and read it, but I can't do that. I have to read it word, word, word, and sometimes even half a word. I can't broaden my thinking, and I lose the meaning of what I'm reading. I read *The Red Badge of Courage* over the summer. It took me a long time, but I read it word for word. I got a good feeling out of it and I knew what I was doing, but I couldn't read it fast. You see, I'm awfully slow in my reading.

People tell me to speed up my reading by taking a whole sentence at a time, but I just can't do that because I keep reading just words and don't know what I'm reading. . . . I go too slowly to think. . . . I'll start getting tired and then I quit. Actually I want to read the book but it takes too long.

Teacher: That is all very interesting. You analyze your reading problem much better than most students do. Is there anything else you'd like to tell me?

Carl: I think my major problem is distraction. I get distracted very easily. I will be reading along and I put myself in the character's place and ask, "What would I do in that case?" Then I go on dreaming. If I'm reading about the Civil War, the next thing I know I'll be thinking about painting. Or I'll hear my sister playing the guitar and first thing I'll be tapping the tune on the table and forget about the book. . . . Things like these bother me all the time. . . .

Teacher: What about vocabulary?

Carl: Well, if I don't know a word, I usually figure it out by the sentences.

Teacher: You use context clues?

Carl: Yes, and if I don't know it completely—I'm lazy—I say, "Well, maybe I'll figure it out tomorrow. . . ."

You have noted that although Carl rates a little above the average range in total IQ on an individual intelligence test, his performance IQ, which involves little or no reading, is 16 points higher than his verbal IQ. This degree of discrepancy usually indicates a reading problem. Although a relatively low verbal score may sometimes indicate a general verbal deficiency or a lack of verbal stimulation in the home, this is not the case here: Carl's conversation shows that he is verbally fluent, and he scores above average on vocabulary tests. His relatively high score on the arithmetic test and his lower score on the group intelligence test, which requires reading, furnish further evidence of a reading problem.

In the interview Carl gives a plausible explanation of his reading retardation. Like so many adolescents, he has difficulty in concentrating on school assignments that are remote from his present concerns. Although his description of the effect of word-by-word reading is reasonable, and his comments about his methods show insight, it will take deeper diagnosis to learn how and why he adopted this inefficient method and why distraction is his "major problem."

Reading could be presented to him as an art or as an occasion for using his artistic skill. To focus his attention on comprehension, the teacher might ask him to read a number of stories with a view to making illustrations for them. As Carl discovers his difficulties in word recognition and comprehension skills, he may become receptive to instruction and practice that would correct his specific reading deficiencies. If inner conflicts are preventing him from concentrating on his reading, counseling may be necessary before he can profit by reading instruction.

CHARACTERISTICS

In a class of retarded readers you will usually find both slow learners and able retarded readers. The latter are pupils who are performing below their intellectual capacity; they are mentally capable of accomplishing reading tasks appropriate to their age or grade level. They learn better by listening than by reading. If they pass their subjects, it is because they have listened to class discussions and taken part in them. One youngster managed to pass his tests by getting someone in the class that met just before his to tell him the test questions and answers. "And," he slyly added, "I've got good eyes, too." These pupils are often called "lazy" because they do not complete their homework.

Although they may not admit that they have a reading problem, they usually have a nagging feeling of failure and inferiority. They are often afraid of making mistakes and of being different from their peers. To protect their egos and bolster their self-esteem, they may employ various defenses, such as disparaging the importance of reading, or gaining recognition or attention in other ways. Underneath a facade of indifference, they usually really want to read better.

CONDITIONS AND CAUSES

In each case a unique combination of causes and environmental conditions has prevented the retarded reader from developing his reading potentialities. The following factors are often associated with reading retardation: defective hearing or vision, general poor health and low energy level, unfavorable home environment, educational deprivation, emotional problems, and lack of interest in reading. Some of these conditions may, in fact, be either causes or effects of reading difficulty. They are interrelated; success or failure in one line of development may affect several others. Thus, in one case an undetected visual or auditory defect, which may have been the cause of the initial failure in learning to read, may have led to a train of consequences. In another case an unhappy teacher-pupil relationship may have contributed to failure by making the pupil resistant to instruction. Poor instruction has retarded other individuals. In some cases a teacher has expected too little of them so that they have become reconciled to failure though they were capable of average or superior attainment. Or, on the other hand, pupils subjected to too much pressure, too much nagging, too much insistence upon perfection, in defense may become antagonistic toward reading, toward teachers, and toward school in general.

Of pervasive importance in serious reading cases is the way in which the individual regards himself. Repeated experiences of failure, accompanied by disparaging comments from other people, help to create the negative self-concept so often found among poor readers.

Physical Conditions

Visual impairments, especially farsightedness and difficulties in fusion that prevent the reader from getting a clear, unblurred image, account for some of the able students' retardation in reading. These and other visual defects, their correction, and their relation to reading performance are described in Chapters 1 and 4, and in Spache [28, pp. 103–117]. Even though the eye examination has revealed no specific defects, the teacher should not neglect vision as a possible factor in the reading retardation of able learners.

Impairment of auditory acuity may have caused difficulty for the able retarded pupil, especially in beginning reading. If a child cannot hear clearly the sounds in spoken words, he cannot take the first step in identifying words and the sounds in them. It is at best a difficult task for a child to connect sounds with their written symbols. It is doubly difficult if he is hampered by poor auditory acuity. However, if the hearing loss was not too severe, the necessary auditory discrimination could have been developed with practice.

Endocrine disorders, especially hypothyroidism, have been reported to be associated with reading failure in a fourth or more of the cases studied [13]. Hypothyroidism characteristically causes fatigue and inability to put forth effort, which results in underachievement. Treatment of endocrine disorders and other complicated medical problems is not within the province of the reading specialist.

Extreme cases of reading disability—those that involve possible neurological immaturity or brain damage—are discussed in Chapter 15.

Mental Ability

According to our definition, retarded readers score within the normal range of intelligence as measured by tests that do not require reading. However, they may be deficient in one or more of the mental abilities that underlie reading proficiency. If a student can be given special instruction and practice in developing the ability or abilities he lacks, he may be able to succeed in the next stage of the reading process (see Chapter 1).

Educational and Cultural Deprivation

Retardation in reading may be a result of cultural and educational deprivation. Even on the college level, the high and low reading groups are differentiated by such cultural factors as the educational and professional status of the parents, the number of books in the home, and other background items. More subtle factors, such as the treatment the child receives from his parents (see Chapters 4 and 14) may affect his ways of perceiving, thinking, and remembering, as well as his attitude toward reading and toward himself. Unfavorable home conditions are often further complicated by emotional concomitants. It is no wonder that as many as half of the retarded readers may come from homes in which there is little esteem for education in general and reading in particular, and in which parents express little or no understanding or sympathy for the child's reading difficulties. These environmental factors will be described in the section on the disadvantaged in Chapter 14.

In school the child may get off to a poor start in the first grade because of illness or frequent change of residence. The teacher may disregard his lack of readiness for formal instruction or more often the child may show antagonism toward the teacher. Perhaps the retarded reader is simply a student who has not had skillful instruction in reading. Having failed initially, he cannot catch up without help. His later teachers may be too much concerned with teaching the rest of the class to bother with him.

Lack of Motivation and Interest

This is often the most apparent cause of reading retardation among able learners. One might ask: What has become of their basic need to grow, to discover, to explore? Why do some have a negative need to resist reading? How many of these retarded readers may be using their failure in school as a weapon against parents who have rejected them or sacrificed them at the altar of parental ambitions? Why do they try to maintain their self-concept, inadequate as it may be? Why do they expend their energy in the direction of self-sabotage rather than in the direction of self-development?

The whole ego structure of an individual—the network of personal dispositions within the ego—guides his behavior. If being a good reader is contrary to the ego ideal, the youngster may be completely indifferent about his progress in reading or may reject reading altogether.

Some retarded readers from economically secure homes have had all their wants supplied; they have been so overprotected and overindulged that they have never learned to strive toward a goal such as proficiency in reading where effort is necessary.

Faith in the efficacy of a new method of learning reading sometimes causes the retarded reader to put forth the effort he has been withholding. The same is true for personal attention from a teacher he respects and for reading material of high intrinsic interest.

Emotional Difficulties

Retarded readers are usually sensitive about their failure to read acceptably. They may have begun to think of themselves as persons who can't succeed in reading. Every new experience of failure reinforces this idea. The label "remedial reader" makes their difficulty known to classmates from whom they have tried to conceal it and embarrasses them further. Other emotional problems associated with reading difficulty are discussed in Chapter 15.

IDENTIFICATION AND DIAGNOSIS

Methods of diagnosing reading difficulties are described in Chapters 4 and 5. They include continuous classroom observation, additional observation in interview situations, and the use of informal and standardized tests. The aim of the diagnosis is to understand the manner in which the student performs and the nature of his specific difficulties, as well as to measure the level of his performance. Its aim is to find out what is right about an individual—what he can do—as well as what is wrong—what he can't do. To distinguish the able retarded reader from the slow learner, it is also necessary to ascertain his reading potentiality. Having an estimate of a student's reading potential helps the teacher to be realistic in his hopes for improvement. The greatest gains may be expected of those whose mental age is clearly above their present reading age, who comprehend better when they listen than when they read, who read some books voluntarily, and who are present in school more than 80 per cent of the time.

While giving instruction, the classroom teacher can learn a great deal about the retarded reader. Knowing what to observe and how to observe, he is able to recognize the student's assets and deficiencies. There is some evidence of a substantial correlation between pupils' scores on standardized reading tests and teacher's estimates (based on daily observation) of pupils' grasp of language structure, ability to recall ideas or incidents when telling a story, and general reading readiness. If the teacher focuses his attention on the study of one student at a time for a few minutes each day, he will gain new insights into the student's reading problems.

Observation, supplemented by informal and standardized tests of both silent and oral reading, enables the teacher to explore further the student's reading ability. If these tests are used for teaching as well as for testing, diagnosis leads immediately into remediation.

Estimating the student's reading potential is more difficult than appraising his reading proficiency. The instrument that has been most commonly employed in schools and clinics is the intelligence test. Group intelligence tests are useful mainly in predicting a student's achievement in an academic curriculum; they are ineffectual in estimating his reading potential since they require so much reading ability. For example, about half of the Scholastic Aptitude Test consists of exercises requiring reading comprehension.

A better estimate of reading potential may be obtained from individual intelligence tests, especially the Wechsler tests which yield both verbal and performance scores. The retarded reader tends to rate higher on the performance than on the verbal part. On the WISC, the retarded reader is usually low on the subtests of Information and Arithmetic, both of which are related to school learning. These low scores suggest he has not responded well to group instruction and that his fund of information may have been limited by his difficulty in reading. He is also likely to have a low score on Digit Span which requires attention and concentration. High scores on Block Design and Object Assembly suggest adequate perceptual organization and ability to deal with concrete tasks. Low scores on these subtests as well as on Picture Completion suggest possible difficulty in visual perception. Ekwall [14] showed that individual profiles of the subtest scores of retarded readers could be used in diagnosis and remediation.

Strengths indicated by subtests of the WISC give clues as to approaches to instruction for children with reading difficulty: they often respond well to stimuli always at hand and to concrete tasks involving manipulation.

Listening comprehension, or auding, is another indication of reading potential. There is usually a moderate positive relationship between listening and reading comprehension. When listening comprehension is markedly higher than reading comprehension, there is potential reading ability. During the fall in the first grade, a single test of auding predicted a March reading performance as well as or better than either of two reading-readiness tests or an intelligence test [9].

A test of concept formation may prove useful in estimating reading potential. In grades 3, 5, and 7 the results of this kind of test were more closely related to reading achievement than were scores on tests of mental maturity. The "overachievers" obtained relatively high scores on this test [8].

Another test that gives promise of usefulness in estimating both reading achievement and reading potential is the cloze test. Various forms of this test systematically omit in a given passage every fifth or seventh word or certain kinds of words such as basic concepts, nouns or verbs, or structural words that provide clues to grammatical relationships [10]. The individual supplies the missing words. Bormuth [7] found this test to be more valid when the correct reply was the same word that the author had used. High school pupils who made high scores on the cloze test were more likely than low-scoring pupils to see the relationships between ideas, to understand language structure, to use grammatical and syntactical clues to meaning, and to avoid undue subjectivity [18]. These are all indications of reading potential.

Statistical methods of identifying underachievers were thoroughly and concretely reviewed by Winkley [34]. The mental-age discrepancy index compares the reading age with the mental age, preferably the highest. For elementary school children, this is often expressed in terms of grade placement by subtracting five years from the mental age. Tables of expected achievement grade placement have been computed by Alice Horn for the Los Angeles City School Districts. An "Anticipated Achievement Calculator" was published by the California Test Bureau. Bond and Tinker [6] developed a relatively simple formula for classifying students as "disabled readers." In their formula, the reading-expectancy grade = (years in school × IQ/100) + 1.0. The stanine score is quite popular for school use. It is based on a scale of nine segments of the total range of performance on a test. An individual's score may be from 1 (low) to 9 (high). The technique for computing *stanines* is described in *Test Service Notebook*, No. 23, distributed by Harcourt, Brace & World, Inc., New York. Underachievement is indicated by simply noting the discrepancy of two stanine points between the measure of potential and the measure of reading achievement. The difficult and time-consuming procedure of computing a regression line "is probably not worth all the effort when other, simpler techniques yield comparable results" [34, p. 160]. In concluding her study of the various statistical methods of selecting underachievers, Winkley seems to favor the Bond and Tinker formula or some other objective method supplemented by "the subjective judgment of reliable and experienced teachers [which] is of inestimable value" [34, p. 162].

Some able retarded readers need more intensive diagnosis of underlying causes of their reading difficulty. Ideally they would be sent to the reading specialist in the school. Otherwise they would be referred to a reading or psychodiagnostic clinic..

SPECIAL READING GROUPS

In my ninth-grade English class where (1) the pupils range from the well-read to nonreaders who cannot recognize as many as twenty-five words, (2) the subject matter is far too extensive, and (3) much of the material in the textbooks is beyond the pupils' comprehension, what would be your step-by-step procedure in setting up an efficient reading program?

Whether or not to form special reading groups is the first question. And the answer depends on conditions in the particular school or college. If the regular classes are small, if the teachers are skillful in individualizing instruction within their classes, if they can provide suitable reading material and experiences for all, then special reading groups are not needed. If, on the other hand, classes are large, if rigid grade standards are maintained, if teachers let the poor readers just sit and do busy work and the able learners languish in idleness, if the range of reading materials and equipment is too narrow to meet varied needs, and if the students cannot read well enough to profit by the regular class work— then there is need for special groups. In other words, if the teachers cannot, in regular classes, give all the retarded readers the stimulation, instruction, and practice they need, then special groups should be formed.

However, since individual patterns of skills and needs are so different, even among students who make similar scores on reading tests, it is impossible to achieve completely homogeneous grouping. For this reason, teachers are giving more and more attention to devising ways of meeting a wide range of needs in regular classes and in developmental reading courses for all students. A competent reading teacher must be available for small remedial groups and there must be a budget for the necessary books and other instructional materials.

Need for help in reading is reflected in the eagerness with which many students take advantage of offers of help. For example, in one school even when the school day was lengthened and no grades were given, there was a great demand for a course in Reading Enrichment [32]. The special features of this course included an informal, encouraging atmosphere, freedom from required reading and reports, individual help to meet the needs of each student, and a close tie-up between the reading class and the other subjects. Students could bring their textbooks to the reading class; if the text was too difficult, the teacher would try to find another book dealing with the same topic. Many important outcomes were observed by the teacher or reported by the students—reduced anxiety in reading aloud, increased voluntary reading, and improved class work.

Physical Setting and Classroom Atmosphere

In many schools physical facilities for working with small groups of retarded readers are poor or nonexistent. When no special room is assigned for reading instruction, the reading teacher must carry all his materials from room to room; he has no place to keep his confidential case material.

Sometimes a converted stockroom or a cleaned-out closet is the only space available for remedial reading. One reading teacher described this kind of situation:

At present I'm working with fifty-three children, who come to me in groups of five to eight and meet daily for forty minutes. I have eight periods a day. Fortunately I have the last period of the day for testing and preparation.

My quarters are limited to two closets. The smaller of the two is my office. It just barely holds my desk. I share this closet with the off-season kindergarten decorations and the extra textbooks. Needless to say, if I gain any weight I'll not be able to get into my office!

My "big" closet serves as the reading room. It has shelves, blackboard, bulletin board, two large tables and eight chairs. The tables are in the center leaving only walking space around the edges of the room. Fortunately all of our poor readers are skinny! Actually this room is quite cheery. It also has the advantage that it will not hold more than eight pupils, thus making more individualized instruction possible.

With the present overcrowded school conditions, any available space must be used. In one school, a basement room that had formerly been used for storage was transformed into the most attractive room in the building. The dark, frosted windowpanes were replaced with clear glass through which the sun poured in. Cherry-colored curtains, pale blue walls, and yellow bookcases added to the cheeriness. There were library tables and chairs and room dividers that provided freedom from distraction for small groups. Bookcases on three sides of the room were filled with reading material arranged according to grade level. A section of shelves held reference books and guides for teachers. Vertical files contained folders of reading material of varying difficulty on numerous topics.

In many other schools it has been possible to convert a good-sized classroom into an attractive, highly functional reading laboratory or center.

Retarded readers are especially affected by the general tone or atmosphere of the school environment—the attitudes and personal relationships of the teachers and the other students, the appearance of the halls and classrooms, and a certain spirit in the air that makes one school an exciting place to be and gives another a deadening effect.

Referral to Special Classes

Every member of the school staff should be careful not to attach any stigma to membership in the special reading group. The morale of the poor reader is usually low enough already without increasing his sense of inferiority by segregating him in a class labeled "remedial reading." For this reason, honorific names like "reading club," "reading homeroom," "special English," or "reading laboratory" can designate the special class for retarded readers, and the class should live up to its name. Nor should the special reading class become a dumping ground for the school's unwanted disciplinary problems.

Teachers should present the reading class to students as an opportunity to get the most out of their high school or college years. In these days of speed and efficiency, students do not want to lag behind in the horse-and-buggy stage of reading. The special group will help them to attack their immediate study and reading problems more effectively and thus gain time for other activities.

The attitude that students take toward the special reading group also depends on the experience of previous members of the class and the attitude the teachers have toward the work. Students who have been happy and successful in the special reading group spread the idea that being in the reading class is a privilege. Teachers, too, by favorable comments may make students feel that membership is a privilege. A waiting list reinforces this feeling. One boy asked to be enrolled in "the immediate reading class." The way the class is described to the students in their first meeting is also important. In the small English classes in South Philadelphia High School for Girls, the reading teachers used to tell the students truthfully, "You have been chosen for this small English class because you have average or above-average ability; you are not working up to your ability; you can profit by this special instruction."

Forming the Groups

How large should these groups be? A class may be too small to allow the optimum interaction among its members. On the other hand, it may be too large to allow for individualized instruction. Although something can be accomplished in classes of any size, the instruction is most effective in groups of ten to twenty students or in groups structured for many individual contacts.

How much time should be devoted to the group? Seriously retarded readers need instruction that has day-to-day continuity. When the reading instruction is substituted for a regular class, the group usually meets three to five times a week for the entire semester. If it is a special class, the time is frequently limited to one or two periods a week, sometimes with an additional individual conference period.

When should the groups be scheduled? When scheduling special reading groups, one should be cautious about interfering with students' other activities. The special reading groups should not supplant classes that the students particularly enjoy. It is also best not to take students out of their regular classes for two reasons: the regular teachers sometimes resent it and the students may miss instruction that they need. Nor should reading classes be held after school if this deprives students of recreation or valuable part-time work experiences.

How are the members of a group selected? It is important to place a student in a group with others whom he has chosen, to balance aggressive and submissive personalities, and to include some especially articulate members in each group who can stimulate discussion. These are some of the factors that should be considered in forming small groups. Whitney [33] developed a procedure by which students chose the groups they wanted to join. He described to the students three types of groups:

Group I will go to the library for independent reading. To join this group you should be a responsible person who can set reading goals for himself and work toward them with very little help from the librarian or teacher.

Group II is best for those who want to improve their reading skills and would work on practice exercises for this purpose.

Group III is an opportunity for pupils who have lost out somewhere in their school years and need special instruction in basic vocabulary, word recognition, and sentence and paragraph reading so they will be "on their own in reading" and be able to gain ideas from the books they are expected to read.

Students are commonly selected for remedial classes because they are one or more years retarded in grade placement, because their mental age is greater than their reading age, and because their school marks are below expectation, and because their teachers recognize that they need special help.

With individualized instruction the student may remain in the special reading group until he has acquired the desired proficiency. He is graduated from the class when he has achieved his goal.

EXAMPLES OF PROCEDURES

After the teacher has obtained some preliminary diagnostic information, as described earlier in this chapter and in Chapters 4 and 5, he continues to study the students and help them study their own reading process. Stressing their potential and especially their successes, he bases his instruction on what the students know and what they need to know. Whenever possible he relates his reading instruction to the actual problems that the students face. In selecting materials, he avoids those causing frustration.

Self-appraisal

The teacher encourages various forms of self-appraisal, having the students take the initiative and responsibility for analyzing their reading needs and difficulties. A gifted college student wrote the following introspective report:

My main reason for taking this course in the improvement of reading is to speed up my reading rate. Probably one thing which retards it is the fact that I find it difficult to concentrate on the reading matter before me. Therefore, if this course can increase my power of concentration, it will undoubtedly help speed up my reading rate. My fastest rate, when I concentrate as well as I know how, is twenty pages an hour of the average book. Tests do not show up my deficiency because, first of all, tests introduce a special situation in which I am under pressure. I always do anything more efficiently under pressure than when I am left to myself. Secondly, tests usually give short reading passages. . . . With a short passage there is, you see, no problem of concentration, whereas concentration can become a problem when one has several pages to read at a sitting.

Another aspect of my problem is, I think, that I have only one reading method, the intensive reading method. I suppose that I should have at least two reading methods, the intensive and the extensive. . . . One reason for my difficulty in concentrating is the fact that I have an imagination which is too active. As I read along in a novel, for instance, I come across a word or a phrase which recalls something in my past experience. I stop to enjoy that sensation, and usually the recalled experience will remind me of something else and so on *ad infinitum.* Thus my creative imagination makes of the book a sort of instigator of a series of pleasant, or sometimes unpleasant, memories. This sort of creative or re-creative reading is pleasant, but it uses up precious time when it intrudes into all my reading. And, in extreme cases, it slows up my reading to such an extent that by the time I reach the end I have forgotten the beginning of the book.

To obtain perspective on their present reading status, students may write reading autobiographies, starting with their earliest recollections of interest and proficiency in reading, and continuing up to the present [29]. Lefevre [20] approaches self-analysis through language, suggesting the student write a "linguistic" autobiography.

Students should analyze their purposes in coming to a reading class and review their difficulties in reading as well as their strong points so that they will actively participate in the kind of instruction and practice best for them. To make their goals clearer, they mark on a check list the skills they would like to improve, for example, "I should like to learn the best methods of building a bigger and better vocabulary." "I should like to know how to read critically."

They might write the teacher a letter summarizing their deficiencies and the skills to aim at. Next, they select one of the skills on which they need practice. The teacher can then refer them to a number of different pages in different workbooks for practice in the skill they have specified. They record their progress on an assignment sheet, which becomes their individual reading program.

Group Planning

Once they have recognized their needs, the students can frequently work in groups with the reading teacher as a resource and consultant.

One special reading class which met five days a week decided on the following weekly program: On the first two days the periods were spent in free reading. During these periods individual pupils had conferences with the teacher to receive help with their specific reading difficulties. On the third day the pupils discussed books they had read. On the fourth day the pupils had a "work period," ironing out a common problem, such as an unnecessarily slow habit of reading. Sometimes the class used timed exercises differing in material and purposes. One group particularly enjoyed this exercise: "You have only five minutes to read the major news in the daily paper. See how many important facts you can obtain." After the reading, the pupils listed the facts they had obtained and made a composite list. They asked classmates who had done exceptionally well to tell how they had managed to get so much information in so short a time. There are variations of this exercise: "You have two minutes to find out on page 10 what the critics think of the new play—or movie." "A friend just phoned that she will be ten minutes late. What ideas can you get from this article while you are waiting?" Sometimes they worked individually on books or practice materials dealing with the skills they needed (see Appendix C). The pupils decided to leave the last period of the week open for unfinished activities or for some reading experience in which they had immediate interest. In this program, reading takes its rightful place as a means to an end—reading to learn, reading to understand oneself and others, reading to have experiences to share, reading efficiently so as to have more time for other activities.

Another group of reluctant readers talked about their hobbies, leisure activities, adjustment to the new school, and vocational plans until they themselves became tired of this rather aimless use of time. They began to say, "I thought this was a reading class. When do we begin to read?" Thus the demand came from the group. They began to talk about why people read and "what reading means to me." They thought it would be a good idea to take a test and grade it themselves so that they could find out what their reading problems were. The teacher helped them develop their program as it gained momentum.

Another group in which most of the students were initially resistant to reading spent their first period making the room more attractive and building bookcases out of crates and boxes. They next decided what books they would like to have for their class library. This involved reading reviews for suggestions and then reading the books to decide which ones to buy. To increase the attractiveness of their room, they made arrangements with a publishing house to send them monthly shipments of discarded advertising posters, from which they learned new words and acquired some interest in new books.

Starting with Activities and Interests

A gifted young teacher [12] was discouraged by her first experience in teaching English to ninth-grade pupils who were totally unable to comprehend the books the state course of study prescribed. They were in a fog that showed no sign of lifting. These pupils were from homes where there was little opportunity for reading and little interest in it. Most of them had never read a book voluntarily. In talking with the pupils about their interests, the teacher learned that they liked to read about the adventures of persons like themselves. Why not, then, begin reading about their own experiences? The next day they were to come to class prepared to tell the most exciting and interesting experiences they had had during the summer. These accounts a senior commercial pupil took down in shorthand, typed, and returned to the ninth-grade youngsters. After editing their "stories," they had them retyped and bound into a little booklet of easy, interesting reading material. Two examples demonstrate their content, vocabulary, and sentence structure:

One night my sister and I were walking home from a party. We saw shadows. They weren't ours. Someone was following us. My sister turned around and saw the shadow in back of us, but she could not see whose shadow it was. We started to run; the shadow started to run, too. We ran the rest of the way home and hurried into the house and told my mother. While we were talking, the kitchen door opened, and in walked a man—my father!

I had a dream Friday night. Friday afternoon we had a test about bugs. I didn't know how many legs a spider had, and Mr. Masters told me I had better find out. That night I was sleeping and all of a sudden I thought that a spider was being let down from the ceiling on a string. It stretched its legs out as if trying to grasp hold of someone. It kept coming closer and closer until it grabbed me. I let out one yell and my sister came running in to see what was the matter. I told her there was a giant spider in the room, but she wouldn't believe me. She had to turn on the light to convince me that it was only a dream.

Their next interest was in making books of travel. Each pupil decided upon some place that he would like to visit and obtained pictures and information from a great many sources including library books, copies of the *National Geographic Magazine*, etc. The project involved writing letters to travel agencies, reading magazines and books about the country chosen, and writing a day-by-day imaginary account of what he did and saw. Each of these travel diaries served as reading material for the other youngsters as well.

Another activity that led to reading was a class visit to places of historic interest in the vicinity. The town librarian supplied a number of books on local history. One of the youngsters found a picture of his own house in one of them. These reading experiences, growing out of pupil-initiated activities, led to practice in the reading of assignments for other classes. The pupils transferred information and skill to other classes with a success that they had never before experienced.

At the end of the year the pupils showed gains in their reading scores and, even more important, improvement in their attitude toward reading. In the words of one pupil, "I enjoy reading now because when I get through I know what I have been reading about, instead of being in a fog."

A group of delinquent adolescents who had a negative attitude toward reading rejected an approach usually appealing to these youngsters, that of learning to read road signs, directions for constructing model airplanes, and so on. However, they responded to instruction based on information on the jackets and labels of the phonograph records they brought to school. They identified the few words they knew in the titles and eventually learned how to recognize the rest. Before long, they were reading.

A class newspaper stimulates both reading and writing, students contributing such items as original tall stories, book reviews, school news, and personals. One boy who had never written any original material discovered his bent for poetry. Writing articles for their classmates made students aware of the need for a colorful vocabulary and a command of sentence and paragraph structure. For retarded readers, accounts of the experiences of their contemporaries, written in a familiar vocabulary with easy sentence structure, are a source of excellent reading material.

There is growing evidence of the value of a less serious and more creative approach to reading improvement of able retarded readers. Sometimes teachers correct and drill too much. Children who are permitted to select their own books become competent by reading easy material; they read more difficult books as they become ready for them and want to read them. The teacher gives instruction along with the reading. The more natural, spontaneous, and happy the situation, the more readily the children learn.

Practice with Instruction

In the work of the special reading class there is a place for drill, though it is not as exalted as it once was. Skill-drill courses that depend largely on a single textbook do not offer adequate provision for individuals and do not integrate the practice. Nor is there any assurance that the student will transfer his newly acquired skills from the workbook to his other reading. Students too frequently spend their time in special reading classes mainly in working exercises and taking tests, while continuing poor reading methods which merely reinforce errors. Instruction is necessary. There should be time for discussing the specific reading methods that are appropriate to a given passage before and after each period of practice. Teaching suggestions for many reading skills in which retarded readers lack competence are given in Chapters 6 and 7.

For example, a teacher may give the students typed daily assignments, such as the following, which incidentally provide extra practice in reading and in following directions:

Our reading selection for today, "The Law of Club and Fang," starts on page 401. The selection has four parts, which fit together like links in a chain. First skim the story from beginning to end. Then go over it again to try to decide what the four parts are. Make a brief note about each part to aid you in the discussion that we shall have when the entire class has finished reading. Find the place and begin now.

Using Mechanical Devices

Certain of the various machines briefly described and evaluated in Chapter 17 are often used in remedial reading classes. For retarded readers who have failed to learn by other methods, machine instruction may arouse a spark of interest and hope.

Counseling

At the opposite pole from the machine approach is the program with the accent on counseling. The reading teacher who recognizes that emotional difficulties and personality factors are closely related to reading achievement is alert to evidences of apathy, hostility, frustration, and inner conflicts that may be usurping the attention and effort that are necessary for effective reading (see Chapter 15).

Making Progress Evident

The retarded reader needs to see the progress he is making; otherwise he will ask, "Why should I keep going to this class?" Objective evidence of progress includes lists of words that the student has learned to spell correctly, vocabulary cards containing words he can now recognize at sight, graphs and charts of his scores in speed and comprehension on daily exercises of comparable difficulty. His individual record should remind him of a growing list of books that he has read, improved marks in other subjects, and favorable specific comments about his reading from teachers and classmates. It is well for the teacher to conclude a period by asking, "What did you learn today," or "What progress did you make today?" At the end of each term, members of reading classes should write an evaluation of their progress. Each student should include a comparison of his attitudes and difficulties before and after taking the course, should mention the most helpful reading experiences and materials he has encountered both in class and outside, and should describe the progress he has made.

To achieve a sense of progress, the student should come in contact with reading material, its scope and difficulty increasing as rapidly as he is ready to cope with it successfully. He should become acquainted with more reading skills, acquire greater speed and accuracy in using each skill, and move upward from comics and light fiction to biography, popular science, and other more serious reading. A balanced program of reading should include at each stage some books that are hard enough to challenge his skill and some books that are easy enough to promote fluency.

Follow-up in Regular Classes

One of the problems of the special reading class is to bridge the gap between special instruction and the regular class. This may be done in many ways. The reading teacher may use the students' assignment in a given subject as practice material in the reading class. Thus retarded readers are able to shine in their regular class as they have never done before. Linking the reading in the special class with regular class activities has several advantages: it affords the students further practice in the reading methods they have been taught; it appeals to the students as practical and timesaving; it gives them the satisfaction of knowing success in subjects in which they have previously felt inferior. For example, students in one reading class who had made a study of the dictionary and its uses assumed leadership for the first time in their regular English class when this topic was introduced.

A pupil in the reading class reads material on his own level about a topic or problem that is currently being studied by his subject class. He prepares his report and presents it orally to the other members of his small group. In this way he gains self-confidence and assurance. When the pupil is ready to report in the large class, the reading teacher sends a note to the subject teacher to the effect that the pupil has prepared a report for extra credit. The subject teacher accordingly plans to give the pupil an opportunity to present his report. The subject teacher also provides easier reading material for the retarded pupils. When a pupil is discharged from the remedial reading group, his official teacher is given his latest test results and a check list of his competencies and difficulties in basic reading skills. This list is sent to all subject teachers, so that they can continue the work of the remedial teachers.

IMPROVEMENT IS POSSIBLE

All teachers should try to remedy certain weaknesses common in programs for able retarded readers. One is using methods and books appropriate only to the lower grades. These bore or embarrass the retarded reader, reminding him of his previous frustrations and failures. Another weakness is to assign undifferentiated repetitive exercises rather than to offer instruction based on pertinent materials and to continue to diagnose the effect on the pupil's reading progress. The importance of continuity in instruction between the regular class and the special reading class has already been mentioned. Finally, too many remedial reading classes emphasize the acquisition of isolated skills rather than the comprehension which demands these skills. Unremitting drill confirms the poor reader's conviction that reading is drudgery.

To correct these weaknesses, H. Alan Robinson [24, pp. 176–178] has suggested that remedial classes put more emphasis on the reading skills that are needed in the content fields and give much more instruction and practice in these skills. He would give remedial students access to reading materials on many levels of difficulty in the content fields as well as to materials that are immediately related to their interests and developmental tasks. He would emphasize the importance of helping each pupil determine his specific purposes and of making sure that all pupils are successful in achieving these personal goals.

REFERENCES

1. Anderson, Harold M., and Robert J. Baldauf: "A Study of a Measure of Listening," *Journal of Educational Research,* vol. 57, pp. 197–200, December, 1963.
2. Barbe, Walter B.: "Effectiveness of Work in Remedial Reading at the College Level," *Journal of Educational Psychology,* vol. 43, pp. 229–237, April, 1952.
3. Blair, Glenn N.: *Diagnostic and Remedial Teaching,* The Macmillan Company, New York, 1956.
4. Bliesmer, Emery P.: "Methods of Evaluating Progress of Retarded Readers in Remedial Reading Programs," Fifteenth Yearbook of the National Council on Measurement Used in Education, New York, 1958, pp. 128–134.
5. Bloomer, Richard H.: "The Cloze Procedure as a Remedial Reading Exercise," *Journal of Developmental Reading,* vol. 5, pp. 173–181, Spring, 1962.
6. Bond, Guy L., and Miles A. Tinker: *Reading Difficulties, Their Diagnosis and Correction,* Appleton-Century-Crofts, Inc., 1957, pp. 76–81.
7. Bormuth, John R.: "Validities of Grammatical and Semantic Classifications of Cloze Test Scores," in J. Allen Figurel (ed.), *Reading and Inquiry,* International Reading Association Conference Proceedings, vol. 10, Newark, Del., 1965, pp. 283–285.
8. Braun, Jean S.: "Relation between Concept Formation Ability and Reading Achievement at Three Developmental Levels," *Child Development,* vol. 34, pp. 675–682, September, 1963.
9. Budoff, Milton, and Donald Quinlan: "Reading Progress as Related to Efficiency of Visual and Aural Learning in the Primary Grades," *Journal of Educational Psychology,* vol. 55, pp. 247–252, October, 1964.
10. Coleman, E. B., and J. P. Blumenfeld: "Cloze Scores of Nominalizations and Their Grammatical Transformations Using Active Verbs," *Psychological Reports,* vol. 13, pp. 651–654, December, 1963.
11. Collins, J. E.: *The Effects of Remedial Education,* Educational Monographs, no. 4, University of Birmingham, Institute of Education, Oliver and Boyd Ltd., Edinburgh, 1961, p. 154.
12. Collyer, M. Arlene: "Improving Reading in the Ninth Grade," *English Journal,* vol. 29, pp. 37–43, January, 1940.
13. Eames, Thomas H.: "The Effect of Endocrine Disorders on Reading," *The Reading Teacher,* vol. 12, pp. 263–265, April, 1959.
14. Ekwall, Eldon E.: "The Use of WISC Subtest Profile in the Diagnosis of Reading Difficulties," unpublished doctoral dissertation, University of Arizona, Tucson, Ariz., 1966.
15. *English S, Communication Skills,* Detroit Public Schools, Division for Improvement of Instruction, Department of Language Education, Board of Education of the City of Detroit, Detroit, 1962.
16. Friedmann, S.: "A Report on Progress in an I.T.A. Remedial Reading Class," *British Journal of Educational Psychology,* vol. 28, pp. 258–261, November, 1958.
17. Hall, John Fry: *The Psychology of Motivation,* J. B. Lippincott Company, Philadelphia, 1961.
18. Jenkinson, Marion Dixon: "Selected Processes and Difficulties of Reading

Comprehension," unpublished doctoral dissertation, Department of Education, University of Chicago, Chicago, 1957.

19. Kottmeyer, William: *Handbook of Remedial Reading,* 2d ed., McGraw-Hill Book Company, New York, 1960.

20. Lefevre, Carl: "Language and Self: Fulfillment or Trauma?" part I, *Elementary English,* vol. 43, pp. 124–128, February, 1966.

21. Loretan, Joseph O.: "The Decline and Fall of Group Intelligence Testing," *Teachers College Record,* vol. 67, pp. 10–17, October, 1965.

22. Lovell, K., D. Shapton, and N. S. Warren: "A Study of Some Cognitive and Other Disabilities in Backward Readers of Average Intelligence as Assessed by a Non-verbal Test," *British Journal of Educational Psychology,* vol. 34, pp. 58–64, February, 1964.

23. Mouly, George J.: "A Study of the Effects of a Remedial Reading Program on Academic Grades at the College Level," *Journal of Educational Psychology,* vol. 43, pp. 459–466, December, 1952.

24. Robinson, H. Alan: "A New Concept of Remedial Reading," in J. Allen Figurel (ed.), *Reading and Inquiry,* International Reading Association Conference Proceedings, vol. 10, Newark, Del., 1965, pp. 176–178.

25. Robinson, H. Alan (comp. and ed.): *The Underachiever in Reading,* Supplementary Educational Monographs, no. 92, University of Chicago Press, Chicago, 1962, pp. 33–61.

26. Robinson, Helen M.: "Understanding the Able Retarded Reader," in Ruth Strang (ed.), *Understanding and Helping the Retarded Reader,* University of Arizona Press, Tucson, Ariz., 1965, pp. 20–26.

27. Sipay, Edward R.: "A Comparison of Standardized Reading Scores and Functional Reading Levels," *The Reading Teacher,* vol. 17, pp. 265–268, January, 1964.

28. Spache, George D.: *Toward Better Reading,* The Garrard Press, Champaign, Ill., 1963.

29. Strang, Ruth: *Diagnostic Teaching of Reading,* McGraw-Hill Book Company, New York, 1964.

30. Strang, Ruth (ed): *Understanding and Helping the Retarded Reader,* University of Arizona Press, Tucson, Ariz., 1965.

31. Taylor, Wilson L.: "Recent Developments in the Use of Cloze Procedure," *Journalism Quarterly,* vol. 33, pp. 42–48, Winter, 1956.

32. Turner, Carla S.: "Remedial Reading Pays Dividends in the Junior High School," *English Journal,* vol. 48, pp. 136–140, March, 1959.

33. Whitney, Algard: "The Reading Consultant," unpublished doctoral dissertation, Teachers College, Columbia University, New York, 1955.

34. Winkley, Carol K.: "Building Staff Competence in Identifying Underachievers," in H. Alan Robinson (comp. and ed.), *The Underachiever in Reading,* Supplementary Educational Monographs, no. 92, University of Chicago Press, Chicago, 1962.

reading problems
of slow learners

chapter 13

In your classes you will usually have some slow learners among average and gifted pupils. Or you may be given a whole class of slow-learning pupils. Against a background understanding of the common characteristics of these pupils you will observe the unique behavior pattern of each one. You will discover that most of them are higher in some prerequisites for success in reading than in others. This variability requires accurate diagnosis. Only when you know their strengths and weaknesses can you direct instruction toward building their competencies and correcting their deficiencies. Your knowledge of the sequential development of reading ability will tell you where to begin with an individual pupil and the direction to take.

Empathy, or the ability to feel with these pupils, to put yourself in their place, to see things from their point of view, is essential to successful teaching. Equally important are a repertory of teaching procedures and appropriate instructional material.

SEVERAL SLOW–LEARNING PUPILS

Several brief case studies of slow-learning pupils will illustrate some of their characteristics and the methods used by different workers in handling their special difficulties. Steve [24] illustrates a fairly typical case of slow maturation and slow rate of learning. Tommy was a slow learner particularly dependent upon encouragement and personal relationship. John had social assets and responded to the appeal to read for social purposes. Terry's retarded mental development was complicated by secondary emotional problems.

Steve

Steve, whose IQ test scores were 56, 48, and 56—measured at different times by competent psychologists, had potential ability to read better, although it was not developed until he was almost seventeen years old and was still very limited. He was timid and unaggressive, with marked feelings of inferiority and inadequacy. He said he was the only child in his family who had difficulty in reading. The others used to remind him of his reading inability and this made him mad. He had a slight speech defect, slow and halting diction, a meager vocabulary, and little conversational ability. His errors in word recognition tended to persist. He was quite skillful in handwork and was a substitute on the basketball team. He was tall and thin, walking with a slow, shambling gait.

During his seven years at various public schools he had not learned to read or write. He had become a chronic truant with a record of petty theft. During the first two and a half years at the training school he was given the usual instruction in the "three Rs" but remained practically a nonreader.

When he was sixteen years, ten months old, he was given individual help in reading. A combination of methods used with him included the kinesthetic method of pronouncing, tracing, and writing words as wholes and simple phonics to figure out unfamiliar words. He learned words that were exceptions to the simplest phonic rules by associating them with pictures and later used the "look-and-say" method. The phonic and kinesthetic methods were helpful in correcting reversal errors and the confusion of similar letter and word forms. Steve showed excellent retention of words.

Since the reading of first- and second-grade books would never be of much value to this boy, he was taught a special practical vocabulary of 500

to 600 words and phrases found in signs and notices, directions, advertisements, labels, and the like. This kind of reading interested Steve, and the
progress he made gave him much satisfaction.

During the first twelve months of this individual work he made a gain
on a standardized reading test of one year, four months. In the next fifty-five
lessons he made only two months' further progress and in the following fifty
lessons only one month's. At the end of the individual work he was reading on
almost a third-grade level. Either he had reached the limit of his learning ability
for the time being, or the methods used were not such as to promote further
learning. Other students at the training school who did not have Steve's
emotional problems made greater progress. In no case was there a miraculous
solution of the reading problem, but many students slowly acquired sufficient
reading ability to serve their life needs.

Tommy

Twelve-year-old Tommy seemed in special need of affection. He sat close
to the reading teacher and put his arm around her sometimes.

One day Tommy came into the reading room saying, "I wonder if I'll get
it right today. Last time I got mixed up with two of the words." The reading
teacher responded to his enthusiasm and encouraged his active thinking by
such comments as these: "What do you think will be happening in the story
today?" "Let's see if you can find the title of the story." Looking at the picture
she asked, "What's happening here?"

Tommy: The sky is getting very dark.
Teacher: Who is running away?
Tommy: Dick and his dog.
Teacher: Why are they running?
Tommy: It's beginning to rain.
Teacher: I think Dick is talking. Let's see what he is saying.
         Read it the way he would say it.

With this kind of orientation, Tommy read beginning reading material that
was not too childish with expression and enjoyment.

Tommy next worked on a page of the practice book used in connection
with the story. When he had completed it, the teacher commented, "You got
that page all correct." Tommy next did a page of exercises on initial consonants—words beginning with *f*. The teacher read the words out loud:

"How about *letter*, does it begin with the same sound as *fork*? . . . *Talk*—does
the beginning of *talk* sound like the beginning of *fork*?" The teacher continued
with other similar questions. Tommy responded correctly to this informal test
of auditory perception.

Then he read another story from the book, with the teacher directing his attention to the thought conveyed through the words. Throughout the entire period, with its variety of activities, he maintained interest and concentration. At one point he said, "It's important to read, isn't it?" and added, "It's fun to read, too. Would one get a prize for reading?"

The teacher replied, "You don't need a prize; you get fun from reading itself. That's much better than a prize, isn't it?"

There was something about Tommy's performance that was difficult to describe—a certain detachment or aloofness—as though someone else were talking through him. For example, his comment, "It's important to learn to read," seemed like an echo of a remark that his parents had made. His pleasure in reading and in being with the reading teacher grew more spontaneous as his reading lessons continued. One got the impression of higher mental ability than the Binet test indicated and good functioning of his ability in an emotionally favorable environment. Despite a discouraging medical report of organic deficiency and some evidence of deterioration, he seemed to be progressing in reading.

John

John, a large boy, seventeen years old, had a friendly manner of greeting people. He made a good appearance, was good-humored and sympathetic, and showed genuine kindness toward people. He seemed to have considerable social intelligence. All these qualities would be useful in the vocation in which he was most interested—assisting his father in his business. Apparently there were good home relationships. He was a member of a happy family which accepted him as he was and gave him confidence in himself.

Although the *Reader's Digest* was a little beyond his current reading level, the reading teacher helped him read some of the stories and articles. He enjoyed them because they were more in line with his interests than most of the material in his reading books. At first he read word by word, not in phrase or thought units. The reading teacher encouraged him to give more expression to his reading by asking such questions as this: "If *you* were eager to go, as the boy in the story is, how would you say it?" When he met an unfamiliar word, the teacher helped him to acquire word recognition skills by asking: "What do you think the word might mean? What would make sense here?" She helped him to divide the word into syllables and to pronounce it. If a new word was composed of two familiar words, she called his attention to the familiar components. After he had puzzled out the meaning of a new word, he pronounced it, wrote it, divided it into syllables, gave sentences in which it was used, included it in his card file of words he knew by sight, and reviewed it from time to time. To encourage him to read for meaning, she asked questions that called for prediction or interpretation and focused his attention on the content: "What do you think happened next? What kind of boy was Tom? How do you think finding his dog made him feel?" After a while he began to read with more expression and understanding.

Since people were important to John, the teacher encouraged him to read for social purposes—to dramatize a story with other boys, to tell someone about it, to write a review for the school newspaper or bulletin board, to enrich his conversation at home. Instead of using formal tests of comprehension, the reading teacher considered these social applications as evidence of John's functional comprehension of the material he read.

Terry

Terry's mental retardation was so interwoven with emotional difficulties that it was difficult to be sure of her real ability. Her performance in reading fluctuated with her mood. Terry would give the impression one day that she did not know any of the words the reading teacher thought she had learned in previous weeks. When the teacher held up the charts with sentences for her to read, she did not even attempt to read them. But when stimulated by playing teacher, holding up the chart for the teacher to read, she showed great glee in correcting the mistakes the teacher purposely made. Under these conditions of heightened motivation, she read every sentence correctly. After that successful experience she responded very well in supplying the missing words as the teacher read parts of sentences from a book. This lesson had vitality and interest. Under these conditions of heightened motivation, Terry had the immediate purpose of correcting the teacher's mistakes and the exhilaration of exchanging roles with the teacher. On other occasions the teacher asked her to serve as an assistant in making reading material for the other pupils. Objective evidence that she could learn and make progress in reading was particularly important to Terry because underlying all her activity was her fear of disappointing her parents.

Many slow-learning pupils are reading slightly above expectation, according to standardized tests. But the marked fluctuations in their performance in reading indicate greater potential than they ordinarily show. Motivation is crucial. Success in reading may increase their general self-confidence and self-esteem; this may later result in higher performance on intelligence tests. Therapy sessions often help these pupils gain a more hopeful idea of themselves; skillful instruction in reading gives them a tool for self-realization.

CHARACTERISTICS OF SLOW LEARNERS

The slow learner has been variously defined. According to Kirk in 1949, "The term 'slow learner' should be restricted to the child who does not have the capacity or potentiality to learn intellectual things, such as reading, at the same rate as average children. It should not be used to refer to educational retardation regardless of the cause" [14, p. 172]. The slow learner develops later and learns more slowly than the average child. He has his own natural rate of maturation and less potential for improvement than the able retarded reader. He is a child who learns slowly.

On verbal intelligence tests the slow learner in school would score approximately 75 to 90 IQ or even as low as 60. According to this criterion, about 10 per cent of our secondary school population would be classified as slow learners. The slow learner ranks high enough in intelligence to escape the classification "mentally retarded" but too low to be called "average." Thus he is in a kind of neglected no-man's-land.

The slow learner is difficult to describe because within this broad classification you may have children who vary in specific abilities and who learn at widely different rates. "One child with an IQ of 75 may be learning to read at a more rapid rate than would be expected from his mental age. Another with an IQ of 90 may be performing in school far below his expectancy" [15, p. 62]. The slow learner is rarely slow in every respect. His profile shows ups and downs.

Although his slow rate of learning may be the primary underlying factor in the slow learner's retardation in reading, a number of other factors may have influenced the utilization of his mental abilities. Some slow learners have been handicapped by defective hearing or vision, by unfavorable home conditions, by emotional conflicts, or by lack of opportunities for language development. Habits of perceiving, reasoning, and remembering, while initially determined by the individual's quality of mind, may be influenced, as shown in Chapter 6, by the way adults respond toward him. It is difficult to say whether these conditions are causes or results of the individual's mental retardation. Intelligence is depressed by deprivation of various kinds, and this in turn makes the individual less competent to cope with his environment. If teachers are aware of this interaction between intelligence and environmental conditions, they will not take a fatalistic attitude toward a low IQ. Rather, they will try to understand the slow-learning child's mental processes and his strengths as well as his weaknesses. Knowing these, they will give him appropriate instruction.

In general, slow learners seem to be "slightly inferior physically to children of average intelligence" [14, p. 173] and to have more minor illnesses and defects of sight, hearing, and speech. Their emotional and social behavior is usually influenced by their poor health and by continual failure to measure up to unrealistic expectations of them at home and at school. Being labeled as "slow learners," "retarded readers," or "remedial reading cases" often increases their feelings of inferiority. Under such conditions it is only natural that they should dislike school, miss frequently, sometimes become behavior problems, and drop out of school as soon as the law allows. However, some of them try so hard that they achieve more than their measured intelligence would indicate. In some instances the teacher may expect too little of them and neglect to give them the instruction they need.

They are slow in learning to read. It is difficult for them to perform the complex cognitive acts involved in reading: to concentrate, organize, understand abstract ideas, and remember. They read with less adequate understanding than the brighter children. As slow-learning pupils advanced from grade 3 to 6, Wozencraft [30] found, they had increasing difficulty with word meaning; they often used words without really understanding them. Backwardness in language development is an important factor in their reading retardation.

DIAGNOSIS OF THEIR DIFFICULTIES

Accurate diagnosis is the first step in helping slow learners. Standardized test results alone are not a sufficient basis for identifying and understanding them. Test results should be supplemented by histories of early development and by observation of responses to learning in a school situation.

Diagnosis should be differential; it should give information about the individual's specific mental and reading abilities. In addition to the WISC subtests and other diagnostic methods already described, the Illinois Test of Psycholinguistic Abilities (ITPA) [18] is particularly valuable in the diagnosis of reading retardation. It is designed to detect a sequential series of specific disabilities in the reading process, affecting [15, pp. 64 66]:

Auditory reception
Visual reception
Visual discrimination
Perceptual speed—lack of "ability to see and identify details rapidly"
Sound blending
Visual closure—difficulty in recognizing the whole from seeing a few parts
Association
Vocal expression
Motor expression

The ITPA and the WISC make possible a detailed diagnosis of the underlying mental abilities of slow learners as well as of other retarded readers and allow the exploration of an individual's specific learning difficulties, his pattern of difficulties, and his ability to function within his capacity. Marianne Frostig's Developmental Test of Visual Perception [19] estimates the visual perception, and Wepman's Auditory Discrimination Test [28], auditory perception. A diagnosis of these supplements the study of the reading habits and physical, social, and emotional conditions of the slow learner that may be interfering with the best functioning of both mental abilities and reading skills. By means of differential diagnosis, the reading teacher may be able to detect the specific strengths that can be reinforced and the specific abilities that need to be developed. Marianne Frostig has prepared practice exercises to develop specific aspects of visual perception. The Winter Haven Lions Research Foundation [29] has perceptual training forms. Starting where they are, slow learners, too, can follow a sequential development of reading skills but more slowly, step by step, than the average or superior reader.

ESSENTIALS IN TEACHING READING TO SLOW LEARNERS

When a group of retarded readers were asked to give their best advice to teachers, they made these suggestions, appropriate for all pupils as well as for the slow learners:

Explain more. A little bit of work explained is better than a lot of work without explanation.
Don't get cross right away if the pupils don't understand.
Try to find out the reasons for their difficulty and give individual help.
Teacher should understand the pupils as well as the pupils understand the teacher.

One boy summed up his advice to teachers in three well-chosen words: "Take it easy." Like many other slow learners, he was tired of being pushed and hurried and harassed. Slow learners especially need short assignments, lots of varied repetition using all sensory avenues, concrete tasks involving manipulation, reading materials that will hold their interest and that have personal significance to them, and immediate applicability. Reading has special significance for them when the teacher writes their own thoughts for them to read.

Since most slow learners do not read before the age of seven or eight, reading instruction for these children should be delayed until the prerequisites for success are built up. It is much more difficult to teach a "burnt" child— a child who has tried to learn to read and failed—than a child who begins when he is intellectually ready and can succeed. For slow learners the preacademic program should be lengthened. Whatever the pupil's ability, the teacher must begin where the pupil is.

Activities Preparatory to Reading

Learning starts with a problem which the children want to solve or an activity in which they are interested. Such activities offer opportunities for them to think concretely, solve practical problems, and follow verbal directions. Various enjoyable games and activities give training in the prerequisites for reading. Many of these activities are described in the books by Kephart [13] and by Radler and Kephart [22]. Matching animal pictures, colors, geometric designs, letters, and words develops visual perception and discrimination. Putting together simple jigsaw puzzles requires perception of forms in the setting of a total configuration. Identifying details and relationships in magazine illustrations, picture postcards, greeting cards, and picture books gives practice in identifying "figure on ground" details in a larger whole. Spontaneous conversation, oral reports, choral speaking, and simple dramatization, supplemented by exercises in distinguishing between the sounds of words and sentences, develop auditory perception and discrimination as well as language ability. Telling about a trip and recounting the events in a story develops ability to relate events in sequence. These activities are important for the average child at an earlier stage in his development.

Coloring, first within a cardboard frame, then within lines without the aid of a stencil, and cutting out simple shapes at first, then gradually more complex pictures give practice in eye-hand coordination, which eventuates in ability to copy designs and to write their names and all letters of the alphabet from models. Since research has shown a positive relationship in some cases between gross motor integration and the reading process, physical education activities such as walking a board, imitating movements, using stepping stones, and writing on the chalkboard are included in the readiness program.

Appropriate Methods of Instruction

Many special methods have been helpful to the slow learners. The concreteness and thoroughness of the Montessori method, the intensive use of filmstrips and concentration on phonics, the reading about their own experiences, the basic vocabulary and pictorial emphasis of the Richards-Gibson approach, certain features of the linguistic approach, programmed learning materials, and the Initial Teaching Alphabet have all had success with slow learners.

Many teachers tend to go too fast with slow learners instead of letting them read a great deal of material on their current level before they go on to more difficult books. By reading the same material over and over, they reinforce vocabulary and acquire fluency. Nothing is gained by trying to speed them up. Indeed, much may be lost—their self-confidence, self-esteem, and pleasure in reading. Acting on the *spur fallacy*—attempting to challenge them with material that is over their heads—results in loss of personal confidence and self-acceptance. They need the experience of mastery of each new step. They become interested in tasks that they can complete successfully. Teaching methods should include concrete, specific explanations, many demonstrations, and firsthand experiences.

For slow learners, instruction normally follows the sequence described in

Chapters 3 and 6, with whatever variation in tempo and preferred mode of learning may be indicated by the diagnosis. Of the three approaches to teaching beginning reading—visual, auditory, kinesthetic—Burt and Lewis [4] found the visual best for mentally retarded children, because a combination of methods seemed to cause confusion, in contrast to normal children who benefited from a combination. A vivid first impression is half the battle in learning a new word. These pupils need to hear the word, become familiar with its meaning, look at it while the teacher writes it, say it, write it themselves, and use it in sentences.

A concrete system of phonics is often advocated for slow learners. They can learn by the phonovisual system, which is based on the analysis of speech sounds and represents the sounds in key words. Slow learners have profited by the phonetic drills described by Hegge, Kirk, and Kirk [11]. The success of any phonic method depends, when it is introduced, on the number of sound-letter associations being controlled, the pace being slower than for the average child, and not too much dependence being placed upon facile memory. Also important is immediate application of the word recognition skills learned to easy, interesting reading materials such as the Miami Series [20], which is not too childish for the older slow learner.

Appraisal while teaching helps students to identify the reading processes or methods that they can or cannot use successfullly. For example, when some retarded readers were stumbling over small words, the teacher said, "You can read the big words, but the little words give you trouble." The group then studied the initial sounds of these small words. They mentioned familiar words that began with the same sounds and other words that rhymed with the troublesome words. They discovered similarities and differences among words like *what, when, which,* and tested themselves on word cards they had made. Finally, they reread the story that had originally given them trouble. This time they were able to read it fluently. The teacher then remarked, "You see, the little words that cause trouble can be learned by the methods we have just used. What are these methods?" With a little help, the students described the procedure in their own words. Having acquired command of this method, they were ready to apply it to other reading situations.

Like average pupils, the slow learner is likely to change his attitude toward reading if he manages to master basic reading skills which lead to at least a measure of literal comprehension.

When the slow learner enters high school, he is confronted with many problems. After being in special classes in elementary school where the work is carefully adjusted to his needs and interests, he is usually turned loose in a high school that makes no special provision for him. If he is placed in a special reading group in high school for a semester or two, he is then expected to succeed in regular classes. Retarded readers who have come out of the slough of despond and have started upward on their true developmental curve should be able to make good in the regular classes. But not so the slow learner; the curriculum and methods of instruction must be continuously adjusted to his needs.

The slow learner cannot be expected to do standard high school work. The high school freshman with a Stanford-Binet IQ of 75 cannot be expected to read ninth-grade books. If his instruction in reading has been excellent he should be able to read simple fiction and factual material on about sixth-grade level. Being given high school credit for his work increases his effort and satisfaction.

As the slow learner approaches the time when he will be leaving school, his reading should become increasingly practical. Groelle [8, p. 186] suggests the following kinds of experience:

Learning the specialized vocabulary for the kind of work he is planning to do
Reading and filling out job application blanks
Learning to use telephone books, city directories, road maps and street guides, menus, recipes, directions, radio and theater programs
Reading advertisements, mail-order catalogs, and want ads with understanding and discrimination
Reading newspapers critically, so far as he is able
Using the dictionary to look up unfamiliar words

The following program was developed in a junior high school by Rauch [23]:

Activity 1. Free silent reading (approximately fifteen minutes). This part of the period followed a fairly rigid routine. The writer found that the routine at the beginning of the period gave the pupil a feeling of confidence. Everything was in place. The pupils knew exactly what was expected of them. This also gave them a feeling of shared responsibility with the rest of the group.

Upon entering the room, each pupil picked up his reading folder, selected the book or magazine of his choice from the class library, then sat down. On his reading record he would write the title of his book, the day's date, and the page number at which he started to read. At the end of the fifteen minutes, he would enter the number of the last page he read. In this way there would be no confusion as to book title or page number when the class met again. After completing each book or story, the pupil usually made a simple written report which the teacher and he checked during the free silent reading period. These written reports were not compulsory.

The writer made a special effort to supply reading materials for the class library at or slightly below the pupil's reading level. For those readers on the third-grade level and below, the free silent reading alternated with pairs of pupils working on the Dolch word cards.

Activity 2. Oral reading and discussion of "Today's Headlines" (approximately fifteen minutes). This consisted of two important headlines under the caption, "Today's Headlines," which the teacher wrote on the chalkboard before the pupils entered the room. They came to expect them. Many times as a headline was read aloud in class a pupil would say, "I knew that headline would be on the board." This anticipation of oral reading and discussion of news headlines prompted many of them to look at newspapers beforehand or to listen to radio broadcasts. One seriously retarded reader seemed to do exceedingly well during the discussion following the oral reading of the headlines explained, "At breakfast I always ask my father what he thinks is the most important news of the day. That way I get a head start."

Activity 3. Special reading exercise (twenty-five minutes). The greatest variation in the planning of the class period came during this final twenty-five minutes. The general pattern was to select a short exercise (one or two pages) from a workbook or reader that dealt with a specific reading skill. Preparation for each type of reading skill exercises included the following steps:

1. Motivation, followed by one pivotal question to give the pupils direction to their reading.
2. Anticipation of the difficult vocabulary. There were no word lists on the blackboard beforehand because the word list grew out of the motivation and subsequent class discussion.

Every third period the special reading exercises were alternated with other activities.

Reading guidance. At least thirty minutes were allowed for this type of exercise. The free silent reading portion of the period was usually omitted on these days to provide ample time for study and discussion of the topics. The topics chosen were those that interested and affected these youngsters, with no attempt to avoid reality and to pick innocuous, meaningless subjects. The three examples selected to illustrate this type of lesson bear directly or indirectly on these topics: the use and danger of narcotics, behavior during examinations, and the recent athletic scandals. The pupils attempted to analyze a person's action. Key questions were: "Why did he do it? Put yourself in his place. Would you do the same thing?" "Was it worth it?" "How would you help that boy?" "How can we prevent such things from happening?"

Suitable Instructional Materials

Films and filmstrips, radio and recordings are good devices to introduce a story or article, to teach vocabulary, to reinforce points made in a lesson, and to create a desire to read. Through puppets, shy pupils may be induced to communicate first to the teacher and then to larger audiences.

Too often slow learners are given books on their grade level that are too difficult. To develop speed and fluency, they need to read many books on their own level before they go ahead to the next. Up-to-date, attractive, interesting books a little below their current reading level give them the experience of reading with ease and pleasure (see Appendix C). Many a teacher has seen the magical effect of giving a slow-learning pupil a book that captivates his interest and makes sense to him. Enjoyment and use are key conditions for improvement. On the other hand, books that are abstract and too difficult, or too childish, intensify his dislike of reading.

Since the way a story is presented as well as its content and readability determines the pupils' response, the teacher is wise to take the time to choose the right presentation for his class and for the particular selection [5, 23]. Some possibilities are describing vividly the setting of the story, referring to its humor, mystery, or suspense, giving some interpretation of the characters, reading a page or two aloud each day, putting questions on the board to guide the students' silent reading, giving help with vocabulary when necessary, and using filmstrips or stills from the motion picture of the book. These are ways which create interest. Play writing and play reading, too, can be fun [4]. It appeals to the pupils' interest in dramatics, improves their phrasing, oral expression, and comprehension, and provides for individual differences.

In addition to using published books, teachers have prepared special reading material for their classes. Quinn [21] prepared three types of reading material for his classes of slow learners: (1) simplified news events in which pupils expressed interest, (2) simplified shop manuals, and (3) original stories and accounts of their experiences that they wrote or dictated. He asked students to bring in news stories and articles of special interest to them. He then simplified the newspaper account so that all the pupils could read it. The pupils would draw illustrations for the story. When mimeographed, these stories supplied highly interesting, readable materials for the class.

Recognizing that the manuals used in the shop courses were far too difficult for the slow learners to read, another teacher let the pupils write their own manuals. After he had demonstrated a process and the pupils had carried it out, they described what they had done. The teacher then wrote their statements on the board as the pupils dictated them. After they had arranged the ideas in proper sequence, they copied them in their notebook. This manual written in their own vocabulary and sentence structure was easy for these pupils to read and comprehend. A similar procedure has been used in history and science classes.

Original stories written or dictated by themselves are a kind of creative reading material enjoyed by these pupils. In one class the pupils made books illustrating their summer adventures. Each page consisted of a picture and an explanatory sentence or two that the pupils had dictated and the teacher had printed. Another "volume" consisted of other stories which the class had written and illustrated. These are not always the kind of incidents and humor that the teacher expects. They reveal a great deal about the content of these students' minds. The following stories [1] were written by slow-learning tenth-grade pupils in a large city vocational high school:

[1] The teacher and the students corrected the spelling and grammar to a degree before having the stories typed.

John always wanted to join the Air Force so he could fly a plane and buy an airplane when he got out. He always liked to fly. So he went to a school where they taught him everything about a plane so he would know how to fix any parts that were broken.

After he got out of the vocational high school, he got a job in the Air Force waving a flag. One day he had to bail out of the plane. But he had forgotten to bring his parachute. So he landed on a carrier pigeon, and they lived happily ever after in the bird's nest.

At least this story had a surprise ending!

My first job was to deliver newspapers, and I did not like it. So I took another job selling. This job was too easy and I wanted a harder job. So I got a job with a plumber as his assistant and put in pipe with him.

After a while I got tired of being a plumber's assistant, so I quit and got a job in an office. I had to know how to type and to file important papers. After a while I quit and got another job somewhere. Soon after I quit again and decided to join the WAVES. He spent the rest of his life in the WAVES because he was the only man.

This vocational biography is quite typical of slow-learning adolescents. Other stories deal with crime in a melodramatic way.

When asked how they liked the idea of writing and reading these original stories, the pupils made such comments as:

I think it was very interesting because it shows how the class can work together.

It gave all the boys a chance to think up their own ideas.

The stories were exciting and pitiful in some ways.

It was exciting—the day we changed papers. It was something new to me and I hope we can do it again.

We all had fun doing it.

It might teach you how to write a story.

The "incomplete story" is another technique used by a teacher of seventh- and eighth-grade slow learners [23]. The pupils read the story written or selected by the teacher, answered the questions, and discussed their answers and method of reading [23, pp. 42–44].

Instruction: This is the beginning of a short story. Read it carefully and answer the questions at the end.

It was one of those warm summer afternoons. Fred and Tony were standing in the shade in front of the drug store. Both boys were dripping with perspiration.

"What shall we do today?" asked Fred.

"Don't ask me," yawned Tony. "It's too hot to do anything but sleep."

"Don't you sleep enough in class?" answered his friend.

"Okay, Okay, so Mrs. Franklin caught me sleeping in the assembly. But it still doesn't solve our problem of what to do."

While the two boys were talking, they noticed a familiar figure strolling towards them. It was Frankie, the neighborhood "wise guy." Frankie, as usual, was dressed "sharp." A cigarette hung from the corner of his mouth. He sneered at the boys and said, "You two dopes still hanging around? Why don't you stick with me? I'll show you some excitement. How's about it?"

Fred and Tony looked at one another. They couldn't make up their minds.

Questions (answers to be written on this paper):

1. Does the beginning of this story interest you? (Yes—No)
2. Answer either one:

   Why is this a good beginning for a story?

   Why is this a poor beginning for a story?
3. Imagine you are the author. What will happen next?
4. What would be a good title for the story?

   Note: If you need more space for your answers, use the other side of the paper.

Sampling of Pupil Response [2]

Question 1: Does the beginning of this story interest you?

Yes—48   No—7

Question 2: Why is this a good (poor) beginning for a story?

Reasons for good beginning: "It tells that wise guys can get you into trouble." "It tells all the facts." "It talks about something what happens in school."

Reasons for poor beginning: "It wasn't a good story because they couldn't make up their minds." "The boys were dopes for hanging around. They should have gone swimming." "I like to know what happened in the end. The story doesn't tell you."

Question 3: Imagine you are the author. What will happen next?

"They will go with him and rob and become a dope attic."

"They may have to steal or kill or something that is very bad. They will join his gang. They have to do everything that he does even smoke narcotics or something."

"They would go with the boy because they have nothing to do."

"They went with Frankie and got into trouble. And went to jail for the whole summer."

"They are not going with the other boy because he is well dressed. They smell of perspiration."

"I think that maybe next time Tony won't go to sleep in the assembly."

"I would try to write another story."

Question 4: What would be a good title for this story?

"The Boys Who Got into Trouble"

"A Summer Afternoon"

"The Wise Guy"

[2] The wording, spelling, and diction were left unchanged.

"A Bad Summer"
"Two Boys Who Would Not Make Up Their Minds"
"The Wandering Bums"
"Nothing to Do" [3]

By listening and speaking, writing and reading, slow learners learn to communicate with others. As they become more fluent, they get along with people better and acquire a necessary foundation for reading. They expand their vocabulary with conversation and group discussion, informal dramatization and role playing. By participating in social-personal activities such as assuming responsibility for greeting and guiding school visitors, answering the telephone, taking messages by word of mouth from one teacher to another, they slowly expand the perimeter of their language abilities.

Personalized Instruction

If reading has some personal reference, if the slow learner can see the relation of reading to his present life and immediate goals, he will be more willing to acquire the necessary skills. For example, reading and writing for a class newspaper seem worthwhile. Slow-learning pupils get a thrill from seeing their names in print. Finding stories to read to younger children is another purposeful activity that builds their self-esteem. If a pupil lacks the skill to write a story, poem, joke, review of a book or movie, or description of an experience, he may dictate it to the teacher who will transcribe it.

A group of twelve- to fourteen-year-old slow learners were especially interested and happy when they were acting out sentences written specifically for each pupil, e.g., "The boy with red hair will sing a song." "The boy with the red and blue sweater will go to the door." Sentences such as these were effective because they were personal. The redheaded boy was proud of his singing ability and delighted to use it in carrying out his direction.

They next read sentences about daily events and their activities and interests which the teacher had written on the board.

Then subgroups were formed. The more able boys chose appropriate books or articles on their independent reading level. Some played games such as word lotto—matching word forms with illustrative pictures. Another favorite game was building sentences from words already learned. The teacher worked with a group reading *My Weekly Reader*. She asked questions to arouse the pupils' curiosity and desire to read the article and direct their thinking about each paragraph. For example, before they began to read the second paragraph the teacher said, "The second paragraph gives a common name for our government. What is it?"

[3] Quoted with the permission of Dr. Sydney Bauch, Hofstra College, Hempstead, N.Y.

Pupil: (after reading the paragraph) Uncle Sam.
Teacher: Yes. Now see if you can find out what Uncle Sam is doing to save the buffalo.
Pupil: He's giving them places to live.
Teacher: What does he keep other people from doing to them?

The pupil found the sentences containing the answer. The teacher understood and accepted what these boys could do and showed no disappointment when one of them did not read so well as she had hoped.

This was an excellent period from the standpoint of group work—a friendly atmosphere of learning and succeeding; subgrouping within the class; reading material that was personal, meaningful, and enjoyable to the students and within their range of comprehension; use of daily experiences as reading material; a variety of activities to prevent fatigue or boredom; and skillful, immediate motivation to read each paragraph.

A kind and understanding teacher, good social relations in the classroom, and interesting activities are the "big three" of the program for any learner. Slow learners are no exception. In addition, the teacher of slow learners should have special preparation for his work. The group should be small enough for much individual instruction. Instead of a competitive atmosphere, there should be one of helping each other to learn. The child moves, when he is ready, from one subgrouping to another or from easy to slightly more difficult material and gets a sense of progress and success.

Understanding and Respect

Children in general want understanding teachers. One rural youngster expressed his appreciation in the following words: "The teachers in this school seem to understand the pupils and that helps us to get along." It is most important to know what kind of person each child is, how he feels about himself and his reading difficulties, and what his motivations and fears are. For example, one teen-age girl needed to take a more positive, hopeful attitude toward herself; her older brother had recently been committed to an institution for mental defectives, and she was afraid the same thing would happen to her.

Some teachers tend to dislike slow learners; they think of them as a nuisance and would like to get rid of them. Too often teachers take a fatalistic attitude toward retardation in reading. They let the pupil draw or schedule him for shop courses that require little reading. Consequently, he never receives the instruction and practice in reading which he needs. Since many of these children have felt keenly their parents' disappointment over their failure to read, the teacher must be particularly careful not to show disappointment. Instead, he should accept occasional failure as a natural part of life, meanwhile providing an easy progression of reading experiences in which failures are few. He should accept the child, whether he succeeds or fails. If the teacher is overconcerned with his own success in teaching, it may be hard for him not to show annoyance when a slow-learning child fails to recognize words he is supposed to know.

An adolescent, looking back over her early school experiences, said, "My fifth-grade teacher was very, very unqualified as a teacher. She called us dumb-bunnies and other ugly names." When the teacher asks another pupil to help the slow learner read, he feels embarrassed—"All the little kids turn around" [3, p. 112].

It is especially important with slow-learning children to accentuate the positive—to emphasize what they *can* do. They need to set realistic goals for themselves and see objective evidence of progress toward these goals. The child who is failing may not be able to express his feelings in words, but he is uncomfortable and longs to withdraw from the situation. The longer the child has experienced failure and frustration in learning to read, the more intense his negative reaction is likely to be. There are a few simple but fundamental procedures for building more positive attitudes toward the reading situation: (1) the child should be accepted and appreciated as a person; (2) he should be helped to choose books he can understand and read successfully, with real interest; and (3) he should be made aware of and rewarded for each step in the right direction and for his smallest success.

The slow learner who is already reading up to capacity cannot be expected to show any permanent sharp increase in his developmental reading trend as a result of special instruction. The problem here, at a given time, is to increase the breadth of his reading achievement rather than its level—to help him do the kind of reading useful and possible for him on his present level of ability.

REFERENCES

1. Abramowitz, Jack: *Diary of a Slow Learner Class: A Teacher's Experience with a Class of Slow Learners in History,* Follett Publishing Company, Chicago, 1965.

2. Bernstein, Bebe: *Readiness and Reading for the Retarded Child,* The John Day Company, Inc., New York, 1965.

3. Bullock, Harrison: *Helping the Non-reading Pupil in Secondary School,* Teachers College Press, Teachers College, Columbia University, New York, 1955.

4. Burt, Cyril, and H. B. Lewis: "Teaching Backward Males," *British Journal of Educational Psychology,* vol. 16, pp. 116–132, November, 1946.

5. Ebbett, P. F.: "Drama for Slow Learners," *English Journal,* vol. 52, pp. 624–625, November, 1963.

6. Gillingham, Anna, and Bessie Stillman: *Remedial Training for Children with a Special Disability in Reading, Spelling, and Penmanship,* 5th ed., Sackett and Wilhelms Lithographing Company, New York, 1956.

7. Goldstein, Edward: *Selective Audio-visual Instruction for Mentally Retarded Pupils,* Charles C Thomas, Publisher, Springfield, Ill., 1965.

8. Groelle, Marvin C.: "Techniques and Adjustments for Slow Learners with Special Reference to Reading," in William S. Gray (comp. and ed.), *Classroom Techniques in Improving Reading,* Supplementary Educational Monographs, no. 69, University of Chicago Press, Chicago, 1949, pp. 182–186.

9. Hagen, Elizabeth: "Errors in the Interpretation of Test Scores," *Journal of the National Association of Women Deans and Counselors,* vol. 23, pp. 52–55, January, 1960.

10. Harris, Albert J.: *How to Increase Reading Ability,* 4th ed., rev., Longmans, Green & Co., Inc., New York, 1961.

11. Hegge, Thorleif G., Samuel A. Kirk, and Winifred D. Kirk: *Remedial Reading Drills,* George Wahr Publishing Company, Ann Arbor, Mich., 1948.

12. Hermann, Knud: *Reading Disability,* Einar Munksgaard Forlag, Copenhagen, Denmark, 1959.

13. Kephart, N. C.: *The Slow Learner in the Classroom,* Charles E. Merrill Books, Inc., Columbus, Ohio, 1960.

14. Kirk, Samuel A.: "Characteristics of Slow Learners and Needed Adjustments in Reading," in William S. Gray (comp. and ed.), *Classroom Techniques in Improving Reading,* Supplementary Educational Monographs, no. 69, University of Chicago Press, Chicago, 1949, pp. 172–176.

15. Kirk, Samuel A.: "Reading Problems of Slow Learners," in H. Alan Robinson (comp. and ed.), *The Underachiever in Reading,* Supplementary Educational Monographs, no. 92, University of Chicago Press, Chicago, 1962, pp. 62–69.

16. Kirk, Samul A.: *Teaching Reading to Slow-learning Children,* Houghton Mifflin Company, Boston, 1940.

17. Kirk, Samuel A., and Barbara Bateman: "Diagnosis and Remediation of Learning Disabilities," *Exceptional Children,* vol. 29, pp. 73–78, October, 1962.

18. Kirk, Samuel A., and James J. McCarthy: "The Illinois Test of Psycholinguistic Abilities: An Approach to Differential Diagnosis," *American Journal of Mental Deficiency,* vol. 56, pp. 399–412, November, 1961.

19. Marianne Frostig: *Developmental Test of Visual Perception,* 3d ed., Consulting Psychologists Press, Palo Alto, Calif., 1961–1964.

20. The Miami Reading Series, D. C. Heath and Company, Boston, 1965.

21. Quinn, Thomas J.: "A Reading Program for a Group of 14–17 year old CRMD Pupils in a New York City School," unpublished doctoral project, Teachers College, Columbia University, New York, 1955.

22. Radler, D. H., and N. C. Kephart: *Success through Play,* Harper & Row, Publishers, Incorporated, New York, 1960.

23. Rauch, Sydney J.: "The Organization and Instruction of Special Reading Classes in a New York City Junior High School," unpublished doctoral dissertation, Teachers College, Columbia University, New York, 1952.

24. Sears, Richard: "Characteristics and Trainability of a Case of Special Reading Disability at the Moron Level," *Journal of Juvenile Research,* vol. 19, pp. 135–145, July, 1935.

25. Sniff, William F.: *A Curriculum for the Mentally Retarded Young Adult,* Charles C Thomas, Publisher, Springfield, Ill., 1962.

26. Strang, Ruth: "Step by Step Instructing in Beginning Reading for Slow Learners," *Exceptional Children,* vol. 32, pp. 31–36, September, 1965.

27. Vernon, M. D.: *Backwardness in Reading,* Cambridge University Press, New York, 1957.

28. Wepman, J. M.: *Auditory Discrimination Test,* University of Chicago Press, Chicago, 1958.

29. Winter Haven Lions Research Foundation: *Procedure Manual: Perceptual Training Forms,* Winter Haven Lions Research Foundation, Winter Haven, Fla., 1960.

30. Wozencraft, M.: "Word Meaning Difficulties," *Elementary English,* vol. 41, pp. 44–46, January, 1964.

other disabled readers

chapter 14

In the previous chapters you have focused your attention on the reading problem and its multiple causation. In this chapter, severe reading disability is considered as secondary to other problems. You will see how cultural and economic deprivation and lack of early opportunity to learn the English language may prevent a child from learning to read. Failure in reading, in turn, causes anxiety, feelings of inadequacy and inferiority, or hostility which further intensifies the initial handicap and increases the difficulty of treatment.

After studying this chapter you will become more aware of behavioral indications of these problems, as you observe students, day by day. The chapter will also suggest principles, methods, and materials especially appropriate in teaching the disadvantaged and those with non-English-speaking backgrounds.

You will draw on your previous knowledge of the goals of reading instruction, the development of reading abilities, diagnostic and remedial techniques, and materials of instruction.

As you read, relate the information about characteristics and needs to individual pupils whom you have known. Question the applicability of the procedures and materials described to the particular group with whom you are working, adapt the suggestions given here, and devise new methods and materials to meet their needs.

THE DISADVANTAGED RETARDED READER [20]

Among retarded readers are individuals who are economically impoverished, "culturally deprived," "culturally different," or otherwise disadvantaged [1] because of environmental conditions. Although some of these pupils will also be intellectually limited, many have potential ability which can be developed if the debilitating effects of cultural deprivation are reversed. Thus teachers will guard against the danger of class labels, which conceal individual differences. Most children who are "culturally deprived" are unique in some ways; there is no typical "socially disadvantaged" child [18].

Case of a Disadvantaged Nonreader

George was one of five children whose mother said that she and the father were divorced. With no knowledge of where the father was, the family lived on welfare funds. Disorder and dissension characterized the home. During his preschool years George had had none of the prereading experiences described in Chapter 3. Although his general health was good, he suffered from earaches which may have contributed to his low level of auditory-perception skills.

At eleven years of age he was practically a nonreader, able to pronounce only half the words in a preprimer. When told a word, he could remember it for a page or two. Although able to recognize many beginning and ending sounds, he was lacking in knowledge of vowels and consonant blends and in other word attack skills. Tested on seventy Dolch basic sight words, he recognized only eight. But on the listening comprehension subtest of the Durrell Analysis of Reading Difficulty his score was comparable to that of fourth-grade children. He expressed himself on a concrete level but was often confused about the pronunciation of words.

On the first of two individual intelligence tests he tested within the average

[1] In general, the word *disadvantaged* will be used here in referring to these individuals. Two collections of articles in paperback editions will give background for this section: Joe L. Frost and Glenn R. Hawkes, *The Disadvantaged Child,* and Frank W. Lanning and Wesley A. Many, *Basic Education for the Disadvantaged Adult,* both published by Houghton Mifflin Company, Boston, 1966.

range, but two years later he had dropped to the dull-normal rating. The low score on the Digit-Span subtest of the Wechsler Intelligence Scale for Children suggested difficulty in paying attention and anxiety that interfered with his performance. When words were placed in meaningful context, he was quick to learn them; for unfamiliar words he used a spelling approach.

There were also other indications of an increase in anxiety about his reading difficulty. He was sensitive to criticism and, facing failure, gave up. To maintain his self-esteem, he tried to avoid situations involving reading that for him had no personal meaning or satisfaction. He was troubled by nightmares and enuresis, and teachers reported that he was untruthful and had been caught stealing.

His lack of prereading language experiences explains his limited vocabulary and conversational ability. No one had read to him; no one had often talked or listened to him; he had had few interesting experiences to talk about.

It is probable that his intelligence-test scores were depressed by educational deprivation, for in other situations he showed insights and abilities not compatible with the IQ score obtained. He was cooperative and friendly. He wanted to improve his reading because it would help him get a job. He reacted favorably to genuine praise and the experience of success. After he had learned three words, he said to the worker, "If I keep this up, I'll get real smart."

The worker in this case began with a trip to the zoo. There they talked about the animals they saw. To help George establish his identity and build a happier self-image, the worker took photographs of him when he was enjoying some experience. Later, George dictated simple sentences about each picture for a book about his visit, which he read and reread. He also wrote a book about his life—anything that he wanted to tell. In addition to the reading material he dictated, he read very easy books about his major interests— sports, hunting, and animals. Unfamiliar words and concepts became opportunities to practice word recognition skills.

Conditions and Characteristics

Certain conditions seem to promote characteristics which, in turn, may lead to success or failure in reading. At present it is possible only to infer the relationship of these conditions and characteristics to reading retardation [20]. While recognizing the obvious unfavorable home conditions, teachers should also seek out some aspect in these children's environment that has positive implications and use it to good advantage. An anthology by Celeste Edell, *The Family Is a Way of Feeling*, includes stories that portray genuine strengths in Negro and Puerto Rican families. Despite poverty, some families do provide an intellectually stimulating home environment for their children and are concerned about their education. As Congreve pointed out, "Not all the disadvantaged are poor" [9]. If teachers understood the home and school conditions contributing to retardation in reading, they would be better able to help disadvantaged pupils capitalize on their assets and minimize their liabilities.

Physical Limitations. The poverty, overcrowding, poor eating habits, and unsanitary conditions in many disadvantaged children's homes may result in children who are physically below par, low in energy output, and high in auditory and visual defects. In large, impoverished families, crowded rooms, confusion, and noise interfere with children's concentration, deprive them of necessary sleep, and a place or time for reading. All of these conditions may adversely affect their learning to read.

Deficient Verbal Communication. In the educationally disadvantaged homes there is meager verbal communication between parents and children. As in the case of George, parents seldom answer the children's questions, encourage them to ask questions, listen and talk to them, or read aloud to them. A home where poor English is spoken may be as detrimental to language development as a silent home. Many parents from the subculture of poverty speak what is commonly called "nonstandard" English. If the children have become accustomed to different speech sounds, different idioms, and different sentence patterns from those they hear in the classroom, they may make errors in spelling and reading comprehension as well as in pronunciation. Actually their speech often resembles a second language. It would be of great value to the teacher of reading in a non-English-speaking community to know specific characteristics of the student's speech patterns. On the basis of this knowledge he would be able to judge better what is true dialectical variation and what is carelessness in speech.

Their vocabulary is limited in extent and precision. Many of the words they have learned have unique meaning within their own culture; for many of their concepts they do not have the English words [15]. These pupils may talk freely among themselves in their own language. They are *not* nonverbal; they do not have apparent verbal ability in classroom situations for a number of reasons:

1. Some pupils may be genuinely retarded in their language development.
2. Some may have learned a language that is not accepted by the school. They can talk freely with their parents and with other children like themselves, but not to their teachers.
3. The culturally different child may not have had the experiences which are discussed in school, consequently he has nothing to say.
4. Some children hesitate to speak up in class because they fear that their experiences will not be acceptable.
5. Some speak freely in small congenial groups but not in a formal class discussion.

6. Many children do not talk much because the questions asked require only brief answers.

7. Many children will verbalize better in response to pictures or other concrete experiences than to words alone [37, pp. 552–556].

Loban's study [31] of children in the kindergarten through first grade showed small differences in structural patterns of sentences between the low and high socioeconomic groups but marked superiority in the children of high socioeconomic status in the dexterity with which they used clauses, infinitives and verbals, and in their reading, writing, and oral language.

The listening habits of disadvantaged children are poor; they tune in and out on what the teacher is saying. Instead of listening to the class discussion, they are often thinking about what their gang will be doing that evening. Deutsch [14] and Bateman [3] hypothesized that specific training in listening, in talking, and in visual and auditory discrimination would improve the intellectual development and achievement of preschool children deprived of the cultural advantages of better homes.

Ways of Perceiving and Thinking.   Habits of perceiving, reasoning, thinking and remembering, cognitive style, and self-concepts or self-image are formed early in the home. More pervasive than social status in their effect on children's language, cognition, and intelligence are the subtle aspects of adults' manner of responding to children. In the deprived family the communication is often "restricted," i.e., limited to short, simple, often unfinished sentences with few subordinate clauses. Children are given little chance to develop their ideas. Hess and Shipman [24, p. 872] illustrate these differences in style of communication by two examples of mother-child communication:

A child is playing noisily in the kitchen with an assortment of jars and pans when the telephone rings. In one home the mother says, "Be quiet" or "Shut up" or issues any one of several short, peremptory commands. In the other home the mother says "Would you keep quiet a minute? I want to talk on the phone." In one instance the child is asked for a simple mental response. . . . He is not called upon to reflect or to make mental discriminations. In the other example, the child is required to follow two or three ideas. He is asked to relate his behavior to a time dimension; he must think of his behavior in relation to its effect upon another person. He must perform a more complicated task to follow the communication of his mother in that his relationship to her is mediated in part through concepts and shared ideas; his mind is stimulated or exercised (in an elementary fashion) by a more elaborate and complex verbal communication initiated by the mother.

Insofar as socially disadvantaged children are often criticized, disparaged, and arbitrarily punished rather than reasoned with, their self-concepts as molded by parental behavior are unfavorable. "Of the many critical dimensions in which the advantaged differ from the disadvantaged, the one that over-shadows all others is the self-image, or self-concept" [9, p. 15].

Although most research has found a relationship between intelligence and economic status, it has not yet proved that this relationship is permanent or irreversible [20]. The impact of social class will vary with the student's level of achievement, ability, and personal characteristics. By the time students get to college, high achievers share a common subculture despite diverse social origins.

Values and Aspirations. The parents of many of these children seem less concerned about their children's education than the average parent. Although many of the values by which they live are alien to those accepted in the school, they have aspirations and goals of their own that can be used as motivation for reading improvement. In an extremely disorderly junior high school class, one of the girls begged the teacher, "Please, Mr. —, teach me to read. I want to be a nurse when I grow up. And you have to know how to read." The discouraged teacher thought, "If we just could teach them to read and figure, they might respond."

Not being successful in reading, they naturally dislike school, become discouraged, and read less and less. Some are hostile to the authority represented by the teacher. Some individuals turn their aggression inward against themselves in a kind of self-sabotage.

Briefly, as a result of combinations of unfavorable conditions at home and at school, disadvantaged children and young people may be physically below par, substandard in their speech, and restricted in their experiences. They are frequently weak in abstract thinking, conceptualization, auditory discrimination, and perceptual styles necessary for success in reading. Their feelings of inadequacy and inferiority may determine how they approach any reading task.

These attitudes and behaviors may be either reinforced or modified by their school experiences. They need acceptance and success in school. Yet giving acceptance, approval, and praise is not so simple as it seems. Acceptance is often confused with complete permissiveness. Some disadvantaged pupils are likely to interpret the teacher's effort to build up their self-esteem as an attempt to control their behavior.

Difficulties in Diagnosis

Disadvantaged pupils in rural as well as in urban areas are handicapped on reading and intelligence tests by their immature and nonstandard language, by their poor vocabulary and low level of comprehension, and by their social background. The diagnosis and correction of specific weaknesses in the mental processes involved in reading offers a more promising approach than the effort to develop "culture-free" tests [28] for disadvantaged groups. Tests should be used for diagnosis rather than for prediction; their main purpose is to improve status rather than determine status [22]. More information is needed about the high achievers in disadvantaged groups and how they achieved and maintained their superior level of achievement in reading.

Effective Methods of Instruction

Ways to improve reading ability of disadvantaged and culturally different pupils are suggested by the analysis of their strengths and deficiencies. Planned instruction, practice to decrease deficiencies in mental abilities, and a work-study program have been effective [22].

Preschool activities will help to develop language learning during the formative years. The modified Montessori approach may be especially suitable for preschool disadvantaged children because of its emphasis on sense-stimulating materials and step-by-step activities that require use of their hands and their minds. Other experiences usually provided in preschool and kinder-garten programs help these children to adjust to social aspects of the classroom situation, understand what the teacher is saying, communicate with one another, and interpret the words they see in beginning reading [11].

Informal school situations offer many opportunities for learning to listen and speak, to think more precisely, to compare their speech with that of children from different backgrounds. Ponder [40] suggests role playing as a method of understanding the language of the disadvantaged child and making him aware of other levels of language as it relates to different real-life situations. In this activity he learns the language that is appropriate at different times and in different places.

These children need instruction to overcome specific difficulties in pronunciation and sentence structure. Opportunity to talk in small, informal groups encourages the shy pupil to participate. Role playing, dramatized reading, puppet shows, choral speaking, dialogues, and similar methods stimulate these pupils to speak more freely and effectively with natural intonation, stress, and rhythm.

Betty Frey, a junior high school teacher in the Amphitheatre public schools, Tucson, Arizona, and her pupils have written dialogues based on science lessons. The following is one dealing with rocks and minerals:

First pupil: Have you ever wondered about how mountains were formed?
Second pupil: Yes, I have. Also how so many different kinds of rocks were formed.
First: When the earth cooled, it became smaller and parts that were pushed up became mountains.

Second:	Didn't volcanoes make mountains, too?
First:	Volcanoes formed many different kinds of rocks. They're what we call *igneous* rocks.
Second:	That's easy to remember because it begins like *ignite*, which means to catch on fire. What are some of the igneous rocks?
First:	All of the familiar crystals. Many birthstones were volcanic rock bubbles that cooled very slowly with crystals forming inside.
Second:	What if the lava cooled quickly?
First:	It was full of gas bubbles. It made a very light rock called *featherstone* or *pumice.*
Second:	What other kinds of rocks are there?
First:	Those made when particles of sand, gravel, shells, clay, or plants were washed up by the water. Then when layers upon layers were pressed together, they formed sedimentary rocks. Most of the rocks around here are sedimentary.
Second:	How could water wash across the desert?
First:	This wasn't always desert. In fact, it was once a part of the ocean.
Second:	What happened to it? The water, I mean.
First:	It dried up millions of years ago and left the sands and shells behind.
Second:	Is that why sometimes we find pieces of rock with shells or prints of shells in them?
First:	Sure. They're known as fossils.
Second:	What kind of rock is made when shells are crushed together?
First:	Limestone. You see, shells are made of lime or calcium. That's why this kind of rock is called *limestone.*
Second:	Well, you've certainly learned quite a bit about rocks. Let's get together some time and hunt for the different kinds you've told me about.
First:	That sounds like a good idea. We can be a couple of Rock Hounds.
Second:	See you later.

This technique is very useful with bilingual children.

The teacher first reads the dialogue as a model of pronunciation, natural intonation, and stress. Then the class as a whole reads it, then subgroups, and finally individuals take the parts. In these subject-matter dialogues, the pupils acquire knowledge of science as they obtain practice in speaking and reading.

Teachers use the writing of experience stories to give practice in reading the words and sentences familiar to pupils in their speaking vocabulary. Older children write their own stories and books which they pass around to be read by others.

Starting with an activity or an article of concern to them, they build vocabulary, classify ideas, speak and read before the class, become familiar with sentence structure as described by modern linguists. For example, they find the key sentence in a paragraph, read it aloud, write it on the board, underline the key thought, and tell what each phrase shows—when, how, why, where. Other methods described in Chapters 6 and 7 are also appropriate for the disadvantaged.

Instructional Materials

In homes of disadvantaged pupils there are few books or other reading materials. In school, much of the reading material is too abstract and remote from their interests. Their surface apathy may be partly resistance to and resentment against inappropriate reading material. The kinds of reading material already mentioned in Chapters 12 and 13 work well with the disadvantaged retarded reader: multilevel pamphlets such as the Science Research Laboratories and books at a low level of reading difficulty and high level of interest [47]. Many books are now available that interest adolescents and are on a low level of difficulty (see Appendix D). Some of these deal with life situations that are familiar to the disadvantaged, adolescent backward reader. The biographies and autobiographies of handicapped people who have made good are particularly appealing. Among these are: *The Story of Helen Keller; Hey, I'm Alive* by Helen Klaben; *People to Remember* by Gertrude Moderow; *Victory over Self* by Floyd Patterson; *Opportunity, Please Knock* by Oscar Brown; and *A Present for Rosita* by Celeste Edell. Supplementary reading of a wide range of trade books and magazines enriches basic instruction. More books in the subject-matter areas are appearing for disadvantaged pupils.

The selection of reading material for these pupils is especially important. If the book is too difficult, it intensifies their dislike of reading and their sense of failure. If it seems "babyish" it undermines their feeling of personal dignity. If it is about persons and places completely foreign to them, they find it too remote from their lives and interests and cannot identify with the characters.

Visual and auditory aids are especially useful for disadvantaged pupils who need to broaden their experiences, to hear correct speech, and to have a concrete sensory approach to reading. This whole area has been effectively presented in Spache's *Toward Better Reading* [42, pp. 392–407].

More important than any specific methods, techniques, or materials is a sincere respect for disadvantaged pupils. The sensitive teacher is quick to recognize and applaud any spark of interest and any genuine sign of progress in the students' reading and attitudes.

STUDENTS FROM NON-ENGLISH-SPEAKING BACKGROUND

In many parts of this country today there are large numbers of retarded readers who come from non-English-speaking homes. They are handicapped by their lack of knowledge of the English language. In Texas, for example, approximately 80 per cent of all beginning first graders from a non-English-speaking background fail the first grade because of their inability to read [44]. These children become increasingly retarded as they progress through school and tend to leave school prematurely.

Special Problems

The child from a non-English-speaking home has not had the opportunity during preschool years to acquire the vocabulary and speech patterns prerequisite to learning to read English. Research suggests that ages three and four are especially favorable for language learning. It is then that children have the greatest capacity for imitating sounds accurately without consciousness of rules. Certain sounds in English may be absent from the pupil's native language; he may not even recognize that his speech is different from English [45, 46]. For example, the Navajo language does not form plurals by adding a final *s* to words. Consequently, the Navajo child does not hear the difference between *hand* and *hands.* So he repeats, "I'm washing my hand" even after the teacher has said the sentence correctly. Such a child needs well-designed exercises to train his ear to hear sounds that are not in his own language.

Faulty pronunciation of English words interferes with getting the meaning of words by sounding them out. Unfamiliarity with English syntax and idioms adds to the difficulty of anticipating the meaning and checking interpretation as these children read.

It is also difficult to translate concepts from one language to another, partly because the concepts express the basic philosophy or values of the culture. For example, "in English, one says he missed the bus; in Spanish he says the bus left him. . . . In English the clock *runs;* in Spanish he says it *walks,* in French it *marches,* in German it *functions"* [50, pp. 65–66]. Pupils who speak another language find special difficulties in idiomatic expressions: "He got the axe." "I've let the cat out of the bag." There are many idioms in the basal readers which present no problem for English-speaking children, but increase bilingual children's difficulty in comprehension. Children from non-English-speaking homes are significantly lower than Anglos on tests of common idiomatic expressions, multiple meanings of common works, simple analogies, and opposites [51].

To some children from non-English-speaking homes, learning English means losing their native culture with all its emotional ties. The language and folkways of infancy have such strong roots that pupils may resent and resist attempts to impose an alien culture upon them. To abandon their native language makes it difficult for them to achieve identity. If forbidden to use their language, which they have associated with their parents from early years, they may become emotionally disturbed. This should not be. Teachers should appreciate the best features of the child's culture and help him retain them. This necessitates understanding

> . . . the life values, the cultural beliefs, motivations, and aspirations of the various minority ethnic groups. . . . Pueblo Indian children most likely will be taught at home a harmony-with-nature rather than a mastery-over-nature philosophy; present-time orientation rather than future-time orientation; and a level of aspiration to follow in the ways of the old people. . . . Language is an integral part of a people's culture. It is the way the heritage is transmitted. It is the means by which the attitudes and feelings of the group are made known [50, pp. 64–65].

Relation of Reading to Acculturation

In a literate society, facility in reading may contribute to acculturation in several ways. Being able to read decreases the social distance between children of other cultures and Anglos. Reading is one way in which the individual may achieve his goals as, for example, entrance into a certain vocation. Reading strengthens security on a job. Some books present an objective picture of the two cultures and may suggest solutions to the problem of finding and developing the best in both cultures. Knowledge of his own culture obtained through reading increases the bilingual's awareness of himself as a person.

Case of a Bilingual Student

Anna, fifteen years old and in the ninth grade, comes from a non-English-speaking home. Her verbal IQ on the WISC is 80; her performance IQ, 120; her grade score on the Stanford Achievement, Advanced Paragraph Meaning Test, 5.3; and on the Gray Standardized Oral Reading Tests, 4.0.

She said she did not like factual-type articles and would rather read about people than animals, and her lack of interest in the content of most of the assigned books cut down her effort to comprehend and remember. She had no incentive to read other than that of immediate school requirements.

In reading aloud a selection that did not interest her, she tended to substitute for an unfamiliar word any word that began with the same letter, regardless of whether it made sense in the sentence. For example, in the sentence, "The winning team left the field in triumph," she read "trumpet" instead of "triumph."

If the content of an article interested her, however, she worked away at the meaning rather successfully despite many errors. Under pressure to read fluently, she often substituted her own ideas for the author's or made up her own unrelated conclusions; but she recognized the author's purpose and remembered details that were of special interest. She sometimes looked ahead to see whether the word she was reading fitted into the rest of the sentence. Her attempts to sound out words were often not rewarding because, even though she might sound them out correctly, they were not in her speaking vocabulary. Sometimes she used her previous knowledge and experience, limited as it was, to interpret a word or sentence. At other times she obtained the meaning through reasoning by analogy. When concerned with reading for meaning, she willingly used the dictionary to help her get the meaning of unfamiliar words.

If given sufficient incentive for reading, Anna could quite readily acquire the necessary skills. Learning common syllables and other clusters of letters that have consistent sound-letter associations would be more efficient for her than sounding out separate letters. By reading stories and factual material to younger children in her family she could contribute to their language development as well as to her own vocabulary and reading fluency. By listening to radio and television programs with the intent to learn, she could increase her vocabulary, improve her oral language, and build up her background of experience.

Suggestions for Diagnosis

Since students from non-English-speaking backgrounds are definitely handicapped on the verbal parts of standardized tests, interpretation of their test results must be adjusted accordingly. Relatively higher arithmetic and performance test scores indicate potential ability. If they can read in their native language, the test may be given to them in that language or they may simply read a short selection in their native language.

Holland [26] suggested the following modification of the standard method of administering the Wechsler Intelligence Scale for Children:

1. Give the instructions for selected WISC subtests in English.
2. Then repeat the instructions in the native language if the English instructions are not fully understood.
3. Accept and give credit for correct answers in either language.

Thus three scores are obtained: an English verbal IQ, which represents the current level of functioning in English language skills; a bilingual verbal IQ, which suggests potential for verbal skills when knowledge of English is approximately equal to that of the native language; a performance IQ, which gives the approximate intellectual potential under optimal social and cultural conditions [26].

The language barrier = bilingual verbal IQ − English verbal IQ. This adaptation of the WISC may be a promising method of distinguishing between the mentally retarded and those whose opportunity to learn to speak English has been limited.

Other methods of obtaining an understanding of the mental ability of children from non-English-speaking homes follow:

1. The Goodenough Draw-a-Man Test, or some modification of this technique.
2. A learning capacity test; for example, present a series of learning tasks that are within the individual's experience, give instruction in doing them, and observe his success in learning.
3. Observation of the individual's ability to solve practical problems within his range of experience and the framework of the culture with which he is familiar.
4. Observation of the pupil's ability to profit by the best instruction that the teacher can give.
5. Arithmetic section of Stanford Achievement Test, (a) given according to directions, (b) read to the individual in English, (c) read to him in his native language.
6. Other standardized performance tests and tests of visual and auditory perception (see Chapters 4 and 5).
7. A vocabulary test to show which of the basic sight-vocabulary words the bilingual child knows and on which he needs more practice. Such a test, plus a phonics inventory, would identify the sound-letter associations he has mastered and those that are still giving him trouble.
8. An informal, individual inventory to indicate other assets and liabilities in word attack skills, phrasing, and interpretation.

In view of the many possible sources of error, teachers and psychologists should be especially cautious in giving, interpreting and using the results of tests with bilingual pupils.

Programs and Methods of Instruction

Since the reading problems of bilingual children have much in common with those of other retarded readers, many methods which can be used with them to advantage are discussed in other parts of this book. The suggestions that follow include only those having special relevance to instruction of bilinguals.

Acquiring Spoken Language. In teaching sentence patterns, the more elements that are alike and the fewer that are different, the more easily the analogy between similar patterns can be perceived. Many children learn English as a second language by imitation, by reasoning, and by analogy. Instead of memorizing a number of English sentence patterns, they derive one pattern from another by analogy. Elizabeth Willink of Shiprock Boarding School for Indians describes the process as follows:

The children would be taught a simple sentence such as "I like to play" and the plural form of "I." From this knowledge they can produce the sentence "We like to play." If, in a two-term relationship the first term and the relationship are known, they can arrive at the other term. Or if they know two sentences, they can by comparison observe the relationship between them. The sentences may consist of the same words but in a different order: "He should be here" and "Should he be here?" This is a statement-question relationship. Or the sentences may consist of different words but have the same structure: "He loves girls." "She hates boys." Having acquired informally and intuitively a sense of the structure of the language, the children work to produce well-formed sentences of their own, not primarily by the slow, laborious process of applying consciously memorized verbalized rules but by spontaneously using their internalized knowledge of the structure of the language.

They progress from the simplest to the more complex analogies. In the first stage the referent may be dramatized:

"Play—I'm playing."

"Read—I'm reading."

"Eat—I'm eating."

Most children will soon catch on and be able to handle a new element themselves: "Walk—I'm walking." More complex analogies are gradually introduced: "There is Daddy" when they see Daddy coming; "There is Bobby" when they see Bobby coming. If they say "There is Susie" when they see Susie coming, they have become aware of this sentence form. After learning kernel sentences, they can learn to transform one sentence into another as, for example:

"He is a scout."

"He is not a scout."

"Is he a scout?"

"Yes, he is."

"They are scouts," etc.

Thus bilingual pupils acquire a sense of language structure and a feeling of how language works. The more easily and spontaneously this practice is given, the better. The children learn to generalize from the examples given.

The teacher should introduce only one contrasting element at a time, a closely supervised practice stage. The children's attention should be focused on the specific task of learning the forms of the language. The teacher tries to prevent errors by insisting on facile imitation first. If the children err, they repeat the key sentences.

After the practice period, the children have opportunities to apply the newly learned sentence structure to sentences that they produce. This practice helps to increase familiarity with sentence structure, even while the learner's attention is focused on vocabulary. Each interesting situation provides the pupil with one more opportunity to use the language he has learned. It also provides the teacher with a check on how well the pupils have learned the structural forms and their manipulation. Taught in this way, language study is meaningful, purposeful, and functional, with pupils getting a sense of accomplishment and progress.

The children go through these stages:

1. Imitating and memorizing a number of analogous sentences and phrases
2. Perceiving the analogy and the appropriate linguistic forms
3. Structuring the language by analogy in new analogous situations by making sentences of their own
4. Applying their newly acquired skill to real-life situations

Common sentence patterns can be introduced in connection with action. Children are able to understand sentences used in the classroom such as "Put your papers on the table." Action songs and dramatization make more vivid the meaning of the story as well as acquainting children with the sound of literary language.

Learning Both Languages. There are several advantages in employing a teacher who can speak the children's native language. Just to hear the teacher say something in their mother tongue is comforting to little children for whom the school is a strange and alien environment. Sometimes the teacher saves time and clarifies meaning by explaining in their native language an abstract word or a direction that the children cannot understand in English. If a teacher understands the sound system and syntax of the pupils' native language as compared with English, he will be better able to recognize their difficulties.

Combining Speaking, Reading, and Writing. Some second-grade children who initially knew no English but had the advantage of coming from homes where the parents talked a great deal with the children and showed affection for them and respect for education, learned from the following method:

The teacher [2] chose a story and selected ten or more key nouns. She wrote them one by one on the board, illustrating each with her own sketches. Once the children had identified the object and related it to their experience, a pupil wrote the word on the board. The teacher then used the word for language-skills development, asking such questions as: "What words sound like this?" "What words have similar meanings?" "What words begin in the same way?" etc. If the word had a strong verb or adjective association, for example, *open door, shut gate, bird flies,* she discussed the related word and wrote it as well. At the end of this introduction the separate pictures represented the story as a whole. When the word has been thus fully explored, the teacher told or read the story while the children looked at the chalkboard to clarify the meaning of particular words. After the teacher had told the story, the children drew a scene from it and wrote a few sentences with the help of the words still on the chalkboard. While the class was writing in the relaxed

[2] Mrs. Helen von Randow, who taught reading to non-English-speaking Chinese children in New Zealand.

and happy atmosphere, the teacher helped individual children with the pronunciation or understanding of any of the new words.

There are many opportunities for successfully introducing reading and writing. An inherent unity exists among the communication skills, each reinforcing the other, for the efficient teacher to capitalize on.

Beginning Reading Procedures

As with other retarded readers, the teacher builds on the bilingual pupil's assets and begins instruction with something that he wants to read. In the process of reading, the pupil gets help in overcoming his difficulties as he meets them.

With José, who finds his chief satisfaction and success in sports, the teacher begins by writing José's account of the baseball game. Some of the words that José has mispronounced are easily corrected; others require detailed and patient instruction in how to produce the difficult English sounds. To develop proper rhythm, intonation, and stress, the teacher reads aloud José's story; then they read it together. After José has learned to read it well, the teacher records his reading so that José may listen many times to it. After watching the teacher write his story in manuscript writing, José copies it in his own book of original sports stories.

There are many advantages for children from non-English-speaking homes in this integrated approach that involves listening, speaking, reading, and writing. The content is interesting and meaningful to the pupil. The vocabulary and sentence structure are familiar to him. He has immediate motivation to profit by speech instruction. He is beginning to learn to read the same as the English-speaking children in his class.

In the intermediate grades, the pupil should put to use vocabulary and reading comprehension skills he has already acquired. These should not be allowed to lie fallow while he is concentrating exclusively on acquiring oral language. Instead, he should acquire the reading skills he so desperately needs to maintain his self-esteem and to gain knowledge in all of his subjects.

The Need for Both Languages

In a community in which there is a need for educated bilingual clerks, doctors, secretaries, lawyers, policemen, and other workers, it is desirable for children from non-English-speaking homes to be truly bilingual, to be able to speak and read two languages. This has been the goal of a bilingual school in a middle-class community in Dade County, Florida [4]. Approximately half of the pupils in this school are Spanish speaking and half English speaking. From the beginning, parents were invited to participate in the program. Six native speakers of Spanish, who are bilingual, form teams with six English teachers. The English-teacher team member is responsible for developing the usual English curriculum during half of the school day, and the Spanish-speaking teacher develops the second language program for the same pupils during the other half of the day. The teacher aides provide released time for the teachers to plan their program. Preliminary examination indicates that the pupils are making progress comparable to that made by previous classes. The response of parents has also been favorable.

Recent research tends to stress the advantages of knowing two languages. For example, a study in Montreal showed that ten-year-old French children appear to have a better concept formation and a greater flexibility and range in mental abilities than do their monolingual classmates. They also have a more friendly attitude toward the people whose language they have learned [39]. Bilingualism can be an asset in speech and language development, intellectual development, educational progress, emotional and vocational adjustment.

Results of investigations on the effects of childhood bilingualism have been conflicting. According to some studies, children who attempt to learn two languages are retarded in both. However, pupils from non-English-speaking homes who have not been to school before and do not know how to speak English or read or write their native language need special systematic instruction in English. One program consists of an hour of oral practice in carefully selected language patterns, an hour of reading and writing the language patterns they have just learned to speak, and at least a third of the day devoted to informal language activities related to their other school subjects. By listening and talking, they learn the vocabulary and concepts of each subject.

Instructional Materials

Audiovisual aids are especially helpful to pupils from non-English-speaking homes. Individual earphones or listening posts give these students unlimited opportunity to become familiar with the sounds of English. Tape-recording their own oral reading enables them to recognize errors in pronunciation. Opaque projectors, films, filmstrips, pictures, and field trips supply experience background that they lack.

Bilingual pupils spend many hours viewing television or listening to the radio. Have they learned to listen? What do these programs communicate to them? Do they neglect the verbal aspects and merely focus on the action in the lovemaking, the violence, the tumult, and the shouting? How do they appraise the culture they view? The teacher can direct the pupils' attention to the way the characters speak. He may ask them to report what the characters say and their manner of speaking. He may ask pupils to repeat—with the same phrasing, stress, and intonation—the commercials they hear repeatedly.

Many experiences outside the classroom can reinforce reading. Pupils need to read television and movie captions, road signs, maps, menus, labels, directions, notices. Illustrated magazines, mail-order catalogs, newspaper headlines, advertisements, and want ads develop vocabulary and reading skills needed in everyday life. Books prepared for adult illiterates and special magazines and newspapers appeal to adolescents (see Appendix D). Books about children of other races and nationalities help primary children to understand their own culture and their relationship to other peoples (see Appendix E). Linguistic readers such as the Miami Series [35] are very useful in giving practice in sound-letter associations as they are introduced to beginning readers.

REFERENCES

1. Allen, Virginia French (ed.): *On Teaching English to Speakers of Other Languages*, National Council of Teachers of English, Champaign, Ill., 1965.

2. Ausubel, David P.: "A Teaching Strategy for Culturally Deprived Pupils," *School Review*, vol. 71, pp. 454–463, Winter, 1963.

3. Bateman, Barbara: "Learning Disabilities—Yesterday, Today, and Tomorrow," *Exceptional Children*, vol. 31, pp. 167–177, December, 1964.

4. Bell, Paul W.: "The Bilingual School," in J. Allen Figurel (ed.), *Reading and Inquiry*, International Reading Association Conference Proceedings, vol. 10, Newark, Del., 1965, pp. 271–274.

5. Brooks, Nelson: *Language and Language Learning: Practice and Theory*, Harcourt, Brace & World, Inc., New York, 1964.

6. Bumpas, Faye L.: *Teaching Young Students English as a Foreign Language*, American Book Company, New York, 1963.

7. Ching, Doris C.: "Methods for the Bilingual Child," *Elementary English*, vol. 42, pp. 22–27, January, 1965.

8. Coffman, William: "Principles of Developing Tests for the Culturally Different," *Proceedings of the 1964 Invitational Conference on Testing Problems*, Educational Testing Service, Princeton, N.J., 1965, pp. 82–92.

9. Congreve, Willard J.: "Not All the Disadvantaged Are Poor," *PTA Magazine*, vol. 60, pp. 15–17, February, 1966.

10. Crosby, Muriel: *Reading Ladders for Human Relations*, 4th ed., American Council on Education, Washington, D.C., 1963.

11. Cutts, Warren G.: "Reading Unreadiness in the Underprivileged," *NEA Journal*, vol. 52, pp. 23–24, April, 1963.

12. Davis, Allison: "Teaching Language and Reading to Disadvantaged Negro Children," *Elementary English*, vol. 42, pp. 791–797, November, 1965.

13. DeBoer, John S.: "Structure in Relation to Reading," *Education*, vol. 84, pp. 525–530, May, 1964.

14. Deutsch, Martin: "Early Social Environment and School Adaptation," *Teachers College Record*, vol. 66, pp. 699–706, May, 1965.

15. Edwards, Thomas J.: "The Language-experience Attack on Cultural Deprivation," *The Reading Teacher*, vol. 18, pp. 546–551, April, 1965.

16. English 900 Series, English Books 1–6 and Workbooks 1–6, with accompanying tapes, The Macmillan Company, New York, 1964.

17. Finochehiaro, Mary: *English as a Second Language: From Theory to Practice,* Regents Publishing Company, Inc., New York, 1964.

18. Glatt, Charles A.: "Who Are the Deprived Children?" *Elementary School Journal,* vol. 65, pp. 407–413, May, 1965.

19. Goldberg, Herman R., and Winifred T. Brumber (eds.): The Rochester Occupational Reading Series, The Job Ahead, Levels I, II, III, Science Research Associates, Inc., Chicago, 1963.

20. Gordon, Edmund W.: "Characteristics of Socially Disadvantaged Children," *Review of Educational Research,* vol. 35, pp. 377–388, December, 1965.

21. Gray, Susan W., and Rupert A. Klaus: "An Experimental Preschool Program for Culturally Deprived Children," *Child Development,* vol. 36, pp. 887–898, December, 1965.

22. Hamburger, Martin: "Measurement Issues in the Counseling of the Culturally Disadvantaged," *Proceedings of the 1964 Invitational Conference on Testing Problems,* Educational Testing Service, Princeton, N.J., 1965, pp. 71–81.

23. Harris, Albert J.: "Teaching Reading to Culturally Different Children," in *Improvement of Reading through Classroom Practice,* International Reading Association Conference Proceedings, vol. 9, Newark, Del., 1964, pp. 24–26.

24. Hess, Robert D., and Virginia Shipman: "Early Experience and the Socialization of Cognitive Modes in Children," *Child Development,* vol. 36, pp. 869–886, December, 1965.

25. Holbrook, David: *English for the Rejected: Training Literacy in the Lower Streams of the Secondary School,* Cambridge University Press, New York, 1964.

26. Holland, William R.: "Language Barrier as an Educational Problem of Spanish-speaking Children," *Exceptional Children,* vol. 27, pp. 42–44, 46–50, September, 1960.

27. Isenberg, Irwin: *The Drive Against Illiteracy* (The Reference Shelf), vol. 30, no. 5, The H. W. Wilson Company, New York, 1964.

28. Karp, Joan M., and Irving Sigel: "Psychoeducational Appraisal of Disadvantaged Children," *Review of Educational Research,* vol. 35, pp. 401–412, December, 1965.

29. Lado, Robert: *Language Teaching: A Scientific Approach,* McGraw-Hill Book Company, New York, 1964.

30. Lee, Maurice A.: "Improving the Reading of the Negro Rural Teacher in the South," *Journal of Negro Education,* vol. 13, pp. 47–56, Winter, 1944.

31. Loban, Walter: "Language Ability in the Elementary School: Implications of Findings Pertaining to the Culturally Disadvantaged," in Arno Jewett, Joseph Mersand, and Doris V. Gunderson (eds.), *Improving English Skills of Culturally Different Youth in Large Cities,* Office of Education Bulletin 1964, no. 5, 1964, pp. 62–68.

32. Lovell, K., and M. Woolsey: "Reading Disability, Non-verbal Reasoning, and Social Class," *Educational Research,* vol. 6, pp. 226–229, June, 1964.

33. Mackintosh, Helen K., Lillian Gore, and Gertrude M. Lewis: *Educating Disadvantaged Children under Six,* Disadvantaged Children Series, no. 1, U.S. Government Printing Office, 1965.

34. Metz, F. Elizabeth: "Poverty, Early Language Deprivation, and Learning Ability," *Elementary English,* vol. 43, pp. 129–133, February, 1966.

35. Miami Linguistic Readers, D. C. Heath and Company, Boston, 1965.

36. Niemeyer, John H.: "The Bank Street Readers: Support for Movement toward an Integrated Society," *The Reading Teacher,* vol. 18, pp. 542–545, April, 1965.

37. Olsen, James: "The Verbal Ability of the Culturally Different," *The Reading Teacher,* vol. 18, pp. 552–556, April, 1965.

38. *On Teaching English to Speakers of Other Languages,* Papers Read at the TESOL Conference, Tucson, Ariz., National Council of Teachers of English, Champaign, Ill., 1965.

39. Peal, Elizabeth, and Wallace E. Lambert: "The Relation of Bilingualism to Intelligence," *Psychological Monographs: General and Applied,* vol. 76, no. 546, American Psychological Association, Inc., Washington, D.C., 1962.

40. Ponder, Eddie G.: "Understanding the Language of the Culturally Disadvantaged Child," *Elementary English,* vol. 42, pp. 769ff., November, 1965.

41. *Review of Educational Research,* vol. 35, no. 5, December, 1965. (Issue on education for socially disadvantaged children.)

42. Spache, George D.: *Toward Better Reading,* The Garrard Press, Champaign, Ill., 1963.

43. Staats, Arthur W., and William Butterfield: "Treatment of Nonreading in a Culturally Deprived Juvenile Delinquent: An Application of Reinforcement Principles," *Child Development,* vol. 36, pp. 926–942, December, 1965.

44. Stemmler, Anne O.: "An Experimental Approach to the Teaching of Oral Language and Reading," *Harvard Educational Review,* vol. 36, pp. 42–59, Winter, 1966.

45. Stockwell, Robert P., and J. Donald Bowen: *The Sounds of English and Spanish,* University of Chicago Press, Chicago, 1965.

46. Stockwell, Robert P., J. Donald Bowen, and John W. Martin: *The Grammatical Structures of English and Spanish,* University of Chicago Press, Chicago, 1965.

47. Strang, Ruth, Ethlyne Phelps, and Dorothy Withrow: *Gateways to Readable Books,* 4th ed., The H. W. Wilson Company, New York, 1966.

48. Timothy, M. (Sister): "The Reading Problem of a Bilingual Child," *Elementary English,* vol. 41, pp. 235–237, 241, March, 1964.

49. Witty, Paul A. (guest ed.): "Reading and the Underprivileged," *Education,* vol. 85, pp. 450–506, April, 1965.

50. Zintz, Miles V.: "Developing a Communication Skills Program for Bilinguals," in Ruth Strang (ed.), *Understanding and Helping the Retarded Reader,* University of Arizona Press, Tucson, Ariz., 1965, pp. 64–75.

51. Zintz, Miles V., and Maurine Yandell: "Some Difficulties Which Indian Children Encounter with Idioms in Reading," *The Reading Teacher,* vol. 14, pp. 256–259, March, 1961.

severe reading

disability

chapter 15

Some reading problems seem to be secondary to emotional or neurological problems. The classroom teacher uses his best methods of guidance and instruction, but without apparent success. The pupil's inability to concentrate, to comprehend, and to remember are external evidences of his basic inability to cope with social and emotional stress or to respond to instruction. These cases usually involve a complex of constitutional, environmental, and psychological factors. In the effort to create the most favorable classroom conditions possible, the teacher may seek the assistance of an educational or clinical psychologist or a child psychiatrist, if such help is available.

This chapter will point out symptoms of severe reading disability that can be observed in the classroom and will offer suggestions for carrying out an educational program for these pupils. It will also call to your attention the basic importance of a constructive, meaningful relationship between the teacher and the pupil.

From the repertory of teaching techniques that you have already acquired, you will select those that seem most appropriate in the light of understanding of these severe learning disorders.

READING DIFFICULTIES STEMMING FROM EMOTIONAL PROBLEMS

Among retarded readers we find many different types of disturbances; these children should not be lumped together under the label of "emotionally handicapped." We find passive children who simply give up in the face of a reading task. They think of themselves as children who cannot learn to read; this self-concept is central to their reading problem. They often say, "I'm just an average kid," "I'm no good," "Why try? I can't do it." These children are often called lazy. Some may have started life with a low energy level; some may have been deprived of perceptual stimulation at a crucial stage of their development; others may have had their curiosity suppressed; still others may have lacked opportunities for normal language development. Their parents may have been either overdemanding or overindulgent.

Children who are extremely aggressive or hyperactive expend their energy in "acting out" their tensions rather than in trying to reach a goal. They have difficulty in adjusting to school. Their difficulty in learning is explained in part by their tendency to respond on a perceptual-motor level rather than on a symbolic level. Failure in beginning reading only serves to increase their antagonism toward school and teachers.

"Withdrawn" children are highly disturbed in their social relations. They live in a fantasy world of their own. Unless they learn at an early stage to cope successfully with school tasks, their marks will decline as they go through the grades.

In some cases emotional difficulties have prevented the child from learning to read; in other cases they are preventing him from using the reading ability he has; in a few cases they are at present making him inaccessible to reading instruction. In the study of emotional problems, less emphasis is now being placed on unconscious motivation. Instead, investigators seek evidence of (1) a failure at some stage of the child's development and/or (2) a confusion in his thought pattern or cognitive structure, which is an important determinant of what he learns from his environmental experiences.

Two Cases of Emotional Disturbance

Lois, a bright-eyed ten-year-old who was popular with her classmates, was two years retarded in reading. She was excellent in arithmetic and other kinds of school work that did not involve much reading. Her reading level was barely equal to that of a second grader.

A history of her reading problem disclosed the fact that her father had attempted to teach her to read before she started school. He had bought a copy of a beginning reader; he would sit down with Lois each day to give her a reading lesson. The lesson invariably ended in tears; she became violently angry and upset because she could not learn to read as rapidly as her father thought she should. By the time she started school, she had grown so emotionally disturbed about reading that she could not accept the guidance of her teachers or keep up with her classmates.

The solution of the problem involved, first of all, reducing her emotional reaction to reading by selecting tasks that she could perform successfully in a secure pupil-teacher relationship. After building on her strengths for a while, the reading teacher found that Lois was able to attack her difficulties step by step with little failure or frustration. In an interview with the father, the teacher tactfully enlisted his cooperation in an "experiment": he agreed to leave reading instruction to the school, and, if reading were mentioned at all, to associate it only with pleasant experiences.

Aarenson has described a child who was much more seriously disturbed. Eugene was diagnosed as having "an intense passive-aggressive personality trait disorder with possible underlay of schizophrenia and a suggestion of organic impairment" [1, p. 92]. At nine years of age he was functionally a non-reader. Though he scored within the normal limits on the Wechsler Intelligence Scale for Children, his verbal and performance scores showed a discrepancy of 33 IQ points.

It was then decided that Eugene was to receive help twice weekly—in two 50-minute periods. He was extremely anxious in a learning situation; he communicated with difficulty, in monosyllables. He either guessed impulsively or failed to respond at all. It seemed as though he found words so loaded with personal emotional content that he could not even look at them.

In the initial treatments he chose stories for the worker to read to him and frequently played with blocks, clay, or other manipulative materials. As his anxiety decreased, he gained greater physical control and soon began to engage in reading activities. Using the Fernald kinesthetic approach, the teacher wrote his first reading material—stories embodying the words he had learned. From these, he progressed to preprimers. He began to learn specific phonic elements "by a combined auditory, visual, and kinesthetic approach, using games, puzzles, etc., to enhance interest and focus attention" [1, p. 93].

After eight months of work in this program, he had learned most of the initial consonant sounds and had developed an adequate basic vocabulary. Although his progress in reading was uneven and slow, "the change in his attitude was quite dramatic" [1, p. 93]. After he had learned to work successfully with another child—an ability he had lacked in the beginning—he began to improve in all areas.

After two and a half years of remedial help "he could read with fluency and ease on the second grade level." He increased 20 points in IQ on the WISC and "appears to be making an adequate adjustment to his situation at home and school" [1, p. 94].

Characteristics of Emotionally Blocked Readers

Among the characteristics that have been most observed in reading cases are anxiety, fear, tension, withdrawal of effort, lack of sustained attention, antagonism to school, compensatory interests, and general lack of emotional and social responsiveness. The majority of the severe reading cases that have been reported seem to be shy and withdrawn; they lack drive, initiative, and interest in reading. They are often submissive, insecure, and apprehensive. A few show aggressive behavior [46]. Any of these emotional responses may be either a cause or a result of failure in reading.

Anxiety seems to be a dominant characteristic. It may be reflected in slow reading, little understanding, and poor recall of content. In Gregory's [20] study of children eight to ten years old, anxiety and restlessness appeared to be contributing causes of reading failure. Among the children whose reading problems were not very severe, he found few symptoms of anxiety. On a higher level, the Minnesota Multiphasic Personality Inventory suggested a marked personality difference between men and women college students. The men showed many characteristics of poor adjustment, especially difficulty in social relations. The poor readers among the women students, on the other hand, seemed somewhat better adjusted than typical freshmen women [41].

Although the Rorschach test does not always distinguish good readers from poor readers [27], it has been valuable in studying personality patterns. Gann [18] studied superior, average, and retarded readers in grades 3 to 6 who were matched as to chronological age, IQ, mental age, school experience, and sex. Using the Rorschach method as the main measure of personality organization, she found indications that the retarded readers were less stable than the good readers, not so well adjusted emotionally, less adaptable socially, more fearful and less secure in the face of challenges, less efficient in the use of their potential mental capacity, and more concerned with small detail.

From an analysis of Rorschach tests administered to 309 boys and girls between the ages of six to fifteen, all of whom were retarded readers, Vorhaus

[61] found four unique configurations or patterns of response, each of which occurred in 72 per cent of all the test results. These configurations were as follows:

1. The individual's principal way of adapting to life is to repress his inner drives. This inhibits growth; he lacks spontaneity.
2. The individual lacks emotional responsiveness to the external world. The pleasure drives he feels are not acted out.
3. The creativity which the individual possesses has no outlet. He may respond submissively but feel rebellious. He can achieve but refuses to do so.
4. The individual is responsive to stimulation but feels that it is necessary to repress these strong feelings. He is afraid of his feelings of anger and may turn them inward against himself.

Similar characteristics were reported in a study of thirty-five fourth-grade children [51]. When aggressive drives are disciplined away, the impulse to read may also vanish. When children cannot express their feelings openly, they may channel them into resistance to learning. These clinical cases of reading deficiency appeared to be predominantly passive and unable to put forth the effort that reading demands. On the Rosenzweig Picture-Frustration Study, however, retarded readers revealed more than average hostility and aggression toward others [52].

These two apparently conflicting clinical pictures—one showing passivity and the other hostility—may actually be complementary. The retarded reader is one whose self-esteem has been damaged by experiences with adults. He would naturally feel resentful and hostile. But he would also feel weak and incapable—passive and in need of being told what to do. Some situations would evoke the passivity-dependency pattern and others the hostility-resistance pattern.

Relation between Emotional Difficulty and Reading

Reading difficulty may be a symptom of underlying emotional conflict. On the other hand, inability to read may itself create emotional problems. The incidence of emotional involvement in reading cases has been variously estimated at 6 to 75 per cent or even higher. Severe cases of reading disability show some degree of emotional involvement. Of the 114 emotionally disturbed children in a mental hospital, 75 per cent were from one month to three years below their mental ages in reading [48]. In interpreting clinical findings one must remember that children referred to clinics are not a representative sampling. They may be referred primarily because of emotional problems rather than reading difficulties.

Emotional problems may have as surface manifestations complaints such as, "I read too slow," "I can't remember what I read," "I can't concentrate," "I read word by word," I feel tired when I begin to read," "I don't understand what I read." On a deeper level these children may have fears of making mistakes, of failing, of having people know how poorly they read, of growing up; they may lack self-confidence; they may conceive of themselves as persons who cannot learn; they may be suppressing feelings or be unable to take responsibility for choices; they may be resistant to learning, may refuse to allow another will to be superimposed upon them; they may be determined to be themselves; they may be unwilling to do anything unless it can be perfect; they may have a chronic feeling of failure and a consequent reluctance to attempt anything; they may have fear of success, or a greater need for attention than for achievement [16].

Challman [12] suggested three principal ways of accounting for the relationship between emotional difficulties and reading problems:

1. Frequently, unfavorable conditions cause reading failure and consequent emotional problems:

Unfavorable home and school conditions $\longrightarrow$ Reading failure $\longrightarrow$ Emotional problems

Unfavorable school and home conditions or physical defects may give rise to an initial reading difficulty which soon begins to have emotional repercussions. The potential reading failure "may enter school as an unhappy child who cannot free his energies for learning, or he may enter as a happy, well-adjusted child who fails to learn to read and becomes maladjusted because of his failure" [47, p. 25].

Initial failure to learn to read may affect the child's relations with his parents, depending upon how much value they place on reading achievement. To fail in reading is to fail in one of the most important developmental tasks, as many parents and teachers see it. Sensing this, the child becomes insecure, anxious, tense—conditions that further defeat his attempts to read. Being labeled "a retarded reader" or sent prematurely to a reading clinic may even make a reading case out of a child who has really shown only normal errors in the process of learning to read. The anxiety that parents and teachers feel about a child who does not learn to read may be transferred to the child himself; this will further retard his learning processes.

The child's social relations with his classmates may also be affected; if the school atmosphere is highly competitive, the poor reader feels humiliated. In his efforts to get his studying done, he may be deprived of normal social activities.

As the child continues to fail in reading, he becomes more and more emotionally disturbed; the reading in each grade becomes more difficult, and other children show greater and greater superiority. When the causative factors are educational, it is not suprising that children respond well to an educational approach.

2. The second situation is one in which emotional factors lead to reading failure:

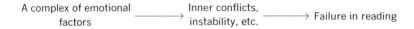

In some situations, inner conflicts and emotional instability may prevent an individual from concentrating on the reading process. He may not be accessible to instruction in reading until the emotional block has been removed. Resistance to reading may be a means of expressing hostility toward someone in the environment. This symptom calls attention to conditions that should be changed. Both reading difficulty and emotional disturbance may reflect underlying conditions that can be uncovered only by a thorough diagnostic study.

3. Reading disability and emotional problems usually have a reciprocal relation. There is a circular process:

Personality is a dynamic unity, a gestalt that embraces both emotional factors and reading performance. On the basis of a study of thirty-four children in residential treatment for emotional disturbance, Tamkin [56] suggested that the emotional problems and the educational disabilities may both have resulted from the same underlying conditions.

We must remember, too, that emotional responses are learned. If a given response causes tension or anxiety the individual tries to change it. If it is satisfying, he tends to persist in it.

Hewett [24] outlined a hierarchy of educational tasks suitable for emotionally disturbed children. The first essential is to establish meaningful contact between the teacher and the child. This is possible only when the child is finding some reward in the learning situation. Rewards range from the most basic and tangible—a piece of candy—to the most subtle and intangible—the respect of the teacher and one's classmates. Unlike other children, the disturbed child may be frightened by a competitive situation. The teacher's control may vary "from permissiveness in structuring to careful setting of behavioral limits and academic expectations" [24, p. 208]. Hewett describes the following levels on which teacher and child may interact:

1. When the child is "inaccessible to social controls or totally resistant to learning" the task he needs is the easiest task he can accomplish. For the older pupil the reward may be money, or tokens that will buy something he wants; for the younger child, candy or a toy. In their efforts to acquire such extrinsic rewards, many of these pupils learn to read.

2. When it is necessary to signify complete acceptance of the pupil, "the teacher sets few behavioral limits and usually works on a one-to-one basis with the child. The student competes only with his own records; no grades are given." The sessions include a variety of activities such as playing games and taking trips.

3. As the child begins to feel accepted and secure in his relationship with the teacher, the teacher can gradually increase his control; the child is ready to accept certain routine restrictions on the learning situation. Order and routine are particularly important for hyperactive childen who are easily distracted.

4. On the next higher level, exploratory tasks have a place. Teacher and child explore together the basic perceptual-motor responses involved in concrete learning experiences with arts and crafts, music, simple games, imaginative play, and story dramatizations. The Fernald method of kinesthetic word tracing and the daily writing of an experience story are also appropriate on this level.

5. On the next level, the child is concerned with gaining the recognition and approval of the teacher with whom he has established a genuine interpersonal relationship. To promote the development of peer relationships, the teacher may pair students and give more group instruction.

6. On the master level, the student is ready to deal with his deficiencies and begin acquiring the knowledge and skills he needs for a good life.

7. The highest level is reached when the student has become self-motivated and is able to realize his intellectual potential.

Reading and the Dynamics of Personality

Some reading difficulties seem to have their roots in infancy. Some seem to originate during the years when the child is struggling to move away from the complete dependency of babyhood. Other reading difficulties can be traced to home and school conditions that prevailed at about the time the child was learning to read. Still others stem from various disturbed family and school relationships. Let us attempt here to suggest the dynamics that obtain in some of these patterns.

Pattern 1. During the first few months of life the infant gains impressions that may affect his later modes of response. For example, let us suppose that during his first six months he cries and cries—the only method he knows to relieve his physical or psychological discomfort—and no one comes. He may in some vague way become convinced that it is futile for him to put forth effort; he may become apathetic. If his subsequent life experiences reinforce this initial impression, apathy may become his habitual response.

That this feeling of inadequacy and dependency may be related to reading inability is suggested in a number of reading cases. For example, at sixteen years of age Jane was shy and extremely apathetic about reading. Since she had experienced nothing but failure, she disliked school and teachers. She took no initiative about overcoming her reading and writing difficulties. Nothing the worker suggested aroused any interest or effort. This apathy seemed to be beyond her conscious control. She liked the worker but seemed unable to establish any fundamental relationship with her [55, p. 131].

Pattern 2. The child who fails to develop the independence that is normal for his age may reflect a general immaturity in his reading [55, pp. 131–132]:

Sooner or later, perhaps around three years of age, the child who thus far has enjoyed his dependency and freedom to follow his own natural rhythms meets with greater pressure to conform to the ways of civilized life and to his parents' expectations. The way in which he adjusts to this deflation of his idea of his own omnipotence may affect his future learning. When faced with the necessary restrictions of life, he may respond in either of two extreme ways: (a) accept dependency on his parents to keep his sense of security or (b) try to maintain his exalted self-concept by his own efforts, at the expense of security. The person who has a healthy personality achieves a gradual revision of his sense of omnipotence in the framework of a supportive relationship. He attains security through self-realization, not through submissive dependency. This kind of security is fostered by parents who help the child to do things for himself; thus he comes to regard himself as a competent person who is able to incorporate new values into his old value system.

Reading problems seem to arise predominantly from the submissive pattern— in children who have clung to this dependent relation for security. Since they do not feel obliged to maintain a flaunted independence or a high level of aspiration, these individuals assume an attitude of emotional subordination and conform passively to the demands of their parents and teachers.

Pattern 3. The dynamics of family attitudes and relationships throw light on reading problems. One pattern has as its central feature a home that withholds love from the child or rejects him unless he meets its high standards with respect to learning to read. Sometimes, by extreme effort, a child may achieve status in such a home. More frequently he outwardly conforms to its demands while resisting inwardly. This inner conflict produces an apathy that prevents him from putting forth the necessary effort. In suppressing his rebellion, he also suppresses spontaneity and enthusiasm. Nonreading may become an expresssion of unconscious resistance to learning, a symbol of his will to assert himself [30, 61].

Pattern 4. The child is from a home where the mother is openly hostile, critical, nervous, easily angered; she punishes the child for his school failures.

The father seldom shows fondness for the child. In addition, the child may be jealous of a baby who came at about the time he was learning to read [37].

Pattern 5. The child has a mother who, while not openly hostile, is tense and overprotective. Overprotection tends to suppress a child's natural eagerness to learn. When too little is expected of him, he grows to expect little of himself. The child may have been overindulged during the preschool years and neglected when he reached school age. The mother may also be insidiously coercive; she demands perfect obedience. Any attempt to force a child to be a credit to the family may evoke resistance if it is not accompanied by real affection and concern for the child as a person. A slow child whose parents or teachers constantly prod him to hurry will tend to develop either anxiety or negativistic attitudes toward reading. In most of these cases the father shows little fondness for the child. Missildine studied thirty children with reading disabilities who were normal in intelligence, sight, and hearing; all were emotionally upset by their relations with someone in the family [37]. Failure to read may be a neurotic symptom rather than inability to learn. The child who suppresses his curiosity may be suppressing his potential reading ability [30].

Pattern 6. A great variety of conditions may make a child unhappy. He may be bothered by his parents' quarreling, concerned over a possible or actual divorce, upset by rivalry with a brighter brother or sister. Missildine [37, p. 266] reported the case of a ten-year-old boy with an IQ of 117 in the low fourth grade who misbehaved in class, talked out of turn, continuously annoyed the teacher, was sent to the principal's office twice a week. Since the first grade he had stuttered and had difficulty in reading. He read slowly and uncertainly, with no reversals but with many errors and spontaneous corrections. According to the physician's summary, the problem originated when the child was between five and six years old. Until then he had been overprotected by a cold, rejecting mother and had had all the attention of his maternal grandparents; just when a new baby was born, he was pushed off to school. He showed his resentment by his behavior. "His reaction of remonstrance had started a campaign of condemnation which completely cowed and crushed the boy. He lost all confidence in himself. The child's difficulties are the result of, and reactions to, a maternal attitude of cold hostility" [37, p. 266].

The cause of Helen's problem was more obscure [55, p. 133]:

Her background was socially, economically, and culturally favorable. She could carry on an interesting, pleasant conversation; her oral vocabulary was superior; her IQ on the Stanford-Binet test was 111. Yet, at sixteen years of age, she was reading below the fourth-grade level. The central factors interfering with her improvement in reading seemed to be deep-seated anxiety, complete confusion in word recognition, and a concept of herself as a person who could not learn to read. In school she was greatly embarrassed by her poor oral reading; in the individual conferences at the Reading Center she constantly tried to cover up her inability to recognize words, making wild guesses in preference to admitting that she did not know the word. Her mother and some of her teachers took a hopeless attitude toward her. In school she was passed from grade to grade without showing evidence of achievement. Accordingly, problems accumulated as texts increased in difficulty, and everything combined to increase her own feeling of hopelessness and her anxiety to maintain her social position in her family and with her age group. To all outward appearances, Helen was a charming, well-adjusted adolescent, but her severe reading and spelling disability and one response on the Rorschach test indicated some serious disturbance of what otherwise seemed to be a healthy personality.

Reading difficulties in this case may be considered as symptoms of underlying emotional tensions that blocked learning [35, p. 33].[1]

It seems, therefore, that these failures in the language arts, no matter which personality syndrome they show, are basically insecure, worried, anxious children who are more concerned, often on an unconscious level, about basic emotional problems in their lives, than they are about the difference between a "b" and a "d" or between "was" and "saw." As one very immature ten-year-old boy said in one of his therapeutic sessions, in which he frankly verbalized about his jealousy of his preschool sister, "I just can't wait to get home from school to see what my mother and sister are doing. I'm afraid they will do something behind my back. I just can't think with all these things on my mind.

Pattern 7. Parental attitudes, social pressures, and poor social adjustment may combine to produce an overemphasis on reading that interferes with the development of a healthy personality [55, pp. 133–134].

Initially testing high in mental ability, Joan had attained by 12 years 8 months a mental age of 17 years 2 months, IQ 183, and a score of 113 on the Iowa Silent Reading Test, the highest in her class and equivalent to a percentile rank of 99 in grade eleven. Her own comment, "I read everything. I can't tell if it's good, but I read it anyway. . . . My reading is and always has been almost omnivorous, if not quite," was borne out by her reading record. She entitled her reading autobiography, "Bred on Books." Her preschool years were rich in intellectual stimulation; very poor in human relations. She early turned to books as a solace. Unsuccessful in making friends in school, and lacking social acceptance by the group, she withdrew still further into books. In the fourth grade she was very unpopular; in the seventh and eighth grades she was respected for her mental ability, but was not a participant in the social life of the group. This unusual case illustrates how excessive reading as well as retarded reading may be a symptom of personality disturbance.

Wollner [63] described this case in more detail.

[1] Reprinted with permission of Dorothea McCarthy and the International Reading Association.

There are innumerable variations in the patterns of causation that underlie both reading and personality problems. In fact, each case is unique. However, the experience of clinical workers will help others to gain a better understanding of the individual who has reading and/or personality problems and to create more favorable conditions for him.

The Role of the Self-concept. Many reading cases feel hopeless about themselves and about learning to read. We get clues to their feelings in such comments as these:

I can't read, I can't write, I can't learn words.
I just can't get the words, I guess at them and then they are wrong.
I'm the black sheep of the family; I guess every family has to have one black sheep.

Such self-concepts are learned. They are built up in many subtle ways. They derive, in part, from the negative comments of parents, teachers, and classmates and from repeated experiences of failure. The child or young person becomes fearful of making mistakes, afraid and ashamed to be wrong again. Self-confidence, on the other hand, arises when others show a positive expectancy that the individual can close the gap between his present performance and his potential; it is reinforced by experiences of success.

The individual's approach to reading is profoundly affected by his self-concept. By helping students to change their self-concepts we can help them to change their ways. However, this is more easily said than done; one's self-concept is deep-rooted and persistent. It can be changed only by repeated experiences of success. The role of the reading teacher is to provide materials and instruction that will enable the student to see his own progress and gain recognition and approval from the persons who are significant in his life. In a study of the members of a college reading class, Roth [50] reported significant differences in the self-perceptions of those who improved, those who did not improve, and those who dropped out of the course. It seems that both those who achieve and those who fail to achieve "do so as a result of the needs of their own self system" [50, p. 281].

Individual Treatment of Reading Cases

Referral of Cases. The manner in which the student is referred to the reading specialist or clinic largely determines the success of the first interview. The reading service should be presented to the individual as an opportunity to understand his reading—to find out how he reads, what is preventing him from reading better, and how he may improve. He decides whether to take advantage of the opportunity. The attitude of teachers and other students toward the reading service strongly affects its reputation. Those who are scheduled for individual work should never feel inferior or deficient because of the referral.

The recognition that a reading difficulty is accompanied by emotional disturbances does not necessarily imply that the case should be referred to a psychologist or a psychiatrist. Most problems are not severe enough to warrant this. They can be treated by the psychologically oriented reading specialist. Over a period of time he helps the individual to gain some understanding of the conditions that are contributing to his reading difficulties and to learn techniques for handling them. He talks with the student's teacher about adjustments she can make in the classroom. If the emotional problems are beyond his competence, referral is indicated. If the requisite service cannot be obtained within the school system, the specialist should investigate community resources, such as a nearby university, a mental hospital, or a county or state cooperative board.

Initial Interviews with Parents. A student is frequently referred by a parent, a counselor, or a teacher who is concerned about his reading. The adult who comes with the client in his first interview should usually be interviewed alone. Otherwise he may pour forth all his criticisms of the child in the child's presence and thus intensify his feeling of inferiority and inadequacy. This kind of unfortunate introduction makes it more difficult for the worker to win the client's acceptance and confidence.

When the worker interviews the adult privately, he may obtain considerable understanding of the case. In an interview with the intelligent father of a tenth-grade pupil the worker learned much about the girl's reading problem. Mr. R had brought his daughter to the reading center for a study of her reading difficulty. The worker gave him the opportunity to present the problem in his own way by asking what it was that concerned him.

Mr. R: She reads very slowly, in fact, far too slowly to get anywhere with her studies or anything of that sort. She passes her work, but it requires a great deal of her time on things where there is much reading involved. We know that we should have done something about it much sooner. In her last year in grammar school she came home and reported to us that in the reading tests they had given at the school, she was far below the average of the class. Her speed of reading in the eighth grade was the equivalent of the fifth- or sixth-grade student. . . . We thought at first that it was mainly because she hadn't done as much reading as she should have. When she was much younger, she was constantly urged to read more. She didn't enjoy reading, probably because she read slowly. By the time she got anywhere, she'd lost interest. . . . I think she is a bright enough child. . . . As the matter stands now, she is just not able to complete the homework assignments that she is given.

Worker: Does that upset her? Does it bother her when she can't do them?

Mr. R: Well, naturally is does. She is conscientious. It isn't that it's causing a psychological difficulty if that is what you are driving at. I don't think it is causing her to become a psychological misfit.

Worker: I don't mean anything abnormal. Worry does take away from one's energy. It is energy spent in a not very fruitful way. If she worries, then it takes energy away from her work. . . .

Mr. R: I'm sure that anyone making the diagnosis would have her complete cooperation. I think she is much older in her actions than most. She is more mature.

Worker: What makes you say that? Could you give me a better idea?

Mr. R: She takes much greater individual responsibility than most girls do. She is quite a leader. I think it is because of home environment. She is the youngest of four and enters into the family conversation on social, political, and other subjects.

Worker: Is she the only one of your four who has had difficulty with reading?

Mr. R: Her sisters and brothers who went to the school to which she is now going made excellent records for themselves, and I do believe that she is under pressure a bit because of this.

Worker: They made standards for her to follow? Is that it?

Mr. R: Sometimes the teachers throw it up to her. Even now, although it is some years since her sisters were there, some of the teachers who knew them expect wonderful things immediately upon seeing her in the class. One sister was valedictorian. Both sisters were not only very capable in school work, but were also leaders in extracurricular activities and were very popular there.

Worker: Is there anything else that you think would be of help for us to know?

Mr. R: No, I think I've probably described her as well as I can. I do think that you would agree with me that she is much more mature than her age indicates. . . . Her interests are quite mature. Of course, we have quite a group of young people about the same age. She conducts herself with as much decorum as the average. I mean, where it is necessary, for instance, almost to step on the necks of some of the kids to maintain any discipline, she will be the one to maintain the discipline. She has a more mature interest. She will take an interest in such things as a housing problem or a social problem, or things that the average person of that age isn't concerned with, and she will be able to discuss them fairly intelligently.

Worker: Thank you very much for explaining it so clearly, and I'll write to you soon.

Mr. R: I'm happy to have had the chance to talk it over with you.

This conference with the father brought out several factors that had a possible relationship to B's reading difficulty. Perhaps the father overcame some of his anxiety by talking about B objectively to an understanding listener. He obtained an idea of the nature of the service offered and could present it to B in such a way as to win her interest and cooperation. He also obtained the necessary specific information as to time, place, and fees. At the end of the interview the worker's word of appreciation strengthened the friendly relation that had developed.

In conferences of this type, parents often pass through three phases. First they pour forth a flood of negative comments about everything that is wrong with the child and with the school. In this phase they are usually thinking of themselves and their disappointment that the child is not being a credit to them. If the interviewer is able to direct their attention to the child by skillful interpretation, the parents will often begin to speak of some of the child's good qualities. Toward the end of the interview they may, with or without the interviewer's suggestions, decide on one or two desirable changes they can make in their behavior. Even though this is all that can be accomplished in the single contact, it often produces good results with parents who are genuinely fond of their children. They may begin to shift their attention from themselves to the child; they may perceive him differently. And when they later make some favorable change in their behavior, they set up a beneficial circular response—the child responds to their changed behavior and they, in turn, respond to the improvement in the child.

Initial Interviews with Clients. There is no one best approach. The approach varies with the client's attitude and also with the personality and orientation of the worker. Every individual has different expectations and different needs. Some are antagonistic to reading or deeply anxious about their inability to read. The worker encourages them to bring these negative feelings out in the open, as in this first interview with Jim, a nineteen-old boy.

Jim: I have to learn how to express myself. I just can't express myself. . . . I always stress the least important thing. I read slowly, very slowly. (Pause.) But I get down to it. A lot of times I do! I am at my desk for hours but I can't concentrate.

Worker: What are you thinking about when you can't concentrate?

Jim: Everything I have to do is on my mind until I finish it. . . . I have great satisfaction in finishing things. I like to finish things and be prepared for my work. If I go to class unprepared, I concentrate on being afraid rather than on what goes on in class. (Pause.) So, you don't know what to say if the teacher calls on you. And if he doesn't call on you, you're listening to what they're saying but you don't know what they mean.

Fears and anxieties are somewhat alleviated if they are discussed in a secure relationship. Such discussion also gives the worker a better understanding of the problem. If the client's fear of reading is very great, the worker may start with a visual screening test; this will establish a friendly relation without bringing into the situation the emotional feelings associated with previous failures in reading. Boys and girls usually respond with interest to these tests.

Some clients forget their anxieties and gain new hope that improvement is possible as they turn their attention to visual factors or use an unfamiliar gadget.

An approach that is effective with individuals who like books is to place on a table a number of books on different subjects and on varying levels of reading difficulty and let the client browse through them; meanwhile the worker busies himself with something else but also notes the client's responses. After the client has examined the books, he may be asked to read a few paragraphs from the book he has selected. If he reads these fluently, he can be tested on a more difficult book until his level of reading ability is approximately ascertained. This procedure is also valuable in establishing a friendly relationship and in supplying information on reading interests and attitudes. Discussion of these books may lead to conversation about the student's interests in general, the way he uses his time, and his reading difficulty as he sees it.

If the individual comes with the idea that he is going to take reading tests and find out what his reading ability is, the worker may begin the interview with an oral-reading test and follow it with a silent-reading test. In this interview, if time permits—if not, in the next—the worker can score the tests with the client, study the errors, encourage him to figure out how he happened to make these errors, and give him a few suggestions about reading this kind of material more effectively. The client's interest in his test results often increases his eagerness to do something about them.

A mature, intelligent student may want to spend the first interview thinking through his reading problem for himself. The role of the worker then becomes that of a sympathetic listener who occasionally asks a question or offers an interpretation when the client seems ready for it.

A good approach with seriously retarded readers who are deeply discouraged about their reading but very anxious to improve may be to give them the experience of success in the first interview. This was done in the case of a boy seventeen and a half years old who had good oral vocabulary and conversational ability but was practically a nonreader. Excerpts from the first interview follow:

Worker: Mr. L tells me you're interested in learning to read.
E: Yes, I'll be in the Army in about five months, and every time I go for a job, I have to do some reading and writing.
Worker: Tell me some word in which you are particularly interested.
E: *Guns*, I guess. Guns are my hobby.
Worker: Fine. Let's learn to write *guns*. (Worker writes *guns* with crayon in large letters on card. E traces letters with finger, pronouncing the word correctly as he does so. He repeats this process several times [Fernald method].) Now you can write it without looking at the copy. (E writes word correctly.) That's just fine. Now let's try *are*. (E traces this word four times and then writes it correctly. He does the same with *my*.) The next word is *hobby*.

E: Oh, I don't think I can do that one.

Worker: Sure you can. Try it. (Worker pronounces it clearly in syllables as he writes it. Then E traces it five times.)

E: Now I think I can write it. (Does so correctly.)

Worker: That's *very* good. Do you want to write it again without looking? (E does so correctly.) Now you know the whole sentence. You can write it all now.

E: Without looking?

Worker: Sure. . . .

E: OK. (Writes entire sentence omitting *my.*)

(They talked for a little while; E told about his collection of matches and the collection of gun catalogs that he had made while he was in the hospital. He had been hospitalized for a number of years for infantile paralysis.)

Worker: Would you like to write another sentence today about getting the catalogs or would you rather wait until next time?

E: Let's go. (Using the same method, he learns the words of the next sentence—*I had catalogs from every gun industry in the country.*)

Worker: Now, for the whole sentence. (E writes the first two words and hesitates on *catalogs.*) Just skip that and go on with the rest of the sentence. (He finishes the sentence correctly except for putting *g* instead of *n* in *gun* and *nu* instead of *un* in *country.* After practicing *catalogs* again, he writes it correctly.) Now the sentence is 100 per cent perfect. Will you file the cards while I have your three sentences typed?

E: Sure. I know how to file them in the card catalog. (He does this correctly.)

(The worker had the three sentences typed in booklet form with the title "Guns" and the boy's name on the outside page. The "book" read—

    Guns are my hobby.
    I would like
    to make a collection.
      I had catalogs
    from every gun industry
    in the country.)

Worker: Now, here's your book in typed form. Let's hear you read it just as though you were talking to me. (E reads it fluently and with great pleasure.)

(They talked for a few minutes about skeet shooting. The worker was interested and said he had never known so much about that before.)

E: Gee, you learned something, too.

In this interview the objective was to help E acquire an initial feeling of confidence and success in reading and writing, beginning with words that had special interest for him and that would be a start toward a basic sight vocabulary. By using his own conversation as reading material, he gained a sense of reading fluency. His interest and enjoyment in the learning process were indicated by such comments as, "Ain't we got fun!" which he repeated several time, and, "Now I think I can do it." The casual conversation about his interests and future plans not only prevented fatigue but helped to give

E a sense of direction and a more accurate and hopeful appraisal of himself. The Wechsler-Bellevue test indicated that this nonreader had potential ability to read at about the fourth-grade level. The changed self-concept that arose from the counseling relation and from his success in learning to read made it possible for him to realize his reading potentialities.

The client may gain understanding of himself by trying to express his thoughts and feelings. This is illustrated in the case of Gene. Despite the counselor's overinsistence that Gene think things through himself, the boy nevertheless was able to analyze his reading problem far better than he had thought possible. Here are a few excerpts from the first interview.

Worker: Well, suppose we begin by your telling me why you're here, Gene.
Gene: Well, I guess I'm here to learn something—how to read.
Worker: What else?
Gene: That's about all I know.
Worker: How do you feel about coming here?
Gene: How do I feel about coming? Let's see. I don't know what to say. . . .
Worker: What are you thinking?
Gene: I'm not thinking of nothing now. Just relaxing. . . . What do you usually teach the children?
Worker: It depends on what they need. You would need some things; others would need something else. That's the way it goes.
Gene: Yeah.
Worker: That's why I wondered if we could get at what you feel you need.
Gene: You know, it's funny. Sometimes when I'm reading there isn't any word there. I put 'em in there, like small words, like *we* and all that.
Worker: You stick them in?
Gene: Yeah, it sounds better to me. . . .
Worker: Tell me more.
Gene: Sometimes when I'm reading there I come to the end of a sentence. You know, instead of stopping for a few seconds I go right on. When I come to a question mark, I just keep on going. . . .
Worker: That's good to know. You notice these things yourself?
Gene: Yeah.
Worker: What else have you noticed?
Gene: Let me think. (Pause.) Sometimes I'm reading . . . a word like *there* and *their*. I don't see the difference there. So they both sound the same to me. . . .
Worker: Uh-hum.
Gene: Let me see. Of course, there's one thing I don't like. When you're reading out loud, and come to a word and you can't pronounce it, and the teacher tells me what it is.
Worker: Oh yes.
Gene: I'd like to figure it out myself.
Worker: How do you feel when this happens?
Gene: Well, with the kids in my class I don't feel much ashamed, 'cause they

can hardly even read. Some of them can't read little words. It's true that when you're reading, you get it all mixed up, like oh, some of those little words.

Worker: Sometimes little words are more troublesome than big.

Gene: Yeah, big words you can get little by little.

Worker: Those were very good observations. Not many people can see their own reading as clearly as that. Anything else you can think of?

In the course of this interview the boy made progress, which became apparent to him as the worker praised his efforts to understand his reading. This newly acquired skill in thinking about his problems was more important than the actual information he gained.

Some clients are too much disturbed emotionally to begin work right away on the reading problem. Initial interviews with these cases focus on why they are coming for help; how they feel about themselves, their families, and school; what they are thinking. This approach is well illustrated by four initial interviews presented and discussed by Ephron in her book *Emotional Difficulties in Reading* [16], a *must* for everyone who wants to improve the quality of his reading casework.

These are only a few examples of the great variety of possible approaches to individual reading difficulties. There is no general principle except to maintain sensitivity to the person who is being helped to realize his best potentialities. The objectives of the first interview, in general, are:

To establish a friendly relationship

To feel with the client when he indicates anxiety about coming for help, or shame about being teased and laughed at because of his poor reading

To gain some understanding of his reading difficulty, oral vocabulary, and interests

To obtain some clues as to the reasons for his retardation in reading

To be sure that the client has, at the end of the interview, a feeling of satisfaction and a sense of having accomplished something

These objectives may be accomplished in many ways. Try to make physical conditions, such as lighting, pleasant and comfortable. It is good practice to sit beside the client rather than across the table from him. It is most important in any interview to treat him with courtesy and consideration; let him present himself and his reading problem in his own way; encourage his spontaneous comments; be continuously sensitive to his feelings, such as anxiety about being different or deficient; and be relaxed and confident, not insecure, about your ability to help him. If the client feels anxious or uncertain about the situation or associates you with repressive authority, it is necessary to describe or structure the situation, briefly explaining your role and his responsibility.

Subsequent Interviews.   The interviews following the first contact will be as diverse as the needs of the clients. Many different approaches are presented in the detailed reports of cases that are given in the references at the end of this chapter. Here we shall get only a few glimpses of reading cases.

Use of the reading autobiography [31, 54]. A history of the student's reading development as he views it—either orally or in writing, depending on which avenue of communication is preferred—often throws light on the best procedures to use. In some cases the autobiography may be limited primarily to reading per se; in other cases, as in the following, the child's interests and family relationships have a most important bearing on her reading development.[2]

Fifteen years ago a baby girl was born to a school principal and his wife. When the baby's sister, who was about ten, first viewed this little red ball, her reaction was a grown of disappointment. That homely, red baby was I.

Of the town of my birth I remember very little as we soon moved to another town. There I played in our great, big yard for four years. I had short, straight hair and was seldom seen, when not wearing overalls. I did not play with girls, as boys games, and toys appealed to me more. The boy across the street, was my best pal. We played with his electric trains and made airplanes together.

I played mostly with boys until I was about eight years old when I joined the Sunshine Club. It was a girls' organization. They served cocoa every meeting. That was the only reason I attended. It was always I that would not obey. Probably this was dew to the fact that the heads of the organization always told me to set a good example as I was the principal's daughter. I resented this very much and still do.

I attended public school for eight years. I always had a dislike for education and teachers. Consequently, I would never obey them. I walked out of the class several times. I was sent out of classes by three different teachers. One teacher literally through me out. She took me by the neck, opened the door and gave me a shove. I cannot account for my attitude toward teachers, except that one kept me until four thirty, after school, telling me I should be good because of my father's position.

I have been brought up in a family that is mentally allert, a family of broad minded people. I have always eaten at a table at which, problems of economics were discussed often. I've heard my brothers discuss contriversial subjects by the hour. It is only natural that I too would be somewhat interested in these things.

When I was fourteen years old one of my sisters was engaged to be married. She asked me to be Maid of Honnor. The wedding was held in the church. I received my first evening dress and high heals. I had a permanent wave too. You would not have known me that day. At the wedding I met a boy who invited me to attend a formal dance with him. It was my first dance. That summer he took me other places too. By fall practically all of my tomboy characteristics had vanished. I believe my sister's wedding was the beginning of a great change in me.

[2] This is the girl whose father's conference with a clinician was reported earlier in this chapter. Spelling, punctuation, and style are unchanged. As in reporting any case, names have been changed and identifying details omitted.

Now I am in high school. There are a great many things I regret. I wish that I had not waisted my time, fooling in grammar school. If I could live those years over, I would attend school with the purpose of obtaining everything I could possibly receive from it. I would spend my spare time reading masterpieces and not trash. . . .

Within me there seems to be a desire to serve mankind. I would like to do Social Service Work. If I did this, it would put me in a better position to do my part in abolishing slums. I realize this is a hard, depressing task. I would like to give those people an ideal, a reason for living well. Perhaps to some of the homes I might bring a note of Religion. I feel that the making of a man, and of a nation is based upon a strong, enduring faith in God.

Social Service or perhaps Religious Education work, would be the occupation I would choose if any. But I don't think I am unlike any other girl, when I would like to have a home. Most any other person would like to own there home, and bring up a family, they can be prowd of. This is something of course that cannot be counted on therefore I will train myself for Social Service. Unfortunately the future can not be foreseen.

In this autobiography the need for instruction in spelling first attracts our attention. Since the client recognized poor spelling as an academic handicap, she was glad to work on the words she misspelled in her written work and letters. The autobiography also indicated emerging interests and motivations which would make her receptive to reading instruction. A psychologically astute counselor might infer that she feels resentment toward people who want to make her different. Her interest in social service might stem from a personal need or reflect normal adolescent idealism. The worker began by trying to meet the girl's desire for help in reading and spelling, but was also alert to clues that might lead to a counseling relation.

Use of tests and observation of client's reading (see Chapters 4 and 5). If the client wants an appraisal of his reading, tests may be given. Standardized tests may be used more flexibly in a clinical setting than in a group, since the aim is to study the reading process. By analyzing the client's errors and his reflections on the causes or conditions that give rise to the difficulties, worker and client both gain insights into the reading problem. Specific instruction may also be based upon the analysis of test results.

Observation of the client as he reads an assignment accomplishes several ends. It helps both worker and client to understand the reading process; it gives the worker opportunity to give specific instruction; and it helps to lighten the load of an overburdened student.

Introducing instruction and practice. In most cases there is a place in the interview for instruction in reading or the other language arts. When a student is worried about his poor marks and fears failure, he wants expert help in reading and study methods. He is willing to talk about his problem up to a certain point; then he becomes impatient and wants to know what to do. Giving the instruction he needs helps to relieve his immediate distress. For example, in an interview with B, the worker asked her what she would like to do next; B laughed, a little puzzled, and said she would like to know where to begin—by trying to improve her spelling or by trying to improve her reading. The worker suggested the following procedure, which she could use independently to improve her spelling:

1. Ask someone to find the misspelled words in a letter or composition you have written, and make a list of them, all spelled correctly.
2. Study each of the misspelled words. Pronounce each correctly: write it one syllable at a time, saying the syllables distinctly as you write them; note the parts of the word that are hard for you and give special attention to them; write the word several times to get the feeling of how it is written correctly; close your eyes and write the word the way you feel it should be written, then check to see if you are correct; close your eyes and see if you can see how the word looked. When you are sure that you know how to spell the word, write it and check it for correctness. Practice until you have written the word correctly without help at least three times. Test yourself again each week until you never make a mistake.
3. Form the habit of looking closely at unfamiliar words; break them into syllables that you can spell easily.
4. If certain letters or letter combinations give you special difficulty, make a column for each item and fill the column with words that contain it, being sure that each word is spelled correctly—for example:

oa	*al*	*a*	*ou*
groan	alert	permanent	proud
moan	alternate	testament	loud

5. Play word-building games—anagrams, crossword puzzles—combining small words that you know into larger words.
6. Overpronounce some words that cause special difficulty:

perm *a* nent

priv *i* lege

Overburdened students especially appreciate instruction that is given in connection with their school or college assignments. For example, Miss M wanted help on writing a book report. When she tried to recall the main ideas, she showed some tendency to enlarge on trivial points. The worker helped her to see their subordinate relationship. After she had written the report, she said that it was the best and easiest review she had ever written.

In another period Miss M expressed dissatisfaction with her newspaper reading. "You see, I don't actually have time to read my newspaper thoroughly. I'd like to have help on that because I feel that so many important things are happening and I'm just not 'up' on them." The worker asked her if she would like to appraise her newspaper reading and radio and television listening according to a form used for analyzing attitudes toward reading and listening.

This they did, the worker asking the questions and presenting the alternative answers and Miss M replying orally. From this analysis, Miss M discovered that she did not cover enough ground because she read everything with equal care. She also did very little critical reading. Without a purpose for reading and listening, she did not select and remember important ideas.

The question might be raised: Why use interview time for instruction that could be given in a group? To be sure, the kind of instruction described here can also be given in the classroom. But many students, especially those who are emotionally disturbed, learn best in the highly personalized relation with the reading teacher. In the case of Miss M, instruction and practice were given in response to her recognized needs. Using some of the interview time to do class assignments is particularly helpful to students who are carrying heavy schedules; getting some of their studying done during the interview period helps to decrease their anxiety and tension.

Almost any procedure may be woven into an interview. The reading counselor needs a repertory of techniques and methods that he can use or adapt as they are appropriate and useful in the individual case.

Getting information needed to make and do things. With a nonacademic youngster who comes to the reading center with a strong aversion to reading, the opportunity to make a model airplane, construct a reading game, make a bookcase for the reading room, or engage in some other activity that does not involve reading is often disarming. Working with this client on something he can do successfully is an effective way of establishing a friendly relationship. Moreover, almost any activity requires reading—making a model plane requires ability to read directions; making a reading game involves writing and understanding certain words. And what good is an empty bookcase! Beginning with an interesting activity is one of the best ways to demonstrate to reluctant readers that reading has meaning, use, and purpose for them.

Finger painting and clay modeling. For some clients, finger painting or the free use of any plastic material helps to relieve tension; it provides an outlet for suppressed feeling; it also gives the psychologically trained worker clues to the emotional factors that may be contributing to the reading disability. Finger painting is a medium of expression, a way of saying things, a conscious or unconscious manifestation of personality, a starting point for free association. An individual will frequently express in the painting things that are bothering him in reading, in school, or in his family relations. The worker notes the way the client approaches the finger painting, whether gingerly with just a small dab, or in a big way with a great gob of color. He may derive some meaning from the lines, rhythms, colors, and content of each picture, or from the recurrence of themes in a series of pictures. He may learn most of all from the free associations stimulated by the projective media.

Puppetry. In work with individual cases as well as with groups, puppetry may contribute to the improvement of reading. It has the values already mentioned for finger painting and clay modeling and is especially useful in helping the emotionally disturbed child to express himself verbally. Several other children may be invited to share the interview time so that he may give a certain puppet play. The way the client spontaneously uses puppets also gives the worker more understanding of the content of his mind. The following excerpt from an original puppet play by emotionally disturbed boys shows how remote their thoughts may be from the polite, childish content of the usual reading material on their level [48, p. 58]:

SCENE ONE

(Man Standing beside Table)

Participants: Radio Voice, Man, Bookie, Woman

R: There is a blizzard. People are snowed in. We must fly food to them. (Man moves away from table.)

M: I got to get some money to send to my family. They are snowed in. Where can I get money? I'll find a bookie.
(Man exits as two other men enter.)

M: I want to place a bet, Bookie.

B: How much? (Man runs as a woman enters.)

W: How did you become a bookie?

B: Widow Brown, it goes way back to when I was a "wittie-bittie" child. I was hungry, Widow Brown.

W: Why don't you sing for money?

B: I can't, my voice is froggy. Listen. (He sings in a deep voice.)

When Al started to sing, Charles, who had been observing the show, started tap dancing and clowning to the tune that the bookie in the puppet show was singing. There was no complaint from Al, who continued as if he were the only person in the room.

Although puppetry lends itself best to small groups, it may sometimes be used effectively in individual conferences. With a hand puppet, a child may communicate to the worker thoughts and feelings he could not express in his own character. Doing this helps him to accept and clarify his feelings and work out acceptable ways of behaving.

Dramatization. Though dramatization, like puppetry, lends itself best to group situations, it can be used in individual conferences. Dramatization may take many forms: the reading of parts in a story, the reading of published plays, the reading of plays written especially for the client, and the acting out of original plays written by the client and transcribed from a role-playing situation. Dramatizing a story with the worker gives the client an opportunity to follow the worker's correct phrasing; it also gives him a stimulus to read with expression the conversation of the character he has chosen to represent.

Dramatizations that deal with personal problems often serve as a springboard for bringing out the client's feelings about his own problems. There are now available some mental-hygiene [53] and guidance plays [62] that contribute both to reading development and to personal development through reading. Role playing may be used effectively to help a client work out realistic ways of handling life situations.

Experience reading. With reading cases of any age it has repeatedly proved effective to have the client relate an interesting experience which the worker records and later types and uses as reading material for him.

Games. Preadolescents have a strong interest in games. The worker can take advantage of this to increase the client's satisfaction with the period as a whole. One or more other young clients may be invited to take part.

Finding the right reading material. With clinical cases, the improvement of reading depends to a large extent on finding suitable reading material. Workers must often spend a good deal of time looking for, or even writing, material that will meet the needs of an individual. For example, when one nineteen-year-old boy who was reading on the second-grade level expressed an interest in the Navy, the worker gave him the *Navy Life Reader* [39], which he could read successfully. Another worker gained rapport with a Puerto Rican boy who could read Spanish but not English by giving him a simple story that contained some Spanish words and phrases. Since the worker did not know Spanish, the boy assumed the role of teacher when they came to the Spanish words. Another boy, who was keenly interested in snakes and reptiles, felt that his worker really liked him when he took the trouble to find interesting books on this subject. Many workers take time to rewrite newspaper or magazine paragraphs that are of special interest to the client or to write original stories and practice material.

The wire or tape recorder. This piece of equipment may be used in many ways. For example, Mary Ann read several stanzas of "The Lady of Shalott" in her usual singsong, expressionless way. Then she was given a little instruction in oral reading:

To see pictures in her mind's eye of the river, the castle, the people going up and down, etc.
To say the lines as though talking with someone in a conversational way
To carry over the idea from one line to the next
To stress and hold on to the words that seem most important
To read each phrase as a whole, rather than as separate words

After practicing the poem with these things in mind, she recited it for recording; when it was played back she was delighted, for her voice was clear and young and expressed the feeling of the poem. Recordings may also be used to take before-and-after pictures of the client's interpretation of passages of different kinds. For the worker, the recorder is an invaluable aid to the objective study of his interviewing technique.

A chance to be creative. We have described only a few procedures that have proved successful in reading interviews. The worker has infinite opportunities to adapt these or to devise new ones. However, any procedure should have the sanction of sound theory and should be geared to the interests, needs, and ability of the individual client.

Psychotherapeutic Interviews. In some cases emotional difficulties have prevented the client from learning to read; in other cases they are preventing him from using the reading ability he has; in a few cases they are making him inaccessible to reading instruction. As far as possible, emotional difficulties must be recognized, consciously faced, and coped with in a rational rather than an irrational way. While meeting the client's primary expectation—and that of his parents—that he will receive instruction and practice in reading, the worker who is qualified may have to delve more or less deeply into emotional involvements as they are related to the reading problem.

The detailed records presented by Ephron [16] show how certain of the emotional difficulties that are related to reading may be handled by a worker with a warm personality, an understanding of the dynamics of behavior, and skill in interviewing. Although each case is unique, many follow a common pattern: first the client describes general symptoms of reading difficulty; then he gives a more detailed analysis of his reading problem; and finally he reveals to some extent his fears and/or compulsions—fear of making decisions, of taking initiative, of competing with his father or his siblings; compulsion to do everything perfectly, or to repress his real feelings or his true self-image. The therapy helps him to gain a new way of looking at his problems.

The question may be asked: Can therapy and reading instruction be interwoven? Perhaps not, in cases of the most serious emotional disturbance. "Sometimes the skillful employment of reading techniques may implement the therapeutic process" [16, p. 268].

What does the therapist do? He gives the client his full attention, undistracted by telephone calls and other interruptions. By his voice, facial expression, and expressive movements, he encourages the client to try to understand himself. Comments such as, "Tell me more," "Yes?" "And then?" "And how did you feel?" and "What are you thinking?" evoke the client's efforts to clarify his problems. The therapist listens creatively and with the "third ear," seeing relations that the client has not found. But he does not rush in with suggestions for a solution; that would defeat his aim of helping the client learn how to think about himself. He is constantly alert to recognize clues to the client's difficulties, but he gives his interpretation only when he feels quite sure that he is right and that the client is ready for it. He also helps the client to see his needs in relation to the needs of others. As the client learns to cope with some of his emotional difficulties, he is free to attack his reading and study problems. When this happened in one case, the boy said, of his own accord, "Hadn't we better get started on this reading business?"

Harris [23] raised the question: Should remedial help be replaced by therapy aimed directly at the child's emotional problems? His answer is "no" for these reasons: (1) good remedial assistance does help most poor readers to improve in reading; (2) improvement in reading contributes to self-confidence, stability, and social adjustment; and (3) facilities for psychotherapy for children are too limited to meet the needs of a large proportion of the poor readers [23, p. 574]. A combination of group therapy and appropriate remedial instruction has been found to be most effective.

How certain therapeutic principles may be translated into classroom procedures used in teaching a high school class in American literature was delightfully described by Dorothy Bratton [9].

The Comprehensive Case-study Approach. The case study is the best method of understanding the individual as a whole. It helps the reading teacher to appraise the client's growth in reading ability. It shows the conditions within the individual and in his environment that combine to produce certain kinds of development.

The trend in case studies of reading difficulty is to start with the person as he wants to present himself and to use whatever approach and techniques may be helpful to him in moving toward emotional maturity and realizing his reading potential. Thus the case study unfolds as the worker continues with the client. The real difficulties lie in understanding the dynamics of the case and in translating into practice the understanding that is obtained.

Concluding Statement

Berlin [8, pp. 56–58] has stated the value of skillful instruction in working with emotionally disturbed pupils:

Often teachers appear amazed when I relate how long it may take us at Langley Porter Children's Service to be helpful to children and parents. I want to emphasize that while teachers cannot hold themselves responsible for psychotherapeutic efforts, they must recognize that learning has a vital therapeutic effect on disturbed children. Seventeen years of experience at Langley Porter Neuropsychiatric Institute Inpatient Service has convinced all of our staff that the educative efforts of our skilled teachers play an important part in the recovery of even psychotic children. Beginning to learn academic material is one way of beginning to deal with the real world. The successes in the mastery of subject matter mean a great deal to a sick child's concept of himself. I would, therefore, again emphasize that the teacher expect of herself that she learn to teach as effectively and skillfully as possible and that, in teaching, she is performing an important mental health task.

NEUROLOGICAL FACTORS IN SEVERE READING DISABILITY

When a child fails to respond to the usual remedial treatment, he is sometimes referred to the neurologist as part of a comprehensive clinical evaluation to determine whether there is evidence of a structural lesion of the nervous system. In some cases there is gross or obvious brain injury. In other cases there are certain clinical findings that have been ascribed to "minimal" brain damage. To attribute reading disability to "minimal brain damage" is misleading for several reasons: (1) neurologists do not agree on what is "minimal"; (2) clinical signs do not necessarily indicate actual brain injury; (3) minimal neurological findings may not be associated with reading disability in some cases; and (4) the minimal clinical signs vary with the tests used by the neurologist and their interpretations [13]. There is danger in labeling without a total systematic study of biological, social, and psychological factors that may be involved in severe cases of reading disability.

Two Cases of Severe Language Disorder (Dyslexia)

A severe case of reading inability of a nine-year-old boy studied by de Hirsch at the Pediatric Language Disorder Clinic at the Columbia Presbyterian Medical Center was described in detail in an article in *The New Yorker* [58]. The first year of treatment this boy's anger was so intense and his fear of words so painful that there was no attempt to teach him to read. Instead, he was allowed to express himself in physical activities such as dart throwing.

The second year, when he began to calm down, he worked on phonics fifteen minutes at a time, drew pictures, and talked with the worker. He was beginning to learn words and word families in isolation and sometimes in sentences. The third year he progressed more rapidly, though he still had trouble with visual perception and continued to confuse words. But his resistance to reading was now ebbing and he could talk frankly about his problem. During the fourth year he caught up with his class.

Another case of reading impairment involving the consequences of possible brain lesions was reported to Reitan [43, pp. 109–110] by Drs. Kathleen and Loren Fitzhugh, research psychologist and chief psychologist, respectively, at the New Castle State Hospital, New Castle, Indiana.

D. L. was first seen when he was eight years of age. His difficulty in learning to read had been noted early, and for two years previously he had been receiving private remedial reading training with very poor results. Because of this very limited progress, his reading tutor had begun to despair of teaching D. L. to read and the school authorities, although allowing him to be promoted to the third grade, felt that there was little chance of passing him to the fourth grade at the end of the school year.

Our neurological test battery for children from five through eight years of age was administered to this child in September, 1963. The Wechsler Intelligence Scale for Children yielded IQ results in the normal range. The neurological battery, however, gave evidence of definite, chronic brain dysfunction, especially involving the right cerebral hemisphere. The evidence for this conclusion was the consistently poorer performance with the left hand than with the right hand, taking into consideration the expected proficiency of the right hand, since the child was right-handed. The psychological correlates of this picture amounted to deficiencies, demonstrated in various ways, of ability to deal with problems requiring the differential perception and manipulation of spatial configurations. This finding suggested the hypothesis that D. L.'s failure to learn to read might be a function of a basic difficulty in visual form perception in conjunction with damage of the right cerebral hemisphere.

The Fitzhughs have developed two six-month courses of programmed instruction . . . aimed at improving the communicational uses of language symbols and the ability to effect meaningful discriminations among visuo-spatial configurations. . . .

At the end of this six-month program, D. L. was again tested. The performance IQ as measured by the WISC had risen from 104 to 118. Evidence of lateralized dysfunction of the left hand (which was a substantial part of the evidence for inferring damage of the right cerebral hemisphere) had essentially disappeared. . . . On the Wide Range Achievement Test the reading-grade placement had risen from 0.9 to 3.1 years, spelling from 1.8 to 2.6 years, and arithmetic from 2.9 to 4.4 years. These gains of 2.2 years in reading, 0.8 years in spelling, and 1.5 years in arithmetic took place in a period of seven months. The reading gain may be even more significant considering the lack of progress during two previous years of conventional remedial training. In fact, his reading instructor had given up trying to teach D. L. to read just before he was started in the visuo-spatial training program that has been described. The continuing progress of D. L. has been so striking that his school officials have reversed their previous position and have decided to promote D. L. to the fourth grade.[3]

Relation of Lateral Dominance to Reading Disability

At one time severe reading disability was attributed simply to left-handedness or "mixed dominance." This explanation of retardation in reading has aroused much popular interest. A person with *strephosymbolia*, which merely means "twisted symbols," sees certain words and letters reversed, or upside down, or both: *was* as *saw*, and *b* as *d*. He may also transpose letters within a word, as *stop* for *spot*, or words within a sentence.

Most first-grade children occasionally read and write letters and words

[3] Reprinted by permission from Ralph M. Reitan, "Relationships between Neurological and Psychological Variables and Their Implications for Reading Instruction," in H. Alan Robinson, (ed.), *Meeting Individual Differences in Reading*, The University of Chicago Press, Copyright 1964 by The University of Chicago, Chicago, Ill., 1964.

backward or upside down. They look at words as they look at pictures. Most of these inaccuracies in perception "seem to die out naturally as the child matures" [60, p. 549].

If the tendency toward reversals persists into the second and third grades despite careful teaching of the left-right direction, it may indicate a deficiency in the child's "powers of reasoning about words" [60, p. 549] or a neurological immaturity in which neither side of the brain has become clearly dominant in controlling the perception of symbols. Such immaturity may affect reading.

Anderson [2] presented the point of view that "it does not appear that mixed dominance is a factor of any great importance in reading disability. Even more uncertain is the evidence linking errors of reversal to mixed dominance. Fortunately, the reversal problem can be understood without involving any assumption about brain physiology" [2, p. 2]. After a thorough, insightful review of experimental studies, Vernon concluded that "relationship to reading disability of incomplete lateralization and cerebral dominance is extremely obscure" [59, p. 115].

These conclusions have been supported by more recent investigations. Among populations of normal children the incidence of left-handedness has been found to be as high among normal as among retarded readers [28]. A recent control-group experiment further confirmed the conclusion that laterality is not a factor in reading disability [57]. Balow and Balow [5] reported that no combination of hand and eye dominance or knowledge of left or right was significantly related to the reading of first- and second-grade school children. However, Belmont and Birch [7] found that a larger proportion of nine- and ten-year-old retarded readers were unable to distinguish their right from their left hands and were generally confused in their right-left orientation.

Lateral dominance may be checked informally when the child has opportunities to throw darts, kick a ball, sight a toy rifle, and insert pegs in a board. The observer notes whether the child uses his right arm for throwing and his left foot for kicking; whether he closes his right eye and looks through the left when shooting, and whether he starts inserting pegs with his right hand then switches to his left. The Harris Tests of Lateral Dominance [22], designed for children aged seven years and older, give more systematic evidence. The results of these and other tests of laterality are influenced by the varied amount of practice different children have had in exercises of these kinds.

Neurological Impairment or Dysfunction

Far more complicated and difficult to diagnose is the relationship between severe reading disability (dyslexia) and neurological impairment or brain damage. Among the behavioral manifestations of possible neurological impairment are "learning deficits and inability to sustain concentrated attention and motivation; a loss in the ability to appreciate the significance of language symbols; impairment in the ability to form and generalize rational concepts; and deficits in the perception and manipulation of visuo-spatial configurations" [43, p. 109].

The theory that reading disability is a function of neurological organization [15] is more widely presented in the popular press than by authorities in the fields of medicine, psychology, and reading. In a carefully designed experiment, Robbins [44] obtained no support for Delacato's theory of the relationship between neurological organization, as measured by creeping and laterality, and reading achievement, nor for Delacato's experimental program carried on in addition to the ongoing curriculum of second graders.

Authorities agree on the importance of early identification of neurological dysfunction as a preventive of secondary emotional disturbance that often results from subjecting a child to learning tasks too difficult for him. Instead of attempting to categorize the type of brain damage, Reitan would recommend "explicit and detailed diagnosis of the specific difficulties underlying reading retardation" [43, p. 110]. Kass [26] considers that the most fruitful approach for the educator is to try to discover psychological correlates of reading disability, such as those measured by the Illinois Test of Psycholinguistic Abilities. Cohn [13] and Cruickshank [14] advocate the identification of relatively intact normal channels through which language can be developed.

Diagnosis. To date there are no fool-proof methods of diagnosing neurological causes of severe reading disability although new ways of detecting brain functioning are constantly being tested. The electroencephalograph (EEG) is not the last word.

Psychological testing may be of great practical value when combined with neurological examination. Reitan [43] suggested a combination of the Halstead battery, the appropriate Wechsler test, and simple neurological techniques, with special attention to comparison of low and high scores on the Wechsler subtests. The draw-a-person technique and the Bender Visual Motor Gestalt Test are often used in cases of severe reading disability. Krippner [29], in his study of thirty clinic cases, included in his diagnostic procedure developmental data, the Vineland Social Maturity quotient, Peabody Picture Vocabulary quotient, WISC total and subtest scores, and total percentile on the Mental Health Analysis.

One negative side of extensive neurological and psychological examinations is the effect on the individual, who may become more fearful, anxious, and preoccupied with his defect. Such feelings tend to decrease his concentration and ability to resist distraction.

Treatment. With children having pervasive, persistent, severe reading disability, it is especially important for the teacher to emphasize training in left-to-right progression, in seeing resemblances and distinguishing differences, in making generalizations, and in moving from the concrete to the abstract. In writing, such children progress best from simple sentences to paragraphs, reports, and original stories.

Like other children, cases of severe reading disability respond differently to various methods. If the child's visual memory is unreliable, teaching him to learn words as wholes may increase his frustration. But if he can learn by the whole-word method, it would be foolish not to give him the opportunity. Although phonetic analysis is usually recommended for these children, the method may be difficult for them because they lack auditory perception to grasp the sound adequately, or ability to learn and apply sound-symbol associations, or verbal memory to cope with the inconsistencies of English orthography. They often fear the printed word. The Gillingham and Stillman remedial training manual [19] has been used with success in groups or with individuals. Three-dimensional letters and the Fernald tracing or kinesthetic method have proved to be especially useful. When a child seems to know a word one day but forgets it the next, when he identifies it on an experience chart but not in a book or on a flash card, he needs to get a clearer image of the word in the first place. The teacher helps him by:

1. Calling his attention to the sequence of letters within a word as she writes the word for him
2. Having him write or trace it
3. Asking him to fill in missing letters within words
4. Giving him practice with flash cards or other tachistoscopic devices to insure rapid recognition
5. Preparing practice exercises that require discrimination of one word from other similar words

When a child repeatedly errs in associating sounds with letters or clusters of letters, the teacher helps him by:

1. Presenting the letter as part of a familiar word, to be quickly blended with other sounds in the word like connecting cars on a train
2. Pronouncing a word for a child if he does not immediately pronounce it correctly
3. Focusing his attention on single associations until each becomes automatic

The teacher should help these children to avoid making incorrect responses, which cause confusion and decrease their confidence and motivation. The Miami Series and other linguistic readers provide much repetition of each vowel sound as it is introduced. Children learn by contrast as well as by similar associations. Children learn short *a* and short *o* separately, and then they can be presented in pairs of words: *cat* and *cot*, *hat* and *hot*. Cases of severe reading disability are particularly vulnerable to confusion. "If a child who is trying makes several errors in a row, it is likely that the teacher has made an incorrect judgment in selecting materials or tasks" [11, p. 569]. The teacher should try to obtain or construct reading exercises which require only the skills the child has already learned, thus avoiding confusing him with the need for skills he has not yet developed [11].

When a child is confused about two words such as *what* and *when*, he should:

1. Learn first one then the other, thoroughly
2. Review the first briefly
3. Discriminate between the two words when they are presented together
4. Distinguish between the two words in a sentence
5. Identify the words correctly in stories

Other aspects of word recognition are taught in the usual way, with frequent reviews of basic perceptual associations and blending skills applied in reading sentences, directions, and stories. The teacher should introduce one task at a time, underlining or blocking off the words for the child, to focus his attention on words he is reading. Many features of the Montessori method are appropriate for these children.

Instruction should be as free from distractions as possible. Consistently maintaining a warm, friendly interest, the teacher should capitalize on the individual's immediate interest and transient enthusiasms.

Motivation is extremely important for these children, who, responding to a specific incentive, may replace apathy with effort.

Cohn [13] advocated the detailed study of the child's behavior in social settings so as to make the child's learning experience as realistic and concrete as possible. Instead of merely attempting to correct the disturbances, the teacher would emphasize continuous development and growth, using all the relatively intact channels open to learning. Thus the child would achieve success rather than failure and gain self-respect and security in the abilities he does possess.

Parents may participate in the treatment by helping the child set suitable goals for himself. They can praise and encourage his successful efforts while avoiding overprotecting him; they can guard him from the experience of repeated failure. When he does fail, they can show him how to learn from mistakes.

Evaluation. How effective is remedial reading instruction with severe reading problems? Studies of children of elementary school age show that they make substantial gains while actively receiving assistance. They are also able to progress in reading skills after their return to regular classes. But despite this continued progress, they increasingly fall behind. After they discontinue the remedial reading instruction, they do not progress according to the normal rate. Balow's recent research with very severely disabled clinic cases ten to twelve years of age was consistent with previously reported studies. He concluded that severe reading disability is a chronic condition that needs long-term treatment [3, pp. 581–586].

REFERENCES

1. Aarenson, Shirley: "Changes in IQ and Reading Performance of a Disturbed Child," *The Reading Teacher,* vol. 19, pp. 71–95, November, 1965.

2. Anderson, Irving H.: "An Interpretation of Reversal Errors in Reading," *University of Michigan, School of Education Bulletin,* vol. 30, pp. 1–5, October, 1958.

3. Balow, Bruce: "The Long-term Effect of Remedial Reading Instruction," *The Reading Teacher,* vol. 18, pp. 581–586, April, 1965.

4. Balow, Bruce: "A Program of Preparation for Teachers of Disturbed Children," *Exceptional Children,* vol. 32, pp. 455–560, March, 1966.

5. Balow, Irving H., and Bruce Balow: "Lateral Dominance and Reading Achievement in the Second Grade," *American Educational Research Journal,* vol. 1, pp. 139–143, May, 1964.

6. Bateman, Barbara: *Reading and Psycholinguistic Processes of Partially Seeing Children,* Council for Exceptional Children, Research Monographs, ser. A, no. 5, Washington, D.C., 1963.

7. Belmont, Lillian, and Herbert G. Birch: "Lateral Dominance, Lateral Awareness, and Reading Disability," *Child Development,* vol. 36, pp. 57–72, March, 1965.

8. Berlin, I. N.: "Unrealities in Teacher Education," *Saturday Review,* vol. 19, pp. 56–58, December 19, 1964.

9. Bratton, Dorothy: "Reading for Therapy," *English Journal,* vol. 46, pp. 339–346, September, 1957.

10. Bryant, N. Dale: "Characteristics of Dyslexia and Their Remedial Implication," *Exceptional Children,* vol. 31, pp. 195–199, December, 1964.

11. Bryant, N. Dale: "Some Principles of Remedial Instruction for Dyslexia," *The Reading Teacher,* vol. 18, pp. 567–572, April, 1965.

12. Challman, Robert C.: "Personality Maladjustments and Remedial Reading," *Journal of Exceptional Children,* vol. 6, pp. 7–11, October, 1939.

13. Cohn, Robert: "The Neurological Study of Children with Learning Disabilities," *Exceptional Children,* vol. 31, pp. 179–185, December, 1964.

14. Cruickshank, William M. (ed.): *The Teacher of Brain-injured Children: A Discussion of the Bases for Competency,* Syracuse University Press, Syracuse, N.Y., 1966.

15. Delacato, Carl H.: *The Diagnosis and Treatment of Speech and Reading Problems,* Charles C Thomas, Publisher, Springfield, Ill., 1963.

16. Ephron, Beulah Kanter: *Emotional Difficulties in Reading,* Julian Press, New York, 1953.

17. Fernald, Grace: *Remedial Techniques in Basic School Subjects,* McGraw-Hill Book Company, New York, 1943.

18. Gann, Edith: *Reading Difficulty and Personality Organization,* King's Crown Press, New York, 1945.

19. Gillingham, Anna, and Bessie Stillman: *Remedial Training for Children with a Special Disability in Reading, Spelling, Penmanship,* Sackett and Wilhelms Company, New York, 1956.

20. Gregory, Robin E.: "Unsettledness, Maladjustment and Reading Failure: A Village Study," *British Journal of Educational Psychology,* vol. 35, pp. 63–68, February, 1965.

21. Haring, Norris, and Lakin Phillips: *Educating Emotionally Disturbed Children,* McGraw-Hill Book Company, New York, 1962.

22. Harris, Albert J.: *Harris Tests of Lateral Dominance: Manual of Directions for Administration and Interpretation,* The Psychological Corporation, New York, 1958.

23. Harris, Albert J.: "Motivating the Poor Reader," *Education,* vol. 73, pp. 566–574, May, 1953.

24. Hewett, Frank M.: "A Hierarchy of Educational Tasks for Children with Learning Disorders," *Exceptional Children,* vol. 31, pp. 207–214, December, 1964.

25. Hillerich, Robert L.: "Eye-hand Dominance and Reading Achievement," *American Educational Research Journal,* vol. 1, pp. 121–126, March, 1964.

26. Kass, Corinne: "Some Psycholinguistic Disabilities of Children with Reading Problems," *Exceptional Children,* vol. 32, pp. 533–539, April, 1966.

27. Knoblock, Peter: "A Rorschach Investigation of the Reading Process," *Journal of Experimental Education,* vol. 33, pp. 277–282, Spring, 1965.

28. Koos, Eugenia M.: "Manifestations of Cerebral Dominance and Reading Retardation in Primary-grade Children," *Journal of Genetic Psychology,* vol. 104, pp. 155–166, March, 1964.

29. Krippner, Stanley: "Correlates of Reading Improvement," *Journal of Developmental Reading,* vol. 7, pp. 29–39, Autumn, 1963.

30. Kunst, Mary S.: "Psychological Treatment in Reading Disability," *Clinical Studies in Reading I,* Supplementary Educational Monographs, no. 68, University of Chicago Press, Chicago, 1949, pp. 133–140.

31. Lefevre, Carl A.: "Language and Self: Fulfillment or Trauma?" *Elementary English,* vol. 43, pp. 124–128, February, 1966.

32. Levi, Aurelia: "Treatment of Disorders of Perceptual and Conceptual Formation in a Case of School Failure," *Journal of Consulting Psychology,* vol. 29, pp. 289–295, August, 1965.

33. Lewis, Richard S., Alfred A. Strauss, and Laura E. Lehtinen: *The Other Child: The Brain Injured Child,* Grune & Stratton, Inc., New York, 1951.

34. Long, Nicholas J., William C. Morse, and Ruth G. Newman: *Conflict in the Classroom: The Diagnosis and Education of Emotionally Disturbed Children,* Wadsworth Publishing Company, Inc., Belmont, Calif., 1965.

35. McCarthy, Dorothea: "Language and Personality Development," *The Reading Teacher,* vol. 6, pp. 28–37, November, 1952.

36. Miller, Nandeen L.: "Teaching an Emotionally Disturbed, Brain-injured Child," *The Reading Teacher,* vol. 18, pp. 460–465, March, 1964.

37. Missildine, W. H.: "Emotional Background of Thirty Children with Reading Disabilities with Emphasis on Its Coercive Elements," *Nervous Child,* vol. 5, pp. 263–272, July, 1946.

38. Money, John (ed.): *Reading Disability: Progress and Research Needs in Dyslexia,* The Johns Hopkins Press, Baltimore, 1962.

39. *Navy Life Reader, Book 1* (restricted), Bureau of Naval Personnel Training, Standards and Curriculum Division, NAVPERS 15180, 1945.

40. Rabinovich, Ralph D.: "Neuropsychiatric Considerations in Children's Reading Problems," in Ruth Strang (ed.), *Understanding and Helping the Retarded Reader,* University of Arizona Press, Tucson, Ariz., 1965, pp. 46–52.

41. Raygor, Alton L., and David M. Work: "Personality Patterns of Poor Readers Compared with College Freshmen," *Journal of Reading,* vol. 7, pp. 40–46, October, 1964.

42. Reed, H. B. C.: "Some Relationships between Neurological Dysfunction and Behavioral Deficits in Children," *Conference on Children with Minimal Brain Impairment,* The University of Illinois Press, Urbana, Ill., 1963.

43. Reitan, Ralph M.: "Relationships between Neurological and Psychological Variables and Their Implications for Reading Instruction," in H. Alan Robinson (ed.), *Meeting Individual Differences in Reading,* Supplementary Educational Monographs, no. 94, University of Chicago Press, Chicago, 1964, pp. 100–110.

44. Robbins, Melvyn P.: "A Study of the Validity of Delacato's Theory of Neurological Organization," *Exceptional Children,* vol. 32, pp. 517–523, April, 1966.

45. Robinson, H. Alan (comp. and ed.): *Meeting Individual Differences in Reading,* Supplementary Educational Monographs, no. 94, University of Chicago Press, Chicago, 1964, pp. 83–99.

46. Robinson, Helen M.: "Manifestations of Emotional Maladjustments," *Clinical Studies in Reading I,* Supplementary Educational Monographs, no. 68, University of Chicago Press, Chicago, 1949, pp. 114–122.

47. Robinson, Helen M.: "Some Poor Readers Have Emotional Problems," *The Reading Teacher,* vol. 6, pp. 25–33, May, 1953.

48. Robles, Louise: "A Teacher's Use of Puppetry to Improve the Reading Skills of Emotionally Disturbed Children," unpublished doctoral dissertation, Teachers College, Columbia University, New York, 1954.

49. Roswell, Florence, and Gladys Natchez: *Reading Disability: Diagnosis and Treatment,* Basic Books, Inc., Publishers, New York, 1964.

50. Roth, Robert M.: "The Role of Self-concept in Achievement," *Journal of Experimental Education,* vol. 27, pp. 265–281, June, 1959.

51. Silverman, Jerome S., Margaretta Fite, and Margaret M. Mosher: "Clinical Findings in Reading Disability Children: Special Cases of Intellectual Inhibition," *American Journal of Orthopsychiatry,* vol. 29, pp. 298–314, April, 1959.

52. Spache, George D.: "Personality Patterns of Retarded Readers," *Journal of Educational Research,* vol. 50, pp. 461–469, February, 1957.

53. Stirling, Nora: *The Ins and Outs,* National Association for Mental Health, Inc., New York, 1949.

54. Strang, Ruth: *Diagnostic Teaching of Reading,* McGraw-Hill Book Company, New York, 1964.

55. Strang, Ruth: "Reading and Personality Formation," *Personality,* vol. 1, pp. 131–140, April, 1951.

56. Tamkin, Arthur S.: "A Survey of Educational Disabilities in Emotionally

Disturbed Children," *Journal of Educational Research,* vol. 53, pp. 313–315, April, 1960.

57. Tinker, Karen J.: "The Role of Laterality in Reading Disability," in J. Allen Figurel (ed.), *Reading and Inquiry,* International Reading Association Conference Proceedings, vol. 10, Newark, Del., 1965.

58. Tompkins, Calvin: "A Reporter at Large: The Last Skill Acquired," *The New Yorker,* vol. 39, pp. 127ff, September 14, 1963.

59. Vernon, M. D.: *Backwardness in Reading: A Study of Its Nature and Origin,* Cambridge University Press, New York, 1957.

60. Vernon, M. D.: "The Development of Visual Perception in Children," *Education,* vol. 78, pp. 547–549, May, 1958.

61. Vorhaus, Pauline G.: "Rorschach Configurations Associated with Reading Disability," *Journal of Projective Techniques,* vol. 16, pp. 2–19, March, 1952.

62. Weiss, M. Jerry: *Guidance through Drama,* Whiteside, Inc., New York, 1954.

63. Wollner, Mary Hayden Bowen: *Children's Voluntary Reading as an Expression of Individuality,* Teachers College Press, Teachers College, Columbia University, New York, 1949.

special problems of
able learners

chapter 16

Recall some of the gifted children and adolescents whom you have known. Compare these characteristics with those briefly described in this chapter. Which of these characteristics would naturally lead to superior reading ability?

Why, then, are there many bright students in our schools who are underachieving in certain subjects and reading below their potential ability? It has been found that the intelligence-test scores of high school students who were failing in one or more subjects were distributed over the entire range of intelligence instead of piling up at the lower end. Gifted students were failing in subjects that they should have passed easily. Many more were merely getting by when they should have been doing superior work [19, 20]. From a review of research, Gowan concluded that nearly all gifted children are, to some extent, underachievers [12].

What are some possible causes of this discrepancy between mental ability and achievement? The conditions underlying underachievement are complex and appear to be of early origin.

Review the methods of appraising a student's reading ability and apply them to the identification of gifted children and the appraisal of their reading proficiency. Any of the factors or combination of factors—physiological, sociological, and psychological—described in previous chapters may account for, or contribute to, the underachievement of gifted children [5]. An understanding of conditions is essential for the prevention and correction of reading difficulties. Prevention forestalls failure; correction repairs weak skills and removes blocks to progress.

The most positive emphasis is the focus on developing the child's reading potentials and creating conditions conducive to learning. If you were to provide the ideal home and school environment for the development of gifted children's reading ability, what experiences would you include? How would you translate into connected experiences such general goals as parental interest and encouragement free from domination; tasks that are challenging but commensurate with the child's ability; social interaction and concern for others, self-confidence and enthusiasm, efficient use of time [12].

THE GIFTED AND THEIR IDENTIFICATION

As defined here, the gifted are able learners [1] who constitute about 15 to 20 per cent of the school population; the highly gifted, about 1 or 2 per cent. The latter are "old for their age." With an IQ of 117, a twelve-year-old enters junior high school with a mental age of fourteen. If his IQ is 133, his mental age is four years beyond his chronological age. He learns rapidly. Consequently, he is often ahead of his class and becomes bored with waiting for them to catch up with him. Routine and drill irk him. Textbooks crammed with disorganized facts make reading unrewarding.

It is important to keep able learners' initial interest in reading alive by making it a rewarding experience. If the teacher is unaware of their high reading proficiency, they are likely to find reading a disappointing experience. One bright boy was given the sentence, "The boy can run." His comment was, "You don't have to learn to read to know that." A docile little girl in the first grade who was already reading on the third-grade level, after dutifully reading several pages of a very dull primer, looked up at the teacher and said, "Boring, isn't it?" A less tractable little boy, under similar circumstances, said to the teacher, "Take that pusillanimous primer away!" When the books they are given to read are dull and boring, when the teacher forces reading drills on them

[1] The *gifted* and *able learners* are terms that are often used synonymously.

or a reading-readiness program they do not need, and when they have to sit and wait while other children stumble through a story, gifted children lose their initial enthusiasm for reading and turn their active minds to mischief or other activities.

Able learners are good at comprehending abstract material and making generalizations. They will read eagerly to answer a significant question or to solve a challenging problem. Their insatiable curiosity and eagerness to learn motivate them to explore, enjoy the world of books, and read for pleasure.

Bright children learn to read by almost any method, although the visual seems somewhat superior to the kinesthetic. They respond to somewhat informal methods, rather than a well-planned, systematic program which suits pupils of lower ability. They prefer to discover the principle underlying phonetic and structural analysis for themselves; they enjoy inductively designed work and its subsequent application [31]. Techniques of critical and creative reading will amplify their enjoyment of reading.

They like to work independently. Interested in science, travel, and social problems earlier than the other pupils, on their own accord they will frequently make an intensive study of a topic of interest. "Give us books and other materials to work with and don't interfere with us," was the advice one gifted youngster gave to teachers.

Although they have special verbal facility, they can also do well in subjects that require motor and manipulative ability, especially if these subjects demand intricate planning and a grasp of general principles. Some individuals, only average in abstract verbal ability, have special talent in music, drama, and the dance.

Gifted children usually do not resemble the stereotyped caricature of the round-shouldered, pale, thin, bespectacled, precocious child, but usually have superior health and an attractive appearance. They tend to be socially sensitive and to engage in an average number of extraclass activities.

Gifted children learn to read early, almost half of them before they come to school [21]. A few begin before they are four years old and continue their exceptional interest in reading. They tackle adult books earlier than other children. They come from homes in which the parents enjoy reading, have many suitable books, and often read aloud to their children.

These are central tendencies; there are, of course, many individual differences within the gifted group [21].

First-grade teachers should promptly identify those children who know how to read when they enter school. The gifted child usually stands out to the observing teacher because of his interest in and accurate use of words, his interest in reading, his ability to organize and relate ideas gained from a number of sources, his eagerness to explore new fields. On standardized tests of intelligence he rates high. On standardized tests of achievement he is likely to score one or more years above grade level. However, a gifted student may score high in mathematics and science and yet fail social science and English because of poor reading skills.

To appraise a student's reading potentialities is not easy because to get an accurate measure of his general mental ability is difficult. Scores on a group test of intelligence depend a great deal on the individual's reading proficiency. Moreover, other factors that are lowering his reading score may also affect his intelligence test results.

THEIR READING DEVELOPMENT

As with all students, there are two main goals for the gifted—reading development and personal development through reading. Problems in connection with reading development involve the early identification of proficient readers, appraisal of their reading potentialities, and provision of progressive experiences conducive to reading development. A surprisingly large number of these able learners mention difficulty in concentrating—a difficulty that may be due to poor environmental conditions, inner conflicts, lack of purpose, or hopelessly dull and meaningless reading material.

Problems in connection with personal development through reading involve understanding of the developmental tasks to which reading may contribute— the achievement of self-esteem, understanding of oneself and others, a balanced leisure-time program, insight into different kinds of life situations and problems, appreciation of the prevalence of problems that one may have thought peculiar to oneself, and development of a sense of direction or destiny and social responsibility [23]. Reading may also contribute to the development of special talents and vocational goals.

How Do They Learn to Read?

Teachers know that many gifted children acquire flexible, rapid, effective habits of reading. If they knew more about the psychological process involved, they might be able to teach other children to learn to read in the same way. Some information on this question came from the introspective reports of gifted children. Apparently they learn to read in many different ways [21, 35]. Some seem to learn to read all by themselves. "I got interested in books and read them; that was all there was to it," one gifted boy said. For many, this interest in books stems from having had the best literature read to them very early, even before they understood. Some learn by noticing the words underneath pictures. One youngster said, "I was a comic book enthusiast before I went to the first grade and I learned to notice small words together with the pictures and remembered them. If I could not make out a word I would ask my mother." Others say members of the family taught them to read by various methods, but favor the phonetic approach. The preferred learning pattern seems to be listening to stories, looking at the book being read and distinguishing certain words, and learning some common words by sight. Soon they begin to take an analytical approach, sounding out words "by syllables and the letter's sound."

Gifted pupils like to be on their own in reading. One sixth-grader said, "In the second grade I would take some books home and Daddy would help me read them, but I liked it better when I could read them myself." Another sixth-grader expressed the feeling of many able learners of her age when she said, "I just love our library periods." They want some guidance in learning at first, but "when you get started, you can go ahead at your own speed."

With special interests of his own, Don said, "From the first to the fourth grades I read the books that they had in school—when I had to. But I would take Daddy's science books to school to read when I got ahead of the others. Sometimes I couldn't read them but I liked to look at the pictures and sometimes I could read parts of them. In the fifth and sixth grades I liked aviation books, but now, in the twelfth grade, I am interested in nuclear physics." These able learners are capable of attaining the reading maturity described by Gray and Rogers [14].

In describing their methods of reading science material, high school students frequently say something of this sort: "I read the lesson fairly rapidly but carefully, slowing up over difficult parts." "I read fairly slowly. If there is a complicated section, I read it over until I do understand it." One student who read with excellent comprehension a science article about the method of chromatographic adsorption described his method as follows:

I read more slowly than usual because the material was not very familiar. I fixed in mind as well as possible the materials used in the method decribed and the facts about its invention and use. I tried to recall some of the work I had done in biochemistry and remembered using the method described in testing for vitamins. I tried to understand what the author had in mind, using my own background, and tried to get a picture of the whole sense of the article with the main ideas in the foreground. When I came to details I thought important, I stopped and tried to fix them in mind.

From the beginning, personal relations exert a strong influence on a child's reading. If his first attempts evoke approval from a loved parent or teacher or classmates, his interest and effort will be reinforced.

What Does Reading Mean to Them?

Gifted children often become completely absorbed in books. One girl said that when she was reading *Heidi* no one could come into her room until she had finished it. A vivid example of the complete absorption of a very exceptional child is given in the following quotation from Somerset Maugham's *Of Human Bondage*. It describes the small boy's first experience with books:

One day a good fortune befell him, for he hit upon Lane's translation of *The Thousand Nights and a Night*. He was captured at first by the illustrations, and then he began to read, to start with, the stories that dealt with magic, and then the others; and those he liked he read again and again. He could think of nothing else. He forgot the life around him. He had to be called two or three times before he would come to his dinner. Insensibly he formed the most delightful habit in the world, the habit of reading; he did not know that thus he was providing himself with a refuge from all the distress of life; he did not know either that he was creating for himself an unreal world which would make the real world of every day a source of bitter disappointment.[2]

In their early years these exceptional children often respond to the wonder of books by living what they read. One girl, who mentioned *The Wizard of Oz* as her first book, said, "I loved the magicalness of it and the wonderful adventures. I always repeated the magic phrases to see if they would work for me." Another said she thought of her stuffed animals in the same way that Christopher Robin did. One boy said he found the Dr. Dolittle books charming until he was about fifteen. He reread them five or six times and found different things in them each time. To one person a book may be just a good story; to another it may be an interpretation of character. Each book leaves its personal residue of meaning. Sometimes children get from a book something quite different from what an adult expects them to get. Each book speaks to them in accord with their own needs and purposes.

Gifted children and young people are often clearly aware of the personal values of reading—for enjoyment, for building vocabulary, for broadening interests, for acquiring information, and, most important of all, for gaining understanding of themselves and other persons. A high school boy said:

In reading *Silas Marner*, you get an idea of what the life of a miser is like and how he feels; in reading Dickens, you gain understanding of how a poor person lived in his times. From other books you learn what is involved in making a decision, and how to handle certain kinds of situations. You make applications to yourself: "Am I doing this with my life? How can I make myself a better person?"

Under favorable conditions reading continues to be one of "life's inexhaustible pleasures." As a leisure activity it is not crowded out even by the many other adolescent interests [37]. This is what two gifted junior high school pupils say about their interest in reading:

[2] From W. Somerset Maugham, *Of Human Bondage*, p. 37. Copyright 1917 by Doubleday & Company, New York. Reprinted by permission.

I love to read; I spend much more time in reading than I do in other pleasurable recreations.

Now in the seventh grade, I belong to Revelers, Campfire Girls, Y-teens, 3 Star Club; write to about twenty people and take knitting, piano and oboe lessons, so my interest in reading is slowing down. But I still say, give me a good book any time.

In addition to the enjoyment that reading affords, gifted students realize that it fulfills other needs. The academically ambitious know that school success and admission to college depend on it. The socially minded find reading useful in carrying on a conversation. The vocationally oriented are aware of the importance of reading in most vocations.

Gifted children sometimes find the world of books more satisfying than the real world. Consequently they use reading as an escape from thinking, desirable physical activities, or developmental tasks. One youngster who was unable to win social acceptance turned more and more to reading. In other instances parents and teachers unwittingly intensify an already overintellectual tendency.

EXPERIENCES NEEDED

In planning a reading program, one should keep in mind the characteristics of gifted pupils and make every effort to meet their needs. Although the able learners love and cherish independence and want to take initiative, they also recognize the value of some guidance in learning. In one high school a number of seniors—all A students—requested special help in reading. They were concerned with where they were and where they wanted to go in reading. Competent readers in college are often surprised at the progress they make in reading-improvement classes. Graduate students working for doctorates find that they can improve their reading. Nearly all capable students can learn to read better and faster. Sometimes they develop more effective reading methods themselves in response to an intellectually stimulating environment.

Provide for Creative Activities

Superior students respond to stimuli to creative expression. Among the stimuli Rinker [29] presented to a high school English class were quotations, proverbs, and epigrams jotted on the board to read or not, as they pleased; the "Poet and Peasant Overture" played over and over until the class had filled the chalkboard with words suggested by the music; and suggestions that the students write stories for younger children and then read them to these young critics.

Give Them the Instruction They Need

Although gifted children often need help themselves to gain proficiency in reading, they can be saved unnecessary trial and error by appropriate instruction. Those with higher IQs usually show the greater improvement. A reading program for able learners described by Bond [3] produced gains on the reading tests of from eight to forty-eight months for all but two pupils and favorable reactions on the part of pupils, parents, and members of the faculty.

If superior learners are given more difficult reading material, they should also have help in meeting the difficulties they will encounter. They will need skill in detecting subtle propaganda and in reading poetry which leaves much unsaid —much that must be inferred by the reader. Even gifted pupils need help in finding clues that lead to hidden meanings.

Early instruction in the use of indexes, tables of contents, periodical indexes, and other aids to locating information on a particular topic is especially valuable for gifted children who want to work independently on some project or problem. Many of them also profit by suggestions on how to study, how to read different kinds of material, how to take notes, and how to write reports.

In addition to the basic reading skills, they need to develop ability to make a critical evaluation of what they have read, to assess ideas from the reading, and to analyze their own responses. Above average learners will find effective, mature reading methods advantageous all through school and college. They will also profit by them in later life when, as business executives or professional people, they have to extract the ideas they need from a vast amount of reading material.

Gifted students can reach higher levels of appreciation and interpretation of meaning than they usually do. Donahue [7] described the procedures she used in a junior high school class in which there were a number of children whose intelligence and reading ability were far above their chronological age. She began by letting them analyze cartoons in some of which the implications were not obvious. Next they tried to understand dramatic characters by noticing what they said and did in one-act plays such as Susan Glaspell's *Trifles*. From plays they made the transition to poems that unfold their meaning by revealing what the characters do and say, e.g., Lowell's "Yussouf," old English ballads, Daniel Sargent's "It's the Rain," and Robert Frost's "The Fear." Next they noted symbolism in poetry, as lilacs associated with New England spring. After a poem had been read aloud, questions of interpretation were raised for class discussion and for independent analysis. The pupils began to look for key lines and their comprehension and appreciation of poetry increased.

The creative aspects of reading—reflecting on what one reads and finding the hidden meaning, anticipating outcomes—especially appeal to gifted students. They learn by hunting for the truth in great books. For a combination of independent reading, creative writing, and study of mass media, students get a sense of the role of words in world affairs. They are eager to use reading to solve problems. They may use ideas gained from reading in preparing stories to tell younger children; in giving plays and puppet shows; in making posters, collections, displays of favorite books; in writing tall tales, poems, letters to their favorite authors, book reviews; in preparing bulletin-board exhibits and files of information on different subjects; in selecting books to buy or request for their class library.

Don't Waste Their Time

In many classrooms a great deal of the gifted student's time is wasted. "The worst thing," one child said, "is oral reading. It is boring to listen to all the slow pokes drawling it out. I should listen, but I am usually drawing pictures." She was referring to the practice of having each pupil in turn read aloud a paragraph or two from the same book. One can easily understand why this procedure is distressing to gifted children who read fluently. If they follow along with the class, they cannot help becoming impatient with the slow, stumbling reading; if they read ahead and are called on, they are scolded for losing the place. One sixth-grade youngster said: "The teacher worked with the slow ones and I read ahead and got into trouble because I would be two or three chapters ahead and when the teacher asked me a question I would answer her from where I was and not from where the class was." Because some able children are sensitive to the feelings of others in the class, they want to "keep with the other kids." This social motive keeps them from reading ahead and slows down their reading rate.

The teacher can do much to avoid this inexcusable waste of time. If the students are not resourceful in finding worthwhile things to do, the teacher may plan with them individually ways to spend their unassigned time. Subgroups within the regular class help to solve this problem. "Now," said Kay, "we are not in one big group, but each group goes as fast as it wants to." Jane said, "I think the teacher need not spend too much time with the smart ones—give them interesting things to do and let them go ahead and do them."

Enrich Their Curriculum

As able learners progress through the grades, the opportunities for curriculum enrichment are unlimited. They often want to read intensively on a particular problem. Books on that subject should be available to them. When asked about his problems, one gifted boy said, "The librarian is my problem. When I asked for the book on science I needed, she said, "That is an adult book, and you are a juvenile.'" Fortunately this is an atypical situation; most librarians are very helpful about providing suitable books for individuals of all levels of reading ability and interest.

However, making interesting literature available is not quite enough. Even ardent readers need some help in choosing books and in using reading to ascertain and develop their interests. One pupil paid tribute to the teachers who had influenced her interests in reading: one teacher had interested her in composers' lives, and another had encouraged her to read a variety of biography and fiction.

Group projects requiring wide reading are even more valuable for gifted students than are individual pursuits. Group activities are the ideal way to combine reading with the social experience needed by the intellectually superior student. Writing and producing a play or radio script, serving as editor of a school paper, being a sports columnist on the local paper, working on a class committee responsible for giving a report—activities like these involve human relations as well as reading. Even an individual who has not learned to relate himself to other persons may become interested in a few who share his intellectual interests. This experience serves as an entering wedge to wider social relations.

Enriching the reading experience of the gifted involves more than recommending the right books to the right child and making them easily available, not that these measures are unimportant. However, a teacher can lead a child to a book, but he can't make him read it. In fact, too much pressure can increase his resistance to reading it. One gifted adolescent, for example, rebelled against her mother's attempts to make her read Shakespeare. "Although at first I had no objection to Shakespeare," she said, "my mother was so insistent that I began to hate it. In fact, I called *everything* I especially disliked 'Shakespearean'; later, when I began to read his plays of my own accord, I became deeply interested." Others express similar reactions to adults' attempts to dictate their reading experiences.

Both negative and positive drives may influence a child's receptivity toward efforts to enrich his reading. Perhaps the competition of reading with television and other media of communication is not so serious a deterrent to reading as is the philosophy of life to which people are being conditioned by continual repetition of certain ideas and values such as "Pleasure up," "Take it easy," "Dream your troubles away." Reading requires effort; it is not an easy, passive way of spending time.

Give Them a Chance to Match Wits

These children love to talk. They especially enjoy group discussion about their favorite books—laughing over funny parts, sharing the thrills of suspenseful incidents, and wondering why the characters behaved as they did.

If able pupils are together in a number of special classes—creative writing, literature, science, and social problems—they do not have to mark or waste time. They can go ahead as fast and as far as they wish. These classes should provide challenging books, equipment for experimentation, and opportunities to communicate through art, music, and rhythms as well as through spoken and written words.

Because they like to share their reading experiences with others, reading clubs are popular. These clubs are most successful when the members themselves decide on the purpose of the club and evolve a satisfying club procedure. In the Cleveland Major Work Classes, the pupils read first to understand and enjoy the story; they read a second time to answer any questions that might be asked; in a third reading they noted new words and parts of the story which they particularly liked. With such preparation their discussion periods were exceptional [27].

Allow More Time for Reading in School

Gifted children like to have more free reading—unhurried periods to enjoy reading with no strings attached. They can make good use of these periods if they have proper guidance and have had instruction in the deeper levels of interpretation and critical reading. While some are reading without supervision, the teacher can instruct others individually or in small groups. An advanced reading course, slightly beyond their present reading ability and interests, with no credits, no written book reports, and no grades, proved to be most challenging to the bright children invited to join it. They enjoyed the experience and profited by it. One girl said, "I never read so many books in so little time." And a boy remarked, "I like the way we come into the room and just sit down and talk things over."

Help Them to Evaluate Their Reading

What difference has reading made in their lives? Has it widened their interests? Has it brought them a better understanding of themselves, of others, and of the world in which they live? Have they used any ideas gained from reading to meet practical situations? Have they gained in ability to interpret what they read? Can they detect more quickly an author's intent to influence the reader? Have words acquired richer meanings? Have they become more critical in their choice of books? Discussions of questions like these are stimulating to gifted pupils and help them to plan a still finer reading program for themselves.

Let Them Follow Their Interests

With a little guidance they can plan their individual reading lists, making a kind of contract for the year's reading. Gifted children are capable of a two-way appreciation of poetry—reading and writing it. At first, of course, they listen to the poems read to them and often remember parts after they have heard them several times.

Many gifted boys, especially, are interested in science, often as early as the primary grades. Through pictures and simple, accurate science material they can build a good foundation. They learn the word *experiment* by performing simple experiments. They learn the names of elements by seeing and handling samples of them and using them in experiments. Older pupils may help with younger children's science clubs and discussion groups.

Any topic may invite intensive reading. A second-grade youngster became interested in people who write books. His interest spread to his friends and other members of the class. For a while they used all their available time in reading about famous people. The Bobbs-Merrill Childhood of Famous Americans Series was especially helpful. They read their book reviews to the group and rewrote them in the light of the criticism received. Their reading culminated in a program for parents in which they represented some of the famous people about whom they had been reading [13].

A group of able high school seniors, thinking back over their experiences in school, made comments such as the following:

The happiest experience I had in elementary school was in the fifth grade. . . . We were not limited to a regular schedule of study. If we were slow in certain fields we had time to catch up. If we were faster than most in other particular fields we were given a chance to go ahead and make as much advancement as we could safely. Another important factor was that we were given a chance to develop our ingenuity and use our ideas instead of our teacher's plans.

Give Them Freedom to Choose Their Reading

Although youngsters frequently appreciate guidance in their reading, they do not want adults to dominate their choice of reading. Some take a negativistic attitude: "I didn't want to read books my mother wanted me to read. That scared me off of fairy-tales." The youngsters' advice to parents is, "Don't worry. If you start opposing a child's choice, you may make an issue out of it." It is no use trying to make children read certain books before they are intellectually and emotionally ready. Children themselves believe that if a child's natural curiosity has play, he will come around to good books. One boy suggested it might be a good idea "to go through a stage of reading comic books and get them out of your system." Many speak of outgrowing comic books. The important thing is to get an interest in reading and to feel free to make one's own choices.

Their resistance to required reading seems to stem from the fact that they want to read what they want, when they want to read it. Required reading seems to be a symbol of forced labor. They prefer to pace themselves, avoiding the typical assignment "to read two more chapters." Some of them dislike having to dissect a book in class and object strenuously to having to go over and over it until everyone comprehends. However, they are fair-minded enough to admit that sometimes when they have read a required book they enjoyed it and got out of it what they needed at that particular time.

Some read whatever happens to be in their environment—"I used to read my brother's books, mostly haphazardly." Parents can often make a book seem like something special. They should also be ready to share their reading with the children and be willing to discuss the books the children want to talk about. To do this effectively, parents must keep up with the younger generation— their times, tempo, interests, needs.

Social influences may be negative, as well as positive. Some children read the books their friends are reading just to be accepted. One girl said, "All my friends were discussing what Nancy Drew did, so I read *Nancy Drew*. But I disliked it so much I got other friends." In reading some of the poor-quality books the other boys were reading, one youngster discovered that the characters were not true to life—they were either all good or all bad. The reading of these children seems to be most influenced by friends older than themselves.

Turn Them Loose in the Library

Many go to the public library of their own accord. One youngster tells of getting her first library card "at the ripe old age of five." Children in the elementary school can learn about the public library through a class visit at its storytelling hours. Older students may take responsibility for the story hour for young children. Both older and younger children are members of a library council that plans the program for these story hours. After each story hour the children evaluate the program with a view to improving it.

In the Long Beach public schools, small groups of fifth- and sixth-grade children whose reading ability was seventh-grade level or above were offered a special program under the instruction of the school librarian and the classroom teacher. The librarian's purpose was to acquaint these children with the history of various forms of literature and to make available many kinds of books— biography, mythology, folklore, poetry, and translations. Each group spent one 40-minute period a week in the school library, where they had the individual guidance of the librarian. She also arranged an introduction and exhibit for each assigned area. With such a vivid introduction, each child found a book that he wanted to take home. The next week they met with their classroom teacher for another forty-minute period to discuss their interpretations of and reactions to the books they had read [33]. Both the measurable and the intangible results of this program were gratifying.

Provide a Wealth of Reading Material

Recognizing that able learners have wide reading interests, teachers, parents, and librarians will try to provide books in many fields. Recognizing that these students read to find out, they will select authentic, informative books. Recognizing the potentialities for appreciation of literary quality, they will be sure to include children's classics in the collection. They will remember that the reading interests of gifted children are not very different from those of other children, except that they are usually accelerated in their interests, as in other aspects of their development. One junior high school student summed up his idea of a good book as follows: "It should be about something you like, interesting and well put together, with action and appeal to our age group." They dislike books that are "boring, childish, and far-fetched." Some of the gifted students say that "illustrations do not seem to matter." Others think that poor pictures may be a deterrent to comprehension and enjoyment. Said one girl: "The illustrator sometimes pictures the characters and events as I hadn't imagined them, and then I wonder whether I've read the story badly."

Resources of the school and community often provide suitable reading material for able learners of all ages. Librarians are great allies in supplying book lists, selecting classroom libraries, and arranging other reading opportunities for these children. An annotated book list of sources of reading materials for gifted children, compiled by Miriam E. Peterson, was published in the February, 1954, issue of *The Reading Teacher*. Members of the National Association for Research in Science Teaching ranked highest books that "suggest further problems," "stimulate further reading," and are "accurate and authoritative" [2]. (See also Appendixes A and C.)

When able learners have suitable reading material at hand, they will not languish in idleness waiting for the slower pupils to finish the asssignment. Able learners are in their element when they have a wealth of reading material, freedom of choice, and opportunity to discuss what they have read [18].

Help Them to Plan a Balanced Daily Program

Excessive absorption in reading may be avoided if gifted children are helped to plan a balanced daily program of reading, social experiences, outdoor and creative activities, radio and television, and unscheduled time. This balance among activities is particularly important around twelve and thirteen years of age when the majority of children tend to reach a peak in their voluntary reading.

So many children today see television shows and listen to radio programs that these avenues of learning cannot be ignored. Able learners often associate these experiences with reading. They hear new words and concepts which they want to discuss and understand more fully. They see a type of story or play and seek further examples in books. They readily appreciate the relative values of reading and other avenues of communication, but generally prefer reading because, as they say, "You can read at your own speed. You can choose what you want to read. You can form your own opinion. You can use your imagination." With a little guidance they will put television in its place and achieve a balanced daily program.

SHOULD GIFTED STUDENTS BE SET APART?

Every learner needs challenging experiences to stretch his reading abilities and experiences easy enough to increase his fluency. He needs success, he needs creative outlet, he needs discipline, whether he is bright or dull [17, 39]. In the elementary grades the able learner should engage in the activities of a reading group unless they are a needless repetition for him. Perhaps the pupils are delving for the first time into the intricacies of outlining or learning the technique of syllabizing. If the gifted student is not in the group, he will miss these new learnings; he will lose the opportunity of discussing a story's deeper meanings and matters of style in a group under the guidance of a teacher.

In their heterogeneous groups, able learners work with pupils of less ability— to help and be helped by them in various activities. This, too, is an important part of the education of gifted children. In any class they may also make a special contribution to their group and sometimes to groups of younger children. They can help other children find the answers to questions. They can locate stories and other reading material needed for a project or unit. They may contribute original poems, drawings, and other creative products needed by the group.

CONCLUDING STATEMENT

Although Gallagher and Rogge [9], in their review of research from February, 1963, to June, 1965, found only one study specifically on the reading ability of the gifted, they reported many factors that might be related to reading achievement. Gifted children's superior mental ability may make it possible for them to appraise their environment and use the reading opportunities it offers more effectively. Their tendency to persist, to use a logical approach instead of guessing, and to verify their results would be assets in critical reading. Their ability to predict outcomes is one characteristic necessary in creative reading.

Certain attitudes and personality traits of gifted individuals may also be conducive to reading proficiency. Among these are independence, positive self-concepts, positive attitudes toward school, and ability to think in more original and creative ways. Independence and industry, however, were viewed by teachers and peers as more appropriate for boys than for girls. For the gifted pupil, the classroom environment seemed less influential than the reward gained from superior performance.

Research has repeatedly shown that acceleration has, in general, no negative results. Gifted children, partly because of their superior reading ability, can gain a year in academic achievement without detrimental social, emotional, or physical consequences. They also profit personally as well as academically by independent study and enrollment in honors classes. The characteristics of successful students in honors courses are similar to those of the mature reader.

The low self-concept of gifted underachievers has been well established, but it is still not clear "how he got that way or what can be done about it" [9].

REFERENCES

1. American Association for Gifted Children, Paul A. Witty (ed.): *The Gifted Child*, D. C. Heath and Company, Boston, 1951.

2. Barnes, Cyrus W., and others: "Criteria for Selecting Supplementary Reading Science Books for Intellectually Gifted High School Students," *Science Education*, vol. 42, pp. 215–218, April, 1958.

3. Bond, George W.: "A Program for Improving Reading in the Secondary Schools," *School Review*, vol. 60, pp. 338–342, September, 1952.

4. Cappa, Dan, and Delwyn G. Schubert: "Do Parents Help Gifted Children Read?" *Journal of Educational Research*, vol. 56, pp. 33–36, September, 1962.

5. Carey, Helen B.: "The Bright Underachiever in Reading: Causes of Underachievement," in H. Alan Robinson (comp. and ed.), *The Underachiever in Reading*, Supplementary Educational Monographs, no. 92, University of Chicago Press, Chicago, 1962, pp. 70–78.

6. DeBoer, John J.: "Creative Reading and the Gifted Student," *The Reading Teacher*, vol. 16, pp. 435–441, May, 1963.

7. Donahue, Rosemary S.: "A Problem in Developmental Reading," *English Journal*, vol. 42, pp. 142–147, March, 1953.

8. Durkin, Dolores: "The Achievement of Preschool Readers: Two Longitudinal Studies," *Reading Research Quarterly*, vol. 1, pp. 5–35, Summer, 1966.

9. Gallagher, James J., and William Rogge: "The Gifted," *Review of Educational Research*, vol. 36, pp. 37–55, February, 1966.

10. Gladstein, Gerald A.: "Study Behavior of Gifted Stereotype and Nonstereotype College Students," *Personnel and Guidance Journal*, vol. 38, pp. 470–474, February, 1960.

11. Gomberg, Adeline W.: "The Lighthouse Day Camp Reading Experiment with Disadvantaged Children," *The Reading Teacher*, vol. 19, pp. 242ff., January, 1966.

12. Gowan, John Curtis: "Dynamics of the Underachievement of Gifted Students," *Exceptional Children,* vol. 24, pp. 98–101, November, 1957.

13. Granger, Grace A.: "Techniques in Stimulating and Guiding the Reading Activities of Superior Readers in the Primary Grades," in William S. Gray (comp. and ed.), *Classroom Techniques in Improving Reading,* Supplementary Educational Monographs, no. 69, University of Chicago Press, Chicago, 1949, pp. 158–162.

14. Gray, William S., and Bernice Rogers: *Maturity in Reading,* University of Chicago Press, Chicago, 1956.

15. Gregory, Margaret, and William J. McLaughlin: "Advanced Reading for the Bright Child," *Clearing House,* vol. 26, pp. 203–205, December, 1951.

16. Haggard, Ernest A.: "Socialization, Personality, and Academic Achievement of Gifted Children," *School Review,* vol. 65, pp. 388–414, December, 1957.

17. Havighurst, Robert (chm.): *Education for the Gifted,* Fifty-seventh Yearbook of the National Society for the Study of Education, University of Chicago Press, Chicago, 1958.

18. Jacobs, Leland B.: "Books for the Gifted," *The Reading Teacher,* vol. 16, pp. 429–434, May, 1963.

19. Josephina (Sister): "Actual and Expected Reading Scores of Gifted and Average Pupils," *Peabody Journal of Education,* vol. 42, pp. 28–31, July, 1964.

20. Josephina (Sister): "Survey of the Research Related to the Reading Ability of the Gifted," *Journal of Educational Research,* vol. 53, pp. 237–239, February, 1960.

21. Kasdon, Lawrence M.: "Early Reading Background of Some Superior Readers among College Freshmen," *Journal of Educational Research,* vol. 52, pp. 151–153, December, 1958.

22. Krippner, Stanley, and Clare Herald: "Reading Disabilities among the Academically Talented," *Gifted Child Quarterly,* vol. 8, pp. 12–20, Spring, 1964.

23. LaPlante, Effie, and Thelma O'Donnell: "Developmental Values through Library Books," *Chicago Schools Journal,* vol. 31, pp. 1–21, March–April, 1950.

24. Larrick, Nancy: *A Parent's Guide to Children's Reading,* Pocket Books, Inc., New York, 1958.

25. Maugham, W. Somerset: *Of Human Bondage,* Doubleday & Company, Inc., Garden City, N.Y., 1917.

26. Moe, Iver L., and Nania Frank: "Reading Deficiencies among Able Pupils," *Journal of Developmental Reading,* vol. 3, pp. 11–26, Autumn, 1959.

27. Norris, Dorothy: "Planning for Your Gifted Children," *Instructor,* vol. 61, p. 83, September, 1951.

28. "Reading and the Gifted Child," *The Reading Teacher,* vol. 16, pp. 417–451, May, 1963.

29. Rinker, Floyd: "Stimulating Creative Expression," *English Journal,* vol. 42, pp. 551–552, December, 1953.

30. Robinson, F. P.: "Study Skills for Superior Students in Secondary School," *The Reading Teacher,* vol. 15, pp. 29–33, September, 1961.

31. Sabaroff, Rose E.: "Challenge in Reading for the Gifted," *Elementary English,* vol. 42, pp. 393–400, April, 1965.

32. Sears, Pauline S.: *The Effect of Classroom Conditions on the Strength of Achievement Motive and Work Output of Elementary School Children,* U.S. Office of Education Cooperative Research Project 873, Stanford University, Stanford, Calif., 1963.

33. Shearer, Elga M., and Lois Fannin: "Reading for the Bright Child," *Library Journal,* vol. 74, pp. 1289–1291, November, 1949.

34. Strang, Ruth: "Helping Gifted Students Develop Their Reading Potentialities," *Selection and Guidance of Gifted Students for National Survival,* Report of the Twentieth Educational Conference, New York, October 27–28, 1955, American Council on Education, Washington, D.C., 1956, pp. 115–121.

35. Strang, Ruth: *Helping Your Gifted Child,* E. P. Dutton & Co., Inc., New York, 1960.

36. Strang, Ruth: "Prevention and Correction of Underachievement," in H. Alan Robinson (comp. and ed.), *The Underachiever in Reading,* Supplementary Educational Monographs, no. 92, University of Chicago Press, Chicago, 1962, pp. 70–78.

37. Wang, James D.: "The Relationship between Children's Play Interests and Their Mental Aibility," *Journal of Genetic Psychology,* vol. 93, pp. 119–131, September, 1958.

38. Witty, Paul A.: "A Balanced Reading Program for the Gifted," *The Reading Teacher,* vol. 17, pp. 418–424, May, 1963.

39. Witty, Paul A.: "Reading for Potential Leaders and Future Scientists," *Nation's Schools,* vol. 61, pp. 57–59, February, 1958.

part V

AN INTEGRATED APPROACH

synthesis of

controversial issues

chapter 17

The purpose of this chapter is to help you combine
the best features of various theories and procedures,
some of which may be mutually contradictory, into a
reading program that will be appropriate for a
particular school.

You will again meet certain major controversial
issues that have already been discussed; you may
learn of a few that have not. Each of these controversies affects practice in the teaching of reading;
each has given rise to all sorts of materials and
methods that are persuasively presented by their
originators or advocates. Literally hundreds of research studies have attempted to prove that one
method or one set of instructional materials is better
than another without asking the essential questions:
better for what purpose? with what age group? with
what kind of pupils? under what classroom conditions? Proponents of conflicting methods of teaching
reading often cite only the results of a single standardized test as evidence that their method will improve the reading of your pupils.

You would be wise to replace this either-or attitude with efforts to define the essential features of effective learner-centered reading programs. This will help to stabilize the pendulum which tends to swing from one extreme to the other.

The major controversial issues in each area of reading instruction are summarized below.

THE READING PROCESS

Reading as an act of synthesizing ideas versus reading as an act of merely pronouncing printed words. Actually, reading involves decoding word forms, analyzing their relations to each other, and determining their meanings. The emphasis changes with the child's stage of development. In the beginning, the child gives most of his attention to the process of decoding words in sentences. As he becomes a more mature reader, he focuses on interpreting the meaning. However, one activity interlocks with the other.

Extrinsic versus intrinsic motivation. Although the individual should ideally be motivated by a basic desire to learn, there is a place for extrinsic rewards in the initial stage of learning and especially with pupils of below-average mental ability and with the emotionally disturbed. A reward that immediately follows a move in the right direction spurs these pupils on to greater effort and higher achievement—provided that the teacher understands the purpose of the reward and knows what constitutes a reward for the individual pupil. The process using such rewards is known as operant conditioning: the individual's feeling response to one stimulus affects his response to the next. His success strengthens his concept of himself as a competent person and helps him to overcome the idea that he is set apart from classmates who can read. Thus viewed, motivation becomes part of the dynamic personality.

PRESCHOOL AND KINDERGARTEN EXPERIENCES

Formal reading instruction versus spontaneous preschool activities. This controversy has been discussed in previous chapters. A reasonable way to resolve it is to *permit* but not to force a preschool or kindergarten child to learn to read. If parents and teachers provide a verbally stimulating environment and respond appropriately to the child's initiative, the chances are that he will learn to read before he enters school. If the first-grade teacher adjusts her program to his needs, he is likely to maintain his initial superiority in reading without incurring any physical, social, or emotional problems [23]. Children who do not show this initiative need prereading experiences for success in beginning reading.

The resolution of this controversy depends upon longitudinal studies designed to provide detailed information on the ways in which many children are affected by either an early or a late start. In the meantime each teacher should observe what effect various procedures have on the responses of his pupils.

DIAGNOSIS OF READING DISABILITY

Focusing diagnostic study on actual reading performance and its causation versus "discovering psychological correlates of reading disability" [13, p. 533]. Both are important considerations. The teacher should continue to assess the child's actual performance—his correct pronunciation and interpretation as well as his errors—and to use this information in helping him to improve. At the same time tests such as the Wechsler tests and the Illinois Test of Psycholinguistic Abilities enable us to discover strengths and deficits in underlying mental abilities, the most obscure of which are the integrative processes. Both prevention and remediation of specific deficiencies stem from such diagnostic information.

Diagnosis before treatment versus diagnosis that accompanies treatment from the beginning. Although the procedure would vary with the individual and the situation, it is best to use all available diagnostic information prior to treatment; then begin immediately to try to solve the problem that most concerns the individual and collect further diagnostic information as he progresses.

METHODS OF TEACHING READING

There have been many recent innovations in teaching beginning reading (see Chapter 6). Each has been compared experimentally with one or more procedures with inconclusive results.

A new alphabet versus the traditional orthography in beginning reading. The Initial Teaching Alphabet aims to protect the child from the confusion that occurs when he finds that a single letter represents different sounds. Beginning readers should not be confronted with incomprehensible irregularities in pronunciation; they may lose confidence in their ability to build rational phonic skills. Experiments have shown that with the i.t.a. children are more confident in the beginning stages, learn to read more quickly and to write more fluently, and sooner or later make a successful transition to traditional orthography. Before this controversy can be resolved, certain questions must be answered: Is it theoretically sound to teach something that has to be corrected later? What is the long-term effect of the i.t.a.? Could the same purpose be accomplished without using beginners' books written in the new alphabet?

Beginning with consonants versus beginning with vowel sounds. Beginning with consonants, which for most practical purposes have constant sounds, has the advantage of introducing the child at first to consistent sound-letter associations. He soon makes the pleasant discovery that he can read many new words by simply acquiring a single vowel sound. Beginning phonic instruction with the vowels also has certain advantages which must be weighed against the disadvantages. In any case, it is always important to start with words that are in the children's speaking vocabulary and apply their knowledge of phonics immediately to phrases and sentences.

Programmed reading materials versus basal reader instruction. Programmed reading materials are based on two sound psychological principles: (1) the child gains immediate knowledge of the results he is achieving—one aspect of operant conditioning; and (2) the structural or other learnings to be derived from the particular selection or assignment have been thoroughly analyzed. However, it is not necessary to use teaching machines in order to apply these principles; comparable results can be obtained when the content is presented in book form.

We should have a basis for evaluating the linear type of programmed material in which the learner is led through a series of steps to the desired goal, if we knew the answers to several questions: Does programmed learning provide for individualization of other factors than rate of progress? Are able learners bored or slowed down by having to go through all the specific steps that are needed for slower learners? Do they actually need the reinforcement that comes from immediate knowledge of results? What opportunities does programmed learning offer for student initiative, critical thinking, originality, and communication with others? Certain of these questions also apply to another type of program far less common—the intrinsic program in which the student's choice in a multiple-choice exercise is used to direct him to new material [33]. In addition, there still remains the question as to whether the learning acquired by the use of programmed material is transferred to the solving of other problems [11].

These questions suggest that programmed material is best used at certain stages of the learning process, for certain purposes, and with certain pupils. Pupils who are socially inclined may learn better in classes with a teacher and classmates. Even though pupils who are shy or withdrawn may learn much content from programmed material, this technique may deprive them of the social experience they need. Well-designed programmed material might be excellent as a supplement, for review or additional practice. It would also give teachers valuable examples for analyzing their own steps in presenting subject matter.

Individualized reading versus basal reading instruction [27]. At one time certain enthusiasts advocated making individualized reading the total reading program. Those days are past. Individualized reading is now recognized as an essential part, but only a part, of a successful reading program. Enthusiasts for individualized reading have tended to include more and more systematic instruction, while advocates of the basal reader have incorporated more and more individualized reading procedures. The problem now, as Duker [6] pointed out, is to find out more about the long-term effectiveness of individualized reading for pupils of different ages, backgrounds, and abilities. Especially important is a study of methods to increase the effectiveness of teacher-pupil conferences.

THE RELATED ROLES OF TEACHER AND SPECIALIST
IN THE TREATMENT OF EXCEPTIONAL CHILDREN

Teacher's responsibility versus specialist's responsibility. These two approaches to the treatment of emotionally disturbed children stem from two different conceptions of behavior disorders in children. One is that emotional disturbance is a function of underlying pathology. After identifying the disturbance, the teacher refers the case to professionals who have a psychotherapeutic orientation. The teacher modifies his classroom procedure in accord with the specialist's recommendations.

If, on the other hand, the disordered behavior is owing to specific educational deprivation or inadequate social learning, the teacher is the best person to help the child overcome the deficiencies that have made him apathetic, aggressive, or withdrawn.

There is a middle ground here. As we have already pointed out in Chapter 15, reading disability may either cause or result from emotional disturbance. The role of the psychologist or psychiatrist, therefore, may be to interpret the child's behavior in the light of the teacher's own observations and to assist the teacher in providing classroom experiences that will help to remedy the emotional difficulties [24].

LINGUISTICS [1]

Structural linguists have enlightened teachers' understanding of the internal composition of language. They emphasize three main components of communications: the *phonemes,* the basic sound unit by which the hearer is able to identify word patterns; *morphemes,* the basic meaning-bearing patterns of language, represented by words and word parts; and *syntax,* the various patternings of morphemes into larger structural units. They are also con-

[1] Written with the assistance of Dr. Margueritte Caldwell.

cerned with the deeper level of meaning as related to structure, namely, with psycholinguistics, which is a more recent field for investigation.

One of the basic assertions of the linguists is that speech is the first mode of communication and that the written language is only a representation of it. In learning to read, the child must associate the printed word with its oral counterpart which in turn he associates with meaning. This process is a form of conditioning which results in a good reader's making the associations almost instantaneously. Eventually the intermediate step of translating the written symbol into the spoken symbol occurs so quickly that it appears to be bypassed.

To what extent pronunciation intervenes between visual perception and comprehension is a matter of controversy. Perhaps it is primarily a matter of reading proficiency. Some beginners may depend upon pronunciation to get the meaning; the highly skilled reader seems to get the meaning directly from his visual impression.

It seems reasonable, therefore, to pronounce words whenever pronunciation aids the apprehension of meaning as in beginning reading or in attacking an unfamiliar word. Otherwise teachers should encourage the student to minimize as early as feasible the intervening step of vocalization between visual association and meaning, to promote efficiency in reading. It may be a primary part of beginning reading since oral language is the child's initial language, but once the reading process has begun, the primacy of sound over sight in seeking meaning should be subordinated or practically omitted.

There is disagreement among the linguists as to what the basic unit of meaning is. Some of them maintain that the letters are the basic units; others feel that words are; but Lefevre asserts that sentences are the building blocks of meaning [15]. He concedes that the phonemes in word analysis and spelling and morphemes (words or parts of words) in structural word analysis and vocabulary are important; but he still considers the syntax of the sentence to be the fundamental source of meaning and hence primary for reading comprehension. Fries [9], too, recommends that the child be introduced to meaningful sentences in the early stage of reading.

From these different points of view stem different approaches to beginning reading: the alphabet and the phonic method, the word method, and the sentence method. Teachers have used these approaches over the years successfully for many students, but each grade still has its poor readers.

Since most approaches work well with some students, teachers should move toward a synthesis of the effective features in all these methods. To stress meaningful sentences will help the child focus on reading as a thought-getting process. To use small words with consistent sound-letter associations of high frequency in these sentences will enable the child to acquire a sight vocabulary. To point out to the child the sound-letter associations for single letters or for clusters will give him one tool for attacking unfamiliar words.

Other linguists, who are systematizing the processes of language in another way, are the transformationalists or generative grammarians. They are attempting to make the relationship of syntax more explicit and to transcribe native linguistic intuition into a set of rules, initially for machine translations. Native speakers apparently do not need these rules since they are able "to invent and interpret new sentences without recourse to rules" [15, p. 654]. As yet there is no direct application of the principles of generative grammar to reading, although the intensive theoretical exploration of syntax has given the teacher a greater understanding of his language if not immediate practical suggestions for classroom procedures in teaching reading.

To teach English to speakers of other languages there are several possible courses of action: (1) teach them to speak English fluently so that they too will have an intuitive feeling for the syntax of English sentences, (2) give instruction in the rules of transformational grammar which have been formulated, or (3) teach the discovery of grammatical generalizations concomitantly with their learning to speak the language. Here, too, it is not either-or. In the early years, language can be learned most readily. Facility in speaking provides a basis for later intuitive verification of correct intonation and syntax.

There is strong advocacy for spending some months teaching children brought up with another language to speak English before introducing reading. One study showed that exposure to the written word accompanying audio-lingual drill during the early stage of foreign language instruction has an adverse effect upon pronunciation. Whether this would be true with Spanish-speaking children in an Anglo environment has not been determined. Although theoretically there may be interference with speech if pupils' attention is directed to the printed word, there might also be reinforcement. Other factors may make reading in small blocks, after the students have learned to pronounce the words accurately, the more effective approach.

Introducing single sound-letter associations one at a time until thoroughly learned, as is done in several new linguistic series, may build confidence as already suggested, but it may make the student less flexible when he later meets irregularities in his reading.

USE OF MECHANICAL DEVICES

The controversy over machines continues. It flares up noticeably when a school system installs a pressure type of machine that may increase speed of reading without regard for the content of the material or the purpose for which it is read. How can skills and content be separated when reading is a thought-getting process? The content and purpose determine the skills to be used. Although it is desirable to read any material as rapidly as possible while still maintaining the necessary comprehension, many students today read too fast; they skim when they should read thoughtfully, critically, deliberately, creatively.

What most of them need to learn is to adjust their speed and method of reading to the particular material and to their purpose in reading it. Superior reading technique requires not mere speed but a greater flexibility.

Machines designed to promote reading rate are of two main types—"those that pace the speed of the reader and those that control his span of perception in reading" [30, p. 255]. Machines of the first type merely push the reader until he acquires the habit of more rapid reading. Those of the second type claim to reduce the number of eye fixations and regressive movements and to increase the number of words read during one fixation.

Extensive research has shown that training with these devices does increase rate of reading for some students; it does not show that machine training per se "markedly modifies eye movement or the span of recognition or produces permanent changes in eye-movement characteristics" [30, p. 256]. Spache [30, pp. 258–259] gives an excellent answer to whether or not one should use reading machines:

. . . gains in reading rate or speed of word recognition can be achieved equally well by ordinary motivated practice or carefully planned classroom activities. Machines add variety, additional motivation, economy in dealing with large groups, and a certain attitude toward improvement for those who read slowly simply because of habit, lack of confidence, or perfectionism. They will help some students to read faster when other methods fail to provide sufficient motivation or impetus. But, like all other methods, they are not successful with all students and cannot be used indiscriminately.

Individuals who have timed themselves while reading have shown as much improvement in comprehension as those who used a reading-rate controller. However, both machine training and nonmachine techniques have produced greater improvement in reading than no training at all. One disadvantage of machine methods is that some students may become so dependent upon the machine that they fail to develop inner motivation.

THE INSTRUCTIONAL MATERIALS EXPLOSION

Reading materials and equipment are of central importance in the reading program. Basic readers can be used to provide a common core and continuity of reading experience year by year. Workbooks and programmed material may reinforce essential skills and give additional practice where needed. Textbooks in each of the content fields provide a framework and sequence of knowledge which make supplementary reading more meaningful and easier to remember. Models and samples, pictures, slide films, and motion pictures, as well as conversations, excursions, and other firsthand experiences may supplement and clarify a person's reading. At all age levels suitable reading material helps children and young people to develop skill in reading and contributes to their personal and social development.

On the other hand, unsuitable material may cause or intensify reading problems. When the books given students are too difficult, they may confirm their impressions of the drudgery of reading and of themselves as failures. When the books are obviously childish, the poor reader is embarrassed to be reading them. When the books are dull and remote from students' interests, they offer no immediate reward for reading; when they present an untrue or sordid view of life, their influence on children and young people is degrading.

There are controversies in the area of reading materials and equipment which can be only briefly mentioned here. Vocabulary control and control of sound-letter associations increase ease of learning to read at the same time that they make the content stilted and uninteresting. The all-white cast of characters in traditional reading material is in conflict with the need to introduce Negro characters and members of diverse ethnic and socioeconomic groups, which will provide a background of experience for all children and more personal significance for nonwhite children [14]. Anthologies of stories and essays selected by the compiler are now competing with thousands of fiction and non-fiction paperbacks.

Conflicts in the area of reading materials should be resolved by reference to the nature of reading (Chapter 1), curriculum trends (Chapters 2 and 3), and student interests. Reading interests have been studied by many ingenious methods. The interests of first-grade children have been ascertained by recording their oral reports during "share-and-tell" periods [4]. These were found to be quite different from the content of primers they were reading. Stanchfield [31] interviewed eighth-grade boys, each for more than an hour, about their general reading interests and specific preferences in type of content and quality of writing. Simpson and Soares [29] obtained junior high school pupils' appraisals of stories from thirty-five junior high school anthologies. Pupils read each story and indicated on a scale how much they had liked it. Many forms of questionnaires and check lists have also been used [32].

From these studies several generalizations may be made. The difference in reading interests between boys and girls is quite marked. Boys tend to prefer exploration, outdoor adventure, physical action, science and science fiction, and sports, while girls prefer romance, milder adventure, poetry, home and family life, and stories about teen-agers and their problems. Both boys and girls like mystery stories. Gifted children have interest patterns similar to those of their peers but often arrive at a given pattern earlier. Science articles, biographies, and other nonfiction are becoming more popular than fiction. There is often a gap between what children want to read and what the teacher assigns or recommends. In general, they like fast-moving narrative, illustrations, clear and concrete language.

Conflicts with respect to reading materials can be resolved in several ways.

By beginning reading instruction with familiar, personally meaningful words, phrases, and sentences that the child dictates and then reads, the teacher introduces reading as a thought-getting process and bridges the gap between the alien world of reading and the child's own thoughts, feelings, and experiences. The teacher next teaches consistent sound-letter associations in already familiar reading material. At this stage the child's satisfaction in mastering the new skill of decoding printed symbols into familiar sounds and meaning is so keen that he does not need highly interesting material. Once he has mastered basic word recognition skills, he is able to read and enjoy a wider variety of reading material. Stories, science, biography, and other reading material must then be intrinsically interesting and rewarding, going beyond his own experience to a wider world. For youngsters having special needs, selected reading material should be provided. Retarded readers need books of high interest and low difficulty. Bilinguals need readable books that build appreciation of both cultures. Emotionally disturbed children and young people can gain insight into their own problems of adjustment by reading stories about characters who solve their personal and social problems. Thus their fluency increases and reading becomes an enrichment of their daily lives. Teacher-sponsored reading clubs, in which members read and discuss books of current interest to them, arouse keen interest in reading on the part of secondary school pupils [20].

These are only a few examples of the possibilities a teacher has to incorporate psychologically sound and practical features of any innovation into his total reading program. Instead of trying to find out which of two programs is better, investigators should select the features in each method that prove to be most effective in helping certain pupils under certain conditions to learn without unnecessary failure or frustration.

REFERENCES

1. Blakely, W. Paul, and Beverly McKay: "Individualized Reading as Part of an Eclectic Reading Program," *Elementary English,* vol. 43, pp. 214–219, March, 1966.

2. Brzeinski, Joseph E.: "Beginning Reading in Denver," *The Reading Teacher,* vol. 18, pp. 16–21, October, 1964.

3. Burton, William H.: "Some Arguments about Reading," *Education,* vol. 84, pp. 387–392, March, 1964.

4. Byers, Loretta: "Pupils' Interests and the Content of Primary Reading Texts," *The Reading Teacher,* vol. 17, pp. 227–233, January, 1964.

5. Campbell, C. S.: "Leisure Reading in the Senior High Schools of Alberta," *Alberta Journal of Educational Research,* vol. 10, pp. 46–55, March, 1964.

6. Duker, Sam: "Needed Research on Individualized Reading," *Elementary English,* vol. 43, pp. 220ff., March, 1966.

7. Durkin, Dolores:"The Achievement of Preschool Readers: Two Longitudinal Studies," *Reading Research Quarterly*, vol. 1, pp. 5–35, Summer, 1966.

8. "Emerging Practices in Modern Reading," *Education*, vol. 85, pp. 515–561, May, 1965.

9. Fries, Charles C.: "Linguistic Approaches to First Grade Reading Programs," in James F. Kerfoot (comp. and ed.), *First Grade Reading Programs*, International Reading Association Conference Proceedings, vol. 9, Newark, Del., 1965.

10. Furness, Edna L.: "Pupils, Teachers and 'Sentence Sense,'" *Education*, vol. 86, pp. 12–17, September, 1965.

11. Gagné, Robert M., and Larry T. Brown: "Some Factors in the Programing of Conceptual Learning," *Journal of Experimental Psychology*, vol. 62, pp. 313–321, October, 1961.

12. Goodman, Kenneth S.: "The Linguistics of Reading," *Elementary School Journal*, vol. 64, pp. 355–361, April, 1964.

13. Kass, Corinne E.: "Psycholinguistic Disabilities of Children with Reading Problems," *Exceptional Children*, vol. 32, pp. 533–539, April, 1966.

14. Larrick, Nancy: "The All-white World of Children's Books," *Saturday Review*, vol. 1, pp. 63ff., September 11, 1965.

15. Lefevre, Carl A.: "A Comprehensive Linguistic Approach to Reading," *Elementary English*, vol. 42, pp. 651–659, October, 1965.

16. Lefevre, Carl A.: "The Contribution of Linguistics," *Instructor*, vol. 74, pp. 77, 103–105, March, 1965.

17. Levin, Harry: "Reading Research: What, Why, and for Whom?" *Elementary English*, vol. 43, pp. 138–147, February, 1966.

18. Marquardt, William F.: "Language Interference in Reading," *The Reading Teacher*, vol. 18, pp. 214–218, December, 1964.

19. Newman, Robert E.: "The Kindergarten Reading Controversy," *Elementary English*, vol. 43, pp. 235ff., March, 1966.

20. Paul, William (Sister): "Surf's Up—And So Is Reading Interest," *English Journal*, vol. 55, pp. 93–94, January, 1966.

21. Perry, William G., Jr., and Charles P. Whitlock: "A Clinical Rationale for a Reading Film," *Harvard Educational Review*, vol. 24, pp. 6–27, Winter, 1954.

22. Perry, William G., Jr., and Charles P. Whitlock: "The Right to Read Rapidly," *Atlantic Monthly*, vol. 190, pp. 88–96, November, 1952.

23. "Preschool and Beginning Reading," *The Reading Teacher*, vol. 18, pp. 3–42, October, 1964.

24. Quay, Herbert C., and others: "Remediation of the Conduct of the Problem Child in the Special Class Setting," *Exceptional Children*, vol. 32, pp. 509–515, April, 1966.

25. Robinson, H. Alan (comp. and ed.): *Recent Developments in Reading*, Supplementary Educational Monographs, no. 95, University of Chicago Press, Chicago, 1965.

26. Robinson, Helen M. (comp. and ed.): *Controversial Issues in Reading and Promising Solutions*, Supplementary Educational Monographs, no. 91, University of Chicago Press, Chicago, 1961.

27. Sartain, Harry W.: "Individualized Reading," in H. Alan Robinson (comp.

and ed.), *Recent Developments in Reading,* Supplementary Educational Mono-graphs, no. 95, University of Chicago Press, Chicago, 1965, pp. 81–85.

28. Shores, J. Harlan: "Reading Interests and Informational Needs of High School Students," *The Reading Teacher,* vol. 17, pp. 536–544, April, 1964.

29. Simpson, Ray H., and Anthony Soares: "Best and Least Liked Short Stories in Junior High School," *English Journal,* vol. 54, pp. 108–111, February, 1965.

30. Spache, George D.: *Toward Better Reading,* The Garrard Press, Champaign, Ill., 1963.

31. Stanchfield, John: "The Reading Interests of Eighth-grade Boys," *Journal of Developmental Reading,* vol. 5, pp. 256–265, Summer, 1962.

32. Vaughn, Beryl I.: "Reading Interests of Eighth-grade Students," *Journal of Developmental Reading,* vol. 6, pp. 149–155, Spring, 1963.

33. Weintraub, Samuel: "Programed Reading Material," in H. Alan Robinson (comp. and ed.), *Recent Developments in Reading,* Supplementary Educational Monographs, no. 95, University of Chicago Press, Chicago, 1965, pp. 64–69.

bibliographies of books
for different purposes

appendix A

1. Baker, Augusta: *Books about Negro Life for Children,* New York Public Library, New York, 1961.

2. *Bulletin of the Center for Children's Books,* University of Chicago Press, Chicago. Published monthly by the Graduate Library School, 5835 Kimbark Avenue, Chicago, Ill. 60637.

3. Crosby, Muriel (ed.): *Reading Ladders for Human Relations,* 4th ed., American Council on Education, Washington, D.C., 1963.

4. Dunn, Anita E., Mabel E. Jackman, and J. Roy Newton: *Fare for the Reluctant Reader,* 3d ed., Capital Area School Development Association, State University of New York at Albany, New York, 1964.

5. Huus, Helen: *Children's Books to Enrich Social Studies,* National Council for the Social Studies, Washington, D.C., 1961.

6. Korey, Ruth Anne: "Children's Literature for Integrated Classes," *Elementary English,* vol. 43, pp. 39–42, January, 1966.

7. Logasa, Hannah: *An Index to One-act Plays,* Faxton Publishing Company, Boston, 1958.

8. Nealon, Thomas E.: "The Adapted Classic in the Junior High School," *Journal of Reading,* vol. 9, pp. 256–262, March, 1966.

9. Simmons, John S., and Helen O'Hara Rosenblum: *The Reading Improvement Handbook,* 1966, Reading Improvement, Box 75, College Station, Pullman, Washington 99163.

10. Smilananich, Helen, and Wilson Pecot (comps.): "Bibliotherapy: Stories with a purpose," 1963, Bridge Street School, Los Angeles School District, Los Angeles, Calif. (Mimeographed.)

11. Spache, George D.: *Good Reading for Poor Readers,* The Garrard Press, Champaign, Ill., 1958.

12. Strang, Ruth, Ethlyne Phelps, and Dorothy Withrow: *Gateways to Readable Books,* The H. W. Wilson Company, New York, 1966.

films in the

reading program

appendix B

The following films are intended to help teachers and pupils understand and appreciate the reading process as well as related processes, such as efficient study and use of the library. This list of films does not include those designed to be used in training pupils in the mechanics of reading, such as rhythmic eye movements, increased recognition span, and so forth.

All motion picture films listed are designed to be used with 16-mm sound projectors. (There is a recent trend toward the use of 8-mm films, but this is still somewhat experimental and is something for the future so far as regular school use is concerned.) The information given includes the level or levels for which each film is suitable (p, primary; i, intermediate; jh, junior high school; sh, senior high school; c, college; ad, adult); the length of the reel or set of reels in minutes; and whether available in black and white (BW) or color (C). The date the film was released is also indicated where available.

Video tapes and closed-circuit television systems will enable each classroom to utilize materials that can be made available to every school.

FILMS AND FILMSTRIPS FOR TEACHERS AND PROSPECTIVE TEACHERS OF READING [1]

Films

1. "Eyes That Learn," Educational Developmental Laboratories, 1958 (c, ad; 17 min, BW).
2. "Gregory Learns to Read," Wayne State University, 1957 (c, ad; 28 min; BW and C).
3. "Individualizing Reading Instruction in the Classroom," Teachers College Press, Teachers College, Columbia University, 1957 (c, ad; 20 min; BW; 2 reels).
4. "Mike Makes His Mark," National Education Association, 1955 (c, ad; 29 min; BW and C).
5. "Phonovisual in Action," The Film Center, 1961 (p, i, jh, sh, c, ad; 29 min; C).
6. "Skippy and the Three R's," National Education Association, 1953 (c, ad; 29 min; BW and C).
7. "They All Learn to Read," International Film Bureau, 1955 (sh, c, ad; long version: 26 min, standard version: 22 min; BW).
8. "Who Is Pete?" International Film Bureau, 1961 (c, ad; 27 min; BW and C).
9. "Why Can't Jimmy Read?" International Film Bureau, 1961 (c, ad; 15 min; BW).

Filmstrips

1. "Reading Improvement," Learning through Seeing, 1957 (set of 3 filmstrips; c, ad; silent; BW: "In the Elementary School," 41 frames; "In the Secondary School," 43 frames; "College and Adult," 47 frames).
2. "Teacher Training: Reading" (K-6), The Jam Handy Organization, 1955 (set of 13 filmstrips, 19 to 83 frames each; c, ad; sound; C; prereading experiences, learning to read printed symbols, reading as a continuous experience, study skills, reading experiences).

[1] See also Anthony P. Witham, "In-service Films for the Reading Teacher," *Elementary English,* vol. 40, pp. 542–552, May, 1963; and George D. Spache, "Auditory and Visual Materials in Reading Instruction," *Development in and through Reading,* Sixtieth Yearbook of the National Society for the Study of Education, University of Chicago Press, Chicago, 1961, pp. 209–225.

FILMS AND FILMSTRIPS FOR PUPILS

How to Improve Reading and Study: Films

1. "A Book for You," McGraw-Hill Book Company, 1959 (jh; 17 min; BW).

2. "Reading Improvement: Defining the Good Reader," Coronet Instructional Films, 1965 (i, jh, sh; 11 min; BW and C).

3. "Reading Improvement: Word Recognition Skills," Coronet Instructional Films, 1965 (i, jh, sh; 11 min; BW and C).

4. "Reading Improvement: Comprehension Skills," Coronet Instructional Films, 1965 (i, jh, sh; 11 min; BW and C).

5. "Reading Improvement: Effective Speeds," Coronet Instructional Films, 1965 (i, jh, sh; 11 min; BW and C).

6. "Improving Study Habits," McGraw-Hill Book Company (jh; 14 min; BW and C).

7. "Learning to Study," Encyclopaedia Britannica Films, Inc., 1954 (jh, sh; 14 min; BW).

8. "Reading Maps," Encyclopaedia Britannica Films, Inc., 1955 (i, jh; 11 min; BW).

9. "Developing Reading Maturity: The Mature Reader," Coronet Instructional Films, 1965 (jh, sh, c; 11 min; BW and C).

10. "Developing Reading Maturity: Critical Evaluation," Coronet Instructional Films, 1965 (jh, sh, c; 11 min; BW and C).

11. "Developing Reading Maturity: Interpreting Meaning," Coronet Instructional Films, 1965 (jh, sh, c; 11 min; BW and C).

12. "Developing Reading Maturity: Understanding Style," Coronet Instructional Films, 1965 (jh, sh, c; 11 min; BW and C).

13. "Developing Reading Maturity: Comparative Reading," Coronet Instructional Films, 1965 (jh, sh, c; 11 min; BW and C).

14. "How Effective Is Your Reading," Coronet Instructional Films, 1954 (jh, sh, c; 11 min; BW and C).

Filmstrips

1. "How to Study," Curriculum Films, Inc., 1951 (3 filmstrips, each 25 frames; i, jh; silent with captions; C).

2. "Improve Your Study Habits," Young America Films, 1951 (45 frames; i, jh; silent with captions; C).

How to Improve Vocabulary

1. "Reading Improvement: Vocabulary Skills," Coronet Instructional Films, 1965 (i, jh, sh; 11 min; BW and C).

How to Read Specific Kinds of Literature and Do Specific Kinds of Study: Films

1. "Educational Guidance: Basic Study Skills," Coronet Instructional Films, 1950–1964 (13 films, chosen from a longer list; each 1 reel; 11 min; BW and C):

"Building an Outline" (jh, sh)
"Find the Information" (jh, sh)
"Homework: Studying on Your Own" (jh, sh, c)
"How to Concentrate" (jh, sh, c)
"How to Develop Interest" (jh, sh)
"How to Judge Authority" (jh, sh)
"How to Judge Facts" (jh, sh)
"How to Read a Book," 2d ed. (jh, sh)
"How to Study," 2d ed. (jh, sh)
"Importance of Making Notes" (jh, sh)
"Know Your Library," 2d ed. (jh, sh)
"Library Organization" (jh, sh, c)
"Look It Up! Dictionary Habits" (jh, sh, c)

2. "Literature Appreciation Series," Coronet Instructional Films, 1952–1965 (7 films; jh, sh, c; BW and C):

"English Lyrics" (11 min)
"How to Read Biographies" (13½ min)
"How to Read Essays" (13½ min)
"How to Read Poetry" (11 min)
"Stories" (13½ min)

3. "How to Read Newspapers," Coronet Instructional Films, 1951 (jh, sh; 11 min; BW and C).

Filmstrips

1. "Learning to Study," The Jam Handy Organization, 1952 (7 filmstrips; jh, sh, c; silent with captions; BW and C):

"Study Headquarters" (33 frames)
"Getting Down to Work" (34 frames)
"Using a Textbook" (26 frames)
"Taking Notes in Class" (29 frames)
"Giving a Book Report" (29 frames)
"Writing a Research Paper" (32 frames)
"Reviewing" (27 frames)

2. "Reading a Newspaper," Your Lesson Plan Filmstrips, 1955 (52 frames; i, jh; silent with captions; C).

3. "Reading for Understanding," Pacific Productions, Inc., 1960 (5 filmstrips; i, jh; silent with captions; C):

"Content Clues" (32 frames)
"Main Ideas" (27 frames)
"Details" (27 frames)

"Details" (26 frames)
"Inferring Meanings" (23 frames)

Background of Reading and Expression: Films

1. "Discovering the Library," Coronet Instructional Films, 1954 (p, i; 11 min; BW and C).
2. "Fun with Speech Sounds," Coronet Instructional Films, 1954 (p; 11 min; BW and C).
3. "Reading for Beginners: Word Sounds," Coronet Instructional Films, 1954 (p, i; 11 min; BW and C).
4. "Sentences That Ask and Tell," Coronet Instructional Films, 1961 (p; 11 min; BW and C).

Filmstrips

1. "Syllabication and Structure," The Jam Handy Organization, 1965 (p; 7 filmstrips averaging about 33 frames each; individual pictures reproduced in a manual).

ADDRESSES OF FILM COMPANIES

1. Coronet Instructional Films
65 East South Water Street
Chicago, Ill. 60601

2. Curriculum Films, Inc.
Curriculum Materials Corporation
1319 Vine Street
Philadelphia, Pa.

3. Educational Developmental Laboratories
284 East Pulaski Road
Huntington, L.I., N.Y.

4. Encyclopaedia Britannica Films, Inc.
1150 Wilmette Avenue
Wilmette, Ill.

5. The Film Center
915 12th Street N.W.
Washington, D.C. 20005

6. International Film Bureau
332 S. Michigan Avenue
Chicago, Ill.

7. The Jam Handy Organization
2821 East Grand Boulevard
Detroit, Mich.

8. Learning through Seeing
   Chadron, Nebraska and
   Sunland, Calif.

9. McGraw-Hill Book Company
   330 West 42d Street
   New York, N.Y. 10036

10. National Education Association
    1201 16th Street N.W.
    Washington, D.C. 20006

11. Pacific Productions, Inc.
    414 Mason Street
    San Francisco, Calif.

12. Teachers College Press
    Teachers College
    Columbia University
    New York, N.Y. 10027

13. Wayne State University
    Detroit, Mich.

14. Young America Films
    18 East 42d Street
    New York, N.Y. 10017

15. Your Lesson Plan Filmstrips
    1319 Vine Street
    Philadelphia, Pa.

reading materials for the junior and senior high school grades and for college

The teacher of reading at the high school or college level must be able to choose materials appropriate for use with individuals or groups at varying stages of reading maturity. Before 1935, there was available to teachers of reading very little material that was specifically designed or selected for use in reading instruction in high schools. This kind of material was nonexistent in the colleges. Consequently, it was necessary for teachers of reading to spend much time locating and duplicating materials suitable for their objectives and for the reading interests and abilities of their students.

During the last thirty years, there has been rapid multiplication of reading materials for both high school and college. It is no longer necessary to depend on one reading workbook or textbook alone. The use of a large amount of supplementary material is highly desirable. This keeps the work of the reading course from becoming stereotyped and routinized and enables the teacher to take account of individual interests and needs. The development of readability formulas in recent years provides an objective basis for the selection of appropriate materials from different sources.

The sources of materials for remedial, corrective, or developmental reading in the high school and college are of the following types: (1) reading workbooks, (2) reading textbooks or textbook series for the secondary school or college, (3) materials for vocabulary training, (4) procedures and materials to facilitate word recognition, (5) study-habits workbooks and guides, (6) materials for use with reading films, and (7) books for free reading. Let us consider each of these sources and note some of the titles that are available in each category.

READING WORKBOOKS

Secondary School. Several well-designed and widely used reading workbooks for the secondary school have been published within the last fifteen years. Many of these are revisions of earlier workbooks. Most of them are in the nature of workbook series designed to cover a rather wide range of grade levels and reading abilities.

Two workbooks made available in the latter 1950s by Gray, Monroe, and Artley are suitable for use in grades 7 to 12. These are *Basic Reading Skills for Junior High School Use* [17] and *Basic Reading Skills for High School Use* [18]. Each of these workbooks exists in a pupil's edition and a teacher's edition and provides a refresher program of reading skills for pupils not reading up to grade level.

Another workbook series for junior and senior high schools is the Be a Better Reader Series, Books I–VI, by Nila Banton Smith [45]. This set of materials may serve as the basis of a developmental reading program in high school. It covers common reading skills and the reading skills of literature, social studies, science, and mathematics.

The SRA Better Reading Books Series, books 1, 2, and 3, by Elizabeth A. Simpson [44] has been available for some years. Each book is attractively prepared and is based on practical experience in teaching reading to high school students. Each workbook contains twenty practice exercises, twenty reading selections, and twenty tests, and is accompanied by a progress folder in which the pupil may keep a record of his growth in reading achievement. This series is suitable for use with junior and senior high school pupils and may also be used with college students and adults who are slow readers.

Among the earlier published workbooks is *Study Type of Reading Exercises for Secondary Schools* by Strang and others [48], which consists of 1,000-word articles on the reading process, used for practice in reading for secondary school students. A more advanced book with a similar title is available for the college level [49].

A long-used series, Diagnostic Reading Workbooks, by Eleanor M. Johnson and others [26], contains a workbook suitable for retarded readers in high school, as well as workbooks for the elementary grades. There is a set of achievement tests to be used with the workbooks. A more recent set of materials prepared by the same author is Modern Reading Skilltexts [25], a three-book series for reading improvement of junior and senior high school pupils. The series is aimed at these reading-study skills: understanding ideas, interpreting ideas, organizing ideas, word analysis and dictionary skill, and understanding words.

A popular workbook series, Reading for Meaning by Guiler and Coleman [19], is being extensively revised by Coleman and Jungeblut [7]. Separate workbooks were issued for grades 4 through 6 in 1962 and for grades 7 through 9 in 1964. Plans are under way for new workbooks covering grades 10 through 12. Each of the Guiler and Coleman workbooks, which, incidentally, are still in print, contains twenty-four units. The workbooks in the new series by Coleman and Jungeblut have thirty-two units at each grade level. Each unit consists of a short passage, usually two or three paragraphs, followed by six types of questions relating to: getting word meanings, choosing the best title, getting the main idea, getting the facts, making an outline, and drawing conclusions. The questions are objective, and percentile norms for the appropriate grade level are given for each lesson. All exercises are either revised from the Guiler and Coleman series or are new. Each exercise covers two pages and is untimed, but it is estimated that about half an hour is required for each unit. Recent research by the authors offers favorable indications for the selections used at the seventh-, eighth-, and ninth-grade levels.[1]

Perhaps the longest-used of all the workbooks in the field of reading are the Standard Test Lessons in Reading Series by McCall and Crabbs [34], first published in 1926 and revised in 1950 and 1961. The first four of these booklets, A, B, C, and D, are designed mainly for the elementary grades, and book E is planned for grades 7 to 12. Scores on the questions in the various lessons are translated into G scores or grade scores. The keeping by the pupils of graphic records of their achievement on the lessons stimulates interest in their progress from day to day.

Other useful workbooks for the high school level are Reading Skills by Bamman [2] and New Adventures in Reading by Leavell and Davis [31].

College. Several very useful manuals for college students have been prepared by reading specialists with experience at the college level. A manual that is well designed for the improvement of the basic reading skills is *Power and Speed in Reading* by Doris W. Gilbert [14]. It contains twelve selections designed for a course of twelve weeks that involves twenty-four hours of instruction, although the plan is flexible. The reading selections and vocabulary exercises are well chosen. At intervals throughout the manual there are reading tests, the results of which may be recorded on progress charts in the appendix. Although this manual is intended primarily as a guide for college students and adults, it should also be useful in developmental and corrective reading programs in secondary schools where the general level of scholastic aptitude is comparatively high.

Somewhat in contrast to the Gilbert manual, where the reading selections are fairly long, is the *College Reading Manual* by Shaw and Townsend [43] which contains 106 exercises, most of which are rather brief. The reading selections are similar to those found in college textbooks in English, science, and social studies. Questions at the end of each reading passage check the ability of the student to

[1] Ann Jungeblut and John H. Coleman, "Reading Content That Interests Seventh-, Eighth-, and Ninth-grade Students," *Journal of Educational Research*, vol. 58, pp. 393–401, May–June, 1965.

comprehend main ideas. For about half the exercises, check tests on the ability of the student to grasp details are also given.

A rather recent workbook designed especially for college students is *Improving Reading Skills in College Subjects* by Cherington [6], with an introduction by Strang, under whose sponsorship the manual was undertaken. While use of this manual will no doubt help to improve general reading efficiency, its attention is centered on reading skills in different college subjects—history, sociology, economics, government, psychology, philosophy, chemistry, and physics. The booklet contains seventeen selections, each numbering several hundred words. Each selection is timed and is followed by a number of questions, most of which are multiple choice, although questions calling for explanation are also included. Since the answers to some of the questions cannot readily be scored objectively, no norms for the questions have been published; nevertheless, the questions should be useful in appraising the students' grasp and understanding of ideas.

A revision of Triggs's *Improve Your Reading* [51], which was one of the first manuals of remedial reading exercises for college students, is available. This book is concerned with the following topics: "What Is Good Reading?"; "Streamline Your Reading"; "Get Acquainted with Strange Words"; "To Understand What You Read, Think as You Read."

Other promising workbooks or manuals for use by college students are *Improving Reading Ability*, second edition, by Stroud, Ammons, and Bamman [50]; *Toward Better Reading Skills*, second edition, by Cosper and Griffin [8]; *Better Reading in College* by Dallmann and Sheridan [12]; and *The Art of Efficient Reading* by Spache and Berg [46].

READING TEXTBOOKS AND TEXTBOOK SERIES

There is no clear dividing line between workbooks and textbooks which are designed as guides for high school and college students in improving their reading skill. In general, workbooks tend to be comparatively brief, to be oriented around a series of specific skills, to be issued in flexible covers, and to be consumable, although not all workbooks may be characterized in this way. On the whole, textbooks tend to be longer than workbooks, to contain more explanatory material to help the student understand the reading process, to be published in hard covers, and not to be consumable. Some textbooks, however, are published both in a hard-cover, permanent edition and in a soft-cover edition which may be used up by the student. A reading textbook is usually intended to meet the needs of reading classes that are set up as an integral part of the curriculum.

Secondary School. Among the earliest secondary school reading textbooks to find their way into print was the series by Carol Hovious, the first book of which, *Following Printed Trails,* appeared in 1936. The Hovious books did a great deal to give practical application to remedial and developmental reading programs for secondary school pupils, but all of them except *Wings for Reading* [22] are now out of print.

A two-book series that has been used in junior and senior high schools for a good many years is *Develop Your Reading* [28] and *Read and Comprehend* [29] by Knight and Traxler. Each book contains two parts designed to provide practice respectively in extensive and intensive reading. The latter book is available in a revised edition and contains chapters on such questions as "How Much Fun Can You Find in Books?"; "Can You Get the Main Idea?"; "How Rapidly Do You Read?"; "Do You Need Winged Words?"; "Do You Believe All You Read?"; and "How Shall We Read the Newspaper?" The last subject is dealt with more extensively in a book, *How to Read a Newspaper* by Edgar Dale [11], which has been used in high schools for about twenty-five years.

Another of the earlier textbooks is *Improving Your Reading* by Wilkinson and Brown [53], which is now available in a second revision. This book is intended for pupils in the elementary grades and for those in the junior high school who are seriously retarded in reading. The first of the four parts contains a series of tests which are called experiments in reading; the second and third parts are devoted respectively to oral reading and silent reading; and the fourth part includes experiments or tests to show improvement.

Another reading textbook which has been used widely at the high school level for many years is *Experiences in Reading and Thinking* by Center and Persons [5]. This was formerly the easiest of a well-written, but comparatively difficult, three-book series of reading textbooks for the secondary school. The two more difficult books have been discontinued.

One of the best-known series of books for use in improving the reading ability of junior and senior high school pupils is the Let's Read Series by Murphy and others [37]. In contrast to reading textbooks which contain a large number of very short selections, the four books under the title "Let's Read" contain interesting stories and articles, each of which is several pages in length. The selections are followed by instructions to the students and by questions. The materials are well chosen to appeal to the interests of high school pupils. In case some other book is used as the basic text, the Let's Read Series could well be employed for supplementary work or be placed on the list for free reading.

The Reading for Enjoyment Series by Jewett and others [24] is a comparatively recent set of books for junior high school use. The three books in the series are *Adventure Bound,* for grade 7, *Journeys into America,* for grade 8, and *Literature for Life,* for grade 9. A workbook and a teacher's guide are available for each of the three titles.

The Mastery of Reading Series by Bailey and Leavell [1] may be used in grades 7 to 12. This is an impressive series, with extensive material and good illustrations.

Other reading textbooks for the high school are *Reading Skills* by Wood and Barrows [55] and the Better Reading Series by Blair and Gerber [3]. The latter consists of two volumes, *Factual Prose* and *Literature.* The first of these volumes, which is in its fifth edition, contains well-chosen reading exercises and an integrated program for developing student reading and writing abilities. The volume on literature is intended to help students develop skill in understanding and appreciating fiction, drama, and poetry. There is also a single-volume edition, *Repertory,* which represents a combination of materials from *Factual Prose* and *Literature.*

College and Adult. At the college level, an especially practical and helpful reading textbook is *Effective Reading and Learning* by Shaw [42]. This book is based on a course in reading taught in Brooklyn College. It is concerned with improving reading speed and versatility, reading college textbooks, reading assignments in various subjects, improving vocabulary, improving concentration, using the dictionary, taking notes, and preparing for and taking tests.

Witty's *How to Become a Better Reader* [54] is a well-known guide for high school pupils, college students, and adults. Other books designed to help mature readers are *Improvement of College Reading* by Glock [16] and *Reading Improvement for Adults* by Leedy [32].

Triggs has published a book, *Reading: Its Creative Teaching and Testing, Kindergarten through College* [52]. The first part is largely theoretical; the second part is in the nature of a teacher's manual on how to teach reading in the subject-matter fields, how to determine the level of difficulty of reading material, and so forth. It is not intended that this book be placed in the hands of students, but it is mentioned here because it is designed as a guide for teachers in their day-to-day work with students at all levels.

MATERIALS FOR VOCABULARY BUILDING

A number of books and pamphlets containing useful vocabulary-teaching materials are available. One of the most interesting of these is *Building Your Vocabulary*, with revisions, by Gilmartin [15]. This is a rather mature book, suitable for use in senior high schools and colleges. The book challenges the student in the very beginning with "Sixty Snags in Pronunciation" and then takes up a variety of procedures for improving vocabulary. It maintains a flexible organization through the use of short units. Vocabulary tests and quizzes are included.

An easier book, one designed for remedial reading classes at the high school level, is *Word Attack: A Way to Better Reading* by Roberts [39].

An interesting vocabulary textbook that has been available for many years is *Twelve Ways to Build a Vocabulary* by Hart [20]. Designed for use in high school and college, this little book contains twelve chapters, some of which carry such intriguing titles as "Weary Words," "The Poison Well," "Malapropisms or What Did She Mean?" and "Fun with the Dictionary."

A somewhat easier book by Hart and Lejeune, *The Growing Vocabulary* [21], is intended for pupils twelve to sixteen years of age, and uses a word list based on the *Thorndike-Century Junior Dictionary.*

Secondary schools attempting to correlate instruction in reading with the teaching of spelling may be interested in two books in this area. One of these is *Vocabulary-Building Speller* by Meyer [35]. Spelling lists are accompanied by definitions and illustrations of the use of the words, and most of the words are repeated several times in the definitions of other words. The other book is *Spelling and Word Power* by Malsbary [33]. It includes units on basic words, everyday business words, advanced words, study helps, and special vocabularies of various fields. It is accompanied by a workbook. A revised edition of the book was published in 1965.

PROCEDURES AND MATERIALS TO FACILITATE WORD RECOGNITION

Instruction in reading the English language has always been made difficult by problems inherent in spelling and writing. In recent years, the linguists have turned their attention to problems of reading, and in some schools close working relationships between teachers and linguists have been developed. It is not a function of this section of the present book to discuss the theory and technique of linguistics nor to provide a critique of different systems of linguistics as a foundation to reading instruction. This has been capably presented in a recent article by Betts.[2] Some schools report good success in applying the ideas expressed in a book by Fries.[3] Other schools have used the practice exercises in *Let's Read*, a linguistic approach to reading developed by Bloomfield and Barnhart.[4]

Since 1960, the interest of teachers of reading in both England and the United States has been captured to an unusual degree by the Initial Teaching Alphabet devised by Sir James Pitman.[5]

Until very recently, teaching materials printed in the i.t.a. were not readily available to American schools, but a reading series of this kind is now being published in the United States [23]. This series consists of pupil readers and workbooks, teachers' manuals, and additional materials.

Although the i.t.a. was devised primarily as a method for teaching beginners to read, it has been suggested that this method has uses for remedial reading with individuals at all levels, particularly with emotionally disturbed persons, and evidence on this point is beginning to become available.[6] The i.t.a. method is also being promoted for use in teaching English as a foreign language in underdeveloped countries. Much more research on the values and long-term benefits of the i.t.a. is needed.

A "package deal" including flash cards, pads, and recordings of letter sounds as they occur in words in the pupils' vocabulary is available for a class of 35 pupils.[7]

---

[2] Emmett A. Betts, "Linguistics and Reading: A Critique," *Innovation and Experiment in Modern Education,* Report of Twenty-ninth Educational Conference Sponsored by Educational Records Bureau, American Council on Education, Washington, D.C., 1965, pp. 130–140.

[3] Charles C. Fries, *Linguistics and Reading*, Holt, Rinehart and Winston, Inc., New York, 1963.

[4] Leonard Bloomfield and Clarence L. Barnhart, *Let's Read: A Linguistic Approach,* Wayne State University Press, Detroit, Mich., 1961.

[5] Sir James Pitman, "The Future of the Teaching of Reading," *Keeping Abreast of the Revolution in Education,* Report of the Twenty-eighth Educational Conference Sponsored by the Educational Records Bureau, American Council on Education, Washington, D.C., 1964, pp. 144–178.

[6] Gordon L. Barclay, "i/t/a with Emotionally Disturbed Children," *Modern Educational Developments: Another Look,* Report of the Thirtieth Educational Conference Sponsored by the Educational Records Bureau, Interstate Publishing Company, Danville, Ill., 1966, pp. 135–146.

[7] Donald D. Durrell and Helen A. Murphy, *Speech-to-Print Phonics,* Harcourt, Brace & World, Inc., 1964.

STUDY–HABITS WORKBOOKS AND GUIDES

Closely related to reading textbooks and workbooks are workbooks and aids in the field of study habits. Perhaps the workbook for training in study habits in the secondary school which has been longest in use is *Better Work Habits* by Salisbury [41]. This book, which was revised in 1965, contains many detailed practice exercises on a variety of work and study skills. It is planned especially for the ninth grade, but it may be used in the senior high school as well.

A considerable proportion of the workbooks and manuals planned to help students improve their study procedures are designed for the college level. One of the best known of these is *Effective Study* by Robinson [40]. This workbook was originally developed in how-to-study programs with college freshmen, but it can be used with students in the upper years of high school. An admirable feature of the book is close coordination between diagnostic tests and remedial materials. A revised edition was published in 1961.

A second type of booklet designed to help pupils study better consists not of practice exercises primarily, but of a series of practical suggestions concerning methods of study in different fields. *Improvement of Study Habits* by Jones [27] is a booklet containing helpful suggestions for the senior high school or college student. Among the aspects of study discussed are reading, note taking, improving one's memory, use of the library, the habit of concentration, reading in mathematics and science, mental hygiene, and preparing for and taking examinations.

Another study guide, written primarily for the college student, is *How to Study* by Morgan and Deese [36]. This booklet contains many valuable suggestions and some practice exercises. Among the topics taken up in detail are successful studying, getting work done, reading better and faster, taking notes, taking examinations, studying foreign languages, and mathematical problems.

Teaching Study Habits and Skills by Preston [38] is a practical guide for teachers in helping pupils develop interest in learning, self-discipline, skill in gathering information, and mastery of content from the preschool to the college level.

MATERIALS FOR USE WITH READING FILMS

Although avoidance of overemphasis on the mechanical aspects of training in reading is highly desirable, some schools may feel a need for materials that will furnish guidance in the use of reading films as one aspect of a reading-improvement program.

An instructor's manual is available for the *Advanced Reading Program* [4], produced by the Perceptual Development Laboratories. The manual serves as a guide for the use of the Perceptoscope, a specially designed 16-mm projector which combines the functions of tachistoscope, motion-picture projector, and reading pacer. It outlines an advanced reading course of twenty-four 1-hour sessions.

Some of the techniques discussed in manuals and guides for use with reading films are probably more appropriate for use in reading centers and clinics than in classrooms. Schools needing to refer pupils who are seriously retarded in reading to clinics or service centers outside the school system may be interested in the comprehensive *Directory of Reading Clinics,* prepared by the Educational Developmental Laboratories [13].

BOOKS FOR FREE READING AND PRACTICE IN READING SKILLS

There is an ever-present need for easy, interesting material for seriously retarded readers in high school. A bibliography for adolescents who find reading difficult is available in a revised edition by Strang, Phelps, and Withrow [47]. This bibliography, *Gateways to Readable Books,* includes many titles of about fifth-, sixth-, and seventh-grade levels of difficulty and some still easier.

A pamphlet called *Individualized Reading* by May Lazar [30] contains a book list for an individualized reading program arranged by grade level and subject. This organized book list is helpful, although it is limited to the books of just one publisher.

The National Association of Independent Schools (NAIS) publishes annually for pupils of average and superior ability the *Junior Book List* and *Senior Book List* [9, 10] which are very useful. The *Junior Book List* is primarily for elementary school pupils, but it devotes several pages to an annotated list of books appropriate for pupils in grades 6 to 9. The *Senior Book List* provides an annotated list of books for students in the last four years of secondary school, grouped in the following categories: novels; short stories, poetry, and drama; people; places; ideas; the arts; the world today; history; hobbies; sports and vocations; science; and reference works. Titles of books chosen annually by the NAIS as the ten best adult books for the precollege reader are starred.

READING LABORATORIES AND PROGRAMMED INSTRUCTION

In addition to the foregoing books, workbooks, and study guides for the improvement of reading above the elementary school level, some less-conventional methods and materials have been developed in recent years for all reading levels from primary to adult. These include especially (1) reading laboratories and (2) materials and techniques for programmed instruction of programmed learning. One of the prime advantages of both these approaches is that each one is designed to permit the pupil to begin at the reading level where he functions best and to proceed at his own rate. Immediate feedback and reinforcement of learning are further advantages of these procedures.

Reading laboratories are exemplified by the series of Science Research Associates and the Educational Developmental Laboratories. The SRA Reading Laboratory Series, developed by Don H. Parker with the cooperation of other reading specialists, consists of nine overlapping laboratories covering grades 1 through 12. Laboratories IIIa, IIIb, and IVa span the junior and senior high schools. Word games, power builders, rate builders, and listening-skill builders are features of this laboratory series.

The reading program of the Educational Developmental Laboratories is designed to help develop visual discrimination and visual perception, build a sight vocabulary, strengthen visual memory, contribute to regular eye movements, build up study skills, develop listening ability, and increase skimming efficiency. The various aspects of the program consist of group and individual tachistoscopic training, controlled reader training, a study-skills library program, a listen-and-read program, a word-clues series, and a skimming-and-scanning program. Instruments have a central place in most aspects of the EDL reading program. All levels—kindergarten, primary, intermediate, junior and senior high school, college and adult—are included in the overall EDL program.

Programmed instruction in reading is illustrated by *Programmed Reading,* prepared by M. W. Sullivan and Cynthia Dee Buchanan. This program is based on the science of linguistics, and, like similar programs, consists of a series of small, painstakingly prepared tasks which are designed to lead the child through a gradual developmental sequence in learning to read. Since programming allows each child to work individually at his own rate, each one responds to every "frame" or task, learns immediately whether his response is correct, and is given an opportunity to respond repeatedly to each bit of information, so that mastery of the correct response is fixed in his mind. This program was in the beginning confined to kindergarten and grades 1 and 2, but materials are in the process of being written for several higher levels. The program consists of story books, programmed reading books, tests, and teacher's guides for the different units in the series.

Information concerning other programmed materials and where they may be obtained is obtained in a publication of the National Education Association.

Several other contributions to programmed instruction in reading are among the references at the end of this appendix.

REFERENCES

1. Bailey, Matilda, and Ullin W. Leavell: The Mastery of Reading Series, revised and enlarged, American Book Company, New York, 1956, 503 to 732 pp.

2. Bamman, Henry A., and Robert J. Whitehead: World of Adventure Series, Benefic Press, Chicago, 1964.

3. Blair, Walter, and John C. Gerber: Better Reading Series, vol. I, *Factual Prose,* 5th ed., 1963, 512 pp.; vol. II, *Literature,* 4th ed., 1959, 840 pp.; *Repertory,* 3d ed. (single volume edition of I and II), 1960, 1188 pp., Scott, Foresman and Company, Chicago.

4. Bryant, Norman Dale, and John Michel: *Advanced Reading Program: Instructor Manual,* Perceptual Development Laboratories, Inc., St. Louis, 1957.

5. Center, Stella S., and Gladys L. Persons: *Experiences in Reading and Thinking,* The Macmillan Company, New York, 1940, xi + 305 pp.

6. Cherington, Marie R.: *Improving Reading Skills in College Subjects,* Teachers College Press, Teachers College, Columbia University, New York, 1961, x + 141 pp.

7. Coleman, J. H., and Ann Jungeblut: Reading for Meaning, separate books for grades 4 through 8, books for grades 10 through 12 in preparation, J. B. Lippincott Company, Philadelphia, 1962–1965.

8. Cosper, Russell, and E. Glenn Griffin: *Toward Better Reading Skills,* 2d ed., Appleton-Century-Crofts, Inc., New York, 1959, 299 pp.

9. *Current Books: Junior Book List of the National Association of Independent Schools,* NAIS, Boston, 1965, 109 pp.

10. *Current Books: Senior Book List of the National Association of Independent Schools,* NAIS, Boston, 1965, 95 pp.

11. Dale, Edgar: *How to Read a Newspaper,* Scott, Foresman and Company, Chicago, 1941, xii + 178 pp.

12. Dallmann, Martha, and Alma Sheridan: *Better Reading in College,* The Ronald Press Company, New York, 1954, 308 pp.

13. *Directory of Reading Clinics,* EDL Research and Information Bulletin, Educational Developmental Laboratories, Huntington, N.Y., 1964.

14. Gilbert, Doris Wilcox: *Power and Speed in Reading,* Prentice-Hall, Inc., Englewood Cliffs, N.J., 1956, viii + 246 pp.

15. Gilmartin, John G.: *Building Your Vocabulary,* 2d ed., Prentice-Hall, Inc., Englewood Cliffs, N.J., 1952, 210 pp.

16. Glock, Marvin G.: *Improvement of College Reading,* Houghton Mifflin Company, Boston, 1958, 307 pp.

17. Gray, William S., Marion Monroe, and A. Sterl Artley: *Basic Reading Skills for Junior High School Use,* rev. ed., Scott, Foresman and Company, Chicago, 1957, 192 pp.

18. Gray, William S., Marion Monroe, and A. Sterl Artley: *Basic Reading Skills for High School Use,* rev. ed., Scott, Foresman and Company, Chicago, 1958, 192 pp.

19. Guiler, W. S., and J. H. Coleman: Reading for Meaning, Books 4–12, J. B. Lippincott Company, Philadelphia, 1955.

20. Hart, Archibald: *Twelve Ways to Build a Vocabulary,* E. P. Dutton & Co., Inc., New York, 1939, 183 pp.

21. Hart, Archibald, and F. Arnold Lejeune: *The Growing Vocabulary,* E. P. Dutton & Co., Inc., New York, rev. 1950, 160 pp.

22. Hovious, Carol: *Wings for Reading,* D. C. Heath and Company, Boston, 1952, xiv + 460 pp.

23. ITA Early-to-read Series (prepared by Tanyzer and Mazurkiewicz), Pupil's Workbook, Teachers' Manuals, additional materials, ITA Publications, Inc., New York, 1963–1965.

24. Jewett, Arno, and others: Reading for Enjoyment Series, rev. ed., *Adventure Bound, Journeys into America, Literature for Life,* Houghton Mifflin Company, Boston, 1958–1965, 307 to 726 pp.

25. Johnson, Eleanor M.: Modern Reading Skilltexts, Charles E. Merrill Books, Inc., Columbus, Ohio, rev. 1959.

26. Johnson, Eleanor M., and others: Diagnostic Reading Workbooks, Charles E. Merrill Books, Inc., Columbus, Ohio, 1940.

27. Jones, Edward S.: *Improvement of Study Habits,* Henry Stewart, Incorporated, Buffalo, N.Y., rev. 1951, 126 pp.

28. Knight, Pearle E., and Arthur E. Traxler: *Develop Your Reading,* D. C. Heath and Company, Boston, 1941, 376 pp.

29. Knight, Pearle E., and Arthur E. Traxler: *Read and Comprehend,* rev. ed., D. C. Heath and Company, Boston, 1949, xiii + 298 pp.

30. Lazar, May: *Individualized Reading,* Franklin Watts, Inc., New York, 1959, x + 43 pp.

31. Leavell, Ullin W., and Betty Elise Davis: *New Adventures in Reading,* Steck-Vaughn Co., Austin, Tex., 1953.

32. Leedy, Paul D.: *Reading Improvement for Adults,* McGraw-Hill Book Company, New York, 1956, 475 pp.

33. Malsbary, Dean R.: *Spelling and Word Power,* Prentice-Hall, Inc., Englewood Cliffs, N.J., rev. 1965, 140 pp.

34. McCall, William A., and Lelah Mae Crabbs: Standard Test Lessons in Reading, rev. ed., Books A, B, C, D, E, Teachers College Press, Teachers College, Columbia University, New York, 1961.

35. Meyer, Alma: *Vocabulary-Building Speller,* The Macmillan Company, New York, rev. 1950, 160 pp.

36. Morgan, Clifford T., and James Deese: *How to Study,* McGraw-Hill Book Company, New York, 1957, vii + 130 pp.

37. Murphy, George, and others: Let's Read Series, Third Series, Book 1, Book 2, Book 3; New Series, Book 4, Holt, Rinehart and Winston, Inc., New York, 1955–1962, 302 to 662 pp.

38. Preston, Ralph C.: *Teaching Study Habits and Skills,* Holt, Rinehart and Winston, Inc., New York, 1959, vii + 55 pp.

39. Roberts, Clyde: *Word Attack: A Way to Better Reading,* Harcourt, Brace & World, Inc., New York, 1956, teacher's ed. 163 pp., students' ed. 139 pp.

40. Robinson, Francis P.: *Effective Study,* rev. ed., Harper & Row, Publishers, Incorporated, New York, 1961, 278 pp.

41. Salisbury, Rachel: *Better Work Habits,* Scott, Foresman and Company, Chicago, rev. 1965.

42. Shaw, Phillip B.: *Effective Reading and Learning,* Thomas Y. Crowell Company, New York, 1959, x + 447 pp.

43. Shaw, Phillip B., and Agatha Townsend: *College Reading Manual,* Thomas Y. Crowell Company, New York, 1959, xiii + 237 pp.

44. Simpson, Elizabeth A: SRA Better Reading Books Series, 1, 2, and 3, Science Research Associates, Inc., Chicago, rev. 1962, each 90 pp.

45. Smith, Nila Banton: Be a Better Reader Series, Books I–VI, Prentice-Hall, Inc., Englewood Cliffs, N.J., rev. 1960–1963, 128 to 218 pp.

46. Spache, George D., and Paul C. Berg: *The Art of Efficient Reading,* The Macmillan Company, New York, 1955, 273 pp.

47. Strang, Ruth, Ethlyne Phelps, and Dorothy E. Withrow: *Gateways to Readable Books,* The H. W. Wilson Company, New York, rev. 1966.

48. Strang, Ruth, and others: *Study Type of Reading Exercises for Secondary Schools,* rev. ed., Teachers College Press, Teachers College, Columbia University, New York, 1956, 128 pp.

49. Strang, Ruth, and others: *Study Type of Reading Exercises: College Level,* Teachers College Press, Teachers College, Columbia University, New York, 1951, 152 pp.

50. Stroud, James B., Robert A. Ammons, and Henry A. Bamman: *Improving Reading Ability,* 2d ed., Appleton-Century-Crofts, Inc., New York, 1956, 187 pp.

51. Triggs, Frances Oralind: *Improve Your Reading,* University of Minnesota Press, Minneapolis, rev. 1960.

52. Triggs, Frances Oralind: *Reading: Its Creative Teaching and Testing, Kindergarten through College,* published by the author, Mountain Home, N.C., 1960, 150 pp.

53. Wilkinson, Helen S., and Bertha D. Brown: *Improving Your Reading,* Noble and Noble Publishers, Inc., New York, rev. 1964, 352 pp.

54. Witty, Paul A.: *How to Become a Better Reader,* Science Research Associates, Inc., Chicago, 1953, 275 pp.

55. Wood, Evelyn N., and Marjorie W. Barrows: *Reading Skills,* rev. ed., Holt, Rinehart and Winston, Inc., New York, 1958, 256 pp.

REFERENCES FOR "READING LABORATORIES AND PROGRAMMED INSTRUCTION"

1. Blumenthal, Joseph C.: *English 2600,* rev. ed., Harcourt, Brace & World, Inc., New York, 1962.

2. *Educational Developmental Laboratories Reading Program,* Educational Developmental Laboratories, Huntington, N.Y.

3. Markle, Susan Meyer: *Words,* Center for Programmed Instruction, Inc., New York, 1962.

4. Markle, Susan Meyer: *Good Frames and Bad: A Grammar of Frame Writing,* John Wiley & Sons, Inc., New York, 1964.

5. Parker, Don H., and others: *Reading Laboratory Series,* Science Research Associates, Inc., Chicago.

6. *Selection and Use of Programed Materials: A Handbook for Teachers,* Division of Audiovisual Instructional Service, National Education Association, Washington, D.C., 1964.

7. Sullivan, M. W., and Cynthia Dee Buchanan: *Programmed Reading,* Webster Division of McGraw-Hill Book Company, St. Louis, Mo.

selected bibliography of low difficulty books and magazines for severely retarded adolescent readers

appendix D

1. Bamman, Henry A., and Robert J. Whitehead: World of Adventure Series, Benefic Press, Chicago, 1964.

2. Botel, Morton (ed.): Interesting Reading Series, Follett Publishing Company, Chicago.

3. Cass, A., and others: *Adult Education Reader,* Educational Division, Reader's Digest Services, Inc., Pleasantville, N.Y.

4. Coleman, James C., and others: The Deep-sea Adventure Series, Harr Wagner Publishing Company, San Francisco, 1959, 1962.

5. Dale, Edgar: *Stories for Today,* United States Armed Forces Institute, U.S. Government Printing Office, catalog no. D1.10:MC002.

6. Dale, Edgar: *Stories Worth Knowing,* United States Armed Forces Institute, U.S. Government Printing Office, catalog no. D1.10:2003.

7. English 900 Series, The Macmillan Compay, New York, 1964.

8. Frontiers of America Books, Children's Press, Inc., Chicago.

9. Goldberg, Herman R., and Winifred T. Brumber (eds.): *The Job Ahead,* Science Research Associates, Inc., Chicago, 1963.

10. Goldberg, Herman R., and Winifred T. Brumber (eds.): Rochester Occupational Reading Series, Science Research Associates, Inc., Chicago, 1963.

11. Guyton, M. L., and M. E. Kelty: *From Words to Stories,* Noble and Noble, Publishers, Inc., New York, 1961.

12. Hader, Berta, and Elmer Hader: *Snow in the City,* The Macmillan Company, New York, 1963.

13. Heffernan, Helen, and others: The Reading-motivated Series, rev. ed., Harr Wagner Publishing Company, San Francisco, 1965, 1966.

14. Justus, May: *New Boy in School,* Hastings House, Publishers, Inc., New York, 1963.

15. Kitchin, A. T., and V. F. Allen: *Reader's Digest Readings: English as a Second Language,* Educational Division, Reader's Digest Services, Inc., Pleasantville, N.Y.

16. Kohan, Frances A., and Trude Weil: *Juan's Adventures in Mexico,* Noble and Noble, Publishers, Inc., New York, 1961.

17. Kottmeyer, William A., and others: The Everyreader Series, McGraw-Hill Book Company, New York, 1952–1962.

18. Larrick, Nancy (ed.): *Junior Science Books,* The Garrard Press, Champaign, Ill.

19. Laubach, Frank C.: *Streamlined English,* rev. ed., The Macmillan Company, New York, 1955.

20. Leavell, Ullin W., and Adda Mai Sharp: *Work Time,* Steck-Vaughn Co., Austin, Tex.

21. Leonard, Rhoda, and William S. Briscoe: Wildlife Adventure Series, Harr Wagner Publishing Company, San Francisco.

22. Lerner, Lillian, and Margaret C. Moller: Follett Vocational Reading Series, Follett Publishing Company, Chicago.

23. Montgomery, Elizabeth Rider: *The Mystery of Edison Brown,* Scott, Foresman and Company, Chicago, 1960.

24. Neville, Emily: *It's Like This, Cat,* Harper & Row, Publishers, Incorporated, New York, 1963.

25. *News for You,* Robert S. Laubach (pub.), Syracuse, N.Y. A weekly newspaper published on three levels: AA—very easy, A—easy, B—harder.

26. Piper Books, Houghton Mifflin Company, Boston.

27. Rambeau, John, and Nancy Rambeau: The Jim Forest Readers, Harr Wagner Publishing Company, San Francisco, 1959.

28. Rambeau, John, and Nancy Rambeau: *Morgan Bay Mysteries,* Harr Wagner Publishing Company, San Francisco, 1962, 1965.

29. Ramono, Louis G., and Nicholas P. Georgiady: *This Is a Department Store,* Follett Publishing Company, Chicago, 1962.

30. *Reader's Choice,* Scholastic Magazines, Inc., New York.

31. *Reader's Digest Skill Builders,* Educational Division, Reader's Digest Services, Inc., Pleasantville, N.Y.

32. *Reader's Digest Science Readers,* Educational Division, Reader's Digest Services, Inc., Pleasantville, N.Y.

33. *Reading Adventures,* by the editors of *My Weekly Reader,* Charles E. Merrill Books, Inc., Columbus, Ohio.

34. *Scholastic Scope,* Scholastic Magazines, Inc., Dayton, Ohio. A national magazine for high school students.

35. Signal Books, Doubleday & Company, Inc., Garden City, N.Y.

36. Smith, Harley A., and Ida King Wilbert: *I Want to Read and Write,* rev. ed., Steck-Vaughn Co., Austin, Tex.

37. Stone, Clarence R., and others: New Practice Readers, McGraw-Hill Book Company, New York.

38. Strang, Ruth, and others: *Teen-age Tales,* D. C. Heath and Company, Boston, 1959.

39. Tom, Judith J., and John A. Hurst: "and hereby hangs the tale . . ." Series, Children's Press, Inc., Chicago.

40. Tripp, Fern: *Reading for Safety,* published by the author, Dinuba, Calif., 1962.

41. Turner, Richard H.: *On the Telephone,* Teachers College Press, Teachers College, Columbia University, New York, 1964.

42. Turner, Richard H.: The Turner-Livingston Reading Series, New York University Press, New York.

43. Warner, Gertrude Chandler: *Mystery Ranch,* Scott, Foresman and Company, Chicago, 1958.

44. We Were There Books, Grosset & Dunlap, Inc., New York.

45. Zolotow, Charlotte: *The Quarreling Book,* Harper & Row, Publishers, Incorporated, New York, 1963.

bibliography of books for primary children with Indian, Mexican-American, or Negro characters[1]

appendix E

1. Acker, Helen: *Lee Natoni: Young Navajo,* illus. by Richard Kennedy, Abelard-Schuman, Limited, New York, 1958, 7–10 years.

2. Baker, Betty: *The Shaman's Last Raid,* illus. by Leonard Shortall, Harper & Row, Publishers, Incorporated, New York, 1963, 8–10 years.

3. Baker, Betty: *The Treasure of the Padres,* illus. by Leonard Shortall, Harper & Row, Publishers, Incorporated, New York, 1964, 8–10 years.

4. Beim, Lorraine, and Jerrold Beim: *Two Is a Team,* illus. by Ernest Crichlow, Harcourt, Brace & World, Inc., New York, 1945, 4–7 years.

5. Beyer, Ernestine Cobern: *The Story of Little Big,* illus. by Vee Guthrie, Reilly & Lee Company, Chicago, 1962, 5–8 years.

6. Bontempts, Arna: *Sad-faced Boy,* illus. by Virginia Lee Burton, Houghton Mifflin Company, Boston, 1937, 8–10 years.

[1] Compiled by Mrs. Kenneth L. Keating and published with annotations by Pima Printing Company, Tucson, Ariz.

7. Brock, Emma L.: *One Little Indian Boy,* illus. by the author, Alfred A. Knopf, Inc., New York, 1932, 6–8 years.

8. Buff, Conrad, and Mary Buff: *Dancing Cloud: The Navajo Boy,* rev. ed., illus. by Conrad Buff, The Viking Press, Inc., New York, 1957, 9–11 years.

9. Bulla, Clyde Robert: *Eagle Feather,* illus. by Tom Two Arrows, Thomas Y. Crowell Company, New York, 1953, 7–10 years.

10. Carroll, Ruth, and Latrobe Carroll: *Tough Enough's Indians,* illus. by the authors, Henry Z. Walck, Inc., New York, 1960, 8–10 years.

11. Clark, Ann Nolan: *The Desert People,* illus. by Allan Houser, The Viking Press, Inc., New York, 1962, 6–8 years.

12. Clark, Ann Nolan: *In My Mother's House,* illus. by Velino Herrera, The Viking Press, Inc., New York, 1941, 8–11 years.

13. Clark, Ann Nolan: *The Little Indian Basket Maker,* illus. by Harrison Begay, Melmont Publishers, La Puente, Calif., 1957, 6–8 years.

14. Clark, Ann Nolan: *The Little Indian Pottery Maker,* illus. by Don Percival, Melmont Publishers, La Puente, Calif., 1955, 6–8 years.

15. Clark, Ann Nolan: *Little Navajo Bluebird,* illus. by Paul Lantz, The Viking Press, Inc., 1943, 8–11 years.

16. de Angeli, Marguerite: *Bright April,* illus. by the author, Doubleday & Company, Inc., Garden City, N.Y., 1946, 8–10 years.

17. Deming, Therese O., and Thelma Shaw: *Little Eagle,* illus. by Edwin W. Deming, Laidlaw Brothers, Publishers, River Forest, Ill., 1958, 5–7 years.

18. Ets, Marie Hall, and Aurora Labastida: *Nine Days to Christmas,* illus. by Marie Hall Ets, The Viking Press, Inc., New York, 1959, 5–8 years.

19. Evans, Eva Knox: *Araminta,* illus. by Erick Berry, G. P. Putnam's Sons, New York, 1935, 5–8 years.

20. Evans, Eva Knox: *Jerome Anthony,* illus. by Erick Berry, G. P. Putnam's Sons, New York, 1936, 5–8 years.

21. Faulkner, Georgene: *Melindy's Happy Summer,* illus. by Elton C. Fax, Julian Messner, Publishers, Inc., New York, 1949, 8–12 years.

22. Faulkner, Georgene, and John Becker: *Melindy's Medal,* illus. by Elton C. Fax, Julian Messner, Publishers, Inc., 1945, 8–10 years.

23. Friskey, Margaret: *Indian Two Feet and His Horse,* illus. by Katherine Evans, Children's Press, Inc., Chicago, 1959, 4–7 years.

24. Gates, Doris: *Blue Willow,* illus. by Paul Lantz, The Viking Press, Inc., New York, 1940, 9–12 years.

25. Gates, Doris: *Little Vic,* illus. by Kate Seredy, The Viking Press, Inc., New York, 1951, 8–12 years.

26. Hoffine, Lyla: *Jennie's Mandan Bowl,* illus. by Larry Toschik, Longmans, Green & Co., Inc., New York, 1960, 8–10 years.

27. Hoffine, Lyla: *Running Elk,* illus. by Patricia Boodell, The Bobbs-Merrill Company, Inc., Indianapolis, 1957, 6–9 years.

28. Hoffine, Lyla: *Sioux Trail Adventure,* illus. by the author, American Book Company, New York, 1936, 8–10 years.

29. Hunt, Mabel Leigh: *Ladycake Farm,* illus. by Clotilde Embree Funk, J. B. Lippincott Company, Philadelphia, 1952, 8–10 years.

30. Justus, May: *New Boy in School,* illus. by Joan Balfour Payne, Hastings House, Publishers, Inc., New York, 1963, 6–8 years.

31. Keats, Ezra Jack: *The Snowy Day,* illus. by the author, The Viking Press, Inc., New York, 1962, 4–7 years, Caldecott medal.

32. Keats, Ezra Jack: *Whistle for Willie,* illus. by the author, The Viking Press, Inc., New York, 1964, 4–7 years.

33. Lattimore, Eleanor Frances: *Jasper,* illus. by the author, William Morrow and Company, Inc., New York, 1953, 6–8 years.

34. Lenski, Lois: *We Live in the Southwest,* illus. by the author, J. B. Lippincott Company, Philadelphia, 1962, 8–10 years.

35. Lewis, Mary: *The Halloween Kangaroo,* illus. by Richard Lewis, Ives Washburn, Inc., New York, 1964, 6–8 years.

36. Lexau, Joan M.: *Benjie,* illus. by Don Bolognese, The Dial Press, Inc., New York, 1964, 6–8 years.

37. Meigs, Cornelia: *The Willow Whistle,* illus. by E. Boyd Smith, The Macmillan Company, New York, 1931, 8–12 years.

38. Politi, Leo: *Juanita,* illus. by the author, Charles Scribner's Sons, New York, 1948, 6–8 years.

39. Politi, Leo: *Song of the Swallows,* illus. by the author, Charles Scribner's Sons, New York, 1949, 6–8 years.

40. Randall, Blossom E.: *Fun for Chris,* illus. by Eunice Young Smith, Whitman Publishing Company, Racine, Wis., 1956, 5–8 years.

41. Schweitzer, Byrd Baylor: *Amigo,* illus. by Garth Williams, The Macmillan Company, New York, 1963, 5–8 years.

42. Schweitzer, Byrd Baylor: *One Small Blue Bead,* illus. by Symeon Shimin, The Macmillan Company, New York, 1965, 6–9 years.

43. Shotwell, Louisa R.: *Roosevelt Grady,* illus. by Peter Burchard, Harcourt, Brace & World, Inc., New York, 1963, 8–10 years.

44. Steele, William O.: *Wayah of the Real People,* illus. by Isa Barnett, Holt, Rinehart and Winston, Inc., New York, 1964, 9–11 years.

45. Sterling, Dorothy: *Mary Jane,* illus. by Ernest Crichlow, Doubleday & Company, Inc., Garden City, N.Y., 9–12 years.

several outstanding sources

of comprehensive knowledge

specifically about reading

appendix F

PROCEEDINGS

International Reading Association Conference Proceedings, vols. 1–11, Newark, Del. 19711.

 Articles in every area of reading on all educational levels written by outstanding persons in the reading field.

Proceedings of the Annual Conference on Reading Held at the University of Chicago, Supplementary Educational Monographs, University of Chicago Press, Chicago, from 1925 to present.

 Each volume deals with a particular theme; basic theory is followed by concrete application on all grade levels from beginners to adults.

PROFESSIONAL JOURNALS

Education, 4300 W. 62d Street, Indianapolis.
  Contains a large proportion of articles on reading.
Elementary English, National Council of Teachers of English, 508 South Sixth Street, Champaign, Ill.
Journal of Reading, published six times a year by the International Reading Association, P.O. Box 695, Newark, Del. 19711.
  A journal for the improvement of reading in high school, college, and adult programs; formerly the *Journal of Developmental Reading.*
Reading in High School, A Quarterly Journal for the Improvement of Reading Teaching, P.O. Box 75, College Station, Pullman, Wash.
Reading Research Quarterly, published four times a year by the International Reading Association, P.O. Box 695, Newark, Del. 19711.

name index

subject index

Textbooks, for college use, 528
  in home economics, 370, 373
  in industrial arts, 375
  in mathematics, 339–341
  for science, 327–329
  for secondary schools, 526–528
  (*See also* Materials)
Thai language, learning, 367
Thorndike-McCall Reading Scales, 188
Trade schools (*see* Vocational high
  school)
Traxler Reading Tests, 189, 191–192,
  202–204
Tucson High School, 77
Typewriter, use of, in reading, 218
Typewriting, reading and, 364

Underachievers (*see* Able retarded
  readers)
Ungraded primary unit, 56
U.S. Army, illiteracy rate of, 6

Vernon Sentence Reading Test, 250
Visual defects (*see* Defects)
Visual factors in reading, 16–18
Visual memory, 221
Visual perception, 15
Vocabulary, development of, 241–245
  of disadvantaged child, 429
  in foreign languages, 368
  growth of, in preschool child, 116–117
  in home economics, 372–373
  in industrial arts, 374–375
  materials for buildings, 528
  principles applying to, 240–241
  problems of, 301–302
  as reading goal, 11

Vocabulary, in reading tests, 183
  in science, 323–327
  size of, 240
  for slow learner, 407–408, 416
  teaching, 238–248
  tests of, 200
Vocabulary cards, use of, 246
Vocational high school, reading program
  for, 63–65
Vocations, reading and, 4

Walton High School, 72, 106
Watts Sentence Reading Test, 250
Wepman's Auditory Discrimination Test,
  412
Wechsler-Bellevue Test, 463
Wechsler Intelligence Scale for Children
  (WISC), 20–21, 221, 386, 391, 392,
  412, 437, 448, 505
"Whole-word" approach, 222
Winter Haven Lions Research Founda-
  tion, 413
WISC (*see* Wechsler Intelligence Scale
  for Children)
Word clusters, 232–233, 236
Word comprehension, levels of, 10–11
  studies in, 304–309
Word recognition, analysis of, 227–229
  materials to facilitate, 529
  skills in, 11
  teaching, 226
Workbooks, for college students, 525–
  526
  criticisms of, 238
  for secondary schools, 524–526
  for study habits, 530
Workshop, reading, described, 83–84
Writing and reading ability, 31–32